The SAGE Handbook of

Curriculum, Pedagogy
and Assessment

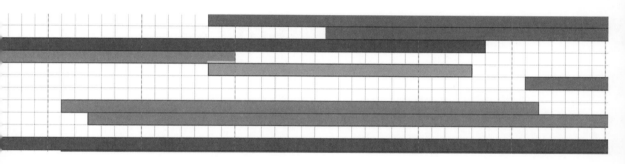

The SAGE Handbook of

Curriculum, Pedagogy and Assessment

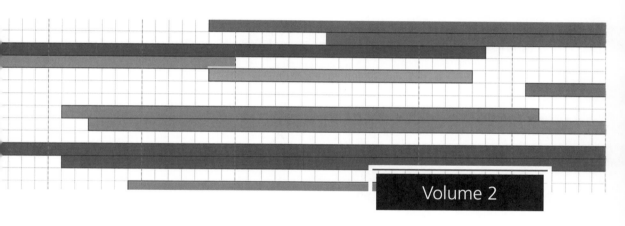

Volume 2

Edited by

Dominic Wyse, Louise Hayward
and Jessica Pandya

$SAGE reference

Los Angeles | London | New Delhi
Singapore | Washington DC

Los Angeles | London | New Delhi
Singapore | Washington DC

SAGE Publications Ltd
1 Oliver's Yard
55 City Road
London EC1Y 1SP

SAGE Publications Inc.
2455 Teller Road
Thousand Oaks, California 91320

SAGE Publications India Pvt Ltd
B 1/I 1 Mohan Cooperative Industrial Area
Mathura Road
New Delhi 110 044

SAGE Publications Asia-Pacific Pte Ltd
3 Church Street
#10-04 Samsung Hub
Singapore 049483

Editor: Jude Bowen
Editorial assistant: Matthew Oldfield
Production editor: Shikha Jain
Copyeditor: Sunrise Setting Limited
Proofreader: Sunrise Setting Limited
Indexer: Cathryn Pritchard
Marketing manager: Dilhara Attygalle
Cover design: Wendy Scott
Typeset by: Cenveo Publisher Services
Printed and bound by CPI Group (UK) Ltd,
Croydon, CR0 4YY [for Antony Rowe]

MIX
Paper from
responsible sources
FSC www.fsc.org FSC® C013604

At SAGE we take sustainability seriously.
Most of our products are printed in the UK
using FSC papers and boards. When we
print overseas we ensure sustainable
papers are used as measured by the
PREPS grading system. We undertake an
annual audit to monitor our sustainability.

Library of Congress Control Number: 2015941576

British Library Cataloguing in Publication data

A catalogue record for this book is available from the British Library

ISBN 978-1-4462-9702-5

Contents

Volume 2

PART IV

Areas of the Curriculum

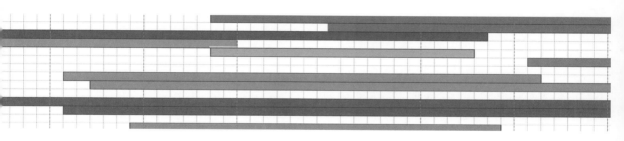

Transdisciplinarity in Curricular Theory and Practice

James Albright

Transdisciplinarity may be understood as one of a number of related challenges to what is a shared characterization of narrow disciplinary approaches to curriculum theorizing and development. Although notions of interdisciplinarity are likely to be more familiar to students of curriculum theory, transdisciplinarity shares long-established and often well-rehearsed critiques of disciplinary approaches to curriculum, pedagogy, and assessment. Transdisciplinary discourse participates in ongoing curriculum theorizing debates, which argue that disciplinary approaches promote curriculum proliferation, a contestation about what is to be valued within the curriculum, an elision of the interdisciplinary nature of most school subjects, and an inability to address complex scientific and social problems (Tanner, 1971). Throughout this debate, cognitivist, and problem-solving approaches have been allied to interdisciplinary and transdisciplinary challenges to curricular disciplinarity (Tanner and Tanner, 1990). Consequently, an outline

of the various emergent conceptions of transdisciplinarity's stances toward notions of disciplinarity is important to understanding its viability in curriculum theorizing and development. Similarly, any analysis of transdisciplarity within curriculum theorizing and development requires some discussion of its theoretical and pragmatic relations to contending inter-, cross-, and multi-disciplinary approaches to knowledge production and transfer (Klein, 2006). But, as Julie Thompson Klein, one of the foremost scholars on the subject, notes, 'Clearly, transdisciplinarity means more than one thing. It is perceived as a vision of knowledge, a particular theory or concept, a particular method, and an essential strategy for addressing complex problems of the contemporary world' (Klein cited in Lattanzi, 1998: 59).

This chapter begins by tracing transdisciplinarity's origins as an epistemology of knowledge production 'beyond the disciplines'. The translation of Transdisciplinarity into the fields of scientific research, tertiary education, and, ultimately, schooling are also discussed. Along the way, confounding shifts in meaning and relation to other overlapping curricular discourses (Klein, 2014) and practices are noted.

TRANSDISCIPLINARITY AS EPISTEMOLOGICAL STANDPOINT

As with many innovations in curriculum theorizing, transdisciplinarity is derivative from discourses outside the field. It arose in debates primarily focused on the future of research. For curriculum theorists in the Anglosphere, it is important to note that the origins of transdisciplinary theorizing and much of its current applications in research and education, especially in universities, are European. Jean Piaget (1896–1980) is often attributed with coining the term 'transdisciplinarity' at the international workshop 'Interdisciplinarity: Teaching and Research Problems in Universities', which was organized by the Organization for Economic Co-operation and Development (OECD) in collaboration with the French Ministry of National Education and the University of Nice in 1970. Austrian astrophysicist, Erich Jantsch was another early proponent of transdisciplinarity (Jantsch, 1972), but the Romanian/French theoretical physicist, Basarab Nicolescu, author of transdisciplinarity's manifesto (2000) and co-author of its charter (1994), is most frequently associated with transdisciplinary theorizing, particularly as an epistemological concept. He is the founder (1987) and director of the International Center for Transdisciplinary Research and Studies (CIRET, http://ciret-transdisciplinarity.org/index.php). Aligned with UNESCO, CIRET promotes transdisciplinary theorizing and adoption through conferences and publishing. By the end of the century, transdisciplinarity, as a philosophical and epistemological concept and understood as a space beyond disciplines, posited an understanding of the fundamental unity of knowledge, and held currency with important international sponsors, such as UNESCO.

Early definitions of transdisciplinarity attempted to make a distinction from interdisciplinarity as a move from the 'interaction of two or more disciplines [to] a more comprehensive and systematic integration' (Klein, 2002a: 49). An early defining tension arose on how knowledge production might be integrated and what distinctions could be made in the substitution of the prefixes (inter/multi/cross/trans) as they relate to the base (disciplinarity).

Interdisciplinarity has a longer history in curriculum theorizing. Dewey (1938) argued that the structure of the disciplines should not dictate curriculum and that learning should be experiential. Interdisciplinarity was also a hallmark of early progressive curricular reforms, such as Kilpatrick's (1918) 'Project Method'. There is a legitimate worry that, as with interdisciplinary approaches, unfamiliarity with discipline-centered discourses in transdisciplinary education may share the same problem:

> What tends to happen with such curricula is that disciplines become storehouses containing topics for classroom activities; typically, however, only one part of the disciplinary storehouse is raided while another is systematically ignored.... [T]he 'disciplined' part of the disciplinary tends to fall away, leaving a body of information without the tools for evaluating its quality or warrant. (Wineburg and Grossman, 2000: 13)

This is the 'disciplinary paradox' (Klein, 1990), 'on the one hand, the fragmentation of knowledge into the disciplines leads to the necessity for interdisciplinary approaches, yet, on the other hand, interdisciplinary approaches to knowledge can only receive an epistemic justification for knowledge claims' (Petrie, 1992: 305). Interdisciplinarity faces the 'burden of comprehension', with the disciplines marshaled to study a particular phenomena and the additional responsibility of maintaining intra- and inter-disciplinary standards and confidence (Klein, 1990).

From its inception, two discursive warrants emerged in transdisciplinarity theorizing, 'one highlighting epistemological transcendence and the other problem solving' (Klein, 2014: 69). Commenting on these early attempts to define this new approach to knowledge, Nicolescu notes that Piaget retained only the meanings 'across' and 'between' disciplines to distinguish transdisciplinarity from interdisciplinarity, and proposed the inclusion of the meaning 'beyond disciplines' (Nicolescu, 2010: 18).

This tension between the prepositional metaphors of 'across' and 'above' plays though the transcripts of international proceedings; however, both transdisciplinary positions – 'across' or 'above' narrow disciplinarity – promise to 'transcend' the disciplines 'while at the same time maintaining the advantages of creativity and initiative peculiar to each specific field of knowledge' (Lattanzi, 1998: 13).

As a vision of knowledge, a clear line of argument regarding transcendent transdisciplinarity emerged and is evident in the literature since its inception (Klein, 2014). Nicolescu defined epistemological transdisciplinarity as a holistic conceptual framework that transcends the narrow scope of disciplinary worldviews that '... metaphorically encompass parts of the material fields that disciplines usually handle separately' (Miller, 1982, cited in Klein, 2002a: 50). Following CIRET's manifesto and charter, UNESCO's 1998 symposium positioned transdisciplinarity as a redirection of the object of scientific study 'within the framework of the fundamental unity underlying all forms of knowledge' (Lattanzi, 1998: iv). Less metaphysically, other orientations to transdisciplinarity, framed as a concept or method and focused on collaborative knowledge integration as an approach to problem solving, enjoyed considerable currency at these meetings. In 1997, Yersu Kim, UNESCO's Director Division of Philosophy and Ethics, characterized transdisciplinarity as a happy meeting point of people and minds, an '"intellectual space" where the

concrete daily work of UNESCO has to be rethought in a dimension of "synergy" and "integration" of efforts' (Lattanzi, 1998: iv).

Since its inception, proponents of both warrants have contended that transdisciplinary collaboration is different and more revolutionarily hopeful than interdisciplinary cooperation, arguing that interdisciplinarity is weak in face of the strong institutional pull of disciplinary structures in research and teaching. Transdisciplinary theorists posit that, 'Nearly nothing is known about the question if, how and why interdisciplinary knowledge and competencies are superior to disciplinary knowledge and competencies, be that in understanding the social worlds and/or to act successfully and responsibility in them' (Hedtke, 2006: 3). Such arguments are supported by contentions that disciplinarity and interdisciplinarity produce a lack of coherence and fragmentation of understanding of complex scientific and social problems. Consequently,

> The difference between an interdisciplinary and a transdisciplinary approach is as follows: in the former, disciplines offer a parallel analysis of problems (...); in the latter, disciplines offer their specific approaches and even basic assumptions, to a dialogue, in order to address complex issues together. In the case of transdisciplinarity, approaches and even methods are developed in a joint effort, something, which is indeed difficult in complex societies, but very necessary. (Masini, Pontificia Universita Gregoriana, Italy, cited in Lattanzi, 1998: 33)

The holistic epistemological conceptualization of some proponents of the transdisciplinary project is open to critique. Transdisciplinary theorizing in its contestation with disciplinarity and, to some extent, interdisciplinarity posits that narrow disciplinarity is unable to address complex contemporary scientific and social problems, 'whose solution would at once necessitate and provide a better understanding of reality' (Lattanzi, 1998: 15). The transdisciplinary hope is 'a quest for a wider and deeper knowledge of a compound reality' (Lattanzi, 1998: 15). This transcendental premise that 'a discipline is not constitutive but just instrumental' (Lattanzi, 1998: 15) can be questioned. Transdisciplinary theorizing and, by implication, transdisciplinary curriculum theory and development are rehearsals of classic debates concerning epistemological and ontological holisms. Just as in debates about disciplinarity within curriculum theorizing during this period, transdisciplinarity's holistic transcendental promise is seen by critics as 'utopian' and 'contradictory' (Janz, 2006: 2). Even sympathetic chroniclers of transdisciplinarity note that, 'Campaigns for unified knowledge, transdisciplinary schemes, and holistic thought promote a metaphysical model that is an interrelated conception of the world. Ironically, though, holisms have proved contradictory both within and among themselves…' (Klein, cited in Lattanzi, 1998: 60). The mystical tone and ideological claims within some transdisciplinary theorizing (Janz, 2006: 5–6) have been questioned.

The epistemological status of transdisciplinarity theorists' desire for new forms of collaboration have led its critics to see contradictions in establishing parameters of dialogue and ground rules on which dialogue beyond disciplines should take place. Such conversations are:

> [A]lways rooted in a life-world, and its terms spring from that world. It is not necessarily a negotiation prior to meaningful conversation, but the meaning shows itself forth in the discussion of difference and similarity. It seems that in giving a description of the attitude of transdisciplinarity before the fact, the writers have tried to circumscribe the conversation and, ironically, distance the program from any discussion. (Janz, 2006: 7)

Two contending positions about the perceived unity of knowledge: ontologically transcendental discovery of a common unity in the order of being versus subjective construction of unified subject can be posited (Hadorn, 2002). Consequently, transdisciplinarity can only be entered into by those predisposed to participate in research founded on either claim. This condition of entry implies the adoption of one of two normative claims or hard and soft epistemological conceptions.

TRANSDISCIPLINARITY AS A CONCEPT AND METHOD FOR COLLABORATIVE PROBLEM SOLVING IN RESEARCH

Advocates who foreground problem solving over more transcendent transdisciplinary warrants implicitly draw on social epistemology (Fuller, 1988) and the sociology of late modernity, which describes how knowledge production has changed and is facilitated by new institutional structures that have developed in response to the increasing hybridity and complexity of social life at the beginning of the third millennia (Gibbons et al., 1994). Problem-solving orientated transdisciplinarity theorizing shares concerns about the number of specialized knowledge fields and sub-fields that have proliferated in late modernity (Crane and Small, 1992), especially because traditional disciplinary forms of knowledge production have lost market value and pragmatic research focusing on utility and commercial benefit is now encouraged within neoliberal oriented research institutions (Gibbons et al., 1994). Given the complexity of contemporary life, they argue that the problems facing humanity 'such as water, forced migrations, poverty, environmental crises, violence, terrorism, neo-imperialism, destruction of social fabric' can only be adequately addressed by transdisciplinary approaches to research and education (Max-Neef, 2005). They contend that although technical problems may be solved within disciplines, contemporary social problems require a transdisciplinary approach (Ravetz, 1971).

Transdisciplinarity's advocates (Doty, 1994; Klein and Newell, 1997) argue that the history of interdisciplinarity research teaches that it is crucial to create a 'transdisciplinary attitude' or 'gaze' capable of developing its own modes to enable researchers from different fields to collaborate together to develop new concepts, theories, and methods to solve complex problems. In an effort to facilitate transdisciplinary collaborations, Klein (2008b) suggests an evaluative framework: (1) variability of goals; (2) variability of criteria and indicators; (3) leveraging of integration; (4) interaction of social and cognitive factors in collaboration; (5) management, leadership, and coaching; (6) iteration in a comprehensive and transparent system; and (7) effectiveness and impact. This notion of a transdisciplinary 'common dialogue', based on shared approaches and methods to understand complex systems and problems, emerged at the UNESCO'S 1998 symposium. Again, Klein observes that 'a "transdisciplinary" research team participates in more thorough assimilation of knowledge. [Team members] work together, rather than in a sequential separation, to assimilate their knowledge and perspectives...' (Klein, cited in Lattanzi, 1998: 18).

One response to the pragmatic needs to develop transdisciplinary collaborations for problem solving that is exemplary of the growth in transdisciplinary research and development is the *Handbook of Transdisciplinary Research* (Hoffmann-Riem et al., 2008). Reflecting the European leadership within transdisciplinarity theorizing, this project grew out of the Swiss Academies of Arts and Sciences' capacity-building initiatives over a 40-year period. The handbook provides examples of transdisciplinary research with the aim of identifying some cross-cutting issues around: (1) problem identification and structuring; (2) problem analysis; and (3) bringing results to fruition. The handbook's editors are aware of implicit tension within their project of presenting transdisciplinary research in a paradigmatic manner.

Many reflections on recent transdisciplinary research literature (Lang et al., 2012; Pohl and Hirsch Hadorn, 2008) demonstrate this tension. In illustrating the 'challenges of problem identification, problem structuring, problem analysis' in order to produce

productive solutions, the authors hope to provide grounds for 'systematisation and formalisation' of transdisciplinary research practices (Hoffmann-Riem et al., 2008: 23). These efforts to establish concepts, methods, tools, and standards for research, as well as building a transdisciplinary scientific community and institutions, have the potential to create a new discipline – transdisciplinary studies, which is housed in new transdisciplinary institutions (Whittington, 2011); however, it may be that the centrifugal forces of late modernity will prevent this from happening.

This brief account of transdisciplinarity's origins and definitional tensions may appear somewhat removed from the field of curriculum theorizing. The predominant concerns of transdisciplinarity's proponents, since its inception, were and remain about research. In the intervening years since the 1970s, transdisciplinary research has grown to include emerging social concerns. The breadth of these problems includes climate change and sustainability (Huutoniemi and Tapio, 2014), health sciences (The Third Revolution, 2011), design (Doucet and Janssens, 2011), and human rights and development (Baxi, 2000). Additionally, those engaged in transdisciplinary research are beginning to publish comparative methodological studies in knowledge integration. For example, researchers from the Institute for Social-Ecological Research in Frankfurt, Germany (Bergmann et al., 2012; Jahn et al., 2012), have published accounts of the generative and recursive process of transdisciplinary 'methods, instruments, tools, and strategies that includes hypothesis and model building, integrative assessment procedures, boundary objects and concepts, heuristics, research questions, artifacts, and products, mutual learning, and stakeholder participation' (Klein, 2014).

Philosophers of transdisciplinarity and transdisciplinary researchers were also aware of the connection of research to education, most specifically at the tertiary level. CIRET has proposed 'a new universality of thought and type of education informed by a world-view of complexity in science' (Klein, 2014: 70). Researchers concerned with developing methods to identify and structure problems about transdisciplinary tertiary education suggest a transdisciplinary curriculum where complex problems frame learning, knowledge is unknown or uncertain, the curriculum is set in real world context, it is contested, and there are consequences for learners. They argue for a problem-oriented curriculum where students conceptually, empirically, methodologically and collaboratively engage with and are open to any potentially relevant domain of human knowledge (Hoffmann-Riem et al., 2008). Augsburg nominates what may be termed the curricular attributes of the transdisciplinary student: an orientation to multiple realties and views, risk-taking, transgressive, and creative (Augsburg, 2014).

CONCEPTUALIZING TRANSDISCIPLINARITY IN EDUCATION

Curriculum theorizing has little verticality (pace Pinar, 2007), as Bernstein's sociology of knowledge would suggest. As we have seen, derived from philosophical, ethical, and pragmatic concerns about the production and transfer of knowledge in late modernity, the idea of transdisciplinarity arose at international venues addressing the future of knowledge production in the face of increasing complexity and challenge, especially when institutionally located in universities. As transdisciplinary thinking emerged in curriculum theorizing, definitional tensions developed in its relation to disciplinarity and interdisciplinarity. Consequently, it is no surprise that much transdisciplinary curriculum theorizing arose in tertiary education. As noted, early promoters of transdisciplinarity research were also concerned about education in late modernity (Jantsch, 1970, 1972). Since the 1970s, CIRET and UNESCO have collaborated and initiated several forums encouraging new

models of university education and training; however, Klein observes that,

> [E]xplicit models of [transdisciplinary] education are more recent. Generally speaking, academic programmes tend to be located within discipline-dominated institutions rather than autonomous institutions. Beyond the university, [transdisciplinary] education also occurs in situ, in the workplace and in projects with community stakeholders. There is no systematic compilation of models and practices, but the literature is growing. (Klein, 2008a: 54)

Her examples are predominantly European tertiary transdisciplinary programs. Importantly, she notes that in most tertiary transdisciplinary programs, the disciplines do not disappear.

Tertiary transdisciplinary education has a tense and ambiguous relationship with disciplinarity. Sometimes, transdisciplinarity and interdisciplinarity, valued for their utility, are positioned as enhancing disciplinary education. As discussions of transdisciplinarity shift to issues of education, the positions regarding disciplinarity and interdisciplinarity become even more complicated. As a recent review of EU university partnerships concludes, 'In many cases, strong mono-disciplinary knowledge is the precondition for new cross-cutting knowledge; conversely, interdisciplinary knowledge can contribute to creating the necessary dynamic within the individual fields' (Muravska and Berlin, 2014: 147). Disciplines are integrated to provide students with both the breadth and depth to have 'a contemporary view of disciplines that bridges traditional knowledge and the new developments and skills needed for complex problem solving' (Klein, 2008a: 406). What makes transdisciplinary education different from interdisciplinary education in these cases is that in addition to fostering students' ability to locate and work with pertinent information, to compare and contrast different methods and approaches, to clarify how differences and similarities relate to a designated task, and to generate a synthesis, integrative framework or more holistic understanding of a particular theme, question or problem (Klein, 2002b), transdisciplinary education assists students in 'knowing how to organize and participate in inter- or transdisciplinary processes and projects and knowing how to communicate across academic disciplines and with external stakeholders' (Klein, 2008a: 407). This is accomplished through 'modelling, scenario analysis, systems approaches, integrated risk assessment, group facilitation, and participatory models that foster joint decision making' (Klein, 2008a: 407). Students must learn to orchestrate these transdisciplinary competencies negotiated within problem-oriented collaborations. Klein underscores that the transdisciplinary curriculum engages students beyond the confines of disciplinary expertise to include:

[A] deep understanding of the nature of communities, effective communication, metacognitive skills, and mindsets for engaging in [transdiciplinary] work and study;…the mindsets and metacognitive skills that enable lifelong learning, including critical thinking skills, learning on demand, and self directed learning;…the ability to understand, exploit, and design innovative sociotechnical environments, requiring fluency in using digital media;…the ability to develop, fund, and guide knowledge building communities as contexts of teaching and learning; and …a concern about real world needs, manifested in a willingness to become an engaged citizen. (Klein, 2008a: 408)

Transdisciplinary education has broadened out to include the humanities, the social sciences, technology, professional, and doctoral education. Increasingly, non-European tertiary educationalists have joined the conversation. For example, Canadian university administrators note that the promotion of transdisciplinary collaboration is one of the key challenges facing them as they respond to new trends in graduate education (Carr, 2014). Tertiary transdisciplinary education is promoted as a means of increasing labor force competencies and international competitiveness.

A description of an Australian transdisciplinary teacher education program is illustrative of its spread into professional training

(Paige et al., 2008). In this program, undergraduate primary and lower secondary science and mathematics pre-service teachers engage in professional training with a focus on educating for ecological sustainability. The program's intent is clearly transformative and is informed by futures (Toffler, 1974), placed-based (Gruenewald and Smith, 2008), and problem-based learning (Barrows, 1980). The program designers' desired graduate outcomes include a commitment to social justice and equity, futures thinking, sustainability, education for community living, well-being and relationships development, and professional competence within the knowledge, understandings and dispositions needed for teaching (Paige et al., 2008: 20).

As with other avowedly transdisciplinary programs, students' disciplinary knowledge is important. The program emphasizes 'the need to be "disciplinary" before "transdisciplinary" in the three courses by focusing upon discipline specific aspects and identifying the epistemological commitments for each of the disciplines' (Paige et al., 2008: 27). Their orientation is pragmatic:

[W]hilst learning in context and connecting to students' world views is important,…that you cannot integrate various ways of knowing effectively until differentiation has been accomplished, even if to a limited degree. It is therefore essential that teachers and students be introduced to the various disciplines and their uniqueness, but also how they can complement each other when addressing complex issues. Each discipline contributes important concepts, ways of thinking and working, skills and values that students need to explore to satisfy their curiosity and become informed citizens … (Paige et al., 2008: 20–1)

Students in the program develop holistic systems-style thinking to tackle complex real-world problems, ranging from land rights to the politics of food. The program is taught in a three-course sequence (which was developed and trialed in 2005) that includes specific course modules and assessments, combined with two strands of course work in science, mathematics, and society and environment. They are encouraged to contribute to the solution of local and global issues through its emphasis on inclusive and authentic assessment practices. Topics in the program are developed that build from interdisciplinarity to transdisciplinarity. For example, initial mathematics workshops on measurement and science workshops related to soil are taught as foundation for a study of belonging to a place. Through a series of activities, students are challenged to construct a futures scenario of their place in 50 years time and make suggestions about how to work towards a preferred future. They also use a range of strategies and multimedia tools to generate a pamphlet as part of their summative assessment to demonstrate their use of mathematics and science outside the classroom for engaging with their local environment. Collaboration is fostered through group work and peer evaluation (Paige et al., 2008: 27–30).

TRANSDISCIPLINARITY IN SCHOOLING

Primary and secondary school curricula serve different functions from those of universities, which are oriented towards careers and research. School subjects have broader cognitive, personal, social, cultural, and political goals. The curriculum is notionally organized to reflect generally the disciplinarity of aligned fields of knowledge production; it is a historical and institutional consensus that varies across jurisdictional contexts. The disciplinarily organized curriculum found in most schools facilitates the selection of what is to be taught, constructs teachers' identity and professionalism, and orients students into multiple worlds of knowledge production. School subjects are constitutively interdisciplinary, for example English brings together literary studies, composition, rhetoric; and mathematics and science survey and provide introductions to a range of allied fields. Traditionally, school subjects provide greater specificity and focus on disciplinarity

knowledge as students move from primary to secondary school, but the trend in the organization of school subjects appears to be towards greater curricular differentiation and proliferation (Audigier, 2006; Klein, 2006).

What is disciplinary in any school subject is its general coherence to key determinants. School subjects disciplinarily cohere to sets of topics, concepts, and conceptual relations. They orient students toward a particular mode of knowledge (explaining, interpreting, predicting, etc.), and they introduce procedures to make knowledge, and disciplinary conventions for verifying or judging knowledge claims. Importantly, they induct students into specific dispositions toward various specific forms of thinking, meaning making, and texts. Subjects move students away from commonsensical to more abstracted and specialized ways of knowing as they progress from primary to secondary school.

It is necessary to note that effective teaching is implicitly transdisciplinary. Experienced teachers make transdisciplinary-like connections to other subjects and to the world outside the classroom (Ladwig, 2009; Newmann, 1996). Teachers implicitly and sometimes explicitly signal differences between commonsensical and disciplinary knowledge, and between the disciplinary knowledge of their subject in relation to another. Teachers provide subtle transdisciplinary understandings 'across and between' subjects by describing, explaining, and providing meta-commentary about the key determinants that shape their subject's particularities – 'boundary marking'. Teachers also make 'accountability moves' (Heap, 1997) where they discursively mark out the knowledge and processes for which students are to be held responsible. These are often opportunities for student to infer potentially important distinctions between types of work and assessments across subject-specific curricula. Quite commonly, teachers' transdisciplinary work is accomplished through 'shuttling' (Freebody et al., 2008), which often occurs when teachers begin and end lessons or when they signal a shift in class work during a lesson. Using either anecdote or exposition, teachers provide their students with insights into levels of abstraction and technicality in relation to common sense and disciplinary knowledge. Further, they often accomplish this through recasting students' knowledge and language in more disciplinary appropriate terms in short and long sequences of initiation/response/evaluation sequences of classroom talk (Freebody et al., 2008). Again, this is sometimes done by contrasting what is particularly disciplinary in their subject to that of others.

The tensions between transdisciplinarity and disciplinarity persist through conceptual translation as schooling attempts to conceive and enact a transdisciplinary curriculum. In the cases of tertiary transdisciplinary education presented here, disciplinary knowledge is seen to be foundational, although how much more than in primary and secondary schooling is arguable. Looking at systemic and more modest transdisciplinary innovations in schooling is productive in understanding the problems and possibilities of the various commingling conceptions of transdisciplinarity as epistemological conception of either knowledge discovery or construction, transformational future-oriented practice, or pragmatic choice to responding to complexity in curriculum theorizing.

Announcing a 'big change' in Finnish education, recent news reports (Garner, *The Independent*, 20 March 2015) signal a move in the direction of transdisciplinary curriculum in one of the world's most successful education systems. Characterized as a 'radical' change, Finland is replacing its subject-based curriculum with one organized by 'topic'. Justified by appeals that students need to be better prepared for contemporary life, the traditional division of the high school day will be phased out and replaced by 'phenomenon' teaching. 'For instance, a teenager studying a vocational course might take "cafeteria services" lessons, which would include elements of maths, languages (to help serve foreign customers), writing skills and communication

skills' or 'cross-subject topics such as the European Union – which would merge elements of economics, history (of the countries involved), languages and geography' (2015: n.p.). More emphasis will be placed on collaborative group problem solving and communication skills. Anticipating some reluctance from teachers and administrators, Finnish education will provide professional development, and schools are required to introduce at least one period of 'phenomenon-based teaching' at least once a year, two periods a week in Helsinki. Full adoption of this reform is slated for 2020.

Another systemic reform from the other side of the globe preceded this recent change in Finnish education. Initiated between 1998 and 2001, the Queensland's Department of Education and Training (DET) commissioned the Queensland Longitudinal Study of Teaching and Learning (QSTL) project. The QSTL project researched how issues of pedagogy, assessment, and broader school organization influenced student learning (Lingard and Ladwig, 2001). Australian researchers observed approximately 1000 classrooms to examine the links between classroom practices and improved learning (Lingard et al., 2003). The study's principal finding showed generally low levels in quality pedagogy in Queensland classrooms. The QSTL study formed the basis for two systemic transdisciplinary innovation projects, New Basics and Rich Tasks.

The New Basics Project was trialed in 38 Queensland schools and sought to align curriculum, assessment, and pedagogies (Lingard and Ladwig, 2001). New Basics focused on four themes: life pathways and social futures, multiliteracies and communications media, active citizenship, and environments and technologies. Similar to the Finnish reforms, New Basics was a response to shifts in late-modern identities, technologies, work places, economies, and communities (Education Queensland, 2004a). High quality learning would be achieved through the employment of what was termed 'productive pedagogies', which focused on intellectual quality, connectedness to the world, supportive classroom environments, and the recognition of differences, and were developed from Newmann et al.'s (1996) concept of 'authentic pedagogy' (Lingard et al., 2003).

The Rich Tasks Innovation focused on assessment practices that aligned to student engagement with the New Basics and productive pedagogies (Education Queensland, 2004a, 2004b). They were designed to be the assessable and reportable outcomes of a 3-year curriculum plan. Students would display their understandings, knowledge, and skills through performances in transdisciplinary activities that had an obvious connection to the wide world (Education Queensland, 2004a, 2004b). Students would complete Rich Task assessments at the end of Years 3, 6, and 9. For example, between Years 1 and 3, Rich Tasks would require students to create a webpage, plan a travel itinerary, and develop a personal health plan, adapting collaboratively the task to students' interests and contexts (Matters, 2005).

These initiatives were not realized because of the structures and systems of schools in Queensland. Their failure may be attributable to political factors (Wyse et al., 2013). Some have argued that students' expectations of what is 'real' schooling were not 'necessarily consistent' with the reform (Macdonald et al., 2007), such that responsibility for their failure was placed on systemic and teachers' attachments to disciplinary,

> While on the one hand disciplinary regimes can hold teachers accountable for rich task outcomes through this self and peer surveillance, on the other, rich tasks challenge traditional disciplinary knowledge boundaries with which secondary specialists are comfortable. When engaging with their colleagues, secondary specialists should be ready to relinquish their subject allegiance and position students' holistic learning as central….Ideologically, teachers need to be ready to move from their often longstanding commitments to the primacy of particular subject specialisations at the level of curriculum implementation while also being ready to represent their specialisation in transdisciplinary planning and teaching. (Macdonald, 2003: 250)

In contrast to these Finnish and Queensland examples, a collaborative research study, set in a small public middle school in New York City's Chinatown, which ran from 2000–4, took a novel approach to transdisciplinarity. The innovation project worked with yearly cohorts of sixty 8th grade students, most of them first or second-generation Chinese immigrants. The projects collaborators taught within and across school subjects whilst situating curricula in students' subjectivities as poor urban youth and competent users of computer-based technologies and media. The study's participants became to be seen as 'artful actors within semiotic systems', able to meld disciplinary knowledge with the strategic employment of design adapted to the particular discursive demands of a variety of tasks (Albright et al., 2007b). This innovation combined inquiry into what is disciplinary in the means by which subjects construct knowledge with the skills and understands that emerged in that inquiry to facilitate students' learning and its application to context related problems, for example the representation of Asians in American history and culture. Rather than beginning with presumptions about student learning oriented to beyond the disciplines, the project engaged students in their deconstruction from the inside out.

The project adopted a multiliteracies approach because of its emphasis on the importance of critical language skills and the social semiotics in school subjects (The New London Group, 1996; Cope and Kalantzis, 2000). Multiliteracies provided a framework (Situated Practice, Overt Instruction, Critical Framing, and Transformed Practice) that assisted in learning the tools and 'grammars' for understanding disciplinary meaning-making in order to eventually use that learning to (re)construct powerful texts that act in their world. The innovation positioned students as living in economies and cultures that are 'complex, multiple, and characterized by rapid change, uncertainty, and complexity. The teaching of [multi] literacy is an introduction to semiotic economy where identities, artifacts, texts, and tokens are exchanged in predictable and unpredictable ways' (Luke, 2001: xiii).

In the humanities and science curriculum – and to a smaller extent in mathematics – the innovation introduced new critical perspectives and modes of analysis. To connect the work in different disciplines, the collaborators cobbled together analytical strategies and approaches to do what multiliteracies' pedagogy terms 'critique' and 'design' work. Table 33.1 shows how in a transdisciplinary curriculum, such as this, certain kinds of critique work enable students' competency for design. Drawing heavily upon systemic functional linguistics (Fairclough, 1995a; Halliday, 1994; Martin and Veel, 1998) to think about grammars facilitated students' capacity for design tasks. For instance, work in systemics informed visual critique and design, emphasizing text production and social uses (Kress and van Leeuwen, 1996, 2001). Visual literacy and genre-focused inquiry (Kamler, 2001; Lemke, 2000; Unsworth, 2001) helped students connect what they learned about textuality when representing their learning within and across disciplines (Fairclough, 1995b; Kress and van Leeuwen, 2001; Lemke, 2004; Peim, 1993). An extensive elaboration of the project can be found in Albright et al. (2006), Albright et al. (2007a), Albright et al. (2007b), and Walsh and Albright (2006).

SUMMATION AND CHALLENGE

This chapter has traced the development of transdisciplinarity as a form of curriculum theorizing from its high level origins as a philosophical and pragmatic concern for knowledge production in late modernity to curricular examples from all stages of education. Definitional tensions in what transdisciplinarity means were forged at its inception. Transdisciplinarity contends to be an answer to disciplinarity's inability to access relevant knowledge in the face of increasing social, cultural, economic, political, technical, and ecological complexity and danger. How transdisciplinarity finds or constructs new knowledge is posited as a way of moving 'beyond' disciplines or 'between' and 'across' them but, as transdisciplinarity was translated from research into education, two complications arose. The shift in the transdisciplinary curriculum imaginary along the cline of theorist to practitioner raises problematic issues concerning the importance of foundational disciplinary knowledge, modes of representation, and dispositions taught in university courses to school subjects. Various and competing critiques have also been raised about transdisciplinary in relation to interdisciplinarity. Does it supplant or supplement? From its inauguration, transdisciplinary curriculum theorizing has valued collaboration and transformational learning, but evaluating the quality and accessibility of the learning in transdisciplinary curriculum and pedagogy remains an open question.

The push that transdisciplinarity shares with interdisciplinary is a promise of meaningful integration of knowledge; the pull is the trope that disciplinary boundaries are static (Lyon, 1992). Transdisciplinary shares with interdisciplinarity the argument that academic disciplines and, to a greater extent, school subjects do not have a coherent conceptual structure in terms of a unified body of concepts and interrelationships, and that the separation of conceptual (substantive) and methodological (syntactic) aspects of knowledge may be artificial. Early proponents of transdisciplinarity have argued that disciplinarily focused curriculum reifies formal and frozen abstractions of knowledge, synchronically captured (Phillips, 1987), and yet these positions 'fail to allow for either changing aims and actions *within* a discipline or overlapping aims and actions among disciplines' (Lyon, 1992: 682). This 'two-dimensional' metaphor 'fail[s] to describe adequately the role of language' (Lyon, 1992: 682). As we have seen in these critiques of disciplinarity, what counts as subject matter is fundamentally epistemic, rather than conceived as normative or pragmatically and ethically oriented to pedagogy and learning.

Table 33.1   Connection of critique to design

Transdisciplinary Work	Critique Examples	Design Examples
Critical language work, for example: – nominalization – modality and mood – collocations – ordering	In science, students looked at the use of collocations in texts about penguins. They moved from language analysis to a consideration of how language is used in different science genres.	In humanities, students did argumentative writing about historical events (such as Japanese internment), using nominalization and modality to produce effective academic writing.
Investigating genres and intertextuality, for example: – gaps and silences – construction of authority – register and modality – degree of nominalization – cultural production of texts	In social studies, students considered the gaps and silences in texts around Chinese immigration and exclusionary legislation.	In science, students drew on understandings of position and vectors to design water cycle diagrams. Through these diagrams, students communicated positions about water resource use, through their choices of information, placement of processes, use of size and color, and organization of vectors.
Visual and media grammars, such as: – vectors and positioning in visual texts – anchoring; relation of visuals to print texts	In social studies, students represented ways of reading propaganda from the Spanish-American War. They analyzed the use of vectors and placement of participants in the posters to front certain ideas of war and position the viewer.	
Multimodal work	In humanities and science, students investigated the ways in which textbooks, like online sites, invite particular ways to navigate, and thereby generate particular narratives and ways of reading.	In science, students adapted PowerPoint presentations about plate tectonics to interactive, non-linear websites that could be navigated by readers.
		In social studies, students re-wrote history textbook chapters about Chinese immigration history and racism. Responding to readings from common history texts, they integrated photos, images, and print texts to create paper and online chapters/sites that were critical of dominant representations of the Chinese experience in the United States.

Source: Albright, Walsh, and Purohit, 2007b: 103

The 'structure-of-the-discipline' (Schwab, 1964) has been the principle rationale for curriculum theorizing (Pinar, 1975). There may be a logic to that because disciplines are historical and future-oriented social institutions, with conventions and standards to evaluate and arbitrate. They conserve and change – none are the same and some may differ radically in how they function. Etymologically, discipline derives from words meaning both to teach and to learn (Hoskin and Macve, 1986: 106, cited in Shumway and Messer-Davidow, 1991: 202). Modern disciplines are not arbitrary 'administrative categories' but cosmopolitan communities of practice (Shumway and Messer-Davidow, 1991: 208). Understanding disciplines as social practices can help relate the disciplinary organization of knowledge to other social practices (1991: 211). Disciplinary knowledge in the sciences and humanities in representing the world also intervenes (Fuller, 1988). A discipline has 'an agenda, an attitude, and a language' (Shumway and Messer-Davidow, 1991: 219).

As illustrated here, transdisciplinary curriculum, in similar fashion to inter-, cross-, or multi-disciplinary teaching, is often organized around a topic, issue, period, institution, or place, focusing on a theme rather than on a particular body of knowledge or skill, but the taken-for-granted nature of the discursive formation of any theme may assume that the knowledge exists outside the interactions and contexts that create it. Theme-based transdisciplinary instruction may lead to students learning different bits of information, but they may be left on their own to make sense of these bits. This transdisciplinary curriculum could lead to knowledge learned decoupled from its formation, applications, and dispositions.

What tends to happen with such curricula is that disciplines become storehouses containing topics for classroom activities. Typically, however, only one part of the disciplinary storehouse is raided whilst another is systematically ignored. The 'disciplined' part of the disciplinary tends to fall away, leaving a body of information without the tools for evaluating its quality or warrant (Wineburg and Grossman, (2000: 1). This is the 'disciplinary paradox' (Klein, 1990) – 'on the one hand, the fragmentation of knowledge into the disciplines leads to the necessity for interdisciplinary approaches, yet, on the other hand, interdisciplinary approaches to knowledge can only receive an epistemic justification for knowledge claims' (Petrie, 1992: 305). Interdisciplinarity faces the 'burden of comprehension' with the disciplines marshaled to study a particular phenomena and the additional responsibility of maintaining intra- and inter-disciplinary standards and confidence (Klein, 1990). Transdisciplinary, as well as disciplinary-focused curriculum theorizing, share the same normative issues about the selection of what knowledge is to be taught, which is based implicitly or explicitly on a meta-disciplinary standpoint (Deng

and Luke, 2008). Transdisciplinarity in curriculum theorizing raises questions about normative justifications for curricular innovation and reform. Like much of what enters curriculum theorizing, transdisciplinarity is an appropriation and translation.

The way in which the field appropriates and translates new concepts and their warrants may be somewhat unreflexive. An answer to this problem may be found in Bourdieu's (1984) theoretical and empirical contributions to curriculum studies and his pragmatic recommendations about pedagogical reform. In 1984, responding to Mitterrand's (the first socialist president of France's Fifth Republic) commissioned reports on the future of education, Bourdieu led colleagues (comprised of leading College de France professors) to author a set of guiding principles for educational change. First published as *Proposition pour l'ensignment de l'avenir* (College de France, 1985) and later as the *Principes pour une réflexion sur les contenus d'enseignment* (Bourdieu, 1989), the principles set out to restructure the division of knowledge; provide a new definition of the transmission of knowledge; eliminate outdated or outmoded notions; and introduce 'new knowledge that stems from research as well as economic, technical and social changes' (Bourdieu, 1989: 309).

At the core of these recommendations was the call for a curriculum that focused on the 'genealogy of concepts, ways of thinking, mental structures…to give everyone the means to re-appropriate the structures of their own thinking' (Grenfell and James, 2004: 75). Although *Principes pour une réflexion sur les contenus d'enseignment* (Bourdieu, 1989) may have had little lasting effect on the course of French educational policy, many aspects of Bourdieu's principles for reflecting on the curriculum resonate with the theoretical and practical desires for transdisciplinary education.

Despite being over 25 years old, many students of curriculum theorizing may still find the College de France committee's highly pragmatic and prescient principles quite timely. Written as an introduction to new knowledge stemming from research, and reflective of contemporary economic, technical, and social changes, the principles were not intended to define the ideal content of an ideal curriculum (Bourdieu, 1989). Rather, the principles' curricular ends value explicit teaching, active learning, creativity, critical abilities, and imagination. Eschewing 'haphazard examination' the committee argue for continuous assessment and evaluation of pupil learning with a focus on essential knowledge. They argued for a curriculum that focuses on providing 'the [technologies] of intellectual enquiry' and developing 'rational ways of working' (Bourdieu, 1989: 308), therefore 'reducing inequalities based on cultural inheritance' (1989: 309).

The overarching curricular goals envisioned in these principles will be achieved through regular review of content. A constant re-balancing of the curriculum and pedagogy that reflects the influence of the past and the necessary adaptations to the future is necessary. Any additions to the curriculum must be compensated by a reduction elsewhere. What must be avoided are gaps in curriculum 'where knowledge could be acquired just as efficiently (and sometimes more pleasantly) through other means' (Bourdieu, 1989: 309). The principles argue for clear, well-paced, coherent, progressive, and culturally sensitive curricular objectives. Knowledge taught and learned should be seen to have both vertical and horizontal transdisciplinary connections across the curriculum. Much is made in the principles of the importance of collaboration and teacher autonomy to produce methodological diversity. The principles argue for the flexible and intensive use of learning materials and buildings, organization of the day, and the flexible grouping of pupils (Bourdieu, 1989).

The curriculum envisioned in the principles is implicitly transdisciplinary. Pupils are to be invited to study the 'deductive, experimental, the historical as well as the critical and reflective' fields of human knowledge transmission and production, privileging 'experimental thinking', arguing for 'a

positive reassessment of qualitative reasoning', 'a clear recognition of the temporary nature of explanatory models', and providing pupils with training in 'practical forms of research enquiry' (Bourdieu, 1989: 312).

As noted earlier, Bourdieu argues that across the breadth of the school curriculum, 'techniques or cognitive tools, which are totally indispensible in promoting rigorous and reflective reasoning' (Bourdieu, 1989: 312) should be the focus:

> The opposition between art and science, which continues to dominate the organisation of schooling and the mentality of teachers, pupils, and parents must be surmounted. The curriculum should be capable of addressing simultaneously science and the history of science or epistemology. It should also promote art and literature, and literature, philosophy, and science, but also the active process of logical procedures and rhetoric that engagement with these subjects requires. The apparent abstractness of these areas could be removed if common programmes were developed where the teacher of mathematics (or physics) and teachers of language or philosophy made clear that general competencies were required in the reading of scientific texts, technical briefs or approaches to argument and discourse. A similar effort should be made to articulate the rational, critical thinking mode which all sciences teach, and to ensure that these are based on historical and cultural roots that reflect the range of scientific and cultural knowledge. In this way the pupil will develop a comprehensive respect for diversity in time and space and for civilization, lifestyles, and cultural traditions. (Bourdieu, 1989: 312)

Bourdieu implies in the principles that school subjects are 'interpretations' of disciplines. As such, researchers and teachers must be mindful of the 'logic and traditions of certain specialisms…where they are located in the curriculum' and how each 'contribute[s] to different thought processes' (Bourdieu, 1989: 312). Arguing that the curriculum of the day seldom did this and, when it did, only tacitly, Bourdieu argues that transdisciplinary inquiry where teachers from various subject areas are brought together to collaborate in curriculum design may remedy this absence.

The principles reflect the continental tradition of educational didactics (see chapter 7 on Didactics, this volume.) Didactics is broadly theorized as 'not a normative theory…nor is it descriptive but reflective… an explication of how instructional processes in the institutionalized school may be experienced…useful as a thought model and a research model (Uljens, 1997: v). It may be interesting to English-speaking curriculum theorists to note that didactics is often broadly posited by European researchers as a science that focuses on the institutionally bounded 'diffusion' of knowledge (Chevallard, 1991).

For almost four decades American curriculum theorists and, to some extent, curriculum theory from other English-speaking countries, with the likely exception of that of Basil Bernstein (1999), has been dominated by a reconceptualist theoretical break with an institutional focus on schooling and empiricism. Reconceptualism in Anglo–American curriculum has adopted broad perspectives from a wide range of philosophical, psychoanalytical, aesthetical and ethical standpoints, which runs counter to the didactics 'down-to-earth, realistic point of departure' (Bjerg et al. 1995: 33). Criticism has ranged from its need for greater verticality and disciplinarity (Pinar, 2007) to its loss of scientific authority and marginalization in the field of education (Ladwig, 1996). Consequently, it may be reflexively important in keeping with the Bourdieusian principles that future transdisciplinarity theorizing should be carried out in conversation with the continental didactic tradition.

REFERENCES

Albright, J., Purohit, K. and Walsh, C. (2006) 'Multimodal reading and design in a cross-disciplinary curriculum theorizing', in W. Bokhorst-Heng, M. Osborne, and K. Lee (eds.), *Redesigning Pedagogy: Reflections on Theory and Praxis*. Rotterdam: Sense Publishers. pp. 3–18.

Albright, J., Purohit, K. and Walsh, C. (2007a) 'Hybridity, globalisation and literacy education in the context of New York City', *Pedagogies: An International Journal*, 1(4): 221–42.

Albright, J., Walsh, C. and Purohit, K. (2007b) 'Towards a theory of practice: critical transdisciplinarity multiliteracies', in D. M. McInerney, S. Van Etten and M. Dowson (eds.), *Standards in Education*. Charlotte, NC: Information Age Publishing. pp. 93–118.

Audigier, F. (2006) 'Interdisciplinarity at school: theoretical and practical questions regarding history, geography and civic education', *Journal of Social Science Education*, 5(2): 37–50.

Augsburg, T. (2014) 'Becoming transdisciplinary: the emergence of the transdisciplinary individual', *World Futures*, 70(3–4): 233–47.

Barrows, H. S. (1980) *Problem-Based Learning: An Approach to Medical Education*. New York, NY: Springer.

Baxi, U. (2000) 'Transdisciplinarity and transformative praxis', in M. Somerville and D. Rapport (eds.), *Transdisciplinarity: Recreating Integrated Knowledge*. Oxford: Encyclopedia of Life Support Systems. pp. 77–85.

Bergmann, M., Jahn, T., Knobloch, T., Krohn, W., Pohl, C. and Schramm, E. (2012) *Methoden transdisziplinarer forschung: Ein uberblick mit anwendungsbeispielen. [Methods for Transdisciplinary Research: A Primer for Practice]*. Frankfurt: Campus Verlag.

Bernstein, B. (1999) 'Vertical and horizontal discourse: an essay', *British Journal of Sociology of Education*, 20(2): 157–73.

Bjerg, J., Callewaert, S., Elle, B., Mylov, P., Nissen, T., & Silberbrandt, H. (1995) 'Danish Education, Pedagogical Theory in Denmark and in Europe, and Modernity', *Comparative Education*, 31(1): 31–47.

Bourdieu, P. (1984) *Distinction: A Social Critique of the Judgment of Taste*. Cambridge, MA: Harvard University Press.

Bourdieu, P. (1989) 'Principles for reflecting on the curriculum', *The Curriculum Journal*, 1(3): 307–14.

Carr, G. (2014) 'Promoting research and graduate studies in the university of the future: the roles of deans and vice-presidents', in C. Scholz and V. Stein (eds.), *The Dean in the University of the Future*. Munich: Rainer Hampp Verlag. pp. 41–51.

Chevellard, Y. (1991) *La Transposition Didactique – Du Savoir Savant au Savoir Enseigné*, 2nd edn. Grenoble: La Pensée Sauvage.

College de France (1985) *Proposition pour l'enseignement de l'avenir (Commision Bourdieu-Gros)*. Paris: Documentation Française.

Cope, B. and Kalantzis, M. (eds.) (2000) *Multiliteracies: Literacy Learning and the Design of Social Futures*. New York, NY: Routledge.

Crane, D. and Small, H. (1992) 'American sociology since the seventies: the emerging identity crisis', in T. C. Halliday and M. Janowitz (eds.), *Sociology and Its Publics: The Forms and Fates of Disciplinary Organization*. Chicago: University of Chicago Press. pp. 197–234.

Deng, Z. and Luke, A. (2008) 'Subject matter: defining and theorizing school subjects', in F. M. Connelly, M. F., He and J. A. Phillion (eds.), *The SAGE Handbook of Curriculum and Instruction*. Thousand Oaks, CA: Sage Publications. pp 66–87.

Dewey, J. (1938) *Logic: The Theory of Inquiry*. New York: Holt, Rinehart and Winston.

Doty, W. G. (1994) *Interdisciplinary Studies Today*. San Francisco: Jossey-Bass.

Doucet, I. and Janssens, N. (2011) 'Editorial: transdisciplinarity, the hybridization of knowledge production and space-related research', in I. Doucet and N. Janssens (eds.), *Transdisciplinary Knowledge Production in Architecture and Urbanism: Towards Hybrid Modes of Inquiry*. Dordrecht: Springer. pp. 1–14.

Education Queensland (2004a) *New Basics: Rich Tasks*. Brisbane: Queensland Department of Education (Assessment and New Basics Branch). Available from http://www.qtu.asn.au/files/8713/2268/2363/vol21_matters.pdf (accessed 28 July 2015).

Education Queensland (2004b) *The New Basics Research Report*. Available from http://education.qld.gov.au/corporate/newbasics/html/research/research.htm (accessed 6 December 2014).

Fairclough, N. (1995a) *Critical Discourse Analysis: The Critical Study of Language*. New York, NY: Longman.

Fairclough, N. (1995b) *Media Discourse*. London: Edward Arnold.

Freebody, P., Maton, K. and Martin, J. R. (2008) 'Talk, text, and knowledge in cumulative, integrated learning: a response to "intellectual challenge"', *Australian Journal of Language and Literacy*, 31(2): 188.

Fuller, S. (1988) *Social Epistemology*. Bloomington, IN: Indiana University Press.

Garner, R. (2015) 'Finland schools: subjects scrapped and replaced with "topics" as country reforms its education system', *The Independent*, 20 March 2015 . Available from http://www.independent.co.uk/news/world/europe/finland-schools-subjects-are-out-and-topics-are-in-as-country-reforms-its-education-system-10123911.html (accessed 30 March 2015).

Gibbons, M., Limoges, C., Nowotny, H., Schwartzman, S., Scott, P. and Trow, M. (1994) *The New Production of Knowledge: The Dynamics of Science and Research in Contemporary Societies*. London: Sage Publications.

Grenfell, M. and James, D. (2004) 'Change in the field – changing the field: Bourdieu and the methodological practice of educational research', *British Journal of Sociology of Education*, 25(4): 507–23.

Gruenewald, D. A. and Smith, G. A. (eds.) (2008) *Place-Based Education in the Global Age: Local Diversity*. New York, NY: Lawrence Erlbaum Associates.

Hadorn, G. H. (2002) 'Unity of knowledge in transdisciplinary research for sustainability', in *Encyclopedia of Life Support Systems*. Oxford: Encyclopedia of Life Support Systems.

Halliday, M. A. K. (1994) *An Introduction to Functional Grammar*. 2nd edn. London: Edward Arnold.

Heap, J. L. (1997) 'Conversation analysis methods in researching language and education', in N. H. Hornberger and D. Corson (eds.), *Encyclopedia of Language and Education. Vol. 8: Research Methods in Language and Education*. Amsterdam: Kluwer Academic. pp. 217–25.

Hedtke, R. (2006) 'The social interplay of disciplinarity and interdisciplinarity. Some introductory remarks', *Journal of Social Science Education*, 5(4): 1–9.

Hoffmann-Riem, H., Biber-Klemm, S., Grossenbacher-Mansuy, W., Joye, D., Pohl, C., Wiesmann, U. and Zemp, E. (eds.) (2008)

Handbook of Transdisciplinary Research. Zurich: Springer.

Hoskin, K. W. and Macve, R. H. (1986), 'Accounting and the examination: a genealogy of disciplinary power', *Accounting, Organizations and Society*, 11(2): 105–136.

Huutoniemi, K. and Tapio, P. (eds.) (2014) *Transdisciplinary Sustainability Studies: A Heuristic Approach*. New York, NY: Routledge.

Jahn, T., Bergmann, M., and Keil, F. (2012) 'Transdisciplinarity: between mainstreaming and marginalization', *Ecological Economics*, 79: 1–10.

Jantsch, E. (1970) 'Inter- and transdisciplinary university: a systems approach to education and innovation', *Policy Sciences*, 1: 403–28.

Jantsch, E. (1972) 'Towards interdisciplinarity and transdisciplinarity in education and innovation', in G. Berger, A. Briggs and G. M. L. Apostel (eds.), *Interdisciplinarity. Problems of Teaching and Research in Universities*. Paris: Organization for Economic Co-operation and Development. pp. 97–121.

Janz, B. B. (2006) *Transdisciplinarity as a Model of Post/Disciplinarity*. Available from https://pegasus.cc.ucf.edu/~janzb/papers/transdisciplinarity.pdf 'Integration, evaluation and disciplinarity'.

Kamler, B. (2001) *Relocating the Personal: A Critical Writing Pedagogy*. Albany, NY: State University of New York Press.

Kilpatrick, W. (1918) 'The project method', *The Teachers College Record*, 19(4): 319–335.

Klein, J. T. (1990) *Interdisciplinarity: History, Theory, and Practice*. Detroit, MI: Wayne State University Press.

Klein, J. T. (2002a) 'Integration, evaluation and disciplinarity', in M. A. Sommerville and D. J. Rapport (eds.), *Transdisciplinarity: Recreating Integrated Knowledge*. Montreal: McGill-Queen's Press. pp. 49–51.

Klein, J. T. (2002b) 'Introduction: interdisciplinarity today: who? what? and how?', in J.T. Klein (ed.), *Interdisciplinary Education in K-12 and College: A Foundation for K-16 Dialogue*. New York, NY: The College Board. pp. 1–17.

Klein, J. T. (2006) 'A platform for a shared discourse of interdisciplinary education', *Journal of Social Science Education*, 5(4): 10–18.

Klein, J. T (2008a) 'Education', in H. Hoffmann-Riem, S. Biber-Klemm, W. Grossenbacher-Mansuy, D. Joye, C, Pohl, U. Wiesmann and E. Zemp, (eds.), *Handbook of Transdisciplinary Research*. Zurich: Springer. pp. 399–410.

Klein, J. T. (2008b) 'Evaluation of interdisciplinary and transdisciplinary research: a literature review', *American Journal of Preventive Medicine*, 35(2): S116–23.

Klein, J. T. (2014) 'Discourses of transdisciplinarity: looking back to the future', *Futures*, 63: 68–74.

Klein, J. T. and Newell, W. (1997) 'Interdisciplinary studies', in J. G. Gaff and J. L. Ratcliff (eds.), *Handbook of the Undergraduate Curriculum: A Comprehensive Guide to the Purposes, Structures, Practices, and Change*. San Francisco, CA: Jossey-Bass. pp. 393–415.

Kress, G. and van Leeuwen, T. (1996) *Reading Images: The Grammar of Visual Design*. London: Routledge.

Kress, G. and van Leeuwen, T. (2001) *Multimodal Discourse: The Modes and Media of Contemporary Communication*. London: Oxford University Press.

Ladwig, J. G. (1996) *Academic Distinctions: Theory and Methodology in the Sociology of School Knowledge*. New York, NY: Routledge.

Ladwig, J. G. (2009) 'Working backwards towards curriculum: on the curricular implications of Quality Teaching', *The Curriculum Journal*, 20(3): 271–86.

Lang, D. J., Wiek, A., Bergmann, M., Stauffacher, M., Martens, P., Moll, P. and Thomas, C. J. (2012) 'Transdisciplinary research in sustainability science: practice, principles, and challenges', *Sustainability Science*, 7(1): 25–43.

Lattanzi, M. (1998) Transdisciplinarity: Stimulating Synergies, Integrating Knowledge. Paris: UNESCO. Available from http://unesdoc.unesco.org/images/0011/001146/114694eo.pdf (Accessed 10 September 2010).

Lemke, J. (2000) *Multimedia Genres for Science Education and Scientific Literacy*. Available from http://www-personal.umich.edu/~jaylemke/webs/nasa/Davis-NASA.htm (Accessed 5 February 2015).

Lemke, J. (2004) The literacies of science. in S. E Wendy, *Crossing borders in literacy and science instruction: Perspectives on theory and practice*. Newark, NJ: International Reading Association, 33–47.

Lingard, B. and Ladwig, J. (2001) *The Queensland School Reform Longitudinal Study.* Brisbane: Education Queensland. Available from http://trove.nla.gov.au/version/44996064 (accessed 30 March 2015).

Lingard, B., Hayes, D., Mills, M. and Christie, P. (2003) *Leading Learning.* Maidenhead, UK: Open University Press.

Luke, A. (2001) 'Foreword', in E. B. Moje and D. G. O'Brien (eds.), *Constructions Of Literacy: Studies of Teaching and Learning In and Out of Secondary Schools.* Mahwah, NJ: Lawrence Erlbaum. pp. ix–xiii.

Lyon, A. (1992) 'Interdisciplinarity: giving up territory', *College English,* 54(6): 681–93.

Macdonald, D. (2003) 'Rich task implementation: modernism meets postmodernism', *Discourse*, 24(2): 247–62.

Macdonald, D., Hunter, L. and Tinning, R. (2007) 'Curriculum construction: a critical analysis of rich tasks in the recontextualisation field', *Australian Journal of Education*, 51(2): 112–28.

Martin, J. R., and Veel, R. (eds.) (1998) *Reading Science: Critical and Functional Perspectives on Discourses of Science.* New York, NY: Routledge.

Matters, G. (2005) *Good data, bad news, good policy making...* Melbourne, ACER. Available from http://research.acer.edu.au/research_conference_2005/5 (accessed 30 March 2015).

Max-Neef, M. A. (2005) 'Foundations of transdisciplinarity', *Ecological Economics*, 53(1): 5–16.

Miller, R. (1982) 'Varieties of interdisciplinary approaches in the social sciences', *Issues in Integrative Studies*, 1: 1–37.

Muravska, T. and Berlin, A. (2014) 'The EU–Eastern Partnership Countries: association agreements and transdisciplinarity in studies, training and research', *Baltic Journal of European Studies*, 4(2): 134–49.

New London Group (1996) 'A pedagogy of multiliteracies: designing social futures', *Harvard Educational Review*, 66(1): 60–92.

Newmann, F. M. (1996) *Authentic Achievement: Restructuring Schools for Intellectual Quality.* San Francisco, CA: Jossey-Bass.

Newman, M. (2003) *The designs of academic literacy: A multiliteracies examination of academic achievement.* Westport, CT: Bergen and Garvey.

Nicolescu, B. and Morin, E. (1994, November) 'Charter of Transdisciplinarity'. In *First World Congress on Transdisciplinarity.* Portugal: Convento de Arrabida.

Nicolescu, B. (2000) *Manifesto of Transdisciplinarity* [trans. K. Claire Voss]. Albany, NY: State University of New York Press.

Nicolescu, B. (2010) 'Methodology of transdisciplinarity: levels of reality, logic of the included middle and complexity', *Transdisciplinary Journal of Engineering and Science*, 1: 17–32.

Paige, K., Lloyd, D. and Chartres, M. (2008) 'Moving towards transdisciplinarity: an ecological sustainable focus for science and mathematics pre-service education in the primary/middle years', *Asia-Pacific Journal of Teacher Education*, 36(1): 19–33.

Peim, N. (1993) *Critical Theory and the English Teacher: Transforming the Subject.* New York, NY: Routledge.

Petrie, H. G. (1992) 'Interdisciplinary education: are we faced with insurmountable opportunities?', *Review of Research in Education*, 18: 299–333.

Phillips, D. C. (1987) *Philosophy, Science and Social Inquiry: Contemporary Methodological Controversies in Social Science and Related Applied Fields of Research.* Oxford: Pergamon Press.

Pinar, W. F. (1975) *Curriculum Theorizing: The Reconceptualists.* Berkeley, CA: McCutchan Publishing Corporation.

Pinar, W. F. (2007) *Intellectual Advancement Through Disciplinarity: Verticality and Horizontality in Curriculum Studies.* Rotterdam: Sense Publishers.

Pohl, C. and Hirsch Hadorn, G. (2008) 'Methodological challenges of transdisciplinary research', *Natures Sciences Sociétés*, 16(2): 111–21.

Ravetz, J. R. (1971) *Scientific Knowledge and Its Social Problems.* Oxford: Clarendon Press.

Schwab, J. J. (1964) 'The structure of the disciplines: meanings and significances', in G. W. Ford & L. Pugno (eds.), *The Structure of Knowledge and the Curriculum.* Chicago: Rand McNally, pp. 1–30.

Shumway, D. R. and Messer-Davidow, E. (1991) 'Disciplinarily: an introduction', *Poetics Today*, 12(2): 201–25.

Tanner, D. (1971) 'Evaluation and modification of the comprehensive curriculum', *The High School Journal*, 54(5): 312–20.

Tanner, D. and Tanner, L. (1990) *History of School Curriculum.* New York, NY: Macmillan.

The Third Revolution (2011) *The Convergence of the Life Sciences, Physical Sciences, and Engineering*. Washington, DC: MIT Press. Available from web.mit.edu/dc/Policy/MIT%20White%20Paper%20on%20Convergence.pdf (30 March 2015).

Toffler, A. (1974) *Learning for Tomorrow: The Role of the Future in Education*. New York, NY: Vintage Books/Random House.

Uljens, M. (1997) *Didactics and Learning*. New York, NY: Psychology Press.

UNESCO (n.d.) *Education for Sustainable Development Program*. Available from http://www.unescobkk.org/index.php?id=4237 (accessed 4 November 2014).

Unsworth, L. (2001) *Teaching Multiliteracies across the Curriculum: Changing Contexts of Text and Image in Classroom Practice*. Philadelphia, PA: Open University Press.

Walsh, C. and Albright, J. (2006) 'Re-envisioning teacher education in the new media age: multiliteracies, multimodality and Internet communication technologies', in J. Gray (ed.), *Making Teaching Public: Reforms in Teacher Education: Proceedings of the 2006 Australian Teacher Education Association National Conference*. ATEA, Australia. pp. 389–98.

Whittington, R. (2011) 'The practice turn in organization research: towards a disciplined transdisciplinarity', *Accounting, Organizations and Society*, 36(3): 183–6.

Wineburg, S. and Grossman, P. (2000) *Interdisciplinary Curriculum: Challenges to Implementation*. New York: Teachers College Press.

Wyse, D., Baumfield, V., Egan, D., Gallagher, C., Hayward, L., Hulme, M., Leitch, R., Livingston, K., Menter, I. and Lingard, B. (2013) *Creating the Curriculum*. London: Routledge.

34

Language Policies and Planning for English Education in Post-Olympic China

Lin Pan

LANGUAGE SPREAD IN THE AGE OF GLOBALIZATION

Globalization penetrates cultures and transforms localities, and the cultural impact of globalization on locality has become the topic of intense debate among scholars. First, there is the 'homogenization' point of view, which claims that there is an ever-greater global uniformity of lifestyles, cultural forms and behavioural patterns, in which the American culture of consumerism constitutes the dominant centre (Barber, 1995; Ritzer, 2000, 2006). To counter-argue against this 'homogenization' view, many other scholars (Appadurai, 1996; Giddens, 1990, 2000; Massey, 1994) have contended that globalization is not a one-way flow: it does not impact the whole world to an equal extent; rather, a dialectical process is involved in that local happenings may shape the global flow. Based on this understanding, some scholars, such as Giddens (2000) and Tomlinson (1999), argue that globalization actually means greater

diversity, and that cultural heterogenization has emerged and local cultures are strengthened. Appadurai (1996), Robertson (1995) and Pieterse (2004) argue that the discussion of globalization should transcend the polarities of homogenization and heterogenization because syntheses of cultures often emerge through the ever-increasing contacts between the global and the local. As Robertson (1995: 27) asserted, 'it is not a question of either awareness of both their home country and homogenization or heterogenization, but rather of the ways in which both of these two tendencies have become features of life across much of the late-twentieth-century world'. Hence, cultural homogenization and heterogenization are seen as happening simultaneously, making localities seemingly different from each other. This process is a result of the hybridization of culture (Wyse et al., 2012).

Pieterse (2004) writes extensively on the topic of hybridization. He defines cultural hybridization as the mixing of Asian, African,

American and European cultures, and uses the term 'global mélange' to describe this long-term global intercultural penetration. In his discussion of the 'global mélange', he argues that no matter what terms (for example, 'cre-olization', 'mestizaje' or 'the orientalization of the world') are used to describe global hybridization, what is often missing in the discussion is its differential impact on different localities and an acknowledgement of the actual unevenness, asymmetry and inequality of global relations. What Pieterse has indicated is that the process of globalization is a localizing one, in which different societies appropriate the materials of modernity differently due to their varied historical, cultural and social conditions. Similarly, Appadurai (1990) described the actual form of cultural globalization as deeply historical and uneven, and advocated a deep study of specific geographies, histories and languages undergoing this process. Appadurai (1990) urged that a sense of locality must be maintained in the examination and understanding of all aspects of our everyday life. This chapter is therefore going to focus on one case, China, with its range of local and global contexts.

According to the hybridization view, the global and the local are always 'intertwined' and 'mutually constitutive', that is, 'local actions shape global flows, while global processes, in turn, mould local actions' (Swyngedouw, 1997: 137). However, what I want to emphasize here is that this type of mutual influence does not happen in a random way, and it should be viewed as a rational process of deterritorialization (delo-cation) and reterritorialization (relocation). According to Tomlinson (2007), deterritori-alization means that a culture or a language is no longer 'tied' to the constraints of local circumstances in terms of physical envi-ronment, ethnic boundaries and delimiting practices. He also carefully points out that this does not simply mean a loss of culture or language because localities also thrive in globalization through a process of reterrito-rialization. Deterritorialization and reterrito-rialization, when taken together, may have

a number of different consequences, either negative (with respect to emotions, social relations and cultural identity) or positive (for example, a demand for a new sensibility of cultural openness, human mutuality and global ethical responsibility).

In terms of language spread, the processes of deterritorialization (delocation) and reter-ritorialization (relocation) also apply. In other words, when a language (for example, English as used in England) travels to a new place, it is delocated out of its original cir-cumstances (England) and superimposed on another native language and culture. It becomes a 'deterritorialized' language in that, in the process of spread, the language travels to and across places that are often structurally, historically and culturally dif-ferent. Consequently, when English arrives at a different location, it will be understood, learnt and appreciated differently as part of an active reterritorialization process. This pro-cess involves the relocation (reterritorializa-tion) of values, functions and even language forms. For example, English in Singapore, Hong Kong or South Africa is perceived as having developed as different or distinct vari-eties of English because the language, when it travels to these places, is filtered differently in accordance with the particularities of the places. We therefore see local variations of English with their relocated forms, functions and values around the world. In a reverse way, as pointed out by Blommaert (2005), once the 'global' resource has gained 'the official and the civil permit' to settle down, it will gradually affect the 'local' economies and cultures and have an impact on locally valid patterns of functions, value attribution systems and distribution of resources.

When the notion is applied in the field of language education, the traditional way of viewing language spread or distribution as 'natural', ahistorical and apolitical seems inadequate. People's perceptions about lan-guages are constructed, reproduced and manifested in their discourses differently at various levels, either in government poli-cies and institutional or non-institutional discourses or exhibited in various other forms in social life. That is why attitudes towards global English vary greatly across the world and why some countries view English as a 'natural, neutral and beneficial' language (McCrum et al., 2002) whilst others view its spread as linguistic imperialism and learning English as linguistic genocide (Phillipson and Skutnabb-Kangas, 1995, 1996). I suggest that in discussing the local politics of global English, two general scales need to be taken into account. One scale can be seen as that of globalization from above, which is often manifested as state governance and state hegemony in language policies. Another scale is that of globalization from levels below the state, which shows how agentive powers react to or resist hegemony. Later in this chapter I will endeavour to explore language ideology issues by investigating the discourse from the upper level – the foreign language education policies of China.

Block and Cameron (2002) puts forward the relationship of globalization and language education in the following words:

> Global communication requires not only a shared channel (like the internet or video conferencing) but also a shared linguistic code. For many participants in global exchanges, the relevant code(s) will have been learned rather than natively acquired. In many contexts, then, the 'intensification of worldwide social relations' also intensifies the need for members of global networks to develop competence in one or more additional languages, and/or to master new ways of using languages they know already. At the same time, globalization changes the condition in which language learning and language teaching take place. (Block and Cameron, 2002: 1–2)

Issues regarding globalization in language education in many countries are closely related to the global domination of English, resulting from its status as a former colonial language and now a global language. Nevertheless, language education can benefit from an enhanced understanding of the dialectic between the global and the local, and from an understanding that the local ideologies of English are not just imposed, but are constructed through local discourses at different levels of society.

In the new millennium, English language education in China has also been marked by a transition from a context of liberation to one of globalization (Bolton, 2006; Zheng and Davison, 2008). English has been formally introduced and promoted as part of the school curriculum in modern language education in China as a result of the country's modernization and internationalization and is embraced in China by the public in general; therefore it is worth examining the foreign language education policies in China in the context of globalization from a local perspective.

LANGUAGE POLICIES AND PLANNING WITH REGARD TO ENGLISH IN CHINA

The status of English in Chinese society has changed at an incredible speed in the last century and a half (Pan, 2014, 2015). In China, modern history, politics and international relations with Western countries formerly defined English as 'a barbarian language' in the late 1840s, 'the language of our enemies' in the 1960s and 'a language which brings spiritual pollution' in the 1970s and 80s, and until the late 1970s English had no serious practical value to most people in China (Pan, 2014, 2015). At a more recent stage in history, before and during the 1980s, the acquisition of the skills of English would be seen as showing disloyalty to the political system, and listening to BBC English programmes was regarded as a crime of espionage (Qu, 2012). However, in the last three decades China has been undergoing rapid changes, one of the most astonishing and phenomenal has been the embrace and promotion of English in schooling. Particularly in the last decade, the learning of English has become a national endeavour, with the school English curriculum permeating schools from kindergarten to university entrance, and private English language schools booming (Niu and Wolff, 2003).

With over 400 million school or after-school English learners in China[1], the continuous popularization of the English language, alongside China's emergence as a world power, has evoked enormous changes in ideology and posed intriguing ideological questions. The same is true globally. The global spread of English is a phenomenon whose causes and effects continue to be widely debated (Pan, 2015), and this phenomenon is taken into account by policymakers worldwide. How they do so varies considerably, depending on the political and sociolinguistic situation of individual countries and on how English is perceived – as a threat to linguistic diversity and the vitality of national languages, as a means of accessing technological knowledge, as a useful lingua franca, or all of these simultaneously. However, according to Ferguson (2006, 2010), in the majority of instances national governments, even those like France which are historically the most anxious about the spread of English, have felt obliged to accommodate their language education policies to the massive popular demand for English language skills, illustrating in the process the limited control that the makers of language policy can exert over the dynamics of language spread.

Although English is generally embraced around the world as a global language, it is particularly significant to investigate the issue of English language education in China because Chinese is the language spoken by the greatest number of people in the world and English is the most widely spoken language in the world. The issue is even more important in view of the swift and significant changes in the status of English in China's history. The overarching questions to be investigated in this chapter are: what role does English play in language planning and language policies in China? And what are the ideologies embedded in the current language policies?

This chapter hopes to unpack the state ideologies of languages in post-Olympic China by investigating how the teaching and learning of English was presented in a new language policy document – the 2011 version of the *English Curriculum Standards at Compulsory Education Stage* – hereafter 2011

ECS (Ministry of Education (MOE), 2012) in comparison with its predecessor – the 2003 trial version. The extracts from syllabus discussed in this chapter were translated by the author and proofread by a certified translator. It is to be noted that I choose the language policy of the period of post-Olympic China because it is newly issued and the most up-to-date foreign language education policy, and includes the most authoritative guidelines that reflect the changes in policymakers' fundamental assumptions about the nature, functions and processes of language teaching and learning. These assumptions will be the guiding principles that will be widely promoted and implemented over the next few years nationwide, and the basis and guidelines for updating language policies at other levels of English teaching in China.

Language planning in China has always been done by groups of education specialists commissioned by the MOE in a top–down manner, and language policies are of paramount importance as guiding principles to be followed by schools and teachers. Taking the *English Curriculum Standards at Compulsory Education Stage (2003 trial version)*[2] as an example, since its implementation almost all primary and junior high schools and about 80 per cent of senior high schools were using the new standards by September 2009 (Cheng, 2011). This marks English as the most widely learned and used foreign language in China, which is the state in the world that has the greatest number of English learners. Cheng (2011), a major expert amongst the education specialists who drafted the *English Curriculum Standards (2003 trial version)*, explains that the underlying ideology behind the promotion of learning English is that English enables China to strengthen its economy and participate in international affairs more effectively; it enables the Chinese people to have an international vision in research and development and to contribute to the development of the country; and because it is a global language, it is an important medium for communication with other countries.

However, the past decade has witnessed tremendous social and economic changes in the modern world system, and the rise of China as the world's second largest economic entity and an important international player has made it necessary for China to reconsider its language education policies. It was against this background that the new ECS for the compulsory education stage (age 6–15) was announced in 2011 and it was to be implemented in place of the 2003 version. It can be predicted that based upon the principles and ideologies of the new ECS, language policies above the compulsory stage – that is, at the senior high school and tertiary education levels – will be promulgated and announced soon (Pan, 2015).

The 2011 version of the ECS (MOE, 2012) was a revision based on the previous curriculum standards, which were the guiding principles for English education in China at the compulsory stage (age 6–15). This new version of ECS further highlights the significance of English to the development of both the students and the state. It clearly emphasizes the instrumental and humanistic nature of English education in the curriculum, underlines the goal that students should cultivate comprehensive English ability and fulfil self-development (of values, characters and learning ability) and accentuates that learning English is a way to help retain and promote China's language and culture in the globalizing world (Cai, 2014).

THE TEACHING AND LEARNING OF ENGLISH AS PRESENTED IN THE 2011 ECS

The new ECS starts with an overall introduction of rationales for the teaching and learning of English and it states its aims and objectives. It then points out five aspects that the teaching of English should cover: students' linguistic skills, linguistic knowledge, emotional attitude, learning strategies and cultural awareness. The teaching of linguistic skills includes listening, speaking, writing and reading skills; linguistic knowledge points to knowledge of phonology, grammar and semantics in general. These two aspects are regarded as the basis for good language competence (Byram and Risager, 1999). In discussing learning strategies, the ECS points out that students should be trained to develop cognitive, management, and communication and resources strategies to make their learning more effective. In addition, ECS suggests that positive emotions and attitudes play a decisive role in helping students implement learning strategies, and that cultural awareness may also play an important role in facilitating language learning. The next section will explore some of these statements in the 2011 ECS and investigate the role of English in the language policy in post-Olympic China and how the Chinese state processes the English language – the global material in its education system for its own purpose of meeting the needs of globalization and internationalization.

General Aims and Objectives

The new ECS reflects the state ideologies of language education in China in the coming years and sheds new lights on the status of English and the objectives of teaching it. Concerning the status of English, it states that:

> The world today is undergoing great transformation and development. This can be seen from its multipolar global trend, its economic globalization and its informatization of social life. China is a big and peaceful country and is shouldering an important historical mission, international responsibility and obligation. English as one of the most widely spoken languages used in the world has become an important tool for international communication, science and cultural exchanges. (MOE, 2012: 1)

This statement opens with a claim that we are in a transforming world. It recognizes that all countries are interconnected and play important parts in a multipolar global scene, with economic globalization and the informatization of social life. It also highlights the role of China in the world, and points to English as 'an important tool' that enables China to communicate and play an important role in the world. This pragmatic role of English laid out in the new ECS is in contrast to previous eras when English was associated with imperialism and colonialism in the nineteenth century; when until the late nineteenth century the learning of English was encouraged by the state as a means to resist imperialism; and when after the People's Republic of China had been founded in 1949, it was used to serve nation-building and state-consolidation. Since then, the role accorded to English has been transformed again and is now supported as a modern language with significant social, economic and political value (Pan, 2011).

Essentially, the ECS recognizes that the world is changing economically, including the advancement of technologies. In this modern world system, the positions of states are being transformed. The world is no longer single-centred. At the state level, China recognizes itself as a large and peaceful country, and therefore believes that it shoulders important responsibilities. The instrumental role of English is pointed out as a resource for China's communication and participation with the world and its affairs. It can be seen that in the 2011 ECS, the pragmatic ideology of the usefulness of English remains one of the objectives of learning English (Pan, 2011). At the same time, the humanistic nature of the study of English is put forward and highlighted:

> The English course at compulsory education stage has both instrumental and humanistic natures. The instrumental nature means that the English course should improve the students' basic English competence and develop their thinking. That is, students should gain knowledge of the English language and develop their skills of listening, speaking and writing. They should be able to communicate with others in English and improve their thinking. This will lay a foundation for the continued learning of English and other subjects via English. The humanistic nature of the English course refers to the mission that it carries to improve the overall quality of the students, help formulate their cross-cultural awareness, strengthen their patriotism and abilities to innovate and form correct personalities, a world outlook and value system. Together the instrumental and humanistic nature of the English course can help lay a good foundation for the students' lifelong development. (MOE, 2012: 2)

The embedded ideology expressed is that English is a practical 'tool', and that learning English should strengthen students' patriotism and enable the use of English to spread Chinese culture. This is in line with the previous version published in 2003. I recently argued (Pan, 2011) that the way that English language education is prescribed as a tool for cultivating patriotism and spreading Chinese culture is a way for the state to conduct cultural governance. This is because our identity is constructed by the language(s) we use, and, in turn, our language use is in one way or another regulated by language policy (Blommaert, 2006). We may therefore suggest that the state, by underscoring the necessity of cultivating patriotism and promoting Chinese culture via English education, may be contending that within the trend of cultural globalization, individuals' identities can be constructed and reconstructed only by developing their global cultural consciousness, and that the state's governance can be reinforced and strengthened via English Language Teaching (ELT). The assumption may be that this way of prescribing 'culture' in the ECS will help students to cultivate a sense of 'interculturality' (Kramsch, 1993, cited in McKay, 2009) through the learning process and will facilitate students' reflections on their own culture(s) (Pan, 2011). The extract from the ECS discussed previously elevates the importance of culture and cultural issues to the humanistic dimension of teaching, and reflects how the Chinese state deals with the cultural connotations embedded in the English language. The 2011 ECS (MOE, 2012) therefore retains the previous connotation of the importance of teaching culture and the ways to address culture in language teaching.

Language skills and knowledge

The 2011 ECS defines language skills and language knowledge as:

> Language skills are an important part of one's language competence. It refers to listening, speaking, reading and writing skills and the integrated skills to apply them in communication. Listening and reading are for comprehension and speaking and writing are for expression. All these skills are integrated in communication. Students should formulate language communication competence by participating in all kinds of specialized or comprehensive language practices so as to lay a solid foundation for real life communication. Therefore, listening, speaking, reading and writing are both subjects for study and means for study (MOE, 2012: 12).
>
> Language knowledge refers to pronunciation, vocabulary, grammar and functional expressions used in talking about common topics. Language knowledge is important for communication and the basis for communication. (MOE, 2012: 18)

The ECS therefore specifies in detail what specific skills need to be developed, and what knowledge should be acquired; however, it is worth pointing out that throughout this section of ECS there is no mention of what kind of English should be learnt and there is no clear privilege for any type or variety of English as the 'prestige variety' (Seargeant, 2012: 28). It might be true that this absence just continues the 'traditional practice' because in the former version of the language policy (the 2001 version of English Curriculum Standards) no prestige variety was specified as the legitimate form, and the general statement that '(students should learn) the language of the English speaking countries' was adopted. However, the new version of ECS goes a step further in avoiding saying that students should learn the 'English of English speaking countries', but it only adopts the term 'English' in general. In Johnson's (2009) study, her research participants, who were Chinese educators, pointed out that they were very careful to always use or write 'international English' because English is increasingly being treated as a tool, rather than a carrier of culture. The ECS distances itself from any particular cultural model and tries

to maintain a functionalist perspective that stresses the usefulness of English, and seems to present ELT as natural (unrelated to colonialism), neutral (unconnected to cultural and political issues) and beneficial (to people's personal development and the country's implementation of the opening-up policies). Not specifying a particular variety of English as the legitimate form is therefore a deliberate effort to neutralize the role and function that the language plays; nevertheless, such language policies may not be successfully fulfilled in implementation, as illustrated later in this chapter). The ideology reflected in this way of handling the issue of the form of English is that a language can operate for international communication without unduly politically advantaging one group over another. By doing so, the so-called 'neutrality of English' is established because it is what is ideal to the state and state governance.

Emotional Attitude

The 2011 ECS defines emotional attitude as:

> Emotional attitude refers to interest, motivation, confidence, perseverance, the team spirit and other related factors that influence the progress and effectiveness of learning. It also refers to the motherland awareness and international perspectives which are formed during the learning progress. Maintaining an active learning attitude is the key for learning English successfully. (MOE, 2012: 20)

It can be seen that one goal of English teaching is to help students form their awareness of their motherland, as well as awareness of international perspectives, to meet the needs created by internationalization and globalization. It also emphasizes that the students should learn English in order to form a positive emotional attitude towards their home culture. Yashima (2009) found that a positive international perspective helps learners to establish ideal selves in their learning of the target language, which brings about positive changes to the process of language learning. 'Self' can be defined as the learners' own behaviour in language learning. It not only includes self-motivation towards language learning, but it also refers to interests, confidence, willingness and a sense of team spirit, which are all aspects of emotional attitude (Coffey, 1999; Dörnyei and Csizér, 2006; Goetz et al., 2003; Murray, 2011). However, teachers play an important role in helping and encouraging the students to acquire positive 'self' and positive emotional attitudes. The ECS specifies:

> In the teaching process, teachers should constantly arouse and strengthen students' interests in language learning, and turn the interests of the students into a solid motivation for learning. In this way, student confidence will be built, and they will develop a strong will to overcome difficulties, recognize their strength and weakness in learning, be willing to cooperate with others and foster harmonious qualities and positive attitudes. By learning English, students will increase their motherland awareness and develop their international perspectives. (MOE, 2012: 20)

It is worth noting that the appreciation of the motherland and the cultivation of an international perspective are once again emphasized; maintaining patriotism while learning about foreign languages and cultures is further specified in the next section on cultural awareness. In the ECS, 'emotional attitude' and 'cultural awareness' are separated parts. A learner's emotional attitude should stimulate their enthusiasm towards English, and their cultural awareness is raised through the development of intercultural communicative competence and by cultivating students' positive attitudes towards Chinese culture. These two aspects are therefore closely connected with each other and could influence each other. Students' emotional attitude could be the premise for their cultural awareness; in return, cultural awareness might motivate the L2 students' learning process. Cultural awareness as specified in the 2011 ECS (MOE, 2012) is discussed next.

Cultural Awareness

Culture not only encompasses the traditions of everyday life, but it is also connected with politics, history and religion. Byram and Morgan (1994) state that language and culture are inseparable, and to master any language thoroughly, knowledge of the culture that is embedded in the language is crucial. In the 2011 ECS, 'culture' is clearly defined and 'cultural awareness' is related to patriotism (MOE, 2012). The standards require learners to master the target culture in the process of learning the language and to be aware of the similarities and differences between the local and foreign cultures.

> Language is with rich cultural connotations. In foreign language teaching, 'culture' refers to the history, geography, local customs, tradition, life styles, code of conduct, literature and arts, value system etc. of a target country. In the process of learning English, to get to know and to understand the culture of the other countries can help students appreciate the language and to use the language, deepen their understanding and love of their home culture, make them exposed to the advanced culture of the world, and cultivate their global outlook. (MOE, 2012: 23)

Calling for students to have cultural awareness of both their home country and that of other countries is a way to respond to the globalizing world (Houghton, 2012). Byram and Risager (1999: 4) point out that 'cultural awareness is used to refer to a range of phenomena from knowledge about other countries to positive attitudes towards speakers of other languages, to a heightened sensitivity to "otherness" of any kind'. They argue that cultural awareness helps language learners understand other cultures in greater depth, which in turn helps with language learning. It is evident that this line of thinking is reflected in the 2011 ECS. The 'other' contrasts with 'us' and it helps language learners identify the disparities between two different languages (Holliday, 2010). It therefore assists them in formulating their own cultural awareness during the process of learning. Wen (2012: 88) explains that 'students are required to be exposed to three kinds of cultures: target language cultures, the cultures of other non-native speakers, and the learner's own culture or the local culture', and she explicitly points out the official ideology of having the cultural component of language learning presented in the Chinese foreign language education policies:

> by doing so, we hope our students can not only learn about the various cultures of other countries but can also use English to share Chinese culture with people from the other countries. In other words, it is expected that by using English our students can 'introduce the world to China and introduce China to the world' (in Chinese: 把世界介绍给中国, 把中国介绍给世界), by means of a two-way cultural exchange. (Wen, 2012: 88)

It is often argued that the English language carries within itself the Western culture, values and ways of thinking, and that ELT today is still quite often recognized as a way to promote the global expansion of English and its embedded cultural values (Pennycook, 1994). The issue of teaching about target-language culture is often a sensitive and complex one; however, it is noteworthy that the ECS statement presented earlier is clear in accentuating the need to teach cultural knowledge and to raise students' awareness of the cultures of other countries. Although we cannot make the judgment that there is no anxiety in the current ELT about the influence of foreign cultures and languages, the increased 'liberalization' of official thinking is apparent in these official policy statements, and the constructive and instrumental role that English can play in Chinese society and culture is highlighted.

The 2011 ECS further illustrates how cultural awareness should be fostered:

> In teaching, teachers should gradually expand cultural content and coverage to keep up with students' age and cognitive competence. At the initial stage, students should have a general understanding of the cultures of China and other countries and the cultural differences between China and the other countries. The cultural knowledge to be introduced should be related to students' daily lives and arouse more interest in English study. At more advanced levels of English learning, teachers should help broaden the students' horizon by introducing more aspects of foreign culture, helping them broaden their horizons, and should enhance students' cross-cultural/ intercultural communication competence through fostering the awareness and appreciation of cultural differences. (MOE, 2012: 23)

This statement clearly points out that it is important for the students to distinguish between Chinese culture and foreign culture, and that learning about a foreign culture can help students develop deeper understandings of Chinese culture and foster patriotism. Byram and Risager (1999) contend that foreign language learning should mirror students' home cultures because it can facilitate students' grasp of the language and require the use of the language in familiar contexts. Moreover, language learners can improve their own communication skills by distinguishing the differences between the two cultures. In the same way, Tong and Cheung (2011) claim that intercultural communicative competence is an indispensable factor in learning a foreign language because it involves much linguistic knowledge and sophisticated cultural contexts.

The previous ECS statement outlines the critical role of teachers in teaching culture. A good understanding of the foreign culture by teachers is therefore a prerequisite for foreign language education. According to Byram and Risager (1999), a teacher's awareness of the target language can encourage students to interact with others and understand the foreign (target) culture through their own communication. As depicted in the ECS, the way to learn English culture is through cultivating students' intercultural communicative competence in the language classroom. Teachers are given the role of mediators between cultures and students, and they need to take English, Chinese and foreign culture, and the government's needs, into consideration all at the same time; however, to what degree teachers should understand and teach foreign cultures is undefined and uncertain. Teachers might have differing attitudes and different degrees of understanding of other cultures. Their ways of balancing Chinese and foreign culture and their recognition of where culture should be applied to teaching may also vary. Furthermore, Byram (1997) may be correct in believing that foreign language teaching requires teachers to hold impartial attitudes towards learners' national cultures. It is difficult for teachers to operationalize this in reality without any prejudice towards other cultures or without overemphasizing the home culture.

Read (2008) states that intercultural communication may have an impact on the power of a country. The ECS's emphasis on intercultural communicative competence is related to cultivating individuals' competence so that they can disseminate their ideology to other countries and expand the influence of China, and strengthen its position on the global stage. Nonetheless, proficiency in English varies from one student to another. Faced with students who are at different levels of English proficiency, it is hard for teachers to make plans for teaching intercultural communication. The cultural awareness that the policymakers formulate is included in the rationales prepared by some scholars, and although these rationales have been put into practice or proved by previous practice, different contexts can produce unexpected outcomes.

Equity Issues

In my (Pan, 2011) discussion of a previous language policy – the 2003 ECS – I pointed out that social inequity might be generated by this foreign language education policy because in the 2003 ECS, English has been prescribed since 2001 as a compulsory subject in primary schools from Grade Three (age 8) onwards, whereas in some big cities, such as Beijing, Shanghai and Guangzhou, it has been offered as early as Grade One (age 6) (Cheng, 2011). Although there are many benefits of learning English as early as age 8, social problems and controversies also arise. For example, 'the targets specified in the ECS are said to be unattainable uniformly given the size of the country, and the approaches and methods advocated in the ECS are not fully accepted and practised by teachers' (Cheng, 2011). What is more, in the past 10 years some regions have been competing to start English courses as early as possible. Some primary schools started their English courses at Grade One (age 6) when they had neither the qualified teachers nor the resources needed to teach English (Cheng, 2011; MOE, 2012). These limitations have given the students extra study burdens and caused poor learning quality (MOE, 2012). It seems that the stakeholders have realized the difficulties of implementation and the inequality issues generated by the compulsory learning of English. The new 2011 ECS, as the successor of the 2003 version, takes these issues into account and addresses the inequality generated by the previous ones.

> Considering that our country is vast in area, with many ethnic groups and with regional differences in economic and education development, different regions can have their own plans for the implementation for English courses. The plans for implementation should take into consideration the availability of teachers and resources when plans to open English courses are made and when the students' desired levels of achievement by the time of their graduation are decided. Particularly, the opening of English courses in primary schools should take into consideration factors such as the availability of teachers and teaching conditions. The teaching research organizations should improve their classification of teachers and their guidance and assessment methods, help schools to implement teaching plans based on their conditions and help students make smooth transitions from primary to junior high school and in learning in general. Efforts should be made to achieve a balanced development of English teaching in different regions. (MOE, 2012: 7)

It seems that the state is trying to avoid admitting that good knowledge of English may well become a mark of privilege in China, and that the possession of this kind of linguistic capital possibly generates social and economic stratification. As more and more scholars have begun to point out, students' quests to put English to use for the good of their country is now splitting the state into class strata and undermining the validity of China's governmental system (Johnson, 2009: 150). The state is, however, becoming more careful about the widening gap between China's rich and poor, and more cautious about the side effects that English has brought, along with its benefits for national development and internationalization.

CONCLUSION

This chapter has analyzed the recently issued language policy document – the 2011 version of *English Curriculum Standards at Compulsory Education Stage* – and has interpreted the state ideologies of post-Olympic China reflected in this policy. In discussing the language policy, my position is that globalization has changed the conditions in which language learning and teaching takes place. The global domination of English is debated in many countries, and language education can benefit from an enhanced understanding of the dialectic between the global and the local. In the 2011 ECS, the status and the use of English in Chinese society is related to the development of the country, and its teaching/learning is meant to help China reassert its position in world affairs. The general aims and objectives emphasize that English is of both instrumental and humanistic value. The learning of English is prescribed as a 'tool' and as a way to enhance patriotism and spread Chinese culture. In endorsing the kinds of language skills and language knowledge students should acquire, this 2011 version of the ECS continues to avoid the explicit assignment of any cultural models as examples for learning (such as US English or British English). Furthermore, references to the knowledge and skills of English-speaking countries are also avoided. This way of maintaining the neutrality of English is intended to reinforce the instrumental value of English and to maintain state governance. The new policy also clearly states that students should cultivate (or be taught to cultivate) positive emotions and attitudes towards English, and to have cultural awareness. Their cultural awareness should include understanding and appreciation of their home culture, the advanced cultures of the world

and the global outlook. Even the preface of the ECS stresses that the English curriculum is designed to foster talents for China and to improve the comprehensive strength of the state. Besides guiding students' English learning, the English curriculum does not hide its intention that it is designed to meet the national interests, and the five aspects of English education discussed earlier are designed to serve these purposes. The 2011 ECS is processing English and English education to create a desirable societal scenario for cultural governance by bringing foreign language and cultures into close contact and by taking foreign language education and policies as opportunities to help learners consolidate their own subjectivity and cultural identity. My analysis confirms that language policies are an apparatus for the state's political and cultural governance. The policy items reflect the state's ideologies and are 'an outcome of power struggles and an arena for those struggles' (Tollefson, 1991: 14).

ACKNOWLEDGEMENT

This discussion on globalization and language spread, and also language policies in post-Olympic China is an extension of my ideas in my book *English as a Global Language in China: Deconstructing the Ideological Discourses of English in Language Education* (Pan, 2015) and my paper 'English language ideologies in the Chinese foreign language education policies: a world-system perspective' (Pan, 2011) both published by Springer. Readers can refer to these resources if they are interested in reading more on these issues.

NOTES

1   The figure composed about one-third of the overall Chinese population.
2   This is the predecessor of the 2011 English Curriculum Standards.

REFERENCES

Appadurai, A. (1990) 'Disjuncture and difference in the global cultural economy', in M. Featherstone (ed.), *Global Culture: Nationalism, Globalization and Modernity*. London: Sage Publications. pp. 295–310.

Appadurai, A. (1996) '*Modernity At Large: Cultural Dimensions of Globalization*. Minneapolis, MN: University of Minnesota Press.

Barber, B. R. (1995) *Jihad vs. McWorld*. New York, NY: Random House.

Block, D. (2004) 'Globalization, transnational communication and the internet', *International Journal on Multicultural Societies*, 6(1): 22–36.

Block, D. and Cameron, D. (2002) 'Introduction', in D. Block and D. Cameron (eds.), *Globalization and Language Teaching*. London: Routledge. pp. 1–10.

Blommaert, J. (2005) *Discourse: A Critical Introduction*. Cambridge: Cambridge University Press.

Blommaert, J. (2006) 'Language policy and national identity', in T. Ricento (ed.), *An Introduction to Language Policy: Theory and Method*. London: Blackwell. pp. 238–54.

Bolton, K. (2006) *Chinese Englishes: A Sociolinguistic History*. Cambridge: Cambridge University Press.

Byram, M. (1997) *Teaching and Assessing Intercultural Communicative Competence*. Bristol, UK: Multilingual Matters.

Byram, M. and Risager, K. (1999) *Language Teachers, Politics and Cultures*. Bristol, UK: Multilingual Matters.

Byram, M. and Morgan C. (1994) *Teaching-and-Learning Language-and-Culture*. Bristol, UK: Multilingual Matters.

Cai, J. Y. (2014) *Chinese characteristics in the context of globalisation: 'emotion and attitude' and 'cultural awareness' in the Chinese English Curriculum Standards*, unpublished MA dissertation, Institute of Education, University of London.

Cheng, X. T. (2011) 'The "English curriculum standards" in China: rationale and issues', in A. W. Feng (ed.), *English Language Education Across Greater China*. Bristol, UK: Multilingual Matters. pp. 133–50.

Coffey, A. (1999) *The Ethnographic Self: Fieldwork and the Representation of Identity*. London: Sage Publications.

Dörnyei, Z. and Csizér, K. (2006) *Motivation, Language Attitudes and Globalisation: A Hungarian Perspective*. Vol. 18. Bristol, UK: Multilingual Matters.

Ferguson, G. (2006) *Language Planning and Education*. Edinburgh: Edinburgh University Press.

Ferguson, G. (2010) 'English in language policy and management', in B. Spolsky (ed.), *Cambridge Handbook of Language Policy*. Cambridge: Cambridge University Press. pp. 475–98.

Giddens, A. (1990) *The Consequences of Modernity*. Cambridge: Polity Press.

Giddens, A. (2000) *Runaway World*. New York, NY: Routledge.

Goetz, T., Zirngibl, A. and Hall, N. (2003) 'Emotions, learning and achievement from an educational–psychological perspective', in P. Mayring and C. van Rhoeneck (eds.), *Learning Emotions: The Influence of Affective Factors on Classroom Learning*. Frankfurt: Peter Lang. pp. 9–28.

Holliday, A. (2010) *Intercultural Communication and Ideology*. London: Sage Publications.

Houghton, S. A. (2012) *Intercultural Dialogue in Practice: Managing Value Judgment through Foreign Language Education*. Bristol, UK: Multilingual Matters.

Johnson, A. (2009) 'The rise of English: the language of globalization in China and the European Union. *Macalester International*, 22(1): 12.

Kramsch, C. (1993) *Context and Culture in Language Teaching*. Oxford: Oxford University Press.

Massey, D. B. (1994) *Space, Place and Gender*. Cambridge: Polity Press.

McCrum, R., MacNeil, R. and Cran, W. (2002) *The Story of English*. London: Faber & Faber.

Ministry of Education (MOE) (2012) *Yi wu jiao yu ying yu ke cheng biao zhun 2011 nian ban jie du [Interpretation of English Curriculum Standards at Compulsory Education stage 2011]*. Beijing: Beijing Normal University Publishing Group.

Murray, G. (2011) 'Imagination, metacognition and the self in a self-access learning environment', in G. Murray, X. Gao and T. Lamb (eds.), *Identity, Motivation and Autonomy in*

Language Learning. Bristol: Multilingual Matters. pp. 75–90.

Niu, Q. and Wolff, M. (2003) 'The Chinglish syndrome: do recent developments endanger the language policy of China?', *English Today*, 19(4): 30–5.

Pan, L. (2011) 'English language ideologies in the Chinese foreign language education policies: a world-system perspective', *Language Policy*, 10: 245–63.

Pan, L. (2014) State ideologies of language education in China', in S. Cowan (ed.), *New Directions in Education Research in China*. London: Institute of Education Press. pp. 6–27.

Pan, L. (2015) *English as a Global Language in China: Deconstructing the Ideological Discourses of English in Language Education*. Cham, Switzerland: Springer International Publishing.

Pennycook, A. (1994) *The Cultural Politics of English as an International Language*. London: Longman.

Phillipson, R. and Skutnabb-Kangas, T. (1995) *Papers in European Language Policy*. ROLIG papir, Vol. 53. Roskilde, Denmark: Roskilde Universitets Center.

Phillipson, R. and Skutnabb-Kangas, T. (1996) 'English only worldwide or language ecology?', *TESOL Quarterly*, 30(3): 429–52.

Pieterse, J. N. (2004) *Globalization and Culture: Global Mélange*. Oxford: Rowman & Littlefield.

Qu, W. G. (2012) 'Practical' English and the crisis of English studies', *English Today,* 28(3): 15–20.

Read, B. (2008) '"The world must stop when I'm talking": gender and power relations in primary teachers' classroom talk', *British Journal of Sociology of Education*, 29(6): 609–21.

Ritzer, G. (2000) *The McDonaldization of Society.* Thousand Oaks, CA: Pine Forge Press.

Ritzer, G. (2006) *McDonaldization: The Reader.* 2nd edn. Thousand Oaks, CA: Pine Forge Press.

Roberston, R. (1995) 'Glocalization: time-space and homogeneity-heterogeneity', in M. Featherstone, S. Lash and R. Robertson (eds.), *Global Modernities*. London: Sage. pp. 25–44.

Seargeant, P. (2012) *Exploring World Englishes: Language in a Global Context*. Abingdon, UK: Routledge.

Swyngedouw, E. (1997) 'Neither global nor local: "glocalization" and the politics of scale', in K. R. Cox (ed.), *Spaces of Globalization: Reasserting the Power of the Local*. New York, NY: Guilford Press. pp. 137–66.

Tollefson, J. W. (1991) *Planning Language, Planning Inequality: Language Policy in the Community*. London: Longman.

Tomlinson, J. (1999) *Globalization and Culture*. Cambridge: Polity Press.

Tomlinson, J. (2007) 'Cultural globalization', in G. Ritzer (ed.), *The Blackwell Companion to Globalization*. Oxford: Blackwell. pp. 352–66.

Tong, H. K. and Cheung, L. H. (2011) 'Cultural identity and language: a proposed framework for cultural globalisation and glocalisation', *Journal of Multilingual and Multicultural Development*, 32(1): 55–69.

Wen, Q. F. (2012) 'Teaching English as an international language in mainland China', in A. Kirkpatrick and R. Sussex (eds.), *English as an International Language in Asia: Implications for Language Education*. Dordrecht: Springer. pp. 79–96.

Wyse, D., Nikolajeva, M., Charlton, E., Cliff Hodges, G., Pointon, P. and Taylor, L. (2012) 'Place-related identity, texts, and transcultural meanings', *British Educational Research Journal*, 38(6): 1019–39.

Yashima, T. (2009) 'International posture and the ideal L2 self in the Japanese EFL Context', in Z. Dörnyei and E. Ushioda (eds.), *Motivation, Language Identity and the L2 Self*. Bristol, UK: Multilingual Matters. pp. 144–63.

Zheng, X. M. and Davison, C. (2008) *Changing Pedagogy: Analysing ELT Teachers in China*. London: Continuum.

Multilingual Education for All (MEFA): Empowering Non-Dominant Languages and Cultures Through Multilingual Curriculum Development

Carol Benson and Itziar Elorza

INTRODUCTION

As the world becomes more connected, and interpersonal communication must bridge the local, regional, national and international, the forces of globalization bring about aspirations for high proficiency in widely spoken dominant languages. Some believe that the global linguistic market is a case of survival of the fittest, inevitably bringing about the abandonment and loss of non-dominant languages (see, for example, Crystal (1997) and Graddol (2000) in the case of English). This presupposes that individuals must give up one language to acquire another, which is a myth that represents a monolingual, subtractive way of thinking. On the contrary, language learning theory finds that the learning of new languages is most efficient when it builds upon the language(s) in which people are most proficient. The fact that diverse human languages continue to co-exist at all levels from local to global means that people will increasingly need certain languages for certain purposes. Those best adapted to bridging local and global worlds will be those who speak, read and write a repertoire of languages and who can, in addition, promote intercultural understandings. Educational curricula of the present and future should therefore maximize learners' existing linguistic and cultural resources and build on them, not attempt to erase them only to impose a single dominant 'standard' language and its referent culture. This also means that educational curricula should not leave dominant language speakers monolingual. The position we take in this chapter is captured by the slogan Multilingual Education for All (MEFA), a perspective that we share with other scholars (for example, García et al. 2006). We will demonstrate how MEFA can be and is being accomplished in a range of settings.

The central purpose of this chapter is to describe current theory and practice in multilingual curriculum development, demonstrating its effectiveness in maximizing learners' linguistic resources whilst protecting and promoting non-dominant languages and cultures and learners' self-esteem. We base our points on well-established principles of language learning and cognitive development. Our perspective is a comparative one, using examples from different parts of the world, with a focus on the Integrated Plurilingual School model, as practised in the Spanish Basque Country. Some examples come from educational development contexts where learners' own languages are being brought into the curriculum or expanded to permit access to quality basic education. Other examples come from revitalization contexts where community languages brought close to extinction by suppression are brought back into use through educational programs. What these contexts have in common is the recognition, promotion and protection of non-dominant local or heritage languages in combination with the teaching of regional and international languages – for all learners.

TERMS AND CONCEPTS

We use the term 'non-dominant languages' (abbreviated as NDL) to refer to the languages or language varieties spoken in a certain context that are not considered the most prominent in terms of number, prestige or official use by the government and/or the education system (Kosonen, 2010). A 'dominant language' (DL) is a language with official status and high prestige, spoken by dominant group members and learned by others (Benson and Kosonen, 2012). We acknowledge that these terms are not fixed nor are they completely dichotomous. They are relative – that is, there are degrees of dominance or non-dominance within these categories – and they are dynamic and subject to change based on social, educational, economic and other activities. Further, they must be contextualized, particularly in terms of time and place, for example languages that are dominant in one context may be

non-dominant in another. With these caveats, we adopt these terms to highlight the power differentials that educational programs must address if they are to maximize learners' linguistic and cognitive resources.

Bilingual or multilingual education (MLE) programs are defined by García (2009) as those that intentionally and explicitly teach more than one language; they usually teach using more than one language as medium of instruction, either sequentially or simultaneously. Scholars and practitioners working in low-income contexts use the term 'L1-based MLE' (Kosonen and Benson, 2013), also known as 'mother tongue-based bilingual or multilingual education' (Alexander, 2005; Heugh, 2008) or 'first language first' (UNESCO, 2005), to call attention to the need to use learners' home languages (L1) rather than unfamiliar languages as the basis for beginning literacy and learning. L1 is admittedly an imprecise term where learners have two or more home languages, but the point is to use a language in which learners are highly proficient for initial literacy and learning to optimize comprehension.

Bi- and multilingual education approaches are based on the well-established concept of *common underlying proficiency* (Cummins, 1981), where literacy and cognitive skills and knowledge developed in one language become available to the learner in another language as it is acquired. MLE programs often teach additional (second or foreign) languages orally for the first few years of school, after which learners are encouraged to *transfer* literacy skills from the more familiar language to the new language(s). Transfer of literacy skills across languages is a semi-automatic process that can be facilitated by teachers through explicit comparison and contrast exercises (Cummins, 2009). There is strong evidence that transfer occurs even if the languages are not linguistically related (Cenoz, 2009) or do not use the same writing system (Kenner, 2004). Further, transfer is multidirectional, so all of an individual's languages contribute to her/ his linguistic and cognitive development

(Bialystock, 2001). We return to the concept of transfer later because it is key to the effectiveness of multilingual curricula.

As noted earlier, L1-based MLE uses (one of) the learner's strongest language(s) as the foundation for literacy and learning, after which skills are transferred to additional languages. In contrast, immersion and revitalization programs may use second or foreign languages as a springboard for early learning. In the case of an immersion approach, the goal is to expose learners to a new language at an early age; the L1 is not ignored, but the second/additional/foreign language (Lx) is in focus (Genesee, 1994; Pavlenko, 2014). A revitalization approach focuses on the heritage language of a community that used to be an L1, but which learners may or may not have heard or used at home. In both cases, early learning begins in languages in which learners are not proficient, requiring teachers who are well trained, using communicative and language-across-the-curriculum approaches in well-resourced classrooms (Baker, 2006). It should be noted that the conditions under which such programs are educationally successful are not realistically replicable in low-income or immigrant situations. These conditions include high literacy levels and educational involvement on the part of families and community members, and relatively high status of both the L1 of learners and the additional language(s) taught. For most speakers of NDLs, the use of the L1 provides a solid foundation of comprehensible literacy and cognitive skills upon which additional languages can be built, as well as promoting learner identity and positive self-esteem (Cummins, 2009).

According to UNESCO (2003: 12), bilingualism or multilingualism is 'the use of more than one language in daily life'. The Council of Europe (2006) differentiates between the multilingualism of societies or schools and the plurilingualism of the individual. Plurilingualism refers to the development of communicative competence in multiple languages over one's lifetime according to one's needs. Interestingly, in the European context, plurilingualism is seen not necessarily for its pedagogical benefits but for promoting democratic citizenship, pluralist attitudes, social coherence and mutual understanding:

> Developing and optimising plurilingual competencies can become a common linguistic matrix that will give the European political and cultural area a form of plural linguistic identity rooted in the diversity of its communities and compatible with its values of openness to the world. (Council of Europe, 2007: 39)

Multilingualism has frequently been considered an extension of bilingualism, thus applying many of the basic concepts drawn from research on bilingualism such as those mentioned earlier. However, scholars are increasingly defending the specificity of multilingualism as a distinct phenomenon that can only be approached through a holistic perspective (Cook, 1995; Grosjean, 1989; Herdina and Jessner, 2002). For example, it is argued that the very complex interactions between languages that go on in the mind of a multilingual individual build upon a qualitatively different linguistic system from that of a monolingual or even a bilingual. As Jessner points out:

> [I]n contrast to the hypotheses of Cummins, and Kecskes and Papp, all of whom describe a kind of overlap between the two language systems, DST [dynamic systems theory]...presupposes a complete metamorphosis of the system involved and not merely an overlap between two subsystems. If this is applied to multilingual development, it means that the interaction between the three systems results in different abilities and skills that the learners develop due to their prior learning experience. (Jessner, 2006: 35)

The distinct way in which multilinguals use their languages is also taken into consideration. Multilinguals do not use all their languages in the same way and for the same functions. They will draw from their varied language repertoire and switch from one language to another in a dynamic process reflecting their language needs (Herdina and Jessner, 2002). In consequence, the language proficiency of multilinguals will develop and change as a reflection of the sociocultural conditions in which they live, depending on the domains of use and the functions of the various languages in their everyday lives.

DIFFERENT CONTEXTS OF MULTILINGUAL CURRICULUM DEVELOPMENT AND WHAT LINKS THEM

To illustrate this discussion of theory and practice in multilingual curriculum development, we take a comparative perspective, drawing on our own and others' experiences in two main situations. One situation is where learners are speakers of NDLs and are being educated in these languages whilst learning more widely spoken ones; our examples are from multilingual countries like Ethiopia, Cambodia and Bolivia, where Benson (2012, 2013) has been involved in the application of L1-based MLE to improve student achievement and opportunities. The second situation is where learners have not had the opportunity to develop proficiency in their families' (heritage, often autochthonous non-dominant) languages and where educational programs are designed to help the linguistic community regain youthful speakers whilst using languages with which they are familiar; our examples are from programs for revitalization of regional languages in Europe. As mentioned, our main inspiration comes from the innovative Integrated Plurilingual School model practiced in the *Ikastolas* of the Spanish Basque Country, with which Elorza has been involved (EHIK, 2009; Elorza, 2012; Elorza and Muñoa, 2008). Our examples, taken together, reveal a set of progressive practices designed to protect and promote non-dominant languages and cultures and learner self-esteem whilst maximizing their multi-linguistic repertoires.

Underlying all of the principles and practices discussed here is Cummins' (1981)

thoroughly researched and now axiomatic Interdependence Hypothesis, which states:

> To the extent that instruction in Lx is effective in promoting proficiency in Lx, transfer of this proficiency to Ly will occur provided there is adequate exposure to Ly (either in school or environment) and adequate motivation to learn Ly. (Cummins, 1981: 29)

The multi-directionality of cross-linguistic transfer provides a theoretical link between the two situations described earlier because regardless of whether Lx is the learner's most proficient language, it can be used for learning, given adequate sociolinguistic conditions, enabling educational language policies and appropriate classroom strategies. The social policy link between them is the recognition of NDLs, and their promotion and protection through multilingual education, which has the potential to transform learners' lives as well as their entire societal milieu.

Effective MLE of any kind should promote learners' metalinguistic awareness, or understanding of the explicit properties of human language. Researchers like Bialystock (2001) have found that such understanding facilitates the learning of additional languages and promotes critical and flexible thinking. This would imply that all learners could benefit cognitively from programs that aim for bi-/multilingualism and bi-/multiliteracy (Cummins, 2009; Hermanto et al., 2012).

ADOPTING A MULTILINGUAL HABITUS IN EDUCATIONAL THEORY AND PRACTICE

In the context of educating speakers of NDLs in Europe, Gogolin (2002) characterizes most programs as being representations of a monolingual habitus. She is referring to Bourdieu's (1991) concept of the *habitus* as a set of sociocultural dispositions that tend to go unquestioned, and the *linguistic habitus* as a set of attitudes related to discussing, valuing and using language(s). Despite the fact that human languages are essentially equal in terms of their ability to express speakers' needs, linguistic markets are inevitably hierarchical, giving different values to different languages and people's competence in them (Bourdieu, 1991). There are obvious but essential critiques of dominant monolingual practices, for example Hélot's (2008) work showing how talented bi- or multilingual learners from non-dominant groups in France are considered merely deficient in French, a phenomenon she calls 'ignored bilingualism'. Gogolin (2002) criticizes even bilingual programs, which she sees as reinforcing and reproducing dominant attitudes. Examples would be hiring paraprofessionals rather than qualified teachers to teach NDLs, teaching standard rather than local varieties of the NDL, switching to the DL as medium of instruction as soon as possible, and testing only in the DL. Although these practices can at least in part be explained by limitations in human, technical or economic resources, they are marginalizing just the same, and they raise the question of why multilingual programs should be so under-resourced.

Other scholars have joined Gogolin in questioning these and other practices in bi- or multilingual and immersion programs. Traditional bilingual approaches, such as a linear L1-to-L2 sequence, as well as the strict separation of languages – what Cummins (2007) calls the 'two solitudes assumption' – have been challenged based on new understandings of transfer (Cenoz and Genesee, 1998; Hoffman and Ytsma, 2003). The same approaches have been challenged from the perspective of the fluid communicative practices of multilinguals, discussed by García (2009) in terms of 'translanguaging'. According to García, schools should be embracing rather than stigmatizing translanguaging, and teachers should be role models of multilingual behaviour rather than being enforcers of 'Lx only'.

The 'Lx only' strategy, still unquestioned in most second and foreign language classrooms, seems to be an outgrowth of communicative methodology as part of the 'natural method' pedagogy, which originated in North America in the 1970s. According to the natural method, the L2 learning environment should imitate home language acquisition by surrounding learners with comprehensible input in the 'target language' (Krashen, 1981; Krashen and Terrell, 1983). Although there are certainly good pedagogical reasons for helping learners learn to think in the target language, the overgeneralization has led teachers to forbid and even penalize learners for speaking anything other than the language in which they are least competent, instead of allowing them to call on their linguistic resources. By ignoring all but the target language in teaching and assessment, 'Lx only' has contributed to the expectation that learners should acquire native-like proficiency in the new language. This is not an entirely realistic goal in most Lx learning situations, even in highly resourced ones like the Canadian immersion programs (for example, Genesee, 2004). We would argue that the scholarly discourse around 'native-like' proficiency (for example, White and Genesee, 1996) has taken both practitioners and the public in the direction of how early to expose learners to 'target' languages, instead of calling for development of bi- and multilingual curricula that will expand on learners' linguistic and cognitive resources for work and life.

International evidence suggests that the most effective approaches are simultaneously additive (Baker, 2006) – building languages upon languages without taking any out of the equation – and dynamic, like practices in multilingual families, where all linguistic resources are applied to tasks like discussing an issue or solving a problem (García, 2009). Based on Hymes' (1972) concept of 'communicative competence', multilingual curricula aim for learners to gain appropriate and effective oral and written competencies in two or more languages by the end of the program, competencies that can be sustained and further developed over people's life-times. Effective approaches aim not only to build upon learners' strongest language(s) but also to work multidirectionally on their entire linguistic repertoire. Learners should not be assessed monolingually and compared to native speakers in each language, but should rather be assessed in all of their languages according to the different levels and types of competencies that have been developed (Cenoz and Genesee, 1998; Cenoz and Gorter, 2011).

The term 'multiliteracies' represents new conceptions of literacy as going well beyond the acquisition of reading and writing skills in multiple languages. Multiliteracies pedagogy builds upon the rich cultural and linguistic identities that learners bring to the classroom, exposing them to new modalities like information technologies and helping them gain critical insights into how knowledge and society are constructed (Cummins, 2009; New London Group, 1996). The development of critical literacies has been proposed to problematize the dominance or non-dominance of languages in society. Critical literacies are linked to multiculturalism, which promotes respect for all languages, cultures and people, and also intercultural awareness (Luke, 2013). Interculturalism, the ability to mediate between languages, cultures and peoples, is an integral feature of Latin American bilingual programs, and has been operationalized to emphasize Indigenous knowledge and values whilst challenging existing inequities between groups (López, 2006).

As mentioned earlier, our different contexts for multilingual curriculum development are similar in that they aim to maximize learners' multiple linguistic resources and they also prioritize NDLs. Because there is diversity even within the two contexts, a range of strategies has been developed for promoting multilingualism and multiliteracies. In the next two sections we highlight promising policies and practices in MLE as functional, under specific conditions for specific aims.

MULTILINGUAL CURRICULUM DEVELOPMENT IN LOW-INCOME MULTILINGUAL CONTEXTS

This section discusses contexts where learners' home languages are NDLs that are gradually being brought into education systems where more prestigious languages have long dominated. DL-based education systems exist due to (post-)colonial policies favouring exogenous languages (such as Portuguese in Mozambique, Spanish in Bolivia), or due to monolingual state policies favouring dominant groups (such as Khmer in Cambodia). Those multilingual countries that have traditions of educational use of NDLs have tended to use widely spoken regional languages like Kiswahili in Tanzania or state languages in India; see for example, Mohanty's (2006) critique of India's three-language formula – and only for lower primary, after which there is an abrupt 'transition' (adopting a term from bilingual education which was meant to represent a systematic, staged switch from L1 to Lx medium) to a dominant language. The more common practice has been for informal (oral) use of local languages where teachers share learners' NDLs, but this practice is admitted only with shame and the conviction that it is against the official policies of education ministries (Mohanty, 2006; see also Benson, 2004).

The contexts from which we draw can be characterized as low-income, rural and non-dominant. When these factors further overlap with gender and Indigenous status, large numbers of people are prevented from getting basic education of a reasonable quality that will help them lead healthy, secure lives. The gaps in educational access, quality and achievement between non-dominant and dominant groups has become a main concern of development organizations like UNESCO, which in turn has led donors, governments and non-governmental organizations (NGOs) in efforts to achieve Education for All (according to the Jomtien Accords[1]) and monitor accomplishment of the Millennium

Development Goals.[2] The relationship between medium of instruction and achievement of these goals has increasingly come under discussion in the past two decades, with a landmark conference in 2010[3] bringing a large number of scholars, policymakers, politicians and educators to the table. US-driven efforts to reform the teaching of early literacy through large-scale testing of a limited set of reading skills has admittedly brought attention to language of instruction issues, despite raising concerns about assessing literacy in context (Hoffman, 2012) and according to particular linguistic features of the NDLs in question (Schroeder, 2013). Increasingly, educators are recognizing that learners from non-dominant linguistic and cultural backgrounds can be offered more equitable educational services, particularly in basic literacy, if their own languages are used. In some countries, this approach works in parallel with democratic social or political movements to develop policies and practices that bring NDLs into schools through bi- and multilingual and intercultural curricula.

Two examples of educational policy favouring MEFA are South Africa and Bolivia. In the first case, with democracy and the removal of apartheid in 1994 came a designation of 11 official languages, nine of which are Indigenous African languages (Republic of South Africa, 1996). Educational policies that followed called for the use of people's own languages as mediums of instruction at the primary basic level and, in the case of African language speakers, access to competence in Afrikaans and/or English, the nationally and internationally dominant languages, respectively. Interestingly, the policy went further to call for speakers of the two DLs to have access to competence in at least one of the nine NDLs (Heugh, 2009). At about the same time in 1994, Bolivia was undergoing a social and educational revolution, passing the Education Reform Law, along with laws implementing democratic ('popular') participation and decentralization of education (López, 2005). Although this approach was clearly directed toward the Indigenous majority of the country, there was a clause in the Reform policy calling for the Spanish-speaking dominant elite to learn an Indigenous language. In both South Africa and Bolivia, there is anecdotal evidence that learners from dominant groups have actually had some opportunities to learn NDLs, particularly if they attend progressive private schools; however, the literature also reveals fears that elite schools take much-needed Indigenous language speakers away from L1-based school programs, where they are desperately needed (see, for example, López, 2005).

The strongest NDL-based educational policies in low-income countries today are being implemented in Ethiopia and Eritrea, but they stop short of promoting NDL competence on the part of speakers of the nationally dominant (Amharic and Tigrinha, respectively) or internationally dominant (English) languages. Both call for L1-based teaching and learning during the entire 8-year primary school cycle, with the DLs taught as subjects in the curriculum. This 8-year L1 policy is effectively practiced for the most widely spoken NDLs, and partially practiced for others, with documented success in terms of student achievement (Heugh et al., 2012; Walter and Davis, 2005). It is unfortunate that both policies require trilingualism for NDL speakers, but only bilingualism (with English) for speakers of the national DLs (Benson et al., 2012).

Along with policies enabling or promoting MEFA, a range of practices are documented in the literature on multilingual education in low-income settings, particularly in teacher professional development. When NDLs are entering the curriculum for the first time, attention must be paid to teachers' oral and written language proficiency in both NDLs and DLs, as well as to their use of language teaching methodologies. In contexts where NDLs are widely spoken, for example in multilingual African countries, it is often possible to mobilize an adequate supply of qualified teachers who are NDL speakers, as long as they are offered some training in writing their own languages and in teaching them, and assuming they can be placed with learners who share their language (Benson, 2004). However, when NDL communities have not traditionally had access to formal education, there may not be teachers who speak, read or write these languages. This raises the question of how to initiate an L1-based MLE program – with NDL speakers who are not qualified teachers, or with qualified teachers who are not from the NDL community?

There are a number of strategies designed to address NDL teacher shortages, most of which are stopgap measures. It should be noted that once the first generation of bi- or multilingual learners complete their education cycle, there will be a pool from which to draw qualified NDL-speaking teachers. One common practice, the use of parent volunteers or NDL para-professionals to help non-NDL-speaking teachers interpret the curriculum, may facilitate classroom communication but tends to keep the NDL in a subordinate position (Vu, 2010). Another practice, that of attempting to give qualified teachers enough proficiency in the NDL to teach, requires a great deal of training and raises issues of cultural compatibility between teachers and learners. In our experience, the most promising practices promote the education and training of NDL community members who have the appropriate linguistic and cultural background. One example is Bolivia's development of *bachilleratos pedagógicos*, or pedagogical secondary schools, where Indigenous girls were trained in L1-based bilingual education methods whilst learning the secondary curriculum (Benson, 2004). An even more successful model empowering local community teachers has been developed by CARE in Cambodia and is in the process of being adopted by the Cambodian government for certain non-dominant groups. In this model, community volunteers are given training that is tailored to provide L1 literacy and pedagogical skills alongside academic content, so that teachers can eventually be recognized

as qualified by the Ministry of Education and Training (Lee et al., 2014).

Planning for multilingual teacher trainer needs, the University of Limpopo in South Africa has developed a highly innovative Multilingual Studies BA program that prepares bilingual teachers and other professionals using Sesotho sa Leboa/Sepedi and English, alongside additional South African NDLs and world languages (Ramani and Joseph, 2010). These and other measures are being developed to allow for multilingual educational opportunities to be offered in low-income contexts, where admittedly the first priority is to provide access to basic education and literacy for people from ND linguistic and cultural communities.

MULTILINGUAL CURRICULUM DEVELOPMENT IN REVITALIZATION CONTEXTS

This section discusses contexts that are generally better resourced, where NDL communities are striving to revitalize their languages and cultures. These communities face the complex and multifaceted challenge of developing multilingual education models that answer to the needs of the globalized world without compromising the recovery and promotion of languages that have been lost or partially lost due to political and/or social repression. Educational models for these communities should, as Fishman (2001: 43) puts it, 'counterbalance [globalization] by a greater emphasis on cultural values, skills, attitudes and beliefs that stem from and reinforce their own identity'. In such contexts, schools are active agents in 'reversing language shift' (Fishman, 2001) because they are engaged not only in ensuring knowledge and transmission of the NDL, but also in promoting its social use in the educational context, as well as in the surrounding community.

Such a perspective of multilingual education including the promotion of the NDL can now be found in bi- and multilingual communities all across Europe and has been especially developed in the officially bilingual autonomous communities of Spain (Galicia, Catalonia, Valencia, Balearic Islands, Navarre and the Basque Autonomous Community). In all of these communities, multilingual education is increasingly being generalized, and the earlier bilingual models involving the NDL heritage language and the state dominant language have been extended to include English as a language of international communication, as well as major languages such as French.

Multilingual models in revitalization contexts need to address a variety of sociolinguistic settings and types of learners depending on their contact with the NDL. For some learners, the NDL is their L1, still preserved and used in their homes and/or their local environments. In other cases, learners' identities and origins correspond to the nondominant group, but the NDL is no longer spoken by them or their families. Finally, there might be learners belonging to the dominant group, or to other incoming non-dominant groups, who choose to be educated in the heritage NDL of the local community for diverse reasons ranging from identity factors to instrumental motivation. Revitalization models have not traditionally engaged with all of these types of learners in equitable ways; they include total immersion (monolingual in the NDL), partial immersion/bilingual (NDL and DL), or NDL taught as a second or foreign language within a mostly DL curriculum (Grenoble and Whaley, 2006). We need to point out that even these models tend to represent a monolingual habitus in that they are separated in the curriculum and do not necessarily draw upon learners' own linguistic resources.

The *Common European Framework of Reference for Languages* (Council of Europe, 2001) defines multilingual competence in a social and action-based manner: proficiency in multiple languages with the capacity to efficiently use the appropriate language to fulfil the tasks necessary in each specific context and situation of the learner's life. With this definition in mind, a well-designed multilingual model needs to embrace a broad perspective of the learner's language development, one that is not limited to the teaching and learning of languages or to their vehicular use inside the classroom, but that extends to all actions and interactions happening in the school community, and that particularly takes into account the sociolinguistic context and levels of usage of the NDL in learners' school, social and familial environments. This demands a comprehensive framework for language planning and treatment: the School Language Project. The following paragraphs will describe the School Language Project model as designed by the Basque-medium *Ikastola*[4] school network in the Spanish Basque Country. We will expand on one of its main features, the Integrated Language Curriculum for the teaching and learning of all the languages in the school program.

The School Language Project of the Basque Ikastolas

The Language Project of the *Ikastolas* is an illustrative example of an integrated multilingual framework in which both the treatment of language(s) in the teaching and learning process and the social promotion of the NDL are addressed (EHIK, 2009; Elorza and Muñoa, 2008). This framework analyzes the school setting holistically to identify the different communicative fields at the school, each with its own specific functions that require a certain language repertoire. This analysis results in a description of all possible 'fields of intervention in language development' (EHIK, 2009), which becomes the basis for an all-encompassing plan for the development of multilingual competence centred on the NDL (see Figure 35.1).

Looking specifically at the teaching and learning processes that happen within the classroom, this plan includes three dimensions:

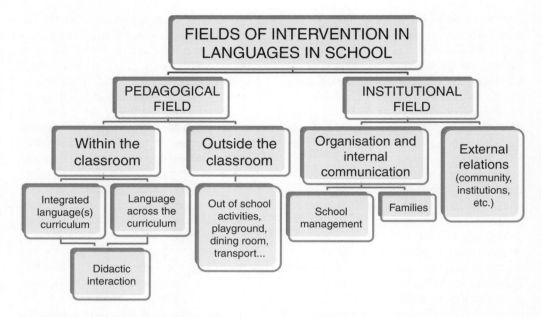

Figure 35.1   Fields of intervention in languages in school

Source: EHIK (2009) *The Ikastola Language Project*. Donostia Spain: Confederation of Ikastolas of the Basque Country.

- An integrated language curriculum, that is, a holistic language program bringing together all languages in the school and aiming for multilingual competence;
- multilingual language-enhanced instruction in all areas across the curriculum, in which each subject will take charge of the teaching and learning of its own specific language repertoire, and all will contribute to the development of the common key competence of 'learning to communicate'; and
- common methodological guidelines that emphasize the importance of interaction and student participation in the classroom. The aim will be to maximize learner language production – in any given language – and to improve the quality of communication in the teaching and learning process.

The following section describes how the language curriculum is integrated.

The Integrated Language Curriculum

The School Language Project of the *Ikastolas* (EHIK, 2009) integrates four languages:

Basque (the NDL) as the main language of education (through immersion or maintenance depending on the learner's background), Spanish (the state DL), English (the international *lingua franca*) and French (neighbouring language). These languages are given varying degrees of use and differing roles depending on their presence in the learners' environment outside school, the linguistic proximity between languages and the level of learners' cognitive development at each level of schooling (Elorza and Muñoa, 2008: 92). Consistent with the principle of interdependence (Cummins, 1981) and the holistic and dynamic nature of multilingualism (for example, Cook, 1995; Grosjean 1989; Herdina and Jessner, 2002), as explained earlier, the teaching and learning programs for all four languages have been integrated into a common curriculum that makes the best of, as well as fosters and nurtures, the unique proficiency of the multilingual student (Elorza, 2012). The axis of this integrated curriculum is the learners' common underlying proficiency (Cummins,

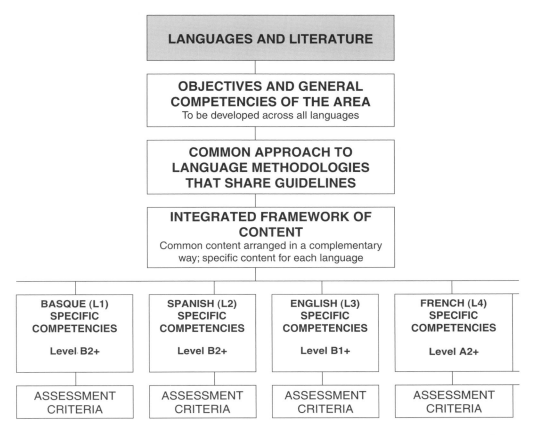

Figure 35.2   Structure of the integrated language curriculum of the Basque Curriculum for Compulsory Education

Source: EHIK (2009) *The Ikastola Language Project.* Donostia, Spain: Confederation of *Ikastolas* of the Basque Country.

1981), which facilitates comparison, contrast and interaction amongst languages, and allows for the transfer of skills and metalinguistic knowledge acquired in one language into the learners' additional languages.

For these reasons, the syllabi of all four languages are defined within a single Languages and Literature area. The main competencies of this common area, all related to oral and written communication and metalinguistic awareness, will be developed across all languages. In order to allow for this complementary work, a common methodological approach has been devised, focused on language usage and communication. Likewise, the main teaching content available to be transferred from one language to others

(Cummins, 1981) is planned in a complementary way for all languages included in the curriculum (see later). In addition, each language has its own set of differentiated specific content. The expected level of acquisition of competencies in each language by the end of compulsory schooling is specified using the language levels stated by the *Common European Framework of Reference for Languages* (Council of Europe, 2001) and defined by means of assessment criteria (EHIK, 2009), as illustrated in Figure 35.2.

Integrated framework of language content

To establish the integrated framework of content, the language content that would be most likely to promote language transfer is selected. The following categories are taken into account when defining this complementary framework (Elorza, 2012):

1 *Development of oral and written skills for comprehension and production.* General procedures and strategies for listening, speaking, reading and writing are shared and taught similarly in the different languages. The introduction of new skills will be done in the main school language (Basque) to be then transferred and generalized to the other languages.

2 *Knowledge of discursive situations and text genres.* Despite certain differences between cultures, a set of common characteristics can be defined relating to structure, organization of content, functions and rhetorical resources within text genres. This allows for complementary planning of text work. For instance, the structure of a story, a letter or an encyclopaedia entry will be presented in one language to be applied and developed further in other languages.

3 *Interdependence of metalinguistic awareness and language usage.* Processes of observation, analysis and conceptualization of the language system, as well as basic linguistic concepts needed to talk about language, are learned in one language and then transferred to others. Cross-linguistic work, that is, activities involving translation, comparison or contrast between languages, will reinforce metalinguistic awareness, which is an essential feature for the development of multilingual competence (Jessner, 2006, 2008).

4 *Language attitudes and intercultural awareness.* Representations of the different languages and cultures that bring about attitudes towards them, motivation to use or learn them, and personal choices of usage need to be considered in complementary ways. This category is especially relevant where the aim is to empower NDLs through multilingual teaching and learning.

We would argue that the design of an integrated language curriculum of this kind is essential for planning coherent and efficient multilingual language teaching. It allows for new content to be introduced using learners' stronger languages, for the content load to be shared between languages in which learners have more balanced proficiency, and generally for unnecessary repetition or contradiction to

be avoided. This type of curriculum makes the learning of each subsequent language easier and faster because all the previous linguistic knowledge built up by the multilingual learner is taken into account when a new language is introduced.

Although it is essential, the integrated language curriculum cannot on its own answer for the full development of learners' multilingual competencies. As stated previously, the process of acquiring all the languages happens through every activity that is part of the life of the school. Consequently, the integrated language curriculum is only part of a comprehensive plan that comprises the entire communicative environment of the school (inside and outside the classroom) and organizes the work carried out by all members of the school community – educators, families and other professionals – in a systematic and integrated manner.

MULTILINGUALISM AND MULTICULTURALISM

Languages are social products that express the vision of the world of a human community, and they would be empty vessels without the cultures that fill them with meaning. Language and culture must therefore be considered as indivisible realities that need to be tackled together when designing multilingual curricula.

In many cases the school has served as an instrument for imposing dominant culture along with dominant language, and for enforcing uniformity. For ND communities that aim to maintain their identity, the curriculum needs to incorporate a cultural itinerary (Garagorri, 2004) that integrates not only specific elements pertaining to heritage, but also the community's own interpretations of universal cultural elements. The combination of these allows for renewal and adaptation of the traditional culture to modern times in a dynamic approach.

The *Ikastola* network has therefore developed, alongside the Language Project, the

Basque Curriculum (EHIK, 2004, 2006), which consists of basic elements of Basque cultural heritage and world cultural elements selected by experts in a range of fields. The intent is for this curriculum to serve as a common shared reference for all students. This would allow for cultural revival and for a model of inclusive integration because the Basque language and culture would form the basis for coexistence of all cultural groups living in the Basque Country. As explained by Garagorri:

> We propose to follow the path of cultural integration, that is, the path that combines diversity and unification. Unification, considering Basque and Basque culture to be the common heritage of all the cultural groups that come into contact in our daily lives and which, in turn, needs to be open and changeable; and diversity, by making use of intercultural channels as a means of respecting, getting to know and appreciating the identity that each community has. (Garagorri, 2004: 25)

The Basque Curriculum proposal stresses the need to integrate multilingualism and interculturalism to reach two complementary aims: creation of unity and appreciation of diversity.

COOPERATION FOR LINGUISTIC AND CULTURAL REVITALIZATION

The Basque experience in NDL revitalization and cultural recovery has opened up an interesting path for cooperation with NDL communities in low-income contexts. The Basque NGO *Garabide Elkartea*[5] carries out cooperation projects with minoritized Indigenous communities in Latin America, sharing knowledge and skills gained throughout the more than 50-year process of Basque revitalization. The NGO has two main fields of work: research and dissemination of the Basque process of language recovery, and training and counselling in revitalization strategies. In collaboration with the Mondragon University Faculty of Humanities

and Education, a course in Native Language and Identity Recovery is offered for Basque language activists wishing to work in cooperation projects and leaders of Indigenous organizations, with the following aims:

- To reflect on the challenges inherent to the language and identity recovery process.
- To offer sociolinguistic training on language recovery strategies in education, the media, corpora, cultural production, language policy and other areas.
- To foster an exchange of experiences between participants and those working in the field of Basque culture.
- To raise awareness among those involved in Basque culture regarding projects aimed at recovering native languages in the southern hemisphere.
- To create and develop language recovery projects to be carried out in the language communities themselves.

An illustrative example of the outcomes of this cooperation is the pilot school *Tosepan Kalnemaxtiloyan*[6] of the Nahuatl ethnolinguistic community in Cuetzalan, Mexico, in which Elorza was involved. The school, created by the agricultural cooperative *Tosepan Titataniske* ('United we shall win'), is promoting a differentiated education model that builds learners' Indigenous identities and reinforces the culture and values of the community through intercultural and trilingual education in Nahuatl, Spanish and English. Since school leaders participated in the Native Language and Identity Recovery course, the school project has evolved from a Spanish-dominant bilingual programme into a total immersion Nahuatl-based education model, aiming to reverse the language shift already in process in the community. A research project has also been launched to define the Nahuatl cultural curriculum – the basic elements of local culture that should be integrated into the syllabus and transmitted to future generations through schooling. In similar ways, Indigenous communities from Ecuador, Bolivia, Guatemala or Colombia have benefitted from training, counselling or financial support for their own recovery plans, reinforcing their own identities and creating a collaborative network to fulfil their common aims.

RISKS IN MULTILINGUAL CURRICULUM DEVELOPMENT

Although we are highly encouraged by the current directions in multilingual education in both settings we have described, there are some impediments to generating a multilingual habitus and achieving multilingual education for all. This is because a habitus in Bordieuian terms is an unquestioned assumption, and changing from a monolingual to a multilingual habitus involves no less than a paradigm shift, among educators, academics and the public. The greatest risk would be to transplant multilingual models or methods whilst maintaining the status quo, that is, without challenging the power imbalances between dominant and non-dominant cultural and linguistic communities. We note that countries like Bolivia and South Africa have included clauses in their educational language policies to support DL speakers learning NDL, but these policies are far from widely adopted. The progress made by the Basque *Ikastolas* is demonstrably better in terms of promoting NDL proficiency as part of learners' holistic linguistic repertoires.

One risk in schools where the Basque multilingual curriculum is implemented is that English (and to some degree French) may be added before NDL issues are fully confronted. This includes programs that rush to include DLs without focusing on Basque development, as well as programs that promote Basque and the DLs but ignore the existing linguistic proficiency of incoming learners. For example, there has been serious discussion regarding Basque language promotion with immigrant learners who speak Mandarin or Indigenous South American languages at home, and whose own NDLs and cultures should arguably be valorized (for example, Etxeberria and Elosegi, 2008). Another risk

is that the widely promoted methodology known as Content and Language Integrated Learning (CLIL), which gives teachers a way to teach languages across the curriculum, is an extension of 'Lx only' pedagogy. The concept of teaching non-language subjects 'with and through' an unfamiliar language (for example, Marsh, 2002) is not new, but the danger is for certain subjects to be taught exclusively through certain languages, for example English, sidelining other languages in the multilingual repertoire of both learners and their teachers. This highlights the risk in both situations internationally of how multilingual curricula are to be implemented, given the existing linguistic proficiency and methodological understandings of available teachers. Put another way, adopting a multilingual curriculum is one thing; implementing it is another.

CONCLUSION

Multilingual Education for All (MEFA) is the slogan we use to represent our position in this chapter, and we have described a number of concerted efforts on behalf of this aim. We have presented MEFA as a paradigm shift but also as a way to promote learners' own (often non-dominant) languages whilst developing multiple linguistic, cognitive and intercultural resources that will stand them in good stead in this increasingly interconnected world.

Building on learners' existing linguistic repertoires, maximizing the efficiency of cross-linguistic transfer and modelling multilingual behaviours are all aspects of putting a multilingual curriculum into practice. Appropriate aims are not native-like proficiency in each language but multilingual proficiency, that is, a range of proficiency levels in various domains with the resulting overall benefits to communicative and social competence. The multilingual curriculum should leave no one – least of all a DL speaker – monolingual. As a result, MEFA has the potential to transform the lives of all learners, as well as the local, regional, national and global social milieux in which they will interact and thrive.

NOTES

1 See, for example, http://www.unesco.org/new/en/education/themes/leading-the-international-agenda/education-for-all/the-efa-movement/jomtien-1990/ (last accessed July 20, 2015).
2 See, for example, http://www.unesco.org/new/en/culture/achieving-the-millennium-development-goals/mdgs/ (last accessed July 20, 2015).
3 The International Conference on Language, Education and the Millennium Development Goals was held on 9–11 November 2010; see UNESCO (2010, 2012).
4 *Ikastolas* are Basque-medium schools (minority language maintenance and immersion) committed to the promotion and development of the Basque language and culture. The *Ikastolen Elkartea*, a network of over 100 schools, organizes administrative services, curriculum development, publication of Basque-medium materials for all subjects and levels, in-service teacher training programs, evaluation services and programs to foster Basque cultural practices.
5 http://www.garabide.eus/english/ (last accessed July 20, 2015).
6 See http://www.youtube.com/watch?v=4VWBwtJUhaA (last accessed July 20, 2015).

REFERENCES

Alexander, Neville (ed.) (2005) *Mother Tongue-Based Bilingual Education in Southern Africa: The Dynamics of Implementation*. Cape Town: PRAESA.

Baker, Colin (2006) *Foundations of Bilingual Education and Bilingualism* (4th ed.). Bristol, UK: Multilingual Matters.

Benson, Carol (2004) 'Do we expect too much from bilingual teachers? Bilingual teaching in developing countries', in Janina Brutt-Griffler and Manka Varghese (eds.), *Bilingualism and Language Pedagogy*. Bristol, UK: Multilingual Matters. pp. 112–29.

Benson, Carol (2012) 'Curriculum development in multilingual schools', in Carol A. Chapelle (ed.), *The Encyclopedia of Applied Linguistics*. Hoboken, NJ: Wiley-Blackwell.

Benson, Carol (2013) 'Towards adopting a multilingual habitus in educational development', in Carol Benson and Kimmo Kosonen (eds.), *Language Issues in Comparative Education: Inclusive Teaching and Learning in Non-Dominant Languages and Cultures*. Rotterdam: Sense. Chapter 15.

Benson, Carol, Heugh, Kathleen, Bogale, Berhanu and Gebre Yohannes, Mekonnen (2012) 'Multilingual education in Ethiopian primary schools', in Tove Skutnabb-Kangas and Kathleen Heugh (eds.), *Multilingual Education and Sustainable Diversity Work: From Periphery to Center*. New York, NY: Routledge. pp. 32–61.

Benson, Carol and Kosonen, Kimmo (2012) 'A critical comparison of language-in-education policy and practice in four Southeast Asian countries and Ethiopia', in Tove Skutnabb-Kangas and Kathleen Heugh (eds.), *Multilingual Education and Sustainable Diversity Work: From Periphery to Centre*. New York, NY: Routledge. pp. 111–137.

Bialystock, Ellen (2001) *Bilingualism in Development: Language, Literacy and Cognition*. Cambridge: Cambridge University Press.

Bourdieu, Pierre (1991) *Language and Symbolic Power*. Cambridge: Cambridge University Press.

Cenoz, Jasone (2009) *Towards Multilingual Education: Basque Educational Research from an International Perspective*. Bristol, UK: Multilingual Matters.

Cenoz, Jasone and Genesee, Fred (eds.) (1998) *Beyond Bilingualism: Multilingualism and Multilingual Education*. Bristol, UK: Multilingual Matters.

Cenoz, Jasone and Gorter, Durk (2011) 'A holistic approach to multilingual education: introduction', *The Modern Language Journal*, 95(3): 339–43.

Cook, Vivian (1995) 'Multi-competence and the learning of many languages', *Language, Culture and Curriculum*, 8: 93–8.

Council of Europe (2001) *Common European Framework of Reference for Languages*. Available from www.coe.int/t/dg4/linguistic/source/framework_en.pdf (last accessed July 20, 2015)

Council of Europe (Feb 2006) *Plurilingual Education in Europe: 50 Years of International*

Cooperation. Strasbourg, France: Language Policy Division. Available from http://www.coe.int/t/dg4/linguistic/Source/PlurinlingalEducation_En.pdf (last accessed July 20, 2015).

Council of Europe (2007) *Guide for the Development of Language Education Policies in Europe: From Linguistic Diversity to Plurilingual Education.* Strasbourg, France: Language Policy Division. Available from https://www.coe.int/t/dg4/linguistic/Guide_niveau3_EN.asp#TopOfPage (last accessed July 20, 2015).

Crystal, David (1997) *English as a Global Language.* Cambridge: Cambridge University Press.

Cummins, Jim (1981) 'The role of primary language development in promoting educational success for language minority students', in California State Department of Education (ed.) *Schooling and Language Minority Students: A Theoretical Framework.* Los Angeles, CA: Evaluation, Dissemination and Assessment Center California State University. pp. 3–49.

Cummins, Jim (2007) 'Rethinking monolingual instructional strategies in multilingual classrooms', *Canadian Journal of Applied Linguistics/Revue canadienne de linguistique appliquée,* 10(2): 221–40.

Cummins, Jim (2009) 'Fundamental psycholinguistic and sociological principles underlying educational success for linguistic minority students', in A. Mohanty, M. Panda, R. Phillipson, and T. Skutnabb-Kangas (eds.), *Multilingual Education for Social Justice: Globalising the Local.* New Delhi, India: Orient BlackSwan. pp. 21–35.

EHIK (Euskal Herriko Ikastolen Konfederazioa) (2004) *Basque Curriculum: Cultural Itinerary. The experts' proposal.* Zamudio, Spain: Confederation of Ikastolas of the Basque Country.

EHIK (2006) *Derrigorrezko Eskolaldirako* Euskal Curriculuma. [Basque Curriculum for Compulsory Education]. Donostia, Spain: Confederation of Ikastolas of the Basque Country. Available in Spanish and English from http://www.euskalcurriculuma.eus/ (last accessed July 20, 2015)

EHIK (2009) *The Ikastola Language Project.* Donostia Spain: Confederation of Ikastolas of the Basque Country. Available from http://www.ikastola.eus/sites/default/files/page/5167/file/The%20Ikastola%20Language%20Project.pdf (last accessed July 20, 2015).

Elorza, Itziar (2012) 'Materials development for multilingual education', in Carol A. Chapelle (ed.) *The Encyclopedia of Applied Linguistics.* Oxford: Blackwell.

Elorza, Itziar and Muñoa, Inmaculada (2008) 'Promoting the minority language through integrated plurilingual language planning: the case of the *Ikastolas', Language, Culture & Curriculum,* 21(1): 85–101.

Etxeberria, Felix and Elosegi, Kristina (2008) 'Basque, Spanish and immigrant minority languages in the Basque school', *Language Culture and Curriculum,* 21: 69–84.

Fishman, Joshua (2001) *Can Threatened Languages be Saved? Reversing Language Shift Revisited: A 21st Century Perspective.* Bristol, UK: Multilingual Matters.

Garagorri, Xabier (2004) 'Introduction', in EHIK (eds.), *Basque Curriculum. Cultural Itinerary.* Zamudio Spain: EHIK, pp.12–42

García, Ofelia (2009) *Bilingual Education in the 21st Century: A Global Perspective.* Oxford: Wiley-Blackwell.

García, Ofelia, Skutnabb-Kangas, Tove and Torres-Guzmán, María (eds.) (2006) *Imagining Multilingual Schools: Languages in Education and Globalization.* Bristol, UK: Multilingual Matters.

Genesee, Fred (ed.) (1994) *Educating Second Language Children: The Whole Child, the Whole Curriculum, the Whole Community.* Cambridge: Cambridge University Press.

Genesee, Fred (2004) 'What do we know about bilingual education for majority language students?', in Tej K. Bhatia (ed.), *What Do We Know About Bilingual Education for Majority Language Students?* Malden MA: Blackwell. pp. 547–76.

Gogolin, Ingrid (2002) 'Linguistic and cultural diversity in Europe: a challenge for educational research and practice. ECER Keynote', *European Educational Research Journal,* 1(1): 123–38.

Graddol, David (2000) *The Future of English? A Guide to Forecasting the Popularity of the English Language in the 21st Century.* London: The British Council. Available from http://www.teachingenglish.org.uk/sites/

teacheng/files/learning-elt-future.pdf (last accessed July 20, 2015).

Grenoble, Lenore and Whaley, Lindsay (2006) *Saving Languages: An Introduction to Language Revitalization*. Cambridge: Cambridge University Press.

Grosjean, François (1989) 'Neurolinguists, beware! The bilingual is not two monolinguals in one person', *Brain and Language*, 36(1): 3–15.

Hélot, Christine (2008) 'Bilingual education in France: School policies versus home practices', in Christine Hélot and Anne Marie De Mejia (eds.), *Forging Multilingual Spaces: Integrating Majority and Minority Bilingual Education*. Clevedon: Multilingual Matters. pp. 203–227.

Herdina, Philip and Jessner, Ulrike (2002) *A Dynamic Model of Multilingualism: Perspectives of Change in Psycholinguistics*. Bristol, UK: Multilingual Matters.

Hermanto, Nicola, Moreno, Sylvain and Bialystock, Ellen (2012) 'Linguistic and metalinguistic outcomes of intense immersion education: how bilingual?', *International Journal of Bilingual Education and Bilingualism*, 15(2): 131–45.

Heugh, Kathleen (2008) 'Language policy and education in southern Africa', in Stephen May and Nancy Hornberger (eds.), *Volume 1: Language Policy and Political Issues in Education. Encyclopedia of Language and Education*. 2nd edn. New York, NY: Springer. pp. 355–67.

Heugh, Kathleen (2009) 'Literacy and bi/multilingual education in Africa: recovering collective memory and expertise', in Tove Skutnabb-Kangas, Robert Phillipson, Ajit Mohanty and Minati Pana (eds.), *Social Justice Through Multilingual Education*. Bristol, UK: Multilingual Matters. pp. 103–24.

Heugh, Kathleen, Benson, Carol, Bogale, Berhanu and Gebre Yohannes, Mekonnen (2012) 'Implications for multilingual education: student achievement in different models of education in Ethiopia', in Tove Skutnabb-Kangas and Kathleen Heugh, (eds.), *Multilingual Education and Sustainable Diversity Work: From Periphery to Center*. New York, NY: Routledge. pp. 239–62.

Hoffman, James (2012) 'Why EGRA – a clone of DIBELS – will fail to improve literacy in Africa', *Research in the Teaching of English*, 46(4): 340–57.

Hoffman, Charlotte and Ytsma, Jehannes (eds.) (2003) *Trilingualism in Family, School and Community*. Bristol, UK: Multilingual Matters.

Hymes, Dell (1972) 'Communicative competence', in John B. Pride and Janet Holmes (eds.), *Sociolinguistics*. Harmondsworth, UK: Penguin. pp. 269–93.

Jessner, Ulrike (2006) *Linguistic Awareness in Multilinguals: English as a Third Language*. Edinburgh: Edinburgh University Press.

Jessner, Ulrike (2008) 'A DST model of multilingualism and the role of metalinguistic awareness', *The Modern Language Journal*, 92(2): 270–83.

Kenner, Charmian (2004) 'Living in simultaneous worlds: difference and integration in bilingual script learning', *International Journal of Bilingual Education and Bilingualism*, 7(1): 43–61.

Kosonen, Kimmo (2010) 'Ethnolinguistic minorities and non-dominant languages in mainland Southeast Asian language-in-education policies', in MacLeans Geo-JaJa and Suzanne Majhanovich (eds.), *Education, Language, and Economics: Growing National and Global Dilemmas*. Rotterdam: Sense. pp. 73–88.

Kosonen, Kimmo and Benson, Carol (2013) 'Introduction: Inclusive teaching and learning through the use of non-dominant languages and cultures', in Carol Benson and Kimmo Kosonen (eds.), *Language Issues in Comparative Education: Inclusive Teaching and Learning in Non-Dominant Languages and Cultures*. Rotterdam: Sense. pp. 1–16.

Krashen, Stephen (1981) 'Bilingual education and second language acquisition theory', in *Schooling and Language Minority Students: A Theoretical Framework*. Sacramento, CA: California State Department of Education. pp. 51–79.

Krashen, Stephen and Terrell, Tracy (1983) *The Natural Approach: Language Acquisition in the Classroom*. London: Prentice Hall Europe.

Lee, Scott, Watt, Ron and Frawley, Jack (2014) 'Effectiveness of bilingual education in Cambodia: a longitudinal comparative case study of ethnic minority children in bilingual and monolingual schools', *Compare: A Journal of Comparative and International*

Education published online 28 April 2014. Available from: http://dx.doi.org/10.1080/03 057925.2014.909717 (last accessed July 20, 2015)

López, Luis Enrique (2005) *De resquicios a boquerones: La educación intercultural bilingüe en Bolivia*. La Paz: PROEIB Andes/Plural Editores.

López, Luís Enrique (2006) 'Cultural diversity, multilingualism and indigenous education in Latin America', in García et al. (eds.), *Imagining Multilingual Schools* Bristol, UK. Multilingual Matters. pp. 238–261.

Luke, Allan (2013) 'Defining critical literacy', in Jessica Zacher Pandya and JuliAnna Ávila (eds.), *Moving Critical Literacies Forward: A New Look at Praxis Across Contexts*. New York, NY: Routledge. pp. 19–31.

Marsh, David (2002) *CLIL/EMILE–The European Dimension: Actions, Trends and Foresight Potential*. Brussels, Belgium: Director General Education & Culture, European Commission.

Mohanty, Ajit (2006) 'Multilingualism of the unequals and predicaments of education in India: mother tongue or other tongue?', in Ofelia García, Tove Skutnabb-Kangas and María Torres-Guzmán (eds.), *Imagining Multilingual Schools: Languages in Education and Globalization.* Bristol, UK: Multilingual Matters. pp. 262–83.

New London Group (1996) 'A pedagogy of multiliteracies: designing social futures', *Harvard Educational Review*, 66(1): 60–92.

Pavlenko, Aneta (2014) *The Bilingual Mind and What It Tells Us about Language and Thought*. Cambridge: Cambridge University Press.

Ramani, Esther and Joseph, Michael (2010) Developing academic biliteracy: a case study of a bilingual BA degree (in English and Sesotho sa Leboa) at the University of Limpopo.

Republic of South Africa (1996) *The Constitution of the Republic of South Africa 1996*. Cape Town: Constitutional Assembly and National Parliament.

Schroeder, Leila (2013) 'Teaching and assessing independent reading skills in multilingual African countries: Not as simple as ABC', in Carol Benson and Kimmo Kosonen (eds.), *Language Issues in Comparative Education: Inclusive Teaching and Learning in Non-Dominant Languages and Cultures.* Rotterdam: Sense. pp. 245–64.

UNESCO (2003) *Education in a Multilingual World.* UNESCO Education Position Paper. Paris: UNESCO. Available from http://unesdoc.unesco.org/images/0012/001297/129728e.pdf (last accessed July 20, 2015).

UNESCO (2005) *First Language First: Community-Based Literacy Programmes for Minority Language Contexts in Asia.* Bangkok, Thailand: UNESCO.

UNESCO (2010) *International Conference on Language, Education and the Millennium Development Goals (MDGs).* 9–11 November 2010, Bangkok. Available from http://www.seameo.org/LanguageMDGConference 2010/ (last accessed July 20, 2015)

UNESCO (2012) *Why Language Matters for the Millennium Development Goals.* Bangkok: UNESCO. Available from http://unesdoc.unesco.org/images/0021/002152/215296E.pdf (last accessed July 20, 2015).

Vu, Thi Thanh Huong (2010) *Enhancing education quality for ethnic minority children through the use of teaching assistants*, unpublished report written for Save the Children, Hanoi.

Walter, Stephen and Davis, Patricia (2005) *Eritrea National Reading Survey: September 2002. Ministry of Education, Asmara Eritrea.* Dallas, TX: SIL International.

White, Lydia and Genesee, Fred (1996) 'How native is near-native? The issue of ultimate attainment in adult second language acquisition', *Second Language Research*, 12: 233–65.

36

Creativity, Education and Curricula

Anusca Ferrari and Dominic Wyse

Creativity can be viewed as an essential characteristic of human thinking, related to the freedom of the human spirit. More instrumentally, creativity can be valued in relation to its economic impact. Governments around the world have turned their attention to how children and young people might acquire the necessary attributes of creativity as part of their education. This has often been a result of politicians' views that creativity is a driver of economic prosperity. The analysis of survey data and input–output models data from Arts Council and Office for National Statistics in the UK (Centre for Economics and Business Research, 2013) offered a powerful case for the economic benefits of arts and culture, as exemplified in the following points:

- Businesses in the UK arts and culture industry generated turnover of £12.4 billion in 2011… (approx. 0.4 to 1.0% GDP)
- The arts and culture industry employed, on average, about 0.45 per cent of total employment in the UK and 0.48 per cent of all employment in England.

- The greatest contributor to the overall funding of the industry … has been and still is earned income … Arts and culture is experiencing a pincer movement effect, reduced consumer expenditure due to squeezed incomes and reduced public funding.
- Commercial creative industries (as recently defined by Nesta) are estimated to provide nearly five per cent of UK employment, 10 per cent of UK GDP and 11 per cent of the UK's service exports. Arts and culture plays a significant role in supporting these industries (Centre for Economics and Business Research, 2013: 2)

Political emphasis has revealed the view by policymakers that creativity is deemed essential for collective and individual well-being (Blamires and Peterson, 2014; Robinson, 2006) and a student asset for the twenty-first century (Barroso, 2009; Katz-Buonincontro, 2012). As a result of these emphases governments have responded with actions. The Australian government's Melbourne Declaration on Educational Goals for Young Australians (which sets educational priorities for 10 years) committed the nation to developing 'confident and creative individuals' (Ministerial Council on Education, Employment Training and Youth Affairs, 2008). In China, from 2006, creativity in the early years became an educational priority (Vong, 2008). In the special administrative region of Hong Kong, creativity has become the theme of educational reform to prepare for the challenges of a twenty-first-century society (Leong, 2010). In Greece, the Cross-Thematic Curriculum Framework introduced in primary education in 2003 focused on creative abilities and imagination through exploration and discovery (Kampylis, 2010). In the twenty-first-century skills movement, which has global reach but started in the US, creativity is perceived as a core skill to redefine the goals of education in the new millennium (Binkley et al., 2012).

Political actions to fashion school curricula reveal specific educational priorities including priorities for the kind of knowledge to be taught. A curriculum is the way in which domains of knowledge are made available to students (Craft, 2005); curriculum development is a political act, which establishes a vision of the kind of society policymakers envisage for the future (Williamson and Payton, 2009). Indeed the creation of a curriculum depends upon a politics of adjustment and negotiation between prospective competence needs, disciplinary domains and educational traditions. National curricula are built, explicitly and/or implicitly, on societal aims for education, conceptions of knowledge and political control (Wyse et al., 2014).

In this chapter, we discuss how different perceptions of creativity influence its place in the curriculum and some of the consequences that this has for the education of children and young people. Our framing for the chapter is based upon the idea that conceptualisations of creativity are reflected in curriculum development and curriculum policy. We argue for the necessity of a clear and consensual agenda for creativity in education. The first section of the chapter outlines how plural conceptions of creativity have been established through research. Three conceptions in

particular are then related to a discussion of personality traits of creative people and how teachers perceive these traits. The second section of the chapter considers the implications of fostering a creative culture in schools and analyses barriers and enablers, in particular considering how curricula and assessment play a part in fostering or hindering creativity.

CONCEPTIONS OF CREATIVITY

An emerging consensus for the definition of creativity stands on three pillars: originality, value and acceptance (Wyse and Ferrari, 2014). A process, product or output is considered creative when it is original and valuable at the same time (thus contributing to a specific area or domain; Beghetto, 2005). Across diverse fields and disciplines, originality (or novelty) and value (or appropriateness) emerge repeatedly as the hallmarks of creative endeavour (Barron, 1955; Mednick, 1962; Mumford and Simonton, 1997; Stein, 1974; Sternberg and Lubart, 1999; Vernon, 1989). The third pillar of the definition – acceptance – involves the judgment of 'experts' in recognising the originality and value of the output or process, thus generating, as we shall point out, one of the unresolved dilemmas about creativity in the designation of such experts.

Authors have diverged in their precise definitions beyond these three pillars. Meusburger (2009) argues that over a hundred different analyses can be found in the literature. Different research perspectives isolate a specific aspect of creativity, often neglecting to relate the single aspect to the whole (Sternberg and Lubart, 1999).

Despite Laske's (1993) opinion that creativity is impossible to define or explain (and should rather be exemplified), a number of scholars have proposed definitions of creativity, each bringing a different voice and perspective to the debate. At one end of a continuum of levels of creativity, Gardner (1993) suggests that creative works cause a 'refashioning' of the domain they contribute to. At the other end of the continuum, Craft (2005) identifies creativity as the ability to see possibilities that others have not noticed, and Burnard et al. (2006) talk about 'possibility thinking' – the 'what if' and 'as if' driven by questioning and imagination. Among scholars underlining the 'thinking' side of creativity, we include Amabile (1990) for whom a creative response to a task is heuristic rather than algorithmic – a discovery rather than a procedural process – and thus is substantively different to reproduction (Taylor, 1988).

An important dimension of the debate has been the consideration of creativity as the preserve of eminent people versus the kind of creativity that occurs in everyday life. According to Kaufman and Beghetto (2009), most research on creativity takes one of two directions: some scholars focus on major creative breakthroughs (for example, Gardner, 1993; Gruber, 1974; Simonton, 1999), whilst others look at new and valuable contributions from ordinary people (for example, Ward et al., 2004; Wiley, 1998). The distinction between the two strands has been referred to as Big C and little c creativity – a distinction reported in many studies, albeit sometimes with different wordings (Amabile, 2013; Craft et al., 2001; Kaufman and Beghetto, 2009; Kozbelt et al., 2010; Shneiderman, 2000).

Big C creativity refers to the creative accomplishments of geniuses, seen in people such as Curie, Confucius, Dickinson, Mozart, Nureyev or Senghor. Their creative achievements are exemplary and comprise ground-breaking novelty and excellence in their domain, as well as societal recognition and valuation. Little c creativity, on the other hand, can be seen as the ability and attitude that leads to new and effective solutions to everyday 'problems'. A similar distinction can be found in Shneiderman (2000) who differentiates between revolutionary creativity, imputable to Nobel laureates and geniuses, and evolutionary acts of creativity, which can include doctors making unforeseen diagnoses.

The theoretical distinction between the different levels of creativity raises a substantial problem briefly mentioned at the beginning of the chapter: the role and designation of 'experts'. In order to judge whether something is original there needs to be a domain of reference – the idea or product has to be seen in a context from which it differs and in which it is judged to be of value. This requires a field of experts who accept the idea or product as new and valuable (Csikszentmihalyi, 1999). Amabile (2013), however, cautions that although experts will easily recognise the originality of a contribution, they will not necessarily endorse its value, which in some cases requires the test of time to be perceived as authoritative or revolutionary. Here is the paradox: creativity contributes to the advancement of society through the work of eminent people; however, contemporaries might not perceive pioneering contributions as valuable (Van Gogh comes to mind, dying in poverty and disgrace), and yet it is contemporary experts who act as gatekeepers of a domain and who are asked to judge the novelty and relevance of contributions.

In relation to little c creativity, the three pillars of our definition can be further contextualised (Jones and Wyse, 2013). Originality is taken to mean original for the individual, the context or the situation, but not necessarily in comparison with larger norms (Runco, 2003). Value is assessed in the context and field in which the person is acting. Acceptance, we have just seen, may come from educators and/or pupils who are not necessarily eminent experts, and yet although little c creativity might not involve a refashioning of a domain or field, it can contribute to the improvement of processes, products, actions, ideas and practices.

TRAITS OF CREATIVE PEOPLE

A strand of studies on creativity considers the personal traits and characteristics of creative individuals. Significant work has been done in seeking to understand eminent intellectuals and creators, but also research has been carried out on ordinary people, with the identification of several intellectual and personality traits that have been recognised as attributes of creativity. We consider that this strand of research is relevant for a discussion of creativity in education because it sheds some light on specific aspects of creativity, and on traits and attitudes that we believe could be fostered in the classroom in the interest of enhancing creativity. Intelligence and motivation are two central aspects of this line of research because they are central in education – we therefore primarily focus on those two features.

For decades intelligence was misleadingly understood as the central individual characteristic of creative people (Albert and Runco, 1999). We can still hear the echo of this idea in the number of studies that associate creativity with genius or giftedness (Albert and Runco, 1990). However, the relationship between creativity and intelligence is not linear. The 'threshold theory' suggests that there is a required minimum level of intelligence (measured in terms of IQ) to be creative, but above a certain level, intelligence does not influence creativity (Runco, 2007). Other studies conclude that intelligence is a 'necessary but not sufficient component of creativity' (Heilman et al., 2003: 370). For Getzels and Jackson (1962), intelligence plays a smaller role than personality in determining creativity.

Sharp (2004) distinguished creativity from talent, arguing that talent refers to the possession of aptitude and skills in a given area, without necessarily implying originality or creative ability. A comparison with the musical domain will exemplify the complexity of this claim. Talented performing musicians might be judged to be less creative than musical composers; however, we believe it would be more useful to talk of 'gradients' of creativity. It is undoubtedly clear that performers such as pianist Glenn Gould or violinist Jascha Heifetz brought original and valuable aspects to performance, and their

performances might be judged as creative (Wyse, 2014). According to Gardner (1993), although a performance often requires reproduction of musical notation, opportunities for innovation, improvisation and interpretation are also present. This reminds us of Amabile's (1990) point that heuristic rather than algorithmic processes are discriminant of creative acts – a performance is creative when it involves discovery, when the process moves away from more basic procedural reproduction.

Motivation is one of the main factors conducive to creative output. On the basis of her research, Amabile (1998) argued that intrinsic motivation is more important than extrinsic when determining impact on creativity. Intrinsic motivation is about passion and interest, an internal desire to be engaged in a specific activity. This internal push is the stronger driver of creative production: people will be creative when they are driven by their interests and passions, and not by external pressure (extrinsic motivation, which can take the form of a cash incentive or, in education, a good grade from the teacher). Creative people are those who are engaged in a task because they derive pleasure from the task itself. Csikszentmihalyi (1996) described this pleasure as a mental state of 'flow' – being fully immersed in an activity, experiencing an automatic, effortless and yet focused state. Csikszentmihalyi (1990) coined the term 'flow' to describe these pleasurable feelings of complete absorption reported by creative people engaged in their selected activity, during which creation seems to flow naturally and concentration makes them lose perception of time. Csikszentmihalyi holds that this state is the fuel of creativity. Sustained creativity needs sustained and undivided attention to the task at hand (Bohm, 1998).

The undivided dedication derived from intrinsic motivation could relate to another two common characteristics of creative people: work ethic and perseverance (Csikszentmihalyi, 1988; Runco, 2007). Csikszentmihalyi (1996) interviewed creative people from different fields (a sculptor, a physicist, a social scientist, a physician, a painter, an inventor). When talking about their work, they all referred to long periods of hard work and to the fact that their curiosity pushed them to dedicate long hours to the tasks they were involved in. Csikszentmihalyi said that without perseverance novel ideas would not come to completion. For Gardner (1993: 362), the 'Exemplary Creator' 'works nearly all the time' and is obsessed with their work. Their perseverance does not stop at motivation and engagement. Creative people tend to persevere in having their ideas accepted: they are persuasive (Simonton, 1990), analyse which ideas are worth pursuing and will persuade others that their ideas are of value (Sternberg and Lubart, 1999). Their persuasiveness, however, can also create social friction according to Ng and Smith (2004). Although many people tend to agree with group norms, creative persons are often dogmatic and will stand up for their ideas against everything and everyone, for example the case of Galileo Galilei and his conflicts with the Catholic Church. Feist (1998) lists a series of arguably less attractive characteristics of creative people: less conventional, dominant, hostile and impulsive. They are norm-doubting, non-conformist and independent. Although being independent, they can also show a certain immaturity (Csikszentmihalyi, 1996; Gardner, 1993).

Despite undesirable characteristics recognised in a variety of studies, the so-called 'dark side' of creativity is often based on misconceptions. The Romantic period is still casting a shade on the artist and creative person as mad and savage (Csikszentmihalyi, 1996) and the creative process as a mysterious and mystical creation (Rodari, 1973). Csikszentmihalyi argued that every period puts a 'transient mask' on creative people (1996: 56). In ancient times, he asserts, creativity was associated with mystical beliefs (Sternberg and Lubart, 1999) or inspired by the Muses ('Sing, goddess', as Homer opened the *Iliad*). More recently, creativity was believed to be induced by drugs (Plucker and Dana, 1999) and has been linked to mental breakdowns and illness (Beghetto, 2005). Most robust overviews of creativity research reject the link between mental illness and creativity, and between drug use and creativity (Sawyer, 2012); however, there is a commonly held belief that creative people are tortured souls who need their creative acts as a sort of healing process (Sawyer, 2012).

TEACHERS, CREATIVITY AND LEARNING

Creativity is a fundamental part of human information processing (Dietrich, 2004), and central to the construction of personal meaning (Runco, 2003), thus aligned with learning. It has long been recognised that appropriate knowledge and expertise in a field is an essential aspect of creativity (Boden, 2001; Guilford, 1950; Weisberg, 1999). Learning in a creative way is a form of meaning-making. Constructivist approaches to learning involve understanding and making new and valuable connections between old and new knowledge. As Piaget (1973) claimed, 'to understand is to invent'. Without invention, learning mainly involves memorisation, and teaching as a consequence can be viewed as nothing more than transmission.

Teaching practices can sometimes privilege knowledge reproduction of factual information over knowledge creation, thus reducing creative endeavours. In an article on future middle and secondary teachers' preferences for students' responses, Beghetto (2007a) showed there is a tendency among teachers to prefer standard answers to unique ones, and to dismiss creative answers. Sometimes dismissal of ideas can be a teacher's response to what is seen as pupils' attempts to distract attention from the tasks planned for the lesson. As Kennedy (2005) reports, although not being a punishment, dismissal conveys to students the message that some ideas will not be discussed, hence discouraging students from investing intellectual energy in the pursuit of their new idea. In her study on school reform, Kennedy observed that unexpected ideas from students were often dismissed by teachers because they felt the need to maintain the lesson's momentum. Kennedy refers to this process as a 'tension' to be resolved routinely by teachers in engaging with students, a tension created between the objectives of the lesson and the unexpected reflections and outbursts of students, as if students' active participation in their lessons was a 'misplaced' act. Although Kennedy does not refer explicitly to creativity, her description of classroom interactions can be seen as a possible ground for creative engagement. Banaji et al. (2013) talk about a dualist framework in schools, one which sees some knowledge as good and some knowledge as bad. Runco (2004) and Beghetto (2007b) also agree on the detrimental effects on students' creativity of the dismissal of their ideas. One of the personality traits of creative people is their capacity to take risks (Davies, 1999), a quality often hindered in a school environment where the correct standardised answer is the desired response. Some forms of teaching, often regarded as 'traditional teaching', can deter students' individual autonomy (Ng, 2002), which affects their creative performance.

Cropley (2014) found that research in many countries and over many years portrays a majority of teachers who 'disapprove of or even dislike' creative children. Despite this, Feldhusen and Treffinger (1975) showed that 96 per cent of the teachers they surveyed agreed that creativity is a good thing. Runco, Johnson and Bear (1993) reported teachers' favourable attitudes to creativity. The paradox of desirability (that is, creativity being explicitly seen as desirable but in practice avoided) is reflected in teacher views of the ideal student. Teachers seem to prefer learners who have characteristics such as 'conforming' and 'considerate', which are in sharp contrast with creative personality traits (Runco, 1999). Ng and Smith (2004) and Westby and Dawson (1995) came to the same conclusion: teachers dislike personality traits

associated with creativity. Creative behaviour in students is often perceived by teachers with scepticism and viewed as students behaving egotistically.

Teachers are pivotal in students' creative performance because they can build a climate conducive to creative learning (Esquivel, 1995). They provide the balance between structure and freedom of expression (Beghetto, 2005). As Wyse and Spendlove (2007) point out, teachers play an important role in triggering students' creativity because they represent the field of experts who are to judge the creative output; however, it is the 'acceptance' of the original and valuable thinking, process or output that is often not supported by teachers.

CREATIVITY AND THE CURRICULUM

There have been a number of moves in policy to promote creativity in school curricula, albeit with contradictory actions from governments. There is an international tendency to tighten government control of curriculum and assessment (Wyse et al., 2014). At the same time teachers are asked to be creative and innovative, but often feel the pressure to achieve standards (for instance, in literacy and numeracy). Tasks, duties and demands accumulate as new requirements do not substitute others but are added to workload (Christensen et al., 2008). In a comparative study involving teachers from England, France and Denmark, Osborn and McNess (2002) found that teachers from England reported that highly prescribed curriculum and high stakes testing left them little possibility for creativity. The knowledge-burden that teachers are often required to impart has a negative impact on the time that can be allocated to exploring topics in a creative and innovative way (Craft, 2005).

A creative environment, where children and young people feel safe and accepted, can be an aim of education. Openness towards different people (tolerance) is one of the principles of creative environments according to Florida (2002) who studies creative cities but whose analyses can also be applied to school environments. The notion of acceptance of creativity goes hand-in-hand with an understanding of what creativity is. This understanding implies tackling some 'implicit theories' (Runco, 1999), ideas that teachers might have about creativity, which might differ from scholarship on the subject. For instance, although we have wide scholar support for originality and value as key factors of creativity (within a context of consensual judgement), teachers seem to perceive creativity mainly as an original output (Beghetto, 2007a).

As a major geographical area of the world, the nation states of the European Union represent important sites for consideration of creativity in the school curriculum. Creativity is present and mentioned in school curricula. In a previous publication (Wyse and Ferrari, 2014), we reported findings on an analysis of national curriculum texts for primary and secondary schools from the 27 countries that were, at the time, part of the European Union.[1] The focus of the analysis was the frequency of use of the word 'creativity' which was searched through its stem creativ* and calculated per thousand words. The analysis highlighted that creativity was mentioned in national curriculum texts of all European countries albeit with notable frequency differences. Occurrences of creativity ranged from 0.04 per thousand words in the Netherlands and Poland to 1.78 in Northern Ireland. The countries where creativity ranked higher in terms of relative occurrences were UK – Northern Ireland, 1.78 occurrences per thousand words; Estonia, 1.65; and in UK – Scotland, 1.25. The long-lasting tradition of creativity in the UK was evident in the rate of occurrences at or above the mean of the EU 27, and in two of the four UK countries, it was significantly above the mean (Wyse and Ferrari, 2014).

The case of Estonia is interesting. In unpublished interviews with three educational experts from Estonia, collected during the ICEAC study (see Cachia et al., 2010; Banaji et al., 2013), interviewees reported that education in Estonia was very traditional; however, since 2002 there had been reforms in both teacher training and curriculum in order to modernise the education in the Soviet era aftermath (see Moree, 2013 for a fascinating account by teachers of similar curriculum development in the Czech Republic). In the new curriculum, creativity was seen as one of the seven general competences, and a section of the curriculum on cross-curricular themes supported its conceptualisation. The most common collocates (that is, words that appear more frequently together with the searched term) of creativity in the Estonian curriculum were 'students' and 'development'. However, the three experts who were interviewed recognised that practices were likely to differ across schools and classrooms. They argued that although there was evidence of transition from didactic to active teaching methods, it was predicted that it would be not easy or immediate to change teachers' beliefs, especially in this case of radical change.

In terms of relative occurrences, the places where creativity was less frequently mentioned per thousand words in the national curriculum texts of the EU were France, 0.09; Belgium – Wallonia, 0.07; The Netherlands, 0.04; and Poland, 0.04 (Wyse and Ferrari, 2014). The case of the Netherlands stands out for both low absolute and relative occurrences (creativity is mentioned 17 times in curricula for all subjects and all levels of compulsory school). Consultation with experts and the data from the ICEAC survey showed, however, that creativity is highly valued in schools in the Netherlands (Cachia et al., 2010). The discrepancy in the data between occurrences of the terms in national curriculum texts and the views of experts could be a result of the independence that schools in the Netherlands have in their interpretation and implementation of the curriculum. To a certain extent, a similar discrepancy can be seen in the relatively high levels of curriculum prescription in England against continuing determination by some settings, schools and teachers to implement creative approaches (Wyse et al., 2014).

Even if sufficient attention is paid to creativity in national curricula, and if teachers and schools have sufficient freedom, it does not follow that students will foster their creativity. A key factor is the belief about creativity and education that teachers hold. A long-lasting debate considers the domain of creativity: although creativity is commonly perceived as inherently connected to the arts (Sawyer, 2012), some scholarship has argued that creativity is a feature of any domain or area of knowledge (Beghetto, 2007a; Runco, 1999; Sharp, 2004). The analysis of curricula of the EU showed that creativity occurred almost twice as much in the curricula for arts-related subjects than in other subjects (Wyse and Ferrari, 2014). Banaji et al. (2013), who interviewed 80 educational experts and stakeholders from Europe, reported that a third of interviewees perceived that limiting creativity to the Arts was a problem for its development in education. An interviewee from France stated: 'Basically in France creativity is only associated with the arts and maybe advertising. But a scientist would not consider himself creative' (Banaji et al., 2013: 455). But Cachia and Ferrari (2010) found that teachers from Europe held an encompassing view of creativity. Almost all teachers who took part in the survey (98 per cent) believed that creativity can be applied to every domain of knowledge. When asked if they agreed that creativity is only relevant to visual arts, music, drama and artistic performance, 86 per cent disagreed, with 31 per cent strongly disagreeing and 56 per cent disagreeing. This finding was quite a surprise in the context of general agreement and evidence that teachers tend to hold contradictory conceptions of creativity (Kampylis et al., 2009; Runco, 2003; Westby and Dawson, 1995). The issue of the location of creativity in relation to disciplines and/or subjects is a very important one to tackle because understanding creativity as relevant for the arts only allows for teachers' withdrawal from an engagement in developing students' creative potential across the curriculum (Kampylis et al., 2009).

One of the explanatory factors in relation to aligning some subjects more than others with creativity was revealed in the two main ways in which creativity was described in the analysed curriculum texts: as an artistic output or as a thinking skill. The cases of national curricula from Ireland and Lithuania provide typical examples of this distinction (Heilmann and Korte, 2010). In art-related subjects of those curricula (Visual Arts, Music, Drama), creativity was mainly formulated in terms of self-expression, spontaneity and enjoyment, whilst in other subjects the prevalent focus was on thinking skills and problem solving. The distinction is unhelpful because self-expression can be present in scientific subjects (for example, the act of persuading others that one's ideas are of value) and creative problem solving is often a feature of artistic creativity (for example, deciding how a character might behave in a novel).

The relevance of creativity for all school subjects is evident in the number of publications, mainly books, dedicated to the topic, where typically there would be a general introduction on creativity, its meaning and implication for education, and different contributions differentiated on how creativity is relevant for each school subject. This is the structure of *Unlocking Creativity: Teaching Across the Curriculum* (Fisher and Williams, 2004), of *Creativity for a New Curriculum: 5–11* (Newton, 2012) and of *Creativity in the Primary Curriculum* (Jones and Wyse, 2013). In these books, suggestions are given on how to foster creativity across the curriculum and in all school subjects. There are, however, different conceptualisations of creativity that emerge in these books and their chapters, ranging from an emphasis on imagination in literacy and writing to the focus on problem solving in science and mathematics. Given that we perceive creativity as being relevant for every school subject, does being creative in Biology mean something different to being creative in Music? Is the type of creativity fostered through a specific subject transposable to another subject, or field, or domain? Research is polarised on this matter: some studies have promoted a vision of creativity as transferable across domains (Mardell et al., 2008; Woods and Jeffrey, 1996); others argue that creativity occurs in a specific disciplinary area (Amabile, 1990; Chappell, 2006; Csikszentmihalyi, 1999; Gardner, 1993; Miell and Littleton, 2004). We are left with the impression that disciplinary areas or subjects are perceived each in their own uniqueness and each with their own interpretation of creativity, thus contributing to a kaleidoscopic vision of creativity and failing to provide a definition of and approach to creativity across the curriculum as a transversal competence.

The field of mathematics is a thought-provoking case. Mathematics is a discipline where creative thinking and creative problem solving is often claimed to be prominent; however, in their review of the literature, Leikin and Pitta-Pantazi (2013) found that creativity is neglected in mathematics education research. They notice a double lack of interest: mathematics research devotes little space to creativity, and research on creativity devotes little space to mathematics. They claim that in the mathematics field, research on creativity is recent, mainly having been carried out in the last few years, and it still remains a niche area in studies on mathematics. The article is the introductory discussion of a special issue on the role of creativity in mathematics of the *ZDM* journal, which in 1997 dedicated another special issue on creativity and mathematics. From this volume, Kohler (1997) suggests that teachers of mathematics should act like artists and welcome creative solutions and self-expression, 'For creativity must first be *permitted*' (1997: 88, emphasis in the original). Mann (2006), in his inspiring article on creativity as the essence of mathematics, simply points to problems with the standard pedagogy of mathematics, which sees 'learning from the master' as the main educational method: teachers demonstrate and students repeat and practice, which he clearly sees

as a hindrance to developing creativity. He claims that, even at the level of research on mathematics, there is a lack of a satisfactory and accepted definition of mathematical creativity. We see the problem of definition again coming back as a cause that influences practices and adoptions. Mann argues that the essence of Mathematics is thinking creatively, not providing the right answer. Conversely, Beghetto (2007a) reported that prospective teachers of Mathematics at secondary school level prioritised relevance of responses above uniqueness of responses much more than prospective teachers from other subjects, thus dismissing novel ideas.

ASSESSING CREATIVITY

When claiming that creativity should form a strong, coherent, constituent part of the curriculum, we acknowledge that policy texts as curricula are indicative of practice, rather than definitive, in part because policies are mediated by schools and teachers and other actors in education systems (Ball, 1997). This is part of the reason why we consider it relevant to discuss the role of assessment in relation to creativity in curricula in this chapter. Assessment is an essential component of learning and teaching because it allows the quality of both teaching and learning to be judged and improved. Assessment often determines the priorities of education; it has 'back-wash' effects on teaching and learning. As a result, the promotion of creativity at the curriculum level will not be fruitful if assessment is based on the avoidance or dismissal of creativity. The literature recognises a barrier for creative learning in the way in which formal, national assessment, especially in the form of tests, is conducted. Wyse and Jones (2003) maintained that testing had narrowed school provision at the expense of creativity. Notwithstanding the amount of time required to prepare students for examinations, there was little evidence that testing helps to raise standards. On the contrary, the high stakes statutory assessment system has been seen to introduce some undesirable effects (Wyse and Torrance, 2009).

High-stake tests are not the only form of assessment that influence school provision. Classroom interaction is often perceived by teachers and students as a form of informal assessment and direct feedback, and as mentioned earlier, classroom conversations could benefit from the recognition of learners' unique ideas. Simplicio (2000) and Beghetto (2005) agree on the importance of setting goals: both learners and teachers should have a clear understanding on what should be learned and how. Despite the statutory summative role of assessment in many countries, the other two functions of assessment should not be forgotten because they offer wide opportunities for the recognition of creativity. These are (1) the diagnostic, which aims to analyse pupils' capabilities and aptitudes as a basis for planning and (2) the formative, which gathers evidence about pupils' progress to influence teaching methods and priorities (Black and William, 2003; Harlen and James, 1997). As rote-learning cannot be recognised as creative learning, so summative assessment of mainly factual knowledge provides little space for recognition of creativity.

Assessing creativity has long been a challenging area despite pioneering work carried out by Torrance (1988) who tested several components of divergent thinking. Ellis and Barrs (2008) recognised the compounded difficulties of assessing creativity. They offered a framework and a creative learning scale, the latter divided into five levels or attainment targets, accounting for both creative products and processes. Ellis and Barrs propose an assessment that aims to detect creativity. Their framework of Creative Learning Assessment (CLA) encompasses diagnostic, formative and summative assessment, allowing teachers to make informal judgements and also to evaluate children's creative work in several ways, including collecting pupils' work in portfolios and e-portfolios. Blamires and Peterson (2014) present and discuss seven frameworks that are currently in use to assess creativity in school. In their review, they notice two main limits of those frameworks: first, frameworks are decontextualized from the subjects or disciplines; second, some of the frameworks lack some degree of construct validity. They propose the use of assessment 'for' learning instead of assessment 'of' learning to be applied to the domain of creativity. Assessment for Learning (AfL, elaborated by the Assessment Reform Group, 2002), although it does not consider creativity, provides scope and space for recognition of creative endeavours. It recognises the priority of promoting students' learning and understanding, and highlights the impact of self-assessment and peer assessment in raising children's achievement (Black et al., 2004).

The field of assessment of creativity in education does not appear to have provided a satisfying solution or approach. As Munro (2010) points out, discussing assessment of creativity raises a number of questions, for instance on what to assess – the creative person? The creative output? The conditions surrounding the act of creation? Collard and Looney (2014) remind us that assessment is a central aspect of creativity because creative processes or products are described as valuable and original, and are therefore assessed against two sets of standards. They recognise, however, that little attention has been given to assessing learners' creative processes or products and they ascribe this lack of attention to be 'in part due to the lack of a clear definition of creativity' (Collard and Looney, 2014: 356).

CONCLUSIONS: CURRICULA FOR CREATIVE EDUCATION

The idea of a school culture based on acceptance, the possibility of long periods of time to be dedicated to creative engagement, the clarification on what creativity actually means and how it can be fostered could all be transmitted through appropriate, new, well-drafted educational curricula. Curriculum developers should therefore foster the acceptance of creativity for learning throughout the curriculum and in every subject, and should do so with a promotion of a clear, consistent and evident definition of creativity to be enacted through a balanced curriculum with space for experimentation, creation and digression. However, this vision is far from where we stand.

There is agreement in the literature that a prescriptive curriculum hinders creativity and affects the teaching formats. Curricula are often knowledge-driven and often allow little time for exploration. Another pitfall of prescriptiveness is in the distance the curriculum takes from learners' needs, experiences and motivations. Intrinsic motivation, we have seen, is one of the main triggers of creativity and of engagement. A curriculum that facilitates creativity is therefore one that triggers the intrinsic interests of learners, whilst at the same time being appropriate to their cognitive current level of functioning. The ideal curriculum is tailored to the interests and stages of development of a specific and real class, rather than based on a cohort of anonymous learners.

The literature highlights another aspect of the curriculum that hinders some creative engagement, namely the distinction between core and foundation subjects. Even if not all countries have such a clear-cut distinction, there is still a hierarchy of areas of knowledge that is exemplified in the different school subjects. School subjects are not only perceived to have different weight in the schooling of children and young people, but their actualisation in terms of learning outcomes also seems to be built on different parameters. We reported how creativity, which is rhetorically endorsed as a cross-curricular competence, is conceptualised differently across the curriculum and described in quite different terms from one subject to another.

The long-standing debate in the field about how creativity should most appropriately be defined continues. We found evidence of the following: some broad consensus in relation to originality and value in the context of disciplinary differences; implicit theories of teachers insufficiently informed by research; stereotypical traits inappropriately associated with creative people; weak specification of creativity in school curricula; and a lack of systematic assessment of creativity. To foster creativity, there is need for a precise definition of creativity that is subscribed to by educational stakeholders (policymakers, researchers, curricula developers, teachers, ministries of education, pupils, parents). Such a definition should be widely applicable to disciplinary domains and therefore school subjects. The definition should allow for a conceptualisation of creativity as an entity that is strongly recognisable as independent from the domain of application, far from the current situation where creativity implies fairly different processes in different contexts. Although recognising that there are degrees of creativity, and that different disciplines reveal different applications of the concept, a precise definition of creativity would help understanding the underlying process of the creative endeavour in terms that, although difficult to measure, would be clearly identifiable. We conclude that, despite the richness of research on creativity and the relevance of academic work on creativity in education, in order to effectively promote creativity in education, and to do so with serious intentions of its development, creativity has to be more consistently part of the educational objectives of national curricula.

NOTE

1   At the time of the study, Croatia was not yet part of the European Union. Curricula documents could not be retrieved from Cyprus. For Belgium, the curricula of all communities were acquired. In countries such as Spain and Germany, where the national ministries provide general guidelines and the autonomous communities and Landern provide the regional curriculum, three regions per country were chosen. For the UK, the curricula of the four countries were acquired.

REFERENCES

Albert, R. S. and Runco, M. A. (1990) *Theories of Creativity*. London: Sage Publications.

Albert, R. S. and Runco, M. A. (1999) 'A history of research on creativity', in R. J. Sternberg (ed.), *Handbook of Creativity*. Cambridge: Cambridge University Press. pp. 16–31.

Amabile, T. M. (1990) 'Within you, without you: the social psychology of creativity, and beyond', in M. A. Runco, R. S. Albert (eds.), *Theories of Creativity*. London: Sage Publications. pp. 61–91.

Amabile, T. M. (1998) 'How to kill creativity', *Harvard Business Review,* 76(5): 76–87.

Amabile, T. M. (2013) *Big C, Little C, Howard, and Me: Approaches to Understanding Creativity*. Harvard Business School Working Paper No. 12–085.

Assessment Reform Group (2002) *Assessment for Learning: 10 Principles*. London: Assessment Reform Group, Institute of Education.

Ball, S. (1997) 'Policy sociology and critical social research: a personal review of recent education policy and policy research', *British Educational Research Journal*, 23(3): 257–74.

Banaji, S., Cranmer, S., and Perrotta, C. (2013) 'What's stopping us? Barriers to creativity and innovation in schooling across Europe', in K. Thomas and J. Chan (eds.) *Handbook of Research on Creativity*. Cheltenham, UK: Edward Elgar Publishing. pp. 450–463.

Barron, F. X. (1955) 'The disposition toward originality', *Journal of Abnormal Social Psychology*, 51: 478–85.

Barroso, J.-M. (2009) Message to the European Commission Conference: 'Can creativity be measured?'. Brussels, 28 May 2009.

Beghetto, R. A. (2005) 'Does assessment kill student creativity?', *The Educational Forum,* 69: 254–63.

Beghetto, R. A. (2007a) 'Does creativity have a place in classroom discussion? Prospective teachers' response preferences', *Thinking Skills and Creativity,* 2: 1–9.

Beghetto, R. A. (2007b) 'Creativity research and the classroom: from pitfalls to potential', in A. -G. Tan (ed.), *Creativity: A Handbook for Teachers*. Singapore: World Scientific. pp. 101–14.

Binkley, M., Erstad, O., Herman, J., Raizen, S., Ripley M., and Rumble, M. (2012) 'Defining 21st century skills', in P. Griffin, B. McGaw and E. Care (eds.), *Assessment and Teaching of 21st Century Skills*. Dordrecht, Netherlands: Springer. pp. 17–66.

Black, P. and William, D. (2003) 'In praise of educational research: formative assessment', *British Educational Research Journal*, 29: 623–37. doi: 10.1080/0141192032000133721.

Black, P., Harrison, C., Lee, C., Marshall, B. and William, D. (2004) 'Working inside the black box: assessment for learning in the classroom', *Phi Delta Kappan,* 86(1): 9–21.

Blamires, M. and Peterson, A. (2014) 'Can creativity be assessed? Towards an evidence-informed framework for assessing and planning progress in creativity', *Cambridge Journal of Education*, 44(2): 147–62.

Boden, M. (2001) 'Creativity and knowledge', in A. Craft, B. Jeffrey and M. Leibling (eds.), *Creativity in Education*. London: Continuum. pp. 95–102.

Bohm, D. (1998) *On Creativity*. London: Routledge.

Burnard, P., Craft, A. and Grainger, T. et al (2006) 'Documenting "possibility thinking": A journey of collaborative enquiry', *International Journal of Early Years Education*, 14(3): 243–62.

Cachia, R. and Ferrari, A. (2010) *Creativity in Schools: A Survey of Teachers in Europe*. European Commission, Joint Research Centre, Institute for Prospective Technological Studies. Available from http://ftp.jrc.es/EURdoc/JRC59232.pdf (Accessed 7 August 2015).

Cachia, R., Ferrari, A., Ala-Mutka, K. and Punie, Y. (2010) *Creative Learning and Innovative Teaching: Final Report on the Study on Creativity and Innovation in Education in EU Member States*. European Commission, Joint Research Centre, Institute for Prospective and Technological Studies. Available from http://ftp.jrc.es/EURdoc/JRC62370.pdf (Accessed 7 August 2015).

Centre for Economics and Business Research Ltd (2013) *The Contribution of the Arts and Culture to the National Economy: An Analysis of the Macroeconomic Contribution of the Arts and Culture and of Some of Their Indirect Contributions through Spillover Effects Felt in the Wider Economy*. London: Centre for Economics and Business Research.

Chappell, K. (2006) *Creativity within Late Primary Age Dance Education: Unlocking Expert Specialist Dance Teachers Conceptions and Approaches*. PhD thesis, Laban, London. Available from http://kn.open.ac.uk/public/document.cfm?documentid=8627 (Accessed 7 August 2015).

Christensen, C., Johnson, C. W. and Horn, M. B. (2008) *Disrupting Class: How Disruptive Innovation Will Change the Way the World Learns*. New York, NY: McGraw Hill.

Collard, P. and Looney, J. (2014) 'Nurturing creativity in education', *European Journal of Education*, 49: 348–64.

Craft, A. (2005) *Creativity in Schools: Tensions and Dilemmas*. London: Routledge.

Craft, A., Jeffrey, B. and Leibling, M. (eds.) (2001) *Creativity in Education*. Bloomsbury Publishing.

Cropley, A. J. (2014) 'Neglect of creativity in education: a moral issue', in S. Moran, D. H. Cropley, and J. C. Kaufman (eds.), *The Ethics of Creativity*. New York, NY: Palgrave Macmillan. pp. 250–64.

Csikszentmihalyi, M. (1988) 'Motivation and creativity: toward a synthesis of structural and energistic approaches to cognition', *New Ideas in Psychology*, 6(2): 159–76.

Csikszentmihalyi, M. (1990) 'The domain of creativity', in R. S. Albert and M. A. Runco (eds.), *Theories of Creativity*. London: Sage Publications. pp. 190–212.

Csikszentmihalyi, M. (1996) *Creativity: Flow and the Psychology of Discovery and Invention*. New York, NY: HarperCollins.

Csikszentmihalyi, M. (1999) 'Implications of a systems perspective for the study of creativity', in R. J. Sternberg (ed.), *Handbook of Creativity*. Cambridge: Cambridge University Press. pp. 313–35.

Davies, T. (1999) 'Taking risks as a failure of creativity in the teaching and learning of design and technology', *The Journal of Design and Technology*, 4(2): 101–8.

Dietrich, A. (2004) 'The cognitive neuroscience of creativity', *Psychonomic, Bulletin and Review*, 11(6): 1011–26.

Ellis, S. and Barrs, M. (2008) 'The assessment of creative learning', in J. Sefton-Green (ed.), *Creative Learning*. London: Creative Partnerships. pp. 73–89.

Esquivel, G. B. (1995) 'Teacher behaviours that foster creativity', *Educational Psychology Review*, 7(2): 185–202.

Feist G. J. (1998) 'A meta-analysis of personality in scientific and artistic creativity', *Personality and Social Psychology Review*, 2(4): 290–309.

Feldhusen, J. F. and Treffinger, D. J. (1975) 'Teachers' attitudes and practices in teaching creativity and problem-solving to economically disadvantaged and minority children', *Psychological Reports*, 37(3f): 1161–2.

Fisher, R. and Williams, M. (eds.) (2004) *Unlocking Creativity: Teaching Across the Curriculum*. London: Routledge.

Florida, R. L. (2002) *The Rise of the Creative Class: And How It's Transforming Work, Leisure, Community and Everyday Life*. New York, NY: Basic Books.

Gardner, H. (1993) *Creating Minds: An Anatomy of Creativity Seen through the Lives of Freud, Einstein, Picasso, Stravinsky, Eliot, Graham, and Gandhi*. New York, NY: Basic Books.

Getzels, J. W. and Jackson, P. W. (1962) *Creativity and Intelligence: Explorations with Gifted Students*. Oxford: Wiley.

Gruber, H. E. (1974) *Darwin on Man: A Psychological Study of Scientific Creativity*. New York, NY: Dutton.

Guilford, J. P. (1950) 'Creativity', *American Psychologist*, 5: 444–54.

Harlen, W. and James, M. (1997) 'Assessment and learning: differences and relationships between formative and summative assessment', *Assessment in Education*, 4(3): 365–79.

Heilmann, G. and Korte, W. B. (2010) *The Role of Creativity and Innovation in School Curricula in the EU27: A Content Analysis of Curricula Documents*. European Commission, Joint Research Centre, Institute for Prospective Technological Studies. Available from http://ftp.jrc.es/EURdoc/JRC61106_TN.pdf (Accessed 7 August 2015).

Heilman, K. M., Nadeau, S. E. and Beversdorf, D. O. (2003) 'Creative innovation: possible brain mechanisms', *Neurocase*, 9(5): 369–79.

Jones, R. and Wyse, D. (eds.) (2013) *Creativity in the Primary Curriculum*. London: Routledge.

Kampylis, P. (2010) 'Fostering creative thinking: the role of primary teachers', University of Jyväskylä, unpublished PhD thesis.

Kampylis, P., Berki, E. and Saariluoma, P. (2009) 'In-service and prospective teachers' conceptions of creativity', *Thinking Skills and Creativity*, 4(1): 15–29.

Katz-Buonincontro, J. (2012) 'Creativity at the crossroads: pragmatic versus humanist claims in education reform speeches', *Creativity Research Journal*, 24(2): 257–65.

Kaufman, J. C. and Beghetto, R. A. (2009) 'Beyond big and little: the four c model of creativity', *Review of General Psychology*, 13(1): 1–12.

Kennedy, M. (2005) *Inside Teaching: How Classroom Life Undermines Reform*. Cambridge, MA: Harvard University Press.

Köhler, H. (1997) 'Acting artist-like in the classroom', *ZDM*, 29(3): 88–93.

Kozbelt, A., Beghetto, R. A. and Runco, M. A. (2010) 'Theories of creativity', in James C. Kaufman and Robert J. Sternberg (eds.), *The Cambridge Handbook of Creativity*. Cambridge: Cambridge University Press.

Laske, O. E. (1993) 'Creativity: where should we look for it?', paper presented at the Artificial Intelligence & Creativity 1993 Spring Symposium. Stanford, California, March 23–25.

Leikin, R. and Pitta-Pantazi, D. (2013) 'Creativity and mathematics education: the state of the art', *ZDM*, 45(2): 159–66.

Leong, S. (2010) 'Creativity and assessment in Chinese arts education: perspectives of Hong Kong students', *Research Studies in Music Education*, 32(1): 75–92.

Mann, E. L. (2006) 'Creativity: the essence of mathematics', *Journal for the Education of the Gifted*, 30(2): 236–60.

Mardell, B., Otami, S. and Turner, T. (2008) 'Metacognition and creative learning with American 3–8 year-olds', in A. Craft, T. Cremin and P. Burnard (eds.), *Creative Learning 3–11 and How We Document It*. Stoke-on-Trent, UK: Trentham Books.

Mednick, S. (1962) 'The associative basis of the creative process', *Psychological Review*, 69(3): 220–32.

Meusburger, P. (2009) 'Milieus of creativity: the role of places, environments and spatial contexts', in P. Meusburger, J. Funke and E. Wunder (eds.), *Milieus of Creativity: An Interdisciplinary Approach to Spatiality of Creativity*. Dordrecht, Netherlands: Springer. pp. 97–153.

Miell, D. and Littleton, K. S. (eds.) (2004) *Collaborative Creativity*. London: Free Association Books.

Ministerial Council on Education, Employment Training and Youth Affairs (2008) *National Declaration on Educational Goals for Young Australians*. Melbourne: Ministerial Council on Education Employment Training and Youth Affairs.

Moree, D. (2013) 'Teachers and school culture in the Czech Republic before and after 1989', *The Curriculum Journal*, 24(4): 586–608. doi: 10.1080/09585176.2013.831770.

Mumford, M. D. and Simonton, D. K. (1997) 'Creativity in the workplace: people, problems, and structures', *Journal of Creative Behavior*, 31: 1–6.

Munro, J. (2010) *Insights into the Creativity Process*. Available from https://students.education.unimelb.edu.au/selage/pub/readings/creativity/UTC_Assessing__creativity_.pdf (Accessed 7 August 2015).

Newton, L. D. (ed.) (2012) *Creativity for a New Curriculum: 5–11*. London: Routledge.

Ng, A. -K. (2002) 'The development of a new scale to measure Teachers' Attitudes toward Students (TATS)', *Educational Research Journal*, 17(1): 63–77.

Ng, A. -K. and Smith, I. (2004) 'Why is there a paradox in promoting creativity in the Asian classroom?', in S. Lau, A. N. N. Hui and G. Y. C. Ng (eds.), *Creativity: When East Meets West*. Singapore: World Scientific Publishing Company. pp. 87–112.

Osborn, M. and McNess, E. (2002) 'Teachers, creativity and the curriculum: a cross-cultural perspective', *Education Review*, 15(2): 79–84.

Piaget, J. (1973) *To Understand is to Invent: The Future of Education*. New York, NY: Grossman Publishers.

Plucker, J. A. and Dana, R. Q. (1999) 'Drugs and creativity', in M. A. Runco and S. Pritzker (eds.), *Encyclopedia of Creativity*. San Diego, CA: Academic Press. pp. 607–11.

Robinson, K. (2006) *Why Schools Kill Creativity: The Case for an Education System that Nurtures Creativity*. TED Talk. Available from http://www.ted.com/index.php/talks/view/id/66 (Accessed 7 August 2015).

Rodari, G. (1973) *Grammatical della fantasia*. Torino, Italy: Einaudi.

Runco, M. A. (1999) 'Implicit theories', in M. A. Runco and S. R. Pritzker (eds.), *Encyclopedia of Creativity*. Vol. 2. San Diego, CA: Academic. pp. 27–30.

Runco, M. A. (2003) 'Education for creative potential', *Scandinavian Journal of Educational Research*, 47(3): 317–24.

Runco, M. A. (2004) 'Everyone has creative potential', in R. J. Sternberg, E. L. Grigorenko, and J. L. Singer (eds.), *Creativity: From Potential to Realization*. Washington, DC: American Psychological Association. pp. 21–30.

Runco, M. A. (2007) *Creativity: Theories and Themes: Research, Development, and Practice*. Amsterdam: Elsevier Academic Press.

Runco, M. A., Johnson, D. J. and Bear, P. K. (1993) 'Parents' and teachers' implicit theories of children's creativity', *Child Study Journal*, 23(2): 91–113.

Sawyer, R. K. (2012) *Explaining Creativity: The Science of Human Innovation*. Oxford: Oxford University Press.

Sharp, C. (2004) 'Developing young children's creativity: what can we learn from research?', *Topic,* 32: 5–12.

Shneiderman, B. (2000) 'Creating creativity: user interfaces for supporting innovation', *ACM Transactions on Computer-Human Interactions,* 7(1): 114–38.

Simonton, D. K. (1990) 'History, chemistry, psychology, and genius: an intellectual autobiography of historiometry', in R. S. Albert and M. A. Runco (eds.), *Theories of Creativity*. London: Sage Publications. pp. 92–115.

Simonton, D. K. (1999) 'Creativity and genius', in L. A. Pervin and O. John (eds.) *Handbook of Personality Theory and Research*. New York, NY: Guilford Press. pp. 629–52.

Simplicio, J. S. C. (2000) 'Teaching classroom educators how to be more effective and creative teachers', *Education,* 120(4): 675–80.

Stein, M. I. (1974) *Stimulating Creativity*. New York, NY: Academic Press.

Sternberg, R. J. and Lubart, T. I. (1999) 'The concept of creativity: prospects and paradigms', in R. J. Sternberg (ed.), *Handbook of Creativity*. Cambridge: Cambridge University Press. pp. 3–15.

Taylor, C. W. (1988) 'Various approaches to and definitions of creativity', in R. Sternberg (ed.), *The Nature of Creativity: Contemporary Psychological Perspectives*. New York, NY: Cambridge University Press. pp. 99–21.

Torrance, E. P. (1988) 'The nature of creativity as manifest in its testing', in R. J. Sternberg (ed.), *The Nature of Creativity*. New York: Cambridge University Press. pp. 43–75.

Vernon, P. (1989) 'The nature–nurture problem in creativity', in J. Glover, R. Ronning, C. Reynolds (eds.), *Handbook of Creativity*. London: Plenum Press. pp. 93–110.

Vong, K. (2008) *Evolving Creativity: New Pedagogies for Young Children in China*. Stoke-on-Trent, UK: Trentham Books.

Ward, T. B., Patterson, M. J. and Sifonis, C. M. (2004) 'The role of specificity and abstraction in creative idea generation', *Creativity Research Journal*, 16(1): 1–9.

Weisberg, R. W. (1999) 'Creativity and knowledge: a challenge to theories', in R. J. Sternberg (ed.), *Handbook of Creativity*. Cambridge: Cambridge University Press. pp. 226–50.

Westby, E. L. and Dawson, V. L. (1995) 'Creativity: asset or burden in the classroom?', *Creativity Research Journal,* 8(1): 1–10.

Wiley, J. (1998) 'Expertise as mental set: the effects of domain knowledge in creative problem solving', *Memory and Cognition*, 26(4): 716–30.

Williamson, B. and Payton, S. (2009) *Curriculum and Teaching Innovation: Futurlab*. Available from http://www2.futurelab.org.uk/resources/publications-reports-articles/handbooks/Handbook1246 (Accessed 7 August 2015).

Woods, P. and Jeffrey, B. (1996) *Teachable Moments: The Art of Creative Teaching in Primary Schools*. Buckingham, UK: Open University Press.

Wyse, D. (2014) *Creativity and the Curriculum – Inaugural Professorial Lectures*. London: Institute of Education Press.

Wyse, D. and Ferrari, A. (2014) 'Creativity and education: comparing the national curricula of the states of the European Union with the United Kingdom', *British Educational Research Journal.* doi:10.1002/berj.3135.

Wyse, D. and Jones, R. (2003) *Creativity in the Primary Curriculum*. London: David Fulton.

Wyse, D. and Spendlove, D. (2007) 'Partners in creativity: action research and creative partnerships', *Education, 3–13*, 35(2): 181–91.

Wyse, D. and Torrance, H. (2009) 'The development and consequences of national curriculum assessment for primary education in England', *Educational Research,* 15(2): 213–28.

Wyse, D., Hayward, L., Higgins, S. and Livingston, K. (2014) 'Editorial: creating curricula: aims, knowledge, and control, a special edition of the *Curriculum Journal*', *The Curriculum Journal*, 25(1): 2–6. Available from http://dx.doi.org/10.1080/09585176.2014.878545 (Accessed 7 August 2015).

37

Positioning Play in Early Childhood Curriculum Pedagogy and Assessment

Sue Rogers

INTRODUCTION

What is the role of play in early childhood education? How and in what ways does play contribute to learning in educational settings? In spite of a vast international and multidisciplinary literature on the topic of play, answers to these questions are complex and surprisingly difficult to establish. Play is firmly established in curricular frameworks across the globe and there is a general consensus in Westernised educational systems, at least, that active play-based learning should form the basis of children's early educational experience (Pascal and Bertram, 2014). However, relatively few empirical studies show precisely how and the extent to which engagement in play leads to the types of specific learning outcomes that children are required to meet in educational contexts. These learning outcomes are typically aligned to traditional subject knowledge, and are adult-determined and measurable. As

such they lie in opposition to the distinctive characteristics of play: its intrinsic value and child-determined content and outcomes.

In keeping with the focus of this volume, the main aim of this chapter is to consider how play is positioned in relation to preschool and early school curriculum, pedagogy and assessment practices. To do this I distinguish at the outset between play per se and play in school (Guha, 1988) to highlight the differences that clearly exist between the types of play we can observe in everyday life and play that takes place in pre-schools and schools. Much of what we know and, arguably, take for granted about play prioritises perspectives from the former category (play as such) through experimental studies of play in animals and young humans, with relatively limited reference to how children's play is shaped by the specific structural and contextual features of the school environment. The vast body of scientific research has provided critical insights into play as an agent of human cognition and development. But its usefulness in elaborating our understanding of how play is enacted in classrooms and its relation to regulatory curricular and pedagogical frameworks is somewhat limited (Rogers, 2010, 2013). To be clear – that children play, or at least display behaviours that we call play, is not in question here. Play is common to both perspectives but play in education engages with contexts beyond play as such and this is a central distinction in meaning.

In this chapter, the focus is deliberately on the play of the youngest children in the education system because play rarely features in curriculum and pedagogy texts and practices beyond the early years of primary schooling. Indeed, from a policy perspective, play is viewed largely as the province of children in the pre-school years and may be confined to playtimes and playgrounds as they enter into formal schooling. But play features throughout the life course in multiple and diverse ways and might be regarded as a fundamental part of what it is to be human. Harris, for example, argues that the early signs of pretend behaviours seen in the second year of life are 'the first indication of a lifelong capacity to consider alternatives to reality' (Harris, 2000: 28). This ability to move between the here and now, between reality and fantasy, is a uniquely human capacity that underpins many aspects of adult life as in the arts, literature, social games such as flirting, use of irony and joking, in virtual social and fantasy worlds, digital technologies and media games (for a more detailed discussion of pretend play, see Rogers, 2015).

It is not my intention here to give a detailed discussion of the myriad ways in which play permeates our lives or to give an exhaustive review of the literature; that would be neither possible nor desirable and there are already many excellent texts available (see, for example, Henricks, 2006; Smith; 2010; Sutton-Smith, 1997). Rather, I consider the ways in which play has acquired meaning in educational practice in Western society. This in turn shades in some of the wider contexts within which educators and policymakers make decisions or gather assumptions about the meaning of play.

First, I will briefly set out the historical background to the emergence of the idea that play is the principal means by which young children learn. This idea persists in spite of a changing policy landscape and concomitant demands on curriculum and pedagogy for young children to be regulated and accountable. I go on to highlight the need to locate play in education within a broader socio-cultural perspective to allow for a richer understanding of the complexity and diversity of children's play. Finally, the chapter addresses the relationship between play, curriculum and pedagogy, highlighting the relationship between school knowledge and informal knowledge gathered through play.

THE RISE AND FALL OF A PLAY ETHOS

Within the Western early childhood tradition, play is widely understood as a natural, voluntary and intrinsically motivated activity, free from externally imposed goals or rules. In their play, it is argued, children exercise choice, autonomy and independence (Bennett et al., 1997). From this perspective, play is viewed in opposition to work or formal approaches to teaching and learning as process, rather than product-oriented, and as the context for, rather than the content of, learning. This polarizing tendency – play versus work – constitutes a recurring theme in the history of early childhood education (Rogers, 2010). At the same time, a very different perspective is suggested by the often-made claim that 'play is the child's work', a phrase believed to be coined originally by Frederick Froebel, and reiterated several decades later by Susan Isaacs: 'play is indeed the child's work […]' (1929: 9). These contradictory positions frame debates about play in education throughout the twentieth and early twenty-first centuries.

If we trace the history of play in education during this period it is possible to discern two 'grand narratives' in accounts of pedagogical practice in early childhood (Rogers and Lapping, 2012). These are, on the one hand, a liberal-romantic philosophy of education and, on the other, psychological theories of cognitive development (Piaget, 1978). Their convergence had a profound shaping influence on what Smith (1988) termed a 'play ethos' in Western approaches to early childhood education. The liberal-romantic philosophy of education, which took its definitive form in the artistic and intellectual culture of the late eighteenth century, was exemplified in the social theory of Rousseau and, in particular, in his treatise *Emile* (1979), which charts the educational exploits of his eponymous pupil. The ideas contained within this text laid the foundations for a singularly European–American view of childhood, which later in the first half of the twentieth century came to be termed child-centred education, drawing also on the ideas of John Dewey in the US at that time (Fairfield, 2009).

In Rousseau's account, Emile is a curious, playful and active child naturally and freely exploring the (rural) environment on his own terms, following his own interests and natural inclinations. It is no coincidence that Emile is a boy; Rousseau's educational theory was confined to the education of the male child. By contrast, the girl child was destined to a rather less playful life, uneducated and passive in the service of her husband and children (Doddington and Hilton, 2007; see Darling (1986) for a discussion of Rousseau and gender). Emile, a model of childhood innocence, was placed in rural isolation, protected from the corrupting influence of adults and, it would seem, other children; curiously, Emile has no play companions. The highly gendered and exclusionary aspects of Rousseau's proposed approach to education are clearly unacceptable today; however, Rousseau's core ideas on the nature of childhood subsequently had a profound effect on the growth of interest in the potential of children's natural play as an educational force, evident in the work of successive pioneer educators, including Fredrick Froebel,

Rudolph Steiner and Susan Isaacs. Each of these figures in different ways promoted play in educational settings, believing it to be a holistic activity and a way of harnessing and integrating young children's learning and development.

A second influence on the growth of the play ethos is traceable to the emergence of psychology as an established discipline in the late nineteenth century. By contrast to theories of integration proposed by Froebel and Steiner among others, advances in scientific methods of study and the prevailing discourses of modernity and progress resulted in the promotion of the measurement and classification of distinctive and observable human behaviours in ways that were particularly apt for the study of children and their development. Play, viewed as the natural activity of early childhood, provided an ideal site for the quasi-scientific observation of children's interests, behaviours and emotional states. Rather than integration, this approach offered a dissection and categorisation of play into domains of development, skills and behaviours. In England, the emphasis on systematic observation, with its roots in the new scientism and positivism of the late nineteenth century, underpinned the approach taken by subsequent twentieth-century educators. To give an example, while working at the Malting House in Cambridge (an experimental school based on free play), and later as the first Head of Child Development at the Institute of Education in London, Susan Isaacs developed her theory of child development and learning based on systematic and detailed observations of children's social, cognitive and emotional behaviours particularly during their free play. In a documentary analysis of Isaacs' key texts and papers, Willan writes that:

> For Susan Isaacs, the curriculum was less important than the person delivering it. For her, it was axiomatic that teachers should be well-educated people with strong observational skills and a deep understanding of child development in all its aspects – physical, mental, social and spiritual. (2009: 153)

Willan's careful analysis of Isaacs's work concludes that Isaacs was not seeking to establish a universal model of child development or child learning as in the case of Piaget, whom Isaacs knew and whose work she critiqued. She was rather 'looking for a universal strategy that would unlock the complex and unique realities of individual children – and for her that strategy was in-depth observation' (2009: 161). As a historic instance of the coalescence of liberal-progressive ideology and psycho-biological research into human behaviours, Susan Isaacs's work is, arguably, paradigmatic and heralds a privileged period for proponents of play, which culminated in England in the so-called Plowden report (CACE, 1967). The increasing politicization of primary education in England during the 1980s and 1990s placed play, particularly in primary classrooms, in a highly tenuous position. In the wake of the English Education Reform Act of 1988 and the introduction of a National Curriculum, teachers came under unprecedented and increasing pressure to provide measurable evidence of learning and attainment, and the type of unstructured or free play on offer in many nursery and primary schools is notoriously difficult to measure because of its spontaneous, child-led and unpredictable nature (Athey, 1990). In addition, the growing influence of the ideas of Vygotsky, and in particular the concept of the zone of proximal development (ZPD), which promoted the intervention of adults in scaffolding and guiding young children's learning, were also exerting an influence on the field of play research. It was also at this time that the theoretical bases of early childhood education were undergoing a critical re-evaluation internationally, captured by Hultqvist and Dahlberg who asserted that 'There is no natural or evolutionary child, only the historically produced discourses and power relations that constitute the child as an object and subject of knowledge, practice, and political intervention' (Hultqvist and Dahlberg; 2001: 2).

Internationally, there has been a move towards greater political intervention in all areas of curriculum, pedagogy and assessment by government and policymakers, in part a reflection of increasing global competitiveness and concomitant discourses of high-stakes testing and performativity (Ball, 2003). The most recent version of the *Early Years Foundation Stage* (Department for Education (DfE), 2012), an avowedly play-based curriculum that now incorporates an explicit focus on 'school readiness' and policies to intervene in the education of 2-year-olds most at risk of disadvantage, has engendered further debate about the role of play in early learning for children under the age of three.

At the same time, there has been an increasing global appetite on the part of policymakers for evidence-based or -informed policy and practice, and for identifying what makes good teaching and good teachers (see, for example, the influential study by Hattie, 2008); however, the notion of evidence is itself contested. Brown (2014), for example, notes that 'engaging with evidence is socially beneficial since it can help develop our understanding of the world via an exposure to ideas and concepts we might not ordinarily come across' (2014: 2). However, he cautions against an oversimplified application of the notion of being 'evidence-informed' due to the complexities of the policy-making process and nature of professional practice. Clearly, the ways in which research evidence influences policy and practice is subject to the processes of recontextualisation and reinterpretation. Bernstein's concept of the recontextualising principle is helpful here in relation to how knowledge is mobilised. In essence, it is based upon the principle that the knowledge taught and acquired within a school 'subject' is by no means identical to the knowledge produced in the discourse from which the subject derives its identity (Thompson, 2009: 47). In Bernstein's terminology, the transformation of the original discourse of a subject (say, mathematics) into 'school knowledge' is regulated by a process of recontextualisation, which in turn generates a pedagogic discourse by means of a principle for the circulation and reordering of discourses that have been selected and sanctioned (by agents such as the state, professional bodies and individual teachers) as appropriate elements of a curriculum (Bernstein, 2000). By this he means that knowledge has become pedagogised and that, in this process, pedagogic discourse is delocated from its original source and takes on its own unique identity. The application of this idea to play-based curriculum and pedagogy is complicated by the fact that play cannot be viewed as having a particular or agreed 'subject' identity or specific knowledge-base, a point that, for some, is precisely what makes it play. Nevertheless, play is pedagogised in similar ways to the subjects of mathematics or literacy, for example (Rogers, 2013), through its enactment in early childhood settings and the multiple influences that surround it. Play therefore has its own unique pedagogic identity and discourse, derived largely from the 'grand narratives' of Romanticism and developmental psychology.

As the global demand for evidence-informed ways of working with young children increases, it has become more challenging to offer traditional free play approaches observed in many early childhood settings, partly because it is difficult to locate evidence to support the view that it is play per se that leads to the types of learning outcomes that governments are most interested in, notably literacy and numeracy. Evidence for the benefits of play in early learning is therefore often sought in other related areas, such as child development, or in research on effective pedagogical interactions between adults and children, which are learning outcomes that are measurable but are more likely a result of the instructional dialogue that takes place, albeit in the context of play (I will say more about this later in relation to the uptake of Vygotskian theory to play). It might be argued, therefore, that play-based curriculum and pedagogy, harnesses or instrumentalises children's predisposition to play to achieve outcomes that are external to the play itself (Rogers, 2010).

WHAT IS PLAY AND WHAT IS IT FOR?

Definitional questions are always difficult to answer, and so it is with the concept 'play', which resists the closure and finality of meaning that is conventionally offered by analytical definitions. Even as we invoke the concepts that enable such definitions, we find ourselves sliding from a consideration of the activity of play towards a consideration of the uses to which it may be put and the responses it engenders. In other words, we are taken inexorably into the social, contextual domain. Play has proved to be a difficult and elusive concept to define either empirically or conceptually. Rather than identifying a single theoretical definition, multiple characteristics have been identified and applied in research. The most commonly cited criteria are:

- Flexibility
- Positive affect
- Intrinsic motivation
- Attention to means rather than ends
- The capacity to be distinguished from exploratory behaviour
- Non-literality, freedom from externally applied rules
- Active engagement (in contrast to idling or daydreaming)
  Adapted from Rubin et al. (1983)

Others suggest that the more criteria that are present, the more playful a child's behaviour (Pellegrini and Boyd, 1993). Children's actions are therefore conceptualised as a continuum from those that may be regarded as pure play to those identified as non-play. In addition, play has often been described in terms of what it is not, rather than what it is: play is 'not real', 'not serious', 'of no material interest' and 'not for profit' or play is viewed as activities not consciously undertaken for the sake of any outcome beyond themselves (Rogers, 2010). Functional analyses of play seek to establish theories of what play is for or what it can do. These include amongst others, the 'surplus energy theory' attributed to the German poet and philosopher Schiller and the later evolutionary theorist, Spencer, an idea that resurfaces in the ubiquitous 'play-time' in schools. But as Evans and Pellegrini (1997) have pointed out more recently, children's inattention in class is more likely explained by the fact that playtime offers children novelty often lacking in classroom lessons, opportunities to socialize and greater choice and control over their activities. In contrast to the surplus energy theory, the relaxation or 'recreation theory' posits that play is the result of a 'deficit' of energy, a method by which spent energy can be replenished. Some parallels can be drawn here with the practice of viewing play as 'time out' after academic work is completed. If seen in this way, play may function simply as a reward for good work or it may be withdrawn altogether as a punishment for poor work or behaviour (Rogers and Evans, 2008). Arguably, the most influential of these early theories is the practice or 'preparation theory' expounded by Karl Groos, a neo-Darwinian scholar, who proposed that play exists so that the very young of the species can practice skills in later life. The preparation theory emphasizes future developmental goals rather than the immediate benefits play may bestow on the player. The view that the function of play is to equip the young with skills for later life is detectable in the instrumental discourses of 'play as progress' (Sutton-Smith, 1997) and 'play with a purpose' seen in contemporary curricular documents such as the English Early Years Foundation Stage (EYFS; DfE, 2012). 'Play cannot just be'; it has to have purpose (Cohen, 1983: 2). Although largely discredited now, many elements of these early classical theories persist in the imaginations and practices of adults who work with young children (Rogers and Evans, 2008).

One functional distinction in the literature worthy of more detailed discussion because it relates directly to how play contributes to learning is that proposed by the experimental research of Corinne Hutt and colleagues conducted during the 1980s. Children were presented with a novel toy and initially engaged in intense exploratory behaviours. Sustained observation revealed that over a period of six days this exploratory behaviour decreased exponentially and a new set of behaviour patterns began to appear (Hutt et al., 1989: 4). Having acquired important information concerning the properties of the novel toy through exploratory behaviour, children deployed this knowledge in a different kind of behaviour that was more innovative and imaginative. Hutt theorized this distinction in the following way:

> Implicit in the behaviours we termed 'exploration' was the query: What does this *object* do? Whilst implicit in the behaviours we termed 'play' was the query: What can *I* do with this object? (1989: 4, emphasis in original).

According to Hutt et al. (1989) exploration involved the child in visual inspection, active investigation and manipulation of novel toys or objects. Exploration is more likely to occur when the child is faced with the unfamiliar and novel. On the other hand, play is more likely to occur when the child is faced with a familiar situation, event or object. The distinction between exploration and play is potentially useful in early childhood classrooms because it enables us to understand the range of children's amorphous behaviours that we include under the generic heading play. This work might also be taken to suggest that exploration is more worthwhile than play because it is linked with the acquisition of new information. Hutt et al. (1989) therefore revised the original categories under the headings 'epistemic' and 'ludic' behaviour, respectively, as interrelated features of play (1989: 12). Lieberman (1977) writes that 'We can postulate that fact gathering precedes the emergence of the creative. It is at this point that combinatorial play enters aided by the powers of imagination' (1977: 110). Imaginative use of familiar objects, roles and relationships – constitutive of play rather than exploration – transforms existing meanings and imaginatively constructs new meanings. These are processes that may in fact be higher forms of mental functioning than simple 'acquisition of information', and may provide an arena for the development of creative and divergent thinking. In essence, this is 'mimesis':

> a uniquely human faculty that goes beyond the Platonic version of mere 'imitation' (in the sense of making a direct copy of something). Rather *mimesis* in play allows for a constructive reinterpretation of an original, which becomes a creative act in itself. (Rogers, 2015: 283)

The uniquely mimetic faculty we observe in play also forges a link between the self and other, enabling humans to develop empathy, itself a vital life skill because 'it is through empathy that human beings can – if not fully understand each other – at least come ever closer to the other, through the discovery and creation of similarities' (Goldman, 1998).

Understanding the relationship between playing and exploring may be important in ensuring that children have access to a wide range of materials and experiences in order to develop both exploratory and representational play competence (Campbell, 2002). Creative and imaginative play in which children transform the meaning of objects, people and places is intrinsically related to exploratory knowledge-seeking behaviours. That children can acquire and learn new information through their independent exploration of the material world and reapply them in new contexts is an indication of learning through the activity of play. The relationship between this type of knowledge and the knowledge that is imparted in schools from agreed disciplinary fields is discussed in more detail later in this chapter.

PLAY AND CULTURE

So far, the picture of play given is one that stems largely from a European–American legacy of early childhood education. Underpinning these theoretical approaches is the assumption that there are play traits that can be defined universally and generalised across populations of children irrespective of cultural, temporal and physical contexts. Although there is international agreement that play is a universal human driver (Smith, 2010), how play is viewed and valued by adults will vary and depend on the way in which children and childhood are positioned within a culture or society (Goncu and Gaskins, 2007). This point is very clearly illustrated in a study of play in three contrasting cultural contexts reported in Gaskins et al. (2007). The way in which play was enacted varied considerably across and within cultures as a result of differing child-rearing beliefs, values, types of social interaction and the resources made available for play. Children's play was dependent on the extent to which other activities, such as work, worship and caring duties or service to kin took priority (Gaskins et al., 2007). For reasons of safety and protection, whether through a heightened and perhaps exaggerated fear of strangers or more immediate and real risks associated with poverty, pollution, disaster and conflict, children's play may be inadvertently curtailed. Play may also be limited by cultural and social attitudes to participation in certain types of play on the grounds of gender roles and responsibilities. Gupta (2011) writes of the deeply held appreciation of children's play in Indian society, and yet she notes that its place in early childhood education and school is much less valued by adults because schools are viewed as purely academic institutions (2011: 91).

Writing about play in diverse African countries, Marfo and Biersteker (2011) caution against imposing a Westernised approach to play in early education without also taking into account local cultural perspectives and practices. Cultural attitudes towards play are inevitably tied up with wider perceptions of childhood and educational aims. They are not only confined to geographical regions and societies, but they also exist within the cultural attitudes that inhabit societies and communities at a micro-level. Global migration and the culturally diverse populations of children that attend early childhood and primary school settings in the UK and elsewhere require us to understand that the meanings ascribed to play as a vehicle for early learning are complex and variable, and that we should not assume that the value of play will be appreciated by all teachers, parents or, for that matter, all children (Brooker, 2010). That play is a culturally contingent and socially constructed activity, also defined by the players themselves (Rogers and Evans, 2008), is now widely acknowledged and requires a more nuanced consideration of how play is situated in relation to the curriculum and the kind of pedagogy that is deployed to enact it.

PLAY AND CURRICULUM

To overcome some of the divisions between play and other types of activity that take place in educational settings, the idea of a 'play-based' curriculum has become established internationally. For example, the current Australian Early Years Learning Framework (EYLF; Australian Government Department of Education, Employment and Workplace Relations, 2009) places a specific emphasis on play-based learning, defined as 'a context for learning through which children organize and make sense of their social worlds, as they engage actively with people, objects and representations'. (2009: 46). In England, the EYFS is similarly based on play, but this is 'well-planned' and 'purposeful' play with an explicit emphasis on 'school readiness' as children progress through the developmental and learning goals set out in the framework. In research conducted in Belgium, van Oers and Duijkers (2013) describe a play-based curriculum in the following way:

> The teacher constructs the curriculum in close interaction with the children in the classroom, informed by the children's interests, the teacher's mandatory goals and his personal ambitions. The teachers merge their personal and formal goals with the children's interests in order to guide them towards the teaching goals that are mandatory for the schooling at that age. (2013: 516)

These three examples typify the favoured contemporary approaches to play in the curriculum. Here we see the shift from play as child-led, voluntary and free to play with a purpose. The merging of teachers' personal and formal goals with children's interests reflects the move towards greater adult involvement in play and the bridging of different kinds of formal and informal knowledge in the context of play. We can extrapolate from the literature three key features that appear to characterise international approaches to play-based curricular: principles for practice; flexibility and permeability; and integration.

Principles for Practice

Traditionally, early childhood education programmes have been based on sets of principles and guidelines agreed within the field rather than at a national level by governments. An extensive review of the early years curriculum, pedagogical and assessment approaches of 20 different countries, conducted by Bertram and Pascal (2002), reported widespread agreement about the principles underpinning the curriculum for children aged 3–6 years. Taken collectively, most agreed that early childhood education should take into account:

- A child-centred, flexible and individually responsive curriculum;
- The importance of working in partnership with parents;
- The need to offer broad and relevant learning experiences in an integrated manner;
- The importance of play and active, exploratory learning;
- An emphasis on social and emotional development; and
- The need to empower the child to be an autonomous, independent learner.
  (Bertram and Pascal, 2002, 3.3: 21)

Similarly, the National Association for the Education of Young Children (NAYEC) in the US proposes 12 broad principles for developmentally and contextually appropriate practice (NAYEC, 2009). Play is described as an important vehicle for developing self-regulation and promoting language, cognition and social competence. The intention of the principles is to frame and guide practice in early years settings.

In England, the EYFS is based on four main principles:

- Every child is a unique child, who is constantly learning and can be resilient, capable, confident and self-assured;
- Children learn to be strong and independent through positive relationships;
- Children learn and develop well in enabling environments, in which their experiences respond to their individual needs and there is a strong partnership between practitioners and parents and/or carers; and
- Children develop and learn in different ways and at different rates.

Flexibility and Permeability

Play-based curricular frameworks incorporate flexibility and act as 'a guiding structure rather than as a prescriptive straitjacket' (Wood and Attfield, 2005: 123). Early childhood curricular frameworks therefore differ significantly from the more rigid curricular structures found in later phases of education and allow for more permeable boundaries between subjects and between knowledge imparted by schools and the everyday knowledge of the teacher and the child. Bernstein (2000) refers to the relative strength or weakness of categories of knowledge as classification and framing. Applied to subject disciplines, strong classification is characterised by a strong subject identity or voice and 'its own specialised rules of internal relations' (2000: 7). In contrast, weak classification leads to less specialised discourse, identities and voices. Play might be seen as weakly classified and aligned with child-centred education, where there is little direction or delivery of subject content on the part of adults (Rogers, 2013).

Framing refers to the social and discourse relations of pedagogy – the intersubjective relations of teacher and those being taught that frame and mediate the construction of knowledge. Framing is therefore the 'realisation of the form of control, which regulates and legitimises communication in pedagogical relations: the nature of talk and the kinds of [pedagogic] spaces constructed' (Bernstein, 2000: 12). How might we apply these concepts to play pedagogy? In his most recent work, Bernstein proposed two pedagogic styles or modes, which he called 'performance' and 'competence'[1] (Bernstein, 2000: 44). In performance modes, he suggests absences (that is, what is not present or known in/by 'the acquirer' or learner) are evaluated and control (that of the transmitter/teacher) is explicit. By contrast, in the competence pedagogic mode, which we might align with child-centred practices, it is presences or what 'is' known that is evaluated and teacher control is implicit or 'hidden'. In such pedagogic practices, the adult authority is masked, and yet present, and children's activity (for example, play) in which they reveal themselves to the teacher is under surveillance and hence available to regulation (Bernstein, 1975). Extrapolating from Bernstein's work and, more recently, application of this work by Ivinson and Duveen (2006), exclusive or overuse of a performance mode may bewilder children because they may not have the socio-cultural tools to make sense of the teacher's discourse in classroom interactions (Rogers, 2013). They may not be able to recognise the classroom discourse and therefore realise or produce the correct response or product. The potential for shared meaning and understanding therefore breaks down. Similarly, overemphasis of a competence pedagogic mode may exclude those children who need more explicit signposting in order to access bodies of knowledge, and information about how things are done in the classroom. Other children may need support to access or withdraw from groups when peer group culture dominates, particularly in free play environments (Ivinson and Duveen, 2006). Alternatively, play-based curriculum and pedagogies co-constructed between children and between adults and children may be viewed as a potentially integrating mechanism that enables such movement across traditional boundaries of knowledge and across pedagogic divisions (play/work; adult-led/child-led).

Although play lacks a strongly defined subject as such, it could be argued that it derives its identity and hence position in early childhood classrooms from particular disciplinary fields such as developmental and cognitive psychology, Romanticism and (increasingly) neuroscience, amongst others. In play, children draw upon and transform subject knowledge, such as mathematics, science and so on. In this way, 'play' might be thought of as a key signifier in the convergence between a range of different and highly distinctive fields (Rogers and Lapping, 2012). Play is also thought of as the context in which to draw upon children's existing knowledge and experience from which teachers can build, weaving in elements of subject knowledge deemed desirable by society at appropriate moments (van Oers and Duijkers, 2013). Pedagogically, the skill of the early childhood teacher is to know when to introduce new knowledge into the child's repertoire, without disrupting the play to such an extent that it loses its playful qualities.

Knowledge in early childhood is typically organized within areas of learning (EYLF, NAEYC, EYFS). Most commonly cited are personal, social and emotional development; cultural, aesthetic and creative; physical; environmental; language and literacy and numeracy (Bertram and Pascal, 2002). The English EYFS follows this trend based on seven areas split between prime and specific areas of learning. The prime areas of learning are:

- Communication and language
- Physical development
- Personal, social and emotional development

The specific areas of learning are:

- Literacy
- Mathematics
- Understanding the world
- Expressive arts and design

Unique to curricular frameworks in early childhood is the explicit bringing together of learning and development. As part of the maturation process, children develop the capacity to learn specific concepts from key areas of knowledge, and play is a leading way in which they achieve this. Debates about what constitutes an appropriate play-based curriculum in early childhood are also concerned with the extent to which curriculum content should be taught. Subject knowledge and content therefore occupy a tenuous position in relation to early childhood curriculum and pedagogy because they are often viewed negatively, a perception that is not confined to early childhood (Krieg, 2011). If children are to be taught through play, what are they to be taught, what will they learn, and how is this to be assessed? Such questions lie at the heart of curriculum debates in the field.

Integration

I have already mentioned the notion of integration in relation to holistic theories of development proposed by the early pioneer educators. As an extension of this idea, I suggest that integration is still a useful concept for understanding how play operates in curriculum. However, there has been a shift from theories of play as an integrating mechanism for the manifold aspects of children's development to one that engages more explicitly with pedagogic discourses related to teaching and learning. Recent unprecedented interest in national performance data, coupled with research evidence on the long-term social and economic benefits of early education, taken up eagerly by politicians and policymakers across the globe have placed further pressure on early years curricular and pedagogy to prepare children for school. The concept of 'teaching through play' rather than 'learning through play', axiomatic in previous decades, is now part of early childhood discourse, particularly in light of evidence that social constructivist and dialogic pedagogies, where adult and child co-construct meaning, are effective in achieving better learning out-comes for children. Social constructivist per-spectives have largely displaced purely Piagetian interpretations of child develop-ment, contesting images of the child as a 'lone scientist' and paving the way for new approaches to thinking about the interrela-tions between play, child and adult.

PLAY AND PEDAGOGY

Knowledge needs to be brought to life in some way, either through interactions between the child and the more knowledge-able other (in Vygotsky's terms), or through exploration of materials and situations where direct experience 'teaches' the child some-thing new (Hutt et al., 1989). In a brief chap-ter on play in child development, Vygotsky (1978) writes of the way in which play cre-ates its own ZPD. My reading of this work suggests that Vygotsky views play differ-ently from other learning activities that might benefit from the instructional pedagogic rela-tionship with adults or more knowledgeable others. Vygotsky points out that the play-development relationship can be compared to the instruction-development relationship, but he suggests that play provides a much wider background for changes in needs and con-sciousness than is possible in instruction as he conceives it between the child and more knowledgeable other. For Vygotsky, play creates its own ZPD, in which children move forward in their development. Play, there-fore, is of central importance to the young child's development, mainly because it 'con-tinually creates demands on the child to act against immediate impulse' (1978: 99). Imagine the child at play, perhaps enacting the role of a mother. She is bound by the rules of the game of what it means to be a mother, but not in the sense of her own mother nor a particular mother with which she has direct experience; rather, the child plays within the rules of 'maternal behav-iour' (1978: 95). She is positioned in a dialectical relationship between her desire to act spontaneously in the play and by the inherent need to subordinate those desires to the rules of the game. This is why Vygotsky suggests that 'the child's greatest control occurs in play' (1978: 99). Children are com-pelled to self-regulate their behaviour in play in order to meet the overriding desire that the play should continue. Vygotsky argued that play was the 'highest level of pre-school development because of its capacity to help the child to self-manage desires and behav-iours in the social context but also because of how it helps children to understand the rela-tionship between meaning (thought) and action. As he explains:

> In play thought is separated from objects, and action arises from ideas rather than things; a piece of wood begins to be a doll and a stick becomes a horse (Vygotsky, 1978: 96).

In the very young child, action on objects is dominant over meaning; however, an impor-tant developmental shift takes place as the child begins to engage in symbolic activity. This is play rather than pure imitation, char-acterized by the subordination of action to meaning. For Vygotsky, play is a serious busi-ness. He does not subscribe to the view that play is 'the child's world' because it is firmly rooted in the imperative to understand the real world of concepts, materials and people. As he explains, 'Only theories which maintain that a child does not have to satisfy the basic requirements of life but can live in search of pleasure could possibly suggest that a child's world is a play world' (Vygotsky, 1978: 102).

From Vygotsky's social constructiv-ist theory a significant body of work has emerged that examines the potential of instructional play. My contention here is that this approach puts a rather different slant on learning through play than was originally intended by Vygotsky, but that is not to sug-gest that adult intervention in the context of play is not a rich potential source of learning. To illustrate this point, I give three examples of research on approaches to adult interven-tion in play.

First, Siraj-Blatchford has promoted the idea that knowledge in the early years is most effectively created jointly in pedagogic interactions, whether in the context of instructional play or in formal teaching Instructional play, an idea derived from the EPPE longitudinal study of pre-school pedagogy (Siraj-Blatchford and Sylva, 2004) presupposes some intervention on the part of adults; therefore, even when activities are child-led, adults play a much more active role in extending children's thinking via dialogic pedagogies such as Sustained Shared Thinking (SST), an idea with widespread currency in the early childhood community. Drawing on Vygotsky's theory of instruction and ZPD, SST is defined as:

> an episode in which two or more individuals 'work together' in an intellectual way to solve a problem, clarify a concept, evaluate activities, extend a narrative, etc. Both parties must contribute to the thinking and it must develop and extend the understanding. (Siraj-Blatchford and Sylva, 2004: 718)

Second, a study by Payler compared scaffolding with co-construction where the adult role involves 'ascertaining, suggesting or jointly creating a role with a child' (Payler, 2009: 121). Co-construction is viewed here as a more flexible, responsive and participatory approach than scaffolding where the adult may have a clearer learning intention in mind. In this respect, co-construction is more responsive and closely aligned to conceptions of play as child-led and open-ended. Payler's study found that co-construction was common in pre-school settings, whereas scaffolding featured more strongly in teacher pedagogy in the reception classes of primary schools. This study is important because it points to how play-based pedagogy changes as children transition from pre-school to school.

Finally, in the third study under consideration, van Oers and Duijkers (2013) consider teaching in a play-based curriculum in Belgium. Once again, following the work of Vygotsky, the study compared two approaches to teaching vocabulary to children in the early years of primary schooling (4 and 5-year-olds) over a 3-week period. The first approach was described as teacher-led direct instruction, which the authors argue mainly adhered to the so-called Initiation, Response and Evaluation (IRE) model (see Mercer and Littleton, 2007), typical of practice in Belgian schools. The second group of teachers worked within a Developmental Approach described as play-based, but which allowed for teacher involvement. Teacher involvement was guided by a sequence of strategies to ensure that they did not dominate the activity and allowed for children's own ideas to be expressed. Although the findings were presented as tentative, significant gains in vocabulary were made in the play-based group when assessed at the end of the study.

Each of these studies make a strong case for teaching approaches that draw upon children's prior knowledge and experience, in which adults introduce new knowledge to take children beyond what they know already. Application of dialogic pedagogies to children's free play has offered the possibility of overcoming the 'see-saw' approach noted earlier to integrate play more securely within the curriculum and pedagogy of the classroom through the idea of a play-based curriculum and by introducing the idea of teaching through play. What this research cannot do, however, is to address questions about the purpose and value of play that takes place outside the teaching/learning nexus. In the study by van Oers and Duijkers (2013), to what extent was it the playful context that made a difference to the learning outcomes for those children? Or was learning simply an outcome of the pedagogic interaction? When we observe children engaging in play with peers, we see different kinds of learning, which may not be measurable and which are often difficult to manage in the classroom. Rogers and Lapping (2012) write of 'excess' in children's play. Drawing upon Bernstein's conceptualisation of the recontextualising strategies instantiated in different models of pedagogy, they explore how these meanings are invoked to regulate the excesses of children's 'play' activities in observed early years classroom practice. For example, there is no mention in curricular documents or guidelines for pedagogy of the troubling excess, the sex, death and violence that is so prevalent in young children's 'play' (Rogers and Lapping, 2012). All this lies outside of the regulatory framework, which serves to present children's play as palatable, manageable and accountable. Children undoubtedly enjoy the company of adults in their play and respond well to pedagogies that are co-constructed and which value their ideas and contributions (Rogers and Evans, 2008), but equally, studies show that from the perspective of children, play is a child-led, peer group activity that is distinctive and separate from work and often enacted beyond the gaze of adults. Pretending and being with friends is high on the list of priorities for children in the pre-school years particularly at around the time when many children enter primary school classrooms at age 4 and 5 (Rogers and Evans, 2008).

THE STATE OF PLAY: PRESENT AND FUTURE

> Play...does not fit well in the rational, instrumental logic that pervades the abstract conceived spaces of today's world. (Aitken, 2001: 180)

Aitken's words remind us that play cannot be viewed simply as a neutral activity, free from the structural and political forces that surround it in early childhood settings and schools. In earlier research I argued that certain pedagogical practices appropriate the meanings that children bring to their play by negating them in favour of prescribed learning objectives or by subjecting classroom play to frequent interruptions to meet other more mundane tasks, such as changing books (Rogers, 2010; Rogers and Evans, 2008). Within this context, play has increasingly become an instrument for learning

future competencies, emphasizing social realism rather than the transformative, mimetic and life-enhancing qualities of play, which are notoriously difficult to manage and difficult to measure (Rogers, 2010). Assessment measures in pre-schools and schools compel us to evaluate play by particular goals and standards – what is good play/bad play? Summative assessments of progress in play-based curriculum might not represent what children perceive to be of value in their play, but are rather rooted in politically prescribed notions of 'standards' and 'quality' (Rogers, 2010). Play, therefore, is not only a supervised and curricularised activity, as Strandell (2000) argues, but also an institutionalized and politicized activity. Evidence suggests that children's free time is increasingly organised and, as children progress from preschool to statutory school, play is increasingly a marginal and recreational activity often confined to playtimes and playgrounds. As we have seen, instructional play clearly provides opportunities for the integration of play into the curriculum through dialogic pedagogies; however, recreational play, and play that lies beyond the regulatory framework, may offer different and valuable ways of learning and being. I have argued elsewhere that our (re-) definition of play might initially include play as recreation in the sense suggested by Stone (1971) that:

> the symbolic significance of recreation is enormous in providing the fundamental bond that ties the individual to his [sic] society...Play is recreation because it continually re-creates the society in which it is carried out. (1971: 4).

Stone is referring here not simply to children's physical and social activity as experienced in recreation (although these are important), but also to children's symbolic activity (drama). Viewed in this way, recreation is not simply 'time out' or a break from the constraints of work; rather, it is of inherent value in itself and in its relation to other obligatory tasks. Recreation (or re-creation) in Stone's terms may serve to re-locate and recover value in the physical, social and affective, rather than a highly prescribed, externally evaluated, purposeful play regime.

Threaded through this chapter is the vexed issue of play's relationship with curricular content, the knowledge that a given society values and requires to be taught in school. One of the main difficulties in recontextualising play into pedagogical practice – what I term the *pedagogisation* of play following Bernstein (2000) – is the resistance of play to categorisation (Rogers, 2010). What is the 'subject' matter of play? There are both conceptual and practical difficulties in fitting play into categories such as subject, discipline, pedagogy and curriculum because the multiple facets of play transcend these artificial boundaries. The theoretical framing offered by Bernstein has been helpful in conceptualising these relationships in the context of pedagogy. With this in mind, I want to end by suggesting that a play-based curriculum has the potential to bring together the learner's everyday knowledge and experience, or horizontal knowledge in Bernstein's terms, with subject knowledge (vertical knowledge) gleaned from interactions with more knowledgeable others. It is also the case, however, that play provides opportunities to learn through independent investigations of the material world. This epistemic or knowledge-seeking behaviour, described by Hutt et al. (1989), is observable in the play of children from birth. Vertical or subject knowledge is inevitably recontextualised in the process of teaching, cut loose and somewhat distant from its epistemic roots by the time it is delivered to learners in schools. Bridging the gap between vertical and horizontal knowledge is challenging at all levels of the education system. I argue that however we conceive it, play is uniquely placed to occupy the discursive gap described by Bernstein as 'the distance between vertical discourse and the real world', the 'crucial site of the yet to be thought' (Bernstein, 2000: 31). Potentially, this is the most creative curricular and pedagogic space for learning to take place in pre-school or school.

NOTE

1 In earlier work, Bernstein had distinguished two types of pedagogy in infant education – invisible and visible. In later work, these types were rethought to account for the changing political terrain in which there was greater state intervention and an evolving culture of managerialism in schools with much more explicit forms of external regulation and evaluation. Bernstein named these as 'competence' and 'performance' models, which might be thought of as a continuum rather than as polar opposites.

REFERENCES

Aitken, S. (2001) *Geographies of Young People: The Morally Contested Spaces of Young People*. London: Routledge.

Athey, C. (1990/2007) *Extending Thought in Young Children*. London: Paul Chapman.

Australian Government Department of Education Employment and Workplace Relations (2009) *Belonging, Being and Becoming: the Early Years Learning Framework for Australia*. Canberra: Commonwealth of Australia.

Ball, S. (2003) 'The teachers' soul and the terrors of perfomativity', *Journal of Education Policy*, 18(2): 215–228.

Bennett, N. Wood, E. and Rogers, S. (1997) *Teaching Through Play: Teachers' Thinking and Classroom Practice*. Bucks: Open University Press.

Bernstein, B. (1975) *Class, Codes and Control. Volume 3: Towards a Theory of Educational Transmissions*. London: Routledge and Kegan Paul.

Bernstein, B. (2000) *Pedagogy, Symbolic Control and Identity: Theory, Research, Critique*. Rev. edn. Oxford: Rowman & Littlefield.

Bertram, T. and Pascal, C. (2002) *Early Years Education: An International Perspective*. London: Qualifications and Curriculum Authority.

Brown, C. (2014) *Evidence-Informed Policy and Practice in Education: A Sociological Grounding*. London: Bloomsbury.

Campbell, S. (2002) *Behaviour Problems in Pre-school children: Clinical and Developmental Issues*. New York, NY: Guildford Press.

Central Advisory Council for Education (CACE) (1967) *Children and their Primary Schools*. London: HMSO.

Cohen, D. (1983) *The Development of Play*. London: Routledge.

Darling, D. (1986) 'Child-centred, gender-centred: a criticism of progressive curriculum theory from Rousseau to Plowden', *Oxford Review of Education*, 12: 31–40.

Department for Education (DfE) (2012) *Statutory Framework for the Early Years Foundation Stage: Setting the Standards for Learning, Development and Care for Children from Birth to Five*. Available from http://www.education.gov.uk/aboutdfe/statutory/g00213120/eyfs-statutory-framework (accessed 1 January 2013).

Doddington, C. and Hilton, M. (2007) *Child-Centred Education: Reviving the Creative Tradition*. London: Sage Publications.

Evans, J. and Pellegrini, A. (1997) 'Surplus Energy Theory: an enduring but inadequate justification for school break-time', *Educational Review*, 49(3): 229–36.

Fairfield, P. (2009) *Education after Dewey*. London: Continuum.

Gaskins, S., Haight, W. and Lancy, D. (2007) 'The cultural construction of play' in A. Goncu and S. Gaskins (eds.), *Play and Development: Evolutionary, Sociocultural and Functional Perspectives*. Mahwah, NJ: Lawrence Erlbaum Associates. pp. 179–202.

Goldman, L. R. (1998) *Child's Play: Myth, Mimesis and Make-Believe: Explorations in Anthropology.* Oxford: Berg.

Goncu, A. and Gaskins, S. (eds.) (2007) *Play and Development: Evolutionary, Sociocultural and Functional Perspectives*. Mahwah, NJ: Lawrence Erlbaum Associates.

Guha, M. (1988) 'Play in school', in G. Blenkin and A.V. Kelly (eds.), *Early Childhood Curriculum: A Developmental Curriculum*. London: Paul Chapman Press. pp. 15–46.

Gupta, A. (2011) 'Play and pedagogy framed within India's historical, socio-cultural and pedagogical context', in S. Rogers (ed.) *Rethinking Play and Pedagogy in Early Childhood Education: Concepts, Contexts and Cultures*. Oxford, UK: Routledge. pp. 86–99.

Harris, P. (2000) *The Work of the Imagination*. Oxford: Blackwell.

Hattie, J. (2008) *Visible Learning: A Synthesis of Over 800 Meta-Analyses Relating to Achievement*. London: Routledge.

Henricks, T. (2006) *Play Reconsidered: Sociological Perspectives on Human Expression*. Urbana and Chicago, IL: University of Illinois Press.

Hultqvist, K. and Dahlberg, G. (2001) *Governing the Child in the New Millennium.* London: Routledge.

Hutt, S., Hutt, C., Tyler, S. and Christopherson, H. (1989) *Play, Exploration and Learning: A Natural History of the Pre-School*. London: Routledge.

Isaacs, S. (1929) *The Nursery Years*. London: Routledge.

Ivinson, G. and Duveen, G. (2006) 'Children's recontextualisations of pedagogy' in R. Moore, M. Arnot, J. Beck and H. Daniels (eds.), *Knowledge, Power and Educational Reform: Applying the Sociology of Basil Bernstein*. London: Routledge, pp.109–125.

Krieg, S. (2011) 'The Australian Early Years Learning Framework: learning what?', *Contemporary Issues in Early Childhood*, 12(1): 46–55.

Lieberman, J.N. (1977) *Playfulness: Its Relationship to Imagination and Creativity*. New York, NY: Academic Press.

Marfo, K. and Biersteker, L. (2011) 'Exploring culture, play, and early childhood education practice in African contexts' in S. Rogers (ed.) *Rethinking Play and Pedagogy in Early Childhood: Concepts, Contexts and Cultures*. Oxford, UK: Routledge. pp. 73–85.

Mercer, N. and Littleton, K. (2007) *Dialogue and the Development of Children's Thinking: A Sociocultural Approach.* London: Routledge.

National Association for the Education of Young Children (NAEYC) (2009) *Developmentally Appropriate Practice in Early Childhood Programs Serving Children from Birth through Age 8. National Association for the Education of Young Children Position Statement.* Available from http://www.naeyc.org/files/naeyc/file/positions/PSDAP.pdf (accessed December 2014).

Pascal, C. and Bertram, T. (2014) *Early Years Literature Review.* Available from https://www.early-education.org.uk/sites/default/files/CREC%20Early%20Years%20Lit%20Review%202014%20for%20EE.pdf (accessed December 2014).

Payler, J. (2009) 'Co-construction and scaffolding: Guidance strategies and children's meaning-making', in T. Papatheodorou and J. Moyles (eds.) *Learning Together in the Early Years: Exploring Relational Pedagogy.* London: Routledge. pp. 136–156.

Pellegrini, A. and Boyd, B. (1993) 'The role of play in early childhood development and education: issues in definition and function', in B. Spodek (ed.), *Handbook of Research on the Education of Young Children.* New York, NY: Macmillan. pp. 105–121.

Piaget, J. (1978) *The Development of Thought.* Oxford: Blackwell.

Rogers, S. (2010) 'Powerful pedagogies and playful resistance: researching children's perspectives', in E. Brooker, and S. Edwards (eds.), *Engaging Play.* Maidenhead, UK: Open University Press. pp. 152–166.

Rogers, S. (2013) 'The pedagogisation of play in early childhood education: a Bernsteinian perspective', in O.F. Lillemyr, S. Dockett, and B. Perry (eds.), *Varied Perspectives on Play and Learning: Theory and Research on Early Years Education.* Charlotte, NC: Information Age Publishing. pp. 159–175.

Rogers, S. (2015) 'Pretend play and its integrative role in young children's thinking', in S. Quinn and S. Robson (eds.), *The Routledge International Handbook of Young Children's Thinking and Understanding.* London: Routledge. pp. 282–294.

Rogers, S. and Evans, J. (2008) *Inside Role-Play in Early Education.* London: Routledge.

Rogers, S. and Lapping, C. (2012) 'Recontextualising "play" in early years pedagogy: competence, performance and excess in policy and practice', *British Journal of Educational Studies,* 60(3): 243–60.

Rousseau, J. J. (1979) *Emile: or On Education.* *[Trans. and ed. Allan Bloom]* New York, NY: Perseus, Basic Books.

Rubin, K.H., Fein, G.C. and Vandenberg, B. (1983) 'Play', in P.H. Mussen (ed.), *Handbook of Child Psychology.* 4th edn. New York, NY: Wiley. pp. 693–777.

Siraj-Blatchford, I. and Sylva, K. (2004) 'Researching pedagogy in English pre-schools', *British Educational Research Journal,* 30(5): 713–730.

Smith, P.K. (1988) 'Children's play and its role in early development: a re-evaluation of the play ethos', in A.D. Pellegrini (ed.), *Psychological Bases for Early Education.* New York, NY: John Wiley and Sons Ltd. pp. 207–226.

Smith, P.K. (2010) *Children and Play.* Oxford: Wiley-Blackwell.

Strandell, H. (2000) 'What is the use of children's play: preparation or social participation', in H. Penn (ed.), *Early Childhood Services: Theory, Policy and Practice.* Maidenhead, UK: Open University Press. pp. 147–157.

Stone, G. (1971) 'The play of little children', in R.E. Herron and B. Sutton-Smith (eds.), *Child's Play.* New York: John Wiley and Sons.

Sutton-Smith, B. (1997) *The Ambiguity of Play.* Cambridge, MA: Harvard University Press.

Thompson, R. (2009) 'Creativity, knowledge and curriculum in further education: a Bernsteinian perspective', *British Journal of Educational Studies,* 57(1): 37–54.

van Oers, B. and Duijkers, D. (2013) 'Teaching in a play-based curriculum: theory, practice and evidence of developmental education for young children', *Journal of Curriculum Studies,* 45(4): 511–34.

Vygotsky, L.S. (1978) *Mind in Society.* Cambridge, MA: Harvard University Press.

Willan, J. (2009) 'Revisiting Susan Isaacs – a modern educator for the twenty-first century', *International Journal of Early Years Education,* 17(2): 151–65.

Wood, E. and Attfield, J. (2005) *Play and the Early Childhood Curriculum.* London: Sage Publications.

38

Children's Literature in the Classroom and the Curriculum

Vivienne Smith

CHILDREN'S LITERATURE AND THE CURRICULUM

Children's books currently enjoy a relatively high profile in UK popular culture. They are made into films, they are used as categories for questions in popular daytime television quizzes, they are bought and borrowed from libraries in vast quantities, they regarded with affection, nostalgia and passion by both child and adult readers and they are even studied at universities. Yet their place in the curriculum continues to be ambivalent. Why is this?

This chapter explores a number of factors that contribute to the marginalisation of children's literature in nursery, primary and secondary schools in the UK. It considers the effect of legislation and curriculum change and the consequences of this for teachers. It considers the construction of reading, both in the curriculum and in teachers' understanding, and the purposes to which reading and literature are put as a result of this construction. It suggests that a wider understanding of what

reading is good for and what literature could do will enrich and enhance the teaching of literature in all phases of schooling and perhaps do something to close the achievement gap between privileged and less privileged children in schools in the UK, US and Australia.

GAINING MOMENTUM: THE RISE OF CHILDREN'S BOOKS IN POPULAR CULTURE

In the UK, we have been rightly proud of our children's literature for many, many years. We draw a line from Lewis Carroll through to Milne and Grahame, and show how those writers established a safe place where playfulness could thrive in the imaginations of their readers. We trace the line further, through writers such as Lucy Boston and Philippa Pearce, admiring the craft of their writing and the subtle, elusiveness of their plots, and on still to Garner and Mayne, where time-slip and history mingle with the possibilities of adolescence.

Following a different thread, we see how the social realism of John Rowe Townsend and Sylvia Sherry made possible the work of Jacqueline Wilson and Anne Fine, and watch as Fine and Gillian Cross, at their best, stretch their young readers' thinking with postmodern ideas and playful structures.

And then, of course, through John Burningham, Anthony Brown, Lauren Child and Emily Gravett, we celebrate that rich, multi-faceted vein of picture books and note the valuable lessons they afford in reading to those who take them seriously. In children's literature we have so much to be proud of.

By the late 1990s, those relatively few of us booksellers, librarians, academics and teachers who took children's books seriously were proud. We would have said that the children's book world was in a pretty good state. Children's literature was thriving in its own quiet way.

Then Harry Potter happened. With two Smarties Gold awards under its belt in consecutive years (1997, 1998) Bloomsbury set its marketing to hyperdrive and the media sat up and noticed. Within months it was cool for everyone (children and adults) to be seen reading Harry Potter (Rowling, 1997) in public. Readers could not get enough: judicious leaks tantalised those readers who could barely wait for the next volume, and the well-publicised launch of each became a major marketing event. Film rights and audio recording rights were soon sold. Before long, J.K. Rowling was a household name and a millionaire. Her fame was infectious. The media, looking for more fantasy and finding that Rowling needed time to write her increasingly lengthy books, focused on Phillip Pullman. *His Dark Materials* Trilogy had already made a small stir in the literary world, and now *The Amber Spyglass* (Pullman, 2000) was nominated for – and won – the Whitbread Award, the first children's book ever to win a major adult literary prize. Suddenly children's books were major news.

The bandwagon continued to roll and the profile of children's books rose ever higher. Hollywood became fascinated with their filmic possibilities. As well as the Potter movies and *The Golden Compass*, recent years have seen three Narnia films, a Lemony Snicket (1999) romp and an Alex Rider adventure (Horowitz, 2000). An adaptation of *A Monster Calls* (Ness, 2011) is currently in production. *The Hobbit* (Tolkein, 1937), *War Horse* (Morpurgo, 1982), *Esio Trot* (Dahl, 1990), *Paddington Bear* (Bond, 1958) and *How to Train Your Dragon* (Cowell, 2003) attest to the variety of texts that are now considered worth the investment of film makers.

Television was not far behind in realising the potential of children's books. First Jacqueline Wilson's (1991) Tracy Beaker and then the spin off series, *The Dumping Ground*, became permanent fixtures in the BBC schedule. For younger children, Lauren Child's *Charlie and Lola* (2000) was popular for some time, and now, Katie Morag, fully 30 years after she first 'helped' deliver the mail on Struay, in a Picture Lion, has stepped onto the small screen (Hedderwick, 1984). She has become more famous and more popular than ever.

Along with this crescendo in the status of children's books in the popular imagination has come the rise of the celebrity children's author. Jacqueline Wilson, Michael Morpurgo and J.K. Rowling have become household names, and Anthony Horowitz, Philip Reeve and one or two others are not far behind. Eccleshare (2015) writes of the legendary length of queues that the most popular children's writers attract for book signings at literary festivals, and notes how the names themselves have become brands. Young readers these days, it seems, position themselves as followers of the brand quite as they respond to individual texts. They are fans of Wilson, or Stephanie Meyer or whoever it is. So powerful is the attraction of celebrity that we have seen David Walliams move from comic to popular children's author with meteoric speed. Twenty years ago, people who wrote for children were mostly unknown, unheard and unregarded. In those days, a television personality who became a children's writer would have seen his star diminish; these days, it is enhanced. The astonishing fact is that in 2015, a children's writer is a thing to be.

By 2008, children's books were so firmly established in the media and the popular mind that the Nestlé Foundation and The Book Trust decided to withdraw the Smarties Prize. Two decades earlier it had been founded to raise the profile of children's books and children's reading. Now this had been achieved, and the prize had served its purpose. Here is what the organisers say:

> It is timely that both parties move away from the prize, confident that increased importance has been placed on children's books. (The Book Trust, 2008: n.p.)

Children's literature, quite simply, has become mainstream.

CONSEQUENCES: CHANGE AND STASIS

This mainstreaming of children's books in the popular imagination since about 2000 is significant in a number of ways. First, and most obviously, it has meant that books have become more popular, more numerous and more available. Sales of children's books, both paper and electronic, have never been so strong. Seven volumes of Harry Potter have made millions for Bloomsbury, and other publishers have benefited in the wake of their success. Libraries have also done well. Famously, between 2004 and 2006, Jacqueline Wilson was the most-borrowed author of *all* in British public libraries, and, between July 2012 and June 2013, children's writers achieved six of the top ten places in the most-borrowed authors chart (*The Guardian*, 2014) – that translates as hundreds of thousands of children's books leaving libraries and finding their way into children's homes. We might have questions to ask about how many of these books are actually read,

and if they are read, by whom, and whether those children who read them are representative of the whole UK population of putative child readers – but the fact remains: the books are out there.

A second consequence of the general rise of interest in children's books and the strong markets that necessarily follow has been that publishers have been confident enough to encourage new talent and innovation. Alongside all the money spinners – the big names, the Jacqueline Wilson wannabes and the Wimpy Kid-a-likes – a steady stream of young, intelligent, literary writers for children has quietly emerged, including Frances Hardinge, whose first stories, reminiscent of Joan Aiken in concept and character, bristled with words and wit, and whose new novel *Cuckoo Song* (2014) is as good a psychological thriller as any teenager is likely to meet. There is also Gill Lewis, who writes of realistic resourceful children, accessibly and subtly, and Katherine Rundell. Rundell's first novel, *Rooftoppers* (2013), is everything a children's book should be: charming, exciting, funny, just a little sad and beautifully written. For younger children, there are new exciting talents: Louise Yates, quirky, clever and witty; Jo Empson, astute and funny; and Catherine Rayner. Rayner's use of space and page design is delightful. If you want to know how to fit a whole giraffe into a landscape format picture book, then Catherine Rayner is the person to show you. And this list of names is by no means exhaustive; others are just as talented and innovative. But what these few examples show is the richness of the culture in the children's book world at present and its potential for generating talent. Popularity has not resulted in a diminution of quality. The best of those books published today are as good, if not better, as books for children (or adults) have ever been. It is right that there should be so much interest in the field.

It is not surprising, therefore, that there has been a third consequence: the rise of children's literature as an academic subject in universities and colleges. Here children's literature manifests itself in three ways: in courses in writing and illustrating children's books, often in art or creative writing departments; as literature, where children's books are understood as an aspect of English literature, and are taught in English or literature departments; and finally, as part of teacher education, usually, but not exclusively, for students studying to be primary school teachers. It is in the first two of these areas that the rise in interest has been most dramatic, with many institutions offering options as part of undergraduate degrees, and at least eight offering courses at Masters level[1], and some offering supervision for PhDs. In teacher education departments, where one might expect students to display a professional interest in children's literature, the rise in opportunity has been less marked. It is interesting to note, for example, that of the five individuals in the UK who have so far been awarded professorships in Children's Literature, only one has a strong professional interest in teacher education.

Significant publications in children's literature in the UK reflect this. We know, for example, with increasing sophistication how picture books work (Nikolajeva and Scott, 2001; Salisbury and Styles, 2012). We also know that writing for young people has always been at the forefront of societal change (Reynolds, 2006) and that, as adults, we know how to study children's literature (Grenby and Reynolds, 2011). We now know more about children as readers, and especially about their responses to picture books (Arizpe and Styles (2003); Evans (2009). But none of this directly addresses pedagogy. Work in this area has always been sparse. Pioneering texts emerged from Homerton College, Cambridge in the 1990s (Watson et al., 1992, 1996) and there has been some work since (Gamble and Yates, 2002; Goodwin, 2008), but these are rare examples.

With so few texts for teachers about children's literature and even fewer attempts to marry the work of literary scholars with educationalists, it is hardly surprising that children's literature as a curriculum area remains undertheorised and undeveloped in both policy and practice. In a crowded curriculum, it

is all too easy to take it for granted. After all, children's books are for *children*. They are easy by definition. Surely teachers already have the knowledge and expertise to teach them well.

The work of Cremin et al. (2008) strongly suggests that neither expertise nor knowledge can be taken for granted. At the beginning of the Teachers as Readers project, few of the teachers they worked with could name more than six contemporary children's writers and most struggled to name more than one poet. It emerged that they relied heavily on texts they remembered from their own childhoods in their teaching, or on texts they had been using year in and year out in their classrooms. They knew little about new books and less about new writers. It seems, therefore, that although an interest in children's literature had been on the ascendency in the wider culture in the UK for the last 15 years or so, it had made little impact in schools or in the curriculum. Stasis, rather than growth was apparent in both. How had this state of affairs come about?

LITERATURE IN THE CURRICULUM: POLICY AND CONCEPTS

Although the two were entirely unrelated, the rise in the profile of children's books in popular culture exactly coincided with a time of enormous change in schools. In 1998, just as Harry Potter was beginning to win over readers, the National Literacy Strategy (DfEE 1998) was launched in England. Constructed entirely on the premise that the literacy attainment of pupils in England was too low because of patchy teaching, the strategy sought to remedy the situation by providing a structured programme of work that would ensure systematic coverage of the language curriculum from KS1 (5-year-olds) to KS4 (16-year-olds). In a move that was analogous with the No Child Left Behind Act (US Department of Education, 2001) in the US, a detailed, non-negotiable curriculum was provided for teachers, and for the first time in the UK, they were told how to teach it. The implementation of the strategy caused a revolution in classroom practice, especially in the primary school, and this had far reaching consequences for the positioning of children's literature in the curriculum.

First, it is important to note that this was a *Literacy Strategy*, not a strategy for teaching *English*. The name is important. While English, as a subject, assumes the study of English literature (as it would at university), literacy does not. It is much more about the skills needed to read and write. This emphasis was clearly reflected in the structure and content of the strategy, and so, although the writers did provide a range of texts that children were to encounter each term, these texts were positioned as vehicles through which literacy could be achieved, rather than as texts to be studied in their own right as literature. At worst, this meant that *The Highwayman* (Noyes, 1947) was read for its similes, and passages from *Good night Mr Tom* (Magorian, 1981) were used to exemplify the use of the relative clause. In many classrooms, children read extracts rather than whole texts, and reading became atomised and decontextualised. Leading writers of children's books (Powling et al., 2003) and librarians (Elkin et al., 2003) raised objections, but to little avail. Function mattered more than engagement and coverage more than response. This was not a climate that was likely to encourage teachers to develop an interest in children's literature per se.

The new emphasis on phonics in the literacy strategy marginalised the place of literature still further. Teachers as well as pupils had to acquaint themselves with a host of new linguistic terms – morpheme, grapheme, digraph, etc. and new ways of teaching phonics in the classroom. In recognition of this, the strategy team provided extensive in-service training across England and supported this with booklets and videos. It is hardly surprising that many teachers devoted their energies to getting this aspect of language teaching right and so let literature slip. It was nobody's priority, and the assumption – if it was ever articulated

at all – seems to have been that literature could look after itself.

Perhaps if the strategies had lasted longer, teachers in England would have found the time and the energy to carve out a fuller place for children's literature in the curriculum, but they did not last long. The phonics lobby, supported by politicians and the popular press, grew ever stronger. The Rose Report: *Independent Review of the Teaching of Early Reading* (2006) recommended the teaching of systematic (and by implication) synthetic phonics to children in the first years of school, and although Rose was careful to stress that this teaching should take place in the context of a broad and rich literacy environment, these were not the words that the press and many schools heard. More classroom time, especially in the early years, was taken up with phonics and less with books and reading stories. Yet again, literature in the classroom had to take a back seat.

The new Conservative government in 2010 made matters worse. Now children of six had to sound out nonsense words to prove they could read. This practice suggests that reading is a mechanical, meaningless, word recognition process that does not merit thought or understanding. It is hard to imagine a reading activity that is less sympathetic to the spirit of literature teaching: surely finding meaning in text is the whole point of reading.

Given these circumstances, is it any wonder that teachers are unsure about the place of literature in the curriculum?

AMBIGUITY OF PURPOSE: WHAT IS LITERATURE FOR?

Another challenge that teachers face in the teaching of children's literature is that there is no real agreement about why they should do it. The question, of course, is allied to the one that Cox (Department of Education and Science/Welsh Office, 1989) asked as the National Curriculum was launched in England. What do teachers think they are teaching English *for*? It is a question that matters because how teachers imagine the 'end product' of what they do will influence the way they select, position and teach the texts they present to their pupils. Cox identified five ways of seeing English. The *adult needs* and the *cross-curricular* approaches both positioned English as a pragmatic subject: the point of it was to ensure that children developed the literacy skills needed to succeed either across the curriculum or in order to play a full part as an adult in a literate society. The *cultural analysis* approach emphasized the role of reading, particularly in helping learners to develop a critical understanding of the world, past and present, and the cultural environment in which they live. The *personal growth* view focused on the child and his or her personal, intellectual emotional and aesthetic development. *Cultural heritage* emphasized the importance of acquainting children with the literary canon – those texts which had been judged to be influential in the language and culture of the nation.

One of the effects of the tsunami of government-led curriculum change that has engulfed England in the last 30 years has been that the debate that should have arisen from these five propositions never happened. Most teachers were too busy accommodating the demands of new curriculum to think through their position on what they were doing, and the politicians and policymakers who wrote the curricular documents were often so engaged in propagating what they saw as common sense approaches to the curriculum that they did not unpick their assumptions. Even so, faint echoes of all five of Cox's positions can be detected in the thinking of teachers today and I use them here as a framework to analyse the way that children's literature is presented and taught in the classroom.

For many teachers, especially those in nursery and primary schools, the adult needs approach dominates thinking. These teachers see themselves as teachers of reading, rather than as teachers of children's literature, and their argument is that children need to be taught to read in order for them to survive in the modern world and to amuse themselves as adults, and children's books are useful tools to help them achieve this. Good children's books are entertaining and motivating and will make children want to put in the effort to learn to read them; because of this they should be used as much as possible. Teachers who think like this will quote Stanovich's (1966) 'Matthew effect' to demonstrate that reading begets success and are likely to argue that it doesn't matter what children read as long as they read a lot – quantity is more important than quality.

Some of these teachers will also identify another adult skill: the ability to read to amuse oneself. For these teachers, 'reading for enjoyment' will be a mainstay of classroom practice, and much energy will be spent on encouraging children to find books they enjoy and in giving them the time and space to read and talk about them.

There is much to be said for both these ways of positioning reading in the classroom. At best, they result in classrooms where there are lively communities of keen and committed readers. Children enjoy books, share books and network around books. They become readers, not just children who can read, and this is to be applauded. But there are possible problems too. Most problematic for me is the way both these approaches distance the teacher from the texts that the children are actually reading. If it doesn't matter *what* children read, then there is no need for the teacher to monitor or influence the texts children choose. All the teacher needs to be able to do is to point the child towards a source of reading matter and try to make sure the child reads it. As one text is as good as the next, teachers do not need to know about particular texts or particular authors, or even which texts offer which experiences for particular readers. The effect of this is the well-meaning, but deskilled teaching force that Cremin et al. (2008) uncovered in the TARS project: a community of teachers who talk about reading as an activity, but do not see that knowledge about what there is for children to read is part of their professional competence.

Knowledge about text matters because, as Meek (1988) and more recently Smith (2008; 2009) have argued, texts themselves provide the framework that structures the thinking that fuels cognitive development in readers; and some texts do this better than others. This is not to say that enjoyment does not matter – just that alone it is not enough. Even Lockwood (2008) in his eloquent defence of reading for pleasure acknowledges this. When teachers lack the knowledge to help children find the texts that will move their reading on, there is a risk that some children will not move on as readers. They will dwell in a netherworld of unchallenging, formulaic texts that fail to induct them into the wider reading habits of a thinking adult. More serious still in some classrooms, is an overemphasis on enjoyment, rather than thoughtful response. This can persuade children to position reading as an activity that is safe, cosy and undemanding, rather like a warm bath or an indulgent bar of chocolate. Reading certainly can and *should* be like this at times, but if that is all it ever is, it has no power to change lives.

A third adult need that is addressed through children's literature in some classrooms is even more distressing, and this is the need for children to learn to sit still and listen. Story time in the best nurseries and early years classrooms can be a wonderful experience where children learn about the enchantment of story and the power of shared experience. They explore text and illustration, they point, interrupt, question and 'interthink' (Littleton and Mercer (2013). They are active in the process of negotiating sense and making texts mean. In short, they learn to behave like readers. Unfortunately, not all classrooms encourage this. In some, children are trained to sit still and 'wait till the end of the story', regardless of their urgent need to share a new insight or understanding. In others, superficial technical skills, such as identifying capital letters become the focus of the teaching. Dombey (2003) describes such a situation and notes that in these circumstances, responding

to the text and articulating responses become subsidiary skills, rather than the main point of reading. Turn-taking, 'listening skills' and getting it right matter, more than cognitive or emotional engagement, and although it is almost certainly not the teachers' intention, children are taught to be passive receivers of text rather than active makers of meaning.

Less common among teachers is Cox's cross-curricular approach (Department of Education and Science/Welsh Office, 1989). In terms of literature, this approach is mostly seen in the primary school as part of topic work. Thus, early years teachers who are charged with delivering a topic on mini beasts will seek out anthologies of poems about insects to enrich or inform the children's thinking about the topic, and those working with older children on, for instance, Titanic or another historical project will find a novel set in a relevant place or time. Very often they will find that Michael Morpurgo has written a text to oblige (for example, Morpurgo, 2010). Of course there are advantages to this. Texts are contextualised and links and connections are easily made with children's thinking and developing knowledge. At best, this can result in rich and embedded learning – but at times it is hard to see what this learning has to do with an understanding of children as developing readers or with literature per se. This can matter. When it comes to working with topical poems, for example, sometimes a teacher is so pleased to have found a poem about a woodlouse, or whatever, that she fails to notice that the poem has nothing interesting to say about woodlice, uses language in a way that is conventional and lacking in energy, is less than perfect in its technical achievement, and, in short, has only been published because the publisher wanted to include a poem on woodlice for teachers to use when teaching the topic. Oh dear!

Again, the problem is that literature is being conscripted to serve a purpose that is not its own. Although most readers would agree that reading fiction is a splendid way of gaining knowledge about all sorts of things, few would name this as its main purpose. Used in this cross-curricular way, literature becomes a carrier of content, rather than an entity created in its own right, and so, although the message of the text is clear, the medium remains invisible. Literature – and the people who write it – deserve more than this.

Cox's three other approaches are harder to find in the primary and nursery school. In secondary schools, personal growth and cultural analysis have more currency, and teachers are more likely to imagine their work as taking place in fluid cultural space (McIntyre and Jones, 2014) Furthermore, English teachers, many of whom have degrees in English literature and see it as an almost undisputed bedrock of the subject (Goodwyn, 2012) are confident in using texts to help young people explore themselves and the world in which they live. They are also adept at helping young people understand how texts do this, that is, at unpicking the medium as well as the message. The problem for these teachers is not that they do not know what to do with literature, as is sometimes the case with primary school teachers, but that they do not know what to do with *children's* literature.

Perhaps the problem is that children's literature is an ambiguous concept. It is not altogether clear, especially in the secondary school, who counts as a child (rather than a young adult). When does childhood stop? The status of children's books is also unclear. Is it the teacher's job to use children's literature as training texts to draw young people into more difficult adult texts and equip them with the skills to read them, or are children's texts literature in their own right to be read on equal terms with any other? What does literature mean anyway? Are all children's books literature? Are some texts only books? If so, what quality or lack of quality makes them so? In the absence of a literary canon for children, who is to say?

For some secondary teachers, the answer to all this is to sideline children's literature as much as possible. They move young readers on to popular adult texts as soon as they can, and their pupils are often impressed. They want to be treated as adults, and reading books that are marketed for adults makes them feel grown up. But there are problems with this. As Hopper (2006) argues, not all teachers are equipped with enough knowledge of popular genres to ensure progression, and it might be that the adult texts that are accessible to 14-year-olds lack substance and challenge. Perhaps they encourage even committed readers to read without thought. Those teachers who believe that the purpose of reading is to encourage reflection and personal growth will find these texts unsatisfactory. Other teachers, unsure of that to give this age group, rely on a narrow range of old favourites. There is nothing at all wrong with Steinbeck and Harper Lee – but these are novels of more than 50 years ago. Has nothing been written since that will appeal to teenagers? Teachers who are committed to a cultural analysis approach to teaching literature will want to find texts that help their pupils think about society today.

Both these sets of teachers would do well to look to contemporary young adult literature. Here are texts written with modern young people in mind. The best authors know how these young people think and what they are interested in and they can write directly to them. They know how young people use language, and they can match their writing to that language so it is both accessible and enriching. They can use simple language to convey complex ideas. They can make young people think. When *The Fault in our Stars* (Green, 2012) is read alongside *Romeo and Juliet*, contemporary teenagers see the modern world and the medieval world in focus. They see young love and tragedy reflected in the lenses of time and circumstance. They learn about human nature and how it is realised in different societies. In the best classrooms, personal growth and cultural analysis are intertwined.

The fifth of Cox's positional categories, cultural heritage, is perhaps the most controversial and most beloved by politicians. Successive Conservative administrations in England and the Scottish Nationalists in Scotland have seen literature as a place where national and cultural identity can be formed and reinforced. Current curriculum documentation in both countries makes this clear.

In England, in a curriculum that places word reading before text and which categorises all other text work as comprehension, children in KS1 (aged 7–11) are expected to read 'fiction from our literary heritage [p 33]', although this is ameliorated by the next phrase: 'and books from other cultures and traditions'. In the lower secondary school, this expectation is expanded. Children should read 'a wide range of fiction and non-fiction, including in particular…[texts from] historical periods, forms and authors, including high-quality works from English literature, both pre-1914 and contemporary, including prose, poetry and drama' (Department for Education (DfE), 2013).

In Scotland the brief is even more explicit. One of the five overarching aims of the Literacy and English Curriculum for young people between 3 and 18 years is 'I engage with a wide range of texts and am developing *an appreciation of the richness and breadth of Scotland's literary and linguistic heritage*' (Scottish Qualifications Authority (SQA), 2007: 1, emphasis added).

It is difficult to see the place of children's and young people's literature through this heritage lens. To begin with, the history of children's writing is relatively short. Is a syllabus based on R.L Stevenson and Lewis Carroll envisaged? Or perhaps Thackeray's (1854) *The Rose and the Ring?* Does *English Literature* include children's books or is some unspecified English canon being referred to? Do all Scottish teenagers have to read *Sunset Song* (Gibbon, 1932) (very many do and hate it!). Here, the provenance and age of texts seems to matter more than their relevance to young readers, or accessibility, and in the documentation for England especially, there seems to be an assumption that old is necessarily good. Is Dickens inherently better than Jacqueline Wilson, I wonder, and are the policymakers who write these documents able to explain why? The mix of nostalgia and nationalism is unpalatable to my taste, and so is the marginalisation of modern texts that

children, who are still learning to be readers, will actually be able to read.

But the cultural heritage approach to the teaching of literature in schools brings the question back in to focus. What *should* the place of children's literature be in the curriculum and why does it matter?

WHY CHILDREN'S LITERATURE MATTERS: MARGARET MEEK'S LEGACY

Nearly 30 years ago, Margaret Meek (1988) showed us that children's books *mattered*. They were not just places where children learned to read, or to amuse themselves, but places where they learned to be readers. In *How Texts Teach What Readers Learn* (Meek, 1988), a book so short as to be hardly more than a pamphlet – and so wise and radical that it was difficult for teachers and policymakers to accommodate – she outlined some of the persuasive lessons in reading that the best texts give to responsive readers. She showed how *Each Peach Pear Plum* (Ahlberg and Ahlberg, 1978) encouraged young readers to think intertexually and join Frank Smith's literacy club (here is a writer who knows the same stories as me!). She showed how picture books with dual and suggested narratives, such as *Rosie's Walk* (Hutchins, 1968) and *Chips and Jessie* (Hughes, 1985), helped readers develop the ability to juggle multiple lines of plot, see between the words on the page and understand irony. She showed how *The Iron Man* (Hughes, 1968) helped children see the language of the text as well as the story (I love the 'delicacies') and how the subtle writing of Jan Mark opened up to slightly older readers the possibility of responding on multiple levels.

These are the sorts of lessons in reading that young people need if they are to become thoughtful, flexible, critical readers, and they are the lessons that not all young people receive. In classrooms where teachers are happy for children to read anything, or where teachers are not knowledgeable enough to guide children towards the best texts, there is a high chance that these lessons will be missed.

Meek's influence in those institutions that take children's reading and children's literature seriously continues to be felt. The exemplary work of The Centre for Language in Primary Education (CLPE) is an example of this. Their work with in-service teachers in projects such as the Power of Reading inspires teachers to use children's books in ways that are creative and enriching (O'Sullivan and McGonigle, 2010). I would like to see more initiatives like this, and I would like to see Meek's ideas taken further. Particularly, I would like to see a curriculum for Children's Literature in schools that builds upon Meek's understanding that texts themselves are important teachers.

As I have argued elsewhere (Smith, 2011), such a curriculum would require a new approach for many teachers. They would need to become familiar with a much wider range of children's text than is common today, and they would need to know those texts, not just in terms of story, but also in terms of what those texts offer in literary and linguistic experience for young readers. Such a curriculum would require a new vocabulary for many teachers. They would need to be able to articulate what it is that particular texts might teach the children in their classes. In primary schools, this would move the discourse of the teaching of reading away from a focus on whether children *can* read to *how* they read and how they *think* about their reading. In secondary schools, it would help teachers look at texts written for young people as literature, rather than as transitional texts to be used as a training ground for literary competence.

WHY CHILDREN'S LITERATURE MATTERS: CHANGING SELF AND SOCIETY

It used to be possible to argue that reading in adult life did not matter much. As long as one could read enough to function in the social and informational context of one's life, one could live well. Fiction was escapism for the masses and an esoteric luxury for the middle classes. It was no more than a life choice. It is becoming increasingly difficult to maintain this argument.

On the one hand, psychologists, such as Susan Engel (1995), and teachers, such as Vivien Paley (1987) and Anne Haas Dyson (2003), have shown us how important storying is for very young children. They show how children structure their lives and make sense of their experiences through telling stories of true and imaginary events. They order, they assimilate and they accommodate. Ideas and memories are processed and organised, and in this way, personhood and individual identities are formed. In short, children, or perhaps people generally, story themselves in to the people they eventually become. It seems entirely reasonable to assume that literature – the stories children hear and read – are also part of this person-forming process. Indeed, Virginia Lowe (2007) showed how, for her own children at least, this was certainly the case. Surrounded by books from babyhood, they used stories from texts in much the same way as Engel's children used stories from life: they used them to mirror, explain and extend their thinking and their experiences. They talked about books and referred to stories as readily as they talked about their friends and family.

Is this important? I think it is. If we can claim that Lowe's children and others like them, who live and breathe books from babyhood make cognitive gains through acquaintance with story, then we can make a very strong case for including literature more prominently in the curriculum. We can argue that literature needs to be there from the early years and beyond – not simply to amuse the children and to pacify them at the end of the day – but to teach them how to think and to give them the resources to make sense of their lives.

Until quite recently, it has been difficult to substantiate this argument. Evidence to show that literature matters in this way has been anecdotal and partial, but recent work in civics education and cognitive literary criticism begins to show clearer results.

First, Paterson's (2008) systematic analysis of the longitudinal data around social participation in the UK uncovered a startling fact: people who read widely as teenagers are more likely than not to grow up into the sort of adult who votes, volunteers in the community and, in various ways, become socially and politically active. They become, in terms of the Scottish Curriculum for Excellence, responsible citizens. It is, of course, possible to argue that that it is not the reading itself that has had this effect. It might be that teenagers who read are more likely than others to come from the sort of families who encourage socially responsible behaviour and that it is the teenagers' upbringing that has made the difference, or it might be that reading fiction is one of a set of middle-class behaviours like recycling and buying broadsheet newspapers that fit together: being socially responsible is part of the cultural norm. But we cannot rule out the possibility that it is the books themselves because if story teaches children how to think logically, perhaps literature encourages older readers to become more thoughtful, socially aware people.

Evidence to suggest that this might be the case comes from cognitive literary studies. This is a new, interdisciplinary field of research that seeks to marry recent scientific findings about the human brain or mind with literary understandings. Hart defines it as:

An interest in the cognitive, from a literary perspective, is an interest in exploring how both the architecture and the contents of the human brain/mind – both in terms of its on-line processing of information and its evolutionary history – may contribute structurally to the writing, reading and interpretation of texts. (Hart, 2001: 319)

The area of cognition that interested Kidd and Costano (2013) was theory of mind. It has long been suggested that reading helps people develop theory of mind. Reading about other people in other situations quite obviously helps readers understand viewpoints other than their own, and so begins to develop empathy and compassion. What Kidd and Costano wanted to know was whether literary fiction (that is, literature) did this any better than popular fiction, or indeed non-fiction, or even not reading at all. In a series of experiments they demonstrated that all fiction improved subjects' theory of mind, but that the effect of literary fiction was measurably stronger and more sustained. They argued two points. First that the texts changed not just *what* readers thought, but *how they thought about it*, and second, that the literary texts had more effect because they were more difficult to read: they defamiliarised the reader and challenged thinking. The effort needed to make sense of these texts imprinted the thinking more securely on the mind.

Even though this work was carried out with adults and not young people, it is significant to the cause of children's literature in the curriculum. If the texts people read have a real and measurable effect on the thinking that they do, then it is important that children read. If literary texts do the job better than popular fiction, then we need to make sure that some of the books we offer children are high quality literary texts that challenge their thinking. Finally, we can be sure that it *does* matter what children read.

I would like to see a curriculum for children's literature in schools that understands the importance of fiction, and literary fiction in particular, in developing children's cognitive processing. Such a curriculum would place story at the core from the early years to the end of secondary school. Children would read and be read to. Texts would be chosen for their richness in ideas and in language, and children and young people would be encouraged to talk and respond, to think and to speculate about the stories and the characters they read. The demands on teachers would be great and the responsibility onerous for they would need to understand that the reading their pupils do will change their young lives. Teachers will need to develop two particular sets of knowledge: knowledge of children's reading needs – when to challenge, when to reinforce, when to consolidate, when to relax; and the knowledge of books – what the challenges are that particular literary texts offer and how to support readers as they attempt the unfamiliar. Teachers will need to be supported in this. A radical change will be necessary in teacher education – a realignment of children's literature from the edges of the curriculum (where so often it exists as an optional extra) to the very core.

WHY CHILDREN'S LITERATURE MATTERS: EQUITY AND THE ACHIEVEMENT GAP

Does this talk of quality and literary texts mean that Children's Literature is elitist? Would an emphasis on quality texts in the classroom exclude a number, perhaps even a majority of children from participating in the curriculum? Might it not be better for everyone to read and enjoy popular undemanding texts as a matter of equity? My final argument positions Children's Literature as means of achieving equity. I argue that far from being a source of difference, when it is taught well, Children's Literature is *the* engine for social mobility and for closing the achievement gap.

Much has been written about inequality in schools in recent years, especially about the achievement gap between boys and girls (for example, Department for Children, Schools and Families (DCSF), 2009). But in Scotland, the rest of the UK, the US (Hoff, 2013) and Australia (Cobbold, 2010) the biggest gap in achievement is not the difference between boys and girls, but between the haves and the have-nots in society. It is a sorry truth that the clearest indicator of how well a child starting school at five will achieve, is not gender, or ethnicity, or intelligence, but the job of the parents (Ellis, 2015). Children with a professional parent or two adapt to school ways easily, learn to read faster and quickly set off on the path to success.

The reasons for this are complex, but an important factor is that children from professional homes have a number of cultural advantages. Professional parents are more likely to have money to spend on children's books. Because they have been successful at schools themselves they are more likely to have taken on the literary discourse that schools propagate that positions books as sites of exploration and speculation. Like Virginia Lowe, they read to and with their children from babyhood, they share and chat, and make meaning together. Children from homes like this come to school already thinking like readers. The cognitive gains that reading affords are already in development.

Less fortunate children have fewer books and fewer interactions with books. Parents, less sure of literary discourse, are less well equipped to talk, play and speculate around books, and so reading becomes less enjoyable for the child, more rigid and less exploratory. The cognitive advantages of embracing challenge recognised by Kidd and Costano (2013) are less apparent and learning is slower and less sure. These children start school with a disadvantage. If the school they attend values learning to read and decodable text above literature, how will these children ever catch up? How will they learn to think about text, understand the logic of story, develop theory of mind, empathy and good citizenship?

For reasons of equity, I want to see a curriculum that front loads children's literature so that children are flooded with books and stories from nursery throughout the primary school. That way, the cognitive gains that are accessed through reading and story will be available to all children, not just those from bookish homes. A result of this 'flooding' will be that all children would be familiar with a wide variety of texts from early on. Quality literary texts would be part of everyone's everyday diet, not reserved as a particular experience for a supposed elite. All children would grow up expecting books to be challenging and interesting, and because they would have developed through reading a wide range of reference and experience, they would be equal to the challenge. There would be no need for poor books for poor readers.

Indeed, poor readers would be scarce because those many children who struggle to learn to read or fail to become readers because they do not see what reading can do for them will *know*. They will know in their hearts and their heads that reading and story are worthwhile.

Flaubert famously wrote to Mademoiselle Leroyer de Chantepie,

> Do not read, as children do, to amuse yourself, or like the ambitious, for the purpose of instruction. No, read in order to live. (Flaubert, 1857)

Children's literature is one of the places where he was especially right. Children's literature is where children learn to live. It is *that* important and it deserves a central place in the curriculum.

NOTE

1   See http://www.playingbythebook.net/2014/04/22/uk-university-courses-in-childrens-literature-and-book-illustration/ (accessed 1 January 2015).

REFERENCES

Children's and Young Adult texts

Ahlberg, A. and Ahlberg, J. (1978) *Each Peach Pear Plum*. London: Picture Lions.

Bond, M. (1958) *A Bear called Paddington*. London: Collins.

Child, L. (2000) *I Will Not Ever, Never Eat a Tomato*. London: Orchard.

Cowell, C. (2003) *How to Train Your Dragon*. London: Hodder Children's Books.

Dahl, R. (1990) *Esio Trot*. London: Jonathan Cape.

Gibbon, L.G. (1932) *Sunset Song*. Norwich: Jarrolds Publishing.

Green, J. (2012) *The Fault in Our Stars*. New York, NY: Dutton.

Hardinge, F. (2014) *Cuckoo Song*. London: Macmillan Children's Books

Hedderwick, M. (1984) *Katie Morag Delivers the Mail*. London: Picture Lions.

Hughes, S. (1985) *Chips and Jessie*. London: Young Lions.

Hughes, T. (1968) *The Iron Man*. London: Faber & Faber.

Hutchins, P. (1968) *Rosie's Walk*. London: Simon & Schuster.

Magorian, M. (1981) *Goodnight Mr Tom*. London: Puffin.

Morpurgo, M. (1982) *War Horse*. London: Egmont.

Ness, P. (2011) *A Monster Calls*. London: Walker Books.

Pullman, P. (2000) *The Amber Spyglass*. London: Scholastic/David Fickling.

Rowling, J.K. (1997) *Harry Potter and the Philosopher's Stone*. London: Bloomsbury.

Rundell, K. (2013) *Rooftoppers*. London: Faber & Faber.

Thackeray, W.M. (1854) *The Rose and the Ring*. London: Macmillan.

Tolkein, J.R.R. (1937) *The Hobbit*. London: George Allen and Unwin.

Significant authors mentioned in the text with illustrative examples of their work

Boston, L. (1954) *The Children of Green Knowe*. London: Faber.

Brown, A. (1983) *Gorilla*. London: Julia McRae.

Burningham, J. (1970) *Mr. Gumpy's Outing*. London: Cape.

Carroll, Lewis (1865) *Alice in Wonderland*. London: Macmillan.

Child, L. (1999) *Clarice Bean, That's Me*. London: Orchard.

Cross, G. (1990) *Wolf*. Oxford: Oxford University Press.

Fine, A. (1996) *The Tulip Touch*. London: Hamish Hamilton.

Garner, A. (1965) *Elidor*. London: William Collins.

Grahame, K. (1908) *Wind in the Willows*. London: Methuen.

Gravett, E. (2005) *Wolves*. London: Macmillan.

Horowitz, A. (2000) *Stormbreaker (Alex Rider)*. London: Walker Books.

Mayne, W. (1966) *Earthfasts*. London: Hamish Hamilton.

Meyer, S. (2005) *Twilight*. New York, NY: Little, Brown & Co.

Milne, A.A. (1926) *Winnie the Pooh*. London: Methuen.

Morpurgo, M. (1996) *The Butterfly Lion.* London: Collins.

Morpurgo, M. (2010) *Kaspar: Prince of Cats.* London: Harper Collins.

Pearce, P. (1958) *Tom's Midnight Garden.* Oxford: Oxford University Press.

Pullman, P. (1995) Northern Lights. London: Scholastic.

Reeve, P. (2001) *Mortal Engines.* London: Scholastic.

Rayner, C. (2014) Abigail. London: Little Tiger Press.

Sherry, S. (1969) *A Pair of Jesus Boots.* London: Cape.

Snicket, L. (1999) *The Bad Beginning.* New York, NY: Scholastic.

Townsend, J.R. (1961) *Gumbles Yard.* London: Hutchinson.

Walliams, D. (2009) *Mr Stink.* London: Harper Collins.

Wilson, J. (1991) *The Story of Tracy Beaker.* London: Doubleday.

Secondary resources

Arizpe, E. and Styles, M. (2003) *Children Reading Pictures: Interpreting Visual Texts.* London: Routledge.

Book Trust (2008) *Reading Champions: involving boys and men in creating a reading culture.* Available from http://www.literacytrust. org.uk/Campaign/Champions/index.html (accessed 1 January 2015).

Cobbold, T. (2010) 'Closing the Achievement Gaps in Australian Schools', presentation to the Independent Scholars Association of Australia, Annual Conference, National Library, Canberra.

Cremin, T., Mottram, M., Bearne, E. and Goodwin, P. (2008) 'Exploring teachers' knowledge of children's literature', *Cambridge Journal of Education,* 38(4): 449–64.

Department for Children, Schools and Families (DCSF) (2009) *The Gender Agenda Final Report.* Nottingham, UK: Department for Children, Schools and Families.

Department for Education (DfE) (2013) *English programmes of study: key stages 1 and 2.* Available from https://www.gov.uk/ government/uploads/system/uploads/ attachment_data/file/335186/PRIMARY_ national_curriculum_-_English_220714.pdf (accessed 1 January 2015).

Department for Education and Employment (DfEE) (1998) *The National Literacy Strategy: a Framework for Teaching.* London: HMSO.

Department of Education and Science/Welsh Office (1989) *English for Ages 5–16 (The Cox Report).* London: HMSO.

Dombey, H. (2003) 'Teachers, children and texts in three primary classrooms in England', *Journal of Early Childhood Literacy,* 3: 37–58. doi: 10.1177/14687984030031002.

Dyson, A.H. (2003) *The Brothers and Sisters Learn to Write: Popular Literacies in Childhood and School Cultures.* New York, NY: Teachers College Press.

Eccleshare, J. (2015, in press) 'The reader in the writer: how Jacqueline Wilson reflects the essential literacy connection between reading and writing in the context of the current changing role of the authors, including herself', in Arizpe, E. and Smith, V. (eds.), *Children as Readers in Children's Literature.* London: Routledge. pp. 83–92.

Elkin, J, Denham, D. and Train, B. (2003) *Reading and Reader Development: The Pleasure of Reading.* London: Facet Publishing.

Ellis, S. (2015) *Improving Literacy in Scotland: Four Policy Proposals.* Glasgow, UK: University of Strathclyde, International Public Policy Institute.

Engel, S. (1995) *The Stories Children Tell: Making Sense of the Narratives Of Childhood.* New York: W.H. Freeman.

Evans, J. (2009) *Talking Beyond the Page: Reading and Responding to Picture Books.* London: Routledge.

Flaubert, G. (1857) 'Letter to Mademoiselle Leroyer de Chantepie', in F. Steegmuller (ed. and trans.), (1980) *The Letters of Gustave Flaubert 1830–1857. Vol. 1.* London: Faber & Faber.

Gamble, N. and Yates, S. (2002) *Exploring Children's Literature.* London: Paul Chapman Publishing.

Goodwin, P. (2008) *Understanding Children's Books: a Guide for Education Professionals.* London: Sage Publications.

Goodwyn, A. (2012) 'The status of literature: English teaching and the condition of literature teaching in schools', *English in Education,* 46: 212–27. doi: 10.1111/ j.1754-8845.2012.01121.x.

Grenby, M.O and Reynolds, K. (2011) *Children's Literature Studies: A Research Handbook.* London: Palgrave Macmillan.

Hart, F.E. (2001) 'The epistemology of cognitive literary studies', *Philosophy and Literature,* 25(2): 314–34.

Hoff, E. (2013) 'Interpreting the early language trajectories of children from low-SES and language minority homes: implications for closing achievement gaps', *Developmental Psychology,* 49(1): 4–14. doi: 10.1037/a0027238.

Hopper, R. (2006) 'The good, the bad and the ugly: teachers' perception of quality in fiction for adolescent readers', *English in Education,* 40: 55–70. doi: 10.1111/j.1754-8845.2006.tb00791.x.

Kidd, D.C. and Costano, E. (2013) 'Reading literary fiction improves theory of mind', *Science,* 342(6156): 377–80. doi: 10.1126/science.1239918.

Littleton, K. and Mercer, N. (2013) *Interthinking: Putting Talk to Work.* Abingdon, UK: Routledge.

Lockwood, M. (2008) *Promoting Reading for Pleasure in the Primary School.* London: Sage Publications.

Lowe, V. (2007) *Stories, Pictures and Reality: Two Children Tell.* London: Routledge.

McIntyre, J. and Jones, S. (2014) 'Possibility in impossibility? Working with beginning teachers of English in times of change', *English in Education,* 48: 26–40. doi: 10.1111/eie.12029.

Meek, M. (1988) *How Texts Teach What Readers Learn.* Stroud, UK: Thimble Press.

Nikolajeva, M. and Scott, C. (2001) *How Picturebooks Work.* New York, NY: Garland.

Noyes, A. (1947) *The Highwayman.* Available from http://www.poetryfoundation.org/poem/171940 (accessed 26 August 2015).

O'Sullivan, O. and McGonigle, S. (2010) 'Transforming readers: teachers and children in the Centre for Literacy in Primary Education Power of Reading project', *Literacy,* 44: 51–9. doi: 10.1111/j.1741-4369.2010.00555.x.

Paley, V.G. (1987) *Wally's Stories.* Cambridge, MA: Harvard University Press.

Paterson, L. (2008) 'Political attitudes, social participation and social mobility: a longitudinal analysis', *British Journal of Sociology,* 59(3): 413–34. doi: 10.1111/j.1468-4446.2008.00201.x.

Powling, C., Ashley, B., Pullman, P., Fine, A. and Gavin, J. (2003) *Meetings with the Minister: Five Children's Authors on the National Literacy Strategy.* Reading, UK: National Centre for Language and Literacy.

Reynolds, K. (2006) *Radical Children's Literature: Future Visions and Aesthetic Transformations in Juvenile Fiction.* London: Palgrave.

Rose, J. (2006) *Independent Review of the Teaching of Early Reading.* London: Department for Education and Skills.

Salisbury, M. and Styles, M. (2012) *Children's Picturebooks: The Art of Visual Storytelling.* London: Laurence King.

Scottish Qualifications Authority (SQA) (2007) *Curriculum for Excellence: English and Literacy Experiences and Outcomes.* Available from https://www.educationscotland.gov.uk/Images/literacy_english_experiences_outcomes_tcm4-539867.pdf (accessed 1 January 2015).

Smith, V. (2008) 'Learning to be a reader: promoting good textual health', in P. Goodwin (ed.), *Understanding Children's Books: a Guide for Education Professionals.* London: Sage Publications. pp. 33–43.

Smith, V. (2009) 'Making and breaking frames: crossing the borders of expectation in picturebooks', in J. Evans (ed.), *Talking Beyond the Page: Reading and Responding to Picture Books.* London: Routledge. pp. 81–97.

Smith, V. (2011) 'Words and pictures: towards a linguistic understanding of picture books and reading pedagogy', in S. Ellis and E. McCartney (eds.), *Applied Linguistics and Primary School Teaching.* Cambridge: Cambridge University Press. pp. 107–17.

Stanovich, K.E. (1986) 'Matthew effects in reading: some consequences of individual differences in the acquisition of literacy', *Reading Research Quarterly,* 21(4): 360–407.

The Guardian (2014) Crime and Cooking: The Most Borrowed Books of the Year. *The Guardian.* 14 February. Available from http://www.theguardian.com/books/2014/feb/14/most-borrowed-library-books-analysis (accessed 1 January 2015).

US Department of Education (2001) *No Child Left Behind.* Available from http://www2.ed.gov/policy/elsec/leg/esea02/index.html (accessed 30 April 2015).

Watson, V., Bearne, E. and Styles, M. (eds.) (1992) *After Alice: Exploring Children's Literature.* London: Cassell.

Watson, V., Bearne, E. and Styles, M. (eds.) (1996) *Voices Off: Texts, Contexts and Readers.* London: Cassell.

39

The Literacy Curriculum: A Critical Review

Kathy A. Mills and Len Unsworth

INTRODUCTION

This chapter critically reviews the scope of the literacy curriculum in the twenty-first century, uncovering some of the strengths, controversies, and silences that have divided literacy researchers and educators. It begins with the acknowledgment that the constitution of literacy and textual practices is in a constant state of flux in the 'digital turn', and in the context of the transnational flow of people, languages, discourses, and dialects. This has led to a search for theories of representation that account for intermodal relations, and the concomitant reformulating of the literacy curriculum to usefully reflect these transitions.

Here, the political and ideological antecedents of literacy curriculum and schooling as a form of cultural apparatus of the nation-state are acknowledged and historicized before tracing some of the major interpretive paradigms that have influenced the shape of the literacy curriculum in many parts of the world – basic skills, whole language, systemic functional linguistics, and critical literacy. The chapter draws attention to noteworthy advances and shifts in the field over recent decades. The significant challenges for the literacy curriculum, and perennial debates and currents that have surfaced in the changing social and political context of curriculum are acknowledged and debated. Finally, the chapter anticipates the future of the literacy curriculum, particularly in relation to global markets, increased mobility and transnational flows of culture, literacy practices, and curriculum technologization.

Defining the Literacy Curriculum in the Digital Turn

Arguably one of the seismic shifts in the literacy curriculum in the past few decades has been the changing social and technological environment as individuals and communities enact the realities of global connectedness, reshaping the way literacy practices are used to participate in daily social life. A number of theoretical, pedagogical, and empirical research directions have been put forward to address these changes in the 'digital turn' (Mills, 2010a). Some of these theories that have empirical support include New Literacy Studies (Street, 1997), multiliteracies (New London Group, 2000), and multimodal literacy (Kress, 2010; Kress and van Leeuwen, 1996). These theories extended earlier writing and reading research in relation to technology, computers, or hypertext in the 1990s that foregrounded the need to seriously rethink the constitution of conventional literacy curricula. Earlier studies had predominantly concerned alphabetic literacy taught using hard copies of published texts, with an emphasis on linear readings and paper-based writing practices (Reinking, 1997; Selfe, 1999).

The complexity of intermodal relations in texts between words, images, gestures, sound and other modes has taken center stage, which was prompted, in part, by the challenge of Halliday (1991) to include new systems of semiotics, such as images, that are distinct from writing, but which modify the meaning of encoded words. Similarly, in the 1980s, Ulmer (1985: vii) theorized communication as a 'multichannelled performance', orchestrating spoken and written symbols with digital imagery and audio–visual texts in the changing context of media and information technologies. He also proposed a 'teletheory' or grammar for the age of video (Ulmer, 1989). These semiotic theories and discourses have implications for the literacy curriculum and pedagogy and have been resisted, ignored, or taken up by government agencies, universities, schools, and teachers in various literacy curricula around the world (Mills and Exley, 2014).

In the context of this discussion of curriculum, literacy is defined, following Scribner and Cole (1981: 236) as 'socially organised practices [that] make use of a symbol system'. Literacy involves the use of the human body and often a technology for producing it, whether a pencil, computer, or some other means. An important dimension of this definition is the aspect of 'social organization' of practices. The literacy curriculum consists of a particular set of socially organized symbolic practices that are always selective, and which are inextricably connected to the function and organization of schooling.

The literacy curriculum, defined here, is the sequencing of knowledge and application of symbol systems and associated social practices that are valued by the curriculum makers. Any literacy curriculum is organized to take into account time, which pertains to learning trajectories that typically consider the age of learners; space, which refers to the social context of the learning; and text, which concerns the learner's performance of the required text or production of text, and its evaluation (Bernstein, 2000). This chapter situates knowledge of literacy theory in relation to the substance of the curriculum, while considering the social processes of literacy curriculum, or what Bernstein calls the 'pedagogic device' or 'cultural relay' of schooling (Bernstein, 2000).

MAJOR INTERPRETATIVE PARADIGMS OF LITERACY CURRICULUM

The literacy curriculum has long been seen as a political instrument, as a means of 'state-sponsored cultural apparatus', an asset that contributes in symbolic or tangible ways to economic prosperity (Green, 1993: 2). In many respects, although not exclusively, the literacy curriculum has remained caught up in the social reproduction of the political relations that sustain the school curriculum. This is evident in the way in which schooling and literacy curricula functions to maintain hegemony by producing educated subjects, good citizens, logocentric rationality, and disciplined bodies.

Those who are empowered by knowledge of how to write through the literacy curriculum are also serving to sustain the transmission of culture. This is illustrated through Foucault's (1977: 191) 'network of writing' as a means of creating, organizing, and controlling disciplined subjects. An essential feature of schooling is that the function of literacy curricula is to reproduce or transform the social relations of which it is simultaneously an outcome (Bernstein, 2003; Green, 1993). The social structure of schooling can be both enabling and constraining for the recontextualization of literacy practices as curriculum knowledge.

Basic Skills: Letters, Words, and the Literacy Curriculum

One of the ideological–discursive assemblages that have influenced literacy curricula worldwide is the basic skills approach. Ministries of education in many parts of the world, such as North America, the UK, and Australasia, demonstrate a view of literacy as a body of universally applicable reading and writing skills, rather than as a set of social practices that varies according to the changing needs of groups and communities (Mills and Exley, 2014). This approach to the literacy curriculum was prominent in the early establishment of compulsory schooling in many societies, where children were taught basic instruction in literacy, computation, and morality. As Green (1993) argues, the 'insistence of the letter' describes a crucial feature of the nexus between curriculum and literacy historically.

The traditional compartmentalizing of literacy skills into lock-step components, from letter formation, to letter–sound relationships, to vocabulary words, to sentence grammar – the skills-based ideology of literacy – still dictates the constructs that undergird classroom assessment and large-scale literacy tests. Literacy assessments in schooling are often politically driven, increasingly mandated by governments worldwide with an accountability agenda. However, such an emphasis inhibits the scope of curricula and pedagogies that embrace broader conceptualizations

of the literacy competences students are able to demonstrate and those they need to develop (Macken-Horarik, 2009; Zacher Pandya, 2011; Unsworth, 2014).

Advocates of a skills-based approach perceive literacy as something merely technical to be acquired, as a neutral set of skills that remain constant irrespective of the manner in which they are acquired or used. This stands in contradiction to the view that the curriculum incorporates community literacy practices defined by their particular social purposes and contexts (Street, 1995). From a skills-based perspective, reading is described as a combination of visual and perceptual skills, sight vocabulary, phonics or word attack skills, and comprehension (Anstey and Bull, 2004).

An important caveat is that there is empirical evidence supporting the benefits of systematic phonics instruction and contextualized systematic phonics, as opposed to synthetic phonics (Wyse and Goswami, 2008; Wyse and Styles, 2007). Systematic phonics instruction is not synonymous with the ideologies and pedagogies of skills-based approaches, although this has often been the case, and phonics instruction can be supported by a repertoire of methods and aligned to varying educational philosophies. Skills-based literacy curricula are often identifiable by a 'performance model' of curriculum, the discourse of transmission characterized by strong sequencing of literacy skills, predefined rates of student progression, and teacher control over the social action in the classroom, which enables this transmission to take place (Bernstein, 2000).

A problem with a skill-based approach is that reading methods can become practiced in such a way that the social context of the literature, and the assumptions inherent in the meanings of words and images in books and other texts, can be considered immaterial to the learning of reading, or ideologically benign (Luke and Freebody, 1997). For example, students might parse a sentence into its grammatical components, but the content or meaning of the selected sentence, which contains implicit or explicit social values, is arbitrary to the instructional purpose. A further criticism of this approach is that students themselves must figure out how to apply grammatical rules in real world literacy uses, and occasionally, some knowledge remains inert and never used, either in community, occupational, or subsequent endeavors (Mills, 2005).

Whole Language Approaches to the Literacy Curriculum

In the late twentieth century, literacy research and curriculum began to address the semantics of text structure and the importance of students' purposeful making of meaning from reading, rather than reading as recitation. The key theorists included Goodman (1976), Graves (1983) Pearson and Johnson (1978), Cambourne (1988), and Turbill (1983), who advocated top–down and whole language approaches to reading (Emmitt and Pollock, 1997). The whole language approach emerged from psycholinguistic reading research identifying readers' prior knowledge as a factor influencing success in deriving meaning from texts. It was observed that different text types and reading tasks require differing fields of prior knowledge (Coles and Hall, 2002). A key feature of whole language approaches was to attend to the semantic features of literacy experiences within real-world literacy situations that skills based approaches had tended to disregard (Mills, 2005).

However, the pedagogies promoted in teaching materials as 'whole language', such as shared reading, retelling, Uninterrupted Sustained Silent Reading (USSR), and process writing became subjects of controversy and critique. Theorists of systemic functional linguistics, such as Rothery and Stenglin (2000), Martin (1993a), Painter and Martin (2011), Macken-Horarik (2009) emphasized the need for students to gain explicit grounding in the metalanguage of text, including grammatical structures and

linguistic features of texts across a range of genres and social purposes (Mills, 2005). As Unsworth (1988: 127) demonstrated in classroom research, whole language practices can be augmented with a much stronger emphasis on the knowledge of texts and how they function in different social contexts, without which whole language classroom organizational strategies simply become 'procedural display'.

One of the key principles of whole language is the view that the written modes of language can be successfully taught by reproducing the same conditions in which children acquire oral language, such as demonstrating mature language forms and recognizing approximations that work toward language objectives (Cambourne, 1988). However, the theory of natural learning has been criticized for its failure to acknowledge the cultural and linguistically diverse textual practices and conditions for early language acquisition across homes (Muspratt et al., 1997). The ways in which children learn to use language are dependent on community and family roles in the community, home patterns of face-to-face interaction, and child socialization (Heath, 1983). Critics have also argued that the lexico-grammatical structures of written language are similar, but also different in many ways to those of speech (Halliday, 1985). Therefore, a single set of oral language learning conditions for writing success cannot be assumed.

A further criticism of whole language is that the emphasis on acquisition may lead to implicit and incidental instruction in phonics, grammar, and syntax, rather than explicit and comprehensive instruction. Rather than 'acquiring' the dominant discourse of the classroom through 'natural learning', or socializing the child into literacy practices, the question must be asked 'natural for whom?' It has been demonstrated in classroom research that implicit teaching practices advantage the dominant cultural group over minority ethnic groups and social classes (Mills, 2005, 2006, 2011).

Functional Linguistic Approaches to the Literacy Curriculum

Since the 1980s systemic functional linguistics (SFL) has increasingly influenced literacy education in Australia, the UK, the US, Canada, South Africa and several other countries in Asia, Latin America, and Europe. SFL, which was developed by Michael Halliday (for example, Halliday, 1978; Halliday and Matthiessen, 2004) and expanded by Jim Martin (for example, Martin, 1992; Martin and Rose, 2007), describes language as a social semiotic system, including functional grammar, and discourse and genre, connecting language forms with meaning in contexts of use.

An important impetus for the SFL influence on school literacy was the overwhelming emphasis in elementary school writing in the 1970s on what was loosely known as 'story', with attention to correct grammar, punctuation, and spelling on the one hand, and student self-expression on the other. SFL theorists distinguished a range of genres for student writing, including different types of narratives, such as prototypical stories, recounts of experience and observation, as well as 'reports' about dealing with the classification, description and behavior of animals or plants or the characteristics of non-living phenomena, 'procedures' detailing steps in producing something, and explanations of how certain phenomena functioned or came to be (Martin, 1989; Martin and Rothery, 1993).

The identification of these genres led to the development of a pedagogy, known as the curriculum cycle, for explicit teaching of how to write the well-recognized conventional forms of these texts. This cycle emphasized teacher modeling of the writing of target genres, deconstruction of the genre through teacher-led classroom discussion to explicate the rhetorical and grammatical structure, collaborative teacher and whole class creation of a new instance of the genre, and finally, student independent writing of a further instance of the genre (Rose and Martin, 2012). The detailed implementation practices of the curriculum cycle have evolved, and different versions have been described and extended to secondary school writing pedagogy (Christie and Derewianka, 2010; Johns, 2001; Love et al., 2002; Unsworth, 2001).

SFL influenced the literacy curriculum and pedagogy, particularly in Australia and the UK. Most recognizable are the 'accelerated literacy' (Cowey, 2005; Robinson et al., 2009) and 'reading to learn' (Rose and Martin, 2012) approaches, which address both reading and writing. In these approaches, the fundamental aspects of the curriculum cycle have been elaborated and adapted, with a central focus on the development of students' explicit knowledge about language as a resource for meaning. This is based on systemic functional linguistic descriptions of language as a social semiotic, including an emphasis on naming and applying the structure and function of language use for different social purposes.

Critical Literacy Approaches

Critical literacy emerged in the 1980s, teaching students 'habits of mind' when reading, writing, listening or viewing, to challenge assumptions in texts, dominant ideologies, and 'political pronouncements' (Shor, 1999). Critical literacy extends to the very selection of literature used in schools because the use of texts in the literacy curriculum is ideologically value laden, while the criteria for judging the quality of school texts are also shifting in the context of society and culture (Macken-Horarik, 1997). In the 1970s, critical literacy emerged as a powerful theory grounded in Paulo Freire's 'Cultural action and conscientization' (Freire, 1970a) and *Pedagogy of the oppressed* (Freire, 1970b). Later, Freire directly addressed literacy curricula through *Literacy: reading the word and the world* (Freire and Macedo, 1987). Literacy texts began to be regarded within curriculum as key sites where cultural discourses, political ideologies, and economic interests should be contested rather than unquestioningly transmitted (Baker and Luke, 1991). As Knobel and Healy (1998: 3) argue: 'Through the selection of textbooks, genres, children's literature, media, literate tastes and practices, dominant mainstream cultures are assembled, presented and taught as culture. In this way, a selective tradition of culture is naturalized as the way things are...'. The social construction of the literacy curriculum is always selective.

Critical literacy can be seen as a vital part of developing students' 'intellectual agency' within the literacy curriculum. Students must not only comprehend texts within the literacy curriculum and the world, but more importantly, they must be able to think for themselves (Fairfield, 2012: 1). The literacy curriculum has been successful if it does more than teach students how to read and write, and also teach students how to critically analyze, evaluate and subject to scrutiny the authorship, intended audiences, textual meanings, silences and omissions in texts, and the interests that are served by texts and information across modes and media (Zacher Pandya and Ávila, 2014). Students need to be able to problematize assumptions in texts about gender, race, age, class, able bodies, beliefs, and other social identities. Similarly, students need to critically consider why they are being asked to read and use particular books, media, or other texts within the social context of school.

Theorists have cautioned that despite the strengths of critical literacy, there are several caveats regarding its application. The critical analysis of popular and commercial texts in the literacy curriculum may convey the implicit message that adults do not condone certain pleasurable texts (Kenway and Bullen, 2001). Equally, selecting for critique authoritative texts that are important to particular religious, political, or cultural groups can unwittingly create value conflicts for students who are members of those communities (Skerrett, 2014). In essence, taking a critical literacy stance will not neutralize classroom literacy practice because it is driven by its own agenda for social change.

However, few would disagree that cultivating in students the intellectual maturity and capacity to ask questions about texts, technologies, and resources, to engage in democratic and dialogic thinking through language and literacy, or to envisage alternatives to dominant cultural readings of the world, are necessary and often overlooked functions of an overly technologized education system (Fairclough, 1999). A technologized education system is one in which curriculum is driven by an instrumental function for purely economic ends. Furthermore, a technolologized curriculum is typically focused on measurable performance and outcomes.

CONTEMPORARY CONCERNS IN LITERACY CURRICULUM

The literacy curriculum is a discourse in which certain issues remain vital in the new times, more so than ever before. This section debates the role of oral language in the literacy curriculum, in a context in which the oral mode has often been a dominant mode of transmission and a means of access to social mobility. Second, central concerns about home-school community literacy practice and debates about the place of these out-of-school experiences in relation to the formal literacy curriculum are discussed. Third, debates regarding the relevance of teacher and student knowledge of language, including grammar, are critically reviewed. Finally, we evaluate the role of curriculum area literacies, that is, the need for subject-specific language structure, rhetoric, and vocabulary.

Orality Before, Within, and Beyond Literacy Curriculum

Students' oral language proficiency plays a vital role in the acquisition of reading fluency and comprehension (Mills, 2009). There is also a strong association between children's language development and their social and academic competence at school. For example, research with students aged 6–14 years indicates how well-designed classroom talk about books enables students to deepen their comprehension (Wolf et al., 2005). Spoken language is often regarded as an area of language competence in its own right, and in many parts of the world it is fostered alongside listening, reading, viewing, writing, and other forms of receptive or expressive language in the formal literacy curriculum (Stierer and Maybin, 1994). Oral language proficiency is not the only factor associated with reading success; other contributing language skills also play an interactive role, including concepts of print, letter naming, phonemic and phonological awareness, story recall, and speech vocabulary (Hay and Fielding-Barnsley, 2009).

Research evidence points to the need for the literacy curriculum to include oral language experiences that teach verbal expression, listening and responding to others, speech-vocabulary development, and gaining knowledge to talk about the world (Morrow et al., 2007). As young children engage in speech interactions they develop important skills in phonological awareness – hearing and recognizing the individual sounds in words – which provide an important basis for reading and writing. In particular, dyadic reading has been shown to enhance social turn taking, vocabulary, syntax, semantics, and pragmatics. This strategy for reading development involves book-reading conversations with parents, teachers, or other mature readers about story content (Hay and Fielding-Barnsley, 2009; Williams, 1998).

However, orality can be viewed not as a skill that exists prior to the literacy curriculum, but as one of many forms of literacy as a social practice that continues to be important throughout the life course, taking varied ephemeral or permanent forms. The emerging digital age has seen the role of orality as one of multiple modes in digital texts, able to be recorded, modified, saved, and podcasted on the Internet with ease. One of the potential implications of the dissemination of user-generated audio and audio-visual recordings is that students will need to become more socially critical, self-aware, and discerning producers of identity artifacts disseminated on the web. An implication of these changes is that it raises political questions about the function of the literacy curriculum, in particular the need to address critical media literacies and the purposeful and safe construction of online identities.

Home-Community Literacy Practices and the Curriculum

A related concern is a significant body of research that encourages the development of local literacy curricula in a way that integrates data about the 'funds of knowledge' that students bring to school from their home and communities (Moll et al., 2013). Although this issue is not new, it continues to be relevant in an age in which paradoxically, globalization is characterized by increased cultural homogeneity across nations, and local diversity. The New Literacy Studies has contributed significantly to ethnographic studies of literacy practices in homes and among youth in out-of-school contexts, and its relation to the practices and discourses of schooling. Some of the earliest of these include Brian Street's (1975) ethnography in an Iranian village, and Shirley Brice Heath's (1983) ethnography of three communities in the US, which were closely followed by an ethnographic study of reading and writing in a community by Barton and Hamilton (1998).

In these studies, and the progression of work that followed, the shape of communicative practices and discourses in children's homes, and the socio-cultural context in which children use language from birth, became the focus of understanding the relation between the cultural capital of communities and its alignment of the literacy curriculum of schooling (Mills, 2010a; Pahl and Burnett, 2013). Integral to this perspective is the view that literacy curricula, although seemingly normalized as a collection of universal skills within the institution of schooling, is in fact deeply ideological, partial, and selective. Some of the groups most marginalized by the design of the literacy curriculum include those affected by poverty and, since post-colonialism, those who are not of the dominant race and culture of the schooling and curriculum establishment. In addition, the socio-cognitive development of the child is seen as connected to the socio-cultural purposes for communication (Mills, 2008; Rosemberg et al., 2013).

Current research about the multimodal practices of childhood and adolescent literacies emphasizes the way in which the young intuitively grasp or acquire new literacies in their recreational spaces (Mills, 2010a). In particular, the New Literacy Studies (NLS) have specifically drawn attention to the situated ways in which language and communicative practices are shared by groups of people who sustain and modify them (Barton, 1994; Gee, 1996; Street, 2003). In recent years, research in this tradition has investigated the innovative and productive potentials of informal literacies in digital environments that children use outside of schools (Gee, 2003; Lankshear and Knobel, 2003; Nixon, 2003; Sefton-Green, 2006; Street, 2003).

Although an emphasis on out-of-school literacies counterbalanced earlier research that separated literacy learning from the lived experiences of students in their communities, there became a need for research that emphasized scaffolding the multimodal practice of youth by experts in school settings (Mills, 2010b). Over the past decade and a half, research of multimodality in school contexts has increased exponentially across a wide range of populations, geographical contexts, types of modes and media, and foci of investigation (see Mills, 2010a). These studies underscore the fluid way in which youth draw from the multimodal texts and experiences of their life worlds to connect with mature literacy practices in school settings, making permeable the boundaries between home and school (Dyson, 2003). Teachers can incorporate students' predilections while

extending the range of multimodal literacy practices that are already familiar to youth. In this way, teachers can balance the emphasis on multimodal literacies that have value in the local communities with those that afford students status and recognition throughout their formal education, workplaces, and the global communications environment.

Knowledge of Language

Clearly, the construction of the literacy curriculum must take into account students' need for 'knowledge about language' (KAL), frequently interpreted as grammatical knowledge and which encompasses rhetorical forms of extended texts. Nevertheless, much KAL research centered on grammar – and meta-analyses of the efficacy of grammar teaching has concluded that there is no evidence that teaching grammar is beneficial to literacy development (Andrews et al., 2006; Braddock et al., 1963; Hillocks, 1986). Hillocks and Smith (1991) argued that research in this area consistently showed little or no effect of grammar teaching on students; however, the teaching of grammar in the studies reviewed was largely isolated teaching of grammar rules and parsing of texts with little or no direct connection to students' actual writing endeavors. The grammar that was being taught in these studies was overwhelmingly traditional grammar, or in some cases, transformational generative grammar, but did not include the more recently developed, meaning-based systemic functional grammar (Halliday, 1973; Halliday and Matthiessen, 2004).

From the late 1990s a number of studies have shown that children in the early years of schooling could learn aspects of systemic functional grammar (SFG) and use these concepts in their literacy development. For example, children in the first 2 years of school were able to learn about functional description of verbal 'processes' and use this knowledge in learning how to punctuate direct speech (Williams, 1998) and to become more aware of using expression in oral reading of dialogue (French, 2012). Year six children were able to learn about process (verb) types and the 'participant' roles associated with them in SFG, such as Actor and Goal, and they were able use their grammatical knowledge as a resource in discussing how the language of the picture book *Piggybook* (Browne, 1986/1996) constructed certain patterns of meaning associated with particular characters.

Further studies of students for whom English is an additional language show how the children in the early years of schooling are able to distinguish between the grammatical construction of statements, commands, questions, and exclamations, known as sentence moods. They were also able to identity types of processes and participant roles, in contextualized learning experiences, pursuing the disciplinary goals of English language arts (Schleppegrell, 2013). A large-scale study investigating the teaching of grammar in the context of writing lessons to year eight students was based on a descriptive rather than a prescriptive approach to grammar (Carter, 1990), which, consistent with systemic functional grammar, centered on rhetorical understanding of how language works for different purposes and in different contexts (Jones et al., 2013). This study clearly showed the positive impact of teaching systemic functional grammar on the quality of student writing, and also indicated that the quality of the teachers' knowledge of grammar was significant in influencing student outcomes.

A consistent finding in the research since the turn of this century is that many teachers have very limited grammatical knowledge (Hammond and Macken-Horarik, 2001; Harper and Rennie, 2009; Hudson and Walmsley, 2005; Louden et al., 2005; Meyer, 2008) and an important thrust of ongoing research is concerned with determining the kind and extent of grammatical knowledge that teachers need to optimally address disciplinary goals in the teaching of English throughout schooling (Love et al., 2015; Macken-Horarik et al., 2011).

Curriculum-Area Literacies

As the well-established significance of reading to learn in curriculum areas (Herber, 1978; Marland, 1977; Morris and Stewart-Dore, 1984) was complemented by recognition of the concomitant importance of student writing, the notion of writing across the curriculum, or literacy across the curriculum, emerged (Behrens and Rosen, 2010; McLeod et al., 2001). The further recognition of the need to differentiate subject-specific literacies was advanced through systemic functional linguistic research establishing the distinctive discourses of school subject areas (for a detailed account, see Rose and Martin, 2012). This research trajectory has provided detailed explication of the discourses of school subject areas.

Within subject areas, particular structural forms of texts or genres that students are required to read and write were consistently identified, but these varied substantially across subject areas (Martin and Rose, 2008). Grammatical and cohesive resources were deployed in ways characteristic of the particular subject areas, constructing, for example, the technical discourse of science and the less technical but abstract discourse of history (Martin, 1993b; Unsworth, 1999). These detailed accounts of the disciplinary discourses into which students needed to be apprenticed in school subject areas facilitated the refinement of literacy pedagogies embedded in curriculum area teaching that was specifically oriented to progressing student learning in the curriculum areas (Klein and Unsworth, 2014; Unsworth, 1997).

As well as the explicit teaching of genres distinctive to, and common across, subject areas, there is explicit teaching of functional grammatical knowledge that enables students to understand how the structuring of the various genres is achieved through the strategic patterning of grammatical choices, as texts are constructed, and how grammatical resources are typically used within disciplines to construct and communicate specialized knowledge (Christie and Derewianka, 2010;

Quinn, 2004; Unsworth, 2001). This includes the development of critical literacies through explicit teaching of the systems of evaluative language resources (Martin and White, 2005) so that students understand how linguistic choices can color representations of experience through the expression of particular forms of affect, judgment of propriety or social esteem, and appreciation of the relative significance or appeal of natural or artificial phenomena (Coffin, 2003; Humphrey et al., 2012; Macken-Horarik, 1998).

Although earlier curriculum literacies largely focused on the language of curriculum area learning, subsequent work has addressed the multimodal nature of distinctive disciplinary discourses and, correspondingly, curriculum area literacy pedagogies are addressing the development of students' comprehension and creation of multimodal texts. This has focused on the role of images and image interaction in the core school subject areas of science (Lemke, 1998; Unsworth, 2004; Veel, 1998), history (Derewianka and Coffin, 2008; Oteíza, 2003) and mathematics (O'Halloran, 2000, 2003). Ongoing developments include the investigation of new literate practices afforded by digital media resources (Chan and Unsworth, 2011; Jewitt, 2006; Lemke, 2002), and the specification of subject-specific literacies in an expanded range of discipline areas (Barton, 2014).

DIRECTIONS FOR CONTEMPORARY LITERACY CURRICULUM

There are new challenges for education and the literacy curriculum that must be met to transcend the historical acculturation of the young as textual consumers, compliant workers, unthinking citizens, and technologized subjects. Students need to develop a language for thinking, a deep knowledge of language, and an ability to judge texts for quality, credibility, authority, and reliability. The literacy curriculum can lead students to become creative, imaginative, inventive, and discerning producers of knowledge within a world in which digital media and popular culture are reconfiguring the nature and role of curriculum and schooling.

There are new challenges for students as language users and thinkers in online textual environments, where research shows that online readers must draw upon a broadened range of prior knowledge, of the architecture of online informational text structures (for example, web genres), and of Internet application knowledge (for example, web browser features). They require facility to engage in the content-area or world knowledge using malleable bites of searching across multiple websites using what has been called 'schemas of the moment' (Dwyer, 2013). Online reading inquiries encompass new skills, such as generating and revising search strings, use of search engine algorithms, specialized domain and topic knowledge to generate effective key words, and strong vocabulary knowledge.

The online environment can be a challenging landscape for readers, who must make use of self-regulation and persistence to avoid the cognitive overload and disorientation experienced by an endless sea of hyperlinked reading pathways. They must engage in active decision-making processes, engaging in predication of partially obscured web content that is hidden behind navigational links. Online reading requires careful planning, monitoring, predicting, and questioning, and involves moving speedily and efficiently by skimming and summarizing valid findings. These digital contexts for literacy present new challenges for reading comprehension (Coiro, 2012), particularly for those with learning difficulties (Castek et al., 2011).

It is seldom noted that the changing digital environment in which literacy practices are now learned throughout the trajectory of formal schooling and the life course engage the senses and the body differently across modes and media. Literacy practices have always been embodied forms of communication, whether of writing, reading, speaking, dramatizing, viewing, listening, drawing, or engaging in literacy play. Literacy practices are embodied, collective, and acquired through both mind and moving bodies. This includes an important sensorial dimension that has previously been unobserved in most studies of children's digital media production (Mills, 2015). Such a perspective parallels a conceptual shift in the social sciences and humanities towards a sensory revolution that focuses on the body and the senses in social encounters (Howes, 1991).

The sensorial nature of literacy practices are modified, for example, when users engage in literacy practices across modes and media using books, computers, laptops, smart phones, tablets, or video games, particularly with the technical affordances of certain digital communication devices to respond to more than the click of mouse, such as touch, voice, breath, or gaze. As Heath argues (2013) in relation to hands: 'the heuristic power of the hand begins early in life and continues into more creative and controlled representations.... Cognition becomes grounded as young children engage in motor-dependent production...of what they are thinking, imagining and planning...'. The hand is a manipulator of the environment and this appendage cannot be separated from the moving body. The changing features of communication in recreational and other social sites have implications for the way in which the literacy curriculum shapes the bodily experiences of students into the future, and this is only beginning to be explored empirically, such as in relation to digital film production by students (Mills et al., 2013; Ranker and Mills, 2014).

There is a concomitant shift in the changed materiality of literacy practices and the curriculum (Haas, 1996; Marsh, 2010; Ormerod and Ivanic, 2002; Pahl, 2001). Within socio-material approaches to literacy, there are references to the materiality of writing as early as the late 1990s, such as Haas' (1996) volume, *Writing technology: studies on the materiality of writing*. Through original research, Haas demonstrated that the materiality of different computers and their software configurations is important to understanding how writers use technology to produce texts. As Haas (1996: 51) concludes: 'The computer is not an all-powerful monolith...'; rather, findings about how writers use computers for both reading and writing were 'strikingly dissimilar' for different computer systems and digital devices, and when used for different social purposes (1996: 51).

When we consider early literacy learning in homes, kindergartens, libraries, and schools, there are material cultures that play a vital role in this process, from tablets to toys (Nixon and Hately, 2013). In many capitalist societies today, digital media practices are cleverly connected to cultural and material objects for children and youth, creating a circulation of related artifacts, merchandise, and digital literacy practices, and yet socio-material research is currently only marginal in literacy studies. This is despite its well-developed presence across a number of disciplines, such as material culture studies, science and technology studies, social geography, environmental studies, and gender studies (Fenwick and Landri, 2012). Sørensen (2009: 2) has argued that in education more broadly there has been an apparent '...blindness toward the question of how educational practice is affected by materials'.

To conclude, the future of literacy curricula is uncertain in many ways, but what remains potentially unchanged are the general principles that operate within the recontextualizing of language knowledge into literacy curriculum in schools. One of these is that the literacy curriculum involves the classification and distribution of language knowledge. As Bernstein (2000) argues, only a very small number of students who have access to abstract principles will eventually graduate from schooling to 'produce the discourse', and 'will become aware that the mystery of discourse is not order, but disorder, incoherence, the possibility of the unthinkable' (2000: 11). The reproductive transmission of literacy knowledge and basic skills will not liberate students to become critical producers, but will unfortunately serve to '...remove the danger of the unthinkable', that leads to imagining 'alternative realities' (2000: 11).

REFERENCES

Andrews, R., Torgerson, C., Beverton, S., Freeman, A., Locke, T., Low, G., ... and Zhu, D. (2006) 'The effect of grammar teaching on writing development', *British Educational Research Journal,* 32(1): 39–55.

Anstey, M. and Bull, G. (2004) *The Literacy Labyrinth* (2nd edn.). Frenchs Forest, NSW: Pearson.

Baker, C. and Luke, A. (eds.) (1991) *Towards a critical sociology of reading pedagogy: Paper of the XII World Congress on Reading.* (Vol. 28). Amsterdam: John Benjamins.

Barton, D. (1994) *Literacy: An introduction to the ecology of written language.* Oxford, UK: Blackwell.

Barton, D. and Hamilton, M. (1998) *Local literacies: Reading and writing in one community.* London: Routledge.

Barton, G. (ed.) (2014) *Literacy in the arts: Retheorising learning and teaching.* New York, NY: Springer.

Behrens, L. and Rosen, L.J. (2010) *Writing and reading across the curriculum.* (11th ed.). New York, NY: Longman.

Bernstein, B. (2000) *Pedagogy, symbolic control and identity: Theory, research, and critique.* Oxford: Rowman & Littlefield.

Bernstein, B. (2003) *The structuring of pedagogic discourse: Class, codes and control* (Vol. IV). London: Routledge.

Braddock, R., Lloyd-Jones, R. and Schoer, L. (1963) *Research in written composition.* Urbana, IL: National Council of Teachers of English.

Browne, A. (1986/1996) *Piggybook.* London: Julia MacRae.

Cambourne, B. (1988) *The whole story: Natural learning and the acquisition of literacy in the classroom.* Sydney: Ashton Scholastic.

Carter, R. (1990) 'The new grammar teaching', in R. Carter (ed.), *Knowledge about language and the curriculum* (pp. 65–74). London: Hodder and Stoughton.

Castek, J., Zawilinski, L., McVerry, J.G., O'Byrne, W.I. and Leu, D.J. (2011) 'The new literacies of online reading comprehension: New opportunities and challenges for students with learning difficulties', in C. Wyatt-Smith, J. Elkins and S. Gunn (eds.), *Multiple perspectives on difficulties in learning literacy and numeracy* (pp. 91–110). London: Springer.

Chan, E. and Unsworth, L. (2011) 'Image-language interaction in online reading environments: Challenges for students' reading comprehension', *Australian Educational Researcher,* 38(2): 181–202.

Christie, F. and Derewianka, B. (2010) *School discourse: Learning to write across the years of schooling.* London: Bloomsbury Publishing.

Coffin, C. (2003) 'Reconstruals of the past – settlement or invasion? The role of JUDGMENT analysis', in J. R. Martin and R. Wodak (eds.), *Re/reading the past: Critical and functional perspectives on time and value.* Amsterdam: John Benjamins.

Coiro, J. (2012) 'Predicting reading comprehension on the Internet: Contributions of offline reading skills', *Journal of Literacy Research,* 43(4): 352–392.

Coles, M., and Hall, C. (2002) 'Gendered readings: Learning from children's reading choices', *Journal of Research in Reading,* 25(1): 96–108.

Cowey, W. (2005) 'ACTA background paper: A brief description of the National Accelerated Literacy Program', *TESOL in Context,* 15(2): 3–14.

Derewianka, B. and Coffin, C. (2008) 'Time visuals in history textbooks:Some pedagogic issues', in L. Unsworth (ed.), *Multimodal Semiotics: Functional Analysis in Contexts of Education* (pp. 187–200). London: Continuum.

Dwyer, B. (2013) 'Developing online reading comprehension: Changes, challenges, and consequences', in E. T. Hall, T. Cremin, B. Comber and L. Moll (eds.), *The International Handbook of Research on Children's Literacy, Learning and Culture* (pp. 344–358). Oxford: Wiley-Blackwell.

Dyson, A.H. (2003) '"Welcome to the Jam": Popular culture, school literacy, and the making of childhoods', *Harvard Educational Review,* 73(3): 328–361.

Emmitt, M. and Pollock, J. (1997) *Language and learning: An introduction for teaching.* (2nd ed.). Melbourne, Oxford University Press.

Fairclough, N. (1999) 'Global capitalism and a critical awareness of language', *Language Awareness,* 8(2): 71–83.

Fairfield, P. (2012) *Education after Dewey*. New York, NY: Bloomsbury Publishing.

Fenwick, T. and Landri, P. (2012) 'Materialities, textures and pedagogies: Socio-material assemblages in education', *Pedagogy, Culture and Society,* 21(1): 1–7.

Foucault, M. (1977) *Discipline and punish: The birth of the prison* [Trans. A. Sheridan]. London: Penguin Books.

Freire, P. (1970a) 'Cultural action and conscientization', *Harvard Educational Review,* 40(3): 452–477.

Freire, P. (1970b) *Pedagogy of the oppressed* [Trans. M. B. Ramos]. New York, NY: Continuum.

Freire, P. and Macedo, D. (1987) *Literacy: Reading the word and the world*. Hadley, MA: Bergin and Garvey.

French, R. (2012) 'Learning the grammatics of quoted speech: Benefits for punctuation and expressive reading', *Australian Journal of Language and Literacy,* 35(2): 206–222.

Gee, J. (1996) *Social linguistics and literacies: Ideology in discourses*. (2nd ed.). New York, NY: Routledge and Falmer Press.

Gee, J. (2003) *What video games have to teach us about learning and literacy*. New York, NY: Palgrave, Macmillan.

Goodman, K. (1976) 'Reading: A psycholinguistic guessing game', *Journal of Reading Specialist,* 4, 126–135.

Graves, D. (1983) *Writing: Teachers and children at work*. Portsmouth, NH: Heinemann.

Green, B. (1993) *The insistence of the letter: Literacy studies and curriculum theorising*. London: Falmer Press.

Haas, C. (1996) *Writing technology: Studies on the materiality of literacy*. Hillsdale, NJ: Lawrence Erlbaum Associates.

Halliday, M. (1985) *An introduction to functional grammar*. London: Edward Arnold.

Halliday, M. (1991) 'Linguistic perspectives on literacy: A systemic-functional approach', paper presented at the Inaugural Australian Systemics Network Conference, Literacy in Social Porcesses, Deakin University, Geelong, Australia, 18–21 January 1991.

Halliday, M.A.K. (1973) *Explorations in the functions of language*. London: Arnold.

Halliday, M.A.K. (1978) *Language as a social semiotic: The social interpretation of language and meaning*. London: Edward Arnold.

Halliday, M.A.K. and Matthiessen, C. (2004) *An introduction to functional grammar*. 3rd edn. London: Arnold.

Hammond, J. and Macken-Horarik, M. (2001) 'Teachers' voices, teachers' practices: Insider perspectives on literacy education', *Australian Journal of Language and Literacy,* 24(2): 112.

Harper, H. and Rennie, J. (2009) '"I had to go out and get myself a book on grammar": A study of pre-service teachers' knowledge about language', *Australian Journal of Language and Literacy,* 32(1): 22–37.

Hay, I. and Fielding-Barnsley, R. (2009) 'Competencies that underpin children's transition into early literacy', *Australian Journal of Language and Literacy,* 32(2): 148–62.

Heath, S. (1983) *Ways with words: Language, life and work in communities and classrooms*. Cambridge: Cambridge University Press.

Heath, S.B. (2013) 'The hand of play in literacy learning', in K. Hall, T. Cremin, B. Comber and L. Moll (eds.), *International handbook of research in children's literacy, learning and culture*. Chichester, UK: Wiley-Blackwell.

Herber, H.L. (1978) *Teaching reading in content areas*. Englewood Cliffs, NJ: Prentice-Hall.

Hillocks, G. (1986) *Research on written composition*. Urbana, IL: ERIC Clearing House on Reading and Communication Skills.

Hillocks, G. and Smith, M.W. (1991) 'Grammar and usage', in J.M. Flood, D. Jensen, D. Lapp and J.R. Squire (eds.), *Handbook of research on teaching the English language arts*. New York, NY: Macmillan. pp. 591–603.

Howes, D. (1991) *The varieties of sensory experience: A sourcebook in the anthropology of the senses*. Toronto, ON: University of Toronto Press.

Hudson, R. and Walmsley, J. (2005) 'The English patient: English grammar and teaching in the twentieth century', *Journal of Linguistics,* 41(3): 593–622.

Humphrey, S., Droga, L. and Feez, S. (2012) *Grammar and meaning*. Sydney: Primary English Teaching Association Australia.

Jewitt, C. (2006) *Technology, literacy and learning: A multimodal approach*. London and New York, NY: Routledge.

Johns, A.M. (2001) *Genre in the classroom: Multiple perspectives*. London: Routledge.

Jones, S., Myhill, D. and Bailey, T. (2013) 'Grammar for writing? An investigation of the effects of contextualised grammar teaching on students' writing', *Reading and Writing,* 26: 1241–1263. doi: 10.1007/s11145-012-9416-1

Kenway, J. and Bullen, E. (2001) *Consuming children: Education-entertainment-advertising.* Buckingham, UK: Open University Press.

Klein, P. and Unsworth, L. (2014) 'The logogenesis of writing to learn: A systemic functional perspective', *Linguistics and Education,* 26: 1–17.

Knobel, M. and Healy, A. (1998) 'Critical literacies: An introduction', in M. Knobel and A. Healy (ed.), *Critical literacies in the primary classroom.* Brookline, MA: Zephyr Press. pp. 1–12.

Kress, G. (2010) *Multimodality: A social semiotic approach to contemporary communications.* London: Routledge.

Kress, G., and van Leeuwen, T. (1996) *Reading images: The grammar of visual design.* London: Routledge.

Lankshear, C., and Knobel, M. (2003) *New literacies: Changing knowledge and classroom learning.* Philadelphia, PA: Open University Press.

Lemke, J. (1998) 'Multiplying meaning: Visual and verbal semiotics in scientific text', in J. R. Martin and R. Veel (eds.), *Reading science: Critical and functional perspectives on discourses of science.* London: Routledge. pp. 87–113.

Lemke, J. (2002) 'Travels in hypermodality', *Visual Communication,* 1(3): 299–325.

Louden, W., Rohl, M., Gore, J., Greaves, D., McIntosh, A., Wright, R., Siemon, D. and House, H. (2005) *Prepared to teach: An investigation into the preparation of teachers to teach literacy and numeracy.* Canberra: Australian Government.

Love, K., Pigdon, K., Baker, G. and Hamston, J. (2002) BUILT – Building understanding in literacy and teaching [CD ROM]. The University of Melbourne.

Love, K., Sandiford, C., Macken-Horarik, M. and Unsworth, L. (2015) 'From "bored witless" to "rhetorical nous": Teacher orientation to knowledge about language and strengthening student persuasive writing', *English in Australia,* 49(3): 43–56.

Luke, A. and Freebody, P. (1997) 'Shaping the social practices of reading', in S. Muspratt, A. Luke and P. Freebody (eds.), *Constructing critical literacies: Teaching and learning textual practice.* Sydney: Allen and Unwin. pp. 185–225.

Macken-Horarik, M. (1997) 'Relativism in the politics of discourse: Response to James Paul Gee', in S. Muspratt, A. Luke and P. Freebody (eds.), *Constructing critical literacies: Teaching and learning textual practice.* Sydney: Allen and Unwin. pp. 303–314.

Macken-Horarik, M. (1998) 'Exploring the requirements of critical literacy: A view from two classrooms', in F. Christie and R. Misson (eds.), *Literacy and Schooling.* London: Routledge. pp. 74–103.

Macken-Horarik, M. (2009) 'Navigational metalanguages for new territory in English: The potential of grammatics', *English Teaching: Practice and Critique,* 8(3): 55–69.

Macken-Horarik, M., Love, K. and Unsworth, L. (2011) 'A grammatics "good enough" for school English in the 21st century: Four challenges in realizing the potential', *Australian Journal of Language and Literacy,* 34(1): 9–23.

Marland, M. (1977) *Language across the curriculum.* London: Heinemann Educational Books.

Marsh, J. (2010) 'The ghosts of reading, past, present and future: The materiality of reading in homes and schools', in K. Hall, U. Goswami, C. Harrison, S. Ellis and J. Soler (eds.), *Interdisciplinary perspectives in learning to read: culture, cognition and pedagogy.* New York, NY: Routledge. pp. 19–31.

Martin, J.R. (1989) *Factual writing: Exploring and challenging social reality.* Oxford: Oxford University Press.

Martin, J.R. (1992) *English text: System and structure.* Amsterdam: Benjamins.

Martin, J.R (1993a) 'A contextual theory of language', in B. Cope and M. Kalantzis (eds.), *The powers of literacy: A genre approach to teaching writing.* London, UK: Falmer Press. pp. 116–136.

Martin, J.R. (1993b) 'Life as a noun: Arresting the universe in science and humanities', in M. A. K. Halliday and J. R. Martin (eds.), *Writing science: Literacy and discursive power.* London: Falmer Press. pp. 221–67.

Martin, J.R., and Rose, D. (2007) *Working with discourse: Meaning beyond the clause.* 2nd ed., Vol. 1. New York, NY: Continuum.

Martin, J.R. and Rose, D. (2008) *Genre relations: Mapping culture.* London: Equinox.

Martin, J.R. and Rothery, J. (1993) 'Grammar: Making meaning in writing', in B. Cope and M. Kalantzis (eds.), *The powers of literacy.* London: Falmer Press. pp. 137–53.

Martin, J.R. and White, P. (2005) *The language of evaluation: Appraisal in English.* New York, NY: Palgrave Macmillan.

McLeod, S.H., Miraglia, E., Soven, M. and Thaiss, C. (2001) *WAC for the new millennium: Strategies for continuing writing-across-the-curriculum programs.* Urbana, IL: National Council of Teachers of English.

Meyer, H. (2008) '"It's sort of… intuitive, isn't it?"', *English in Aotearoa,* 65: 59–76.

Mills, K.A. (2005) 'Deconstructing binary oppositions in literacy discourse and pedagogy', *Australian Journal of Language and Literacy,* 28(1): 67–82.

Mills, K.A. (2006) 'Mr. Travelling-at-will Ted Doyle: Discourses in a multiliteracies classroom', *Australian Journal of Language and Literacy,* 28(2): 132–49.

Mills, K.A. (2008) 'Transformed practice in a pedagogy of multiliteracies', *Pedagogies: An International Journal,* 3(2): 109–28.

Mills, K.A. (2009) 'Floating on a sea of talk: Reading comprehension through speaking and listening', *The Reading Teacher,* 63(4): 325–29.

Mills, K.A. (2010a) 'A review of the digital turn in the New Literacy Studies', *Review of Educational Research,* 80(2): 246–71.

Mills, K.A. (2010b) 'Shrek meets Vygotsky: Rethinking adolescents' multimodal literacy practices in schools', *Journal of Adolescent and Adult Literacy,* 54(1): 35–45.

Mills, K.A. (2011) *The multiliteracies classroom.* Bristol, UK: Multilingual Matters.

Mills, K.A. (2015, in press) *Literacy theories for the digital age: Social, critical, multimodal, spatial, material, and sensory lenses.* Bristol, UK: Multilingual Matters.

Mills, K.A. and Exley, B. (2014) 'Narrative and multimodality in English language arts curricula: A tale of two nations', *Language Arts,* 92(2): 136–43.

Mills, K.A., Comber, B. and Kelly, P. (2013) 'Sensing place: Embodiment, sensoriality, kinesis, and children behind the camera', *English Teaching: Practice and Critique,* 12(2): 11–27.

Moll, L.C., Soto-Santiago, S.L. and Schwartz, L. (2013) 'Funds of knowledge in changing communities', in K. Hall, T. Cremin, B. Comber and L. C. Moll (eds.), *International handbook of research on children's literacy, learning and culture.* Oxford, UK: Wiley-Blackwell. pp. 172–83.

Morris, A. and Stewart-Dore, N. (1984) *Learning to learn from text: Effective reading in the content areas.* Sydney: Addison-Wesley.

Morrow, L.M., Tracey, D.H., Gambrell, L.M. and Pressley, M. (eds.) (2007) *Best practices in early literacy development in preschool, kindergarten, and first grade.* 3rd edn. New York, NY: Guilford Press.

Muspratt, S., Luke, A. and Freebody, P. (1997) *Constructing critical literacies: Teaching and learning textual practice.* Melbourne: Allen & Unwin.

New London Group (2000) 'A pedagogy of multiliteracies: Designing social futures', in B. Cope and M. Kalantzis (eds.), *Multiliteracies: Literacy learning and the design of social futures.* South Yarra, Australia: Macmillan. pp. 9–38.

Nixon, H. (2003) 'New research literacies for contemporary research into literacy and new media', *Reading Research Quarterly,* 38(3): 407–13.

Nixon, H. and Hately, E. (2013) 'Books, toys, and tablets: Playing and learning in the age of digital media', in K. Hall, T. Cremin, B. Comber and L. Moss (eds.), *International handbook of research on children's literacy, learning and culture.* Malden, MA: John Wiley & Sons. pp. 28–41.

O'Halloran, K. (2000) 'Classroom discourse in mathematics: A multisemiotic analysis', *Linguistics and Education,* 10(3): 359–88.

O'Halloran, K. (2003) 'Implications of mathematics as a multisemiotic discourse', in M. Anderson, A. Saenz-Ludlow, S. Zellweger and V. Cifarelli (eds.), *Educational perspectives on mathematics as semiosis: From thinking to interpreting to knowing.* Brooklyn/Ottawa/Toronto: Legas Publishing. pp. 185–214.

Ormerod, F. and Ivanic, R. (2002) 'Materiality in children's meaning making practices', *Visual Communication,* 1(1): 65–91.

Oteíza, T. (2003) 'How contemporary history is presented in Chilean middle school textbooks', *Discourse and Society,* 14(5): 639–60.

Pahl, K. (2001) 'Texts as artefacts crossing sites: Map making at home and school', *Reading: Literacy and Language,* 35(3): 120–25.

Pahl, K. and Burnett, C. (2013) 'Literacies in homes and communities', in K. Hall, T. Cremin, B. Comber and L. Moll (eds.), *International handbook of research on children's literacy, learning and culture.* Chichester, UK: John Wiley & Sons. pp. 3–14.

Painter, C. and Martin, J.R. (2011) 'Intermodal complementarity: Modelling affordances across image and verbiage in children's picture books', in F. Yan (ed.), *Studies in functional linguistics and discourse analysis.* Beijing: Education Press of China. pp. 132–48.

Pearson, P. and Johnson, D. (1978) *Teaching reading comprehension.* New York, NY: Holt Rinehart Winston.

Quinn, M. (2004) 'Talking with Jess: Looking at how metalanguage assisted explanation writing in the Middle Years', *Australian Journal of Language and Literacy,* 27(3): 245–61.

Ranker, J. and Mills, K.A. (2014) 'New directions for digital video creation in the classroom: Spatiality, embodiment, and creativity', *Journal of Adolescent and Adult Literacy,* 57(6): 440–3.

Reinking, D. (1997) 'Me and my hypertext: A multiple digression analysis of technology and literacy', *The Reading Teacher,* 50(8): 626.

Robinson, G., Bartlett, C., Rivalland, J., Morrison, P. and Lea, T. (2009) 'Implementing the National Accelerated Literacy Program in Northern Territory', *Criterion,* 2, 1.50.

Rose, D. and Martin, J.R. (2012) *Learning to write, reading to learn: Genre, knowledge and pedagogy in the Sydney School.* London: Equinox.

Rosemberg, C.R., Stein, A. and Alam, F. (2013) 'At home and at school: Bridging literacy for children from poor rural or marginalisd urban communities', in K. Hall, T. Cremin, B. Comber and L. Moll (eds.), *International handbook of research on children's literacy, literature and learning.* Malden, MA: John Wiley & Sons. pp. 67–82.

Rothery, J. and Stenglin, M. (2000) 'Interpreting literature: the role of appraisal', in L. Unsworth (ed.), *Researching language in schools and communities: Functional linguistic perspectives.* London: Cassell. pp. 222–44.

Schleppegrell, M. (2013) 'The role of metalanguage in supporting academic language development', *Language Learning,* 63(1): 153–70.

Scribner, S. and Cole, M. (1981) *The psychology of literacy.* Cambridge, MA: Harvard University Press.

Sefton-Green, J. (2006) Youth, technology, and media culture', *Review of Research in Education,* 30(1): 279–306.

Selfe, C. (1999) *Technology and literacy in the twenty-first century: The importance of paying attention.* South Carbondale, IL: Southern Illinois University Press.

Shor, I. (1999) 'What is critical literacy?', *Journal of Pedagogy, Pluralism and Practice,* 4(1): 1–27.

Skerrett, A. (2014) 'Religious literacies in a secular literacy classroom', *Reading Research Quarterly,* 49(2): 233–50.

Sørensen, E. (2009) *The Materiality of Learning: Technology and Knowledge of Educational Practice.* Cambridge: Cambridge University Press.

Stierer, B., and Maybin, J. (1994) *Language, literacy and learning in educational practice.* Bristol, UK: Multilingual Matters.

Street, B. (1975) 'The Mullah, the Shahname and the Madrasseh', *Asian Affairs,* 6(3): 290–306.

Street, B. (1995) *Social literacies: Critical approaches to literacy in development, ethnography and education.* London: Longman.

Street, B. (1997) 'The implications of the 'New Literacy Studies' for literacy education', *English in Education,* 31(3): 45–59.

Street, B. (2003) 'What's "new" in the new literacy studies? Critical approaches to literacy in theory and practice', *Current Issues in Comparative Education,* 5(2): 77–91.

Turbill, J. (1983) *Now we want to write.* Rozelle, Australia: PETA.

Ulmer, G. (1985) *Applied grammatology: Post (e)-Pedagogy from Jacques Derrida to Joseph Beuys.* Baltimore, MD: Johns Hopkins University Press.

Ulmer, G. (1989) *Teletheory: Grammatology in the age of video.* New York, NY: Routledge.

Unsworth, L. (1988) 'Whole language or procedural display? The social context of popular whole language activities', *Australian Journal of Reading,* 11(2): 127–37.

Unsworth, L. (1997) 'Scaffolding reading of science explanations: Accessing the grammatical and visual forms of specialised knowledge', *Reading,* 31(3): 30–42.

Unsworth, L. (1999) 'Developing critical understanding of the specialised language of school science and history: A functional grammatical perspective', *Journal of Adolescent and Adult Literacy,* 42(7): 508–27.

Unsworth, L. (2001) *Teaching multiliteracies across the curriculum: Changing contexts of text and image in classroom practice.* Buckingham, UK: Open University Press.

Unsworth, L. (2004) 'Comparing school science explanations in books and computer-based formats: The role of images, image/text relations and hyperlinks', *International Journal of Instructional Media,* 31(3): 283–301.

Unsworth, L. (2014) 'Multimodal reading comprehension: Curriculum expectations and large-scale literacy testing practices', *Pedagogies: An International Journal,* 9(1): 26–44.

Veel, R. (1998) 'The greening of school science: Ecogenesis in secondary classrooms', in J. R. Martin and R. Veel (eds.), *Reading science: Functional and critical perspectives on the discourses of science.* London: Routledge. pp. 114–51.

Williams, G. (1998) 'Children entering literate worlds', in F. Christi and R. Misson (eds.), *Literacy in schooling.* London: Routledge. pp. 18–46.

Wolf, M.K., Crosson, A.C. and Resnick, L.B. (2005) 'Classroom talk for rigorous reading comprehension instruction', *University of Pittsburgh Reading Psychology,* 26: 27–53.

Wyse, D. and Goswami, U. (2008) 'Synthetic phonics and the teaching of reading', *British Educational Research Journal,* 34(6): 691–710.

Wyse, D. and Styles, M. (2007) 'Synthetic phonics and the teaching of reading: The debate surrounding England's "Rose Report"', *Literacy,* 47(1): 35–42.

Zacher Pandya, J. (2011) *Overtested: How high-stakes accountability fails English language learners.* New York, NY: Teachers College Press.

Zacher Pandya, J. and Ávila, J. (2014) *Moving critical literacies forward: A new look at praxis across contexts.* New York, NY: Routledge.

40

Numeracy In, Across and Beyond the School Curriculum

Kenneth Ruthven

INTRODUCTION

Numeracy is a loosely defined construct covering mathematically related skills relevant to everyday life, employment and citizenship. It has come to prominence internationally with the growth of concern about the capacity of established school curricula to develop such skills in students.

During the 1960s, the Organisation for Economic Co-operation and Development (OECD) played a key part in fostering an international movement for curriculum development, which was influential well beyond its member countries and embraced several aims (which were not always well aligned), including to bring school mathematics closer to contemporary academic mathematics; to improve the mathematical preparation of a growing scientific workforce; and to create a school mathematics 'for all' (Kilpatrick, 2012). The distinctive feature of what became known as 'new math' or 'modern mathematics' was its rewriting of the school mathematics curriculum in terms of fundamental unifying concepts from contemporary pure mathematics; however, by the mid-1970s, this direction for reform was widely seen as having lost touch with the mathematical needs of many students. Amidst calls for the curriculum to get 'back to basics', a period of retrenchment followed.

This ensuing period saw the growing influence of what were at first only sporadic international comparisons of student achievement. In 1995, however, the International Association for the Evaluation of Educational Achievement (IEA) introduced a quadrennial programme of international assessments. In 2000, the OECD launched its rival triennial programme. The specification for this new Programme for International Student Assessment (PISA) contrasted the IEA's emphasis on established curricular content with its own concern for broader forms of literacy:

> Although the domains of reading literacy, mathematical literacy and scientific literacy correspond to

school subjects, the OECD assessments will not primarily examine how well students have mastered the specific curriculum content. Rather, they aim at assessing the extent to which young people have acquired the wider knowledge and skills in these domains that they will need in adult life. (OECD, 1999: 9)

This shift reflected new thinking, critical both of 'new math' and 'back to basics', and drawing on parallels between numeracy and literacy.

Although originating in England, the construct of 'numeracy' has been more widely influential. In particular, from the late 1990s onwards governments, not just in England but also in Australia and New Zealand, launched high profile national initiatives concerned with numeracy in the primary/elementary phase in parallel to similar developments relating to literacy (Council of Australian Governments, 2008; Department for Education and Employment (DfEE), 1998; New Zealand Ministry of Education, 2006).

This chapter reviews the evolution of the construct of numeracy – and its analogues – within curricular thinking. It then examines how numeracy varies across social practices and shows how contextualisation lies at the heart of the challenge of developing functional numeracy through schooling. Against this background, the chapter considers issues of curricular policy and practice.

GENERATIONS OF 'NUMERACY'

Numeracy and Liberal Education

According to the Oxford English Dictionary (OED, 2014), the first recorded use of the words 'numerate' and 'numeracy' occurred in England in a report commonly referred to as the Crowther Report (Central Advisory Council for Education (CACE), 1959). Highlighting a weakness of the specialised academic curriculum at upper-secondary level, Crowther noted that:

little is done to make science specialists more 'literate'…and nothing to make arts specialists more 'numerate', if we may coin a word to represent the mirror image of literacy. (CACE, 1959: para 398)

Reflecting contemporary criticism of an educational divide between the 'two cultures' of humanities and science, which curricular specialisation forced on most students, Crowther examined how best to create 'complementary elements' intended to liberalise this otherwise specialist curriculum. The parallel with literacy underpinned Crowther's efforts to conjure this new idea of 'numeracy' into educational life:

Just as by 'literacy', in this context, we mean much more than its dictionary sense of the ability to read and write, so by 'numeracy' we mean more than mere ability to manipulate the rule of three. When we say that a scientist is 'illiterate', we mean that he is not well enough read to be able to communicate effectively with those who have had a literary education. When we say that a historian or a linguist is 'innumerate' we mean that he cannot even begin to understand what scientists and mathematicians are talking about. (CACE, 1959: para 401)

In this coinage, 'numeracy' denoted a capacity fitting to the educated layperson to comprehend a quantitative and scientific perspective on affairs:

It is perhaps possible to distinguish two different aspects of numeracy…On the one hand is an understanding of the scientific approach to the study of phenomena – observation, hypothesis, experiment, verification. On the other hand, there is the need in the modern world to think quantitatively, to realise how far our problems are problems of degree even when they appear as problems of kind. (CACE, 1959: para 401)

Numeracy and Basic Skills

Nevertheless, 4 years later, the Newsom Report (CACE, 1963) used the term in a way that emphasized mastery of basic arithmetic. Discussing the curriculum of pupils of average to lower ability, Newsom sketched a numeracy concerned with routine applications of basic techniques:

An increasing number of jobs require a reasonable grounding in elementary mathematics…But a lower standard of numeracy than of literacy will do as a bare minimum. For the least able it will be sufficient if they can apply the arithmetical rules, which average children have mastered by the end of the junior school, with confidence and understanding to the situations involved in running a home or earning a living in a simple routine job. (CACE, 1963: para 335)

A generation later, the Cockcroft Report on school mathematics teaching (Department of Education and Science (DES), 1982) challenged the reductive popular usage of 'numeracy' that grew from these roots as 'too restricted because it refers only to ability to perform basic arithmetic operations and not to ability to make use of them with confidence in practical everyday situations' (DES, 1982: para 37).

Numeracy and Functional Competency

Cockcroft sought to reframe numeracy as encompassing the application and interpretation of number, not simply its mechanical manipulation, and to acknowledge the interweaving of arithmetic with other areas of mathematics in functional application. Thus, the definition of numeracy put forward by Cockcroft emphasized the meaningful production and interpretation of quantitative information:

We would wish the word 'numerate' to imply the possession of two attributes. The first of these is an 'at-homeness' with numbers and an ability to make use of mathematical skills which enables an individual to cope with the practical mathematical demands of his everyday life. The second is an ability to have some appreciation and understanding of information which is presented in mathematical terms, for instance in graphs, charts or tables or by reference to percentage increase or decrease (DES, 1982: para 39)

Numeracy and Foundational Capability

However, recognising the wide range of occupations that pupils would enter,

Cockcroft argued that school mathematics should provide them with a 'mathematical foundation' that would subsequently 'enable competence in particular applications to develop within a reasonably short time once the necessary employment situation is encountered' (DES, 1982: para 84). A generation later, a government 'task force', which established a National Numeracy Strategy for primary schools, emphasized this notion of numeracy as a foundation for later mathematics:

Early work in mathematics must begin to lay the foundations for the skills and insights children will use in later life. A solid grounding in numeracy at primary school will also help children with mathematical skills needed in other subjects, and later, to develop the higher order mathematical skills that are indispensable for large areas of higher education and future employment. (Department for Education and Employment (DfEE), 1998: para 7)

Numeracy as Rhetorical Token

These waves of public deliberation on 'numeracy' saw the emergence of four lines of thinking. The first wave preceded (and exercised little influence on) the mathematics reform movement of the 1960s. It developed two contrasting notions: Crowther's 'liberal' educational notion, emphasizing numeracy as an understanding of mathematico–scientific activity appropriate to the educated layperson; and Newsom's 'computational' notion, focusing on numeracy as mastery of arithmetical methods and their application. These notions were predictably stratified, with liberal numeracy an aspiration for the more able pupil and computational numeracy a ceiling of ambition for the least able.

The succeeding wave, represented by the Cockcroft Report, arose in response to criticisms of 'modern mathematics' reforms and dissatisfaction with the ensuing retrenchment. It embraced a 'functional' notion concerned with numeracy as the contextualised use of school mathematics in everyday life and employment. Ultimately, however,

Cockcroft drew back from a strongly functional approach, arguing for a more 'foundational' one intended to prepare pupils to adapt to the range of situations that they might subsequently encounter in a very disparate range of everyday and employment circumstances. Stratification became more nuanced, with Cockcroft proposing:

> a 'foundation list' of mathematical topics which, while it should form part of the mathematics syllabus for all pupils, should in our view constitute by far the greater part of the syllabus of those pupils…in about the lowest 40 per cent of the range of attainment in mathematics. (DES, 1982: para 455)

In this wave, affective dimensions of numeracy also started to receive acknowledgment alongside cognitive:

> Most important of all is the need to have sufficient confidence to make effective use of whatever mathematical skill and understanding is possessed, whether this be little or much. (DES, 1982: para 34)

In the final wave, as attention turned to younger pupils, it was the foundational idea that was developed in the National Numeracy Strategy (DfEE, 1998). In this narrower version of the foundational notion, numeracy concerns understanding of number and measures, and mastery of the associated computational and representational techniques, which are treated as building blocks for more advanced mathematical expertise.

More broadly, as this sketch of its evolving usage demonstrates, 'numeracy' can be appropriated by differing sets of educational concerns and values. Its uptake has surely been encouraged by these protean possibilities. In popular usage, 'numeracy' often functions more as a persuasive device than as a scientific construct. Indeed, what 'numeracy' is presented 'not to be' appears to be as significant as what it is taken 'as being' when the term is used to create a rhetorical opposition, for example in contradistinction to the mechanical, algorithmic connotations of 'arithmetic', or conversely to the decontextualised, abstracted associations of 'mathematics'. Sometimes, the term simply provides a relabelling of one or both of these domains. People identify with the term, or take against it, or choose to eschew it, depending on where they stand in relation to such positionings. A corollary of this proliferation of contested meanings, therefore, is that alternative terms have started to appear.

ALTERNATIVES TO 'NUMERACY'

Although the Cockcroft Report was aimed at an English audience, its innovative analysis of numeracy reached an international audience, particularly across the Anglosphere. Although I have used the term 'functional' for a key notion of numeracy that differentiates Cockcroft from earlier reports, that word occurs only once in the report itself, in a reference to 'functional innumeracy' (DES, 1982: para 13); however, it also features in a contributory research brief on the mathematical needs of adult life (Advisory Council for Adult and Continuing Education (ACACE), 1982: 57; as reported by Evans, 2000: 12), which urged a 'functional approach'. This usage signals the influence of developments in the field of literacy where an initial notion of 'functional illiteracy' had been reframed more positively to establish a notion of 'functional literacy' (Kirsch and Guthrie, 1977), defined by UNESCO in the following terms since 1978:

> A person is functionally literate who can engage in all those activities in which literacy is required for effective functioning of his group and community and also for enabling him to continue to use reading, writing and calculation for his own and the community's development. (UNESCO, 2006: 154)

In effect, Cockcroft was moving towards a more functional notion of numeracy, analogous to the notion of functional literacy; indeed coterminous to a degree by virtue of the mention of 'calculation' in the definition above, although the scope of the 'numeracy' defined by Cockcroft is considerably broader.

Numeracy and Quantitative Literacy

Following the UNESCO precedent, some organisations have explicitly recognised a component of 'quantitative literacy'. Like numeracy, this has attracted a range of definitions. On the one hand, it has been tightly drawn to focus on the numeracy associated with printed forms and documents:

> The knowledge and skills required to apply arithmetic operations, either alone or sequentially, using numbers embedded in printed material (e.g., balancing a checkbook, completing an order form). (National Center for Education Statistics (NCES), 1993; quoted in Quantitative Literacy Design Team (QLDT), 2001: 7)

On the other hand, 'quantitative literacy' has been given more expansive definition similar to comprehensive functional numeracy:

> An aggregate of skills, knowledge, beliefs, dispositions, habits of mind, communication capabilities, and problem solving skills that people need in order to engage effectively in quantitative situations arising in life and work. (International Life Skills Survey (ILSS), 2000; quoted in QLDT, 2001: 7)

However, perhaps the most important point consistently being acknowledged here is the way in which what conventionally have been sharply distinguished as 'literacy' and 'numeracy' skills often become interwoven in meeting the functional demands of everyday life and employment. In particular, in framing quantitative information and interpreting it, particular forms of literacy may be as important as what has been traditionally emphasized under the head of numeracy.

Although the term 'numeracy' has gained some purchase in the US, it is 'quantitative literacy' that has received greater attention there in recent years. An influential report employs the two terms almost interchangeably in identifying a crucial contrast between the curricular framing of 'mathematics' on the one hand and the functional demands of 'numeracy' and 'quantitative literacy' on the other:

Whereas the mathematics curriculum has historically focused on school-based knowledge, quantitative literacy involves mathematics acting in the world. Typical numeracy challenges involve real data and uncertain procedures but require primarily elementary mathematics. In contrast, typical school mathematics problems involve simplified numbers and straightforward procedures but require sophisticated abstract concepts. The test of numeracy, as of any literacy, is whether a person naturally uses appropriate skills in many different contexts. (QLDT, 2001: 6)

This is an important observation because it highlights a tension between foundational and functional conceptions of numeracy, which leads the report to argue that numeracy cannot be adequately developed in school mathematics alone. The QLTD report suggests that school mathematics suffers from a disconnect from meaningful contexts that inhibits many students from employing numerical common sense, and instead that numeracy needs to be learned and used in the multiple contexts provided by other subjects.

Strands of Quantitative Literacy

The components of quantitative literacy identified by the QLDT (2001) have many resonances with the conceptions of numeracy reviewed earlier. First is a component of 'Confidence with Mathematics' that acknowledges an affective dimension above and beyond the remaining cognitive components. Resonances with the liberal educational conception of numeracy are strong in components of 'Cultural Appreciation', 'Interpreting Data' and 'Logical Thinking', which focus on understanding the cultural scope of quantitative reasoning and on developing its critical habits. 'Making Decisions' and 'Practical Skills' resonate with the notion of functional numeracy in everyday life and employment. The remaining components of quantitative literacy relate more closely to a foundational notion of numeracy: 'Prerequisite Knowledge' concerns core knowledge of generic mathematical tools; and 'Number Sense' and 'Symbol Sense' highlight specific foundational capabilities relating to the semiotic tool systems that are central to arithmetic and algebraic mathematics. Nevertheless, these foundational components are accompanied by a component of 'Mathematics in Context' emphasizing that quantitative literacy is not reducible to such core knowledge or generic capabilities alone, and depends on the capacity to make use of them in a contextually appropriate manner. Thus, this model of quantitative literacy incorporates a range of notions similar to those associated with numeracy over its evolution.

From Quantitative to Mathematical Literacy

For some, the use of 'quantitative' in association with 'literacy' implies too exclusive a focus on an important, but only partial, aspect of mathematical capability. Consequently, the term 'mathematical literacy' has acquired currency in recent years, not least because of its adoption by PISA. PISA's definition has evolved to this current state:

> Mathematical literacy is an individual's capacity to formulate, employ, and interpret mathematics in a variety of contexts. It includes reasoning mathematically and using mathematical concepts, procedures, facts and tools to describe, explain and predict phenomena. It assists individuals to recognise the role that mathematics plays in the world and to make the well-founded judgments and decisions needed by constructive, engaged and reflective citizens. (OECD, 2013: 25)

The mainspring of PISA's operationalisation of mathematical literacy is the idea of a mathematical modelling cycle through which an authentic problem in context is solved by being 'mathematised'. In idealised terms, such a cycle consists of the following three stages. In the opening 'formulating' stage, the problem solver tries to identify mathematics relevant to the problem situation, and to explore the assumptions necessary to make this mathematics applicable, and

so eventually to reformulate the contextual problem as a mathematical problem. In the ensuing 'employing' stage, this mathematical problem undergoes mathematical treatment to produce a mathematical solution. In the final 'interpreting' stage, this mathematical solution is interpreted in terms of the original problem situation, and its reasonableness in context evaluated. In the course of the modelling cycle, students make use both of specific 'mathematical concepts, knowledge and skills' and of 'fundamental mathematical capabilities', such as communicating, mathematising, representation, reasoning and argument, and devising strategies (OECD, 2013).

Functional Mathematics

All too predictably in this unfolding exercise in lexical combinatorics, the term 'functional mathematics' has appeared. In the US, it surfaced in association with a proposed high-school mathematics course emphasizing foundational and functional aspects:

> Functional mathematics stresses an in-depth understanding of fundamental topics that are most likely to be used by large numbers of people. By employing concrete tools in settings that are both complex and realistic, functional mathematics pushes students to draw on the full breadth of mathematics. (Forman and Steen, 1999: 11)

In the UK, the term 'functional mathematics' made a reappearance (long after its earlier use in the Cockcroft research on the mathematical needs of adult life) in an official report on the curriculum for young people aged 14–19, alongside 'functional literacy and communication' and 'functional ICT' (DfES, 2004). Following previous waves of reform that sought to develop 'basic', 'core' and 'key' skills of literacy, numeracy and ICT, this turn to 'functional' skills could be interpreted as no more than a convenient relabelling, as might the shift from 'numeracy' (by now associated in England with primary schooling) to 'mathematics'. However, the fuller characterisation of 'functional mathematics' suggests an aspiration to set a more ambitious definition and bring a stronger functional dimension to the mainstream mathematics curriculum (DfES, 2005).

NUMERACY ACROSS PRACTICES

The Cockcroft Report was informed by extensive research into the mathematical needs of employment. Although the approach taken by this research has subsequently been criticised on the grounds that 'attempting crude behavioural classifications based only on the mathematics of school curricula fails to evoke the authentic details of real work practices' (Noss et al., 2002: 18), it was, at its time, unusual and important in providing insights based on field studies conducted in the workplace. However, later research has employed methods of ethnographic observation and/or work simulation that have generated more nuanced findings.

Numeracy in the Workplace

One classic study (Scribner, 1986) examined workplace numeracy for different occupational groups in a milk-processing plant, including product assemblers and delivery drivers. We can think of these as examples of the type of 'routine job' that the Newsom Report envisaged lower-attaining pupils entering, and towards which the Cockcroft Report's 'foundation list' was particularly addressed.

The role of assemblers was to locate and retrieve products from the warehouse to make up orders requested by drivers. In the warehouse, products were stored in crates of standard capacity: such as one-quart containers in crates of 16 and one-pint containers in crates of 32. Orders could specify the number of containers required either directly (such as 10) or as an incomplete crate (such as 1–6), meaning 6 containers short of 1 full crate. Scribner reported that assemblers filled identical orders in different ways, depending on the contents of the partially filled crates available, for example by removing 4 containers from a crate containing 14, or by adding 2 to a crate containing 8. In particular, the assemblers consistently used whatever procedure required the fewest possible transfers from one case to another, and did so with speed and accuracy. By comparison, when the researchers asked members of other occupational groups in the plant to attempt this task, they responded literally to an order, for example by making up 1–6 by removing 6 containers from 1 full case. As these workers gained experience, however, they also developed least effort strategies without instruction.

One role of drivers was to record the number of containers of each product left with a customer and to determine the cost. Pricing problems were solved in a variety of ways, tailored to the values concerned, so as to minimise computational demand and make it possible to solve problems mentally with near perfect accuracy, rather than requiring written or calculator computation. Instead of multiplying number of containers by cost of container, one common strategy was to employ a dual unit system of crates and containers (with the cost of each unit a known fact) to create a simpler addition and/or subtraction computation (so that a purchase of 31 pints of chocolate milk at 0.42 per pint became 1 crate of chocolate milk at 13.44 minus 1 pint at 0.42). By comparison, when the researchers asked members of other occupational groups in the plant to attempt this task, they showed a strong tendency to use algorithmic procedures. Equally, when the researchers set the drivers a pencil and paper arithmetic test, they made many errors on formal decimal multiplication problems, which were analogous to the (number of containers by cost of container) problems that they solved at work.

Characteristics of Informal Numeracy

From this study, Scribner draws out some salient characteristics of this type of informal numeracy. First, she concludes that it goes beyond computational solution of a given problem but extends to formulation or reformulation of the problem, as displayed by both groups of workers in their (re)formulations so as to minimise physical or computational effort. Second, such numeracy is marked by flexibility so that what appear at one level to be examples of the same problem, are solved differently due to situational adaptation at a different level, as displayed for both tasks in the contrast between the flexibility of the 'expert' workers experienced in the task against the algorithmic procedures employed by 'novice' workers who normally carried out other tasks. Third, such numeracy often incorporates features of the task environment into the problem-solving process as in the case when these workers used the crate as a second unit (of varying size according to product in the number of containers that it held/represented) alongside the basic container. Fourth, such numeracy seeks not just accurate solutions but effort-saving ones, in physical terms as shown by the assemblers' minimisation of the need to move containers, or in mental terms as shown by the drivers' minimisation of the demands of calculating costs. Finally, such numeracy depends on the acquisition and use by workers of knowledge particular to the setting, such as the 1–6 type recording system, the capacity of crates for each product and the price of container and crate for each product.

This analysis helps to identify why there is often a gap between the numeracy developed in school and the numeracy called for in a particular occupational role. Typically, as the previous examples illustrate, workplace numeracy is shaped by and adapted to a specific occupational setting so as to optimise performance within that particular niche. Indeed, such numeracy may even appear to conflict with schooled numeracy in some respects, as in the distinctive meaning accorded to symbolic representation of the type 1–6 in order forms in the processing plant. By contrast, schooled numeracy

aspires to transcend any particular occupational setting or task, and so to assume a decontextualised and generic character. In this respect, of course, schooled numeracy offers beginner workers initial resources with which to engage in a wide range of occupations, particularly to the extent that it focuses on aspects that are invariant across contexts. Indeed, this provides the rationale for schooled numeracy to be more foundational than functional in character. At the same time, it shows how school also represents a particular type of setting – one that conditions the form taken by schooled numeracy, particularly when the principal locus of school attention to numeracy is within the mathematics curriculum that introduces important disciplinary shaping factors. The valorisation of formalised knowledge and standard methods that typify school mathematics can act against its acknowledging, and so preparing pupils for the great variation in, and often strong contextualisation of, numeracy practices outside the school. However, this gap is narrowed when schooled numeracy acknowledges the value of alternative methods, supported by flexible mathematical thinking, as for example the Cockcroft Report was at pains to do (DES, 1982: paras 265–66).

The Shift Towards Techno-Mathematical Literacy

A further important factor has been transforming workplace numeracy. Over the last 25 years, digital technologies have become increasing central to the task environment for many working practices. The effect has been to shift many occupational roles away from the execution of routine procedures towards interaction with digital systems, in particular towards interpretation of the information that such systems provide. Moreover this information is increasingly provided in graphic form, not just numeric. Studies suggest that rather than being a decontextualised process of inference from the graph alone, interpretation often involves the reader imbuing a graph with contextual significance derived from practical experience. For example, paediatric nurses asked to interpret a chart of a baby's blood pressure construct a narrative about what the baby might have been doing (for example, in relation to the baby's anxiety or activity) when the readings were taken that would explain the fluctuations in blood pressure data shown by the chart pressure (Noss et al., 1999). The researchers point out that explaining away variation that does not arise from a medical condition is precisely what is required in this context, enabling nurses to home in on any residual variation that might indicate a need for medical attention.

The mathematical practices found in workplaces mediated by digital technologies are sufficiently distinctive that the notion of 'techno-mathematical literacies' has been proposed (Bakker et al., 2006). This focuses not on computation but on a form of modelling that depends on understanding a combination of contextual and mathematical issues, grounded in work experience as well as mathematical expertise. This 'situated modelling' differs from mathematical modelling as conventionally understood. The conventional form involves 'translation' of a real-world situation into a mathematical model that, ignoring what (from a mathematical perspective) is 'noise' from the context, is employed to produce mathematical results, which are then translated back to the real world. By contrast, in 'situated modelling' it is this contextual information that provides much of the meaning of the model and guides much of the thinking, as the example of nurses interpreting a blood-pressure chart illustrates.

Again, this analysis helps to identify why there is often a gap between the numeracy developed in school and the numeracy called for in modern workplaces. Although schooling continues to place a strong emphasis on computation, it rarely gives any systematic attention to modelling. Of the lines of thinking about numeracy and its equivalents reviewed earlier, only the construct of 'quantitative literacy' makes an implicit distinction

between mathematical and situated modelling in the contrast it draws between school mathematics problems and typical numeracy challenges. Only the construct of 'mathematical literacy' places a form of modelling at its – albeit mathematical rather than situated – core. As a later section shows, the school curriculum has also been reluctant to engage with digital technologies as core mathematical tools.

Home and School Numeracies

Studies of children's numeracy experiences have found important differences between home and school, and conceptualised these in terms of differing numeracy practices (Baker et al., 2006). Pupils are more likely to experience difficulties with school numeracy when there are discontinuities between the cultural tools (such as forms of language, systems of measurement and methods of computation) privileged in school and those with which they are familiar from home, particularly if the school devalorises the latter (de Abreu and Cline, 2005). Attention has also focused on the decontextualised treatment of number often found in school mathematics, lacking the links to everyday uses and embedding in social purposes with which children are familiar (Baker et al., 2006). Conversely, when school numeracy does allude to everyday contexts, pupils (particularly those from families less attuned to the rules of the school game) often import realistic considerations, which go beyond those authorised, leading to 'incorrect' practical solutions to what were intended as 'dressed up' mathematical problems (Cooper and Dunne, 2000). Although such situations arise more commonly for pupils from social groups that are disadvantaged/marginalised, they are not confined to such groups. In particular, parents from all social groups find it difficult to support their children's learning when they encounter school numeracy practices very different from those into which they were inducted when themselves at school – differences that arise because of changes over time within one education system or because parents have attended school in another (de Abreu and Cline, 2005).

In order to address such discontinuities, it is often suggested that school numeracy practices should be aligned more closely with the out-of-school practices familiar to pupils, particularly in the early stages of learning. Indeed, recognising that institutionalised forms of school numeracy tend to crystallise the values and practices not just of earlier generations but also of particular social groups, proponents of a more equitable and inclusive approach have called for adaptation to acknowledge the 'funds of knowledge' in minority communities (Civil, 2007). The degree of cultural diversity that increasingly characterises developed societies can, however, make such an approach challenging because it depends on identifying out-of-school practices that are familiar across the social spectrum, or on making more rarefied out-of-school practices accessible to an audience across this spectrum. Although practices of these types represent a resource for school numeracy, the challenge remains of doing justice both to them and to the powerful disciplinary ideas with which an equitable schooling is necessarily concerned (Cobb et al., 2011). Perhaps most fundamental is the recognition that numeracy teaching, whatever its base, needs to acknowledge the kinds of discontinuity that diversity of numeracy practices entails. This calls for a pedagogy that gives priority to identifying where numeracy activities involve culturally marked assumptions that may be foreign to some students, and to taking appropriate action to make such activities accessible (Cobb et al., 2011).

Multiplicity and Functionality

The shift in language from 'numeracy' to 'numeracies' acknowledges the variation in systems of numeracy found in social practices outside the school and the proliferation of modalities of numerate representation. This shift has been encouraged by socio-cultural analyses that focus on how numeracy practices develop contextually situated constructs and procedures, shaped by structuring resources, such as computational tools and notational systems. Although this approach has generated powerful insights into numeracy in practice, it has been criticised on the grounds that it may lead to overestimation of the degree of diversity across, and discontinuity between, practices. Nunes (1992) argues that understanding cultural influences calls not only for analysis of differences across variant mathematisations of similar problems, but also for identification of underlying logical invariants that operate across them. Pursuing this line of thinking leads Noss et al. (2002) to differentiate between situations in which practitioners deal with essentially the same objects and relations as conventional mathematics (although perhaps employing methods and language that differ in some respects) on the one hand and, on the other, situations in which the objects and relationships distinguished by practitioners and the models they conceptualise for their activity differ more fundamentally from conventional mathematics.

In terms of schooling, the thrust of the various conceptions of numeracy and its analogues reviewed earlier is towards optimising the mathematics curriculum as a vehicle for developing a range of capabilities that provide a base for students to engage in 'conventional' situations – in particular, these capabilities go beyond the purely technical to those concerned with adaptation and learning. These latter capabilities will also assist students when they encounter mathematically 'unconventional' situations, but students will lack the necessary technical capability unless that has also been considered sufficiently important to find a place somewhere within the school curriculum. This raises the issue of how best to frame the idea of functional numeracy for educational purposes. For the purposes of inducting someone into a particular practice (as might be a concern of adult or workplace education), functionality clearly implies developing proficiency with the methods and language of that practice; however, for the purposes of preparing someone more broadly for adult life, further study and indeterminate employment (a major concern of school education), the situation is much less clear-cut. That person can expect to participate in multiple and evolving numeracy practices, calling for continuing learning on their part, and assisted by their bringing a foundation of flexible technical capability and capacity to adapt to new situations. Moreover, only a fraction of these practices are ones in which most other people also engage, although that fraction may be particularly valuable for inclusion in the school curriculum because it is important in its own right and exemplary for situated functional numeracy. It is for these reasons that, given the purposes of school education, attention to functional numeracies needs to run alongside development of a foundational numeracy.

NUMERACY AS A SYSTEMIC CONCERN

To what degree has the construct of numeracy permeated curricular thinking across educational systems? In the most recent Trends in International Mathematics and Science Study (TIMSS) Encyclopedia (Mullis et al., 2012), each participating educational system contributed a chapter describing its school mathematics and science curricula. Of the 63 system-specific chapters, 16 make reference to 'numeracy'. Two others make reference to 'mathematical literacy', one to 'functional mathematics' and none to 'quantitative literacy'. In addition, a curriculum questionnaire completed by the TIMSS research coordinator for each participating system included structured questions about emphases of the intended mathematics curriculum, two of which can be related to numeracy. The great majority of systems

reported placing 'strong emphasis' on 'mastering basic skills and procedures', and around half reported placing 'strong emphasis' on 'applying mathematics in real-life contexts' (Mullis et al., 2012).

The TIMSS questionnaire also sought information about system policies on the use of calculators in school mathematics. This can be taken as an index of curricular adaptation to the widespread use of digital tools in numeracy practices outside the school. Many returned questionnaires suggested limited or no use of calculators at primary/elementary level. At the middle/lower-secondary level, although only 4 per cent of systems indicated that calculator use was prohibited, only 9 per cent of systems reported that the development of calculator proficiency was itself a curricular goal. The typical response indicated a policy of qualified permission for calculator use. Often the emphasis was on the calculator more as a pedagogical aid than as a mathematical tool.

NUMERACY THROUGH THE MATHEMATICS CURRICULUM

Given that the mathematics curriculum continues to be seen as the principal vehicle for developing numeracy, what are some of the curricular approaches to mathematics that have engaged seriously with such development?

Realistic Mathematics Education

One approach that has grappled with the challenge of developing a numeracy that is both functional and foundational is Realistic Mathematics Education (RME) (van den Heuvel-Panhuizen, 2003). Developed in the Netherlands, its central aim is to enable students to develop a functional capability through learning to 'mathematise' – to frame in a mathematical way – situations that are realistic to them. In the longer term, this process is managed so as to be 'progressive', in the sense of reshaping students' untutored solutions towards increasingly powerful and efficient solutions and towards the use of conventional mathematical tools.

RME makes an important distinction between 'horizontal' mathematisation (essentially the modelling of realistic situations in mathematical terms) and 'vertical' mathematisation (essentially the organisation of mathematical knowledge and resources in more powerful and systematic terms). Although it might seem that these forms could have been better termed 'external' and 'internal' mathematisation, respectively, the horizontal/vertical distinction helps to convey how vertical mathematisation underpins development of a progressively more powerful repertoire of organising mathematical concepts. In order to lend themselves to both dimensions of mathematisation, the types of mathematical tools or models at the core of this approach must have two characteristics:

> On the one hand they have to be rooted in realistic, imaginable contexts and on the other hand they have to be sufficiently flexible to be applied also on a more advanced, or more general level. This implies that a model should support progression in vertical mathematizing without blocking the way back to the sources from which a strategy originates. (van den Heuvel-Panhuizen, 2003: 13–14)

The Calculator-Aware Number Curriculum

Following a proposal that basic numeracy should be redefined as 'the ability to use a four-function electronic calculator *sensibly*' (Girling, 1977: 4) so that '(w)ith mental methods…as the principal means for doing simple calculations…calculators…are the sensible tool for difficult calculations, the ideal complement to mental arithmetic' (Plunkett, 1979: 5), an English project set out to develop a Calculator-Aware Number (CAN) curriculum for the primary school (Shuard et al., 1991). The CAN approach emphasized informal methods of mental calculation, renounced

standard written methods of arithmetic, and gave pupils access to calculators in their place. In the practical and investigative tasks employed to develop understanding of number, use of a calculator:

> allows children to handle large numbers, beyond those that they could work with mentally or with pencil and paper. Children are able to use 'real life' numbers in 'real life' situations; there is no longer a need to simplify numbers and situations. Children explore and play not only with large numbers, but also with decimals and negative numbers, and in doing so they gradually understand the structure of numbers. (Shuard et al., 1991: 10)

However, the use of a calculator touches directly on prized skills of written calculation that have long been taken as fundamental components of schooled numeracy (Ruthven, 2014), even if these are mastered by only around half of students, consume a substantial proportion of the available curriculum time and are rarely used outside mathematics lessons (Treffers, 1987). In particular, when any use of a calculator is seen as an improper retreat from a personal numeracy 'independent' of technology, school mathematics takes on a moralistic aspect. In effect, numeracy continues to be conceived as the 'residual' capability of an individual when technology is withdrawn, rather than as the joint capacity of a human/machine system. Thus, although the CAN approach had some initial influence on the English national curriculum, the tone of public debate and government intervention became increasingly 'calculator-beware' (Ruthven, 2001). This reflects the reserve towards use of calculators that the TIMSS survey findings suggest is commonplace around the world.

Mathematical Literacy as a Subject

In 2006, a new subject of Mathematical Literacy (ML) was introduced to the South African upper-secondary curriculum as an alternative to conventional Mathematics. The official characterisation of the new subject reflects the broad thrust of the notions reviewed earlier:

> Mathematical Literacy is defined as a subject driven by life-related applications of mathematics that must develop learners' ability and confidence to think numerically and spatially in order to interpret and critically analyze everyday situations and to solve problems. (Graven and Buytenhuys, 2011: 493)

Nevertheless, the official guidance acknowledges the dual mission – and potential internal tension – that teachers face:

> (T)he challenge for you as the teacher is to use situations or contexts to reveal the underlying mathematics while simultaneously using the mathematics to make sense of the situations or contexts, and in so doing develop in your students the habits or attributes of a mathematically literate person (Department of Education [DoE], 2003: 9; quoted by Graven and Buytenhuys, 2011: 493)

The subject is compulsory for any student who, in the official discourse, 'does not perceive Mathematics to be necessary for the career path or study direction chosen' – it is generally students with weak mathematical competence and confidence who are steered towards taking it (Graven and Buytenhuys, 2011: 494).

Venkat (2010) reports a case study of an ML project on 'litter in our school', which asked pupils to consider 'where litter went, how it got there, and whether any recycling occurred', and how to find answers to these questions through collecting and analysing relevant data (Venkat, 2010: 58). Observations of the resulting lessons found activity across all five strands of the Kilpatrick, Swafford and Findell (2001) model of mathematical proficiency, including strategic competence, adaptive reasoning and productive disposition. However, Venkat draws attention to the reorientation of ML lessons towards organisation around the terrain of the situations being investigated rather than the mathematical terrain. This impression of a focus on situated numeracy is reinforced by the conclusions that Venkat draws about the 'localisation of the mathematical work done within the confines of the immediate problem' (Venkat, 2010: 66).

NUMERACY IN THE WIDER CURRICULUM

Although the subject of mathematics is generally perceived as the major site for developing numeracy within the school curriculum, other subjects have potential to make a distinctive contribution through giving students more strongly contextualised numeracy experiences. Within particular school subjects, attention to numeracy is mediated by shifting views on the place of mathematical methods within the wider discipline. For example, comparison of geography textbooks has shown that those that sought to transplant the 'quantitative revolution' in academic geography to the school curriculum were – even in their time – outliers, but that there has been a gentler long-term trend towards greater use of quantitative approaches (Zhang and Foskett, 2003).

Numeracy Across the Curriculum

The idea of 'numeracy across the curriculum' positions all teachers as teachers of numeracy, and seeks to coordinate the development of numeracy across the school:

> All…teachers, regardless of the subject being taught, are responsible for supporting, developing and extending learners' numeracy skills and for ensuring that what a child has learned in earlier years is built upon, practised and refreshed regularly throughout their time at school…All schools… need to have strategies in place to ensure that children and young people develop high levels of numeracy skills. Promoting numeracy across all areas of the curriculum will ensure that all teachers will develop a shared understanding of how children and young people progress in numeracy. (Learning and Teaching Scotland, 2011: 1)

When secondary schools have a policy for numeracy across the curriculum, it typically covers matters such as codifying a common approach to developing numeracy, mapping out areas of skill to be developed and progression through these, and sketching the contribution of each subject area. One widespread assumption is that consistency of approach should be maximised across subjects. However, given that functional numeracy calls for a capacity to adapt to inconsistency of approach between contexts, there is arguably a case for exploiting at least some of the differences between subject contexts to develop this capacity.

Although the research literature in this area is not large, the Australian contribution stands out. Auditing the South Australian middle-school curriculum, Goos, Geiger and Dole (2010) found that numeracy demands were highest in Design & Technology, Science, and the Arts; moderate in Society & Environment and Health & Physical Education; and lowest in English and Languages. 'Exploring, Analysing & Modelling Data' was the strand of mathematical knowledge most strongly represented, followed by 'Measurement', 'Number' and 'Spatial Sense & Geometric Reasoning', with 'Patterns & Algebraic Reasoning' least strongly featured. The audit identified the significance of differences between subjects, highlighting how students would encounter very different approaches, for example to read and create maps in Mathematics versus Society & Environment; or to construct graphs to show relationships between variables in Science versus Health & Physical Education. The report suggests that 'teachers need to be aware of such differences in techniques and terminologies associated with the use of these representational tools and to draw students' attention to important similarities between underlying concepts' (Goos et al., 2010: 216).

Another Australian study throws light on putting 'numeracy across the curriculum' into practice (Thornton and Hogan, 2003). In the Middle Years Numeracy Across the Curriculum Project, participating teachers worked in research circles on activities intended to stimulate reflection on, and development in, numeracy practice in their schools. The participants found that developing a whole school approach to numeracy across the curriculum was challenging because most teachers did not have numeracy

as a priority in their teaching and viewed it as involving low-level school mathematics skills needed for social goals. Nevertheless, many teachers were surprised at the extent of the mathematical demands revealed in the work they asked students to do. Thornton and Hogan also note that, even when teachers do engage with the numeracy agenda, they tend to do so in a school-centred way: 'Most teachers focus more on the possible mathematical demands of their curriculum rather than on the numeracy problems their students are actually having' (2003: 125).

Numeracy in the Science Curriculum

Traditionally, science is the mainstream school subject that has made particular use of mathematical ideas and techniques. On this basis, the science curriculum provides an important site for the development of numeracy, contextualising it in both the syntax of scientific activity and the substance of particular scientific domains. Often, official curricular guidelines contain outline statements such as:

> Many elements of numeracy are evident in the Science Curriculum, particularly in Science Inquiry Skills. These include practical measurement and the collection, representation and interpretation of data from investigations. Students are introduced to measurement, first using informal units then formal units. Later they consider issues of uncertainty and reliability in measurement. As students progress, they collect both qualitative and quantitative data, which is analysed and represented in graphical forms. Students learn data analysis skills, including identifying trends and patterns from numerical data and graphs. In later years, numeracy demands include the statistical analysis of data, including issues relating to accuracy, and linear mathematical relationships to calculate and predict values. (Australian Curriculum, Assessment and Reporting Authority, 2014: n.p.)

Nevertheless, in some countries, concern has been expressed about 'demathematisation' of the school science curriculum. Reviewing science test items at upper-primary and lower-secondary levels in England, Orton and Roper (2000: 129) reported that 'the mathematical demands of the questions were not high except in the area of data handling, and scientific principles were more important than mathematics'. It could be argued, of course, that the character of numeracy is such that one would expect to see relatively elementary mathematics in use and strong reference to the scientific context. Finding, in addition, little attention in the contemporary literature to mathematics in the science curriculum, Orton and Roper concluded that science curricula 'appear to be seeking to manage without mathematics, or at least to function on as little as possible' (2000: 146).

CONCLUSION

As the preceding sections indicate, there has been disappointingly little research attention to the development of numeracy through curricular areas other than mathematics. It may be that researchers on these subjects, or on the curriculum as a whole, are little different from teachers (as reported by Thornton and Hogan) in not viewing numeracy as a priority. Indeed, numeracy in other school subjects has been studied far less than numeracy in employment and everyday life. This indicates an important gap in the research literature.

From the extensive pedagogical research literature on developing numeracy within the mathematics curriculum, constraints of space have permitted this chapter to discuss briefly only three strategically chosen approaches. Equally, there is an extensive body of research on the development of specific mathematical concepts and strategies, lying outside the scope of this chapter, but providing a valuable resource for detailed curriculum design. These literatures have started to recognise the crucial role of context and culture.

The literature on conceptions of numeracy is well developed. Again, this chapter has had to be selective, focusing on conceptions that have been influential on policymakers and practitioners, and not just debated amongst academics and activists. One omission has been discussion within the world of critical mathematics education – of mathematical literacy for cultural identity, social change, environmental awareness and evaluating mathematics – but good coverage can be found elsewhere (Jablonka, 2003).

In summary, this chapter has distinguished liberal, computational, functional and foundational notions of schooled numeracy, showing that these can also be found in analogous constructs such as quantitative literacy, mathematical literacy and functional mathematics. Although analysis of authentic numeracy practices has highlighted their often strongly contextualised character, it has also identified underlying invariants. Such invariants provide the basis for developing foundational numeracy through a school mathematics curriculum that acknowledges functional adaptation. Various approaches along these lines have been developed, but there are some fundamental tensions surrounding the use of the mathematics curriculum as a vehicle for developing numeracy over issues such as the role of digital mathematical tools and the balance between computational, foundational and functional notions. Although other school subjects provide potential sites for developing correspondingly contextualised forms of functional numeracy, this has received little serious attention.

REFERENCES

Advisory Council for Adult and Continuing Education (ACACE) (1982) *Adults' Mathematical Ability and Performance*. Leicester: ACACE.

Australian Curriculum, Assessment and Reporting Authority (2014) *F-10 Curriculum / Science / General capabilities*. Available from http://www.australiancurriculum.edu.au/science/general-capabilities (Accessed 25 July 2015).

Baker, D., Street, B. and Tomlin, A. (2006) 'Navigating schooled numeracies:

explanations for low achievement in mathematics of UK children from low SES background', *Mathematical Thinking and Learning*, 8(3): 287–307.

Bakker, A., Hoyles, C., Kent, P. and Noss, R. (2006) 'Improving work processes by making the invisible visible', *Journal of Education and Work*, 19(4): 343–61.

Central Advisory Council for Education (1959) *15 to 18*. London: HMSO.

Central Advisory Council for Education (1963) *Half our Future*. London: HMSO.

Civil, M. (2007) 'Building on community knowledge: an avenue to equity in mathematics education', in N. Nasir and P. Cobb (eds.), *Improving Access to Mathematics: Diversity and Equity in the Classroom*. New York, NY: Teachers College Press. pp. 105–17.

Cobb, P., Hodge, L. and Gresalfi, M. (2011) 'Diversity and equity: introduction', in E. Yackel, K. Gravemeijer, and A. Sfard (eds.), *A Journey in Mathematics Education Research: Insights from the Work of Paul Cobb*. New York, NY: Springer. pp. 167–77.

Cooper, B. and Dunne, M. (2000) *Assessing Children's Mathematical Knowledge: Social Class, Sex and Problem Solving*. Buckingham, UK: Open University Press.

Council of Australian Governments (2008) *National Numeracy Review Report*. Available from https://www.coag.gov.au/sites/default/files/national_numeracy_review.pdf (Accessed 25 July 2015).

de Abreu, G. and Cline, T. (2005) 'Parents' representations of their children's mathematics learning in multi-ethnic primary schools', *British Educational Research Journal*, 31(6): 697–722.

Department of Education (DoE) (2003). *National Curriculum Statement, Grades 10-12 (General): Mathematical Literacy.* Pretoria, South Africa: DoE.

Department for Education and Employment (DfEE) (1998) *Numeracy Matters*. London: DfEE.

Department of Education and Science (DES) (1982) *Mathematics Counts*. London: HMSO.

Department for Education and Skills (DfES) (2004) *14–19 Curriculum and Qualifications Reform*. London: DfES.

Department for Education and Skills (DfES) (2005) *14–19 Education and Skills Implementation Plan*. London: DfES.

Evans, J. (2000). *Adults' Mathematical Thinking and Emotions: A Study of Numerate Practices*. London: RoutledgeFalmer.

Forman, S. and Steen, L. (1999) *Beyond Eighth Grade: Functional Mathematics for Life and Work*. Berkeley, CA: National Center for Research in Vocational Education.

Girling, M. (1977) 'Towards a definition of basic numeracy', *Mathematics Teaching,* 81: 4–5.

Goos, M., Geiger, V. and Dole, S. (2010) *Auditing the Numeracy Demands of the Middle Years Curriculum*. Available from http://eric.ed.gov/?id=ED520869 (Accessed 25 July 2015).

Graven, M. and Buytenhuys, E. (2011) 'Mathematical literacy in South Africa: increasing access and quality in learners' mathematical participation both in and beyond the classroom', in B. Atweh, M. Graven, W. Secada, and P. Valero (eds.), *Mapping Equity and Quality in Mathematics Education*. New York, NY: Springer. pp. 493–508.

International Life Skills Survey (ILSS) (2000). *Policy Research Initiative*. Statistics Canada.

Jablonka, E. (2003) 'Mathematical literacy', in A. J. Bishop, M.A. Clements, C. Keitel-Kreidt, J. Kilpatrick, and F.K.-S. Leung (eds.), *Second International Handbook of Mathematics Education*. Dordrecht, Netherlands: Kluwer. pp. 75–102.

Kilpatrick, J. (2012) 'The new math as an international phenomenon', *ZDM*, 44(4): 563–71.

Kilpatrick, J., Swafford, J. and Findell, B. (2001) *Adding It Up: Helping Children Learn Mathematics*. Washington, DC: National Academy Press.

Kirsch, I. and Guthrie, J. (1977) 'The concept and measurement of functional literacy', *Reading Research Quarterly*, 13(4): 485–507.

Learning and Teaching Scotland (2011) *Curriculum for Excellence Factfile – Numeracy across Learning*. Available from http://www.educationscotland.gov.uk/Images/FactfileNumeracyAcrossLearning_tcm4-660305.pdf (Accessed 25 July 2015).

Mullis, I., Martin, M., Minnich, C., Stanco, G., Arora, A., Centurino, V. and Castle, C. (2012) *TIMSS 2011 Encyclopedia: Education Policy and Curriculum in Mathematics and Science*. Amsterdam: International Association for the Evaluation of Educational Achievement.

National Center for Education Statistics [NCES] (1993). *Adult Literacy in America.Report of the National Adult Literacy Survey (NALS).* Washington, DC: U.S. Department of Education.

New Zealand Ministry of Education (2006) *Findings from the New Zealand Numeracy Development Projects.* Available from http://numeracydb.nzmaths.co.nz/Numeracy/References/Comp05/Numeracy Compendium05.pdf (Accessed 25 July 2015).

Noss, R., Hoyles, C. and Pozzi, S. (2002) 'Working knowledge: mathematics in use', in A. Bessot and J. Ridgway (eds.), *Education for Mathematics in the Workplace.* Dordrecht, Netherlands: Springer. pp. 17–35.

Noss, R., Pozzi, S. and Hoyles, C. (1999) 'Touching epistemologies: meanings of average and variation in nursing practice', *Educational Studies in Mathematics*, 40(1): 25–51.

Nunes, T. (1992) 'Ethnomathematics and everyday cognition', in D. A. Grouws (ed.), *Handbook of research on mathematics teaching and learning.* New York, NY: Macmillan. pp. 557–74.

Organisation for Economic Co-operation and Development (OECD) (1999) *Measuring New Knowledge and Skills: A Framework for Assessment.* Paris: OECD.

Organisation for Economic Co-operation and Development (OECD) (2013) *PISA 2012 Assessment and Analytical Framework.* Paris: OECD.

Orton, T. and Roper, T. (2000) 'Science and mathematics: a relationship in need of counselling?', *Studies in Science Education,* 35: 123–54.

Oxford English Dictionary (OED) (2014) Online entries for *numeracy* and *numerate.* Available from http://www.oed.com/ (Accessed 25 July 2015).

Plunkett, S. (1979) 'Decomposition and all that rot', *Mathematics in School,* 8(3): 2–5.

Quantitative Literacy Design Team (QLDT) (2001) 'The case for quantitative literacy', in L. Steen (ed.), *Mathematics and Democracy: The case for Quantitative Literacy.* Princeton, NJ: National Council of Educational and the

Disciplines/Woodrow Wilson National Fellowship Foundation. pp. 1–22.

Ruthven, K. (2001) 'Towards a new numeracy: the English experience of a "calculator-aware" number curriculum', in J. Anghileri (ed.), *Principles and Practice in Arithmetic Teaching.* Buckingham, UK: Open University Press. pp. 165–88.

Ruthven, K. (2014) 'System error? Debating digital technologies in mathematics education', in D. Leslie and H. Mendick (eds.), *Debates in Mathematics Education.* London: Routledge. pp. 83–95.

Scribner, S. (1986) 'Thinking in action: some characteristics of practical thought', in R. Sternberg and R. Wagner (eds.), *Practical Intelligence: Nature and Origins of Competence in the Everyday World.* Cambridge: Cambridge University Press. pp. 13–30.

Shuard, H., Walsh, A., Goodwin, J. and Worcester, V. (1991) *Calculators, Children and Mathematics.* London: Simon & Schuster.

Thornton, S. and Hogan, J. (2003) *Numeracy across the Curriculum: Demands and Opportunities.* Available from http://www.acsa.edu.au/pages/images/thornton_-_numeracy_across_the_curriculum.pdf (Accessed 25 July 2015).

Treffers, A. (1987) 'Integrated column arithmetic according to progressive schematisation', *Educational Studies in Mathematics*, 18(2): 125–45.

UNESCO (2006) *Education for All Global Monitoring Report: Literacy for Life.* Paris: UNESCO.

van den Heuvel-Panhuizen, M. (2003) 'The didactical use of models in realistic mathematics education: an example from a longitudinal trajectory on percentage', *Educational Studies in Mathematics*, 54(1): 9–35.

Venkat, H. (2010) 'Exploring the nature and coherence of mathematical work in South African Mathematical Literacy classrooms', *Research in Mathematics Education*, 12(1): 53–68.

Zhang, H. and Foskett, N. (2003) 'Changes in the subject matter of geography textbooks: 1907–1993', *International Research in Geographical and Environmental Education*, 12(4): 312–29.

41

Science, Technology, Engineering and Math (STEM) Curricula in the US and Other Contexts

Susan Gomez-Zwiep

The alliance of science, mathematics, engineering and technology (STEM) domains is not a new concept in education; however, the combination of these STEM disciplines into one unique field was not formalized until the early 1990s when the National Science Foundation (NSF) began using an acronym for the science, mathematics, engineering and technology disciplines. Initially referred to as SMET, the term STEM was first branded in 2001 by Judith A. Ramaley, the former director of NSF's education and human resources division (Sanders, 2009). Other countries have also begun to group these fields in a similar fashion (for example, SET in South Africa). A primary reason for the recent rise of the status of STEM is increased funding opportunities for STEM education. In 2013, the US federal budget included US$3.7 billion for STEM education programs (Johnson, 2011). This included Race to the Top Funds, which required a state commitment to create a variety of STEM-specific programs, including statewide

STEM networks and STEM-specific teacher professional development programs for edibility. The UK has seen similar increases in STEM-related funding in the last decade. For example, £600 million was made available for science and innovation in 2010 with an overall investment in science and research promised from the Department for Business, Innovation & Skills (DBIS) of £5.8bn in cash for the year 2015/16 (DBIS, 2014).

Advances in the STEM fields have brought the US, along with other countries like the UK and China, great prestige and economic health in previous decades. In the US, there has been growing concern that this level of productivity will not be sustainable given some clear and disturbing trends concerning the inability to foster home-grown STEM talent. In 2007 and 2011, US students performed near the middle if not lower on international science and mathematics comparisons (Trends in International Mathematics and Science Study, TIMSS). This concern is further compounded by the consistent high performance of Asian countries, such as Singapore, Korea and China. Similar performances were reported from the Programme for International Student Assessment (PISA) in 2000 and 2006 (President's Council of Advisors on Science and Technology (PCAST), 2010). Whether due to a lack of preparation or interest, US students are not pursing STEM degrees at the same rate as their foreign peers. One-third of bachelor's degrees earned in the US are in STEM fields, compared with over 50 and 60 percent in China and Japan. Much of the current focus on STEM is predicated upon the idea that if STEM educators improve how we teach STEM, we will have more young people pursuing STEM degrees, which means continued prestige for the US in STEM fields. How we improve, and whether such improvement will get those results, remains to be seen. Despite highly ranked programs in STEM fields, US students are not pursuing STEM degree programs at the university level in the US. More than half of all STEM-related doctoral degrees granted in the US were awarded to foreign students (National Science Foundation (NSF), 2009).

The other driver behind the recent prominence of STEM is the development of national standards that emphasize the integration of these disciplines. This includes the Science and Innovation Investment Framework in the UK set up in 2004 and similar frameworks in the US (Common Core State Standards Initiatives (CCSS-ELA), 2010; Next Generation Science Standards (NGSS) Lead States, 2013). The focus on strengthening math and science education dates back to the early 1980s through multiple educational reports in both the US and the UK (Gardner et al., 1983; Her Majesty's Treasury, 2007). Several educational reports have stressed the need for science and mathematics education reform, the most notable being *Rising Above the Gathering Storm* (Rising Above the Gathering Storm Committee, 2010) and the National Research Council's (NRC) *Successful K-12 STEM Education* report (NRC, 2011). In addition

to noting the need for increasing the number of students who pursue advanced STEM degrees and careers, these documents advocate for educational systems that produce a STEM-literate citizenry.

Despite the clear economic benefits of 'STEM' and growing investment in increasing the capacity to do STEM, there is a misalignment between the way STEM is viewed in schools and the reality of industry. Furthermore, there is no clear theoretical framework to support the educational innovations to improve STEM education and align school and workplace goals. Although frameworks are beginning to emerge, no single framework has been widely accepted or used. In fact, there is currently no clear definition of what STEM education encompasses. To understand STEM as an integrated arrangement of once-independent disciplines, we must first consider the historical development of their related educational approaches.

THE DEVELOPMENT OF STEM EDUCATION

Although the term 'STEM' did not arise until recently, the history of the related disciplines has some common themes that can contribute to our understanding of the current STEM movement. There have been previous national movements towards improving student STEM success, with the post-Sputnik race to put a man on the Moon probably the most widely known example. The 1950s saw a rising debate over the structure of science and mathematics courses in US high schools, with the crux of the argument forming around whether curriculum should focus on a general and integrated view of content versus one that is specific and specialized. Courses first began to focus on scientific and mathematical ways of thinking during this time with the support of practicing mathematicians and scientists in course development (DeBoer, 1991).

The educational reforms of the late 1960s and early 1970s continued to define the structure of courses, with an increased focus on in-depth coverage of fewer science concepts and an emphasis on higher cognitive skills. One lasting impact of these programs was the shifting role of the teacher from a direct transmitter of information to that of a facilitator of learning. Inquiry lesson designs emerged, such as the learning cycle (Karplus and Atkin, 1962) that promoted student-centered learning experiences where students are allowed to construct new knowledge through the exploration of materials and ideas. Students' new ideas were refined through social interactions with peers and teachers. This pedagogical model emphasized collaboration on common explanations and students engaged in productive arguments, but required that the teacher is seen as a facilitator of information rather than the source of information and students see the group discussions as valuable in meaning making. It is in these programs that early attempts to integrate science and mathematics emerged, such as the Unified Science and Mathematics For Elementary School (USMES) program (DeBoer, 1991).

The 1990s STEM reforms focused on the elementary level for the first time. Reforms also occurred at the state or local level, rather than through national projects, leading to a higher level of implementation at the local level (Bybee, 1995). The most important innovation was the development of national standards and benchmarks that integrated elements of math, science and technology into a coherent plan for the development of a scientifically literate society. *Science for All Americans* (American Association for the Advancement of Science (AAAS), 1989) made clear recommendations that all citizens should understand how science, math and technology are related to and depend upon each other and to society. The rigid disciplinary categories of traditional subjects such as Physics, Biology, and Chemistry were relaxed, and new themes emerged that emphasized the connections across STEM disciplines (models, systems, change) as well

as issues around ethics and the natures of the disciplines (Confrey, 1990).

Recent STEM reforms (2000–2015) have formally linked S, T, E, and M in an effort to develop students who are capable of solving complex problems in order to increase global competitiveness and economic prosperity. Related to these goals is the priority of increasing the number of students who pursue STEM degrees and careers, which is not a new goal; however, the current STEM reform focuses on the inclusion of more women and currently under-represented minorities in the STEM workforce. This inclusion is necessary for reasons beyond basic equity. Possible talent pools are being neglected from large subsets of our population. What has remained is the goal that STEM knowledge and skills are not just for the best and the brightest – those perceived to have the best chance of advancing the field – but for every student. STEM literacy is a goal for all students so that they may posses an understanding of concepts and habits of mind essential for citizens living in a highly technical world (NRC, 2012). What is unique about the STEM reform movement of the last decade is the coordinated effort across national standards towards these goals. In the US, the current state-led movement for shared standards stresses the importance of preparing all students for an increasingly complex life and work environment (Partnership for 21st Century Skills (P21), 2014). Creativity and innovation, critical thinking, problem solving, communication and collaboration are identifiers of students who are both college and career ready. The *Standards for Technological Literacy* (International Technology Engineering Educators Association (ITEEA), 2007) integrate the technology-related standards from the *National Science Education Standards* (NRC, 1996) into learning opportunities that allow students to combine conceptual ideas learned in technology and science classes whilst utilizing common practices such as mathematical modeling and problem solving.

Developed concurrently, the English Language Arts and Mathematics Common

Core State Standards (CCSS) were developed in the US to support and connect each discipline, moving beyond the traditional skills necessary to be a successful student but toward a comprehensive view of the skills and abilities for successful civic participation (Stage et al., 2013). The development of the Next Generation Science Standards (NGSS Lead States, 2013) followed. The NGSS purposefully incorporates Engineering practices into its design, calling for the explicit connection between science and engineering be taught at K-12. Taken together, the NGSS and CCSS emphasize the higher order thinking skills and real-world application of ideas central to STEM endeavors. Similar curriculum reforms have occurred globally in the last decade, and yet challenges remain. Argentina developed national standards around inquiry pedagogies that emphasized science literacy as a main goal for all students; however, gaps in performance for low socioeconomic status (SES) students remain (Cofré et al., 2015). Turkey released national standards integrating science and math with technology around problem solving (Topçu, Arikan, & Erbilgin, 2014), again with a goal of creating equitable access to education; however, Turkey continues to struggle with achievement gaps based on socioeconomic background (Topçu, Arikan, & Erbilgin, 2014). Many African governments have invested a great deal of their resources to STEM reforms, and yet gaps remain between the demand and supply of qualified teachers as well as necessary resources and equipment (Ogunniyi and Rollnick, 2015).

Countries that consistently perform at the highest levels on international assessments have also reformed their national standards, but these have occurred within a larger systemic reform effort. Finland, Singapore, and South Korea consistently top the performance list on TIMSS and PISA assessments. Despite their geographic and cultural difference, similarities in their reform efforts are clear. All have standards that focus on higher-ordered thinking, inquiry, and problem solving. They also have eliminated exam systems that track

students and limit their access to quality secondary STEM education. These countries use assessments that require deep content knowledge and higher-ordered thinking skills rather than rote knowledge and facts. Schools are fully and equitably funded, with incentives for teaching in high-needs areas eliminating teacher shortages in the most needy schools. Teachers are also highly valued and supported with significant investments made to teacher-education programs, high teacher salaries and ongoing teacher learning opportunities (Darling-Hammond, 2014).

DEFINING STEM

Although a widely used term today, there is little consensus on a specific definition for STEM, even by those working in STEM fields (Breiner, Harkness, Johnson, & Koehler, 2012). In fact, the various stakeholders engaged in STEM education (parents, teachers, government funders, and businesses) may hold slightly different meanings of the term, even within similar contexts. Before understanding how science, technology, engineering and mathematics are connected, the character of each discipline must be considered. Each STEM component has its own unique identity based on different epistemological assumptions. Science seeks to describe and predict the natural world through the collection of empirical evidence (McComas and Olson, 2002). Mathematics is the science of patterns and relationships (AAAS, 1993); however, what constitutes evidence for patterns and relationships differs because science is empirically based whilst mathematics is not. Technology applies scientific and mathematical ideas to new design innovation. Technology provides tools to modify the natural world to meet human wants and needs (ITEEA, 2007). Technology also seeks to develop new knowledge through a design approach where the relevance of knowledge is defined by the nature of the problem (Williams, 2011). Engineering emphasizes the use of mathematics and science knowledge and skills to develop ways to economically utilize the materials and forces of nature for the benefit of mankind (ABET, 2004). What knowledge is relevant in engineering is defined by the context of the problem (chemical, computer, biomedical) rather than the nature of the problem. Similar problems can require very different knowledge if the contexts in which they are placed are dissimilar (Williams, 2011). Although related, science, math, technology, and engineering are unique endeavors guided by different theories of knowledge; however, together, science and mathematics uncover the natural mechanisms of our world, and engineering and technology use that knowledge to influence and design a new world.

The term STEM has often been used to refer to Science and Math only, with Technology and Engineering being left behind or, at best, as after-thoughts (Lederman and Lederman, 2013). Although most schools claim to include technology education, 'there are very few other things that influence our everyday existence more and about which citizens know less' (Bybee, 2010, p. 30). Engineering education has gained some prominence in schools but not on any scale that matches its importance to job markets or societal impacts. Full STEM learning will require more emphasis and understanding about technology and engineering in today's school.

An integrated approach assumes that there is some inherent commonality across these disciplines and that there is some benefit to their integration that is absent from the individual components. There have been several rationales suggested for the connection of the STEM disciplines based on their inherent similarities (ITEEA, 2007; National Council of Teachers of Mathematics (NCTM), 2000; NRC, 2012). The STEM disciplines share a common way of logical thinking around shared habits of mind that are based in creativity and collaboration. There are shared processes and problem-solving skills and critical thinking. All the disciplines use an iterative cycle of inquiry to develop new

ideas and, rather than being directed through rigid steps, are guided by logical and reasoned argument to develop valid and useful ideas. Together these four disciplines have the capability to describe complex issues and interactions. Understanding STEM allows us to make accurate predictions about the current and future impacts of shaping our world through man-made tools and processes (Peters-Burton, 2014). The most recent and widely held conception of the term centers on the integration of the component disciplines.

CHALLENGES INVOLVED IN STEM INTEGRATION

Understanding STEM subjects and their integration requires understanding the distinct nature of each field. These distinctions have implications for pedagogy and curricular development. STEM subjects tend to be cumulative and sequential in nature. Concepts and skills learned in the early years have direct connections to concepts and skills learned later. Teachers need to understand how skills and concepts in their course relate to ideas in the sequence of courses students will take. It is therefore not enough to know the content of their single course or year; STEM teachers need to have knowledge beyond their single grade or course. STEM knowledge is highly technical and specialized; however, students often fail to see connections between STEM topics and their everyday life. Furthermore, students come to the classroom with their own preconceptions that need to be addressed through instruction. Finally, STEM knowledge and technology is rapidly changing and teachers need to remain updated on new developments in their field.

One pedagogical approach is to create STEM experiences that take advantage of the specialized knowledge among science, math, and technology and yet situate the learning in a meaningful context where each area of expertise is utilized. This approach makes use of the inherent links within a particular context, whilst allowing the integrity of each subject area to remain in tact. This context-based science education (Fensham, 2009) requires that teachers collaborate to identify the essential intersection points of the disciplines within each context and scope. As a society, some of our most concerning issues are STEM-related (global climate change, ethics related to biomedical research). If we are to develop citizens adept at addressing such issues, topics related to personal, social, and global problems are advantageous in instructional contexts and have inherent STEM connections. Health, energy, and environmental quality can provide the necessary context for student learning at multiple scales (Organisation for Economic Co-operation and Development (OECD), 2006). For example, health issues have a personal (personal maintenance of health and nutrition), social (community health, social transmission of disease), and global (epidemics, global spread of diseases) context. An indication of the effect of contextual connections to STEM understanding and interests can be found in PISA data from 2006. Real world contexts were used for the 2006 PISA assessment in which students were asked to respond to numerous cognitive and affective items related to scientific and technological issues and were found to be more gender equitable than previous formats (Fensham, 2009). Bybee (2010) suggests that this context-based approach can easily be expanded to a context-based STEM approach through model instructional units that involve an engaging STEM-related problem or issue, similar to those used to frame previous PISA assessments. As students explore the problem they can engage with STEM content and practices to understand the issue and design a solution.

INTEGRATED STEM FRAMEWORKS

Although the integrated approach to STEM education has clear benefits, it requires a broad theoretical framework to identify and align the many complex elements that surround the K-12-educational STEM. Nadelson et al. (2014) identify a continuum from which to approach integrated STEM education. On one end of the continuum is anything that addresses science, technology, engineering, or mathematics. This is the more typical K-12 setting where these topics are taught in isolation and content goals drive instruction. On the other end of the continuum is fully integrated STEM learning where content learning occurs around a central problem or project. On this end of the continuum, the context or problem drives instruction. Moving from teacher-directed, highly structured, and lower order thinking to open-ended and higher order thinking, each place on the continuum has value and educators need to be flexible and purposeful in their use. Nadelson et al. (2014), however, argue for a framework based on context and content alignment. For example, if the students have high level of content knowledge, they should be provided opportunities to apply their knowledge in complex contexts such as inventing or critiquing. If the students are being introduced to concepts for the first time, they should be engaged in activities that are less complex such as modeling or classifying. The depth of STEM knowledge that students bring to the learning experiences should be aligned with the complexity of the context to create a 'zone of optimal learning'.

The National Academies (Honey et al., 2014) provides another framework for a systemic integrated approach to STEM education that includes four essential features of integrated STEM education: goals, outcomes, nature and scope of integration and implementation (Figure 41.1).

These four features frame a complex and multi-layered endeavor. First, the framework encourages the identification of clear goals. Closely related to goals is the identification of realistic and appropriate outcomes, such as the development of a STEM identity in students and educators with increased STEM content and pedagogical content knowledge. The third component of the framework involves

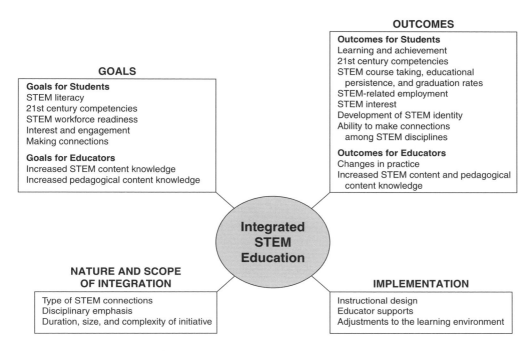

Figure 41.1   A framework for integrated STEM learning

Source: Honey et al. (2014).

the nature and scope of the integration, such as how concepts and practices are connected. The nature of the instructional design being implemented is the final component and is a critical factor because instructional approaches vary from teacher-directed and structured to more student-centered and open inquiry. Implementing an integrated STEM framework requires adjustments to the learning environment that can include time allocation, space use or even teacher collaborative lesson planning/teaching. This framework provides an organizing scheme for a variety of settings and interests engaged in integrated STEM education (Honey et al., 2014).

RESEARCH ON THE EFFECT OF STEM INSTRUCTION

The merging of STEM fields, regardless of the complexity of the integration, benefits

from an understanding of what teaching strategies have been found to be effective in each discipline as well as strategies shown to be effective for integrated approaches. This section will describe the literature related to each area separately and then discuss implications for blending these strategies into STEM instruction.

Effective Instructional Strategies Within and Across Science and Math Instruction

The math and science education have the most substantial research base, including a number of large meta-analyses. This section will describe each area, followed by a discussion of areas of overlap across the two fields of research. Schroeder et al., (2007) conducted a meta-analysis of US research published between 1980 and 2003 of the effect of specific science teaching strategies on student achievement. Sixty-one studies met their inclusion criteria. Enhanced context strategies and collaborative learning strategies were found to have the largest effect sizes on student achievement. Enhanced content strategies were classified as strategies that relate topics to students' previous personal experiences or previous learning.

Presenting material through real-world examples or problems was also a component of this category. Collaborative learning strategies included students engaged in group inquiry projects and heterogeneous and flexible groupings during instruction. Two other categories were also found to have a positive effect on student achievement, although with not as strong of an effect size: questioning strategies and inquiry strategies. Questioning strategies include varying the cognitive level of questions and increasing wait-time. Inquiry strategies were strategies such as student-centered instruction and answering science questions through data collection and analysis. However, the strategies were not treated as distinct strategies and the researchers acknowledge that a great deal of overlap exists between the reported categories, for example enhanced context and questioning are often components of inquiry.

Research on teaching strategies in mathematics indicates the need for some unique instructional strategies for mathematics instruction. Meta-analyses of effective mathematics teaching strategies indicate that direct instruction, computer-assisted instruction, and supplemental instruction, such as small group tutoring, have positive impacts on student learning. Text selected for instruction had no measurable effect on student learning (Slavin and Lake, 2008; Slavin et al., 2007). There were also consistencies with findings from science-specific strategies. Cooperative learning strategies had the strongest effect size on student learning as well as metacognition, which overlaps with the questioning category used in the science research (Slavin et al., 2009). Seidel and Shavelson (2007) conducted an analysis of pedagogical approaches in both mathematics and science.

Their analysis found that domain-specific information processing was the most effective teaching component across all domains (science, mathematics, reading), level of schooling (elementary, middle, high schools) or type of outcome (cognitive, motivational). Domain-specific approaches are content-specific and relate to the knowledge and nature of the domain.

In his synthesis of both the science and mathematics education literature, Ruthven (2010) identified four effective teaching components for the areas of math and science: (1) domain-specific inquiry, which relates to science and mathematics student learning, (2) contextual orientation for science achievement, (3) active teaching in mathematics and (4) cooperative group work on achievement outcomes in math and science. Overall, these studies suggest that although there are strategies that are effective for both science and mathematics instruction, science and math achievement is affected by a unique set of instructional strategies. Blending science, mathematics, technology, and engineering into a STEM discipline requires an understanding of the subtle instructional nuances necessary for each, as well as what methods are effective when the disciplines are taught in combination.

Integrated Math and Science Instruction

The integration of mathematics and science instruction has been researched more than any other form of STEM integration. Hurley (2001) conducted a meta-analysis of 31 studies that compared the effect of integrated math and science instruction to a non-integrated control group on student achievement (math and science). In order to analyze the integration, Hurley created categories for the types of integration: (1) sequenced – when science and mathematics are planned and taught with one before the other, (2) parallel – science and mathematics are taught simultaneously through parallel concepts, (3) partial – science and mathematics are taught partially together and partially separately within the same class, (4) enhanced – one discipline is the major discipline of instruction and the other is apparent throughout the instruction, and (5) total – science and mathematics are equitably taught together. The findings from the meta-analysis of these five forms of integration revealed that the largest student mathematics achievement effects were seen when taught sequentially with science, when they were conceptually planned together but when one was taught before the other. Sequential integration also had a positive effect of science achievement, although the effect was smaller. Total integration had a strong positive effect, and enhanced integration had a medium effect for science, with a small positive effect for both methods on mathematics. Partial integration had small positive effects for both science and mathematics achievement, and parallel integration had negative effects on the achievement of both disciplines.

The benefits of math and science integration have also been examined by grade-level spans. At the middle and high school levels, effect size is often higher for science than mathematics (Hurley, 2001), suggesting that it may be more difficult to improve mathematics achievement by integrating it with other subjects or that the integration interrupts the traditional sequential approach to mathematics instruction (Lehrer and Schauble, 2000). Other studies have suggested that the use of mathematical tools and representations improve the extent students are able to comprehend and represent natural systems, such as forces (Sherin, 2001), electricity (Sengupta and Wilenskey, 2011), and natural selection and population dynamics (Dickes and Sengupta, 2013). Studies have shown that at the elementary levels, mathematics integrations had a positive effect on students' ability to understand complex and challenging science concepts (Lehrer and Schauble, 2006). How much the traditional mathematics and science teaching methods

was changed as a result of these integrations is not clear in this literature. All forms of integration require planning, although it could be argued that parallel instruction requires less collaborative planning than the other integration because there is more flexibility in temporal coordination.

However, caution must be used when interpreting the research on STEM integration. The research is sparse and disconnected in certain areas. Also, rarely do the individual studies explicitly describe the theory that was used to guide the method of integration. The strength of the effect size may also be influenced by the details of the instructional approach, teacher expertise and system supports, such as planning time, which could be lost when studies are combined for meta-analysis. Taken collectively, these findings suggest that there is clear benefit to the integration of mathematics and science, in particular on science achievement. Learning how mathematical patterns and models are used to explain relationships in natural systems is central to learning science concepts.

Engineering Education

The literature on the impact of engineering education is limited compared to that of science and mathematics. Although there is evidence to suggest that engineering education can lead to increases in science and mathematics achievement, the context of these findings must be considered to reconcile inconsistencies in the literature. There is some evidence to suggest that engineering programs have led to increased gains on math and science achievement tests, such as National Assessment of Educational Progress (NAEP) exams, (Bottoms and Uhn, 2007; Hotaling et al., 2007). Other studies found little to no benefit of engineering integration on math achievement, especially for schools serving large numbers of low-income families (Tran and Nathan, 2010). Although these findings may provide further evidence to suggest that mathematics may be more difficult to integrate than other disciplines, other studies which will be discussed here point to benefits that may be difficult to assess on typical achievement tests, such as deeper mathematical knowledge and improved ability to transfer math skills. Participation in engineering programs has shown to improve students' ability to apply mathematical reasoning within the design process (Akins and Burghardt, 2006). Other studies suggest that engineering education participation leads to a broader and more applied understanding of the nature of mathematics, as well a belief that integration had helped them to make more sense of mathematics (Norton, 2007). The design and implementation of the integration were critical to this effect, including a focus on instructional and regulatory discourse and useful integration tools.

The evidence that engineering education has a positive effect on science achievement is more convincing, and yet the circumstances of this integration greatly impact the effect (Fortus et al., 2004; Mehalik et al., 2008; Sadler et al., 2000). The integration of engineering into science is most effective when scientific concepts are introduced along with the design activity, providing a connection between the science concept and a solution to a real world problem. Design failures can provoke conceptual change opportunities in the learner around naïve conceptions (Lehrer and Schauble, 1998) providing an opportunity to develop a more accurate scientific understanding of the phenomena. Applying an inaccurate science concept within a design does not just lead to an incorrect answer, it also means your solution will be less effective or not work at all (Sadler et al., 2000). However, students do not automatically make connections between the science concepts and the engineering design process (Crismond, 2001; Kozma, 2003; Nathan et al., 2013). Students tend to focus on aesthetic or ergonomic aspects of the design rather than the science knowledge being used in the solution. The knowledge related to the design solution is also highly contextualized and students need specific strategies to support the transfer of both existing and new knowledge across contexts (Fortus et al., 2004).

Technology

Few studies have specifically addressed the role of technology in STEM-related instruction. Career and technical education (CTE) courses have been used to uncover the effects of mathematics and technology integration. Substituting CTE courses for academic courses did not impede math achievement (Bozick and Dalton, 2013). With CTE courses designed to incorporate problem solving and logic, students' mathematics were on par with a control group taking the traditional mathematics sequence. In a similar study, Stone et al. (2008) found that students performed better on assessments of general math ability when they experienced math-enhanced technology courses. Engineering/technology courses that introduce mathematical topics at key points in the curriculum to help students make discipline connections have also been shown to improve students performance on mathematics assessments compared to a control group.

A review of the limited literature on engineering education integration makes clear that additional replication and validation of current studies is needed to fully understand its impact on science and mathematics achievement. Teachers, however, need to use strategies to connect the conceptual relationships between mathematical representations, scientific ideas, technologies, and engineering design if the integration is going to successfully improve students' understanding.

STEM INTEREST, IDENTITY, AND PERSISTENCE

Based on the premise that our concern over STEM education is about the lack of students in STEM majors and subsequently STEM fields, student interest in STEM is a primary goal of STEM education, whether that interest leads to the ability to apply a general knowledge of STEM to daily decisions in one's personal life or a STEM career. Interest can mediate learning and is related to other important learning factors, such as self-efficacy, goal setting, and self-regulation (Harackiewicz et al., 2008; Nieswandt, 2007). The development of interest can be cultivated and supported through personal interactions and the design of the learning environment (Renninger and Hidi, 2011). Equally important to interest and goal selection is a student's self-efficacy or their belief that they are capable of achieving in STEM. Math and science academic self-efficacy and outcome expectations have been shown to also influence academic goals. High school students with a high sense of math and science self-efficacy have stronger interests and aspirations towards earning STEM degrees in college (Byars-Winston et al., 2010). The stronger the student interest and self-efficacy beliefs are related to a career choice, the more likely they are to pursue that career path (Tracey, 2010) and the more they will persist in that choice (Lent et al., 2010).

In the middle-school grades (Grades 6 to 8) external factors begin to influence the academic pathway that students will take (Lanzilotti et al., 2009), and student interest in STEM-related subjects is closely related to their likelihood of pursuing a STEM career in the future (Fouad et al., 2002; Tai et al., 2006). Student attitudes are influenced by how topics are presented (Zacharia and Barton, 2004), and working on projects related to issues of power, culture, and ideology can lead to positive attitudes and interest (Zacharia and Barton, 2004). Inquiry-based teaching practices positively impact student motivation interest and motivation (Minner et al., 2010). For example, when science is taught in an engaging, hands-on experience, science often becomes the most situational interesting domain for students, leading to positive science interest (Jones et al., 2000). Studies have shown that activities involving experiments, lab, or project work increase student interest when compared to purely cognitive work, such as reading or listening to lectures (Swarat et al., 2012). Middle-school students involved in a math-infused engineering and technology curriculum saw mathematics as more interesting and having more importance than students participating in the non-math version of the same curriculum (Burghardt et al., 2010). Technology can increase student interest in STEM coursework, but the context and methods of the technology affect the role of technology in increasing student interest (Swarat et al., 2012).

Identity is also related to a student's selection and persistence in STEM fields. Identity refers to who one is or wants to be, as well as how they think others recognize and perceive them (Honey et al., 2014). Identity is transitory and always in the process of construction through social discourse and interactions. The range of a student's aspirations and choices are shaped by the wider social structures within which they operate, even though people themselves often do not consciously recognize these forces (Archer et al., 2012). From this perspective, children's and parents' science aspirations are not simply 'personal' decisions, but are also socially inflected and (partial) products of their social and learning environments.

After decades of reform efforts to broaden and expand the STEM workforce, certain groups of students remain under-represented in STEM fields: women, Hispanics, African Americans and Native Americans. Current research suggests that selection for and persistence in STEM fields may not be a matter of achievement for certain groups. Self-efficacy and identity may account for gender and ethnic disparities in the selection and persistence towards STEM careers.

Women in STEM

Although progress has been made in terms of the number of women in science and engineering fields, men continue to outnumber women, especially in advanced STEM degrees or upper-level positions (Hill et al., 2010). Women represent 30 percent of all STEM researchers worldwide. Regional averages range from 45.2 percent in Latin America to 18.9 percent in Asia (UNESCO, 2012). For example, since the late 1990s, US women have earned less than 30 percent of undergraduate degrees in engineering and computer sciences, and yet they received at least 57 percent of all undergraduate degrees (NSF, 2013). The fact that this disparity is not because of a lack of ability or performance by women has been well documented (Hazari et al., 2007). STEM choices and aspirations of women are greatly affected by social and environmental factors. At the elementary level, there is virtually no gender difference in general attitudes about science (Archer et al., 2012); however, as girls transition to middle school, their identities become more complicated and multi-layered. Although many middle-school girls are high math and science performers and claim to be interested in pursuing STEM-related goals, there is growing evidence of a disconnect between who they are and want to be and what they do and think they should be doing in science class. STEM fields have traditionally been seen as academic (non-social) and masculine. Girls who perform well academically in these fields must navigate around concerns about how their intelligence will cause them to be perceived by others (Skelton et al., 2010).

Factors within and outside traditional classrooms can impact girls' STEM identity. The development and cultivation of a positive science identity requires girls to navigate through the dominant social associations of science. These dominant associations view scientists as masculine, clever, and perceptive, and the field to be an elite one, open to a narrow range of women with very specific characteristics. This narrow space is even smaller for girls from low SES backgrounds or under-represented ethnic groups (Carlone, 2012). Often, inspiration for STEM-related goals is the result of out-of-school experiences when girls engage in

science in a way that makes them feel smart and capable. School-based grades, certificates and awards, and teacher labels can reaffirm or supplant internal STEM identities of girls (Tan et al., 2013).

Interventions that have successfully improved girls' attitudes about STEM have not led to an increase in STEM-related choices (Darke et al., 2002). This is probably due to the complex and mutable nature of identity and the impact that the social climate of the classroom has on girls' STEM identity, which in turn affects their future choices and persistence in those choices. For example, Carlone and Johnson (2007) found that recognition of their STEM ability was central to the development of women's STEM identities. The development of that identity could be disrupted if they fail to receive recognition by meaningful science colleagues. In fact, there is evidence to suggest that there are different sources of STEM self-efficacy and confidence for men and women. Men's STEM self-efficacy is supported through mastery experiences, whilst social persuasions and vicarious experiences are the primary sources of self-efficacy in women (Zeldin et al., 2008). Exposure to female role models has been shown to have a positive impact on girls' STEM identity, but only when there was significant personal connection with these role models. Explicit discussions of the under-representation of women in STEM fields have been positively related to STEM identity for female students (Archer et al., 2012). Simply exposing girls to women in STEM careers, such as guest speakers, does not appear to have a significant impact on their identity formation. Discussions of women scientists' work and frequency of group interactions has also been shown to be ineffective in forming positive STEM identities in girls (Hazari et al., 2010).

Some of the most promising research related to increasing girls STEM participation has been in the area of mindset (Dweck, 2006). Dweck's research findings identified a 'growth mindset' in which individuals perceived intelligence as a changeable and flexible characteristic that could be developed with effort and persistence. Individuals with a growth mindset are likely to persist in the face of struggle and adversity. Other individuals were found to have a 'fixed mindset', believing that intelligence is determined at birth and uncontrollable. Individuals with fixed mindset are more susceptible to loss of confidence in the face of a struggle because they see the need to 'work hard' as an indication that they are not smart enough for the task. Girls who possess a fixed mindset may have difficulty persisting after setbacks in math and science because of the stereotype that girls are not as good at these subjects as boys; however, girls who have a growth mindset are more likely to maintain their confidence and disregard negative stereotypes (Good et al., 2008). Considering mindset sheds light on some of the gender differences observed in STEM. Gender gaps have been found in boys and girls with fixed mindsets, but no gender difference exists among students of growth mindsets (Dweck, 2006; Grant and Dweck, 2003). Girls who believe that they can develop the skills and knowledge needed to be successful in STEM fields are more likely to resist stereotypes and develop positive STEM identities. What is most promising is that growth mindset can be developed. In a related study, girls who were taught that great math thinkers were born with innate math ability and talent performed significantly lower on subsequent math achievement tests compared to their male peers. However, girls who were taught that great math thinkers worked hard and were deeply interested and dedicated to the field performed no differently than their male peers (Good et al., 2008). Growth mindset has been linked not only to higher performance, but also to increased persistence in STEM fields as well.

Equity and Ethnicity

Factors affecting women's selection and persistence in STEM fields are similar to those faced by under-represented minorities (of which women are a subset). Despite a national focus on STEM careers in the US, in 2009, 12 percent of STEM workers were African American and Hispanic; however, African American and Hispanic individuals accounted for 25 percent of overall employment (US Department of Commerce, 2011). African American, Hispanic, or Native American students earned less than 15 percent of undergraduate degrees in engineering, math, and physical science (NSF, 2013). This trend is worse for socioeconomically disadvantaged students, who are less likely to major in STEM fields than students from higher SES levels (Shaw and Barbuti, 2010). Concern over perceived negative stereotypes lower self-assessments of STEM-related abilities, and their performance in STEM tasks (Hill et al., 2010) has been linked to the low numbers of under-represented groups in STEM fields.

Anderson and Ward (2012) used a nationally representative sample of over 1700 ninth-grade students to identify predictors of STEM success amongst high-achieving students from different ethnic backgrounds. Science attainment value, or how well the students' perception of science fits with their own identity, was a common predictor amongst high-achieving White, Hispanic and African American students. However, for Hispanic students, a higher utility value, or perceived connection to future goals, was also an important predictor for STEM success. Mathematics achievement was also found to predict STEM success for African American students. There was no evidence of gender differences with regard to STEM persistence plans; however, the study included life sciences and health sciences in the STEM category, domains that tend to be pursued by larger numbers of females. The results of this study, which focused on high-achieving students, provides further evidence that reasons for the disparity of minorities in STEM fields are not universal and that factors affecting identity and persistence may operate differently for different performance levels, SES backgrounds, gender, and ethnicity.

FUTURE DIRECTIONS

As STEM educators move towards making integrated STEM education a reality, consensus around the term is needed, including clarity regarding what aspects of each discipline are unique and should be preserved versus what inherent overlaps are best taught through a 'nature of STEM' approach. The current evidence suggests that integration improves student learning in all disciplines except for mathematics. Additional research is needed to understand if a lack of evidence pointing to a positive effect for mathematics is because of the discipline's sequential nature or some other undetermined factor. Although there is a great deal of literature on STEM fields, the research on integrated approaches has focused on minimal integrations of the disciplines and remains limited and disjointed, with no common theoretical framework to inform future research. New models are beginning to emerge (Honey et al., 2014; Nadelson et al., 2014), and yet how these frameworks will be interpreted and manifest in the field remains to be seen. New models of integrated curriculum need to be developed using either the few existing frameworks or ones still to be developed.

Several recommendations emerge from the current research regarding effective elements of integrated STEM instruction. Learning occurs when we are able to make connections between concepts and are able to convey those connections through multiple representations. Students need a deep foundation of factual knowledge that is organized in a conceptual framework in order to enable the efficient retrieval of information (Bransford et al., 2000). These 'big ideas' exist in each STEM discipline, but an integrated STEM approach requires that connections across the disciplines be explicitly made and 'big ideas' across STEM identified. Although there are natural overlaps in content and practices in STEM, instruction that makes these connections explicit is necessary for a deep understanding of the disciplines, as well as their relationship to each other. Learning experiences should allow students to make connections between disciplines, but also situate the learning in a real-world context. Real-world settings provide concrete situations that are rich with complex information within a context that students can often relate. It is now clear that interest and persistence play a major part in students' selection of STEM careers; however, school achievement does not explain the under-representation of women and certain ethnic groups in STEM fields. Social and environmental factors affect students' STEM identities, which in turn contribute to their interest in STEM careers and their persistence in these fields.

There has been criticism about the formal acronymization of STEM education based on vocational and economic goals, such as increasing a STEM workforce. Although there is a long history of integrating these fields, the feasibility of a large-scale implementation of integrated STEM is currently unknown. The development of common mathematics and science standards in the US may provide much needed alignment across the disciplines. Technology and engineering are robust and well-defined STEM fields but their role within the K-12 curriculum is still uncertain and their prominence is currently not equal to that of mathematics or science. The educational reform efforts of the past have demonstrated the resilience of educational organizations against systemic change. Integrated STEM curriculum will require schools to consider their organizational structures, and programs are needed to support teachers to navigate through these new STEM learning designs.

REFERENCES

ABET, Engineering Accreditation Commission (2004) *ABET criteria for accrediting engineering programs*. Baltimore, MD: ABET.

Akins, L. and Burghardt, D. (2006) 'Work in progress: Improving K-12 mathematics understanding with engineering design projects', in *Frontiers in education conference, 36th Annual,* San Diego, CA, 27–31 October 2006. New York, NY: IEEE. pp. 13–14.

American Association for the Advancement of Science (AAAS) (1989) *Science for All Americans: Summary Project 2061.* Washington, DC: ERIC Clearinghouse.

American Association for the Advancement of Science (AAAS) (1993) *Benchmarks for Scientific Literacy, Project 2061.* New York, NY: Oxford University Press.

Anderson, L. and Ward, T.J. (2012) 'Expectancy-value models for the STEM persistence plans of ninth-grade, high-ability students: a comparison between Black, Hispanic, and White students', *Science Education*, 98(2): 216–42.

Archer, L., DeWitt, J., Osborne, J., Dillon, J., Willis, B. and Wong, B. (2012) 'Balancing acts': elementary school girls' negotiations of femininity, achievement, and science', *Science Education,* 96(6): 967–89.

Bottoms, G. and Uhn, J. (2007) *Project Lead the Way Works: A new type of career and technical program.* Atlanta, GA: Southern Regional Education Board.

Bozick, R. and Dalton, B. (2013) 'Balancing career and technical education with academic coursework the consequences for mathematics achievement in high school', *Educational Evaluation and Policy Analysis,* 35(2): 123–38.

Bransford, J., Brown, A. and Cocking, R. (eds.) (2000) *How People Learn: Brain, Mind, Experience, and School Committee on Developments in the Science of Learning.* With additional materials from The Committee on Learning Research and Educational Practice, M. Suzanne Donovan, John D. Bransford, and James W. Pellegrino, editors. Commission on Behavioral and Social Sciences and Education of the National Research Council. Washington, DC: National Academy Press.

Breiner, J.M, Harkness, S.S., Johnson, C.C., and Koehler, C. (2012) 'What is STEM? A discussion about conceptions of STEM in education and partnerships', *School Science and Mathematics*, 112(1): 3–1.

Burghardt, M.D., Hecht, D., Russo, M., Lauckhardt, J. and Hacker, M. (2010) 'A study of mathematics infusion in middle school technology education classes', *Journal of Technology Education,* 22(1): 58–74.

Byars-Winston, A., Estrada, Y, Howard, C., David, D. and Zalapa, J. (2010) 'Influence of social cognitive and ethnic variables on academic goals of underrepresented students in science and engineering: a multiple-groups analysis', *Journal of Counseling Psychology*, 57(2): 205–18.

Bybee, R.W. (1995) 'Achieving scientific literacy: using the national science education standards to provide equal opportunities for all students to learn science', *Science Teacher*, 62(7): 28–33.

Bybee, R.W. (2010) 'Advancing STEM education: a 2020 vision', *Technology and Engineering Teacher*, 70(1): 30–35.

Carlone, H.B. (2012) 'Methodological considerations for studying identities in school science', *Identity Construction and Science Education Research,* 35: 9–25.

Carlone, H.B. and Johnson, A. (2007) 'Understanding the science experiences of successful women of color: science identity as an analytic lens', *Journal of Research of Science Teaching,* 44(8): 1187–218.

Cofré, H., González-Weil, C., Vergara, C., Santibáñez, D., Ahumada, G., Furman, M., Podesta, M.E., Gallego, R. and Pérez, R. (2015) 'Science teacher education in South America: the case of Argentina, Colombia and Chile', *Journal of Science Teacher Education*, 26(1): 45–63.

Common Core State Standards Initiatives (2010) *Common Core State Standards for English Language Arts Standards.* (CCSS-ELA). Available from: www.corestandards. org/ELA-Literacy (Accessed 30 July 2015).

Confrey, J. (1990) 'A review of the research on student conceptions in mathematics, science, and programming', *Review of Research in Education*, 16: 3–56.

Crismond, D. (2001) 'Learning and using science ideas when doing investigate-and-redesign tasks: a study of naïve, novice and expert designers doing constrained and scaffolded design work', *Journal of Research in Science Teaching,* 38(7): 791–820.

Darke, K., Clewell, B. and Sevo, R. (2002) 'Meeting the challenge: the impact of the National Science Foundation's program for women and girls', *Journal of Women and Minorities in Science and Engineering,* 8(3–4): 285–303.

Darling-Hammond, L. (2014) 'Closing the achievement gap: a systemic view', in J.V. Clark (ed.), *Closing the Achievement Gap from an International Perspective*. New York, NY: Springer Science & Business Media. pp. 7–19.

DeBoer, G. (1991) *A History of Ideas in Science Education: Implications for Practice*. NewYork, NY: Teachers College Press.

Dickes, A.C. and Sengupta, P. (2013) 'Learning natural selection in 4th Grade with multi-agent-based computational models', *Research in Science Education*, 43(3): 921–53.

Department for Business, Innovation & Skills (DBIS) (2014) *The Allocation of Science and Research Funding 2015/2016: Investing in World-Class Science and Research*. accessed 30 July 2015) https://www.gov.uk/government/uploads/system/uploads/attachment_data/file/293635/bis-14-p188-innovation-report-2014-revised.pdf

Dweck, C. (2006) 'Is math a gift? Beliefs that put females at risk', in S.J. Ceci and W.M. Williams (eds.), *Why Aren't More Women in Science? Top Researchers Debate the Evidence*. Washington, DC: American Psychological Association. pp. 47–55.

Fensham, P. (2009) 'Real world contexts in PISA science: implications for context-based science education', *Journal of Research in Science Teaching*, 46(8): 884–96.

Fortus, D., Dershimer, R.C., Krajcik, J., Marx, R.W. and Mamlok-Naaman, R. (2004) 'Design based science and student learning', *Journal of Research in Science Teaching*, 41(10): 1081–110.

Fouad, N.A., Smith, P.L. and Zao, K.E. (2002) 'Across academic domains: extensions of the social–cognitive career model', *Journal of Counseling Psychology*, 49(2): 164–71.

Gardner, D.P., Larsen, Y.W., Baker, W. and Campbell, A. (1983) *A Nation at Risk: The Imperative for Educational Reform*. Washington, DC: US Government Printing Office.

Good, C., Aronson, J. and Harder, J.A. (2008) 'Problems in the pipeline: stereotype threat and women's achievement in high-level math courses', *Journal of Applied Developmental Psychology*, 29(1): 17–28.

Grant, H. and Dweck, C.S. (2003) 'Clarifying achievement goals and their impact', *Journal of Personality and Social Psychology*, 85(3): 541–53.

Hazari, Z., Sonnert, G., Sadler, P.M. and Shanahan, M.C. (2010) 'Connecting high school physics experiences, outcome expectations, physics identity, and physics career choice: a gender study', *Journal of Research in Science Teaching*, 47(8): 978–1003.

Hazari, Z., Tai, R. and Sadler, P. (2007) 'Gender differences in introductory university physics performance', *Science Education*, 91(6): 847–76.

Harackiewicz, J.M., Durik, A.M., Barron, K.E., Linnenbrink, L. and Tauer, J.M. (2008) 'The role of achievement goals in the development of interest: reciprocal relations between achievement goals, interest, and performance', *Journal of Educational Psychology*, 100(1): 105–22.

Her Majesty's Treasury (2007) *The Race to the Top: A Review of Government's Science and Innovation Policies by Lord Sainsbury*. London: HM Treasury.

Hill, C., Corbett, C. and St Rose, A. (2010) *Why So Few? Women in Science, Technology, Engineering, and Mathematics*. Washington, DC: American Association of University Women.

Honey, M., Pearson, G. and Schweingruber, H. (eds.) (2014) *STEM Integration in K-12 Education: Status, Prospects, and an Agenda for Research*. Washington, DC: The National Academies Press.

Hotaling, L., McGrath, B., McKay, M., Shields, C., Lowes, S., Cunningham, C., Lachapelle, C. and Yao, S. (2007) *Engineering Our Future*. American Society for Engineering Education Annual Conference & Exposition Proceedings. Honolulu, HI, June 2007, p. 1349.

Hurley, M. (2001) 'Reviewing integrated science and mathematics: the search for evidence and definitions from new perspectives', *School Science and Mathematics*, 101(5): 259–68.

International Technology Engineering Educators Association (ITEEA) (2007) *Standards for Technological Literacy: Content for the Study of Technology*. Technology for All Americans Project, & International Technology Education Association.

Johnson, C. (2011) 'Implementation of STEM education policy: challenges, progress and lessons learned', *School Science and Mathematics,* 112(1): 45–55.

Jones, M.G., Howe, A. and Rua, M.J. (2000) 'Gender differences in students' experiences, interests, and attitudes toward science and scientists', *Science Education*, 84(2): 180–92.

Karplus, R. and Atkin, J. (1962) 'Discovery or invention', *Science Teacher*, 29(5): 45.

Kozma, R. B. (2003) 'Technology and classroom practices: An international study', *Journal of Research on Technology in Education,* 36(1): 1–14.

Lanzilotti, R., Montinaro, F. and Ardito, C. (2009) 'Influence of Students' Motivation on Their Experience with E-Learning Systems: An Experimental Study', in C. Stephanidis (ed.) *Universal Access in Human-Computer Interaction*. Applications and Services (pp. 63–72). Berlin Heidelberg: Springer.

Lederman, N. and Lederman, J. (2013) 'Is it STEM or "S & M" that we truly love?', *Journal of Science Teacher Education,* 24(8): 1237–40.

Lehrer, R. and Schauble, L. (1998) Reasoning about structure and function: children's conceptions of gears', *Journal of Research in Science Teaching,* 35(1): 3–25.

Lehrer, R. and Schauble, L. (2000) 'Model-based reasoning in mathematics and science', in R. Glaser (ed.), *Advances in Instructional Psychology.* Hillsdale, NJ: Lawrence Erlbaum. pp. 101–59.

Lehrer, R. and Schauble, L. (2006) 'Cultivating model-based reasoning in science education', in R.K. Sawyer (ed.), *Cambridge Handbook of the Learning Sciences.* Cambridge: Cambridge University Press. pp. 371–87.

Lent, R. W., Sheu, H. B., Gloster, C. S. and Wilkins, G. (2010) 'Longitudinal test of the social cognitive model of choice in engineering students at historically Black universities', *Journal of Vocational Behavior*, 76(3): 387–394.

McComas, W.F. and Olson, J.K. (2002) 'The nature of science in international science education standards documents', in W.F. McComas (ed.), *The nature of science in science education* (pp. 41–52). Dordrecht, Netherlands: Springer.

Mehalik, M. M., Doppelt, Y. and Schuun, C. D. (2008) 'Middle-school science through design-based learning versus scripted inquiry: Better overall science concept learning and equity gap reduction', *Journal of Engineering Education-Washington*, 97(1): 71–85.

Minner, D.D., Levy, A.J. and Century, J. (2010) 'Inquiry-based science instruction – what is it and does it matter? Results from a research synthesis years 1984 to 2002', *Journal of Research in Science Teaching,* 47(4): 474–96.

Nadelson, L. S., Seifert, A. L. and McKinney, M. (2014) 'Place based STEM: Leveraging local resources to engage K-12 teachers in teaching integrated STEM and for addressing the local STEM pipeline', *American Society of Engineering Education*, Indianapolis, IN.

Nathan, M. J., Srisurichan, R., Walkington, C., Wolfgram, M., Williams, C., & Alibali, M. W. (2013). 'Building cohesion across representations: A mechanism for STEM integration', *Journal of Engineering Education*, 102(1), 77–116.

National Academy of Engineering and Natural Resource Council (2009) *Engineering in K-12 Education: Understanding the Status and Improving the Prospects.* Washington, DC: The National Academies Press.

National Council of Teachers of Mathematics (NCTM) (2000) *Principals and Standards for School Mathematics.* Washington, DC: The National Academies Press.

National Research Council (NRC) (1996) *National Science Education Standards.* Washington, DC: The National Academies Press.

National Research Council (NRC) Committee on Highly Successful Schools or Programs for K-12 STEM Education (2011) *Successful K-12 STEM education: Identifying effective approaches in science, technology, engineering, and mathematics*. Washington, DC: The National Academies Press.

National Research Council (NRC) (2012) *A Framework for K-12 Science Education: Practices, Crosscutting Concepts, and Core Ideas.* Washington, DC: National Academies Press.

National Science Foundation, Division of Science Resources Statistics (2009) *Numbers of US Doctorates Awarded Rise for Sixth Year, but Growth Slower.* Arlington, VA: National Science Foundation, Division of Science Resources Statistics.

National Science Foundation, National Center for Science and Engineering Statistics (2013) *Women, Minorities, and Persons with*

Disabilities in Science and Engineering: 2013. Special Report NSF 13–304. Arlington, VA. Available from http://www.nsf.gov/statistics/wmpd/ (accessed 26 February 2015).

Next Generation Science Standards (NGSS) Lead States (2013) *Next Generation Science Standards: for States, by States. Vol. 1: The Standards*. Washington, DC: The National Academies Press. Available from http://www.nextgenscience.org/nextgeneration-science-standards (accessed 1 June 2015).

Nieswandt, M. (2007) 'Student affect and conceptual understanding in learning chemistry', *Journal of Research in Science Teaching*, 44: 908–37.

Norton, S. (2007) 'The use of design practice to teach mathematics and science', *International Journal of Technology Design Education,* 18: 19–44.

Ogunniyi, M.B. and Rollnick, M. (2015) 'Preservice science teacher education in Africa: prospects and challenges', *Journal of Science Teacher Education*, 26(1): 65–79.

Organisation for Economic Co-operation and Development (OCED) (2006) *Assessing Scientific, Reading and Mathematical Literacy: A Framework for PISA 2006*. Paris: OCED.

Organisation for Economic Co-operation and Development (OECD) (2013) *PISA 2012 Results in Focus: What 15-year-olds know and what they can do with what they know.* Available from http://www.oecd.org/pisa/keyfindings/pisa-2012-results-overview.pdf (accessed 9 January 2015).

Partnership for 21st Century Skills (P21) (2014) *Framework for 21st Century Learning*. Available from http://www.p21.org/about-us/p21-framework (accessed 22 June 2015).

Peters-Burton, E. (2014) 'Is there a "nature of STEM"?', *School Science and Mathematics,* 114(3): 99–101.

President's Council of Advisors on Science and Technology (PCAST) (2010) *Prepare and Inspire: K-12 Education in Science, Technology, Engineering, and Math (STEM) for America's Future*. Washington, DC: President's Council of Advisors on Science and Technology.

Renninger, K.A. and Hidi, S. (2011) 'Revisiting the conceptualization, measurement, and generation of interest', *Educational Psychologist*, 46(3): 168–84.

Rising Above the Gathering Storm Committee (2010) *Rising above the Gathering Storm, Revisited: Rapidly Approaching Category 5*. Washington, DC: The National Academies Press.

Ruthven, K. (2010) 'Using international study series and meta-analytic research synthesis to scope pedagogical development aimed at improving student attitude and achievement in school mathematics and science', *International Journal of Science and Mathematics Education,* 9: 419–58.

Sadler, P.M., Coyle, H.P. and Schwartz, M. (2000) 'Engineering competitions in the middle school classroom: key elements in developing effective design challenges', *Journal of the Learning Sciences* 9(3): 299–327.

Sanders, M. (2009) 'STEM, STEM education, STEM mania', *Technology Teacher*, 68(4): 20–6.

Schroeder, C.M., Scott, T.P., Tolson, H., Huang, T. and Lee, Y. (2007) 'A meta-analysis of national research: effects of teaching strategies on student achievement in science in the United States', *Journal of Research in Science Teaching*, 44(10): 1436–60.

Seidel, T. and Shavelson, R.J. (2007) 'Teaching effectiveness research in the past decade: the role of theory and research design in disentangling meta-analysis results', *Review of Educational Research,* 77(4): 454–99.

Sengupta, P. and Wilensky, U. (2011) 'Lowering the learning threshold: multi-agent-based models and learning electricity', in M.S. Khine and M. Saleh (eds.), *Models and Modeling*. Dordrecht, Netherlands: Springer. pp. 141–71.

Shaw, E.J. and Barbuti, S. (2010) 'Patterns of persistence in intended college major with a focus on STEM majors', *NACADA Journal*, 30(2): 19–34.

Sherin, B.L. (2001) 'How students understand physics equations', *Cognition and Instruction*, 19(4): 479–541.

Skelton, C., Francis, B. and Read, B. (2010) 'Brains before "beauty"? High achieving girls, school and gender identities', *Educational Studies*, 36(2): 185–94.

Slavin, R. E., Lake, C. and Groff, C. (2007) *Effective programs for middle and high school mathematics: A best-evidence synthesis*. Baltimore: Johns Hopkins University.

Center for Data-Driven Reform in Education. Available at www.bestevidence.org.

Slavin, R.E. and Lake, C. (2008) 'Effective programs in elementary mathematics: a best-evidence synthesis', *Review of Educational Research,* 78(3): 427–515.

Slavin, R.E., Lake, C. and Groff, C. (2009) 'Effective programs in middle and high school mathematics: a best-evidence synthesis', *Review of Educational Research,* 79(2): 839–911.

Stage, E.K., Asturias, H., Cheuk, T., Daro, P.A. and Hampton, S.B. (2013) 'Opportunities and challenges in next generation standards', *Science*, 340(6130): 276–77.

Stone, J.R., Alfeld, C. and Pearson, D. (2008) 'Rigor and relevance: enhancing high school students' math skills through career and technical education', *American Educational Research Journal,* 45(3): 767–95.

Swarat, S., Ortony, A. and Revelle, W. (2012) 'Activity matters: understanding student interest in school science', *Journal of Research in Science Teaching,* 49(4): 515–37.

Tan, E., Calabrese Barton, A., Kang, H. and O'Neil, T. (2013) 'Desiring a career in STEM fields: Girls' Narrated and Embodied Identities-in-practice', *Journal of Research in Science Education*, 50(10): 1143–1179.

Tai, R.H., Liu, C.Q., Maltese, A.V. and Fan, X. (2006) 'Planning early for careers in science', *Science*, 312(5777): 1143–4.

Teaching Institute for Excellence in STEM (2010) *What is STEM Education?* Available from http://www.tiesteach.org/stem-education. aspx (accessed 5 January 2015).

Topçu, M. S., Arıkan, S. and Erbilgin, E. (2015) 'Turkish Students' Science Performance and Related Factors in PISA 2006 and 2009', *The Australian Educational Researcher*, 42(1): 117–132.

Tracey, T.J.G. (2010) 'Relation of interest and self-efficacy occupational congruence and career choice certainty', *Journal of Vocational Behavior*, 76: 441–7.

Tran, N. and Nathan M. (2010) 'Pre-college engineering studies: an investigation of the relationship between pre-college engineering studies and student achievement in science and mathematics', *Journal of Engineering Education*, 99(2): 143–57.

UNESCO Institute for Statistics (2012) *Science Technology and Innovation: Women in Science Fact Sheet*. http://www.uis.unesco. org/FactSheets/Documents/sti-women-in-science-en.pdf (accessed 14 January 2015)

US Department of Commerce (2011) *Education Supports Racial and Ethnic Equality in STEM*. ESA Issue Brief No. 05-11.

Williams, P.J. (2011) 'STEM Education: proceed with caution', *Design and Technology Education: An International Journal*, 16(1): 26–35.

Zacharia, Z. and Barton, A. C. (2004) 'Urban middle-school students' attitudes toward a defined science', *Science Education*, 88(2): 197–222.

Zeldin, A.L., Britner, S.L. and Pajares, F. (2008) 'A comparative study of the self-efficacy beliefs of successful men and women in mathematics, science, and technology careers', *Journal of Research in Science Teaching*, 45(9): 1036–58.

42

College and Career Readiness for all: The Role of Career and Technical Education in the US

Victor M. Hernandez-Gantes

As the global economy and the rapid changes in technology innovations began to take hold in the 1990s, new skillsets were demanded for workers and students graduating from high school and college around the world (Jobs for the Future, 2007; National Academy of Sciences, 2007). In the US, however, the country struggled in preparing youth for productive participation in the workforce as high school students' performance in math and science continue to lag behind in comparison to international peers, and with only 30 percent of young adults completing a bachelor's degree by age 27 (Symonds et al., 2011; US Department of Education, 2013). It is therefore not surprising that employers in the US began to report problems finding workers with adequate preparation underlined by basic academic skills, technical skills, and complementary skills associated with teamwork and problem-solving (Carnevale et al., 2010). This issue was particularly noted in high-tech, high-wage fields in science, technology, engineering, and mathematics (STEM) where the shortage of qualified workers was more acute (Hernandez-Gantes and Fletcher, 2013; Kim, 2011).

Out of this social and economic landscape, calls for education reforms focusing on improved college and career readiness emerged nationally in the US (Stone, 2013); however, unlike other international counterparts, such as Germany, which features a work-based education system for vocational education and training, the US relies on school-based curricula with varying interpretations set at the state level to prepare youth for transitions to further education and/or employment (Gordon, 2014; Stone, 2013). Further, unlike other industrialized nations where academic as well as vocational education are valued, it appears that in the US a college education is often viewed as the only way to prepare students for success in life (Gray, 2010; Symonds et al., 2011). The problem is that, as a society, we continue to view vocational education – now referred to as career and technical education (CTE) in the US – as 'less than' college education (Gray, 2010; Symonds et al., 2011).

With this frame of reference, the notion that college and career readiness needs to be improved has received renewed attention and is the target of initiatives to address it in the US. For example, the Common Core State Standards (CCSS) represent the forefront of a movement with the premise that all students should graduate from high school with the skills and knowledge needed for productive participation in further education, work, and life (Achieve, 2011; Common Core Standards Initiative (CCSI), 2014; Meeder and Suddreth, 2012). In general, academic reforms are seeking to make learning more relevant for students, whilst in CTE the goal is to enhance the academic rigor of courses and programs to promote college and career readiness (Stone, 2013; Symonds et al., 2011).

As part of this quest, the US is implicitly revisiting a question that was at the core of the nascent educational system early in the 1900s: what should be the purpose of education? Should it be to prepare students for work or for college? As the current push for college and career readiness suggests, we should be more interested in redefining this notion beyond an 'either/or' proposition; however, policy reports continue to equate career readiness as college preparation, ignoring the fact that technical and employability skills are also needed for successful participation in the labor force (Gray, 2010; Stone, 2013; Symonds et al., 2011). In this context, what is the role of contemporary CTE in preparing students for productive participation in postsecondary education and/or work in today's economy?

With this frame of reference, the goals of this chapter are to (1) describe the evolution of CTE and its underlying policy and organizational premises, (2) provide an overview of its core theoretical underpinnings, (3) highlight key curricular strategies to promote college and career readiness, and (4) discuss the implications and role for preparing students for further education and work. The scope of the discussion is restricted to career and technical education in the US.

THE EVOLUTION OF CAREER AND TECHNICAL EDUCATION

In the US, CTE has experienced a transformation since the early1990s, moving from a focus on preparation for specific trades to preparation for college and careers. The evolution of the premises underlying CTE is outlined next, followed by an overview of the current organization of the US education system.

From Vocational to Career and Technical Education

CTE in the US had its inception at the turn of the twentieth century under the designation of 'vocational education'. The seminal ideas shaping the original version of CTE – vocational education – in the US were rooted in two schools of thought debated at the onset of the twentieth century. One viewed education as vocational and serving practical and economic purposes to prepare students for jobs, whilst the other advocated a more democratic education allowing students to select their own path blending hands-on learning and academic knowledge (Labaree, 2010). Out of this debate, a two-track system was created in the US that included academic and technical education through the Smith-Hughes Vocational Act of 1917 (Gordon, 2014; Labaree, 2010).

For almost the entire twentieth century, the utilitarian goal of vocational education in the US was to prepare students for specific trades such as agriculture, industrial arts, and business in addition to home economics (Gordon, 2014). However, in the 1990s, amidst calls for better preparation of high school and college graduates, the field adopted the name of 'career and technical education' to reflect a broader emphasis beyond exclusive preparation for specific occupations. This movement promoted the integration of academic and technical education and broader student preparation for careers, as opposed to specific preparation for narrow trades (Gamoran and Nystrand, 1994; Hernández-Gantes et al., 1995). The movement was supported by School-to-Work, Perkins Vocational and Applied Technology Education, and Tech Prep Education legislation, which paved the way for the formal transformation of vocational education into CTE at the sunset of the twentieth century (Stipanovic et al., 2012).

Today, Perkins legislation provides federal guidelines focusing on the improvement of CTE students' academic achievement through the integration of academic and technical education, secondary and postsecondary education articulation, and improvement of state and local accountability systems (Gordon, 2014). In the US, federal guidelines are translated into a variety of initiatives that are then interpreted and enacted at the state and local level based on their respective goals and priorities (Scott and Sarkees-Wircenski, 2004). In this context, although there is no such thing as a national system of CTE, there is a shared agreement that the purpose of CTE is to prepare youth and adults for careers in a wide array of high-wage, high-skill, high-demand fields (Association for Career and Technical Education (ACTE), 2014). In practice, the purpose of CTE has translated into continued support for preparation for work and a broader role promoting preparation for further education in the education system under a variety of curricular designs (Gordon, 2014).

Organization and Student Participation

CTE encompasses a wide variety of curricular formats around 16 career clusters: Agriculture, Food & Natural Resources; Architecture & Construction; Arts, A/V Technology & Communications; Business Management & Administration; Education & Training; Finance; Government & Public Administration; Health Science; Hospitality & Tourism; Human Services; Information Technology; Law, Public Safety, Corrections & Security; Manufacturing; Marketing; Science,

Technology, Engineering & Mathematics; and Transportation, Distribution & Logistics. Collectively, the clusters represent more than 79 occupational pathways available to students in secondary education (National Association of State Directors of Career Technical Education Consortium (NASDCTE), 2014). The career clusters serve as an organizing tool for school districts and schools in the development of programs linking middle and high school curricula, and transition to postsecondary education (NASDCTE, 2012).

In the US, CTE is school-based with courses and programs primarily delivered through classroom and practical instruction in school workshops, studios, or labs. In middle schools, CTE typically focuses on the promotion of career exploration through elective courses, and in high schools students may have a variety of courses and program options providing opportunities for concentration in a career cluster of interest (Gordon, 2014; NASDCTE, 2012). To this end, various 'career pathways' (also referred to as 'programs of study' in the field) are available in each career cluster and provide the means for the articulation of courses from middle to high school and into 2- and 4-year colleges through dual enrollment (Carnevale et al., 2011; NASDCTE, 2012, 2014; Stone and Aliaga, 2003). For example, a school district in Florida offers over 400 middle and high school CTE courses providing career pathways for the 16 career clusters noted earlier (Hillsborough County Public Schools, 2014).

According to assessments of student participation, about 94 percent of all US high school students take CTE courses for a variety of reasons (Silverberg et al., 2004). In the 2011–12 school year, it was reported that more than seven million high school students took at least one CTE credit, whilst about three million students identified as CTE 'concentrators' took three or more credits in a career pathway (Office of Career, Technical and Adult Education, 2014). In recent years, high school students have shown a trend of CTE participation across multiple pathways, and lower participation as 'concentrators' in a particular pathway (Aliaga et al., 2012; Hudson, 2013). Over the past decade, it has also been reported that students who are male, from low-income families, low achieving, and with special needs are more likely to enroll in career and technical education (ACTE, 2014).

THEORETICAL PREMISES UNDERLYING CAREER AND TECHNICAL EDUCATION

Serving an important role in the education system and seeking to promote college and career readiness, what are the theoretical premises of CTE? Contextual teaching and learning principles are at the core of career and technical education, operationally implemented through the integration of academic and technical curricula.

Contextual Teaching and Learning

At its core, contextual teaching and learning seeks to make student learning more meaningful by establishing connections to real-life and occupational situations to increase the relevance of what is being taught (Brown et al., 1989; Hernandez-Gantes and Brendefur, 2003). As such, contextual teaching and learning in CTE builds upon two conceptual premises: the use of occupational contexts and active learning integrating 'knowing and doing' (Hernandez-Gantes and Nieri, 1997).

Traditionally, academic learning has been viewed as an activity associated with the transmission of knowledge (knowing) often separated from practice (doing). From behavioral and cognitive science we have learned that teaching and learning can be accomplished as a process of knowledge reproduction in which context may be useful, but incidental to the process (Brown et al., 1989). That is, in academic education (for example, mathematics), the use of contextual

learning often relies on ad hoc examples to make concepts relevant for students. The problem is that such contextual examples are typically used in isolation, are not connected with subsequent examples, and are presented as hypothetical contextual scenarios. In this case, the goal is for students to 'know' concepts, assuming that conceptual knowledge will transfer to practical use at some point (Porter et al., 1994). In general, this is a rough and simplistic description of the traditional approach to teaching and learning in secondary education, which has fuelled the push to make learning more relevant through education reforms (CCSI, 2014; Meeder and Suddreth, 2012; National Council of Teachers of Mathematics (NCTM), 2000).

In contrast, CTE has been traditionally viewed as focusing too much on practical skills and lacking rigor on conceptual academic knowledge. That is, CTE programs have been typically associated with the notion of engaging students in 'doing' manual work to learn job-specific skills (Gamoran and Nystrand, 1994; Scott and Sarkees-Wircenski, 2004). From this perspective, the occupational contexts and the teaching and learning processes are viewed as the means for the reproduction of practical skills with limited connection to conceptual knowledge.

To address this disconnect in academic and technical education, educational reform since the 1990s has called for academic education to be more contextually relevant to students, and for CTE to be more academically rigorous. This call has been based on research on situated cognition suggesting that when learning occurs in the context of real-world problem situations representing coherent connections between 'knowing' and 'doing', learning is more meaningful (Greeno, Collins and Resnick, 1996; Hernandez-Gantes and Brendefur, 2003). As a result, over the past two decades, curriculum and instruction in CTE has emphasized the integration of academic and technical education as the means for promoting college and career readiness (Stipanovic et al., 2012). The premise is that whether students are engaged in learning about, for, or through work, the authenticity of occupational contexts provides for opportunities to make learning relevant (Castellano et al., 2012; Hernández-Gantes and Brendefur, 2003;).

In CTE, occupational contexts are provided by career clusters that serve as the source for many meaningful and coherent learning situations that can be used in courses on career exploration or courses required in an occupational program of study. In this case, the occupational contexts represent an authentic source of relevant learning tasks and concept applications. As such, these contextual learning situations are authentic representations of what people do in the world of work (Hernández-Gantes and Brendefur, 2003; Hernandez-Gantes and Nieri, 1997). The authenticity of the learning situations is at the core of contextual teaching and learning in CTE, which is often referred to as 'authentic pedagogy' in academic education (see, for example, Newmann et al., 1996).

Further, when teaching and learning is anchored in an occupational context as part of a coherent program of study, it is possible to integrate conceptual knowledge and skills to promote progressive and deep understandings as well as mastery of related skills (Hernandez-Gantes and Brendefur, 2003). From this perspective, the role of occupational contexts is to help students understand concepts and develop problem-solving skills in ways that resemble how people do things in actual work situations (Castellano et al., 2012; Withington et al., 2012).

Active learning is another key tenet of CTE that stems from cognitive science and is often associated with participatory and engaging activities whereby students take charge of their own learning. That is, when students engage in activities requiring them to reason and solve problems, they are more likely to analyze and assess what they know and need to know, and what worked and did not work in the process of testing solutions (Bransford et al., 2010). To this end, it has been found that engaging students in active

learning helps them improve their reasoning ability, retention, and understanding of new concepts, and the transfer of new ideas to different contextual situations (Bransford et al., 2010; Prince, 2004; Schonfeld, 1991). Active learning as a means to integrate knowing and doing is also at the core of CTE courses and programs seeking to engage in learning about, for, and through work. In CTE, active learning is often emphasized through demonstrations, class projects, senior projects, problem solving, and other learning-by-doing type of activities (Hernandez-Gantes and Blank, 2009). Other forms of active learning include group discussions, brainstorming, case studies, role-playing, journal writing, and cooperative learning strategies (Prince, 2004).

As students get progressively acculturated to the knowledge, skills, and attitudes expected in an occupational context, situated and active learning becomes richer for all participating students. Participation in various forms of cognitive apprenticeship (for example, internships, job shadowing, apprenticeships) is an example of immersive contextual and active learning (Berryman, 1995; Bransford et al., 2010; Brown et al., 1989).

Integration of Academic and Technical Curriculum

Based on the promising premises of contextual teaching and learning, reform in CTE specifically called for integration with academic education to promote college and career readiness (Gordon, 2014). Concurrently, in academic education, a similar call was made to make academic subjects more relevant through contextual experiences (Hernandez-Gantes and Nieri, 1997; NCTM, 2000). In general, the term 'curriculum integration' has been referred to in a variety of ways as a method or process to connect skills, themes, concepts, and topics across disciplines and between academic and technical education (Pierce and Hernandez-Gantes, 2014). The term curriculum integration is therefore often used interchangeably as integrated, interdisciplinary, multidisciplinary, thematic, holistic, and applied learning, making it difficult to come to a unified interpretation (Drake, 2007; Etim, 2005). In this regard, it has been suggested that curriculum integration should be defined based on its goals, the role of the disciplines involved, and the extent of integration (Grady, 1996; Klein, 2006). For example, integration may involve concept connections within single subjects (for example, arithmetic, algebra, geometry) or across two or more subjects (for example, mathematics and technical education) (Goodman, 1989; Hernandez-Gantes and Brendefur, 2003). Regarding the extent of integration, related efforts are often viewed as a hierarchal continuum ranging from least integrative (for example, loose integration within a course) to most integrative (for example, cross-disciplinary integration) involving academic and technical content (Drake, 2007; Grubb, 1997; Klein, 2006).

In the US, CTE curriculum integration has been broadly interpreted at the organizational level through career pathways articulating sequences of courses in occupational areas, integrated coursework (for example, within and across courses), and through the implementation of career academies. These approaches to curriculum integration in CTE have allowed for greater equity in student participation, the creation of small learning communities (for example, career academies), and facilitation of postsecondary transitions (Cox et al., 2014; Lekes et al., 2007; Oakes, 2005; Orr et al., 2003). Further, from a psychological and sociological perspective, integration has also been reported to prepare students for life in general, including helping them make informed career choices upon graduation from high school (Kemple, 2008; Maddy-Bernstein, 2000).

Regarding the impact of participation in integrated curriculum, there is an emerging body of research suggesting positive results in academic subjects (for example, mathematics, reading) and in the preparation of students for the workforce and further education

(Cox et al., 2014; Stone et al., 2008; Pierce and Hernandez-Gantes, 2014). In general, research has suggested that students participating in curricula integrating academic and technical education tend to do as well as – and in some cases better than – students in college-prep curricular tracks (Castellano et al., 2012; Kemple, 2008; Pierce and Hernandez-Gantes, 2015; Silverberg et al., 2004; Stone et al., 2008). For example, a middle-school mathematics curriculum connecting disciplinary topics (that is, algebra and geometry) in contextual problem situations was reported to increase student performance (Romberg, 2001). Similarly, in the context of CTE, results from studies also featuring mathematics in contexts resulted in higher student performance compared to students in comparison groups (Pierce & Hernandez-Gantes, 2015; Stone et al., 2006). Comparable results have also been observed using integrated curriculum in the context of language arts (Castellano et al., 2004; National Research Center for Career and Technical Education, 2011).

In sum, using contextual instructional approaches in integrated curriculum, teachers can promote career awareness and exploration to help students begin to identify occupational fields and what people do in related work. That is, the integration of academic concepts and technical skills in work contexts can result in deeper understanding of concepts and the reasoning behind the application of occupational skills (Berryman, 1995; Bransford et al., 2010).

CAREER AND TECHNICAL EDUCATION CURRICULAR STRATEGIES

The idea of college and career readiness implies that an integrated educational system is in place to promote coherent career awareness and development from the early grades to postsecondary education. This is not necessarily the case because college and career readiness is interpreted in many ways and treated loosely in K-12 education in the US (Kantrov, 2014; Stone, 2013). As such, the US education system is often described as being uneven in providing for coherent career development supports to help all students learn about work and careers in their educational experience (Herr and Cramer, 1996). To address this need, it has been suggested that education systems should promote career readiness by systematically helping students understand the importance of career planning and as the basis for making informed postsecondary transitions (Gray, 2010; Kantrov, 2014). In this regard, CTE provides opportunities to promote career awareness, exploration, and preparation at the elementary, middle, and high school level (Lekes et al., 2007; Maddy-Bernstein, 2000; Stone, 2013).

In elementary school, the promotion of career awareness and exploration has been loosely implemented, primarily using guest speakers to share what they do (for example, firefighters, doctors) and field trips to get acquainted with workplaces. These strategies provide students with opportunities to interact with professionals, learn about their work, and see what workplaces look like (Beale and Williams, 2000; Howard and Walsh, 2011; Magnuson and Starr, 2000). In middle school, career awareness is further complemented with opportunities for career exploration allowing students to better understand related interests and begin thinking about career and college planning (ACT, 2005; Howard and Walsh, 2011; Magnuson and Starr, 2000; Orr et al., 2003). For example, some school districts use 'exploratory wheel' classes where students enroll in a class featuring an occupational theme (for example, business technology, agriculture) for a few weeks before they rotate to the next class so they are exposed to different occupational areas. Other activities in middle schools include field trips, career days, and job shadowing opportunities (Maddy-Bernstein, 2000; Palladino Schultheiss, 2005). In turn, in high school, career exploration activities can take many forms, including informational interviews with employers, career-related

guest speakers, workplace visits and tours, job shadowing, career fairs and career days, career camps, hands-on career projects, and career-focused mentoring (ACT, 2006; Lekes et al., 2007; Maddy-Bernstein, 2000). High school students also have the opportunity to participate in CTE programs either as concentrators (that is, completing a program of study) or by taking selected courses about/ related to particular interests. Other students take selected CTE courses to advance their college preparation and/or to earn dual enrollment credit and expedite transition to postsecondary education (Castellano et al., 2012; Hughes and Karp, 2004; Karp et al., 2007; Stone, 2013).

In general, given the nature and role of CTE, it is possible to engage students in coherent college and career readiness in schools depending on their individual interests (Solberg et al., 2012; Stone, 2013). To this end, CTE features two primary curricular strategies: the use of career pathways (or programs of study) and career academies.

CTE Curricular Grounds: Career Pathways

One way that CTE has broadened the focus of programs beyond narrow preparation for work to an emphasis on college and careers is through the use of the career cluster concept. As noted earlier, there are 16 career clusters informing career and technical education programs, each including several career pathways associated with broadly defined occupations (or careers) (Carnevale et al., 2011). For example in the Industrial, Manufacturing, and Engineering Systems career cluster, manufacturing, architecture and construction pathways are found. Students concentrating on a particular pathway in high school can transition to related postsecondary education or pursue employment upon graduation from high school (Hernandez-Gantes and Blank, 2009).

Career pathways (also referred to as 'programs of study') represent the overarching curricular strategy to organize CTE and provide for coherent articulation between secondary and postsecondary education. The use of career clusters and corresponding programs of study can be implemented in response to local workforce demands, and afford students opportunities to pursue related college and career development, earn occupational certifications, and dual-credit (Lekes et al., 2007). As such, career pathways provide a tangible curricular structure for the promotion of college and career readiness through preparation for further education and work. This broad curricular approach stems from the Perkins legislation of 2006 tying school funding to the requirement of having at least one career pathway available for students (Stipanovic et al., 2012).

This organizational curricular approach has its roots in the Tech Prep initiative enacted in the 1980s and 1990s featuring program articulation between secondary and postsecondary education bridging the last 2 years of high school and the first 2 years of college. The basis of Tech Prep programs was the articulation of programs of study making possible the 2+2 approach (Bragg et al., 2002; Hershey et al., 1998). The complementary concepts of career clusters and career pathways emerged out of calls to make sense of occupations in the economy and organize career pathways around them. As such, career pathways provide clear and coherent curricular grounds for students to become academically and technically prepared to pursue related careers or further education. To this end, the career clusters, corresponding pathways, and companion programs of study have become the organizing curricular structure in CTE (Stipanovic et al., 2012; Withington et al., 2012).

For implementation purposes, career pathways require four core components. First, programs of study must establish articulation agreements that map out a coherent sequence of coursework, delivery strategies, and credits to be awarded at the secondary and postsecondary level. Second, career pathways must also emphasize the integration of academic and technical content based on rigorous standards such as the Common Core State Standards. Third, career pathways should involve opportunities for dual enrollment as a means to facilitate and expedite transition to further education. Finally, career pathways should focus on the completion of recognized industry certifications and/or a postsecondary education degree (Stipanovic et al., 2012). In general, the benefits of this approach lie in the opportunity to explore and engage in meaningful career development, earn industry certifications, pursue employment in related fields, and allow for further education upon graduation from high school or beyond (Castellano et al., 2012; Withington et al., 2012).

Career Academies

There are a variety of curricular designs used to help students become college- and career-ready, including programs focusing on specific preparation for work and occupationally theme-based programs emphasizing preparation for further education and work. Programs focusing on preparation for work include comprehensive technical high schools, career centers, and work-based learning programs. In turn, programs focusing on college and career preparation are represented by theme-based occupational designs, such as magnet schools (that is, schools seeking to attract students within and outside the neighborhood boundaries), comprehensive schools (for example, High Schools-that-Work consortium), and career academies. Of these, the career academy concept has become the most prominent curricular strategy implemented across the country (Hernandez-Gantes and Blank, 2009).

Career academies are operationally defined as smaller learning communities featuring a college-preparatory curriculum in the context of a career theme, and active partnerships with employers and postsecondary institutions. Career academies are typically implemented within high schools with the goal to increase student engagement and achievement whilst developing skill sets necessary to pursue further education or work (Orr et al., 2003). At the core of career academies is the integration of academic and technical content to increase rigor and relevance of learning experiences and promote students' career interests (Castellano et al., 2007; Kemple and Snipes, 2000).

By 2004, there were approximately 4800 high schools in the US offering career academies (Castellano et al., 2007; National Center for Educational Statistics (NCES), 2011). In some states, it is mandated by law that high schools offer at least one career academy in the context of an appropriate career cluster to ensure opportunities for students to develop college and career readiness (Cox et al., 2014). However, with the growing popularity of the career academy concept, the quality of implementation may vary as schools and districts have rushed to join the bandwagon. To address this issue, there are national organizations and networks – such as the National Career Academy Coalition (NCAC), the Career Academy Support Network, and the National Academy Foundation – informing related implementation with the development of standards of practice (National Academy Foundation, 2013; Stern et al., 2010).

The career academy model typically features four components (National Academy Foundation, 2013). One requires that academies be organized around small learning communities using student cohorts, career-themed and sequenced coursework, teacher collaboration, career-themed guidance, and ongoing professional development. A second involves an emphasis on integrated curriculum and instruction component to promote career and academic learning around a relevant theme through project-based activities involving classroom and work-based learning experiences, and internships. A third usually involves the support of an advisory board to ensure that academies are locally relevant and supported by community stakeholder groups. Finally, career academies also require a work-based learning component to promote career awareness and exploration activities in 9th (for example, field trips) and 10th (for example, job shadowing) grades, and experiential opportunities (for example, industry certifications, paid internships) in 11th and 12th grades (National Academy Foundation, 2013).

After more than four decades of implementation, and including data from conclusive random-assignment studies, the career academy concept has demonstrated its potential for promoting student success (Stern et al., 2010). According to Kemple (2008), participation in career academies has resulted in positive outcomes, including increased attendance and academic course taking, higher high school graduation rates, and lower dropout rates. In relation to academic performance, there is evidence indicating that career academy students perform as well as counterparts in other college preparatory tracks (Kemple, 2008; Silverberg et al., 2004). In terms of postsecondary outcomes, research has suggested that compared to students who participated in a traditional high school curriculum, a higher number of career academy students have a transitional plan upon graduation from high school (Kemple, 2008; Stern et al., 2010). Further, regarding employment outcomes, it has been reported that academy graduates earn about 11 percent higher than non-academy graduates 8 years after high school graduation (Kemple, 2008; National Academy Foundation, 2013).

ISSUES AND IMPLICATIONS FOR PRACTICE AND STUDENT PARTICIPATION

Even with the promising premises and prospects of CTE, it continues to be overlooked as a viable alternative to help students' transition to successful participation in further education or work. Two underlying issues are often mentioned in the literature as the roots for this phenomenon: the stigma associated with participation in CTE and the fuzzy interpretation of curriculum integration.

The Lingering Stigma of Career and Technical Education

The stigma associated with CTE has been ingrained in the public's mind since the inception of the two-track system early in the 1900s when the role of vocational education was set as preparation for specific jobs (Gordon, 2014). The idea behind the two-track system was to provide students with differential curriculum tracks (academic and vocational) based on their perceived interests and capacity. This idea resulted in a de facto sorting process channeling students with high academic performance into the college-prep track and struggling students into the vocational track (Gamoran and Nystrand, 1994; Oakes, 2005).

The tracking phenomenon in US schools has been well documented in the literature and has been a divisive topic among policymakers, educators, and the general public (Gamoran and Nystrand, 1994; Oakes, 2005). Some researchers have argued that sorting students into distinct curricular tracks actually resulted into three groups: college-bound for high performers, technical education for low performers, and general education for those in the middle (Gray, 2010; Symonds et al., 2011). This sorting system reinforced the stigma attached to technical education in American culture, which appears to linger. To address this issue, education reform in the 1990s called for integrated curriculum initiatives to shift the role of technical education from preparation for work only, to broader preparation for college and careers (Grubb, 1997; Hernandez-Gantes et al., 1995). However, as the integrated designs have grown in popularity (for example, career academies), new forms of tracking have emerged that sort high-performing students into advanced placement and honors courses, whilst middle- and low-performing students are placed into general and technical programs (Castellano et al., 2004; Cox et al., 2014).

Over the past two decades, in light of employment trends, policymakers and researchers have begun to question the value of a college degree and some point to the need for technical skills in the new economy (Carnevale et al., 2010; Symonds et al., 2011). Nevertheless, shortages of workers in STEM-related fields have continued to reinforce the notion of a college education as the primary goal for all students (Hernandez-Gantes and Fletcher, 2013; Stone, 2013). In this context, Gray (2010) has argued that the stigma of technical education will continue unless US society revisits the two-track system as an either/or proposition, and realizes that technical education is a viable alternative for success in life. To this end, a more nuanced definition of college and career readiness should recognize the value of learning academic skills, as well as technical skills, to prepare students for further education and work.

Curriculum Integration Issues

The call for curriculum integration was promoted through academic and technical education reform in the 1990s in the US. On the academics front, the National Council of Teachers of Mathematics (2000) proposed new standards calling for integrated and authentic representations of mathematical concepts in applied contexts. In turn, technical education called for increased academic rigor to make a shift from narrow preparation for work to preparation for college and careers (Hernandez-Gantes et al., 1995). This movement resulted in curriculum initiatives seeking to integrate college preparatory and CTE coursework (Hernandez-Gantes and Brendefur, 2003).

The promising benefits of curriculum integration have been well documented in the literature (Kemple, 2008; Stasz et al., 1994; Stern et al., 2010). In general, it has been reported that integrated curricular designs promote more relevant learning of academic concepts, career awareness, and leads to better preparation for successful transition to further education or work (Castellano et al., 2004; Romberg, 2001; Stone et al., 2006). At issue is the uneven quality of programs as the popularity of integrated initiatives has grown over the past two decades.

As schools and districts have rushed to join the bandwagon, two primary issues have emerged involving the many interpretations of curriculum integration and the difficulties of implementation requiring teacher collaboration (Johnson et al., 2003; Pierce and Hernandez-Gantes, 2014). Integrated curriculum design and development is a complex undertaking requiring the support of the entire organization (that is, schools and districts) to ensure successful implementation. The problem is that curriculum integration may be interpreted in many ways and there is no such thing as a shared understanding of what it means for all schools and teachers (Etim, 2005; Johnson et al., 2003; Pierce and Hernandez-Gantes, 2014). The lack of a unified definition and interpretation has led to a variety of implementation efforts ranging from informal integration into single courses to district-wide initiatives. The question is, what are the unifying conceptual principles supporting the design and implementation? Further, do the choices of occupational themes make sense in the local contexts? (Hernandez-Gantes and Fletcher, 2013).

Another issue inherent to curriculum integration is the need for organizational support to allow for collaborative curriculum development, common planning periods, team teaching, and the incorporation of integrated projects (Pierce & Hernandez-Gantes, 2014; Stone et al., 2006). To promote effective curriculum integration, it is necessary to engage teams of academic and technical teachers in related design, development, and implementation (Pierce and Hernandez-Gantes, 2015). Research has suggested that in schools where teachers have the opportunity to collaborate, the quality of integrated curriculum and instruction is enhanced (Hernandez-Gantes and Brendefur, 2003). However, given the traditional compartmentalization of teaching work in schools, teacher collaboration and related supports are often difficult to realize. This issue often leads to integration initiatives that have all the buzzwords, but lack the organizational collaboration and support for efficacy of implementation (Hernandez-Gantes and Brendefur, 2003; Hernandez-Gantes and Fletcher, 2013; Newmann et al., 1996).

Despite the promising premises and prospects of CTE, it is apparent that in the US we are focusing too much on college preparation and not enough on what it means for students to be 'career ready'. The stigma of technical education and issues with the enactment of integrated curricula, also appear to be lingering limitations. In this context, what can we learn from counterpart countries? In some industrialized nations (for example, Germany), there is no issue with the term vocational education, and the education system provides opportunities for youth to choose a college or a vocational pathway, with the latter relying on work-based learning programs. The European apprenticeship in particular, a system built on work-based learning with strong employers' support, has been often referred to as the gold standard of vocational education and training (Jacoby, 2013). For example, in the German system, students learn academics in the classroom half of the time, and spend the other half learning in the workplace under the supervision of a mentor. Under this system, about 60 percent of German youth join the workforce after participation in an apprenticeship, with 60 percent getting hired by the company where the apprenticeship was completed, whilst the rest find work elsewhere in their occupational field (Jacoby, 2013; ReferNet Germany, 2009). Making a complete shift from a school-based to a work-based system in the US may not be realistic, but there is an emerging agreement that work-based learning is as element of CTE that should be enhanced (Symonds et al., 2011).

CONCLUSIONS

CTE has come a long way in the US, from a focus on narrow preparation for work when it was known as vocational education, to a contemporary emphasis on college and career readiness (Gordon, 2014). As such, the benefits of technical education have been well documented, suggesting that, in the new economy, CTE is a viable alternative for successful transition to further education and/or work (ACTE, 2014). Research on the outcomes of participation in CTE has indicated that student performance is as good as academic performance of students in college-prep curricula (Stern et al., 2010). In addition, CTE students get the benefit of enhanced college and career readiness because they participate in programs that boost learning relevance and help them acquire skills demanded in the new economy (Kemple, 2008). However, it appears that the more things change, the more they remain the same. Despite the promising prospects of CTE, and the fact that all students need to be college- and career-ready, our society continues to view it as inferior to college education (Gray, 2010).

Given the new skills demands in the new economy and employment trends, it is time to revisit the notion of 'college for all' as the only way to win in life. With only about a third of young US adults completing a bachelor's degree, and 10 percent completing an associate's degree (2 years in the US), it is clear that not everyone ends up with a postsecondary education, and the idea of college as the only way to succeed in life needs an overhaul (Achieve, 2010; Gray, 2010; Symonds et al., 2011). Being college- and career-ready involves both academic knowledge and application skills, and the choice of academic or technical education should not come down to an either/or proposition in a tracking system. College and career readiness should be a goal underlying education for all students.

Some researchers and policymakers have argued that the 'college for all' notion prevents society from seizing the full value of career and technical education as a viable alternative way to win in life (Gray, 2010; Symonds et al., 2011). Grubb and Lazerson (2007) went even further, suggesting that all of US education is, in fact, vocational

education. They reasoned that with the advent of the new economy, education and work connections have become stronger and have progressively pointed to an education system that needs to be more responsive to an economic function. This view has been reinforced in recent years based on employment and economic data questioning the value of a college degree as the primary investment for successful participation in the workforce (Symonds et al., 2011).

With this frame of reference, regardless of students' record of academic achievement and interests, everyone should benefit from opportunities to enhance their college and career readiness – and CTE appears to be well suited for that (ACTE, 2014). Contemporary curricular strategies are yielding promising results promoting enhanced college and career readiness, and there is evidence suggesting that the occupational outlook in the new economy is increasingly calling for technical credentials other than a college degree (Carnevale et al., 2011). As such, the 'college for all' notion should be revisited to become 'further education and work for all'. To get there, we should acknowledge the value of both academic and technical education and work toward a coherent integration in the education system. To that end, some researchers have suggested that we take cues from work-based learning systems in other industrialized countries where vocational education is embraced and valued an as integral part of the education system to prepare students for productive participation in the workforce (Jacoby, 2013).

REFERENCES

Achieve (2010) *Closing The Expectations Gap.* Washington, DC: Author.

Achieve (2011) *Strong Support, Low Awareness: Public Perceptions of the Common Core Standards.* Washington, DC: Author.

ACT (2005) *Career Planning: Students Need Help Starting Early and Staying Focused.* Iowa City, IA: Author.

ACT (2006) *Ready for college and ready for work: Same or different?* Iowa City, IA: Author.

Aliaga, O.A., Kotamraju, P. and Stone, J.R., III. (2012) *A Typology for Understanding the Career and Technical Education Credit-Taking Experience of High School Students.* Louisville, KY: National Research Center for Career and Technical Education, University of Louisville.

Association for Career and Technical Education (ACTE) (2014) *ACTE Today Fact Sheet.* Available from https://www.acteonline.org/CTETodayOct14 (accessed 2 December 2014).

Beale, A.V. and Williams, J.C. (2000) 'The anatomy of an elementary school career day', *Journal of Career Development,* 26(3): 205–13.

Berryman, S.E. (1995) 'Apprenticeship as a paradigm of learning', in W. Norton Grubb (ed.), *Education through Occupations in American High Schools. Vol. 1. Approaches in Integrating Academic and Vocational Education.* New York, NY: Teachers College Press. pp. 192–213.

Bragg, D.D., Loeb, J.W., Gong, Y., Deng, C.P., Yoo, J. and Hill, J. L. (2002) *Transition from High School to College and Work for Tech Prep Participants in Eight Selected Consortia.* St Paul, MN: National Research Center for Career and Technical Education (NRCCTE). Available from http://www.nrccte.org/sites/default/files/publication-files/transition-bragg_all.pdf (accessed 4 December 2014).

Bransford, J.D., Brown, A.L. and Cocking, R.R. (eds.) (2010) *How People Learn: Brain, Mind, Experience and School.* Washington, DC: The National Academies Press.

Brown, J.S., Collins, A. and Duguid, P. (1989) 'Situated cognition and the culture of learning', *Educational Researcher,* 18(l): 32–42.

Carnevale, A.P., Smith, N., Stone, J.R. III, Kotamraju, P., Steuernagel, B. and Green, K. (2011) *Career Clusters: Forecasting Demand for High School through College Jobs, 2008–2018.* Washington, DC: Georgetown University Center on Education and the Workforce.

Carnevale, A.P., Smith, N. and Strohl, J. (2010) *Help Wanted: Projections of Jobs and Education Requirements through 2018.* Washington, DC: Georgetown University Center on Education and the Workforce.

Castellano, M., Stone, J.R. III., Stringfield, S., Farley, E. and Wayman, J. (2004) *The Effect of CTE-Enhanced Whole-School Reform on Student Course Taking and Performance in English And Science.* Available from http://www.nrccte.org/sites/default/files/publication-files/english_science_castellano.pdf (accessed 4 December 2014).

Castellano, M., Stone, J.R. III., Stringfield, S.C., Farley-Ripple, E.N., Overman, L.T. and Hussain, R. (2007) *Career-Based Comprehensive School Reform: Serving Disadvantaged Youth in Minority Communities.* St Paul, MN: National Research Center for Career and Technical Education. Available from http://www.nrccte.org/ (accessed 4 December 2014).

Castellano, M., Sundell, K., Overman, L.T. and Aliaga, O.A. (2012) 'Do career and technical education programs of study improve student achievement? Preliminary analyses from a rigorous longitudinal study', *International Journal of Educational Reform,* 21: 98–118.

Common Core Standards Initiative (CCSI) (2014) *About the Common Core State Standards.* Available from http://www.core-standards.org/about-the-standards/ (accessed 2 December 2014).

Cox, E.D., Hernandez-Gantes, V.M. and Fletcher, E.C. (2014) 'Who participates in high school career academies? A descriptive analysis of six-year enrollment trends in a Southeastern school district', *International Journal of Adult Vocational Education and Technology,* 5(3): 65–81.

Drake, S. (2007) *Creating Standards-Based Integrated Curriculum.* 2nd edn. Thousand Oaks, CA: Corwin Press.

Etim, J.S. (ed.) (2005) *Curriculum Integration K-12: Theory and Practice.* Lanham, MD: University Press of America.

Gamoran, A. and Nystrand, M. (1994) 'Tracking, instruction, and achievement', *International Journal of Educational Research,* 21: 217–231.

Goodman, Y.M. (1989) 'Roots of the whole language movement', *The Elementary School Journal,* 90(2): 113–27. doi:10.1086/461607.

Gordon, H.R. (2014) *The History and Growth of Career And Technical Education in America.* 4th edn. Prospect Heights, IL: Waveland Press.

Grady, J.B. (1996) *Interdisciplinary Curriculum: A Fusion of Reform Ideas.* Available from ERIC database. (ED375980).

Gray, K. (2010) 'Secondary and postsecondary career and technical education: solving the quiet workforce development in Georgia and the nation', presentation conducted at Annual Meeting of the Georgia Association for Career and Technical Education, Atlanta, GA.

Greeno, J., Collins, A. and Resnick, L. (1996) 'Cognition and learning', in D. Berliner and R. Calfee (eds.), *Handbook of Educational Psychology*. New York, NY: Macmillan. pp. 15–46.

Grubb, N. and Lazerson, M. (2007) *The Education Gospel: The Economic Power of Schooling*. Cambridge, MA: Harvard University Press.

Grubb, W.N. (1997) 'Not there yet: prospects and problems for "education through occupations"', *Journal of Vocational Education Research,* 22(2): 77–94. Available from http://scholar.lib.vt.edu/ejournals/JVER (accessed 11 December 2014).

Hernández-Gantes, V.M and Blank, W. (2009) *Teaching English Language Learners in Career and Technical Education Programs*. New York, NY: Routledge.

Hernández-Gantes, V.M. and Brendefur, J. (2003) 'Developing authentic, integrated, standards-based mathematics curriculum: [more than just] an interdisciplinary collaborative approach', *Journal of Vocational Education Research,* 28(3): 259–84.

Hernandez-Gantes, V.M. and Fletcher, E. (2013) 'The need for integrated workforce development systems to broaden the participation of underrepresented students in STEM-related fields', in R. Palmer and L. Wood (eds.), *Community College and STEM: Examining Underrepresented Racial and Ethnic Minorities*. New York, NY: Routledge.

Hernández-Gantes, V.M. and Nieri, L.A. (1997) *Linking the NCTM Standards to Emerging Vocationalism*. Berkeley, CA: National Center for Research in Vocational Education.

Hernández-Gantes, V.M., Phelps, L.A., Jones, J. and Holub, T. (1995) 'School climate in emerging career-oriented programs: students' perspectives', *Journal of Vocational Education Research,* 20(2): 5–26.

Herr, E.L. and Cramer. S.H. (1996) *Career Guidance and Counseling through the Lifespan: Systematic Approaches.* 5th edn. New York, NY: Harper Collins.

Hershey, A.M., Silverberg, M.K., Owens, T. and Hulsey, L.K. (1998) *Focus for the Future: The Final Report of the National Tech-Prep Evaluation*. Princeton, NJ: Mathematica Policy Research.

Hillsborough County Public Schools (2014) *Career and Technical Education Secondary Guide 2013–2014*. Available from http://www.sdhc.k12.fl.us/doc/648/secondaryprogramguide (accessed 2 December 2014).

Howard, K.A. and Walsh, M.E. (2011) 'Children's conceptions of career choice and attainment: Model development', *Journal of Career Development,* 38(3): 256–71.

Hudson, L. (2013) *Data Point: Trends in CTE Coursetaking*. Washington, DC: National Center for Education Statistics.

Hughes, K. and Karp, M. (2004) *School-Based Career Development: A Synthesis of the Literature*. New York, NY: Teachers College, Columbia University.

Jacoby, T. (2013) 'Vocational education 2.0: Employers hold key to better career training', *Civic Report,* 83. Available from http://www.manhattan-institute.org/html/cr_83.htm#.VUOHCM4SMbA (accessed 2 December 2014).

Jobs for the Future (2007) *The STEM Workforce Challenge: The Role of the Public Workforce System in a National Solution for a Competitive Science, Technology, Engineering, and Mathematics Workforce*. Washington, DC: US Department of Labor, Employment and Training Administration.

Johnson, A.B., Charner, I. and White, R. (2003) *Curriculum Integration in Context: An Exploration of How Structures and Circumstances Affect Design and Implementation*. St Paul, MN: National Research Center for Career and Technical Education.

Kantrov, I. (2014) *Opportunities and Challenges in Secondary Career and Technical Education*. Waltham, MA: Education Development Center, Inc.

Karp, M.M., Calcagno, J.C., Hughes, K.L., Jeong, D.W. and Bailey, T.R. (2007) *The Postsecondary Achievement of Participants in Dual Enrollment: An Analysis of Student Outcomes in Two States*. St Paul, MN: National Research Center for Career and Technical Education.

Kemple, J.J. (2008) *Career Academies: Long-Term Impacts on Labor Market Outcomes,*

Educational Attainment, and Transitions to Adulthood. New York, NY: MDRC.

Kemple, J. J. and Snipes, J. C. (2000, March). *Career academies: Impacts on students' engagement and performance in high school*. Available from http://www.mdrc.org/publications/41/execsum.html (accessed 17 October 2014).

Kim, Y.M. (2011) *Minorities in Higher Education: Twenty-Fourth Status Report, 2011 Supplement*. Washington, DC: American Council on Education.

Klein, J.T. (2006) 'Platform for a shared discourse of interdisciplinary education', *Journal of Social Science Education*, 6(2): 10–18. Available from http://www.jsse.org (accessed 28 November 2014).

Labaree, D.F. (2010) 'How Dewey lost: the victory of David Snedden and social efficiency in the reform of American education', in D. Tröhler, T. Schlag and F. Osterwalder (eds.), *Pragmatism and Modernities*. Boston, MA: Sense Publishers. pp. 163–88.

Lekes, N., Bragg, D. D., Loeb, J. W., Oleksiw, C. A., Marszalek, J., Brooks-LaRaviere, M., Zhu, R., Kremidas, C.C., Akukwe, G., Lee, H, and Hood, L.K. (2007, May). *Career and Technical Education Pathway Programs, Academic Performance, and the Transition to College and Career*. St Paul, MN: National Research Center for Career and Technical Education, University of Minnesota.

Maddy-Bernstein, C. (2000) *Career Development Issues Affecting Secondary Schools*. Columbus, OH: National Dissemination Center for Career and Technical Education.

Magnuson, C. and Starr, M. (2000) 'How early is too early to begin life career planning? The importance of the elementary school years', *Journal of Career Development*, 27(2): 89–101.

Meeder, H. and Suddreth, T. (2012) *Common Core State Standards and Career and Technical Education: Bridging the Divide Between College and Career Readiness*. Washington, DC: Achieve.

National Academy Foundation (2013) *National Academy Foundation Performance Measurement System: 2012 Status Report*. New York, NY: Author.

National Academy of Sciences (2007) *Rising Above the Gathering Storm: Energizing and Employing America for a Brighter Economic Future*. Washington, DC: The National Academies Press.

National Association of State Directors of Career Technical Education Consortium (NASDCTE) (2012) *A Look Inside: A Synopsis of CTE Trends*. Available from http://www.careertech.org/sites/default/files/SynopsisofCTETrends-CareerClusters-2012.pdf (accessed 2 December 2014).

National Association of State Directors of Career Technical Education Consortium (NASDCTE) (2014) *Pathways to College and Career Readiness: Career Clusters*. Available from http://www.careertech.org/career-clusters (accessed 3 December 2014).

National Center for Education Statistics (NCES) (2011) *Career/Technical Education (CTE)*. Available from http://nces.ed.gov/surveys/ctes/index.asp (accessed 2 December 2014).

National Council of Teachers of Mathematics (NCTM) (2000) *Principles and Standards for School Mathematics*. Reston, VA: Author.

National Research Center for Career and Technical Education (NRCCTE) (2011) *Report to the Congress of the United States: Program Year 4, August 1, 2010 to July 31, 2011*. Available from NRCCTE website: http://www.nrccte.org (accessed 4 December 2014).

Newmann, F.M., Secada, W.G. and Wehlage, G.G. (1996) *A Guide to Authentic Instruction and Assessment: Vision, Standards and Scoring*. Madison, WI: Wisconsin Center for Education Research.

Oakes, J. (2005) *Keeping Track: How Schools Structure Inequality*. New Haven, CT: Yale University.

Office of Career, Technical and Adult Education (2014) *Consolidated Annual Reports*. Available from http://cte.ed.gov/accountability/reports.cfm (accessed 4 December 2014).

Orr, M.T., Hughes, K.L. and Karp, M.M. (2003) *Shaping Postsecondary Transitions: Influences of the National Academy Foundation Career Academy*. IEE Brief 29. Available from http://www.tc.columbia.edu/iee/BRIEFS/Brief29.pdf (accessed 28 November 2014).

Palladino Schultheiss, D.E. (2005) 'Elementary career intervention programs: social action initiatives', *Journal of Career Development*, 31(3): 185–94.

Pierce, K. and Hernandez-Gantes, V.M. (2014) 'Revisiting the basics of curriculum integration in CTE: a review of literature', presentation conducted at the Annual Conference of the Association for Career and Technical Education Research (ACTER), Nashville, TN.

Pierce, K. and Hernandez-Gantes, V.M. (2015) 'Do mathematics and reading competencies integrated into career and technical education courses improve high school student scores?', *Career and Technical Education Research,* 39(3): 213–229.

Porter, A.C., Kirst, M.W., Osthoff, E., Smithson, J.L. and Schneider, S.A. (1994) *Reform of High School Mathematics and Science and Opportunity to Learn.* New Brunswick, NJ: Rutgers University, Consortium for Policy Research in Education.

Prince, M. (2004) 'Does active learning work?', *Journal of Engineering Education,* 93(3): 223–31.

ReferNet Germany (2009) *Germany-VET in Europe: Country Report 2009.* Thessaloniki, Greece: European Centre for the Development of Vocational Training.

Romberg, T.A. (2001) *Designing Middle-School Mathematics Materials using Problems Set in Context to Help Students Progress from Informal to Formal Mathematical Reasoning.* Available from http://ncisla.wceruw.org (accessed 24 November 2014).

Schonfeld, A.H. (1991) 'On mathematics as sense making: An informal attack on the unfortunate divorce of formal and informal mathematics', in J.F. Voss, D.N. Perkins, and J.W. Segal (eds.), *Informal Reasoning and Education.* Hillsdale, NJ: Erlbaum. pp. 331–343.

Scott, J.L. and Sarkees-Wircenski, M. (2004) *Overview of Career and Technical Education.* 3rd edn. Homewood, IL: American Technical.

Silverberg, E., Warner, E., Fong, M. and Goodwin, D. (2004) *National Assessment of Vocational Education: Final Report to Congress.* Washington, DC: US Department of Education.

Solberg, S., Phelps, A., Haakenson, K.A., Durham, J.F. and Timmons, J. (2012) 'The nature and use of individualized learning plans as a career intervention strategy', *Journal of Career Development,* 39: 500–14. doi:10.1177/0894845311414571

Stasz, C., Kaganoff, T. and Eden, R.A. (1994) *Integrating Academic and Vocational Education: A Review of Literature, 1987– 1992* (RP-445). Santa Monica, CA: RAND.

Stern, D., Dayton, C. and Raby, M. (2010) *Career Academies: A Proven Strategy to Prepare High School Students for College and Careers.* Berkeley, CA: University of California Berkeley Career Academy Support Network.

Stipanovic, N., Lewis, M.V. and Stringfield, S. (2012) 'Situating programs of study within current and historical career and technical educational reform efforts', *International Journal of Educational Reform,* 21: 80–97.

Stone, J.R. III. (2013) 'Programs of study, college, and career readiness: career and technical education and making high school matter', paper presented at the 2013 Annual Meeting of the American Educational Research Association. Available from http://www.aera.net/Publications/OnlinePaperRepository/AERAOnlinePaperRepository/tabid/12720/Default.aspx (accessed 26 September 2014).

Stone, J.R., III and Aliaga, O.A. (2003) *Career and Technical Education, Career Pathways, and Work-Based Learning: Changes in Participation 1997–1999.* St Paul, MN: National Research Center for Career and Technical Education, University of Minnesota.

Stone, J.R. III, Alfeld, C. and Pearson, D. (2008) 'Rigor and relevance: testing a model of enhanced math learning in career and technical education', *American Educational Research Journal,* 45(3): 767–95.

Stone, J.R. III., Alfeld, C., Pearson, D., Lewis, M. and Jensen, S. (2006) *Building Academic Skills in Context: Testing the Value of Enhanced Mathematics Learning in CTE.* Available from http://www.nrccte.org/resources/publications/building-academic-skills-context-testing-value-enhanced-math-learning-cte (accessed 26 September 2014).

Symonds, W.C., Schwartz, R. and Ferguson, R.F. (2011) *Pathways to Prosperity: Meeting the Challenge of Preparing Young Americans for the 21st Century.* Cambridge, MA: Harvard University.

US Department of Education (2013) *Performance of US 15-Year-Old Students in Mathematics, Science, and Reading Literacy in an International Context: First Look at PISA 2012* (NCES 2014–024). Washington, DC: National Center for Education Statistics.

Withington, C., Hammond, C., Mobley, C., Stipanovic, N., Sharp, J.L., Stringfield, S. and Drew, S. (2012) 'Implementing a statewide mandated career pathways/programs of study school reform model: Select findings from a multisite case study', *International Journal of Educational Reform,* 21: 138–58.

PART V

Assessment and the Curriculum

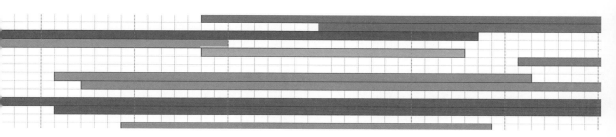

43

Assessment and the Curriculum

Wynne Harlen

INTRODUCTION

The powerful influence of the assessment of students on the curriculum and pedagogy has been a feature of education throughout its history. In recent years the results of student assessment have been used in a range of ways from helping learning to evaluating teachers, schools and national systems. This chapter focuses on student assessment for three main purposes: formative (for helping learning), summative (for reporting on learning) and evaluative (for monitoring performance at school or national levels). After clarifying how various terms relating to the theory and practice of assessment are being used, the main sections focus on the nature, functions and relationship between assessment for formative and summative purposes. Less attention is paid to the role of student assessment in evaluation since this receives attention in other chapters of the handbook.

CLARIFYING TERMS

Many of the terms used in discussing assessment have both technical and commonplace usage, which can impede good communication. Words such as assessment, appraisal, evaluation, testing and measurement are sometimes used interchangeably in everyday discourse, but in the context of education have precise and distinct meanings. Possible confusion of evaluation and assessment is made worse in languages such as French and Spanish in which the same word is used for both. In this chapter, in line with the distinction made by the Organisation for Economic Co-operation and Development (OECD) in its reviews of evaluation and assessment (Nusche et al., 2012: 24), we use the term 'assessment' to refer to judgements about student learning and 'evaluation' when referring to judgements about schools, systems and policies. However, there is no hard and fast usage, even in professional discourse, and the meaning of the term being used in a particular case is generally made clear in the context.

Concepts of Assessment of Students' Learning

The process of assessment is described by Popham (2000) as one of drawing inferences about what students know or can do from their responses in certain situations. These might be naturally occurring or specially created, but are always only a sample of the situations that could be used.

The conception of assessment as a process of drawing inferences from data is built upon by Pellegrino et al. (2001: 42) in describing assessment of all kinds as 'reasoning from evidence' (a phrase also used by Mislevy, 1996). This process of reasoning is described by Pellegrino and colleagues in terms of three key elements:

- A theory or set of beliefs about how students learn
- The tasks to which students respond in order to show what they have learnt
- The reasoning and interpretation that turns data (of what students can do) into information (about what has been achieved). (Pellegrino et al., 2001: 42)

These elements are represented as the corners of a triangle in which each is connected to the others (see Figure 43.1).

Lines linking the performance of tasks and interpretation represent the dependence of what is assessed on the task and also how it

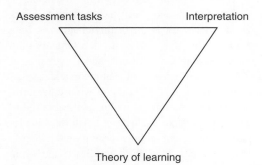

Figure 43.1   The assessment triangle

Source: Adapted from Pellegrino et al., 2001.

is interpreted in terms of achievement. This is particularly clear in the case of items in a test: what a simple test item assesses will depend as much on the mark scheme (rubric) as on the question, but it applies equally to the results of interpreting any form of data about students' performance.

The links between 'assessment tasks' and 'interpretation' and 'theory of learning' indicate that beliefs about how learning takes place will influence the kind of data sought and collected and how it is turned into information about the knowledge and skills being assessed. It underlines the need for the tasks and situations that enable students' performances to be observed to be consistent with the model of learning. Similarly, the methods of interpretation through which inferences are drawn must also reflect the model of how students learn. As Pellegrino et al. (2001) note, the role of theories of learning in decisions about assessment is often overlooked. For instance, issues concerning the acceptability of using assessment results for accountability rest on the understanding of how people learn and how to measure that learning.

Other definitions spell out the processes involved in assessment in more operational detail. For example, Harlen (2013) describes assessment as the generation and collection of data, the interpretation of the data to produce a judgement, and the communication and use of the judgement. The inclusion of 'generation' here is a reminder that decisions are made about what will be taken as evidence of learning and achievement because there has to be a selection from the innumerable possibilities to be found in students' behaviour. There are also numerous decisions (influenced, as indicated in the assessment triangle, by the implicit or explicit view of learning) to be made about:

- The kind of activity in which students are engaged (for example, special task or regular work);
- Who will collect data from that activity (for example, teacher, students or an external agent);
- How the data will be collected (for example, by observation or as writing, drawing or other artefacts);

- How the data will be interpreted (for example, by reference to norms, criteria or to a student's prior performance); and
- How the resulting judgement will be recorded and communicated (for example, as a score, grade, or description).

Different assessment tools – ways of providing evidence from which inferences can be drawn about what students know or can do – are created by different combinations of these various ways of collecting, judging and communicating data. For example, a standardised test is a tool comprising tasks created by an external agency that will have trialled the test during development with a large sample of the appropriate population in order that an individual's score can be expressed in terms of comparison with the 'norm' for that population. The result will indicate whether a student's performance is above or below average but not what he or she can do. A criterion-referenced test differs from a norm-referenced test by being designed to give information about what a student can do in relation to specified outcomes. The items will be chosen for their relevance to the curriculum so that the results can be used in establishing, not how a student compares with others, but how his or her performance compares with the intended performance. When tests are used the data are restricted to the items in the test, whereas if the assessment is carried out by teachers there is the potential to use evidence from a wider range of activities in making judgements.

The basis for choosing what are the most appropriate methods and tools depends on the purpose of the assessment and what is required in terms of validity and reliability to serve that purpose. Before discussing various purposes and uses of assessment, we therefore need to consider the meaning of these properties.

VALIDITY, RELIABILITY AND DEPENDABILITY

One obvious desirable property of any assessment tool is that it should enable valid inferences to be drawn – that it assesses what it is intended to assess. Another is that it should provide reliable or trustworthy data. These properties are not independent of one another, but interact – making changes that affect one property has implications for another. There is a trade-off between them, as we see later.

Validity

There are various ways of judging the validity of an assessment tool. One way is just to look to see if it appears to require the use of the knowledge or skill that it is intended to assess. This is described as 'face validity'. A more formal version of this is 'content validity', where there is some analysis of what content is covered by the assessment and what is found, is checked to see if it reflects the range of content intended to be assessed. 'Construct validity' is a broader concept relating to the full range of skills, knowledge or attitudes – the constructs – that are being assessed.

Important requirements of an assessment are that it samples all aspects, but only those aspects of students' achievement that are relevant to the particular purpose of the assessment. Including what is irrelevant is as much a threat to validity as omitting relevant aspects. The amount of reading required by a question in a test, where reading ability is not the construct being assessed, is a common problem. Often the attempt to set a question or task in a real context in order to engage students' interest, or to see if they can transfer learning into other contexts, extends the reading demand. What is then assessed is a combination of reading skills and the intended construct, and the validity of the result as a measure of the intended construct is consequently reduced. The assessment is said to suffer from 'construct irrelevance' because the result will depend on things other than the intended construct.

Another form of validity, consequential validity, is not a property only of the assessment tool itself but refers to how appropriate the assessment results are for the uses to which they are put. For example, a test of arithmetic items may be perfectly valid as a test of arithmetic, but not valid if used to make judgements about mathematical ability more generally. This extends the concept of validity beyond the quality of the assessment tool itself to include the uses made of the assessment results for purposes other than, and including, those for which the original assessment was designed and conducted.

Reliability

The reliability of an assessment refers to the extent to which the results can be said to be of acceptable consistency and precision for a particular use. Reliability is defined as (and where possible) estimated quantitatively by the extent to which the assessment, if repeated, would give the same result. There are many factors that can affect the reliability of an assessment. Reliability is reduced if, for instance, the results are influenced by the particular sample of possible items or tasks a student is required to attempt. It will be reduced also if the outcomes are dependent on who conducts the assessment (which teacher or oral examiner), or on who rates the students' performances (which marker or observer). The particular occasion on which the assessment takes place and the circumstances under which it is undertaken can also affect the assessment outcome and contribute to reduced reliability.

Reliability has meaning mostly in the case of summative assessment and particularly for tests. When assessment is used formatively (and no judgement of grade or level is involved, only the judgement of how to help a student take the next steps in learning) reliability in its formal sense is not an issue. However, high reliability is necessary when the results are used by others and when students are being compared or selected.

Tests are often chosen as the assessment tool in the interests of fairness, based on the questionable assumption that giving students all the same items and conditions provides them with equal opportunities. Individual students' responses to the same conditions will vary from day to day and, most importantly, the particular selection of items in a test will be found more difficult by some students than by others equally able. All test items (apart from those in IQ-type tests) present questions in some context and there is research evidence that students who perform well in one item will not necessarily do so in another item that is testing the same concepts or skills but in a different content. The content effect has been shown in the context of practical science assessment (Pine et al., 2006; Qualter, 1985), and it also applies to written tests, where there is generally a large number of possible items of which only a small sample can be included in a test of reasonable length. A different selection would produce a different result, giving rise to what is described as the 'sampling error' (a contributor to low reliability), which is typically greater the fewer items there are in the test. As a result, there is considerable uncertainty about what might be the 'correct' result for individual students. Black and Wiliam (2012: 254) estimated that in the case of a national reading test for 11-year-olds, the score of a student given 64 per cent might vary between 52 per cent and 76 per cent.

Interaction of Reliability and Validity

A way of reducing this source of error would be to increase the range of content included for each competence assessed and therefore the number of items used. But the length of a test cannot be greatly increased without incurring other forms of error (student fatigue, for instance) and so more items per skill or concept would mean fewer skills and concepts included, thus reducing the range of what is assessed and reducing the validity of the test. This illustrates a trade-off between validity and reliability that applies to all assessment tools, but it is most readily identified in relation to using tests. Attempts to increase reliability of tests favour items assessing factual knowledge in a closed item format that can be readily marked as correct or incorrect, limiting the range covered in the test. Attempts to increase validity by widening the range of items (for example, by including more open-response items) where more judgement is needed in marking will mean that the reliability is reduced.

Dependability

The interaction of the concepts of validity and reliability led to the introduction of the term 'dependability' to refer to the 'intersection of reliability and validity' (Wiliam, 1993). Although it has no meaningful numerical value, it can be a convenient term for the overall quality and usefulness of an assessment. Stobart (2008) points out that there are several factors that 'pull against' the development of assessment procedures that provide the most dependable information for a particular purpose. One of these is 'the pull of manageability', which refers to resources of time, expertise and cost to those involved in creating and using the assessment materials and procedures. There is a limit to the time and expertise that can be used in developing and operating, for example, a highly reliable external test or examination.

PURPOSES AND USES
OF ASSESSMENT

According to Atkin and Black (2003), the idea of making a distinction between formative and summative purposes originated in the late 1960s (Tyler et al., 1967) in the context of curriculum evaluation, where formative evaluation described the effort to improve a programme rather than to judge it definitively. The distinction was soon adopted in the context of student assessment to differentiate between classroom assessment as part of learning and teaching and assessment as judging learning outcomes. As the terms

'formative' and 'summative' appeared rather formal and academic, in communicating with teachers the alternative phrases 'assessment *for* learning' and 'assessment *of* learning' were also used by the Assessment Reform Group (ARG, 1999), amongst others.

When national tests and assessments were introduced in England and Wales in 1988 the report of the National Curriculum Task Group on Assessment and Testing (TGAT) discussed four main purposes for which information from student assessment could be used:

1 Formative, so that the positive achievements of a student may be recognised and discussed and the appropriate next steps may be planned;
2 Diagnostic, through which learning difficulties may be scrutinised and classified so that appropriate remedial help and guidance can be provided;
3 Summative, for the recording of the overall achievement of a student in a systematic way;
4 Evaluative, by means of which some aspects of the work of a school, an LEA or other discrete part of the educational service can be assessed and/or reported upon. (TGAT, 1988: para 23)

Having stated these four purposes, however, the Task Group quickly rejected the distinction between formative and diagnostic on the ground that any well designed formative assessment would provide information to help in the diagnosis of strengths and weaknesses (1988: para 27). Although diagnosis of learning difficulties is still seen as distinct by some (for example, Csapó, 2014), it is more generally regarded as a form of formative assessment that is particularly close to learning. This acknowledges that there is a range of practices that can serve a formative purpose rather than a single one, a point that becomes evident later when we discuss the nature of formative assessment and its relationship with summative assessment.

The number of 'purposes' of student assessment is therefore reduced to three: formative, summative and evaluative. There is, however, a possible distinction to be made between the purpose of the assessment – the reasons for conducting it – and the use made of the results. For example, information collected and used for a formative purpose may be used for a summative purpose. Similarly, summative information about individual students may be aggregated into group data for evaluative purposes.

Results of students' summative assessment can used in several ways, not all of which are appropriate or valid uses. Newton (2012) identified 16 uses of the results of national tests in England. These ranged from programme evaluation, target setting for students and schools, school monitoring and student selection to school choice by parents, and even the valuation of property in the areas of schools with high or low test scores. In some cases, it is legitimate to use measures of student performance as part of the data used in making judgements (for instance, as an element in school evaluation), but using it as a sole measure – and particularly where rewards and penalties are attached – invites inappropriate actions to inflate the measured performance, a point to which we return later. It is, however, hard to maintain a distinction between uses, and it is more useful to consider the difference between intended uses and what is actually done with the results (Mansell et al., 2009).

FORMATIVE ASSESSMENT

The processes through which assessment is used to achieve the purpose of helping learning can be represented as a continuing cycle of events, as shown in Figure 43.2. A, B and C represent activities through which students work towards goals of a particular lesson or series of lessons. If we break into the continuing cycle of events at activity A, evidence is gathered during this activity and is interpreted in terms of progress towards the goals of the lesson or topic. Some notion of progression in relation to the goals is needed for this interpretation so that the point students have reached can be used to indicate the next step. Following around the cycle clockwise, the identification of appropriate next steps and decisions about how to take them leads to activity B. The cycle is repeated and the effects of decisions at one time are assessed at

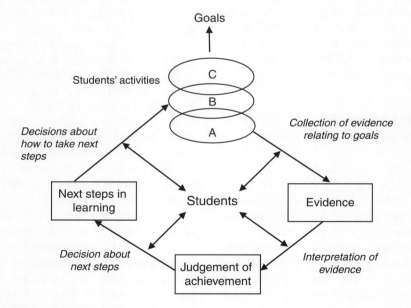

Figure 43.2 Formative assessment as a cyclic process

Source: Adapted from Harlen, 2006a.

a later time as part of the ongoing process. In this way, evidence of current learning is fed back into teaching and learning.

Figure 43.2 represents a framework for thinking about what and how students are learning and using this information to help further learning. Its main features are:

- Clear goals for the lesson or series of lessons that the teacher shares with students.
- Students at the centre of the process, acknowledging that they are the ones who do the learning.
- Students taking part in gathering and interpreting evidence of learning in relation to the goals.
- Teacher and students together making decisions about next steps and how to take them.
- Teachers providing feedback to students and using feedback from students to adjust teaching.

Students have an important role in their own assessment as they come to understand the process, to learn to work towards explicit goals and quality of work and to modify what they do in relation to feedback from teachers (Stiggins, 2001). This role is emphasized in the definition of formative assessment provided by the ARG as 'the process of seeking and interpreting evidence for use by learners and their teachers to decide where the learners are in their learning, where they need to go and how best to get there' (ARG, 2002: n.p.). However, it is the role of feedback that is given prominence in the OECD definition of formative assessment as 'frequent, interactive assessments of student progress and understanding to identify learning needs and adjust teaching appropriately' (OECD, 2005: 21).

Feedback is given to the teacher and also to the students. The information gathered about students' progress provides feedback to the teacher, who can then adjust the pace or challenge of the learning activities – or regulate the teaching – to maximise opportunities for learning. Feedback from teachers to students has been described as 'one of the most powerful influences on learning and achievement' (Hattie and Timperley, 2007). Feedback helps learning when it provides

comments on how students can improve their work but not grades or marks, as revealed in a well-designed study by Butler (1988). One of the outcomes of Butler's study was that feedback in terms of comments-only led to higher achievement for all students and all tasks. An interesting result was that providing both comments and marks was no more effective than marks alone. It appears that students seize upon marks and ignore any comments that accompany them. When marks are absent they engage with what the teacher wants to bring to their attention. The comments can then improve learning as intended by the teacher. Wiliam (2010), in a review of research on feedback, also found that the main features of effective feedback were giving students explanations and specific activities to improve. Although many of the studies of feedback have concerned older students, Wiliam found that 'attitudes to learning are shaped by the feedback that they receive from a very early age' (Wiliam, 2010: 144).

Feedback is also more effective in promoting learning if it involves students in the process of deciding what their next steps should be so they are not the passive recipients of the teacher's judgments of their work. Students will direct their efforts more effectively if they know the purpose of their activities, which means not just knowing what to do but what they are trying to achieve in terms of quality as well as goals.

The practice of formative assessment has been spread more widely since several reviews of classroom assessment provided evidence of its effectiveness in improving learning (Bangert-Drownes et al., 1991; Black, 1993; Black and Wiliam, 1998a; Crooks, 1988; Kulik et al., 1990; Natriello, 1987). The review by Black and Wiliam (1998a) attracted worldwide attention, partly because of the attempt to quantify the impact of using formative assessment. A key finding was that 'improved formative assessment helps the (so-called) low attainers more than the rest, and so reduces the spread of attainment whilst raising it overall' (Black and Wiliam, 1998b: 4).

Varieties of Formative Assessment

Implementation in different contexts has led to different forms of formative assessment being proposed. For example, Carless (2007) has proposed that teachers anticipate students' reactions by using what is known about commonly held misconceptions. He described this as 'pre-emptive' formative assessment and contrasted it with 'reactive' formative assessment, which happens 'after incomplete understanding has occurred' (Carless, 2007: 176). He acknowledges, however, that what is known about misconceptions will not apply to all students. Cowie and Bell (1999) proposed two variants of formative assessment: planned and interactive. They described planned formative assessment as being prepared ahead of time, possibly in the form of a brief classroom test or special tasks given to the whole class. Interactive formative assessment, on the other hand, arose within the learning activities, was used to help the learning of individuals and could include more than only the cognitive aspects of learning. Glover and Thomas (1999) described a rather similar approach as 'dynamic' formative assessment.

These variants serve to underline the point made earlier that formative assessment is not a particular set of actions, but a framework for using information about students' ideas and skills to help further learning. With no prescribed route to follow, implementing formative learning is not easy. It requires knowledge of how to gather and use evidence of students' progress in learning and how to provide effective learning environments to support further progress.

Gathering Evidence in Formative Assessment

Gathering evidence as part of classroom activities involves using strategies for 'making thinking visible' (Michaels et al., 2008).

The main methods for doing this fall under the following:

- Questioning using open questions that encourage students to explain their thinking, rather than closed quiz-type questions to which they are expected to give 'the right answer'.
- Observing students during regular work (this includes listening and discussing with them).
- Studying the products of their regular work (including writing, drawings, artefacts and actions, notebooks).
- Embedding special activities into class work (such as concept-mapping, diagnostic tasks) and observing students and/or studying the resulting products.
- Using computer programs to analyse students' answers to carefully constructed questions and tasks.

Examples of these methods are given in Harlen and Qualter (2014). These methods are carried out by teachers, which is necessary if the teacher is to take action based on the information to help learning. But it is also important to note that it is not the fact of the information being collected by teachers that makes the assessment formative – both formative and summative assessment can be based on teacher-based data, but assessment is only formative when the information is used to decide appropriate next steps for students and to adapt teaching accordingly.

SUMMATIVE ASSESSMENT

Summative assessment has the purpose of summarising and reporting what has been learned at a particular time, and for that reason is also called 'assessment of learning'. It can involve summarising and reviewing learning over a period of time, and/or checking-up by testing learning at a particular time. Although it does not have the direct impact on learning as it takes place, as in the case of formative assessment, it can nevertheless be used to help learning in a less direct way when results are used, for example, to make decisions about courses or teaching.

Summative assessment is important for a number of reasons:

- Providing dependable reports of individual students' achievement and progress in learning.
- Enabling the achievements of groups of students to be monitored (such as higher and lower achieving students, groups formed by gender or ethnicity), providing information that can be used to monitor equity in educational opportunities.
- Providing exemplars and operational definitions of terms such as understanding, applying learning, using skills.
- Making standards and expectations clear to students, teachers and other users.
- Helping learning in the medium and long term.
- Supporting the process of formative assessment.

In addition, it is worth noting that summative assessment cannot usually be avoided because it is part of the teacher's required tasks, which are established at school or national level. By contrast, formative assessment can be considered to be voluntary in that it is part of the teaching process that teachers decide for themselves. Formative assessment can be urged in guidelines and official documents, but cannot be mandated in the same way as summative assessment.

Figure 43.3 represents summative assessment as a process of using evidence to report on achievement. It involves the collection and interpretation of evidence in relation to goals achieved over a period of time, rather than the goals relating to a lesson. The evidence can be gathered from tests, special tasks or regular activities and in a number of different forms, such as written answers, artefacts constructed by students, portfolios, observation of actions, discussion or presentations of work. Achievement is judged by comparison with criteria or standards relating to the goals. The judging (marking or scoring) can be carried out by the teacher or by an external agency, as in the case of some national tests and examinations.

The interpretation of evidence necessarily reduces the richness of the actual performance to something that represents it, such as a score, category or mark, and therefore a great deal of information is lost. When results are used to compare students, particularly when high stakes selection or grading is involved, the procedure will generally include steps for increasing reliability of the result, such as checking marking and moderating judgements by teachers or examiners.

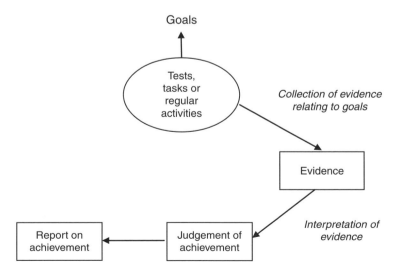

Figure 43.3 Assessment for summative purposes

Source: Adapted from Harlen, 2006a.

Summative assessment in any form has an impact on the content of the curriculum and on pedagogy. What is assessed will inevitably influence decisions about what is to be taught and how. The impact can be to limit or distort what is taught if the assessment tools used do not adequately reflect intended goals, for example using tests of facts when application of ideas is the aim. The impact is exacerbated by use of student outcomes, usually in the form of test scores, for high stakes evaluation of teachers and schools. Pressure on teachers to increase test results is transferred to students, even if the tests are not high stakes of the students. The result can often be that we end up teaching students to pass tests and allowing the assessment to dictate the curriculum.

Gathering Evidence for Summative Assessment

The use of tests to find out what a student knows or can do is a time-honoured approach to summative assessment. It is an attractive approach for certain purposes, particularly when students are effectively in competition with one another because each student can be given the same task or asked the same questions in the same conditions. There is a wide range of types of test, with various kinds of task (written, performance or computer-based) and ways of responding. One of the requirements, if valid inferences are to be drawn from results, is that the method of assessment should be consistent with what is known about the way students learn best (discussed earlier in relation to Figure 43.1) and thus enable them to show what they can do. For some outcomes, a written test may not provide this opportunity if the learning goals required students to work in groups or in collaboration with others.

The emphasis on dialogue and group interaction found in contemporary views of learning (Bransford et al., 2000) reflects a socio-cultural constructivist perspective in which understanding is developed through making sense of new experience with others rather than by working individually; however, as James (2012) points out, much formal testing still relies heavily upon behaviourist approaches to learning. Research has cast some doubt on whether the responses in such formal setting really enable valid inferences to be drawn about what students' can achieve. For example, when Dolin and Krogh (2010) adapted science questions from the OECD's Programme for International Student Assessment (PISA) tests so that students could investigate and discuss the problems posed before giving their answers, they found a 25-per cent increase in students' performance judged using the PISA scoring criteria.

Given the short-comings of tests, we need to consider how to provide information about students' achievements in which the curriculum dictates the assessment, rather than vice versa. Alternatives are based on the recognition of learning activities aimed at developing ideas and abilities that provide opportunities for their progress to be assessed. The teacher can use this information summatively, as well as formatively. The limitation on the range of evidence that can be obtained by testing does not apply when assessment is teacher-based. Evidence from regular activities can be supplemented, if necessary, by evidence from specially devised tasks embedded in the learning activities to provide opportunities for students to use their skills and understanding. Observation during regular work also enables information to be gathered about processes of learning, not only about products. Such information is useful to those selecting students for advanced vocational or academic courses of study where the extent to which students have learned how to learn, and are likely to benefit from further study, is as important as what they have already learned.

The most commonly expressed criticism of assessment by teachers concerns the reliability of the results. It can be the case that when no steps are taken to assure quality, teachers' judgements are prone to a number of potential errors. Research reviewed by Harlen (2004a, 2004b) reports evidence of bias in judging performance in particular tasks because of teachers taking into account information about non-relevant aspects of students' behaviour or being apparently influenced by gender, special educational needs, or the general or verbal ability of a student. However, there are several effective ways in which reliability can be improved to a level equal to and even exceeding that of tests. The main ones are group moderation, using examples, and using a test or task as a check (examples are given in Harlen, 1994).

The absence of reference to students in Figure 43.3 acknowledges that they generally do not have a role in summative assessment, apart from very informal classroom tests. However, if the assessment process is an open one, in which criteria are shared with students and users of the results, there is an opportunity for students to have a role in the process, for example when selecting items in a portfolio. This form of portfolio is not a sample of all a student's work over a period of time, but reflects the best performance at the time of reporting. The evidence is accumulated gradually by retaining what is best at any time in a folder, or other form of portfolio (such as computer files), and replacing pieces with better evidence as it is produced. Such an approach enables students to have a

role in their summative assessment by taking part in the selection of items in the folder or portfolio, a process for which they need some understanding of the broad goals and quality criteria by which their work will be judged. The Queensland portfolio system (Queensland Studies Authority (QSA), 2008) is an example showing how this approach can be used, even for high stakes assessment.

RELATIONSHIP BETWEEN ASSESSMENT FOR FORMATIVE AND SUMMATIVE PURPOSES

From this discussion of assessment for formative and summative purposes, it appears that there are several key differences between them, but there are also some similarities, suggesting that the relationship might be described more as a dimension than a dichotomy. Table 43.1 describes how aspects of practice and use of information vary at points along a dimension from formative to summative.

At the extremes are the practices and uses that most typify assessment for learning and assessment of learning. At the purely formative end is assessment that is integral to student–teacher interaction and in which students have a role. This is the practice

Table 43.1   A dimension of assessment purposes and practices

| | Formative | | Summative | |
	Informal formative	Formal formative	Informal summative	Formal summative
Major focus	Progression towards lesson/topic goals		What has been achieved at a certain time	
Purpose	To inform next steps in learning	To inform next steps in teaching	To monitor progress against plans	To record achievements of individuals
How evidence collected	As normal part of class work	Introduced into normal class work	Introduced into normal class work	Separate task or test
When evidence is collected	During learning	Regularly as part of class work	At intervals during a course	After learning
Judged by	Student and teacher	Teacher	Teacher	Teacher or external marker
Form of judgement	Decision about next steps	Mark or comment	Mark or comment	Score, grade, mark or level
Action taken	Feedback to students and teacher	Feedback into teaching plans	Feedback into teaching plans	Provision of report on achievement

described in Figure 43.2, called 'interactive' by Cowie and Bell (1999) and 'dynamic' by Glover and Thomas (1999). Its main purpose is to enable teachers and students to identify the next steps in learning and know how to take these. At the purely summative right-hand end of the dimension the purpose is to give a measure of what students have achieved at certain times. For this purpose, the assessment should provide a dependable report on the achievements of each individual student. Between these extremes of the dimension it is possible to identify a range of procedures having various roles in teaching and learning. For instance, many teachers begin a new topic by finding out what the students already know – the purpose is to inform the teaching plans rather than to identify the point of development of each individual ('planned' formative assessment). This may not be very different from an informal test that a teacher gives at the end of a section of work to assess whether new ideas have been grasped or need consolidation. The purpose here may also be to guide teaching and it differs from the planned formative assessment only in that formative comes before and summative after teaching, although it also informs further teaching.

Using Evidence for Formative and Summative Purposes

The relationship suggested in Table 43.1 raises questions about whether evidence collected for one purpose can also, in appropriate circumstances, be used for another. Can evidence collected for formative purposes also be used for summative purposes? Can evidence collected for summative assessment be used for formative assessment? If the answer to these questions is positive, then what does that say about the usefulness of distinguishing between formative and summative assessment? Harlen (2006b, 2012) discusses these questions, concluding that there is an asymmetry in using evidence for the two purposes that limits its dual use.

Evidence gathered for formative purposes from observation and experience of innumerable events in the classroom, interpreted in terms of the goals of the lesson, provides information about ongoing learning (see Figure 43.2). If this evidence is also used to report achievement of course or end-of-stage goals, then it has to be reinterpreted in terms of criteria related to these broader goals. This is usually carried out by finding the best fit between the evidence and the criteria for different levels or standards of achievement, giving greater weight to more recent work. In order for the advantages of basing the summative assessment on the wide range of classroom activities, rather than on a test or set of special tasks to be realised, the learning tasks must reflect the full range of intended goals. Working with secondary teachers, Black et al. (2010) found it necessary to help teachers to improve students' learning tasks if they were to provide valid evidence reflecting the learning goals. The answer to the question of whether formative assessment, necessarily gathered by teachers, can also be used in summative assessment is that this is possible, but, as in all assessment, its validity will depend on the evidence gathered and how it is interpreted.

The second question is whether evidence gathered specifically for summative assessment, by tests or special tasks or a summation of coursework grades, can also serve formative purposes. Black et al. (2003) included the formative use of summative assessment as one of four practices that teachers found effective as ways of implementing formative assessment (the others being questioning, feedback by marking, and student peer- and self-assessment). Teachers devised various ways of using classroom tests to enable students to identify their areas of weakness and focus further effort. Using informal summative assessment (Table 43.1) in this way is common practice for many teachers, but whether more formal summative assessment can have a formative role depends upon the frequency and nature of the tests or special tasks. Although the marking of some external tests and examinations can be reviewed (by obtaining marked scripts and discussing them with students), in practice the approach is one that teachers use principally in the context of classroom tests over which they have complete control. Indeed, Black et al. (2003) noted that when external tests are involved, the process could move from developing understanding to 'teaching to the test'. However, although the teachers working with the researchers used their creativity to graft formative value onto summative procedures, in general the evidence available from formal summative assessment is just not sufficiently detailed to support a role in helping learning.

A factor that may well change the relationship between formative and summative assessment is the burgeoning role of information and communications technology (ICT) in all aspects of education, including assessment. A review of developments in computer-based assessment, or eAssessment, by Redecker and Johannessen (2013) suggests that the applications of ICT can go beyond increasing the efficiency of tests and automating scoring. By tracking students' moves in computer-based tasks, not only can the assessment of some twenty-first-century skills (such as problem-solving, risk-taking, collaboration and creativity) be assessed but there is also the potential for formative feedback to learners and teachers, giving real-time information about the needs and progress of each individual learner. However, Redecker and Johannessen also affirm that the effective use of eAssessment requires a paradigm change away from testing to 'a completely new way of learning and assessing', (p. 89) which results from using technology to serve new pedagogical approaches rather than merely supporting existing approaches.

ASSESSMENT FOR EVALUATIVE PURPOSES

The OECD, from its reviews of evaluation and assessment in education in various countries, reports a growing interest in evaluating school performance. There is also a greater focus on using results for accountability of policymakers, school leaders and teachers in response to an increased demand for effectiveness, equity and quality in education. There is, therefore, a need for measures that enable the effect of changes to be monitored and comparisons to be made across systems and countries. Student assessment data, often collected for other reasons such as reporting individual student learning, has a major part in the evaluation of school effectiveness.

The performance of schools based on the average achievement of students is frequently used to make judgements of:

• How performance compares with a set of standards or targets;
• How a school compares with others; and
• Whether performance changes from year to year.

In order to provide a common measure for these comparisons, national tests are used in many countries and targets are set in terms of the levels of achievement to be reached by students at particular ages. Examples are the national tests given to all eligible students in England at ages 7 and 11 and the requirements of the No Child Left Behind Act in the US.

When schools are subject to sanctions if targets are missed, the impact of these tests can be detrimental to the curriculum experienced by students. This negative impact is compounded because what can be included in tests given to all students reflects only what can be most easily and reliably assessed in this way. Research shows that when this happens, teachers focus on the test content, train students in how to pass tests and feel impelled to adopt teaching styles that do not match what is needed to develop real understanding. There is now a large body of research evidence from many countries on the negative impact of high stakes use of test data (for example, Harlen and Deakin Crick, 2003; Nordenbo et al., 2009).

Of course schools have to be held accountable for the learning of their students, but this needs to be conducted in a manner that provides a fair and more complete picture of the curriculum and also takes into account the varied circumstances and nature of the school intake. To serve the evaluative purpose well, the assessment data should include a broad range of outcomes that reflect the aims of twenty-first-century education. Several of these outcomes, such as communication skills, problem solving and critical thinking are not easily measured and require qualitative as well as quantitative data.

Student achievement data are also used for evaluation at system and national levels for making judgements similar to those for schools: comparison with standards, comparison with other countries and trends over time. In this case, however, it is not necessary for all students to be tested; rather, a matrix sampling approach can be used whereby a large number of test items can be used, of which any one student need only attempt a few of those used in a survey. National surveys of this kind, as used in Scotland, New Zealand and France, divide the total number of items into sub-tests given to a random sample of the population. This is the design used in international surveys of Trends in International Mathematics and Science Study (TIMSS) and PISA, and also in national surveys, such as those conducted by the National Assessment of Educational Progress (NAEP) in the US and in the Assessment of Performance Unit (APU) when it operated in England, Wales and Northern Ireland in the 1980s (Foxman et al., 1991). Since 2010, matrix sampling in England is conducted only for students at the end of the primary school in science.

When different items are given to different student samples, there is no need to cram a number of short items into a short test and more time can be given for students to engage with a particular context. Results are only meaningful when aggregated to report at regional or national levels and so cannot be used for individual school evaluation, unless a sufficient sample of students is tested to be representative of a school or district. In this way national data are collected without

adding high stakes to the assessment of students. Wide reporting of results of national sample surveys enables the information to be used formatively at the system level, providing feedback that can be used to identify aspects of the curriculum that may need attention. For schools, the results have value in focusing attention on their own practice in the areas identified as weaknesses nationally.

CONCLUSION

This chapter has been concerned with questions about the nature, purposes and uses of student assessment. In conclusion, it is perhaps appropriate to step back from the detail of specific answers and identify some principles implicit in how these questions have been addressed. Principles convey the values that guide what we do and the standards by which our actions should be judged. The following principles, first identified by Harlen (2010) in Gardner et al. (2010), have implicitly guided the approach we have taken and they constitute a rationale for what has, or has not, been included.

- Assessment of any kind should ultimately improve learning.
- Assessment methods should enable progress in all important learning goals to be facilitated and reported.
- Assessment procedures should include explicit processes to ensure that information is valid and is as reliable as necessary for its purpose.
- Assessment should promote public understanding of learning goals relevant to pupils' current and future lives.
- Assessment of learning outcomes should be treated as approximations, subject to unavoidable errors.
- Assessment should be part of a process of teaching that enables pupils to understand the aims of their learning and how the quality of their work will be judged.
- Assessment methods should promote the active engagement of pupils in their learning and its assessment.
- Assessment should enable and motivate pupils to show what they can do.
- Assessment should combine information of different kinds, including pupils' self-assessments,

- to inform decisions about pupils' learning and achievements.
- Assessment methods should meet standards that reflect a broad consensus on quality at all levels from classroom practice to national policy. (Gardner et al., 2010: 30)

REFERENCES

Assessment Reform Group (ARG) (1999) *Assessment for Learning*. Assessment Reform Group. Available from http://www.aaia.org.uk/content/uploads/2010/06/Assessment-for-Learning-Beyond-the-Black-Box.pdf (accessed 14 July 2015).

Assessment Reform Group (ARG) (2002) *Assessment for Learning: 10 Principles*. Assessment Reform Group. Available from http://www.aaia.org.uk/content/uploads/2010/06/Assessment-for-Learning-10-principles.pdf (accessed 14 July 2015).

Atkin, J.M. and Black, P.J. (2003) *Inside Science Education Reform: A History of Curricular and Policy Change*. New York, NY: Teachers' College Press.

Bangert-Drownes, R.L., Kulik, J.A. and Kulik, C.L.C. (1991) 'Effects of frequent classroom testing', *Journal of Educational Research*, 85: 89–99.

Black, P.J. (1993) 'Formative and summative assessment by teachers', *Studies in Science Education*, 21: 49–97.

Black, P.J. and Wiliam, D. (1998a) 'Assessment and classroom learning', *Assessment in Education*, 5(1): 7–74.

Black. P.J. and Wiliam, D. (1998b) *Inside the Black Box*. London: King's College.

Black, P.J. and Wiliam, D. (2012) 'The reliability of assessments', in J. Gardner (ed.), *Assessment and Learning*. London: Sage Publications. pp. 243–63.

Black, P.J., Harrison, C., Hodgen, J., Marshall, B., Wiliam, D. and Serret, N. (2010) 'Validity in teachers' summative assessment', *Assessment in Education*, 17(2): 215–32.

Black, P.J., Harrison, C., Marshall, B. and Wiliam, D. (2003) *Assessment for Learning: Putting it into Practice*. Buckingham, UK: Open University Press.

Bransford, J.D., Brown, A. and Cocking, R.R. (eds.) (2000) *How People Learn, Brain, Mind,* *Experience and School*. Washington, DC: National Academy Press.

Butler, R. (1988) 'Enhancing and undermining intrinsic motivation: the effects of task-involving and ego-involving evaluation on interest and performance', *British Journal of Educational Psychology*, 58(1): 1–14.

Carless, D. (2007) 'Conceptualising pre-emptive formative assessment', *Assessment in Education*, 14(2): 171–84.

Cowie, B. and Bell, B. (1999) 'A model of formative assessment in science education', *Assessment in Education*, 6(1): 101–16.

Crooks, T.J. (1988) 'The impact of classroom evaluation practices on students', *Review of Educational Research*, 58: 438–81.

Csapó, B. (2014) 'Improving science learning through valid assessments: diagnostics and inquiry', paper presented at the IAP Science Education Programme Biennial Conference, Beijing, China, September 2014.

Dolin, J. and Krogh, L.B. (2010) 'The relevance and consequences of PISA science in a Danish context', *International Journal of Science and Mathematics Education*, 8: 565–92.

Foxman, D., Hutchinson, D. and Bloomfield, B. (1991) *The APU Experience, 1977–1990*. London: Schools Examination and Assessment Council.

Gardner, J., Harlen, W., Hayward, L., Stobart, G. with Montgomery, M. (2010) *Developing Teacher Assessment*. Maidenhead, UK: Open University Press.

Glover, P. and Thomas, R. (1999) 'Coming to grips with continuous assessment', *Assessment in Education*, 4(3): 3–14.

Harlen, W. (ed.) (1994) *Enhancing Quality in Assessment*. London: Paul Chapman.

Harlen, W. (2004a) 'A systematic review of the reliability and validity of assessment by teachers used for summative purposes', in *Research Evidence in Education Library*, Issue 1. London: EPPI-Centre, Social Sciences Research Unit, Institute of Education.

Harlen, W. (2004b) 'Trusting teachers' judgements: research evidence of the reliability and validity of teachers' assessment for summative purposes', *Research Papers in Education*, 20(3): 245–70.

Harlen, W. (2006a) *Teaching, Learning and Assessing Science 5–12*. 4th edn. London: Sage Publications.

Harlen, W. (2006b) 'On the relationship between assessment for formative and summative purposes', in J. Gardner (ed.), *Assessment and Learning*. London: Sage Publications. pp. 103–117.

Harlen, W. (2010) 'What is quality teacher assessment?', in J. Gardner, W. Harlen, L. Hayward, G. Stobart with M. Montgomery (eds.), *Developing Teacher Assessment*. Maidenhead, UK: Open University Press. pp. 29–52.

Harlen, W. (2012) 'On the relationship between assessment for formative and summative purposes', in J. Gardner (ed.) *Assessment and Learning*. 2nd edn. London: Sage Publications. pp. 87–102.

Harlen, W. (2013) *Assessment and Inquiry-Based Science Education: Issues of Policy and Practice*. Trieste, Italy: Global Network of Science Academies (IAP) Science Education Programme.

Harlen, W. and Deakin Crick, R.E. (2003) 'Testing and motivation for learning', *Assessment in Education,* 10(2): 169–207.

Harlen, W. and Qualter, A. (2014) *The Teaching of Science in Primary Schools*. 5th edn. London: Routledge.

Hattie, J. and Timperley, H. (2007) 'The power of feedback', *Review of Educational Research*, 77(1): 81–112.

James, M. (2012) 'Assessment in harmony with our understanding of learning: problems and possibilities', in J. Gardner (ed.), *Assessment and Learning*, 2nd edn. London: Sage Publications. pp. 187–205.

Kulik, C.L.C., Kulik, J.A. and Bangert-Drownes, R.L. (1990) 'Effectiveness of mastery learning programs: a meta-analysis', *Review of Educational Research,* 60: 265–99.

Mansell, W., James, M. and the Assessment Reform Group (2009) *Assessment in Schools: Fit for Purpose? A Commentary by the Teaching and Learning Research Programme.* London: ESRC Teaching and Learning Research Programme. Available from http://www.tlrp.org/pub/commentaries.html (accessed 14 July 2015).

Michaels, S., Shouse, A.W. and Schweingruber, H.A (2008) *Ready, Set, Science! Putting Research to Work in K-8 Science Classrooms.* Washington, DC: National Academies Press.

Mislevy, R.J. (1996) 'Test theory reconceived', *Journal of Educational Measurement*, 33(4): 379–416.

Natriello, G. (1987) 'The impact of evaluation processes on students', *Educational Psychologist,* 22: 155–75.

Newton, P.E. (2012) 'Validity, purpose and the recycling of results from educational assessment', in J. Gardner (ed.), *Assessment and Learning*. 2nd edn. London: Sage Publications. pp. 264–76.

Nordenbo, S.E., Allerup, P., Andersen, H.L., Dolin, J., Korp, H., Larsen, M.S., Olsen, R. V., Svendsen, M. M., Tiftikci, N., Eline Wendt, R. & Østergaard, S. (2009) *Pædagogisk brug af test – Et systematisk review [Pedagogical Use of Tests – A systematic review]*. Copenhagen, Denmark: Aarhus Universitetsforlag.

Nusche, D., Laveault, D., MacBeath, J. and Santiago, P. (2012) *OECD Reviews of Evaluation and Assessment in Education: New Zealand 2011*. Paris: OECD Publishing.

Organisation for Economic Co-operation and Development (OECD) (2005) *Formative Assessment: Improving Learning in Secondary Classrooms*. Paris: OECD.

Pellegrino, J.W., Chudowsky, N. and Glaser, R. (eds.) (2001) *Knowing what Students Know: The Science and Design and Educational Assessment*. Washington, DC: National Academy Press.

Pine, J., Aschbacher, P., Rother, E., Jones, M., McPhee. C., Martin, C., Phelps, S., Kyle, T. and Foley, B. (2006) 'Fifth graders' science inquiry abilities: a comparative study of students in hands-on and textbook curricula', *Journal of Research in Science Teaching,* 43(5): 467–84.

Popham, W.J. (2000) *Modern Educational Measurement: Practical Guidelines for Educational Leaders*. Needham, MA: Allyn & Bacon.

Qualter, A. (1985) 'APU science practical investigations: a study of some problems of measuring practical scientific performance in children', unpublished PhD thesis, University of London.

Queensland Studies Authority (QSA) (2008) *Building Student Success*. Brisbane: QSA.

Redecker, C. and Johannessen, Ø. (2013) 'Changing assessment – towards a new assessment paradigm using ICT', *European Journal of Education,* 48(1): 79–96.

Stiggins, R.J. (2001) *Student-Involved Classroom Assessment*. Upper Saddle River, NJ: Merrill Prentice Hall.

Stobart, G. (2008) *Testing Times: The Uses and Abuses of Assessment*. London: Routledge.

Task Group on Assessment and Testing (TGAT) (1988) *National Curriculum Task Group on Assessment and Testing: A Report*. London: Department of Education and Science and the Welsh Office.

Tyler, R., Gagné, R.M. and Scriven, M. (1967) *Perspectives of Curriculum Evaluation*. American Educational Research Association Monograph Series on Curriculum Evaluation. Chicago, IL: Rand McNally.

Wiliam, D. (1993) 'Reconceptualising validity, dependability and reliability for National Curriculum Assessment', paper presented at the British Educational Research Association Conference, Liverpool, September 1993.

Wiliam, D. (2010) 'The role of formative assessment in effective learning environments', in H. Dumont, D. Istance and F. Benavides (eds.), *The Nature of Learning: Using Research to Inspire Practice*. Paris: OECD. pp. 135–59.

Teachers' Perceptions
of Assessment

John Gardner and Debie Galanouli

TEACHERS' BELIEFS AND PERCEPTIONS

Interest in teachers' beliefs, and their influence on classroom behaviour and practice, has long been a concern of educationalists. For example, as far back as 1953, Oliver (1953/54) was demonstrating a very low correlation (0.31) between the 'professed beliefs' of the 119 elementary teachers in his study and their observed practices in the classroom. Arguably, however, the most important contributions in teachers' beliefs research began to appear in the mid-1980s. The most notable of these (for example, Bandura, 1986; Clark and Peterson, 1986; Nespor, 1987; Pajares, 1992) set the scene by arguing from both theoretical and empirical bases that belief systems are major forces that can promote or hinder the success of any change situation. Such approaches attempt with various degrees of success to develop theory that can generalize across individuals, groups of individuals (for example, pre- and

in-service teachers) and multiple contexts. The theory-behind-the-theories is that they might reasonably be expected to inform planning for the success of new or alternative approaches to classroom practice. As Nespor (1987) put it: 'the contexts and environments within which teachers work, and many of the problems they encounter, are ill-defined and deeply entangled...beliefs are peculiarly suited for making sense of such contexts' (1987: 324).

Arguably much of the research on teachers' beliefs to date has focused on psychological and philosophical approaches designed to address problems of definition and consistency of language, and to illuminate and explain different manifestations of practice. In a recent major review, Fives and Buehl (2012) offered a synthesis of some 627 empirically based articles, variously examining teachers' beliefs. They concluded, perhaps predictably, that teachers hold complex and multi-faceted beliefs, which are related to context and experience, and that these belief systems may act on practice 'in different ways, as filters, frames or guides' (2012: 487). They also concluded that the enactment of teachers' beliefs is related to their practice and student outcomes but could be hindered by contextual constraints. In the context of assessment, it is our view that teachers' practice may be less dependent on their inherent beliefs about education, learning or teaching and more on either their perceptions of the role of assessment in teaching and learning or the perceived imperatives of the policy frameworks within which they work. As one example, in the specific area of promoting new assessment practices, Bliem and Davinroy (1997) spelled out the importance of the teachers' perceptions of measurement as a key dimension of likely success:

> The precise way in which teachers implement new forms of assessment, and whether the reform succeeds or fails, will depend largely on their beliefs and knowledge regarding measurement and its relationship to instruction. (1997: 1)

Working with teachers in the context of assessing the reading skills of second language students in the US, Rueda and Garcia (1994) argued that too much attention had been paid to the technical dimensions of assessment, such as 'measurement', to the detriment of wider literacy issues. At the time of their writing, Rueda and Garcia felt that assessment of reading was in a transitional state. In the face of much literature emphasizing socio-cultural, interactive and multi-faceted approaches, the experience they witnessed was a continuing reliance on 'static, decontextualized, unidimensional standardized tests' (1994: 4). The wider socio-cultural dimensions of, for example, active involvement and authentic contexts were not making ground against these traditional 'reductionist' practices and Rueda and Garcia pointed to the 'underlying paradigmatic belief systems' of teachers as the root cause. Using Tabachnick and Zeichner's (1984) definition of teacher perspectives they defined these belief systems or mental models as 'a combination of beliefs, intentions,

interpretation and behaviour that interact continually' (Rueda and Garcia, 1994: 3). This is a particularly apt definition for our purposes because it recognizes that teachers' engagement with assessment may be less influenced by their internally held beliefs than by external aspects of their or others' purposes and meanings or behaviours. The concept of perception better reflects the result of the forging of this complex mix of influences, including beliefs, which ultimately define how teachers engage with assessment.

ASSESSMENT

It would be remiss of us not to define what is meant by assessment in this chapter, but space dictates that this should be brief (for a comprehensive treatment of the field of assessment, see Gardner, 2012). Broadly speaking there are two poles on the assessment spectrum: summative and formative. At the summative end, the technical definitions of assessment cover processes that seek to establish the extent of knowledge, understanding or skill that the student has acquired at the end of a period of scheduled learning. The assessment may therefore occur at the end of a lesson, module or a full programme of learning, or it may happen at the end of a semester or academic year. The summative extreme of the spectrum could be represented by the simplest test formats, which provide a one-dimensional score, such as a percentage, for the student and teacher (for example, multiple-choice tests). At this extreme, feedback for the students on their test performance (other than the score) or the extent of the learning they have achieved (or not achieved) is unlikely to be available.

At the formative end of the spectrum, assessments tend to be continuous and exist as part of the classroom interactions between the teacher and the students. Effective questioning facilitates a meaningful dialogue and both parties learn from the feedback loop: the teachers adjust teaching tactics by using questions to assess where their students are in their learning and the students identify the next steps in their learning from the teacher's interactions with them. The teachers may also augment the contribution that assessment makes in support of the students' learning by facilitating peer and self-assessment activities.

A parallel conception of this spectrum would be one in which only psychometric assessments (for example, those divorced from the learning context and 'objectively' scored) exist at the summative end whilst situated (for example, classroom-based, teacher-student interactions) and authentic assessments (for example, using judgment contextualized in the learning process) gather at the formative end. However, this conception risks entering a different debate about the ultimate purpose of each type of assessment – that the former should be used only for high-stakes purposes (for example, 'objective' selection for universities or employment) and the latter only for supporting the learning process. We argue instead that each type of assessment can be used to serve the other's purposes. For example, summative assessments can be used to support learning through the students being enabled to review annotated examination scripts, which have been returned to them, or by being offered post-examination debriefings on areas needing improvement.

Formative assessments may also be used summatively but this is a bit trickier because there is a controversial tendency (see, for example, Cech, 2008) for some to interpret formative assessment as repeated occasions of mini-summative assessments, such as weekly class-tests, which aggregate to an assessment profile over time. Many assessment experts reject the notion that these mini-tests represent formative assessment activities because they are usually separate from the teaching–learning interaction, and usually take the form of being time-bounded, structured tests often in multiple-choice formats. In contrast, formative assessments compiled through portfolios or running records, can fulfil both functions: the 'support for learning' in continuous assessment for learning (AfL) fashion and 'assessment *of* learning' in an overall, summative judgement fashion. However, most assessment experts will insist that any process carrying the mantle of 'formative assessment' or 'assessment for learning' must provide a purposeful contribution to supporting the student's learning, during the time they are actually engaged in that learning. We have therefore used the notion of a spectrum deliberately to blur the distinctions and to undermine any tendency to assume that the dichotomy must be absolute in any particular circumstances. Notwithstanding this argument, however, teachers may continue to adopt perceptions of variations in assessment methods as fitting the extremes rather than having the potential to serve a dual purpose. These and various other perceptions that teachers have about assessment are developed later in the chapter.

A FRAME FOR TEACHERS' PERCEPTIONS OF ASSESSMENT

Arguably, the simplest frame in which to structure teachers' perceptions of assessment is based on the concept of dependability of the outcomes of the assessment. Dependability is a complex construct that broadly confers confidence in the outcomes of assessment through assurances of such attributes as fitness for purpose, accuracy, reproducibility and fairness. These features are usually subsumed under the more familiar constructs of reliability and validity, with the expectation that assessments may be 'depended upon' if they are both reliable and valid. Central to this issue, however, is the recognized inevitability of random and systemic errors, which can never be fully eradicated. Rogosa (2003) has shown, for example, that the accuracy of the Californian STAR (Standardized Testing and Reporting) Grade 2 mathematics tests in putting average students within 10 per cent of their 'true' performance is only

57 per cent, and there is a 40 per cent chance that two identically able students will obtain scores 20 per cent apart. There is also always the risk of human (for example, examiner) errors, for which safeguards are possible but not entirely fool proof (for a fuller treatment of how errors are perceived in assessment, see Gardner, 2013). The main pursuit of test agencies is very much focused on ensuring their tests are as reliable as possible, particularly as perceived by teachers, students and the general public. Reliability, however, is only one part of the dependability debate because it is entirely possible to have a technically reliable assessment that misses the point of its purpose (for example, the rifle with the bent barrel will accurately and reliably miss the target at which its sights are aimed). If an assessment process is accurate, but not fit for its purpose, it cannot be deemed valid.

Somewhat paradoxically, an assessment outcome can be valid even if it is unreliable in the technical sense. It is not uncommon, for example, for different students with arguably the same quality of work to receive different grades from the same or different judges. At the cusp of any such judgment threshold there will be a margin of 'human error' above or below which judgments do not predictably fall. Take, for example, the process leading to declaring a person is competent to drive. An assessment comprising the observation of practical driving skills at the wheel of the vehicle is valid compared to a pen-and-paper test that asks questions about driving. It remains valid even if it could be argued that another driving test examiner might deem the same performance to be below passing threshold or if, in similar circumstances on another occasion, the same examiner would fail another candidate on the same level of performance. The lack of reliability in judgment does not necessarily invalidate the assessment.

Teachers' perceptions may or may not be informed by competent knowledge of the technical nuances of reliability and validity but several sources of external influence may shape new perceptions and consolidate or change existing perceptions. The outputs from many academic commentators on the reliability or validity of different types of assessment can be highly influential in shaping perceptions (for example, the work by Black and Wiliam (1998) gave new impetus to the promotion of formative assessment). They may also be influenced by various environmental factors, not least the teachers' experience of examination results that challenge their knowledge of students' performance, or the often sensationalist outputs from the media. In order to expand on the range of perceptions linked to reliability and validity of assessments, and in particular tests, let us consider the following, deliberately stark statement from an imaginary teacher:

> Test results are not dependable indicators of the extent of my students' learning.

Such perceptions of dependability are likely to be prompted, first and foremost, by personal experience. There is a variety of survey evidence that provides proxies of the views of teachers on these matters. For example, the Primary Sources survey (Scholastic, 2012) found that among their 12,212 teacher respondents (pre-K-12), only 44 per cent felt that final examinations were 'essential' or 'very important' for 'measuring student academic achievement' (Scholastic, 2012: 25). Instead, the teachers overwhelmingly (>90 per cent) perceived classroom assessment (including formative assessment, classroom assignments and participation) to be the most important vehicle for assessing student achievement. The proportions for district-required tests, state-required standardized tests and tests from textbooks were 30 per cent, 28 per cent and 26 per cent, respectively. This speaks to perceived doubts about the fitness for purpose (validity) of the test variants in assessing learning (for example, the illustrative quote from the survey report: 'There needs to be less emphasis on mastering a test, and more emphasis on mastering the skills and higher-level concepts in the core subjects', Scholastic, 2012: 26), although 69 per cent did perceive the state-required tests to be fit for the purpose of ensuring every child is treated fairly. Another purpose for external examinations, this time related to teachers' perceptions of the usefulness of tests, formed the basis of an interesting conclusion that Collins et al. (2010) made in the UK. They found that teachers in Wales still valued the use of national science tests for 11-year-olds as a means of calibrating their assessments of their own students, even after the national tests were abolished by the Welsh government.

In the UK, the Office of Qualifications and Examinations Regulation (Ofqual) commissions an annual market research-type survey that specifically addresses teachers' perceptions of reliability in the marking of Advanced-level examinations (A-level, pre-university) and General Certificate of Secondary Education examinations (GCSE, taken at around 16 years of age). The 2011 survey (Ipsos MORI, 2012) reports that 87 per cent and 75 per cent, respectively, of the sampled teachers were confident that most of their students received the A-level and GCSE grades they deserved. These are relatively high expressions of confidence, stable over time in relation to previous surveys, and they suggest that teachers perceive the external assessment system to be reliable. In relation to perceptions of the accuracy and quality of scoring, 73 per cent and 62 per cent of the teachers felt confident about the A-level and GCSE examinations, respectively. These figures indicate lower levels of confidence in the actual marking processes, again relatively stable over time, possibly because it is the scoring rather than the final grade outputs that prompt media interest in relation to system and human errors (for example, see *The Guardian* (2012) newspaper report describing tough action by examination boards in relation to examiner error).

The most recent report from Ofqual (2014) produced more stark results from a survey of 698 teachers in England about their perceptions of the A-level and GCSE examinations. The results showed that only 53 per cent of the teachers surveyed (as opposed to 87 per cent in 2011) believed that A-level students receive the grade they deserve. This decreased to 36 per cent (75 per cent in 2011) for the GCSE students. Sixty-one percent of teachers reported confidence in the accuracy of A-level and GCSE marking, although when asked whether they thought the accuracy of A-level marking had decreased over the last two years, only 28 per cent of teachers agreed that it had indeed decreased, with 34 per cent for the GCSE examinations. Another factor that is likely to affect teachers' perceptions of assessment is the so-called 'accountability agenda' (for a thorough analysis of the situation in England, see Torrance, 2011). This phrase is shorthand for a widespread trend in government policies across the world to use standardized testing and performance standards as means of forcing schools to raise the standards of their student outcomes. In the US the main instrument has been the No Child Left Behind (NCLB) policy, and its mandated state-level standards and standardized tests, and in England it is the assessment of national curriculum outcomes at different stages of a student's schooling. These systems generate judgments on the performance of schools (for example, in meeting targets for different subgroups of pupils and for the school overall) through annual yearly progress (AYP) in the US and contextual value added scores (CVA) in England (used in schools between 2006–11). The phenomenon of teaching to the test is widely perceived by teachers to hinder classroom learning at best and, at worst, to corrupt the whole educational endeavour. Fearing the consequences of negative performance, which may involve the withdrawal of funds or even closure of schools in both jurisdictions, it is not unreasonable to expect that teachers individually and collectively in schools will perceive their students' performance in national or state tests to be the paramount goal of their efforts, no matter how much they might also consider the potentially distorting effects on their students' learning.

The negative social implications of national testing in the US and parts of the UK (primarily England) are widely reported by academic commentators (for example, in the US, Altshuler and Schmautz, 2006; Nichols et al., 2005; and in the UK, Levačić & Marsh, 2007; Strand, 2008) and the mediation of these implications through the professional education literature undoubtedly influences the perceptions of teachers who witness the effects most strikingly 'on the ground'. NCLB, for example, has many detractors amongst the US academic and teaching community because of perceptions of unfairness towards specific types of students, characterized by ethnicity or economic circumstance. The rhetoric of NCLB declares its intention to raise standards and improve outcomes for all children in schools, but its record in reality is very patchy. Taking the state-mandated STAR tests in California, for example, the 2012 results show that 57 per cent and 51 per cent of the students scored at or above proficient level in English-language arts and mathematics, respectively (STAR, 2012), with a slight drop in the English-language arts figure for 2013 (56 per cent) but still 51 per cent for mathematics (STAR, 2013). These do compare favourably with the 35 per cent recorded for the same categories in 2003, but are still a long way off the state target of 100 per cent proficient.

It is interesting to note that there is little or no acknowledgement in most of the official commentaries that this effect may be the result of better test-taking strategies over time and may not have been caused by improved teaching and learning in schools. In addition, the diversity in the fine-grained picture of improvement and regression in NCLB results is often masked by summaries or aggregated reporting. For example, the STAR (2012) county-based results for eight ethnic group categories for the period 2003–12 shows a wide range of changes over time, with the highest positive change (67 per cent) for 'not economically disadvantaged' Filipino students in Tuolumne County (population 54,501) and 31 per cent negative change for 'not economically disadvantaged' Black or African Americans in Inyo County (population 18,546). These overall results may give assurance to state legislators that things are improving, but the effect on many individuals and groups of students is not lost on teachers 'on the ground' – and with the threat of AYP penalties swinging into action, perceptions of what is best for students quite naturally take a back seat to a pragmatic attention to the achievement of targets. In the UK, Levačić & Marsh (2007) argue that schools with high proportions of disadvantaged or disaffected students may suffer from reducing budgets over time as these proportions tend to increase and as their reputation in the hierarchy of local schools begins to fall. The more recent prospect of poor CVA scores (around which there is considerable concern about flawed methods, see for example Dearden et al., 2011) and the threat of state-reduced funding – and even closure – is arguably an inevitable recipe for teachers perceiving outcome targets to be of priority importance to the detriment of student learning outcomes.

Throughout all of these examples, it is hard to escape the conclusion that teachers in 'accountability' systems will not perceive test results to be 'dependable' indicators of the extent of their students' learning. Whether it is the case or not, however, the circumstances of mandated testing processes will likely leave them with no choice other than to comply with them.

TEACHERS' PERCEPTIONS OF ASSESSMENT

In the context of assessment, it is likely that a teacher's behaviour will be influenced by their perceptions of the dimensions of that assessment, whether these are the purposes and dependability of its outcomes, or the procedures and processes used to achieve them. Take, for example, the often-trumpeted exhortations to integrate AfL approaches into classroom teaching. On the occasion that the exhortation is first made in a school, it may be through a school-based professional learning event, perhaps mediated by colleagues or by external experts brought in for the purpose, or it may be the focus of a day out at a professional development course arranged by local authority or district officers and facilitated by an expert in the field.

It is not unreasonable to assume that in any such event, the audience's reaction to the proposal for innovation in classroom assessment practice will be varied and complex. The teachers may be positively or negatively disposed to some or all of the dimensions of the change, and the reactions may vary from enthusiastic engagement through passive compliance to outright rejection. Arguably, this spectrum of reaction will map more widely to the teaching community outside the event in question, with more enthusiastic uptake possible at the level of individual teachers and more resistance as collectivism increases from the whole school through to the schools of a district and on to schools nationally. Examples of this collective resistance to changes in assessment arrangements include the almost total boycott of the introduction of national curriculum testing in England and Wales in 1993 (see, for example, Coles, 1994) and the various challenges that have been aimed at testing related to the NCLB policy since its inauguration in 2002 (see, for example, Fusarelli, 2004; Nichols et al., 2005; Rapp et al., 2006).

The perceptions that give rise to the subsequent behaviour of any one teacher in the audience may be informed by justified beliefs about the assessment proposals. For example, these perceptions may have formed from a competent knowledge base ('I have tried it before and it didn't work'). Alternatively, they may be prompted by unjustified beliefs that are not based on evidence of personal experience, for example, from hearsay, media pronouncements, or political or idealistic positions. Some may perceive assessment to be a separate process that aims only to establish the outcomes of the teaching and learning process; others may see it as an integrated process that acts in support of the teaching and learning, and some may see it as some combination of these. Such perceptions may be promoted by deeply held beliefs, of which the teachers concerned may or may not be conscious and may or may not be able to articulate, or they may simply be descriptions of a routine, unreflective approach to their professional role: 'I teach, they learn, someone else assesses'.

It is worth noting that having any particular perception of assessment cannot imply that the teachers concerned have the competence to carry out new assessment processes effectively; however, not having the necessary competence may precipitate resistant behaviour that is not dependent on the teachers' perceptions, which may or may not be positively disposed. Competence to carry out assessment reforms is therefore a separate concern from the focus on perceptions in this chapter.

REFORMING PERCEPTIONS

Strategies to reform teachers' perceptions of assessment, when these are not contingent with the 'direction of travel' of proposed changes in assessment practice, can be multifaceted. For example, they may seek to improve the teachers' knowledge and understanding of what is proposed, including the outcomes that the changes are designed to deliver. These attempts may capitalize on parallel changes in the curriculum that the teachers deliver, which inherently demand a fresh and different approach to assessment. Such changes have been the focus of curriculum and assessment change in schools in a wide range of countries including Canada, Australia and the four countries of the UK (see, for example, Gardner et al., 2010; Hayward et al., 2004, Sebba, 2012).

A more subtle but longer term strategy to reform perceptions, and consequently practices, may be to nucleate change within the school using key influencers among small faculty groups; the ultimate intention being some form of osmotic transfer to the wider school or a more deliberate form of 'cascaded' dissemination through in-school professional development processes. This peer-influence approach can be very successful or can fail spectacularly depending on the choice of the peer influencers and the approach they take. An evangelistic approach proclaiming the virtues of the change may succeed with some teachers and switch off others. Alternatively, a steady, unobtrusive approach demonstrating improved student outcomes may win over hearts and minds through example and subtle collegiality, but may take considerable time for wider penetration. Perhaps more radical is the potential influence of student 'pester-power'. When students like the learning experience they have with one teacher, they may pester other teachers to adopt the same techniques. Responsive teachers will recognize the impact of the changes on the students and may in turn explore or feel obliged to explore these new techniques in an attempt to improve student learning.

Attempts to change perceptions may also be dependent on the readiness of teachers to change. Teachers who are intrinsically interested or anxious to change existing practices in pursuit of improved learning environments and outcomes would usually represent a fertile base for innovation; however, the worst case is when teachers are susceptible to faddish quick-wins. Regrettably, the educational landscapes of such innovative areas as thinking skills, assessment for learning and multiple intelligences are replete with 'gurus' whose preaching includes plausible sound-bite anecdotes and appealingly simple schema to convince teachers about new ways to solve highly complex and enduring problems.

There is undoubted merit in many of these 'new' educational approaches, including assessment for learning, and the gurus can make them very attractive to teachers in search of change; however, the perceptions of easy integration and immediate results, driven by a plausible set of strategies and tools (tips and tricks) may struggle to achieve

the status of reality in attempts to implement them in each teacher's own complex classroom world. Even when they do, the effects may be short-lived as the teachers fail to register them at more than a relatively superficial level of operation. As Fullan (1993) concluded, 'It's not enough to be exposed to new ideas. We have to know where these ideas fit, and we have to become skilled in them, not just like them' (1993: 16).

THE INFLUENCE OF PERCEPTIONS ON CHANGE SITUATIONS

Much of what we know about teachers' perceptions of assessment processes and outcomes has arisen from studies of change situations, for example where new practices or requirements are presented for assimilation by the teaching community. It is this change situation that is more likely to expose the types of perceptions harboured by teachers who may, up to that point in their careers, have passively followed routine or conventional practices. The major change of the last decade or so is the increasing awareness that assessment should be used to support learning, manifested in the initiatives to introduce or consolidate formative assessment – or as it is commonly called 'assessment for learning' (AfL) – in many nations' schools.

Teachers' perceptions of assessment raise a range of challenges in pursuing the integration of AfL-type changes in their practice, and some of these are illustrated by the following examples. First, Bliem and Davinroy (1997) worked over the course of a year with 14 teachers at three US elementary schools. They identified deeply held beliefs that showed a clear disconnect between the teachers' views on assessment and its relationship to teaching and learning (instruction). The four central propositions were that assessment:

- Is a formal, occasional event with the fundamental purpose of documenting student growth in understanding;

- Provides a tangible product, which the teacher can share with others (for example, the students and their parents);
- Should evaluate student performance on a single discrete target;
- In order to be fair, must be uniform with objective scoring. (Adapted from Bliem and Davinroy, 1997: 30)

The teachers with these beliefs were concluded not to perceive a learning-related (instructional) role for assessment. Instead, they perceived this role to imply that assessment is restricted to offering an objective measure of their students' learning. They were reluctant to use their own subjective assessments of student work, for example in reading, to support the process of learning, and preferred instead to use methods that gave simple quantitative information on numbers of mistakes made.

Dixon et al. (2011) have documented a similar hindrance to changing assessment practices in a project involving 20 teachers in New Zealand. The barriers were caused by tacit beliefs about the relationship between teaching, learning and assessment, and the roles played by the teachers and students in them. On the basis that beliefs do play a significant role in facilitating or hindering changes in assessment practice, and that such beliefs are often 'private, tacit, unarticulated and deeply entrenched' (Dixon et al., 2011: 377), they concluded that it is crucial to raise teachers' awareness of their beliefs and the impact they have on their practice.

Coffey et al. (2005) recount a particularly acute case of counter-productive perceptions of assessment from a project designed to investigate the challenges faced by 25 middle-school teachers in San Francisco in developing AfL-type classroom assessment practices. One teacher's perceptions of fairness in assessment meant that at the outset of the project she put significant weight on the objectivity of tests and gave them high priority in assessing her students' learning. As a consequence of this focus on fairness, she was reluctant to carry out any form of assessment that might be construed to disadvantage

any student. For example, she would not use responses from students to her questions in class as evidence of their learning because other students did not have an opportunity to answer similarly. The outputs from group work were also not an option because of her concerns to establish ownership of the work in a fair manner. Over time, however, she did begin to challenge the consequences of her perceptions of fairness and she began to adopt more effective questioning practices: asking open-ended questions, waiting longer for answers, drawing more students into answering and ultimately creating a richer, more participative learning environment.

Brookhart et al. (2010) reported a similar story of success that includes improved student outcomes. This project involved six US-based remedial reading teachers from a mid-Atlantic US state who participated in a year-long professional development process designed to develop AfL-type classroom practice. In the beginning, the teachers perceived themselves as having to comply with rigidly scripted instructions on how to provide remedial reading support. However, Brookhart et al. (2010) concluded that through a process of questioning their understandings and testing them against evidence from their practice, the teachers were able to transform their beliefs and alter their practices.

The belief that 'measurement' offers objectivity and therefore fairness (fourth bullet for Bliem and Davinroy, 1997) is not uncommon and certainly not surprising in systems that have espoused accountability agendas. In these systems, classroom assessment carried out by teachers is considered to be less trustworthy than externally administered tests, and standardized testing tends to be the assessment approach of government choice. As is argued next, there is reasonable support for external 'objective' testing for high-stakes purposes (for example, selection for employment, university places, etc.) but there is considerably less support for testing as a means of improving student learning and outcomes. In circumstances where there is a push to develop assessment for learning as a means to engage students more effectively in their learning, the clear implication is that contradictory perceptions on assessment and instruction must be addressed. Shepard (2000: 6) argued that the 'power of these enduring and hidden beliefs' about objective and external measurement versus subjective teacher judgment needs to be recognized in any initiative designed to make classroom assessment a part of the learning process.

If these examples show teachers finding it difficult to shake off established perceptions of the role and purpose of assessment, the following example flips the situation to one in which the teachers espouse the tenets of using assessment to support students' learning, but are constrained by circumstances that require schools to demonstrate improved outcomes. Sikka et al. (2007), working with four case study teachers in Texas, explored the effects of having to comply with externally mandated activities when they are clearly perceived to be at odds with the promotion of learning and students' self-esteem and motivation. For example, the teachers considered that multiple-choice tests caused cognitive dissonance for the students in circumstances where more valid assessment would be in the form of essays or performances assessments. Teachers were held accountable by their school administrators for their students' performance in these tests; therefore, they had to comply despite their strongly held perceptions of their inadequacy. This is far from an ideal situation and Sikka et al. (2007) concluded that 'Teachers who believe that such types of tests (for example, multiple choice) play such a small role in instructional decision-making, but still have to implement them in their classrooms, are likely to experience lowered morale and burnout' (2007: 252).

Some aspects of James and Pedder's (2006) work also reflected this compliance situation. They reported on the perceptions of 558 teachers from infant, primary and secondary schools in England in relation to the importance of assessment activities, including AfL-type activities. In a 30-item questionnaire, the teachers were asked to record the level of importance they ascribed to particular assessment activities and, in parallel, record the extent to which these activities formed part of their actual practice.

Although based on self-report (for other aspects of the much larger project, including observations of classroom practice, see James and McCormick, 2009), James and Pedder (2006) were content that the respondents answered candidly and honestly. The research was designed to evaluate the congruence between the teachers' perceptions of the value of different activities and their enactment of them. The values–practices gap was highly significant in a number of activities, for example the AfL-related item 'Students are helped to plan the next steps in their learning' attracted an 83 per cent 'important or crucial' rating, but its enactment was 46 per cent 'often or mostly'. In contrast, the item 'Students' learning objectives are determined mainly by the prescribed curriculum' showed a perceived value level of 63 per cent 'important or crucial' and an enactment level of 92 per cent 'often or mostly'.

Taking into account the range of items, James and Pedder (2006: 132) concluded that over half of the teachers 'believed they were acting in pursuit of ends they clearly do not view as worthwhile or desirable'. However, by the end of the project some of the teachers 'were rebalancing their assessment approaches in order to bring their practices into closer alignment with their values' (James and McCormick, 2009: 978). They achieved this primarily by not blaming external circumstances or student characteristics but by a combination of reflective thinking, taking responsibility for what happened in their classrooms and focusing on improving the learning experience of the students. In particular, James and McCormick (2009) distinguished between those who implemented the superficial 'letter' of the assessment for learning initiative by inserting discrete strategies into their normal classroom processes and those who captured the deeper 'spirit' of the initiative and changed their practices in light of their beliefs in the improvements that would be gained. James and McCormick concluded that '…beliefs and practices are interrelated and need to be developed together. It is not sufficient just to tell the teachers what to do' (2009: 982).

All these examples bear witness, in an assessment context, to Fives and Buehl's (2012) conclusions on challenges to be faced when attempting to modify teachers' beliefs. They illustrate the view that teachers hold complex and multi-faceted beliefs about assessment, and that these beliefs and the teachers' practice can function reciprocally: espoused beliefs hindering enactment in some and struggling against external circumstances in others. Teachers' beliefs or perceptions may be unconsciously held, even when they are deeply entrenched, and may act unconsciously on their practice. Exposing them in the process of professional development may shake them, as some of the previous examples demonstrate, or they may remain steady, forcing the teachers to adopt a compliance approach to those aspects of their professional responsibilities that are not congruent with their own views. Deeply held perceptions of assessment do not develop overnight and as such it is always possible that any changes witnessed will merely ruffle the calm surface of teachers' beliefs, rather than disturb those settled deep below on the sea bed of the sub-conscious (Hayward et al., 2004). As such they can 'decay and disappear when the next initiative comes along' (James and McCormick, 2009: 982).

Arguably this is even more likely in cases where the lived culture is strongly antithetical to the change proposed. Brown et al. (2009) have shown a high correlation between the conceptions of student accountability (through examinations) and improvement in learning for their project sample of 288 Hong Kong secondary school teachers. In addition, the belief system that stems from this high correlation also appears to value effort over ability. Commenting on reforms designed to develop assessment for learning practices (underway in Hong Kong), Brown et al. concluded that it is not merely a question of technical changes, but of fundamental changes

in cultural values. Yung (2002) focused on four teachers in Hong Kong during the early stages of a government initiative to introduce teacher-based assessment. Setting the context as a long-established examination-related culture, he identified a challenge for these teachers in assuming the role of both teacher and assessor. He concluded that to shift the deeply held beliefs about roles of assessment and of teachers, there was a clear need for teachers to have, or to develop, a critical stance in relation to their teaching. This criticality, he argued, is fostered by professional confidence and consciousness directed towards the students' interests and their own. Without these supports, it is more likely that teachers may develop 'a sense of powerlessness and resignation' that is expressed in compliance with 'external prescriptions, even when they judged them to be misguided' (Yung, 2002: 113). Such experiences are not isolated and Berry (2011) has suggested that the deep-rooted examination cultures of the Confucian heritage countries (China, Taiwan, Hong Kong, Japan, Vietnam, etc.) will continue to create tensions between assessment reform policies and the practices of teachers who perceive assessment (specifically examinations) as the ultimate goal for education.

CONCLUDING REMARKS

The thrust of these examples is that many factors may influence how teachers perceive assessment. Some may be influenced by deeply held beliefs that place them in opposition to newly prescribed assessment practices or, conversely, prompt them to embrace the changes enthusiastically. Not all of these beliefs will be held openly or consciously and may have been honed subconsciously into the teacher's world view by previous educational or cultural experiences. Deeply entrenched views, which run counter to ambitions for changes in assessment practice, present considerable obstacles to change in assessment practice and may therefore need to be identified and teased out through challenging engagements with colleagues or professional development facilitators.

There are differences in teachers' roles in assessment across the international landscape, and in some jurisdictions or cultures teachers may perceive their professional role to be solely in support of learning, with the assessment of that learning carried out elsewhere by someone else. In other cases, they may be cast as both facilitator and assessor in continuous assessment processes linked to portfolio and project work. When there is an element of prescription in a role specification that does not match a teacher's espoused beliefs or perceptions of assessment, the alternatives of resistance or compliance will present stark choices for the teachers concerned. The examples illustrate how individual teachers may perceive tests to offer a convenient and external ('objective', 'fair') means of carrying out summative assessments for reporting. Arguably, the more interesting examples are those that illustrate how individual teachers may engage with assessment practices that they perceive to be detrimental to students' learning. It seems that few teachers will have, or will take, the opportunity openly to resist. As was the case in some of the examples, they may feel compelled to act merely as functionaries serving the beliefs and ideals of others.

Even when the individual perceptions and beliefs coalesce into collectively held positions on new assessment arrangements, the outcomes can remain problematic. For example, a somewhat paradoxical situation recently developed in England where individual perceptions and beliefs gathered collectively in opposing positions under the banners of two major teaching trade unions. On the one hand, the National Union of Teachers (NUT), which represents mainly primary school teachers and has over 320,000 members, endorsed boycotts of the national curriculum tests because the 'washback' effect (where teachers feel they have to teach to the tests) is perceived to distort children's education. On the other, the National Association of Schoolmasters/Union of Women Teachers (NASUWT), which represents mainly secondary teachers and has 280,000 members, threatened strike action if the external tests were to be replaced by teacher-based classroom assessments because they are perceived to imply higher workloads for teachers. It is not known what proportions of the two organizations' memberships would feel more comfortable in the 'other camp', but this internecine disagreement played out an interesting illustration of how deeply held beliefs (in the interests of students) can vie with pragmatic behaviours (in the interests of teachers) in establishing perceptions of proposed changes in assessment arrangements.

As indicated at the outset of this chapter, it is difficult to generalize about teachers' perceptions of assessment, particularly changes to assessment processes, and what these might be predicted (theorized) to be for any one person or in any given circumstance. We argue that the formation of these perceptions is subject to a complex combination of the teachers' internal beliefs, the intentions and purposes of the assessment process, and the teachers' or others' interpretations and behaviours. When others' behaviours determine circumstances that demand compliance (whether mandating AfL approaches in the classroom or external testing designed to 'raise standards'), the research suggests that individual teachers' perceptions may or may not lead them to act in the interests either of the mandated changes or the students they are designed to serve. Those contemplating change programmes in the context of assessment should therefore be mindful of the teachers' perceptions of the changes they propose. Change is only likely to proceed effectively if due attention is paid to these 'hearts and minds' perceptions of the teachers concerned.

REFERENCES

Altshuler, S. J. and Schmautz, T. (2006) 'No Hispanic student left behind: the consequences of "high stakes" testing', *Children and Schools,* 28(1): 5–12.

Bandura, A. (1986) *Social Foundations of Thought and Action: A Social Cognitive Theory.* Englewood Cliffs, NJ: Prentice-Hall.

Berry, R. (2011) 'Assessment reforms around the world', in R. Berry and B. Adamson (eds.), *Assessment Reform in Education: Policy and Practice.* New York, NY: Springer. pp. 89–102.

Black, P. and Wiliam, D. (1998) 'Assessment and classroom learning', *Assessment in Education: Principles, Policy and Practice,* 5: 7–71.

Bliem, C. L. and Davinroy, K. H. (1997) *Teachers' Beliefs about Assessment and Instruction in Literacy.* CSE Technical Report 421. CRESST, Graduate School of Education & Information Studies, University of California. Available from https://www.cse.ucla.edu/products/reports/TECH421.pdf (accessed 26 July 2015).

Brookhart, S. M., Moss, C. M. and Long, B. A. (2010) 'Teacher inquiry into formative assessment practices in remedial reading classrooms', *Assessment in Education: Principles, Policy and Practice,* 17(1): 41–58.

Brown, G. T. L., Kennedy, K. J., Fok, P. K., Chan, J. K. S. and Yu, W. M. (2009) 'Assessment for student improvement: understanding Hong Kong teachers' conceptions and practices of assessment', *Assessment in Education: Principles, Policy and Practice,* 16(3): 347–63.

Cech, S. J. (2008) 'Test industry split over "formative" assessment', *Education Week.* Available from http://www.edweek.org/ew/articles/2008/09/17/04formative_ep.h28.html?print=1 (accessed 26 July 2015).

Clark, C. M. and Peterson, P. L. (1986) 'Teachers' thought processes', in M. C. Wittock (ed.), *Handbook of Research on Teaching.* 3rd edn. New York, NY: Macmillan. pp. 255–96.

Coffey, J. E., Sato, M. and Thiebault, M. (2005) 'Classroom assessment up close – and personal', *Teacher Development,* 9(2): 169–83.

Coles, J. (1994) 'Enough was enough: the teachers' boycott of national curriculum testing', *Changing English: Studies in Culture and Education,* 1(2): 16–31.

Collins, S., Reiss, M. and Stobart, G. (2010) 'What happens when high-stakes testing stops? Teachers' perceptions of the impact of compulsory national testing in science of 11-year-olds in England and its abolition in Wales', *Assessment in Education: Principles, Policy and Practice,* 17(3): 273–86.

Dearden, L., Miranda, A. and Rabe-Hesketh, S. (2011) 'Measuring school value added with administrative data: the problem of missing variables', *Fiscal Studies,* 32(2): 263–78.

Dixon, H. R., Hawe, E. and Parr, J. (2011) 'Enacting Assessment for Learning: the beliefs practice nexus', *Assessment in Education: Principles, Policy and Practice,* 18(4): 365–79.

Fives, H. and Buehl, M. M. (2012) 'Spring cleaning for the "messy" construct of teachers' beliefs: what are they? Which have been examined? What can they tell us?', in K. R. Harris, S. Graham and T. Urdan (eds.), *APA Educational Psychology Handbook: Individual Differences and Cultural and contextual Factors.* Vol. 2. Washington: American Psychological Association pp. 471–99.

Fullan, M. (1993) *Change Forces: Probing the Depths of Educational Reform.* London: Falmer Press.

Fusarelli, L. D. (2004) 'The potential impact of the No Child Left Behind Act on equity and diversity in American education', *Education Policy,* 18(1): 71–94.

Gardner, J. (ed.) (2012) *Assessment and Learning.* 2nd edn. Thousand Oaks, CA: Sage Publications.

Gardner, J. (2013) 'The public understanding of error in educational assessment', *Oxford Review of Education,* 39(1): 72–92.

Gardner, J., Harlen, W., Hayward, L., Stobart, G. and Montgomery, M. (2010) *Developing Teacher Assessment.* New York, NY: McGraw Hill/Open University Press.

Hayward, L., Priestley, M. and Young, M. (2004) 'Ruffling the calm of the ocean floor: merging practice, policy and researching assessment in Scotland', *Oxford Review of Education,* 30(3): 397–415.

Ipsos MORI (2102) *Perceptions of A levels, GCSEs and other qualifications: Wave 10*: Report on behalf of Ofqual. Available from http://dera.ioe.ac.uk/14554/1/2012-03-13-ofqual-perceptions-of-a-levels-gcses-wave-10.pdf (accessed 26 July 2015).

James, M. and McCormick, R. (2009) 'Teachers learning how to learn', *Teaching and Teacher Education,* 25: 973–82.

James, M. and Pedder, D. (2006) 'Beyond method: assessment and learning practices and values', *The Curriculum Journal,* 17(2): 109–38.

Levačić, R. and Marsh, A. (2007) 'Secondary modern schools: are their pupils disadvantaged?', *British Educational Research Journal,* 33(2): 155–78.

Nespor, J. (1987) 'The role of beliefs in the practice of teaching', *Journal of Curriculum Studies,* 19(4): 317–28.

Nichols, S. L., Glass, G. V. and Berliner, D. C. (2005) *High stakes testing and student achievement: problems for the No Child Left Behind Act.* Tempe, AZ: Educational Policy Studies Laboratory, Arizona State University. Available from http://epicpolicy.org/files/EPSL-0509-105-EPRU.pdf (accessed 26 July 2015).

Office of Qualifications and Examinations Regulation (Ofqual) (2014) *Perceptions of A-Levels, GCSEs and Other Qualifications in England – Wave 12.* Available from http://webarchive.nationalarchives.gov.uk/20141031163546/http://ofqual.gov.uk/news/publications-notice-ofqual-publishes-perceptions-levels-gcses-qualifications-england-wave-12/ (accessed 26 July 2015).

Oliver, W. A. (1953/1954) 'Teachers' education beliefs versus their classroom practices', *Journal of Educational Research,* 47: 47–55.

Pajares, F. M. (1992) 'Teachers' beliefs and educational research: cleaning up a messy construct', *Review of Educational Research,* 62(3): 307–32.

Rapp, D., Sloan, K. and Hostrop, J. (2006) 'Contesting NCLB and high-stakes accountability: continuing acts of resistance', *Journal of Curriculum and Pedagogy,* 3(1): 95–100.

Rogosa, D. (2003) *How Accurate Are the STAR National Percentile Rank Scores for Individual Students? An Interpretative Guide.* Stanford University, CA. Available from http://www-stat.stanford.edu/~rag/accguide/guide03.pdf (accessed 26 July 2015).

Rueda, R. and Garcia, E. (1994) *Teachers' Beliefs about Reading Assessment with Latino Language Minority Students.* NCRCDSLL Research Reports, Center for Research on Education, Diversity and Excellence, UC Berkeley. Available from http://escholarship.org/uc/item/09v8k3sc (accessed 26 July 2015).

Scholastic (2012) *Primary Sources: 2012: America's Teachers on the Teaching Profession.* A Project of Scholastic and the Bill & Melinda Gates Foundation. Available from http://www.scholastic.com/primarysources/pdfs/Gates2012_full.pdf (accessed 26 July 2015).

Sebba, J. (2012) 'Policy and practice in assessment for learning: the experience of selected OECD countries', in J. Gardner (ed.), *Assessment and Learning.* 2nd edn. Thousand Oaks, CA: Sage Publications. pp. 157–170.

Shepard, L. (2000) 'The role of assessment in a learning culture', *Educational Researcher,* 29(7): 4–14.

Sikka, A., Nath, J. L. and Cohen, M. D. (2007) 'Practicing teachers' beliefs and uses of assessment', *International Journal of Case Method Research and Application,* XIX: 3.

STAR (2012) *County Results: California Standards Test (CST) and California Alternate Performance Assessment (CAPA) Summary Reports by Economic Status and Ethnicity.* Sacramento, CA: California Department of Education. Available from http://star.cde.ca.gov/summaryreports2012.asp (accessed 26 July 2015).

STAR (2013) *County Results: California Standards Test (CST) and California Alternate Performance Assessment (CAPA) Summary Reports by Economic Status and Ethnicity.* Sacramento, CA: California Department of Education. Available from http://star.cde.ca.gov/star2013/index.aspx (accessed 26 July 2015).

Strand, S. (2008) *Minority Ethnic Pupils in the Longitudinal Study of Young People in England.* Cedar Newsletter 20 (Spring). Centre for Educational Development, Appraisal and Research, University of Warwick. Available from http://webarchive.nationalarchives.gov.uk/20130401151715/http://www.education.gov.uk/publications/eOrderingDownload/DCSF-RR002.pdf (accessed 26 July 2015).

Tabachnick, B. R. and Zeichner, K. M. (1984) 'The impact of the student teaching experience on the development of teacher perspectives', *Journal of Teacher Education,* 36(6): 28–36.

The Guardian (2012) Examiners axed after marking mistakes. *The Guardian.* 17 May 2012. Available from http://www.guardian.co.uk/education/2012/may/17/examiners-axed-after-marking-mistakes (accessed 26 July 2015).

Torrance, H. (2011) 'Using assessment to drive the reform of schooling: time to stop pursuing the chimera?', *British Journal of Educational Studies,* 59(4): 459–85.

Yung, B. H. (2002) 'Same assessment, different practice: professional consciousness as a determinant of teachers' practice in a school-based assessment scheme', *Assessment in Education: Principles, Policy and Practice,* 9(1): 97–117.

45

The Role of Assessment in Pedagogy – and Why Validity Matters

Paul Black

INTRODUCTION

Assessment is now more prominent in the educational agenda than ever before. One reason for this is the pressures of accountability testing, which have had a very negative effect on the reputation of assessment and are seen by many as the unpleasant dimension of teaching and learning – at best a tiresome necessity, at worst an enemy of teachers, of schools, and of pupils' learning. In a contrary direction, the practices of formative assessment have come to be valued and are widely promoted, but there is an unfortunate contrast – put simply as 'formative assessment good, summative assessment bad'.

This aversion to summative assessment has two unwelcome effects: teachers have to reconcile a desire to improve their formative assessments with the need to implement their own summative assessments and align their teaching to any externally imposed assessments. The summative priority cannot be neglected because the many stakeholders in education need information about the outcomes of schooling, and yet what type of information do these diverse groups need to have, and how can assessment meet these needs? Valid assessment is the answer to this question – a validity that inheres in the inferences that users make on the basis of assessment outcomes (Newton and Shaw, 2014).

The main argument of this chapter is that the lack of coherence between the formative and summative aims of assessment ought to be resolved by re-appraising their roles within the pedagogy for which each should be the servant and not the master. Such resolution should satisfy several conditions. One is that the validity of assessments should not be compromised. Another is that, in serving their functions within pedagogy, assessments should make positive contribution to the overarching aim of strengthening the learning of pupils. A third is that any such re-appraisal should support practices that teachers will find both practicable and rewarding.

The first step in developing this argument is to explore briefly how some authoritative studies of pedagogy attend to, or neglect, the role of assessment, and how their insights and emphases may contribute to, or provide criteria for, the revision of their models of pedagogy.

The chapter then discusses the role of assessment in pedagogy and proposes a simple model of the steps involved in teaching, the purpose of which is to examine the different levels and types of assessment in each of these steps.

The chapter goes on to explore the link between the aims of formal education and the activities that teachers use to guide progress in meeting those aims. It argues that assumptions about the nature of the learning that teachers should try to develop in their students should be a prominent feature of those activities and should be related to criteria for validity.

Also discussed are the assessment responsibilities of teachers and schools and how the use of formative and summative assessments can support and validly reflect the learning aims of education.

The chapter concludes with a summary of the main findings and explains and justifies the model proposed. It also explains how the model expands on, but does not contradict, previous theories of pedagogy, and how it does not claim to be a theory of pedagogy in the broad sense of that term.

THEORIES OF PEDAGOGY –
A BRIEF OVERVIEW

In the literature about pedagogy, there is a range of ways of regarding the relationship between pedagogy and teaching (or, for US authors, instruction). Alexander (2000) for example, regards teaching as embedded in a broader discussion of educational theories, values, evidence or justifications, so that it 'connects the apparently self-contained act of teaching, with culture, structure and mechanisms of social control' (2000: 540). However, from his study of teaching in five different countries, Alexander also concluded

that although continental practice saw pedagogy as a broad domain within which didactics (the domain of methods of teaching) is contained, in England and the US the relationship between pedagogy and didactics has been more diverse, even confused. A similar range of perspectives also applies to the meaning of curriculum, in particular whether or not pedagogy is subsidiary to curriculum.

A different perspective is presented that describes pedagogy as 'those factors affecting the processes of teaching and learning and the inter-relationships between them' (Hallam and Ireson, 1999: 78). Similar emphasis is found in Shulman (1987) and Tyler (1949). Bruner's (1999) focus was similar in his discussion of the link between models of mind and models of pedagogy, with a four-stage model of learning: from imitative learners, to acquisition of propositional knowledge by didactic exposure, to learning as thinkers with the development of inter-subjective interchange, and finally to being knowledgeable in managing the variety of items of knowledge which they may learn (1999: 10–15). This last example is particularly relevant to the discussion that follows below.

What is striking about all of these writings is that they pay little or no attention to assessment. Tyler (1949) pays more attention than most to 'evaluation', arguing that evaluation is required to check whether the teaching is producing the desired effects. For this purpose, it is necessary to test pupils at the start of the learning and at the end so that the gain may be measured. A later test may also be needed to see whether the gains have been permanent.

A different emphasis appears in a US National Academy's study (Pellegrino et al., 2001), which sets its detailed appraisal of assessment methods and purposes in the context of the triangular relationship between Assessment, Curriculum and Instruction (2001: 51–53). One of the study's 12 recommendations was:

Recommendation 11: The balance of mandates and resources should be shifted from an emphasis on external forms of assessments to an increased emphasis on classroom formative assessment designed to assist learning. (2001: 310)

However, ways to take this further in a revised model of pedagogy were not developed.

In summary, three main themes feature in this literature, namely instruction, learning and curriculum. There is no consensus about an order of priority between these three, although assessment is mainly considered as a marginal or external necessity and not as an intrinsic feature. All the authors cited do pay attention to the central focus of pedagogy, i.e., to the teacher's actions in the classroom.

THE ROLE OF ASSESSMENT IN A MODEL OF PEDAGOGY

Any learning programme has to be implemented in a series of stages and has to be designed with these stages in mind. The following sequence sets a model of this implementation in a series of five stages:

A. *Formulating aims*. Ideally, the learning which a programme aims to achieve should be set out clearly and this specification should guide the steps which follow. This does not always happen. Aims are often taken for granted, and so unexamined, perhaps because it is assumed that others, superior in authority or insight, have determined them. Summative assessment demands, whether by schools or by governments, might be seen as another determinant, in tension with perceptions of the needs of students. However, many teachers live with a compromise, between the aims that they value and the aims that underlie imposed assessments.

B. *Planning activities*. Preparation of a lesson, or of a set of lessons about a topic, is determined, implicitly or explicitly, by the aims, which may mean that it is determined by the need to help students succeed with a final assessment. However, in selecting and adapting activities, teachers should keep in mind the need to engage and motivate the students in ways that will help to promote their learning.

C. *Implementation*. In the implementation of a planned activity in the classroom, the teacher's belief about how to help students to learn will be one guiding factor, alongside such others as keeping control, covering the material within a limited time, and working within those forms of interaction with which the teacher is comfortable.

D. *Review the learning achieved*. Teachers' will naturally check on the learning of their students in a variety of ways. Some will be on-the-fly, using the level of attention of the class, or answers to any questions the class has been asked, or more general contributions to class discussion. Other ways rely on observations of classroom work, and written evidence, produced in class, or as homework, or as responses to written tests. All of these are forms of assessment, and each may function in a formative mode to guide immediate or short-term adaptations within stages B or C, or in a summative mode to keep track of progress towards stage E.

E. *Summing up*. This stage is characterised by the use of the assessment results to inform advice to students, and/or to make decisions with or for them, or with other stakeholders, about their future work. Thus it is a formal, and often a terminal, process. (Black, 2013: 210)

Although these five stages follow a sequence, they also interact in many ways. Difficulties encountered in stage C may lead to an immediate change to the activity being implemented. Teachers' reading of written classwork or homework might lead to a change in the plans of stage B or to the pace and style of implementation in stage C. In some cases, the plans for stage C may be amended to allow time to deal with difficulties revealed in stage D, for example when the results of an end-of-topic test show that a particular concept has been misunderstood by many. All of these are interactions through which evidence about the learning is used to alter the planned learning work, that is, they are forms of formative assessment. The interactions are thereby distinguished in function from assessments used in stage E, which serve to inform firm decisions. Formative and summative assessments are distinguished from one another by how their evidence may be used. It is possible for any evidence to be used for both purposes, for example students' results may advise them about further study, but the same results may be used to advise the student or their future teacher about specific weaknesses that may need attention.

The interaction between stage E and the previous stages, especially stage A, is particularly important. Aims are often set out in very general terms, so that although they may look appealing, their meaning is vague – in such cases, the meaning is inevitably made clear in the summative assessment of stage E. The implication is that stage E should be settled together with stage A so that stages B to D can be aimed at achieving success at stage E. Those who set the assessments may therefore determine the meaning of the aims in explicit detail and guide the whole learning plan. In a situation where teachers are responsible for the whole process, stage E would be entirely within their control and they could ensure it reflects the aims that they value, thereby allowing the five-stage pattern to be coherent and self-consistent. Indeed, the need, in the first stages of the planning of a teaching episode, to make explicit the proposed summative assessments can help identify misunderstanding that might undermine the coherence of teaching. Teachers may appear to agree in a general discussion about their aims, but they may disagree about the meaning of their aims when they look at the test questions, where those meanings will be operationalized.

ALIGNING PEDAGOGY WITH THE LEARNING AIMS

Assessments exert a strong influence on the development of a students' learning. If the aim is to ensure that students have committed certain facts to memory, written tests will reflect these aims and will encourage work to achieve them. Different aims, such

as the ability to select from a student's store of knowledge and apply the selection to tackle a problem, will call for different styles of teaching and of assessment. However, the consideration of learning aims should start from a more general and fundamental level. The following two quotations serve to illustrate my development of an argument about aims. I have selected them because they make different, but complementary, points about priorities in learning. The first is from an article in which the authors were drawing on their experience of the development of teachers' assessments in Australian states:

> ...the teacher is increasingly being seen as the primary assessor in the most important aspects of assessment. The broadening of assessment is based on a view that there are aspects of learning that are important but cannot be adequately assessed by formal external tests. These aspects require human judgment to integrate the many elements of performance behaviours that are required in dealing with authentic assessment tasks. (Stanley et al., 2009: 31)

The second is from a study by Thomas Groome, a Christian lay theologian, in a book entitled *Educating for Life*:

> Educators can take over functions that learners should be doing – learning how to learn, making up their own minds, reaching personal decisions. Such imbalance ill serves learners and can be destructive to educators. There is a fine line between empowering learners as their own people and overpowering them – making them too dependent or indebted to teacher or parent. Walking this tightrope is an aspect of the educator's spiritual discipline of a balanced life. (Groome, 2005: 348)

The first quote emphasizes that a model of transmitting facts and skills, to be learnt by rote, will not equip students to meet the challenges that they have to meet, either in advanced study or in the workplace. It calls for assessment tasks, and by implication the learning work prepared for them, to be 'authentic', serving as preparations for the tasks that life beyond the school will present.

The second quotation evokes a different dimension – if students are to be empowered as learners, school learning must serve as an induction into the role of autonomous and self-confident learning, and assessment should encourage the development of these qualities. Learners who are empowered in this way will be well equipped to select and integrate elements of their learning to deal with tasks that reflect this aim.

Teachers and students must work to achieve these two broad aims in the context of day-to-day classroom activity. Adopting this perspective, I shall discuss five different teaching activities, considering for each both its alignment with my five-stage framework for pedagogy, and its justification in the light of its support for important components of learning. Although these alignments and justifications will guide the presentation of the argument, it will be clear that there are, in practice, diverse inter-actions between all the components.

Classroom Dialogue

A necessary feature of classroom work should be that students are actively involved. An obvious first step is for the teacher to ask questions – but that alone is not enough. As one teacher explained:

> When a question is asked or a problem posed who is thinking of the answer? Is anybody thinking about the problem apart from the teacher? How many pupils are actively engaged in thinking about the problem? Is it just a few well motivated pupils or worse is it just the one the teacher picks out to answer the question? The pupil whose initial reaction is like that of a startled rabbit 'Who me sir?' (Black and Harrison, 2001: 56)

The following account by a teacher illustrates her attempts to overcome such problems:

Questioning

> My whole teaching style has become more interactive. Instead of showing how to find solutions, a question is asked and pupils given time to explore answers together. My Year 8 target class is now well-used to this way of working. I find myself using this method more and more with other groups.

No hands

> Unless specifically asked pupils know not to put their hands up if they know the answer to a question. All pupils are expected to be able to answer at any time even if it is an 'I don't know'.

Supportive climate

> Pupils are comfortable with giving a wrong answer. They know that these can be as useful as correct ones. They are happy for other pupils to help explore their wrong answers further. (Black et al., 2003: 40)

This teacher had implemented several changes to her classroom work to encourage student involvement. One was to allow time for students to think about a question and to explore their ideas together before asking them to respond. Another was to establish a practice of calling on any student to speak, and not just those students who were volunteering to take part. A corollary to this practice was to make clear (by her responses to a student's contribution) that the aim was to explore their ideas, not to find out who had the right answer. Of course, this strategy will only work well if the original question is so chosen that it engages and challenges students by going beyond, but not too far beyond, their established understanding.

This strategy is important for two reasons. First, if the teacher can evoke responses from a range of students, this feedback gives the teacher information of how best to proceed, either to advance in building upon their current understanding, or to retreat and repair gaps in that understanding. A second reason is more fundamental and is explained by Alexander (2008), who argued that talk is 'the true foundation of learning', a view he supports as follows:

> Talk vitally mediates the cognitive and cultural spaces between adult and child, among children themselves, between teacher and learner, between society and the individual, between what the child knows and understands and what he or she has yet to know and understand. (Alexander, 2008: 92)

In this view, involvement in dialogue both helps develop students' understanding of the topic under discussion and also helps develop their capacity to learn. Wood (1998) explains further:

> Vygotsky, as we have already seen, argues that such external and social activities are gradually internalized by the child as he comes to regulate his own internal activity. Such encounters are the source of experiences which eventually create the 'inner dialogues' that form the process of mental self-regulation. Viewed in this way, learning is taking place on at least two levels: the child is learning about the task, developing 'local expertise'; and he is also learning how to structure his own learning and reasoning. (Wood, 1998: 98)

If classroom dialogue is to serve these purposes, it must encourage students to express and exchange their ideas. Such encouragement can be at an elementary level, as in the following extract from a discussion about the effects of light on plant growth:

Teacher: 'What do you think Jamie?
Jamie: 'We thought that...' *(pausing with uncertainty)*
Teacher: 'You thought...?'
Jamie: 'That the big'un had eaten up more light'
Teacher: 'I think I know what Monica and Jamie are getting at, but can anyone put the ideas together? Window-light-plants?' (Black et al., 2003: 38)

Here, the teacher's encouragement supports Jamie in his struggle to compose an expression of his ideas, although the teacher's response to Jamie's explanation illustrates a further strategic move: it does not judge the ideas expressed, but invites others to comment on them. The aim here is to involve as many as possible in expressing and exchanging ideas, and perhaps in developing an argument by proposing alternative explanations (as indeed happened later in the same dialogue). Many teachers find it difficult to play the role of encouraging such involvement of students. It is a difficult role because it involves 'steering' the discussion, achieving a balance between a tendency for it to stray too far from the overall aim of the lesson, and the temptation to close down speculation and argument at too early a stage.

Evidence of this difficulty was found in several surveys of classroom dialogue. For example, a US review of 94 school classes in English found that teacher–pupil discussions lasted, on average, 1.7 minutes in every 60 minutes (Applebee et al., 2003). A survey in 2004 by Smith et al. (2004) of whole class teaching in England found that 15 per cent of the sample did not ask open questions; follow-up questions to encourage further dialogue occurred for about 11 per cent of the questions; and pupils' comments were limited to three words or fewer for 70 per cent of the time. They reported that most of the questions asked were of a low cognitive level 'designed to funnel pupils' responses towards a required answer' (Smith et al., 2004: 408).

One of the problems for the teacher who tries to promote a learning dialogue is how to interpret the students' answers because these can often seem strange, even incomprehensible, and it may be necessary to ask for further explanation of these responses.

In trying to interpret such responses, teachers have to compose their models of the internal processes that led a student to give any particular response because without such a model they cannot give a valid response – one that achieves the desired aim of developing the student's own understanding. Although the issues involved here are complex (see Black and Wiliam, 2009: 13–17), it is clear that in effective classroom discussions, the teacher's contributions have to be interpretative rather than evaluative (Davis, 1997).

Dialogue in Writing

The response of a teacher to students' written work is a different mode of dialogue. It can be focused on the needs of the individual, and the teacher has more time to frame a helpful response than in classroom discussions. A common form of response is to return the work to the student with a mark or grade, with or without a comment. The studies of Butler (1988) and Dweck (2000) showed that such feedback could have a negative effect on the development of the student as an effective learner because students regard the grade as a judgment of their ability, an approach that leads them to look at the grades of others and to check their position in the rank order. The written work may therefore be regarded as a terminal test, rather than as a potential help to developing their learning.

Dweck (2000) explains how the form in which feedback is given influences how students view themselves as learners. One such view is to rank oneself as high or low in the rank order of achievement and to believe that this is a fixed position – some people are 'clever', some are not, and you can do little about it. The other view is to see the feedback as a challenge, in a belief that you can do better by your own efforts. Research studies show that the former mindset is more likely to dominate when grades form part of the feedback, whereas the latter is fostered when the only feedback is from comments encouraging learners to improve their work. These studies also show that those with the former mindset are not able to cope with future changes in their learning environment (for example, moves between schools or to higher education), whereas those who believe they can improve by their own efforts are more confident in coping with change and make better progress. Those in this second category are more likely to achieve the broad aims set out in the statements from Stanley et al. (2009) and Groome (2005).

However, there is more involved here than the avoidance of the negative effects of a diet of grades. The earlier quotation from Wood emphasized that the interactions in dialogue are experiences 'which eventually create the "inner dialogues" that form the process of mental self-regulation' (Wood, 1998: 98). Feedback on written work can be more effective in developing reflection on one's own learning – there is more time to reflect than in oral dialogue, and the feedback can be aligned to the needs of the individual. The teacher's task is to formulate comments on each student's work

that help them understand its strengths and weaknesses, and to work to strengthen the weak aspects. My experience of encouraging teachers to change to comment-only marking has been that, although they have to give more attention to composing comments that can help advance the student's learning, many of them – and their students – find that it is eventually rewarding. Thus, mere praise or criticism is of little value unless complemented, as in the following example:

> Richard, clear method, results, table and graphs, but what does this tell you about the relationship? (Black et al., 2003: 44–5)

Here the teacher's comment suggest a way in which the work could be improved, and the additional work suggested could be checked at a later stage, allowing an interactive dialogue in writing to be developed.

Two further reflections by a teacher highlight the realisation that the new focus on comments is a distinctive contribution to student's learning:

> Students are not good at knowing how much they are learning, often because we as teachers do not tell them in an appropriate way …When asked by a visitor how well she was doing in science, the student clearly stated that the comments in her exercise book and those given verbally provide her with the information she needs. (Black et al., 2003: 45–6)

The last of these is evidence that the student was less dependent on grades and felt more responsible for her own learning, thereby meeting Groome's (2005) criteria.

Testing and Learning

Whereas oral dialogue in the classroom is implemented in stage C of the five-point scheme, interaction in writing is in stage D. Written work assignments can require a review of work already covered, reinforcing it by the repetition and reflection involved. In this respect, they have much in common with informal tests, which a teacher might set at the end of work on a topic to help students review what has been learnt and to expose any gaps in that learning.

If comment-only marking can contribute to each student's development as a learner by activating dialogue in written work, a similar strategy could ensure that informal tests have comparable benefits. The key here is that students should be actively involved in the whole process so that a test is seen as something done for them, and in part by them, to improve their learning. This involvement may be developed in three activities. The first activity is to set up checks and procedures to help students prepare for a test. It has been found that many students do not have a strategy for this purpose (Black et al., 2003: 53) and need help to develop an overview of their learning of a topic in which the relationships between its components are understood. Insofar as this involves reflection on their learning at a more general level than required in the day-to-day activities, it adds a new dimension to the task of developing confident and capable learners.

This overview might also be served by a second activity, in which students are asked to prepare for a test by attempting to set questions that might be used in the test. Two research studies have shown that this can lead to improved performance in the test that follows (King, 1992; Foos et al., 1994). This advantage emerged because, when deciding what should be tested, the students had to reflect on the topic and identify those significant features that ought to be tested, that is, they had to develop an overview of their work.

The third activity is to involve students in marking their own and each other's test scripts. A teacher may mark the scripts first without writing on them and then return the scripts to students, asking them to work in groups marking their scripts – they might even be asked to invent their own mark scheme for this purpose.

In these three activities, students may be involved in interactive dialogue when they – and not their teacher – are in control, thereby taking and developing more

responsibility for their learning. At the same time, they are developing an overview of their learning programme, which helps develop meta-cognition whereby students can take on more responsibility for their learning. Sadler (1989) argued that the three basic elements of any evaluative action are to identify the learner's current achievement, view it in relation to the learning aim, and decide how best to proceed towards that aim. These three steps can be seen either as specifying the teacher's responsibility or as specifying what effective learners ought to be able to do for themselves. The challenge here for learners is to achieve an understanding of an aim that is adequate for the orientation of their next step in working towards it – in fact, when such an understanding of an aim has been achieved, students may be well on the way to achieving it. Debates with peers about what constitutes good test questions or why test answers from some are better than their own, will all serve to clarify the meaning of the aims by relating them to concrete examples.

Overall, activities of this kind can produce the outcome described by one teacher as follows:

> They feel that the pressure to succeed in tests is being replaced by the need to understand the work that has been covered and the test is just an assessment along the way of what needs more work and what seems to be fine. (Black et al., 2003: 56–7)

This outcome makes clear that stage D of the scheme of pedagogy can be seen as helping students develop their ability to take responsibility for their own learning and to become more confident and more autonomous in their learning work.

Collaboration in Group Work

The activities in stage D, and to a more limited extent in stage C, will only succeed if students are able to work effectively in groups. Surveys of such work have shown that peer group work can lead to enhancement of learning, but that it often fails to do so because the group do not interact in a productive way (Johnson et al., 2000; Mercer et al. 2004; Blatchford et al., 2006). It takes time and training to help young learners to see the group activity as a way to learn, especially if the exchange of ideas shows that one has to re-consider one's interpretation of, or attempts at, a particular task: successful schemes are described by Dawes et al. (2004) and Baines et al. (2009). These show that such work can extend and enrich the interactive dialogue that occurs in whole-class discussions.

The use of group work in peer-assessment of written assignments and informal tests can help students see the benefit of such work, and they can develop capacity to reflect on their own work through how it is perceived by peers and to compare their work with their peers' work. It also helps develop their capacity to collaborate in groups. This is of value because group collaborations play an important part in education and in the workplace – employers will often say that the capacity of their staff to work effectively in groups is essential for the progress of many aspects of their work (European Round Table (ERT), 1995; European Commission, 2010).

VALIDITY OF THE ASSESSMENTS BY TEACHERS AND SCHOOLS

In the literature about assessment validity, the main focus is often on such salient points as assessments that inform selection for later stages, whether of further education or of the work-place. However, some stakeholders, notably teachers, parents and students, also have other extensive interests in the validity of assessments, notably those that are made in schools on a yearly basis or more frequently. The formative assessments made by teachers are also used to inform such decisions as the need for teachers to change their teaching, the need for more or different efforts from individual students, decisions by or for a student as to whether or not to

proceed further with study of particular subjects and the use of the results from this year's teacher by next year's teacher. All these decisions should be helped by evidence from assessments, which is the criterion for its validity (Newton and Shaw, 2014: 206–7).

The overall effectiveness of any assessment for learning (AfL) depends on how the tasks reveal what is needed to improve the learning, on the quality of the teacher's decisions about the use of that evidence, and on the effectiveness of any ensuing interventions to further advance the learning.

Summative and Formative Roles

Many implications for assessment have been discussed earlier in the chapter, but they have not been explored because the aim was to maintain an emphasis on assessment as the servant of pedagogy, and therefore of the high quality learning that pedagogy should be designed to foster. Evidence that a range of formative assessment practices can improve learning (Black and Wiliam, 1998) does not necessarily make clear how this improvement is achieved. If the links between these innovations and their effects on students' learning are not understood, adaptation or extension of the practices researched may not replicate the positive effects.

Some of the criteria implied by the earlier discussion can be summarised by stating that assessments overall should help develop:

a) learners' capacity to engage in and learn from interactive dialogue;
b) learners' capacity to reflect critically on the detailed outcomes of their own work and to take initiatives to improve it;
c) learners' capacity to collaborate in group-work;
d) learners' capacity to achieve a broad overview of their progress and to guide their development in the light of its aims;
e) the empowerment of learners to make their own decisions in well-informed and thoughtful ways;
f) the broad aims, of helping learners to integrate the many elements of performance in ways that will be needed to meet real and complex tasks that society will increasingly encounter.

These aims involve, in different proportions, both summative and formative functions of assessments. In what follows, I shall treat these two functions separately, whilst recognising that there are varying degrees of overlap between them.

The alignments of some of this list with the best practices of AfL are quite clear. Aim (a) is related to the use of classroom dialogue in stage C; however, the link is critical – open questions or engaging tasks are but a means to an end that is only secured through the quality of the dialogue generated. If many students contribute, with contributions in the form of sentences rather than single words or phrases, and if these show evidence of thoughtful reasoning, then this aim is being achieved. The criterion for validity of this assessment is that the teacher's inferences (drawn from student contributions) about the learning achieved are justified by the evidence. This criterion can only be met if points raised are challenged and exchanged in order to display more clearly the basis of the students' thinking. Moreover, it should be noted that whilst one-on-one dialogue may be simpler to implement than whole-class discussion, because it aims only to help one respondent, in whole-class discussion teachers' intervention will usually be designed to help both the respondent and, at the same time, the rest of the class by evoking alternative or complementary ideas from other students. Insofar as there is a sequence of contributions and responses, teachers may be making their decisions quite frequently, but they will also be making another type of decision – a meta-decision about when it would be best to sum-up the discussion and/or to change its direction by introducing new ideas or new evidence. Validity overall will depend on the quality of the design and implementation of the initial task and on the decisions about subsequent interventions.

Aim (b) is served by the activity of stage D if the practice of feedback by comment-only marking is similarly thoughtful. The teacher's inferences about how a student's achievement may be improved are more likely to be valid if responses to any comments are followed up in further dialogue, oral or written. Aim (c) is also involved here if peer-assessment forms part of the evaluation of written work and of informal tests.

Aims (d) and (e) are more difficult. Evidence of their achievement may arise from longer term changes in students' approach to learning. More direct evidence can be produced by moving from the closely circumscribed tasks that characterise (a) and (b) to longer and more open-ended tasks in which the learner has to take more responsibility. Such tasks may well involve group collaboration. They can also develop to become more like the complex-real-world tasks with which aim (f) is concerned. The validity of the teacher's feedback on the products of such work will depend on whether the tasks are so designed and presented that students are engaged in taking responsibility for guiding their own work. The capabilities involved, such as researching the background of a problem, seeking new evidence that a task might require, or summing up the findings in a clear and critical report, will only develop if the teacher makes clear that they are required.

It follows that the assessments should cover the whole range of capacities that the learner should have developed through schooling. Whether summative assessments are made at stages within the school system, or are made when the student is about to leave school, the common practice of basing such assessments on a student's performance produced over only a few hours, in isolation, from memory, and responding to demands that they may not have seen before, to which an immediate response in writing is required, is strange. No business enterprise would think of assessing employees' progress in this way. It is hard to justify a decision by a school, which has known about many pieces of work by a student, produced in a range of contexts and on different occasions, to base key decisions on short terminal tests.

In-School Summative Assessments

At this point, it is necessary to consider separately those summative assessments that are controlled by schools because they are for internal uses. These uses include providing information when a class passes from one teacher to the next, informing decisions made by or for students about choices between subjects for further study, and, in aggregate over whole classes, informing longer term decisions by individual teachers or by management groups. For all of these purposes, validity is essential. It can be undermined in the following ways:

- the marking of the assessment may be unreliable because different markers interpret the same criteria in different ways;
- students vary in their performance from day-to-day;
- the assessment uses too narrow a range of tasks, failing to cover important aspects of the learner;
- given that students vary in their response to different types of demand, for example between an essay assignment and an experimental task, the methods of assessment may cover too narrow a range of demands.

These can be seen as threats to the reliability, to the requirement that a parallel version of the assessment tasks, attempted at similar times, would yield the same results. This is a necessary condition for achieving validity, but not a sufficient one because assessments may accurately measure the wrong aspect of the learners' capacities. However, the third and fourth bullet points also involve validity: one cannot, for example, infer from a competent analysis of a set of measurements that the student could select, set up and use the equipment required to produce those measurements.

Black et al.'s (2011, 2013) reports on exploratory work with teachers from three schools revealed some of the problems and potential benefits of work to improve teachers' summative assessments. In this work, a first audit showed that the quality of their existing practices had been neglected so that their policy had to be reconstructed. The first step was to focus on the validity of the assessments by encouraging discussion on what was meant when one teacher told others that a pupil was good at a subject. The following comment, by a teacher of English, shows the value of these discussions:

> The project made me think more critically about what exactly I was assessing. The first question I remember being asked ('what does it mean to be good at English?') gave me a different perspective on assessment. I find myself continually returning to this question. (Black et al., 2013: 8)

Such reflections led teachers to supplement their existing use of formal tests with assessments of other activities. One effect was that as the range covered was expanded, the work revealed new aspects of the students' capabilities. Thus, for a mathematics activity:

> I think it changed the dynamics of the lesson a little bit, in terms of well, in terms of there being much more an element of them getting on trying to find out...they were trying to be more independent, I think, I think some of them struggled with that, and others...some of them, some still find it quite difficult if they are not hand held all the way through. When others were happier to sort of, go their own way. (Black et al., 2013: 19)

To represent diversity of their students' work, the terminal assessment of each was based on a portfolio, a collection of a student's different productions. The variety, of times, of occasions, and of types of activity enriched the validity of the overall results; however, the assessment criteria used, and their application, had to be checked to ensure comparability between students from classes of different teachers of students in the same year and with criteria applied by other stakeholders – notably those who would teach the same students in their next school year.

Two additions to the school's assessment work had to be explored to achieve this aim. The main one was that teachers should work in groups to check one another's grading.

Each group member would select samples of their student's work, make their own assessments privately, and then circulate them to the rest of the group. When all samples had been circulated, the group would meet, share their independent assessment grades with one another and discuss differences in their gradings in order to resolve them. These moderation meetings frequently revealed differences, usually arising from different interpretations of the same criteria. Moderation was only feasible if the work produced by different classes was from similar tasks, and so the second new aspect of the work was that teachers had to agree beforehand on common tasks that were to be included in, and form a large proportion of, every portfolio. These moderation meetings eventually came to be regarded as valuable because the attention to the concrete examples of students' work opened up useful discussions. A typical reflection on this aspect from an English teacher was:

> I think it's quite a healthy thing for a department to be doing because I think it will encourage people to have conversations and it's about teaching and learning...it really provides a discussion hopefully as well to talk about quality and you know what you think of was a success in English. Still really fundamental conversations. (Black et al., 2013: 20)

External Summative Assessments

For the formal summative assessments of stage E, the requirements of validity are different. There is a wider range of stakeholders involved and most stakeholders will look for the ability to apply the abilities that they value. Different countries operate different external assessment systems. At one end of the spectrum are those where all students have to take written tests, externally set and marked, in which their teachers play no part. The results are used to make public judgments of schools so that every school is under pressure to prepare their students for these tests. The current system in England is, for most subjects, an example of this policy. At the other end of the spectrum is a system in which the assessments are entirely in the hands of schools, who are required to work in

groups, with each group taking responsibility for specifying the content requirement for portfolios and for conducting inter-school moderation meetings.

It is clear that assessments based entirely on written tests cannot be valid – the only inferences that their results can support with confidence is that students can respond to the specific demands that they make. Attempts to complement these with a limited range of school-based assessments have not been effective – most of these in England are now being abandoned. There are several reasons for this, including a lack of discrimination because teachers marks are bunched towards the top-end of the mark range, the belief that under the accountability pressures attached to results teachers do not adhere to the rules, and the limited scope of the systems of moderation used to check schools' results.

If assessments by teachers and schools are to claim the validity, which any high-stakes terminal testing should secure, there has to be substantial investment in the means to secure that validity. Such investment must aim to improve teachers' assessment skills, so that they can consider all of the important aims of students' learning, compose activities to assess these, and assemble the outcomes in a student's portfolio that meets the requirement implied by the statements of Stanley at al. (2009) and Groome (2005). Another requirement is to build a system of intra-school and inter-school moderation, with checks of further samples at higher levels to ensure comparability across each national or state assessment authority. Such systems have been established in Ontario, New Zealand and the Australian states of Queensland and New South Wales. These systems take several years to develop, but they can enhance the status and confidence of teachers. Moreover, the work that they require has been seen as enriching the central task of teachers. One modest attempt to develop schools' own assessments in England was eventually welcomed, as found in these other countries, by teachers as a source of professional development, with positive effects on their thinking about their curriculum and about their students' learning (Black et al., 2011).

In summary, this chapter has considered how the concept of validity can be applied to assessments that serve different purposes. For its application to summative assessments, the problem is to achieve optimum compromise between the various inferences that different users of the information need to make: one clear example is that the validity criteria for an assessment made at the end of a year (that is, to make decisions about work for the following year in the school), are quite different from criteria for an assessment at the end of the final year in school.

COHERENT SYSTEMS

This chapter has shown how, in a new model of pedagogy, attention to the learning aims is secured by the ways in which the design of teaching is linked to that of the assessments at all levels from the frequent teacher–learner interactions in the classroom to the formulation of the terminal assessments.

The way the design principles secure validity is discussed, including how the concept is relevant to assessments that serve different purposes. This account is developed in the later discussion of summative assessments by exploring how the outcomes of assessments are used by a wide range of groups who make decisions using the assessment results.

It is not claimed here that the incorporation of the uses of assessments into every stage in the design and implementation of pedagogy helps secure all of the aims of school education, nor that this chapter deals with all of implications of the model that the chapter presents. Such important aims of education as moral education and education for citizenship, and how these should be reflected in the curriculum are not discussed here (see Reiss and White, 2013). Furthermore, the chapter considers only a few aspects of the broader framework of culture, structure and mechanisms of social control, and for this reason it

is presented as a model; a full theory would have to incorporate this model into the wider consideration of the context of education.

The new model that this work highlights is not inconsistent with the theories discussed earlier. As pointed out, the common elements of these theories were instruction, learning and curriculum. The model presented here accepts and incorporates these elements, although in common with earlier theories, has its own way of inter-relating them. It is unique in including assessment in new ways and in claiming that it ought to feature strongly in any theory.

It should also be noted that the model is not 'theoretical' in the pejorative sense of being isolated from the realities of practice. Many of the findings quoted in this chapter emerged from work with teachers and draws upon the experiences of, and reports by, teachers to illustrate how their experiences have guided the formulation of the principles.

REFERENCES

Alexander, R. (2000) *Culture and Pedagogy: International Comparisons In Primary Education.* Oxford: Blackwell.

Alexander, R. (2008) *Essays in Pedagogy.* Abingdon, UK: Routledge.

Applebee, A.N., Langer, J.A., Nystrand, M. and Gamoran, A. (2003) 'Discussion based approaches to developing understanding: classroom instruction and student performance in middle and high school English', *American Educational Research Journal,* 40(3): 685–730.

Baines, E., Blatchford, P. and Kutnick, P. (2009) *Promoting Effective Group Work in the Primary Classroom.* London: Routledge.

Black, P. (2013) 'Pedagogy in theory and in practice: Formative and summative assessments in classrooms and in systems', in D. Corrigan, R. Gunstone and A. Jones (eds.), *Valuing Assessment in Science Education: Pedagogy, Curriculum, Policy.* Dordrecht: Springer. pp. 207–29.

Black, P. and Harrison, C. (2001) 'Feedback in questioning and marking: the science teacher's role in formative assessment', *School Science Review,* 82(301): 55–61.

Black, P. and Wiliam, D. (1998) 'Assessment and classroom learning', *Assessment in Education: Principles Policy and Practice,* 5(1): 7–73.

Black, P. and Wiliam, D. (2009) 'Developing the theory of formative assessment', *Educational Assessment, Evaluation and Accountability,* 21(1): 5–31.

Black, P., Harrison, C., Hodgen, J., Marshall, B. and Serret, N. (2011) 'Can teachers' summative assessments produce dependable results and also enhance classroom learning?', *Assessment in Education: Principles Policy and Practice,* 18(4): 451–69.

Black, P., Harrison, C., Hodgen, J., Marshall, B. and Serret, N. (2013) *Inside the Black Box of Assessment: Assessment of Learning by Teachers and Schools.* London: GL Assessment.

Black, P., Harrison, C., Lee, C., Marshall, B. and Wiliam, D. (2003) *Assessment for Learning – Putting it into practice.* Buckingham, UK: Open University Press.

Blatchford, P., Baines, E., Rubie-Davies, C., Bassett, P., and Chowne, A. (2006) 'The effect of a new approach to group-work on pupil-pupil and teacher-pupil interactions', *Journal of Educational Psychology,* 98(4): 750–65.

Bruner, J.S. (1999) 'Folk pedagogies', in J. Leach and B. Moon (eds.) *Learners and Pedagogy.* London: Paul Chapman. Chapter 1.

Butler, R. (1988) 'Enhancing and undermining intrinsic motivation; the effects of task-involving and ego-involving evaluation on interest and performance', *British Journal of Educational Psychology,* 58(1): 1–14.

Davis, B. (1997) Listening for differences: an evolving conception of mathematics teaching', *Journal for Research in Mathematics Education,* 28(3): 355–76.

Dawes, L., Mercer, N. and Wegerif, R. (2004) *Thinking Together: A Programme of Activities for Developing Speaking, Listening and Thinking Skills for Children aged 8–11.* Birmingham, UK: Questions Publishing Company.

Dweck, C.S. (2000) *Self-Theories: Their Role in Motivation, Personality and Development.* Philadelphia, PA: Psychology Press.

European Commission (2010) *Assessment of Key Competences: Draft Background Paper* for the Belgian Presidency Meeting for Directors-General for School Education. Brussels: European Council of Ministers.

European Round Table (ERT) (1995) *Education for Europeans: Towards the Learning Society.* Brussels: The European Round Table of Industrialists.

Foos, P.W., Mora, J.J. and Tkacz, S. (1994) 'Student study techniques and the generation effect', *Journal of Educational Psychology,* 86(4): 567–76.

Groome, T.H. (2005) *Educating for Life.* New York, NY: Crossroad Publishing Company.

Hallam, S. and Ireson, J. (1999) 'Pedagogy in the secondary school', in P. Mortimore (ed.), *Understanding Pedagogy and Its Impact on Learning.* London: Paul Chapman. pp. 68–97.

Johnson, D.W., Johnson, R.T. and Stanne, M.B. (2000) *Cooperative Learning Methods: A Meta-Analysis.* Minneapolis, MN: University of Minnesota.

King, A. (1992) 'Facilitating elaborative learning through guided student-generated questioning', *Educational Psychologist,* 27(1): 111–26.

Mercer, N., Dawes, L., Wegerif, R. and Sams, C. (2004) 'Reasoning as a scientist: ways of helping children to use language to learn science', *British Educational Research Journal,* 30(3): 359–77.

Newton, P.E. and Shaw, S.D. (2014) *Validity in Educational and Psychological Assessment.* London UK: Sage Publications.

Pellegrino, J.W., Chudowsky, N. and Glaser, R. (2001) *Knowing what Students Know: the Science and Design of Educational Assessement.* Washington, DC: National Academy Press.

Reiss, M.J. and White, J. (2013) *An Aims-based Curriculum: The Significance of Human Flourishing for Schools.* London: Institute of Education Press.

Sadler, D.R. (1989) 'Formative assessment and the design of instructional systems', *Instructional Science,* 18: 119–44.

Shulman, L.S. (1987) 'Knowledge and teaching: foundations of the new reform', *Harvard Educational Review,* 57(1): 1–22.

Smith, F., Hardman, F., Wall, K. and Worz, M. (2004) 'Interactive whole class teaching in the National Literacy and Numeracy strategies', *British Educational Research Journal,* 30(3): 395–411.

Stanley, G., MacCann, R., Gardner, J., Reynolds, L. and Wild, I. (2009). *Review of Teacher Assessment: What Works Best and Issues for Development.* Oxford: Oxford University Centre for Educational Development.

Tyler, R.W. (1949) *Basic Principles of Curriculum and Instruction.* Chicago, IL: University of Chicago Press.

Wood, D. (1998) *How Children Think and Learn* (2nd edn.). Oxford: Blackwell.

46

Assessment for Learning: A Pedagogical Tool

Kari Smith

INTRODUCTION

The title of this chapter is the title of a course I was teaching for many years in in-service as well as in pre-service teacher education programs. Two hours a week in a full semester I talked about the pedagogical values of assessment, not as a judgmental activity at the end of a learning process, but as a pedagogical tool to be used by teachers to enhance learning during the learning process. During the course we discussed theories of learning, emphasizing socio-cultural aspects of learning (Vygotsky, 1978), motivational theories (Bandura, 1997; Deci and Ryan, 2000), self-regulated learning (Zimmerman and Schunk, 2001), and how to apply these in assessment practice. The main purpose of the course was to support teachers in developing a new understanding of the value of assessment in daily teaching and to enhance student learning to achieve better grades on the final exam. My teaching in the course was heavily influenced by the work of Black and Wiliam (Black and Wiliam, 1998a, 1998b), the work of the Assessment Reform Group in the UK (2002) and by Rick Stiggins's (Stiggins, 1988; 2002) and Thomas Guskey's work from the US (Guskey, 2003). Further away geographically, but not less meaningful was the work of David Boud in Australia (Boud, 1995) and Royce Sadler's strong theoretical perspectives on assessment (Sadler, 1989). When I first heard Terry Crooks from New Zealand talk about intelligent accountability at The 2003 AERA annual meeting in Chicago, and the way it was practised in New Zealand through the country's National Monitoring project (Crooks, 2002), I was relieved to learn that at least one country, New Zealand, had at that time not given in to the rapidly developing testing and accountability regimes so widespread internationally. The course curriculum, as well as the reading lists, was truly international, and it was my task to make it all relevant to the teachers and student teachers in that specific context.

If I were to teach the course again, in a different context, I would have developed the course plan based on the same theories and principles, namely that teachers need to have a thorough understanding of the theories on which assessment as a pedagogical tool is built to be able to practise assessment for learning (AfL). There are, however, some basic changes I would make to the course. At that time I viewed assessment of learning (AoL) as a 'no-concept', and I presented tables that clearly illustrated the differences between the 'bad' AoL and the skeleton solution to all pedagogical problems: AfL. My perspectives have changed, and today I believe that AfL has to be preceded by AoL in order to establish a baseline on which AfL is built. In addition, the currently expanded understanding of what assessment includes makes sense to me, and the use of the term assessment 'as' learning (AsL) is a valuable development that I have learned much about from later work by Boud (2001, 2007). Interesting developments taking place in Scotland, where assessment 'is' for learning has become a frequently used concept, caught my attention and triggered my curiosity. Wyatt-Smith et al. (2014) offer an overview of the widespread interest in an expanded perception of assessment as a pedagogical tool. Moreover, the understanding of who the learners are when discussing AsL has also changed, and today I would argue that assessment is just as much about teachers' learning as it is about students' learning in alignment with, for example, the work of Helen Timperley from New Zealand (Timperley, 2011). Students and teachers are partners in contexts where assessment is used as a pedagogical tool. This chapter is structured to mirror my professional journey in understanding the potential of assessment as a pedagogical tool.

I begin by discussing the theoretical foundations for the claim that assessment is a core pedagogical tool for strengthening a broader concept of learning than what can be measured by standardized tests. In the second part of the chapter, some of the challenges in deepening an understanding of the potential of assessment as a pedagogical tool among teachers and other stakeholders will be raised. Finally, I will raise concerns about the implications of global political trends that focus on extensive external accountability demands (Lingard and Sellar, 2013).

ASSESSMENT AND SOCIO-CULTURAL ASPECTS OF LEARNING

Learning takes place in two spheres: in the personal sphere where the individual learner develops new and/or richer understandings and in the social sphere where understanding is heavily influenced by the context in which it takes place (Hodkinson et al., 2008).

In the personal sphere, theoretical principles of constructivism are apposite, where the focus is on the learner and what the learner does when constructing knowledge and the understanding of knowledge. Instruction is about supporting the learner's building of their body of knowledge (Duffy and Cunningham, 1996). The usefulness of new knowledge and understanding is assessed within a certain context, and the learner puts the new knowledge into practice in a real-life context (Rorty, 1991). Thus learning, even in a constructivist view, does not take place in isolation; it takes place within a specific context and will be influenced by the actors in that context, in other words, knowledge becomes contextually dependent. This suggests that learning cannot be seen only from an individual constructivist perspective: a socio-constructivist perspective on learning is more appropriate (Vygotsky, 1962, 1978).

In the broader sphere, learning takes place in a specific context created by the culture, the history of that culture and of the learner, and other participants. The learner is in dialogue with the context as well as with other members of the same context, and individual learning becomes influenced by the socio-cultural environment in which it takes place (Sfard, 1998; Säljö, 2001, 2006; Mason, 2007). There is an ongoing dialogue between the person's internal dialogue (intramental) and the interactive dialogue with other people in the same context (intermental) (Vygotsky, 1978).

Learning, therefore, is not always planned; it is developed within a specific situation with specific people and where some learning is implicit rather than explicit. Vygotsky (1978) claims that learning takes place within the individual learner's zone of proximal development (ZPD), an undefinable zone above the current level of understanding. New understandings develop in interaction between the learner (the subject), what has to be learned (the object) and a mediator or artefact which may include the teacher, other learners, a textbook or Internet site. Vygotsky defined ZPD as:

> The distance between actual developmental level as determined by independent problem solving and the level and potential development as determined through problem solving under adult guidance or in collaboration with more capable peers. (Vygotsky, 1978: s.86)

THE LEARNING DIALOGUE

What, then, is the relation to assessment and the teacher's assessment practices? The Latin root of the word assessment is *assidere,* which means to 'sit beside' (Merriam-Webster, 2003). When I learned about the origin of the word assessment as a schoolteacher (and teacher educator) working on my PhD about self-assessment many years ago, I felt a kind of revelation that has become part of my professional work ever since. It is the teacher's job to 'sit beside the learner' and to support the learner by scaffolding the learning process. The dialogue that develops between the learner and the teacher, the learning dialogue, is essential in AoL as well as in AfL. Freire (1970) talks about the importance of education through respectful dialogues where the interlocutors act on each other's responses and the information found in these responses. Through dialogue, the teacher uses information

volunteered by the learner to assess the current level of understanding and jointly with the learner plans the route to the next milestone in the learning process. The learner and the teacher represent two different worlds, and they have to create a shared space for a true learning dialogue to develop. Rommetveit (1972, 2003) calls this intersubjectivity, which is a shared understanding of the situation true to the here and now. Dov Darom (2000) from Israel was perhaps the first who opened my mind to the importance of educational dialogue. In his lessons he talked about the role of respect in teaching, emphasizing respect for all students as human beings and the teachers' task in supporting student development. In his own teaching and writing he repeatedly emphasized the responsibility of the teacher to develop respectful dialogues with students and to accept them as equals in their humanity:

> Humanistic education is based on dialogue, the 'I' and 'THOU' type of dialogue (Martin Buber). True dialogue can take place only among equals (Freire, 1973). Looking at this issue superficially, one may conclude that there is no equality between teachers and pupils. Their knowledge and life experiences are truly not equal. In their basic humanity, however, in their need to be heard, respected, accepted, never humiliated, there is a large degree of equality. As human beings they are fully equal; their personal needs, aspirations, dreams and hopes, strengths and weaknesses are valued equally. If we can address our pupils in this frame of mind, we create the foundation for meaningful educational dialogue. (Darom, 2000: 20)

This is, in my view, the heart, not only of education, but also of the pedagogy in assessment. The learner and the teacher seek agreement about what the learner can do in order to plan for the next stage and how to get there. The teacher is the mediator of the learning process (Vygotsky, 1978); however, mediation is difficult unless information is volunteered by the learner within a mutually respectful environment.

In more recent assessment literature we find similar ideas related to feedback to the learner. Hattie and Timperley (2007) talk about three basic questions learners should have an answer for: where am I going; where am I; and what am I doing next? The pedagogical principle is, however, that the answers to these questions are not given by the teacher informing the learner, but that the learner and the teacher find the answers in the course of the learning dialogue. Through my meetings with teachers, more recently mainly in Norway where AfL has been on the political education agenda for a decade now, teachers are well acquainted with these three questions, and often feel they act accordingly in their assessment practices. However, recent research suggests that the teacher often assesses students' current level of understanding by using tests, and they provide written and sometimes unclear feedback, and feed forward that is of little use to the students (Havnes et al., 2010; Gamlem and Smith, 2013). The learning dialogue is missing and assessment, perceived to be AfL, is in fact a monologue by the teacher.

Assessment as a pedagogical tool requires a deep understanding of pedagogical principles to be practised beneficially in the instructional encounter (Smith, 2001) and becomes part of teachers' assessment literacy, which is a concept recently used for understanding assessment. Webb defines this as:

> The knowledge of the means for assessing what students know and can do, the interpretation of the results from these assessments, and applications of the assessment results to improve student learning and program effectiveness. (Webb, 2002: 1)

Stiggins (1995) uses the terms sound and unsound assessment, which I choose to understand as pedagogical and unpedagogical assessment focusing on the student and student learning:

> Assessment literates know the difference between sound and unsound assessment. They are not intimidated by the sometimes mysterious and always daunting technical world of assessment. (Stiggins, 1995: 240)

Assessment literacy is more than following recipes; technically it is a well-informed and mindful professional practice that requires teacher learning and professional growth, a theme I shall return to later in the chapter.

MOTIVATIONAL ASPECTS

If AfL is to have the desired effect on learners and their achievements, the individual learner must believe that they capable of reaching the next goal or milestone in the learning process. Through a mindful and pedagogical dialogue, the teacher helps the learner to understand the current level of learning and supports the learner in strengthening the belief in their own competence that they are capable to progress and can reach the next goal. The teacher supports the learner in developing a positive dissatisfaction with the current level of learning, but at the same time the learner is confident that progress is possible. This view builds on Bandura's (1977) notion of self-efficacy, the motivational belief in one's ability to stretch further as an outcome of dialogue with others (Bandura, 1986). In a school situation, the teacher represents a significant other, and the assessment dialogue becomes central to developing self-efficacy within the learner. If the learner perceives the feedback as progress that is unachievable, AfL does not take place because assessment is situated outside the learner's ZPD (Vygotsky, 1978). When this happens, the learner is likely to develop a negative dissatisfaction with the current stage, meaning that they find it too difficult or impossible to proceed, and there is an increased possibility that the learner will become demotivated and may even give up. The demotivating processes the learner experiences are not always made explicit and observed by the teacher; however, inherent in teachers' assessment literacy lies, as I see it, the teacher's skill to balance the feedback to the individual learner in such ways that the learner develops and maintains a positive dissatisfaction with own learning, and yet at the same time develops a strong belief that 'I can do it'. Learners and their learning become the primary focus for assessment in relation to clearly expressed situational goals, and therefore the final goal (summary assessment/exam) is not neglected, but it takes on a secondary focus during the learning process.

In this way, sound pedagogy and sound assessment (AfL) merge to a significant extent.

Much has been written about how assessment impacts learning, and the way assessment as practised often dictates the way learners behave in a learning situation (Snyder, 1971; Gibbs and Simpson, 2003, 2004; Black et al., 2003; Brown, 2004; Gardner, 2006; Stobart, 2008). Assessment becomes, in certain ways, the hidden curriculum (Snyder, 1971; Miller and Parlett, 1974). Since the publication of Black and Wiliam's (1998a) review study 'Inside the Black Box', there are strong claims in the literature that moving away from high stakes standardised tests to ongoing formative assessment (AfL) is preferable when the aim is to enhance learning and, ultimately, to improve grades (Gardner, 2006; Stobart, 2008; Harlen and Gardner, 2010; Hattie, 2009). In this chapter, an additional aspect of the contribution of AfL to the learning process is discussed, more specifically motivation for learning, which is closely related to the learner's belief in themselves, the learner's self-efficacy. The extent to which self-efficacy is developed (or sustained) depends on the way teachers nurture intrinsic and extrinsic motivation for learning.

Ryan and Deci (2000) argue that learning best takes place when three basic needs are being fulfilled: the need for competence, relatedness and autonomy within a social context. 'The inherent tendency to seek out novelty and challenges, to extend one's capacities, to explore, and to learn' (Ryan and Deci, 2000: 70) is defined as intrinsic motivation and found to be conducive to learning (Deci and Ryan, 2000). Its development is, however, dependent on the extent to which these three conditions are being met. Does the learner feel competent in school, in learning a specific subject, and in undertaking a specific task? Does the learner feel related and accepted within the social setting in which learning takes place to take risks that might lead to not succeeding? Does the learner enjoy autonomy, being able to choose among several alternatives in selecting tasks

as well as alternative ways to approach the task? To what extent is it possible for the teacher to create an environment that fosters intrinsic motivation in classes with 25 or more students, with the external pressure of getting through the content, so that external exam requirements can be met? The claim made in this chapter is that when the teacher engages with the class and the individual learner in learning dialogues based on constructive feedback and feed forward, and when assessment activities are varied and created in dialogue with learners, there is a greater likelihood that the learning environment will support, rather than hinder, students' development of intrinsic motivation for learning.

A major goal for schooling is to prepare students for assessments in the form of external examinations, which serve as entrance tickets for further and higher education. It would be unwise to look at examinations as being only harmful and demotivating. Extrinsic motivation, 'the performance of an activity in order to attain some separable outcome' (Ryan and Deci, 2000: 71) is perhaps, the type of motivation that most often initiates activity and production in our daily lives as well as in school. We act and perform because we have to, we are driven by an internal feeling of duty, we want to avoid punishments and gain rewards, and sometimes we have little choice but to do as we are told. Many students are driven by the instrumental value in learning and in studying specific subjects that inherently require external and standardised assessment forms. They have to pass the exam. Ryan and Deci (2000) suggest that extrinsically driven activities are, at times, undertaken because of choices we make, for example in selecting particular courses in higher education because of the doors they will open to a particular professional life. Extrinsic motivation can be a useful driver for learning. However, the question remains – does exposure to external standards foster the conditions for meaningful growth in learning, that is, experiencing a positive dissatisfaction with one's current level of learning and believing in one's capacity to make progress? When looking at my own experience as a schoolteacher and as a university professor, I would say that in both contexts practising AfL is a major pedagogical tool when preparing students for summative AoL. The balance between the two differs greatly. The value of assessment as a pedagogical tool does not lie mainly in preparing learners for exams, but much more in preparing them for a lifelong learning process in which they believe in themselves as capable and contributing members of the society. In higher education the main motivation for learning is often to get a qualification, and yet my experience tells me that practising AfL during the learning process makes the learner not only appreciate and enjoy the process on the way to the extrinsic goal, but also develop a deeper understanding of the concepts (Deci and Ryan, 2000; Gibbs and Simpson, 2004).

SELF-REGULATED LEARNING

In his overview article from 1990, Zimmerman concludes that learners who take initiative activated by intrinsic motivation and who take on responsibility for their learning are successful academically. Zimmerman's claim is supported by others (Andrade, 2010; Pekrun et al., 2011) and by his own later research (Schunk and Zimmerman, 1997; Zimmerman, 2000). Zimmerman (1990) argues that 'self-regulated learners select and use self-regulated learning processes to achieve desired academic outcomes on the basis of feedback about learning effectiveness and skill' (Zimmerman, 1990: 6–7). Feedback as part of assessment plays a key role in self-regulated learning because it is in the light of feedback that learners regulate their learning processes, what Hattie and Timperley (2007) call feedback on process. The communication between the teacher and the learner in light of planned and performed tasks is the foundation of self-regulated learning.

Zimmerman (1990) states that 'students' self-regulated learning involves three features: their use of self-regulated learning strategies, their responsiveness to self-oriented feedback about learning effectiveness, and their interdependent motivational processes' (Zimmerman, 1990: 6). The teacher and other members of the learning community are central dialogue partners in self-regulated learning. But the teacher is not the decision maker. According to Zimmerman (2000) self-regulation can be divided in to three cyclic phases:

1 Forethought – the reflective processes that precede actions, and includes assessing personal competence to undertake the tasks, planning and goal setting.
2 Performance or volitional control – the self-monitoring taking place when working on the task, assessing the effectiveness of chosen strategies, and if the learner finds it necessary, making changes. Affective aspects of the process influence decisions made during this stage, which heavily depend on feedback from self and significant others.
3 Self-reflection – assessment processes that take place when the task is completed and the learner re-examines the learning process as well as the learning outcome.

Self-regulation refers to the learners monitoring the learning process, to look at their own learning in relation to a specific task or to a course from a meta-perspective. These three phases are analogous to the three main processes described in recent theories of formative assessment (Andrade, 2010; Black and Wiliam, 2009), especially in relation to the three questions mentioned previously in this chapter to which learners seek answers: where am I going, where am I, and what am I doing next? (Hattie and Timperley, 2007).

SUSTAINABLE ASSESSMENT

Theories of self-regulation and assessment are also closely linked with the work of

David Boud who has published widely on the relationship between assessment and life-long learning, what he calls sustainable assessment (Boud and Falchikov, 2006; Boud, 2014). Sustainable assessment is not a new form for assessment, but an extension of the functions of assessment, beyond accreditation and assessment for learning. In sustainable assessment learners develop assessment literacy by acting as involved assessors of their own learning processes as well as of the learning outcome, a condition for engaging in life-long learning processes post-formal education. Learners move from being passive recipients of others' opinions to become independent assessors and decision makers about their own development and learning, common characteristics of informal work-based learning (Boud and Falchikov, 2006; Boud, 2014). Sustainable assessment is mainly inherent in formative assessment, relating to feedback on process as well as on outcome; however, the teacher is not the only decision maker and not the main source of feedback. Learners themselves are engaged in goal setting, criteria development and in providing peer- as well as self-feedback, which informs the learning process. Assessment and learning become inseparable, and concepts such as 'assessment as learning', and 'assessment is for learning' start making sense. Formative assessment in the short term strengthens current learning on specific tasks, which is likely to lead to improved performance of learning outcome assessed by summative assessment, including external examinations. When involving learners as assessment partners, a third goal of assessment is addressed, developing assessment literate learners for sustainable assessment. Assessment can therefore be said to have not only a dual function (Boud, 2014), but a third function can be added to prepare learners to be active assessors of their own work and that of others in a learning society, the features of which are unknown to the learner and to the teacher. I would argue that AfL covers various functions

of assessment. The pedagogical role of assessment is not to look at learning from a momentary perspective, but from a life-long and life-wide perspective. The view presented in this chapter is therefore that AfL is a comprehensive concept serving purposes of summative assessment, short-term formative assessment and assessment as learning (involving learners) to support learners in developing sustainable assessment for future learning processes. David Boud defines sustainable assessment as 'assessment that meets the needs of the present without compromising the ability of students to meet their own future learning needs' (Boud, 2000: 151).

AfL AND TEACHER LEARNING

Boud and Falchikov (2006: 406) suggest that 'the use of the label of "assessment" connotes with a job for teachers, whereas the use of the label "learning" connotes a job for students'. In this discussion of sustainable learning, teachers and learners take on both jobs: teachers become learners of student learning and of their own assessment practice as they continue to be assessors, and learners become assessors of their own learning and of teaching and assessment practice at the same time as they keep on being learners. This is a major shift in perceptions and beliefs commonly held by both parties, which requires careful planning, attention, patience and time. The most challenging shift in perspective might lie with the teachers and how they traditionally see their roles and responsibilities. Moreover, in many contexts, accountability issues and competitive rankings of measurable results on standardised testing have become an unpleasant part of reality for many teachers. Engelsen and Smith (2010) suggest that assessment practice is influenced by three poles: teachers' current assessment practice, steering documents and theory and research-based knowledge (Figure 46.1).

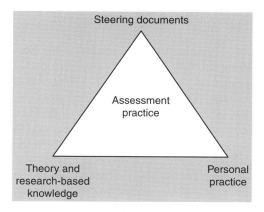

Figure 46.1   Assessment practice

Teachers who are exposed to AfL mainly through policy documents and directives are found to make a strong, rather technical application of AfL, doing as they are instructed in the steering documents (Rønsen and Smith, 2014). AfL can become a set of assessment techniques with little or no understanding of the underlying pedagogical principles. Teachers are less likely to build competence in developing their own AfL practice, adapted to their own teaching context and to individual learners. In several research and development (R&D) projects in which I have been involved, we found that the turning point occurs when teachers become knowledgeable about the pedagogical and research-based literature on AfL which was made accessible through the project (Smith, 2011; Smith, 2013). When teachers develop a deeper understanding of the pedagogics on which AfL and its principles are built, they start to reflect on their own practice. I also noticed that they engage in informed discussions about the directives imposed on them in the guidance documents. Moreover, they jointly develop their own alternatives as a contextualised version of AfL, adapted to their own beliefs as teachers, to the school in which they work and to their own students (Engelsen and Smith, 2010; Smith, 2011; Rønsen and Smith, 2014). When looking at teachers' learning of AfL with the goal of

developing sustainable assessment, literate teachers who are independent creators of their own AfL practice must meet certain conditions. There are no short fixes for sustainable professional development, and in our R&D projects we have found that it takes around 3 years before teachers reach a stage of independent pedagogical practice of AfL (Engelsen and Smith, 2014). The importance of time is also noted by Timperley and her colleagues from New Zealand in a meta-study examining conditions for professional development activities with a positive impact on student learning (Timperley et al., 2007). Another pivotal condition for teacher learning leading to changed beliefs and changed practice is that teachers find the change beneficial to their own students, that they are in charge of the development processes and that they develop a kind of ownership to the change (Ashdown and Hummel-Rossi, 2005; Timperley et al., 2007). Hayward (2010) criticises the commonly used model for teacher learning within educational change programs, claiming that top–down models do not work. Her views align with those of Senge and Schramer (2001) who suggest that teachers have to be in charge of their own professional learning through open critical reflection within communities of practice (Lave and Wenger, 1991).

I strongly believe that teachers want the best for their students, a view that is supported by research on motivation for teaching (Watt and Richardson, 2012). Pedagogical views underpin teachers' professional practice, however, when the teaching profession is subject to strict accountability pressures accompanied by a testing regime, and when teachers' assessment practices tend to be coloured by the external context more than by their own pedagogical beliefs (Amrein and Berliner, 2002). This becomes the case particularly when the operationalisation of AfL has been taken away from the teachers and placed into the hands of policymakers who present their own version – one that fits into a uniform application of AfL adapted to a control system. The following concern about how AfL is perceived and practised internationally was expressed by participants in an international seminar on AfL in Dunedin, New Zealand, with leading researchers from Australia, Canada, Continental Europe, New Zealand, the UK and the US.

> Others (Definitions of AfL, author's insertion) have stemmed from a desire to be seen to be embracing the concept – but in reality implementing a set of practices that are mechanical or superficial without the teacher's, and, most importantly, the students', active engagement with learning as the focal point. While observing the letter of AfL, this does violence to its spirit. Yet others have arisen from deliberate appropriation, for political ends, of principles that have won significant support from educators. (International Assessment Seminar, 2009: 1)

Several of the international participants in this seminar shared experiences from their own contexts, which told about misuses of AfL in ways that had stripped the concept for the underlying pillars of AfL, the pedagogical perspective presented earlier in this chapter. The definition of AfL issued at the end of the seminar was formulated in a way that replaced AfL in the hands of teachers and students:

> Assessment for Learning is part of everyday practice by students, teachers and peers that seeks, reflects upon and responds to information from dialogue, demonstration and observation in ways that enhance ongoing learning. (International Assessment Seminar, 2009: 2)

Inherent in this definition of AfL is that assessment that enhances ongoing learning is context-dependent and in the hands of the actors in the instructional encounter – the teachers and the students. This makes it difficult, if not impossible, to have a set of fixed techniques that dictate assessment practice. The quality of AfL practice is closely related to the assessment literacy of the actors. Teachers learning how to practice AfL should focus on the core pillars of pedagogy and their application in daily assessment practice.

DEVELOPING A CULTURE OF AfL

This argument that AfL addresses the situation in which it occurs, exploiting moments of contingency (Black and Wiliam, 2009), might give the impression that AfL is practised by the individual teacher and their learners in isolation. In early projects in which I was involved the AfL practice of the individual teacher was the main focus, and this was reflected in the topics of our workshops and seminars. We learned that it was difficult, if not impossible, for the individual teacher to practise high quality AfL if they were the only one in the school doing so. External pressures from leadership, colleagues, students, and sometimes also parents, made it an impossible task. In our more recent R&D projects, it became clear that we needed to work with multiple actors to develop an AfL culture in school that allowed for the adaption of the AfL principles by individual teachers with their students (Smith, 2011; Engelsen and Smith, 2014). The driver of introducing an AfL culture in the school is the school leadership, including the principal. The principal does not become the decision maker about what should be done in the name of AfL; the principal is a learner of AfL together with the teachers and the students in school. The leadership provides the conditions and resources for the whole school to engage in the long, and often challenging, process of developing an AfL culture in school. The nature of such a culture is that it provides space for diverse forms for practising AfL, it is dynamic and is continuously under development as the actors gain experience and a deeper understanding of the pedagogies and the practice of these through reflection and sharing of experiences in a community of learning (Engelsen and Smith, 2014). Teacher learning of AfL becomes only one of the many aspects of the process of developing an AfL culture in school.

ASSESSMENT AS A PEDAGOGICAL TOOL IN AN ERA OF ACCOUNTABILITY

A tension frequently expressed in the literature is the tension between a more individualized practice of AfL and the demand for standardized measures of learning for purposes of accountability (Amrein and Berliner, 2002; Crooks, 2011; Hutchinson and Young, 2011). Accountability is a frequently used word, often with notorious connotations for educators, and it can be defined as:

Education: a policy of holding schools and teachers accountable for students' academic progress by linking such progress with funding for salaries, maintenance, etc. (http://www.businessdictionary.com/definition/accountability.html, accessed 23 June 2014)

In other words, accountability in education means that teachers and schools have to deliver what they are expected to deliver in relation to goals, most often set by external authorities, but also by the schools themselves. This is commonly referred to as external accountability. Internal accountability involves greater autonomy for schools where they set their own goals and use an audit system to evaluate to what extent these have been met. Internal accountability is accompanied by a high level of responsibility. Hutchinson and Young (2011) relate the concept assessment to student learning, and evaluation to examining the function of the educational system as a whole. Accountability in education can therefore be said to be an evaluation of the system. It does not have a direct impact on the individual student, but using accountability data for improving the educational system will eventually impact student learning in a long-term general perspective. However, the discussion becomes a sort of chicken-and-egg discussion because the collective improvement of individual learners will be exhibited in the wider evaluation processes of the system. Whereas AfL is clearly located within the assessment concept, AoL as summative assessment by standardised measures is closer to being associated with evaluation.

The interplay between assessment and evaluation is often seen as problematic, especially because measures of student learning for external accountability purposes driven by international and national standardized testing have penetrated educational systems with a negative impact on teachers' professionalism (Valli and Buese, 2007). External pressures on teachers and schools lead to narrowing the curriculum and teaching-to-the-test to prepare students for the best results. This replaces in-depth learning and the time-consuming practice of AfL, and in the US the negative back-wash effect on teaching and learning is widely documented (Amrein and Berliner, 2002; Stiggins, 2002; Sharon et al., 2006). There is little room for practising pedagogically driven AfL at an individual or a class level when not only learners', teachers' and schools' reputation are at risk, but also the country's ranking in the many international competitions of educational achievements. Moreover, financial issues are involved at all three levels, from higher education and job opportunities for the students to tenure and salaries for teachers, and even the closure of schools in the most extreme cases.

Countries that make strong efforts to align AfL with the need for the educational system to evaluate itself are New Zealand (Crooks, 2011) and Scotland (Hutchinson and Young, 2011). Detailed accounts can be found in Crooks's (2011) paper from New Zealand and Hutchinson and Young's (2011) presentation of the Scottish context. In both countries, there are serious attempts to address the need for accountability by developing systems for internal accountability, which to a large extent leaves assessment issues in the hands of the schools and teachers. In these contexts, evaluation emphasizes self-assessment at three levels – student, teacher and school – and includes self-reporting upwards in the system. In both countries, the official policy supports AfL, as documented in the following quote:

The primary purpose of assessment is to improve student-learning and teachers' teaching as both student and teacher respond to the information it provides (New Zealand Ministry of Education, 2007: 38, cited in Crooks, 2011: 73)

Hutchinson and Young (2011) describe the concept 'assessment is for learning' (AifL) in their paper, which incorporates the three functions of assessment presented earlier. The aim was to 'refocus practitioners' attention on assessment as part of pedagogy and sound professional judgments about learning and achievement in the pre-qualifications years, for pupils aged 3–14' (2011: 62), acknowledging the fact that assessment serves other purposes as well.

In both settings, the term 'intelligent accountability' is often used, which, according to Crooks (2003), adheres to specific criteria such as trust among the key participants – students and teachers, teachers and parents, teachers and the school leadership and, above all, the politicians' trust in teachers and their professionalism. The second criterion of intelligent accountability is that all participants experience a strong sense of professional responsibility and initiative, both of which are closely linked to the level of trust in the educational system. The third criterion in Crook's list is that educational challenges encourage participants to engage in deep responses with long-term impact instead of a short-term superficial response. High-stakes tests within a system characterised by extensive control measures are likely to encourage teaching for narrow short-term surface learning. The next criterion, the fourth, relates to feedback, the quality of feedback and the uses of feedback by the system, the schools, the teachers and the learners. By active participation in the assessment processes, feedback becomes meaningful for all actors and can be used for improvement. The last criterion in Crook's list examines the outcome of the accountability process, which should be increased enthusiasm and motivation for further efforts (Crooks, 2003).

In contexts where external accountability is strong and elaborate testing and bureaucracy invade the educational systems, the practice of assessment as a pedagogical tool is endangered. Control takes over from responsibility, and when jobs and financial support disappear, the involved actors are likely to focus on the delivery of measureable achievements, even though it might be in conflict with professional beliefs. Assessment as a pedagogical tool preparing for sustainable learning is endangered in many countries today. There are, however, ways to implement the principles of AfL as well as demands for accountability, and New Zealand and Scotland are examples of this. Knowledgeable, creative and forward-looking policymakers should intensify their efforts to seek innovative ways of how to fully exploit assessment as a pedagogical tool within the need to be well-informed about the quality of the educational system.

In New Zealand (Crooks, 2011) and in Scotland (Hutchinson and Young, 2011), it seems that the main challenge to using assessment as a pedagogical tool is not the policymakers, but teachers' attitude, especially in secondary schools. They have the responsibility for preparing students for school exit (matriculation) and it is stressful in terms of covering the curriculum and preparing students for final exams. School results on these exams in New Zealand are publically available (Crook, 2011) and regional and national 'competitions' between schools move the focus away from AfL and onto how to do well in the final exam.

To me, an immediate comparison can be made to the domain of sports. No athlete will do well in high-stakes competitions if the foundation, built up through tedious daily practice over a number of years with a dedicated coach or team of coaches, is not in place when preparing for the big events. The athlete must develop a trust in the coaches, they need to be confident that the coaches know their job and are professional in planning the route to the finals; however, unless the coach involves the athlete in the goal-setting and in how to fit the practice to the individual athlete by jointly creating the training program, the athlete will not respond with motivation, self-efficacy or self-regulation during practice. It is the athlete who does the hardest work, and they have to be full partners in their own training. There are competitions (tests) along the way, but they are mainly to practise the skill of competing, and are often to check if the immediate personal goals have been reached. The focus is not always on the other competing athletes. An Olympic athlete who won a competition in preparation for the Olympic qualification was congratulated for winning this on-the-way competition. His answer was 'I do not deserve congratulations, have you seen the time? It is not even close to my personal best' (Beeri, 2008). Athletes compete with themselves to see a steady curve of improvement – more than they compete with others. Only in the big events do they focus on outdoing their competitors. All students are athletes in the field of learning, but they do not all have to, or want to, prepare for the Olympics. For most students, personal goals – and achieving them – are what matters, and teachers should coach student learning with this in mind. In fields of sports where the breadth of athletes at the grass-root level is solid, Olympic athletes have a better chance to develop and go on to higher academies of sports. School is for all at the grass-root level, and it is not an academy preparing for winning national and international honour. Schools prepare children and young people for being able to enjoy learning throughout life, to be well functioning members of our current and future society. The important thing is to do as well as you can and want in the professional hands of teachers, who are not compelled to prepare students for repetitive tests and exams, but who can make all students feel special, who know where the students want to go, where the students are in the learning process, what the students have to do to get to the next milestone, and who believe the students are capable of getting there. Using assessment as a pedagogical tool is about all this: it is AfL.

IMPLICATIONS

If we want assessment for learning to be a pedagogical tool, a culture of AfL should be created in schools and in the society. For that to happen, stakeholders of assessment need to develop assessment literacy, understanding what assessment can and cannot do, and what kind of assessment is appropriate for specific purposes. Assessment as a pedagogical tool does not, first and foremost, rest on assessment techniques, but more on deep theoretical and practical knowledge, which provides the stakeholder with a repertoire and creativity in practicing assessment. A major challenge of developing a culture of AfL as a pedagogical tool is the increasing impact of external accountability on students, teachers and schools (Crooks, 2011). There are ways of merging AfL and accountability by developing a system of intelligent accountability (Crooks, 2003), examples of which are found in New Zealand and Scotland.

An additional challenge is the teachers' conception of assessment, and the space in which they can enact pedagogical beliefs and attitudes. If their professionalism is evaluated in light of students' score on external testing, AfL is under severe threat. Teachers should be trusted with autonomy to practice AfL adapted to their context and learners, and empowered to take on the responsibility they have been given. Education is not a competition of measureable results; education is about developing individual human beings who are motivated contributors to maintain and improve a democratic well-functioning society. The way children and young people experience assessment during their education is crucial for achieving this pedagogical goal. The concluding message of this chapter is that all stakeholders of education have to become informed and knowledgeable practitioners of assessment as a pedagogical tool, and this should be a pillar on which future professional development courses are planned.

REFERENCES

Amrein, A.L. and Berliner, D.C. (2002) 'High-stakes testing, uncertainty, and student learning', *Education Policy Analysis Archives,* 10: 1–74.

Andrade, H.L. (2010) 'Students as the definitive source of formative assessment: academic self-assessment and the self-regulation of learning', in H. Andrade and G.J. Cizek (eds.), *Handbook of Formative Assessment.* NY: Routledge. pp. 90–105.

Ashdown, J. and Hummel-Rossi, B. (2005) 'The impact of program adaption on teachers' professional life', in D. Beijard, P. Meijers, G.H. Morine-Dershimer and H. Tillema (eds.), *Teacher Professional Development in Changing Conditions.* Dordrecht: Springer. pp. 213–29.

Assessment Reform Group (2002) *Assessment for Learning: Research-Based Principles to Guide Classroom Practice.* Newcastle, UK: Nuffield Foundation.

Bandura. A. (1977) 'Self-efficacy: toward a unifying theory of behavioral change', *Psychological Review,* 84: 191–215.

Bandura, A. (1986) *Social Foundations of Thought and Action: A Social Cognitive Theory.* Englewood Cliffs, NJ: Prentice Hall.

Bandura, A. (1997) *Self-efficacy: The Exercise of Control.* New York, NY: W.H. Freeman and Co.

Beeri, Tom (2008) Personal communication with Olympic swimmer Tom Beeri (my son), March, 2008.

Black, P. and Wiliam, D. (1998a) 'Inside the black box', *PhiDelta Kappan,* 80(2): 139–48.

Black, P. and Wiliam, D. (1998b) 'Assessment and classroom learning', *Assessment in Education,* 5(1): 7–74.

Black, P. and Wiliam, D. (2009) 'Developing the theory of formative assessment', *Educational Assessment, Evaluation and Accountability,* 21(1): 5–31.

Black, P., Harrison, C., Lee, C., Marshall, B. and Wiliam, D. (2003) *Assessment for Learning: Putting It into Practice.* Buckingham, UK: Open University Press.

Boud, D.J. (1995) 'Assessment and learning: contradictory or complementary?', in P. Knight (ed.), *Assessment for Learning in Higher Education.* London: Kogan Page. pp. 35–48.

Boud, D.J. (2000) 'Sustainable assessment: rethinking assessment for the learning society', *Studies in Continuing Education,* 22(2): 151–67.

Boud, D.J. (2001) *Peer Learning in Higher Education: Learning from and with each other.* London: Kogan Page.

Boud, D.J. (2007) *Rethinking Assessment for Higher Education: Learning for the Longer Term.* London: Routledge.

Boud, D.J. (2014) 'Shifting views of assessment: from secret teachers' business to sustaining learning' in Kreber, C., Anderson, C., Entwhistle, N. and McArthur, J. (eds.), *Advances and Innovations in University Assessment and Feedback.* Edinburgh: Edinburgh University Press. pp. 1–13.

Boud, D.J. and Falchikov, N. (2006) 'Aligning assessment with long-term learning', *Assessment and Evaluation in Higher Education,* 31(4): 399–413.

Brown, S. (2004) 'Assessment for learning', *Learning and Teaching in Higher Education,* 1: 81–9.

Crooks, T.J. (2002) 'Educational assessment in New Zealand schools', *Assessment in Education,* 9: 237–53.

Crooks, T.J. (2003) 'Some criteria for intelligent accountability applied to accountability in New Zealand', paper presented at the Annual Conference of the American Educational Research Association, Chicago, Illinois, 22 April 2003, within Session 36.011 – Accountability from an International Perspective.

Crooks, T.J. (2011) 'Assessment for learning in the accountability era: New Zealand', *Studies in Educational Evaluation,* 37: 71–7.

Darom, D. (2000) 'Humanistic values in education – personal, interpersonal, social and political dimensions', in M. Leicester, C. Modgil and S. Modgil (eds.), *Politics, Education and Citizenship.* London: Falmer Press. pp. 24–40.

Deci, E.L. and Ryan, R.M. (2000) 'The "what" and "why" of goal pursuits: human needs and the self-determination of behavior', *Psychological Inquiry,* 11: 227–68.

Duffy, T.M. and Cunningham, D.J. (1996) 'Constructivism: implications for the design and delivery of instruction', in D.H. Jonassen (ed.). *Handbook of Research for Educational*

Communications and Technology. New York, NY: Macmillan. pp. 170–98.

Engelsen, K.S. and Smith, K. (2010) 'Is "Excellent" good enough?', *Education Inquiry,* 4. Available from http://www.education-inquiry.net/index.php/edui/article/view/21954 (accessed 27 October 2014).

Engelsen, K.S. and Smith, K. (2014) 'Assessment literacy', in C. Wyatt-Smith, V. Klenowski and P. Colbert (eds.), *Designing Assessment for Quality Learning.* Vol. 1. Dordrecht, The Netherlands: Springer International. pp. 91–107.

Freire, P. (1970) *Pedagogy of the Oppressed.* New York, NY: Continuum.

Freire, P. (1973) *Education: The Practice of Freedom.* New York, NY: Writers and Readers.

Gamlem, S.M. and Smith, K. (2013) 'Student perceptions of classroom feedback', *Assessment in Education: Principles, Policy and Practice,* 20(2):150–69. doi: 10.1080/0969594X.2012.749212.

Gardner, J. (ed.) (2006) *Assessment and Learning.* London: Sage Publications.

Gibbs, G. and Simpson, C. (2003) 'Measuring the response of students to assessment: the Assessment Experience Questionnaire', 11th International Symposium Improving Student Learning: Theory, Research and Scholarship, Hinckley, UK 1–3 September.

Gibbs, G. and Simpson, C. (2004) 'Conditions under which assessment supports students' learning', *Learning and Teaching in Higher Education,* 1: 3–31.

Guskey, T.R. (2003) 'How classroom assessments improve learning', *Educational Leadership,* 60(5): 7–11.

Harlen, W. and Gardner, J. (2010) 'Assessment to support learning', in J. Gardner, W. Harlen, L. Hayward, G. Stobart, with M. Montgomery (eds.), *Developing Teacher Assessment.* Maidenhead, UK: Open University Press. pp. 15–28.

Hattie, J. (2009) *Visible Learning: A Synthesis of over 800 Meta-Analyses Relating to Achievement.* London: Routledge.

Hattie, J. and Timperley, H. (2007) 'The power of feedback', *Review of Educational Research,* 77(1): 81–112.

Havnes, A., Smith, K., Dysthe, O. and Ludvigsen, K. (2012) 'Formative assessment and feedback: making learning visible', *Studies in Educational Evaluation,* 38(1): 21–27. doi: dx.doi.org/10.1016/j.stueduc.2012.04.001.

Hayward, L. (2010) 'Moving beyond the classroom', in J. Gardner, W. Harlen, L. Hayward and G. Stobart with M. Montgomery (eds.), *Developing Teacher Assessment.* Maidenhead, UK: Open University Press. pp. 85–99.

Hodkinson, P., Biesta, G. and James, D. (2008) 'Understanding learning culturally: overcoming the dualism between social and individual views of learning', *Vocations and Learning,* 1(1): 27–47. doi: 10.1007/s12186-007-9001-y.

Hutchinson, C. and Young, M. (2011) 'Assessment for learning in the accountability era: empirical evidence from Scotland', *Studies in Educational Evaluation,* 37: 62–70.

International Assessment Seminar (2009) 'Position paper on assessment for learning from the third international conference on assessment for learning', Dunedin, New Zealand, March 2009. Available from http://fairtest.org/sites/default/files/Assess-for-Learning-position-paper.pdf (accessed 23 June 2014).

Lave, J. and Wenger, E. (1991) *Situated Learning: Legitimate Peripheral Participation.* Cambridge: Cambridge University Press.

Lingard, B. and Sellar, C. (2013) '"Catalyst data": perverse systemic effects of audit and accountability in Australian schooling', *Journal of Education Policy,* 28(5): 634–56. doi: 10.1080/02680939.2012.758815.

Mason, L. (2007) 'Introduction. Bridging the cognitive and sociocultural approaches in research on conceptual change: is it feasible?', *Educational Psychologist,* 42(1): 1–7. doi: 10.1080/00461520701190439.

Merriam-Webster (2003) *New Edition of Merriam-Webster's Collegiate Dictionary,* http://www.merriam-webster.com/dictionary/assess (accessed 5 October 2014).

Miller, C.M.I. and Parlett, M. (1974) *Up to the Mark: A Study of the Examination Game.* Guildford, UK: Society for Research into Higher Education.

Pekrun, R., Goetz, T., Frenzel, A.C., Barchfeld, P. and Perry, R.P. (2011) 'Measuring emotions in students' learning and performance: The Achievement Emotions Questionnaire (AEQ)', *Contemporary Educational Psychology,* 36: 36–48.

Rommetveit, R. (1972) *Språk, tanke og kommunikasjon: Ei innføring i språkpsykologi og psykolingvistikk [Language, Thought and Communication: An Introduction to Language Psychology and Psycolinguistics]*. Oslo: Universitetsforlaget.

Rommetveit, R. (2003) 'On the role of "a psychology of the second person" in studies of meaning, language, and mind', *Mind, Culture and Activity*, 10(3): 205–18. doi: 10.1207/s15327884mca1003_3.

Rønsen, A.K. and Smith, K. (2014) 'Influencing and facilitating conditions for developing reflective assessment practice', *Professional Development in Education*, 40(3): 450–66. doi: 10.1080/19415257.2013.836126.

Rorty, R. (1991) *Objectivity, Relativism, and Truth: Philosophical Papers*. Vol. 1. Cambridge, MA: Cambridge University Press.

Ryan, R.M., and Deci, E.L. (2000) 'Self-determination theory and the facilitation of intrinsic motivation, social development, and well-being', *American Psychologist*, 55: 68–78.

Sadler, D.R. (1989) 'Formative assessment and the design of instructional systems', *Instructional Science*, 18(2): 119–44.

Säljö, R. (2001) *Læring i praksis: et sosiokulturelt perspektiv [The Praxis of Learning: A Socio-Cultural Perspective]*. Oslo: Cappelen Akademiske Forlag.

Säljö, R. (2006) *Læring og kulturelle redskaper: Om læreprosesser og den kollektive hukommelsen [Learning and Cultural Artefacts: About Learning Processes and the Collective Memory]*. Oslo: Cappelen Akademisk Forlag.

Schunk, D.H., and Zimmerman, B.J. (1997) 'Social origins of self-regulatory competence', *Educational Psychologist*, 32: 195–208.

Senge, P. and Scharmer, C.O. (2001) 'Community action research', in P. Reason and H. Bradbury (eds.), *Handbook of Action Research*. Thousand Oaks, CA: Sage Publications. pp. 238–49.

Sfard, A. (1998) 'On two metaphors for learning and the dangers of choosing just one', *Educational Researcher*, 27(2): 4–13.

Sharon, L.N., Glass, G.V. and Berliner, D.C. (2006) 'High stakes testing and student achievement: does accountability pressure increase student learning?', *Education Policy Analysis Archives*, 14(1). Available from http://epaa.asu.edu/ojs/article/viewFile/72/198 (accessed 30 October 2014).

Smith, K. (2001) 'Children's rights, assessment, and the digital portfolio: is there a common denominator?', IATEFL Publication, University of Cambridge. pp. 55–68.

Smith, K. (2011) 'Professional development of teachers: a prerequisite for AfL to be successfully implemented in the classroom', *Studies in Educational Evaluation*, 37: 55–61.

Smith, K. (2013) 'Teachers, leaders and local authorities learning together about Assessment-for-Learning (AfL)', paper presented at the ECER Conference, Istanbul, 10–13 September 2013.

Snyder, B.R. (1971) *The Hidden Curriculum*. Cambridge, MA: MIT Press.

Stiggins, R.J. (1988) 'Revitalizing classroom assessment: the high instructional priority', *Phi Delta Kappan*, 69(5): 363–8.

Stiggins, R.J. (1995) 'Assessment literacy for the 21st century', *Phi Delta Kappan*, 77(3): 238–45.

Stiggins, R.J. (2002) 'Assessment crisis: the absence of assessment FOR learning', *Phi Delta Kappan*, 83(10): 758–65.

Stobart, G. (2008) *Testing Times – The Uses and Abuses of Assessment*. New York, NY: Routledge.

Timperley, H. (2011) *Realizing the Power of Professional Learning*. Maidenhead, UK: Open University Press.

Timperley, H., Wilson, A., Barrar, H. and Fung, I. (2007) *Teacher Professional Learning and Development. Best Evidence Synthesis Iteration*. Wellington, New Zealand: Ministry of Education.

Valli, L. and Buese, D. (2007) 'The Changing roles of teachers in an era of high-stakes accountability', *American Educational Research Journal*, 44: 519–58.

Vygotsky, L.S. (1962) *Thought and Language*. Cambridge, MA: MIT Press.

Vygotsky, L.S. (1978) *Mind in Society. The Development of Higher Psychological Processes*. Cambridge: Harvard University Press.

Watt, H.M.G. and Richardson, P.W. (2012) 'An introduction to teaching motivations in different countries: comparisons using the FIT-Choice scale', *Asia-Pacific Journal of Teacher Education*, 40(3): 185–97.

Webb, N.L. (2002) 'Assessment literacy in a standard-based urban education setting', paper presented at the American Educational

Research Association Annual Meeting, New Orleans, Louisiana, 1–5 April.

Wyatt-Smith, C., Klenowski, V. and Colbert, P. (2014) (eds.) *Designing Assessment for Quality Learning*. Vol. 1. Dordrecht, The Netherlands: Springer International. pp. 91–107.

Zimmerman, B.J. (1990) 'Self-regulated learning and academic achievement: an overview', *Educational Psychologist,* 25(1): 3–17.

Zimmerman, B.J. (2000) 'Attaining self-regulation: a social cognitive perspective', in M. Boekaerts, P.R. Pintrich and M. Zeider (eds.), *Handbook of Self-Regulation*. New York, NY: Academic Press.

Zimmerman, B.J., and Schunk, D.H. (2001) *Self-Regulated Learning and Academic Achievement: Theoretical Perspectives.* 2nd edn. Mahwah, NJ: Lawrence Erlbaum Associates.

Implementing Assessment for Learning in a Confucian Context: The Case of Hong Kong 2004–14

Ricky Lam

INTRODUCTION

Since Black and Wiliam (1998) published their seminal work on how assessment can positively impact learning, the Assessment for Learning (AfL) movement has been burgeoning both theoretically and empirically. Despite its educational benefits, research into how AfL can be effectively implemented at the classroom level especially in Confucian Heritage Cultures (CHCs) remains complex and challenging (Berry, 2011; Biggs, 1998; Black and Wiliam, 1998; Carless, 2011). Educational contexts with a legacy of CHCs generally emphasize 'test performance' more than mastery of learning through high-stakes examinations because stakeholders typically possess instrumental views to learning (a means to upward social mobility and success), which pose a sharp contrast with the spirit of AfL (for details, see Carless, 2011; Carless and Lam, 2014a). In Anglophone settings, AfL refers to good teaching that supports learning, and yet it is usually interpreted,

some may say misinterpreted, as an assessment reform initiative in most East Asian jurisdictions such as Hong Kong and Singapore at least during the last decade (Curriculum Development Council, 2001; Ministry of Education Singapore, 2008). Given AfL is situated in such politicized reform environments, its implementation may be in tension with the existing pedagogical and assessment practices, which tend to pay undue attention to the product of learning and results of standardized tests (Chen, 2014; Darling-Hammond and McCloskey, 2008; Marsh, 2007). To this end, this chapter aims to critically review the effectiveness of teacher implementation of various AfL practices as part of teaching and learning processes within a CHC setting during the period 2004–14. The review is concerned with applications of AfL in the English language curriculum with key focuses on writing, speaking and general English at both primary and secondary classroom levels. Pertinent issues arising from the review are analyzed and categorized into themes for discussion. Lastly, implications regarding how AfL could be successfully carried out in the Hong Kong school contexts are proposed.

ASSESSMENT REFORM LANDSCAPE IN HONG KONG

Despite efforts in introducing curricular and assessment reform initiatives since the 1980s (for example, communicative language teaching), the Education Bureau (then Education Department) witnessed continuous failure in changing teaching and learning practices from a product-based and teacher-dominated model emphasizing rote learning to a process-oriented and learner-centred model promoting creativity and independent learning (Berry, 2011; Carless and Harfitt, 2013; Evans, 1996). Introduced in primary education during the early 1990s and faded out after several years of implementation, Target-Oriented Curriculum, which highlighted the centrality of daily observation and stringent record keeping, aimed to promote pupil performance for learning improvement. It was the earliest form of AfL introduced as a system-wide reform policy. Notwithstanding its pedagogically sound intention, Target-Oriented Curriculum was not well received because of strong resistance from teachers (for example, insufficient understanding of the principles), lack of support from school (for example, heavy workload) and incongruence with a larger learning and assessment culture (for example, predominance of CHC and lack of a reform climate) (Morris, 2002; Morris and Adamson, 2010; Poon, 2009).

No sooner had Target-Oriented Curriculum proven to be unsuccessful than the Education Bureau, in 2004, introduced the Basic Competency Assessment in the primary education sector. Basic Competency Assessment, including Territory-wide System Assessment and Student Assessment, is a low-stakes assessment collectively administered in three major subjects, namely English language, Chinese language and mathematics at Grades 3, 6 and 9 across the territory and intends to assist individual schools to make informed decisions about how to improve teaching and learning based upon the assessment information from the Territory-wide System Assessment. Similarly, the secondary education sector has witnessed the implementation of the New Senior Secondary curriculum in 2009, the Hong Kong Diploma of Secondary Education Examination in 2012 (Curriculum Development Council, 2007; 2009) and the integration of School-based Assessment in the key major subjects – English language – since 2005 (see Davison, 2007; Qian, 2008). The rationale for these reform initiatives in the last decade is three-fold, namely the reduction in the number of high-stakes examinations (from two to one at the end of the six-year secondary education), the introduction of a learner-centred curriculum, which principally underscores independent learning rather than teacher-dominated pedagogy, and the dissemination of AfL practices, which synergize learning and testing through Basic Competency Assessment and School-based Assessment (Berry, 2011; Chow and Leung, 2011; Davison, 2007; Davison and Hamp-Lyons, 2010).

AFL MOVEMENT IN HONG KONG: WHERE ARE WE NOW?

As discussed in the previous section, AfL as part of a global educational trend has been intermittently implemented under different labels including Target-Oriented Curriculum, Basic Competency Assessment and School-based Assessment since the 1990s. Despite concerted efforts to encourage innovation in English language assessment practices, policymakers often have failed to take into account diverse socio-cultural factors (for example, CHCs which place a high priority in the standardized examinations) and related learning theories (for example, popularity of rote learning and mechanical drilling) when introducing alternative approaches to classroom-based assessment – such as AfL in the forms of projects, portfolios, self- and peer assessment that emphasize learner agency and process-oriented learning in the Hong Kong school contexts (Carless, 2005; Evans, 1996; Kennedy et al., 2008). From international assessment literature, there has been evidence to support the merits of AfL and to demonstrate how it can be productively utilized to enhance teaching and learning at the classroom level (Black and Wiliam, 1998; Wiliam, 2011; Wiliam and Thompson, 2008). However, this Anglophone concept, if applied in East Asian settings, may encounter incongruence with the current pedagogical and assessment practices where students usually play a subservient role in the learning process and teachers traditionally play an authoritative role, imparting knowledge to learners (Biggs, 1998; Carless, 2011). Such a discrepancy between two opposing assessment ideologies (a learning culture versus a testing culture) can explicate why AfL or other related reform agendas find themselves rather challenged to take root in local classroom environments (Hamp-Lyons, 2007; Inbar-Lourie, 2008).

Over the last decade, it appears that the AfL movement in Hong Kong has begun to take shape in both primary and secondary sectors owing to a larger curriculum reform climate, which has been promulgating concepts, including 'learning how to learn' and 'life-long learning' since the turn of the century (Education Commission, 2000). These educational philosophies underpin the introduction of Basic Competency Assessment at Grades 3, 6 and 9 via Territory-wide System Assessment which, hopefully, not only aims to evaluate students' strengths and weaknesses in learning (as in the case of Assessment of Learning, AoL), but also is supposed to generate useful assessment information for improving teaching and learning (an example of AfL practices). Regardless of its formative potential to support learning, Territory-wide System Assessment was politicized at

least initially because of the fear and cynicism shared by teachers, parents and school administrators about how assessment information is ultimately utilized for purposes such as ranking school performances for accountability (Berry, 2011). As a result, giving students extra after-school lessons about the content and format of Territory-wide System Assessment and sending them to private tutorial schools to master related test-taking skills have become social phenomena because Territory-wide System Assessment is perceived as another high-stakes 'examination' alongside school internal assessments (Bray and Kwok, 2003; Coniam, 2014; Tse, 2014).

From this, it can be argued that the spirit of AfL (in the case of Basic Competency Assessment) seems to have been eroded by entrenched socio-cultural factors, namely the predominance of an examination culture and mistrust between the quasi-governmental agencies and key school-based stakeholders. Additionally, there has been a lack of transparent communication between the Education Bureau and school personnel concerning the theoretical rationale of Basic Competency Assessment and how such a large-scale standardized test – Territory-wide System Assessment – can be used formatively to inform effective teaching and learning at the classroom level (Kennedy et al., 2008; Morris and Scott, 2003; Tong, 2011).

Around the mid-2000s, the reform climate had reached its peak with the inclusion of a School-based Assessment component in English language classrooms in 2005. This happened despite initial teacher resentment that led to the postponement of its full implementation until 2007 and the introduction of the New Senior Secondary curriculum in English language and other subjects in 2009. The English School-based Assessment promotes the integration of classroom-based assessment and standardized testing, the development of teacher judgment, extensive reading and viewing of literary texts and other AfL-related practices, including self- and peer assessment, learning autonomy and sharing of assessment criteria with peers and teachers (Davison, 2007; Davison and Hamp-Lyons, 2010; Davison and Leung, 2009). For the English New Senior Secondary curriculum, the elective component advocates interactive and task-based English learning to help students acquire English both linguistically and communicatively (Curriculum Development Council, 2007). In their study, Carless and Harfitt (2013) reported that students were appreciative of the enjoyable learning experience offered to them, for example, taking electives to develop creativity and having wider exposure to active English learning rather than traditional examination drilling. However, the case study students did not take learning in the elective component seriously because it was not counted in the Hong Kong Diploma of Secondary Education Examination result. To this end, Carless and Harfitt find a palpable tension between enjoyable learning experience and an examination-oriented education.

Unlike the English New Senior Secondary curriculum, the English School-based Assessment received less favourable response at its early stages of implementation. However, since 2005, with the provision of professional training opportunities and enhanced awareness of its theoretical rationale and practices, School-based Assessment has gradually become an indispensable tool to integrate AfL and AoL for learning and grading purposes in the English language classrooms. That said, in his survey, Qian (2014) found that although students were generally receptive to School-based Assessment, teachers had encountered numerous challenges, including asynchronous implementation of School-based Assessment and the Hong Kong Diploma of Secondary Education Examination, unresolved issues of extra workload, incompatibility with an examination culture and failure to integrate School-based Assessment into the regular English curriculum. Notwithstanding these hurdles, compared to other educational reforms, such as communicative language teaching, Target-Oriented Curriculum and Basic Competency Assessment, School-based Assessment could at least achieve its purpose in promoting effective learning, for instance, students had more exposure to extensive reading and in becoming more confident in presenting ideas in front of their peers/teachers (Davison, 2007; Hong Kong Examinations and Assessment Authority, 2010). School-based Assessment, an embodiment of AfL adopted in an examination culture where key stakeholders usually focus on assessment results, may risk sacrificing its formative potential in promoting English learning (Berry, 2011; Chow and Leung, 2011). Nevertheless, if teachers are encouraged to receive ongoing professional training and engage in reflective teaching, they can develop more localized knowledge and skills when administering School-based Assessment (Farrell, 2013; Hamp-Lyons, 2007; Harris and Brown, 2013).

To sum up, it is imperative to review the AfL movement in Hong Kong English classrooms based upon the current assessment scholarship because AfL has become one of the key curricular initiatives that has had a substantial impact on the development of, teaching, learning and assessment in the Hong Kong school context. The next section illustrates how the review was conducted, including use of analytical lens, literature search criteria, databases, choice of publications, categorization of search results and structuring of the review data.

PROCEDURES OF REVIEW

Framework for Review

To provide a conceptual framework for the review, the characteristics of certain Confucian cultural practices, as highlighted in Carless's (2011) book, were utilized to examine the extent to which the implementation of AfL-specific assessment reforms could promote or inhibit learning. Key concepts from CHC settings include (1) teacher beliefs in the traditional pragmatic approach; (2) the centrality of an examination system; and (3) hierarchical power relations in the teaching and learning process. In relation to the first concept, teachers primarily focus on the product of learning rather than the process of learning, particularly in English language because they consider that they hold sole responsibility for students' examination results, which are likely to determine their employability and future career prospects (Biggs, 1996; Hamp-Lyons, 2002; Lee, 2008). Berry (2011) and Hamp-Lyons (2007) have argued that in Hong Kong, accessibility to higher education, particularly undergraduate programmes in eight public-funded universities, remains limited and competitive. Because of that, teaching in English classrooms becomes highly instrumental (that is, teaching to the test) in helping students to be admitted to the university, so that these students stand a better chance to enter favourable professional careers thereafter (Evans, 2011; Lee, 2011a; Poon, 2010).

Likewise, in relation to the second concept, the importance of an examination system in CHC settings is culturally deep-seated, given that in China there has been a long history of utilizing essay examinations to select those who are academically capable of serving the imperial court dating back to the Sung Dynasty, 960–1280 AD (Chen, 2014; Hamp-Lyons, 2002; Zeng, 1999). In order to outperform other candidates in examinations, students would count on memorizing the test syllabus, mechanical drilling past papers, and attending private tutorial centres (Bray and Kwok, 2003; Coniam, 2014). Finally, considering the third concept, hierarchical power relations are one of the prominent features that epitomize the essence of Confucianism, with teachers being knowledgeable experts and students being obedient learners (Brown et al., 2009). Conventionally, teaching and learning takes place in a whole-class manner. The role of teachers is to impart knowledge, whereas students are expected to take a submissive role in learning rather than develop critical and independent thinking. Hence, the CHC-oriented instructional approach tends to be top–down and didactic, rendering students as audience rather than co-participants in the learning process (Biggs, 1998; Carless, 2011).

Selection Criteria and Search Methods

The following describes the four criteria used to select research studies for this review:

- The period of the literature search had to fall between 2004 and 2014, after the release of key governmental assessment reform policies.
- The search was restricted to studies conducted in Hong Kong. Studies related to other educational contexts were excluded.
- Studies were only included on the implementation of AfL practices in English language classrooms. AfL studies published in other subject disciplines were excluded.
- Studies had to include a systematic collection and analysis of empirical data. Conceptual and review papers were excluded.

Regarding the context of the review, studies under review were primarily confined to primary and secondary school settings. AfL studies administered in pre-school contexts, higher education, post-secondary education, vocational training, distance education and other settings were excluded. By adopting the keyword search such as 'assessment for learning', 'assessment of learning', and 'assessment reforms in Hong Kong' in two databases (Google Scholar and Scopus), the initial search results identified more than 150 studies. After repeated keyword search and application of four selection criteria, 21 studies were chosen for further analysis according to themes relating to the aim of this review. To warrant trustworthiness, the author also performed a manual literature search from a range of international assessment and educational journals based upon the selection criteria and relevance of studies.

Analysis of Literature

The 21 studies under review were read and reread by the author and initially classified into broad themes such as the success and failure of AfL initiatives implemented in Hong Kong and how these AfL-related reforms impacted teaching and learning within a larger Confucian cultural setting. The studies were then coded into three themes according to their contexts, results, discussion, contributions and implications for future research. They were broadly categorized into three key issues for in-depth discussion, including (1) teacher beliefs in introducing innovations in the English as a Foreign Language (EFL) writing context; (2) perceived challenges of implementing School-based Assessment in an examination culture; and (3) indigenization of AfL practices in the CHC-oriented classrooms.

ISSUE OF TEACHER BELIEFS IN INTRODUCING INNOVATIONS IN EFL WRITING

In this section focusing on feedback on writing, which should be considered an important aspect of AfL-related reform, feedback studies reviewed included Lee (2007, 2008, 2010, 2011b, 2011c), Lee and Coniam (2013), Lee and Wong (2014), Lo and Hyland (2007), and Mak and Lee (2014).

In EFL writing, Lee (2007) reported that in her study written feedback by 26 teachers on 174 students' compositions primarily emphasized the summative rather than formative function. Other learning-oriented feedback strategies such as multiple drafting, use of self- and peer assessment, and sharing criteria concerning 'good writing' were rarely adopted. Lee (2007) argued that Hong Kong writing teachers generally believed that writing assessment equated to giving grades and was a stand-alone activity independent of teaching and learning of writing, therefore, assessment information provided by them failed to enhance teaching and learning because students were not given adequate opportunities to revise their texts with peer and teacher feedback (that is, the problem of one-shot writing). More recently, Lee and Coniam's (2013) study pointed to the usefulness of introducing AfL practices in EFL

writing classrooms, such as the consolidation of pre-assessment instruction, sharing of learning goals and use of feedback forms to provide feedback. Although some students showed improvements in their texts and became more motivated as learners after the study, there were tensions between innovative and traditional assessment practices. Concerning teacher factors that facilitated AfL innovations in EFL contexts, Lee and Coniam argue that teachers should have a clear picture of what AfL would entail and should consider whether the philosophy of AfL was attuned to their own beliefs and values in terms of assessing writing, namely a learning-oriented approach (AfL) versus a traditional approach to assessment (assessment of learning).

After attending a teacher education seminar on feedback innovation, more than half of the participants became aware that they might need a change in their feedback practices (Lee, 2011b). However, Lee found that the change process was complicated, particularly when there was a disjuncture between what teachers believed they should do in giving constructive feedback and what they actually could do to implementing change in their work contexts. This argument resonates with Lee's (2008) findings in her earlier study where the teacher interview data illustrated how feedback practices were contextually shaped by four critical issues, including accountability culture, teachers' beliefs and values, examination culture and lack of teacher training. The issue of examination culture will be discussed in the next section. Among these issues, Lee (2008) contends that attempts to innovate AfL-related feedback policies are restricted by EFL teachers' entrenched beliefs about production of error-free compositions, for which giving undue attention to error feedback in the writing assessment is prevalent. She continues to argue that against the backdrop of an examination-dominated culture in Hong Kong, where writing practice involuntarily turns into examination preparation (Lee, 2008: 80) because teachers are hard-pressed to cover the rigid examination syllabus rather than spare valuable instructional hours to experiment with AfL feedback strategies (Lee, 2011c). Lee (2010, 2011b) and Lee and Wong (2014) propose that it is not easy to change teachers' mindsets overnight, however, with consistent efforts to provide them with autonomy (opportunities to try out diverse feedback strategies) and professional learning (opportunities to work with teacher educators on action research projects), their beliefs and values may indeed gradually change and become more receptive to those feedback practices that support learning.

In primary education, Lo and Hyland (2007) implemented a new writing programme underscoring creativity and audience awareness through the adoption of process-genre pedagogy in a Grade 5 writing classroom. The results showed that it was low-achieving students who benefitted most in terms of motivation. High-achieving counterparts displayed lower accuracy in their writing. These findings illuminate why writing teachers tend to retain more traditional instructional approaches, given that trying new methods may run counter to helping some students achieve good results in internal and external writing assessments. Similarly, in an effort to innovate AfL strategies in two primary schools from the perspective of an activity theory, Mak and Lee (2014) argue that the contradictions in the activity systems, namely tensions between teacher beliefs, individual school cultures and the larger reform climate in Hong Kong, need to be resolved before the uptake of AfL innovation can be better facilitated.

Based upon these studies, it can be argued that teacher beliefs play a pivotal role in shaping the effectiveness of innovations, because what they believe may inevitably translate into feedback practices that facilitate or impede change (Fullan, 2001; Hamp-Lyons, 2007). Attempts to introduce AfL innovation (for example, self- and peer assessment, comment-only marking) in the local writing classrooms appears to be not as threatening

as it sounds if the change process is initiated by frontline teachers themselves; however, their entrenched beliefs and values may be challenged by the contemporary instructional approaches that emphasize maximum coverage of the examination syllabus, teaching to the test and the use of examination drilling activities (Carless, 2011; Lee and Coniam, 2013; Lee and Wong, 2014). It is imperative to cultivate teacher beliefs about the usefulness of AfL practices, which constructively aligns teaching, learning and assessment of writing because teachers are usually obsessed with a pragmatic view of instruction influenced by a larger CHC setting, namely 'a culture of compliance' within the social norm of an examination culture (Lee, 2007; Littlewood, 2009: 253). It is believed that teachers tend to be more convinced of the merits of AfL practices if presented with practical classroom examples on the implementation of these assessment innovations and given support in setting up their own to promote teaching and learning.

ISSUE OF CHALLENGES WHEN IMPLEMENTING SCHOOL-BASED ASSESSMENT IN AN EXAMINATION CULTURE

The findings from six School-based Assessment studies were used to identify the challenges of its implementation in an examination culture: Cheng et al. (2011), Davison (2007), Davison and Hamp-Lyons (2010), Hong Kong Examinations and Assessment Authority (2010), Mok (2011), and Qian (2014). These studies focus on challenges arising from the implementation of classroom-based speaking assessment as part of system-wide standardized testing.

Drawing upon questionnaires, interviews, observations from 66 teachers and 513 students in 21 schools, Davison (2007) reported the logistics, conceptual rationale, and experimentation of English School-based Assessment introduced in 2005. Students' and teachers' perceptions concerning their School-based Assessment experience in the trial were classified into socio-cultural, technical and practical issues (Davison, 2007). Of relevance to the challenges of implementing School-based Assessment in an examination culture is the inherent socio-cultural concern of impartiality, in other words, teacher scepticism about the fairness of School-based Assessment. Davison (2007) and Qian (2008) have argued that if the rationale of classroom-based assessment (AfL) and the culture of standardized testing remain incompatible, School-based Assessment is less likely to be purposefully integrated into the Hong Kong educational context, which has a deep-seated examination culture emphasizing norm-referenced rather than criteria-referenced assessment. Despite the reported challenges of School-based Assessment, such as heavy workload for teachers and students (Hong Kong Examinations and Assessment Authority, 2010), Mok (2011) found that the four junior students in her study were aware of the benefits of peer assessment (for example, enhancing thinking skills) when practising their speaking skills in a School-based Assessment task. Nonetheless, these low-achieving students felt that they were not adequately briefed and prepared to engage in peer assessment in English when they were asked to give qualitative comments on their peers' oral performance. To overcome these hurdles, students have to be trained and psychologically prepared to take up an active role in the assessment process. Such a drastic shift may pose challenges to their reactive learning mode in the traditional teacher-dominated classrooms.

In another study, Cheng et al. (2011) investigated parents' and students' perceptions of School-based Assessment through a survey because the extent to which School-based Assessment can benefit or impede student English learning remains uncertain, particularly when the School-based Assessment results were not available for the purpose of research at the time of the study. One interesting finding, identified in Cheng et al.'s

(2011) study, is that high-achieving students simply considered School-based Assessment as an examination, although they encountered less difficulties when doing it, whereas their low-achieving counterparts were more appreciative of the merits of School-based Assessment, namely enhanced motivation for learning and improved language awareness, but met with more setbacks, including restricted linguistic abilities when performing School-based Assessment tasks. It appears that low-achieving students generally had a more positive attitude towards School-based Assessment. This point corroborates low-achieving students' increased opportunities for exposure to authentic English, which was also reported in Davison and Hamp-Lyons's (2010) 2-year longitudinal study examining the impacts of School-based Assessment on teachers and students. In their study, Davison and Hamp-Lyons (2010) found that although there were initial teacher concerns about extra workload and the suitability of School-based Assessment being introduced in a CHC context where Chinese learners tend to be examination-driven, the findings showed that teachers became more receptive to the assessment reform and had better conceptual understanding of School-based Assessment towards the end of the study.

Despite improved teacher understandings of School-based Assessment, the Hong Kong Examinations and Assessment Authority report (2010) indicated that student performance in solo presentations and group interactions remained over-rehearsed and note-dependent, with clear evidence of extensive consultations and repeated practice assisted by private tutorial centres before the assessment. This finding illustrates that if students' and their parents' mindsets do not change, the rationale of School-based Assessment (an embodiment of AfL) is less likely to benefit their learning, given that they simply consider School-based Assessment another high-stakes testing and choose an instrumental approach to prepare for it within an examination-oriented educational system (Davison, 2013;

Littlewood, 1999). This is not unique to Confucian backgrounds – it also applies in many Western contexts. In his independent study, Qian (2014) argues that the Hong Kong Examinations and Assessment Authority's (2010) report has included limited coverage of possible challenges that teachers may face when implementing School-based Assessment. He further criticizes that the entire report appears to be too 'optimistic' and the major barrier is mainly caused by insufficient professional development. From the survey data, however, Qian (2014) identifies that within an examination culture such as Hong Kong, teachers did find it demanding to fully integrate School-based Assessment into the regular English curriculum because of limited practical marking skills and overwhelming workload (logistics of administration) and accept it as part of an external examination, in which test fairness remains an unresolved issue. As argued by Davison (2013), the process of an assessment reform like School-based Assessment is complicated, involving a range of system-wide issues in teacher motivation, beliefs, practices, value systems, a larger examination culture, etc. These issues are usually in tension because School-based Assessment, embodying a different set of conceptions of usefulness, reliability and fairness, differs significantly from its immediate examination-driven context where test performance rather than mastery of learning is prioritized (Davison and Leung, 2009).

ISSUE OF ADAPTING AfL PRACTICES IN A CHC-ORIENTED ENVIRONMENT

This section draws on evidence from Bryant and Carless (2010), Carless (2004, 2005), Carless and Lam (2014a, 2014b) and Lam (2013). These studies were all conducted in primary-level English classrooms.

To investigate assessment reform from the socio-cultural perspective, Carless (2005) illustrated how two primary-level teachers, Sue and Winnie, implemented innovative AfL practices, namely constructivist pedagogies promoting problem-solving skills and peer assessment emphasizing collaborative learning and reflection respectively. Carless found that apart from the practical constraints (for example, lack of time), the two teachers received minimal support and encouragement from colleagues, parents and principals because their assessment practices, which promoted learner independence and constructivism, ran counter to the existing educational philosophies of behavioural approaches to assessment, which emphasized extensive practice and memorization of the examination syllabus. To this end, Carless (2011) and Kennedy et al. (2008) suggest that implementing AfL practices relating to the summative assessment, namely pre-test preparation strategies, is more likely to succeed, particularly in a Confucian heritage setting where students usually have restricted autonomy in constructing assessment owing to the rigid hierarchy. In a 2-year exploratory study, Bryant and Carless (2010) examined how two Grade 5 teachers, Nancy and Laurie, implemented self- and peer assessment in their classroom contexts. Near the end of the study, students felt more motivated to participate in peer assessment if it could help them prepare for examinations and develop a learning capacity suitable for secondary schooling. The findings of the study unpredictably revealed the synergetic relationship between peer assessment and examination preparation. Bryant and Carless (2010) therefore commented that peer assessment, like other AfL practices, should be strategically adapted in order not to clash with the local CHC setting where collectivist and teacher-fronted pedagogical approaches remain popular in the primary classrooms. Bryant and Carless (2010) proposed that the implementation of peer assessment should not only highlight its pedagogical potential, namely enhanced learner autonomy, but also relate to how students could utilize this AfL practice to improve internal assessment outcomes.

Following the theme of indigenization of AfL practices, Carless and Lam (2014a) demonstrated how two English teachers linked the implementation of AfL practices with internal school tests in a testing-dominated environment. The first example in their study described how a Grade 3 teacher introduced 'student generation of questions for a mock test'. In groups, students were asked to set mock test items and answers and invite a neighbouring group to complete the student-generated test as a pre-test preparation strategy. The second example concerned 'peer-facilitated test follow up' by inviting high-achieving Year 3 students to share with their classmates what strategies they used when attempting the test. Lam (2013) also reported that Grades 2 and 3 students had moderate improvement in their internal English tests and became more self-regulated after the teachers implemented AfL practices that included self-assessment and student-generated mock papers in their classrooms. Carless and Lam (2014a) argue that adapting AfL practices to suit teachers' work contexts, namely a culture of accountability, may balance seemingly competing purposes of assessment (judging versus supporting learning); however, they warn that students could naturally remain grade-conscious and would be motivated in completing these AfL activities for good results only. Despite this, AfL-related practices, including self- and peer assessment, are generally student-centred and learning-supportive unlike the traditional teacher-dominated instruction. It is hoped that students could eventually develop a 'metacognitive' learning capacity during the course of these alternative methods of study. These adapted AfL practices, for example student generation of test materials, could make global references to comparable senior secondary contexts where the high-stakes examination culture largely reduces learners to passive test-takers rather than considering them as active players in the run-up to knowledge construction and dissemination.

In his research on task-based innovation highlighting AfL, Carless (2004) reported that arising from the issues of (1) use of mother tongue, (2) discipline problems and (3) production of target language in the data sets, the three primary-level teachers had to fine-tune their approaches to task-based teaching for accommodating the socio-cultural demands of traditional Hong Kong classroom contexts in which large class size, teacher-dominated instruction and hierarchy between teachers and learners are evident. The findings implied that in the Hong Kong context, it was more appropriate to implement the 'weak' version of task-based teaching where tasks played auxiliary roles in supporting uptake of target language in primary English classrooms. Carless (2004) further argued that, based upon a larger survey study, the adaptation of AfL practices was more contextually viable because task-based teaching was not favoured by some teachers and had been open to misinterpretations. From this scholarship, it is essential to adapt rather than adopt AfL principles and practices in order to make them contextually suitable for use in the local educational environment where high-stakes testing, traditional pedagogical practices and hierarchical relationship between teachers and students all have a part to play in affecting whether these AfL strategies can promote learning. As shown in the findings of Carless and Lam's (2014b) study, junior primary pupils' perceptions towards assessment tend to be negative and their test anxiety is evident because of a disciplinary aspect of the testing process like threats of punishment, which is common in CHC settings. Nonetheless, by incorporating learner-centred and collaborative assessments into English curriculum, students have more space to develop self-regulated learning capacity and feel less frightened of assessment, particularly if they have sound knowledge of how and what they are assessed for. Through diverse adapted AfL practices, the hierarchical power relationships can be somewhat diminished as students can take up a more proactive role in the teaching and learning process.

DISCUSSION

Three salient themes from the research concerning how AfL practices could be better implemented to support learning will be discussed next.

Changing Teacher Belief

In studies of feedback in EFL writing, it appears that entrenched teacher belief about traditional error correction is a hindrance to innovative AfL practices despite the government rhetoric. According to research on educational change, teacher belief and knowledge is one of the key aspects conducive to the success of any change process (Fullan, 2009; Tang, 2010). From the review, the reality teachers have to encounter – a system of accountability (comprehensive marking of errors) – is incongruent with the theoretical philosophies underpinning those innovative feedback practices (indirect error feedback or peer assessment). Notwithstanding the provision of continuous professional development, teachers remain frustrated and powerless to close the gap between realism and idealism especially in the CHC context where language teaching (for example, teaching of writing) equates to examination preparation (Lee and Coniam, 2013). If there is sound research evidence to corroborate the usefulness of those innovative feedback practices and adequate support from university researchers or quasi-governmental agencies, for example the Education Bureau, teachers are likely to be convinced of adopting those feedback practices in their work contexts (Carless, 2011; Lee and Wong, 2014). After all, implementation of innovative feedback practices will not happen overnight. It takes longer to change teachers' existing beliefs, experiences and practices about how to utilize assessment to promote learning, particularly when they were brought up in a traditional educational context where testing dominates the teaching and learning of writing. However, with collective efforts such as effective communication amongst all stakeholders (subject panel chairpersons, principals and parents) and enhanced teacher conceptual understanding of AfL practices, teachers will become more willing and receptive to experimenting with AfL-oriented feedback strategies (Lee, 2011b).

Promoting a Community of Practice

Although teachers may face numerous challenges when implementing English School-based Assessment including heavy workload, time constraints, etc., students remain appreciative of its benefits, for example improved oral skills (Cheng et al., 2011; Davison, 2007). Other studies showed that students favoured peer assessment (as part of School-based Assessment activities) despite their lack of adequate English proficiency to perform it (Mok, 2011). In all the contextual and system-wide challenges, teacher knowledge and skills about the paradigm of criteria-referenced assessment needs to be reinforced, given that teachers are not used to the new role as teacher-as-assessors in the high-stakes examination, for example a lack of practical marking skills (Qian, 2014). Despite the mandatory professional training, teachers still consider the rationale of School-based Assessment (AfL) and the high-stakes examination (Hong Kong Diploma of Secondary Education Examination, AoL) incompatible (Hamp-Lyons, 2007). As argued by Qian (2014), teachers should be trained to develop alternative notions of fairness, reliability and validity when implementing School-based Assessment because it follows an ethnographic rather than a psychometric approach to assessment (see Davison and Leung, 2009). For School-based Assessment training to be effective, Berry (2011) proposes that the focus of professional development should shift from a top–down orientation to more teacher self-regulating initiatives, for instance, university-school collaboration to investigate how School-based Assessment can support learning, action research projects, workshops on sharing of practical marking skills, etc. Lee (2013) and Poon (2009) also suggest that it is crucial for teachers to foster a community of practice through collaborative projects to develop professional judgment and active engagement in reflective practices for harnessing the learning potential of School-based Assessment, namely using ongoing feedback to inform teaching and learning.

Acculturating AfL Practices

Despite the government reform initiative on AfL, English classrooms remain teacher-dominated and mostly follow the traditional pedagogical approach in a CHC context. AfL practices require a constructivist approach to teaching and learning, therefore its direct adoption may run counter to the product-based instruction in the local educational context. Carless (2004) found that the weak version of task-based learning is more suitable in a setting where students' English proficiency is limited and teachers' pedagogical practices remain traditional. In Confucian-heritage society, it is not surprising to notice that conflicts tend to arise between communicative language teaching approach and examination preparation (for example, Deng and Carless, 2010). Nevertheless, the relationship between assessment innovations like AfL and an examination culture may not be mutually exclusive given that implementation of AfL practices can positively link to either examination preparation or consolidation (Bryant and Carless, 2010; Kennedy et al., 2008). The adaptation of AfL practices to accommodate the instrumental view of learning seems to be inevitable, as in East Asian contexts where a testing culture is usually predominant. Linking AfL practices to the summative assessment is likely to motivate students to actively engage in learning-enhancing activities such as self- and peer assessment, student generation of mock tests and formulation of effective revision strategies in preparing for high-stakes testing.

Such contextualized assessment practices might encourage mastery of test-taking skills and promote surface learning because of their disproportionate focus on test performance. All things considered, teachers from CHC backgrounds should tactfully fine-tune those AfL practices in order to suit the specific needs of student learning disposition given that they are heavily influenced by an examination-driven culture.

CONCLUSION

In this review of research in AfL in the English language classroom, I have attempted to critically evaluate the extent to which AfL has impacted on teaching and learning in an educational context where the local government has financially invested in the upgrade of teacher qualifications, school resources, change of academic structure, reduction in class size and other aspects of the system. Given the small number of empirical studies under review, any conclusions of the usefulness of AfL in a CHC society must be tentative. However, there is emerging evidence to indicate that both teachers and students have become more receptive to innovative assessment practices in some School-based Assessment and classroom-based AfL studies. Despite this, as shown in the review, teachers remain sceptical of the prospects of assessment reform and their new role as change agents. Students find it equally challenging to monitor their learning independently because they are used to the role of being passive learners in the traditional, teacher-centred classrooms.

Davison (2013) argues that the effectiveness of assessment change (such as AfL), particularly within an examination-driven setting, does not only rely on changes in teacher beliefs and practices, but also involves a complex interplay of diverse contextual and socio-cultural factors that are already beyond the scope of this paper. Davison (2013) emphasizes that for AfL to be successfully implemented, the entire assessment culture, including all components within the system, must be changed. Like most education reforms, AfL initiatives are likely to encounter resistance from key stakeholders (Carless, 2005). A learning culture that facilitates uptake of AfL practices in a language education context should therefore be fostered through the development of language assessment literacy amongst pre-service and in-service teachers (for example, Fulcher, 2012); the promulgation of teacher agency in reform contexts (creating space for teacher autonomy, for example, Benson, 2010); and acculturation of AfL climate in CHC settings (Carless, 2011). Despite these future directions, AfL still has a long way to go before it can be fully integrated into the local English language classrooms, unless teachers, parents, principals, school administrators and government personnel are ready to go the extra mile to align teaching, learning and assessment in the wider reform context.

REFERENCES

Berry, R. (2011) 'Assessment trends in Hong Kong: seeking to establish formative assessment in an examination culture', *Assessment in Education: Principles, Policy and Practice*, 18(2): 199–211.

Biggs, J. (1996) *Testing: To Educate or To Select?* Hong Kong: Hong Kong Educational Publishing.

Biggs, J. (1998) 'The assessment scene in Hong Kong', in P. Stimpson and P. Morris (eds.), *Curriculum and Assessment for Hong Kong: Two Components, One System*. Hong Kong: Open University of Hong Kong Press. pp. 315–24.

Benson, P. (2010) 'Teacher education and teacher autonomy: creating spaces for experimentation in secondary school English language teaching', *Language Teaching Research*, 14(3): 259–75.

Black, P. and Wiliam, D. (1998) 'Assessment and classroom learning', *Assessment in Education: Principles, Policy and Practice*, 5(1): 7–74.

Bray, M. and Kwok, P. (2003) 'Demand for private supplementary tutoring: conceptual considerations, and socio-economic patterns in Hong Kong', *Economics of Education Review*, 22(6): 611–20.

Brown, G.T.L., Kennedy, K.J., Fok, P.K., Chan, J.K.S. and Yu, W.M. (2009) 'Assessment for student improvement: understanding Hong Kong teachers' conceptions and practices of assessment', *Assessment in Education: Principles, Policy and Practice*, 16(3): 347–63.

Bryant, D.A. and Carless, D. (2010) 'Peer assessment in a test-dominated setting: Empowering, boring or facilitating examination preparation?', *Educational Research for Policy and Practice*, 9(3): 3–15.

Carless, D. (2004) 'Issues in teachers' reinterpretation of a task-based innovation in primary schools', *TESOL Quarterly*, 38(4): 639–62.

Carless, D. (2005) 'Prospects for the implementation of assessment for learning', *Assessment in Education: Principles, Policy and Practice*, 12(1): 39–54.

Carless, D. (2011) *From Testing to Productive Student Learning: Implementing Formative Assessment in Confucian-Heritage Settings*. New York, NY: Routledge.

Carless, D. and Harfitt, G. (2013) 'Innovation in secondary education: a case of curriculum reform in Hong Kong', in K. Hyland and L.L.C. Wong (eds.), *Innovation and Change in English Language Education*. Abingdon, UK: Routledge. pp. 172–85.

Carless, D. and Lam, R. (2014a) 'Developing assessment for productive learning in Confucian-influenced settings: potentials and challenges', in C. Wyatt-Smith, V. Klenowski and P. Colbert (eds.), *Designing Assessment for Quality Learning*. Dordrecht: Springer. pp. 167–82.

Carless, D. and Lam, R. (2014b) 'The examined life: perspectives of lower primary school students in Hong Kong', *Education 3–13: International Journal of Primary, Elementary and Early Years Education*, 42(3): 313–29.

Chen, R.T.H. (2014) 'East-Asian teaching practices through the eyes of Western learners', *Teaching in Higher Education*, 19(1): 26–37.

Cheng, L., Andrews, S. and Yu, Y. (2011) 'Impact and consequences of school-based assessment (SBA): students' and parents' views of SBA in Hong Kong', *Language Testing*, 28(2): 221–49.

Chow, A. and Leung, P. (2011) 'Assessment for learning in language classrooms', in R. Berry and B. Adamson (eds.), *Assessment Reform in Education: Policy and Practice*. London: Springer. pp. 135–54.

Coniam, D. (2014) 'Private tutorial schools in Hong Kong: an examination of the perceptions of public examination re-takers', *The Asia-Pacific Education Researcher*, 23(3): 379–88.

Curriculum Development Council (2001) *Learning to Learn – The Way Forward in Curriculum*. Hong Kong: Education Bureau.

Curriculum Development Council (2007) *English Language: Curriculum and Assessment Guide (Secondary 4–6)*. Hong Kong: Education Bureau and Hong Kong Examinations and Assessment Authority.

Curriculum Development Council (2009) *Senior Secondary Curriculum Guide. The Future is Now: From Vision to Realization (Secondary 4–6)*. Hong Kong: Education Bureau.

Darling-Hammond, L. and McCloskey, L. (2008) 'Assessment for learning around the world: what would it mean to be internationally competitive?', *Phi Delta Kappan*, 90(4): 263–72.

Davison, D. (2007) 'Views from the chalkface: English language school-based assessment in Hong Kong', *Language Assessment Quarterly*, 4(1): 37–68.

Davison, D. (2013) 'Innovation in assessment: common misconceptions and problems', in K. Hyland and L.L.C. Wong (eds.), *Innovation and Change in English Language Education*. Abingdon: Routledge. pp. 263–75.

Davison, C. and Hamp-Lyons, L. (2010) 'The Hong Kong Certificate of Education: school-based assessment reform in Hong Kong English language education', in L. Cheng and A. Curtis (eds.), *English Language Assessment and the Chinese Learner*. New York, NY: Routledge. pp. 248–62.

Davison, C. and Leung, C. (2009) 'Current issues in English language teacher-based assessment', *TESOL Quarterly*, 43(3): 393–415.

Deng, C. and Carless, D. (2010) 'Examination preparation or effective teaching: conflicting priorities in the implementation of a pedagogic innovation', *Language Assessment Quarterly*, 7(4): 285–302.

Education Commission (2000) *Learning for Life, Learning through Life: Reform Proposals for the Education System in Hong Kong*. Hong Kong: Government Printer.

Evans, S. (1996) 'The context of English language education: the case of Hong Kong', *RELC Journal*, 27(2): 30–55.

Evans, S. (2011) 'Hong Kong English and the professional world', *World Englishes*, 30(3): 293–316.

Farrell, T. (2013) 'Reflecting on ESL teacher expertise: a case study', *System*, 41(4): 1070–82.

Fulcher, G. (2012) 'Assessment literacy for the language classroom', *Language Assessment Quarterly*, 9(2): 113–32.

Fullan, M. (2001) *The New Meaning of Educational Change*. New York, NY: Teacher's College Press.

Fullan, M. (ed.) (2009) *The Challenge of Change: Start School Improvement Now!* 2nd edn. Thousand Oaks, CA: Corwin Press.

Hamp-Lyons, L. (2002) 'The scope of writing assessment', *Assessing Writing*, 8(1): 5–16.

Hamp-Lyons, L. (2007) 'The impact of testing practices on teaching: ideologies and alternatives', in J. Cummins and C. Davison (eds.), *The International Handbook of English Language Teaching*. Vol. 1. Norwell, MA: Springer. pp. 487–504.

Harris, L.R. and Brown, G.T.L. (2013) 'Opportunities and obstacles to consider when using peer- and self-assessment to improve student learning: case studies into teachers' implementation', *Teaching and Teacher Education*, 36: 101–11.

Hong Kong Examinations and Assessment Authority (2010) *Longitudinal Study on the School-Based Assessment of the 2007 Hong Kong Certificate of Education (HKCE) English Language Examination*. Hong Kong: Hong Kong Examinations and Assessment Authority.

Inbar-Lourie, O. (2008) 'Language assessment culture', in E. Shohamy and N.H. Hornberger (eds.), *Encyclopedia of Language and Education. Vol. 7: Language Testing and Assessment*. 2nd edn. New York, NY: Springer. pp. 285–300.

Kennedy, K.J., Chan, J.K.S., Fok, P.K. and Yu, W.M. (2008) 'Forms of assessment and their potential for enhancing learning: conceptual and cultural issues', *Educational Research for Policy and Practice*, 7(3): 197–207.

Lam, R. (2013) 'Formative use of summative tests: using test preparation to promote performance and self-regulation', *The Asia-Pacific Education Researcher*, 22(1): 69–78.

Lee, I. (2007) 'Feedback in Hong Kong secondary writing classrooms: assessment for learning or assessment of learning?', *Assessing Writing*, 12(3): 180–98.

Lee, I. (2008) 'Understanding teachers' written feedback practices in Hong Kong secondary classrooms', *Journal of Second Language Writing*, 17(2): 69–85.

Lee, I. (2010) 'Writing teacher education and teacher learning: testimonies of four EFL teachers', *Journal of Second Language Writing*, 19(3): 143–57.

Lee, I. (2011a) 'Issues and challenges in teaching and learning EFL writing: the case of Hong Kong', in T. Cimasko and M. Reichelt (eds.), *Foreign Language Writing Instruction: Principles and Practices*. Anderson, SC: Parlor Press. pp. 118–37.

Lee, I. (2011b) 'Feedback revolution: what gets in the way?', *ELT Journal*, 65(1): 1–12.

Lee, I. (2011c) 'Working smarter, not working harder: revisiting teacher feedback in the L2 writing classroom', *The Canadian Modern Language Review*, 67(3): 377–99.

Lee, I. (2013) 'Implementing innovative feedback approaches in English as a foreign language context through university-school collaboration', *Journal of Education for Teaching*, 39(5): 602–5.

Lee, I. and Coniam, D. (2013) 'Introducing assessment for learning for EFL writing in an assessment of learning examination-driven system in Hong Kong', *Journal of Second Language Writing*, 22(1): 34–50.

Lee, I. and Wong, K. (2014) 'Bringing innovation to EFL writing: the case of a primary school in Hong Kong', *The Asia-Pacific Education Researcher*, 23(1): 159–63.

Littlewood, W. (1999) 'Defining and developing autonomy in East Asian contexts', *Applied Linguistics*, 20(1): 71–94.

Littlewood, W. (2009) 'Process-oriented pedagogy: facilitation, empowerment, or control?', *ELT Journal*, 63(3): 246–54.

Lo, J. and Hyland, F. (2007) 'Enhancing students' engagement and motivation in writing: the case of primary students in Hong Kong', *Journal of Second Language Writing*, 16(4): 219–37.

Mak, P. and Lee, I. (2014) 'Implementing assessment for learning in L2 writing: an activity theory perspective', *System*, 47: 73–87.

Marsh, C.J. (2007) 'A critical analysis of the use of formative assessment', *Educational Research for Policy and Practice*, 6(1): 25–9.

Ministry of Education Singapore (2008) *2012 English Language Syllabus*. Singapore: Government Printer.

Mok, J. (2011) 'A case study of students' perceptions of peer assessment in Hong Kong', *ELT Journal*, 65(3): 230–9.

Morris, P. (2002) 'Promoting curriculum reforms in the context of a political transition: an analysis of Hong Kong's experience', *Journal of Education Policy*, 17(1): 13–28.

Morris, P. and Adamson, B. (2010) *Curriculum, Schooling and Society in Hong Kong*. Hong Kong: Hong Kong University Press.

Morris, P. and Scott, I. (2003) 'Education reform and policy implementation in Hong Kong', *Journal of Education Policy*, 18(1): 71–84.

Poon, A.Y.K. (2009) 'A review of research in English language education in Hong Kong in the past 25 years: reflections and the way forward', *Educational Research Journal*, 24(1): 7–40.

Poon, A.Y.K. (2010) 'Language use, and language policy and planning in Hong Kong', *Current Issues in Language Planning*, 11(1): 1–66.

Qian, D.D. (2008) 'English language assessment in Hong Kong: a survey of practices, developments and issues', *Language Testing*, 25(1): 85–110.

Qian, D.D. (2014) 'School-based English language assessment as a high-stakes examination component in Hong Kong: insights of frontline assessors', *Assessment in Education: Principles, Policy and Practice*, 21(3): 251–70.

Tang, S.Y.-F. (2010) 'Teachers' professional knowledge construction in assessment for learning', *Teachers and Teaching: Theory and Practice*, 16(6): 665–78.

Tong, S.Y.A. (2011) 'Assessing English language arts in Hong Kong secondary schools', *The Asia-Pacific Education Researcher*, 20(2): 387–94.

Tse, S.K. (2014) 'To what extent does Hong Kong primary school students' Chinese reading comprehension benefit from after-school private tuition?', *Asia Pacific Education Review*, 15(2): 283–97.

Wiliam, D. (2011) 'What is assessment for learning?', *Studies in Educational Evaluation*, 37(1): 3–14.

Wiliam, D. and Thompson, M. (2008) 'Integrating assessment with instruction: what will it take to make it work?', in C.A. Dwyer (ed.), *The Future of Assessment: Shaping Teaching and Learning*. Mahwah, NJ: Lawrence Erlbaum Associates. pp. 53–82.

Zeng, K. (1999) *Dragon Gate: Competitive Examinations and their Consequences*. London: Cassell.

48

Assessment for Learning Community: Learners, Teachers and Policymakers

Mary F. Hill

INTRODUCTION

This chapter interrogates the factors that have been shown to sustain assessment for learning (AfL) practices through learning communities in classrooms, schools and across school systems. Over the 15 years since the term 'assessment for learning' came into popular use, a growing number of studies have explored the claim that 'through a group of teachers' continuous learning in a community…teachers can mutually enhance each others' and their pupils' learning, thus building capacity for sustainable development' (Hargreaves, 2013: 327). This chapter articulates AfL and its connections with learning communities and then provides a short description of the method used to undertake this review and a summary of the studies found. It then draws from these studies to explore how AfL has been successfully sustained through learning communities. The chapter concludes with a discussion of how learning communities were interpreted in these settings and some of the barriers and challenges to sustaining such communities.

ASSESSMENT FOR LEARNING

Assessment for learning emerged as a description of a pedagogical approach in 1999 when the Assessment Reform Group published a pamphlet entitled *Assessment for Learning: Beyond the 'Black Box'*. The term was coined and described by the Group to translate into practice theoretical ideas derived from a review of research of classroom assessment (Black and Wiliam, 1998) that demonstrated the power of using assessment formatively to improve learning and raise standards. In short, the research indicated that improving learning through assessment depended on five key factors:

> the provision of effective feedback to pupils; the active involvement of pupils in their own learning; adjusting teaching to take account of the results of assessment; the recognition of the profound influence assessment has on the motivation and self esteem of pupils; (and), the need for pupils to be able to assess themselves and understand how to improve. (Assessment Reform Group, 1999: 5)

The Assessment Reform Group also summarised the characteristics of assessment that promotes learning in order to clearly differentiate such an approach to teaching from other interpretations of classroom assessment. These are that:

- it is embedded in a view of teaching and learning of which it is an essential part;
- it involves sharing learning goals with the pupils;
- it aims to help pupils to know and to recognise the standards they are aiming for;
- it involves pupils in self-assessment;
- it provides feedback which leads to pupils recognising their next steps and how to take them;
- it is underpinned by confidence that every student can improve; (and)
- it involves both teacher and pupils reviewing and reflecting on assessment data. (Assessment Reform Group, 1999: 7)

These characteristics describe assessment as a learning community in which teachers and learners participate to take learning forward together. The emergence of AfL as a concept signalled the importance of the formative purposes of assessment and helped consolidate, under a label or banner, the assessment for better learning discourses, which were prominent internationally (for example, Hill, 2000; Perrenoud, 1998; Shepard, 2000).

Put another way, assessment for learning involves actively engaging students in assessment processes (including self-, peer- and instructor-based assessment) throughout learning, with the goal of improving achievement, developing metacognition and supporting motivated learning and positive student self-perceptions (DeLuca et al., 2012). Taking the student-centred nature of AfL even further, Earl (2013) fleshes out the student metacognitive and involvement aspects more fully. However, for the sake of clarity in this chapter, these aspects are taken as part of the AfL term used to connote the roles of both teachers and students in the learning and teaching process. As such, AfL promotes a learning community in which teachers and students are actively involved (for a more in depth explanation of assessment for learning, see Chapter 46, this handbook)

LEARNING COMMUNITIES

Assessment for learning therefore puts students at the centre of a learning community where the assessment practices are open to all so that students can fully understand and evaluate their own learning (Elwood and Klenowski, 2002). More generally, learning communities engage together in disciplined inquiry and continuous improvement in order to 'raise the bar' and 'close the gap' of student learning and achievement (Fullan, 2005). In this context, disciplined inquiry means that rather than simply trying out good or popular ideas, following hunches or being driven by political rhetoric, AfL communities investigate and take action to progress learning in systematic ways through establishing goals or priorities, gathering evidence, reflecting on that evidence in light of the planned goals and taking action to move towards goal achievement. 'What is important about disciplined inquiry is that its data, arguments, and reasoning be capable of withstanding careful scrutiny by another member of the…community' (Shulman, 1997: 5). This is the case for AfL communities in the classroom and in professional learning communities within and across schools. In the classroom, students are apprenticed into a learning community through AfL in order to increase their involvement with their own learning where they 'come to share with the teacher a feeling of what counts as success… and move beyond just being able to say *whether* something was good to *why*' (emphasis in original) (Black et al., 2003: 66). In other words, students develop an understanding of what counts as quality (Sadler, 1989) in the process of participating in a learning community.

However, establishing such AfL communities within schooling systems has proved rather challenging. AfL has often been interpreted in ways that fail to engage learners in such self-, peer-, and co-regulated evaluative practices (Dixon, 2008; Marshall and Drummond, 2006). Rather than including learners in assessment as co-assessors, many decisions are made for students by teachers, with student involvement being infrequent at best or involving the learners in low-stakes activities, such as behavioural goal setting (Absolum et al., 2009; Booth, Hill and Dixon, 2014). DeLuca et al. (2012) proffer several main barriers to AfL integration. Readers are encouraged to refer to DeLuca et al. (2012) for more details, and what follows here is a short summary of each of these potential barriers.

In some jurisdictions, teachers and students alike link accountability pressures with a performance view of assessment. High-stakes accountability measures rely on schools instituting self-disciplinary methods that focus on raising achievement levels of students. Such measures have caused teachers to resist the implementation of AfL (DeLuca et al., 2012; Hill, 2000; Shute, 2008). These high-stakes measures tend to cause schools and teachers not to use AfL in their classrooms, but replicate a testing culture instead (DeLuca et al., 2012; Popham, 2008). As DeLuca et al. (2012: 8) point out, '(t)his misalignment is paradoxical as engaging AfL in classroom teaching and learning likely serves to enhance student achievement on summative assessments'.

Fullan (2005: 209) also argues that if we do not align all levels of an education system, at the school, district and state/national levels, 'we will never have more than temporary havens of excellence that come and go'. He refers to these 'tri-level' solutions as necessary to enable professional learning communities at the school level to successfully change practice and influence learning in a sustained and productive way. Carless (2005) also proposes the need for congruence (or at least enough congruence) between personal factors such as AfL being consistent with teachers' pedagogical beliefs and values and being able to implement it, support at the school level for implementation, and societal teaching, learning and assessment cultures conducive to the implementation of AfL.

In addition to the effects of system misalignment, some authors point to teachers having differing conceptual understandings about the nature and meaning of AfL. A critical misconception is 'that assessment for learning and assessment of learning are disconnected processes' (DeLuca et al., 2012: 9), when in fact they are interlinked and of different orders (Bennett, 2011). Furthermore, teachers' conceptions of AfL tend to be driven by their views of learning and teaching (Hargreaves, 2005). Assessment for learning facilitators, school leaders and teachers may also lack the necessary assessment knowledge and understanding (Hill, 2011). Furthermore, it may be difficult to change the views of teachers who perceive AfL negatively and they may be less than willing to commit the necessary effort to make AfL a seamlessly integrated aspect of the teaching and learning process.

Even when teachers hold similar conceptions of AfL, the way they implement it can vary depending upon their 'broader educational beliefs' (DeLuca et al., 2012: 10). Often these variations are referred to as differences in the letter and the spirit (Marshall and Drummond, 2006). Teachers whose beliefs value student involvement in their own assessment and learning as in a community of learners follow the spirit of AfL, whereas teachers who implement AfL 'in a step-by-step fashion with few opportunities to integrate feedback in to learning' (DeLuca et al., 2012: 11) adhere to the 'letter' of assessment for learning.

DeLuca et al. (2012) and Hill (2011) also cite practical difficulties that militate against teachers shifting their practice to incorporate AfL. These include time to learn about and use such approaches, class size, staff turnover, school culture, having appropriate resources and professional support. Finally, a lack of professional learning support in the implementation of assessment for learning can be a real barrier to its use and, as DeLuca et al. (2012) note, in practice all of the barriers listed are often interrelated and co-exist.

In order to establish and sustain AfL communities as envisaged by the Assessment Reform Group (2002), teacher learning communities (Hargreaves, 2013) and professional learning communities have been proffered as a strategy (Birenbaum et al., 2011; Ministry of Education, 2011; Patterson and Rolheiser, 2004, for example). There appears to be some conflation of the terminology in the studies that report the use of learning communities to embed AfL within schooling practices. Hargreaves (2013) makes a distinction between these terms, drawing on the work of Thompson and Wiliam (2008: 328) to state that 'teacher learning communities are distinct from professional learning communities in that their focus is specifically on practice, in this case assessment for learning practice, rather than teaching and learning more generally'. But other sources use the terms learning communities, professional learning communities or school-based professional learning communities when meaning teachers working together collaboratively with a focus on embedding AfL practice. In this chapter the term used is 'learning communities'; however, as Hargreaves (2013: 330) makes clear, such learning communities expect 'teachers to meet together regularly to reflect on their own, and other teachers', expertise in AfL, negotiating the principles underpinning AfL techniques, not just the techniques, so as to be powerful in critiquing which techniques to use, when to use them and why'.

Furthermore, Birenbaum et al. (2011) point out that AfL and school-based professional learning communities (SBPLC) can be linked on several theoretical grounds.

> Both constructs are derived from socio-constructivist approaches to learning…a critically oriented (emancipatory) stance…underlies high level functioning of a SBPLC as well as high-quality AfL practice; and moreover, AfL and SBPLC share the same goal, namely, the advancement of student self-regulated learning…and a similar process of inquiry. (2011: 36)

The terms 'learning communities' and 'professional learning communities' have been used by different authors in different, and sometimes contradictory, ways in AfL literature and more widely, such as in the schooling improvement field (for example, Hord, 1997). Brodie (2013: 6) points out that although, in essence, professionals in these learning communities are 'engaged in ongoing learning for the benefit of their "clients"', this definition allows for a range of meanings and interpretations. She draws on definitions from Stoll and Seashore Louis (2008) and Katz et al. (2009) to pinpoint more accurately a definition for, and the key characteristics of, such learning communities.

> The term 'professional learning community' suggests that the focus is not only on individual teachers' learning but on collective professional learning within the context of a cohesive group that works with an ethic of interpersonal care, which permeates the life of teachers, students and school leaders….Katz, Earl and Ben Jafar (2009) identify four key characteristics:…they have a challenging focus;…they create productive relationships through trust;…they collaborate for joint benefit which requires moderate professional conflict, although not person conflict; and…they engage in rigorous enquiry. (Brodie, 2013: 6)

Brodie (2013: 6) also suggests that to have an effect on student learning (which is the purpose of AfL), 'the focus must relate to the instructional core – the relationship between teacher, student and content, and involve a problem of practice based on learner needs'.

Consistent with Brodie, a synthesis of the best evidence for teacher professional learning and development (Timperley et al., 2007) reported that one of the most consistent findings across the full range of studies reviewed was teacher participation in some form of structured professional group. Two key qualities of learning communities that promoted teacher and student learning (as in AfL) were that 'participants (are) supported to process new understandings and their implications for teaching', and that 'the focus (is) on analysing the impact of teaching on student learning' (Timperley et al., 2007: 203).

LITERATURE REVIEW METHOD

To find evidence of successful implementation of AfL with a focus on sustaining its use through fostering a learning community, two concept maps of search terms were developed after initial searching using Google and Google Scholar. The concept maps used a four-level structure across three subjects to ensure search term combinations were used systematically when searching databases for articles and documents. A list of 39 keywords found in papers relevant to the search terms was compiled and used to assist in locating possible relevant sources. Databases searched included Google Scholar, ERIC, Education Research Journals, and ProQuest education journals. Initially, 65 potential studies were located for consideration; however, many of these studies were not specifically focused on the implementation of AfL or did not contain evidence regarding the extent to which AfL had been sustained. They were therefore either not used or, where they met the criteria regarding learning communities but were not clearly focused on AfL, were used more generally regarding the elements of learning communities that sustained the implementation of AfL.

The studies that shed light on the factors that sustained AfL were included if they clearly indicated that the implementation of AfL was central to the innovation under investigation. When the terminology was described as including practices that fitted within the definitions for AfL used in this chapter (such as assessment for learning, formative assessment, assessment is for learning), these studies were included when the other criteria used for selection were met. For example, one study that used the term 'formative assessment' met this criterion by defining it as: 'Formative classroom assessment is an active and intentional learning process that partners the teacher and the students to continuously and systematically gather evidence of learning with the express goal of improving student achievement' (Moss et al., 2013: 206).

Assessment as learning community interventions were deemed successful and to have been sustained according to a range of factors across the corpus of work. In some, the implementation of AfL was tracked in terms of student achievement results (for example, Hansen et al., 2013), whilst in others success had more to do with sustaining the teacher learning communities where the participants reported positive effects on students' learning (for example, Hallam et al., 2004; Hargreaves, 2013). Nineteen studies were found that reported successfully sustaining AfL through learning communities. All were published after 2000 in line with the fact that the term assessment for learning came into more common use around this time (Assessment Reform Group, 1999, 2002), although it is acknowledged that in some contexts, formative assessment practices matching the AfL definition had been encouraged through the use of professional learning communities before this time (for example, in New Zealand).

ANALYSIS

The studies were read and interrogated for ways in which learning communities were interpreted. Conditions that led to AfL being sustained were then noted. Next, an inductive analysis was conducted across the nineteen studies to identify the factors recognised as important for sustaining the implementation of AfL. Due to the fact that the studies varied hugely in the number of participants, context for change (classroom, school, district, country) and type and scope of the studies, a qualitative analysis was considered most appropriate for this review.

SUSTAINING AND GROWING ASSESSMENT FOR LEARNING THROUGH LEARNING COMMUNITIES

The sources found included research reports and evaluations, including studies from the

UK, Norway, Israel, Hong Kong, Canada, the US, Australia and New Zealand. They were spread across different levels of schooling (both primary and secondary) and ranged from individual case studies of one teacher to system-wide studies in countries where there had been initiatives to embed AfL across schooling (for example, in Norway, Scotland and New Zealand). Studies from nine countries met the criteria for inclusion (see Table 48.1). Seven main themes were identified as sustaining assessment as a learning community.

THEME 1: TEACHERS UNDERSTAND AND COMMIT TO THE USE OF AfL TO IMPROVE STUDENT LEARNING

Almost half (nine) of the 19 studies specifically included the critical role of teachers understanding AfL/formative assessment as building a learning community with learners and committing to build this type of culture within their classrooms; however, this theme was also implicit in the other studies as a condition for successfully sustaining AfL. It is included here as a theme because half of the studies examined demonstrated that how AfL came to be understood and incorporated in pedagogy by the teachers was essential for sustaining classroom learning communities beyond the life of any innovation (Hallam et al., 2004; James and McCormick, 2009).

Furthermore, several of the studies provided evidence that it is ultimately the classroom teachers who spread and grow pedagogical cultures as long as the other themes (see the following themes 2 to 7) are in place (Hallam et al., 2004; Wilson, 2008; Wylie et al., 2009). Speaking about the Assessment is for Learning Initiative in Scotland, Hallam et al. (2004: 14) explained that 'dissemination needs to be undertaken by practising teachers who can convey their enthusiasm and the impact of the project on their pupils in relation to involvement, motivation and improvement in the quality of work'. This type of dissemination

was referred to as 'the importance of "hot" information in generating interest and commitment' (Condie et al., 2005: 149). Such enthusiasm, understanding and commitment links to theories of teacher agency (Priestly, Biesta and Robinson, 2012) and was related to theme 2, collaborative inquiry.

THEME 2: TEACHERS COLLABORATIVELY INQUIRE INTO THEIR USE OF AfL PRACTICES THROUGH PROFESSIONAL EXPERIMENTATION OR CYCLES OF INQUIRY/ACTION RESEARCH

Just over half of the studies (11) highlighted collaborative inquiry into the effectiveness and improvement of their implementation of AfL amongst teachers within and between the schools in which they worked. Sometimes this was referred to as action research (for example, Carless, 2005; Condie et al., 2005; Cooper and Cowie, 2010), whilst others explained the process as collaborative inquiry (Hill, 2011) or experimentation (Wylie et al., 2009). As James and McCormick (2009: 982) explain, 'classroom-based collaborative inquiry practices for teacher learning emerged as the key influence on teachers' capacity to promote learning autonomy with their pupils. These include learning from research as well as working together to plan, try out and evaluate new ideas'. Such collaborative inquiry is not accomplished quickly, but takes time and the commitment signalled in theme 1. In most of the studies, the inquiry process was carried out over an extended period of at least a year, and longer in most cases. It was characterised by successive cycles of trialling new ideas to increase student engagement in, and ownership of, their learning, including initiatives to share learning intentions and success criteria, assist students in understanding what constitutes quality and progression in different aspects of learning and increase self- and peer involvement in setting goals, evaluating

Table 48.1 Empirical studies investigating where assessment for learning has been successfully sustained

Author/s and title	Design	Country	N	Scope	Description of study	Themes that sustained AfL
Birenbaum, M., Kimron, H. and Shilton, H. (2011). Nested contexts that shape assessment for learning: School-based professional learning community and classroom culture.	Quantitative rating response questionnaires; Qualitative case study	Israel	122 teachers surveyed; 6 case study teachers, 6 teachers from the same school as each case study teacher 22 students	Elementary schools	Investigated relationships between assessment for learning (AfL) and attributes of two school-related contexts – the classroom assessment culture (CAC) and the larger context in which CAC is nested, namely the school-based professional learning community (SBPLC). Contrasting case studies that demonstrate how AfL, CAC and SBPLCs are mutually supportive are provided.	1. Teachers understand and commit to AfL to improve student learning 4. School/district leaders understand AfL at deep level and instantiate it through accountability and support 7. Classroom and school AfL practices aligned with macro-level assessment policies
Black, P. and Wiliam, D. (2005). Changing teaching through formative assessment: research and practice. See also Wiliam, D., Lee, C., Harrison, C. and Black, P. (2004).	Multimethod: teacher observations; feedback on teaching; interview data on teachers' perceptions	England	6 schools, 24 teachers	Science and maths in secondary schools	Project helped schools secure the benefits of innovations in formative assessment. No new tests were introduced to measure the outcome. Achievement data from the schools were used and analysed.	4. School/district leaders understand AfL at deep level and instantiate it through accountability and support 5. External facilitation by AfL experts
Carless, D. (2005). Prospects for the implementation of assessment for learning.	Case study	Hong Kong	2 schools	Primary	The author uses two cases (teachers) to illustrate barriers and keys to implementing and sustaining AfL. AfL implementation was successful when the 'innovative approaches' made sense to the teachers and shared links with their training and beliefs; the researcher's collaboration with the teachers.	1. Teachers understand and commit to AfL to improve student learning 5. External facilitation by AfL experts
Condie, R., Livingstone, K. and Seagraves, L. (2005). Evaluation of the assessment is for learning programme: final report and appendices.	Quantitative surveys and Qualitative including case studies	Scotland	32 local authorities, 9 development officers and 11 higher education representatives 102 schools survey 26 case study schools	Primary, secondary, junior high, special school	The study investigated how the Assessment is for Learning Development Programme (AifL) was implemented and sustained in Scotland.	2. Teachers collaboratively inquire into their use of AfL practices 3. Focus on day-to-day practice in teachers' own classrooms 4. School/district leaders understand AfL at deep level and instantiate it through accountability and support 5. External facilitation by AfL experts 6. Regular interactions over time between teachers within and across schools to learn, plan, discuss, evaluate 7. Classroom and school AfL practices aligned with macro-level assessment policies

Reference	Method	Country	Sample	Level	Description	
Cooper, B. and Cowie, B. (2010). Collaborative research for assessment for learning.	Qualitative including reflections, samples of student work, meetings and collaborative discussions	New Zealand	3 teachers	Secondary	Collaborative research between a group of secondary teachers and university researchers, initiated by the teachers, into the practice and impacts of assessment for learning in chemistry, geography and history classes. The findings highlight the importance of external support, shared teacher knowledge and beliefs, professional experimentation, and shared reflection on student responses to classroom innovations.	1. Teachers understand and commit to AfL to improve student learning 2. Teachers collaboratively inquire into their use of AfL practices 3. Focus on day-to-day practice in teachers' own classrooms 4. School/district leaders understand AfL at deep level and instantiate it through accountability and support 6. Regular interactions over time between teachers within and across schools to learn, plan, discuss, evaluate 7. Classroom and school AfL practices aligned with macro-level assessment policies
Geddes (2005). Helping teachers develop formative assessment strategies.	Multimethod and multiphased: surveys; self-assessment; student achievement data	New Zealand	1 school	Primary	A facilitator's view of the changes made to one school's Assessment to Learn (AtoL) professional development programme over several years.	1. Teachers understand and commit to AfL to improve student learning 2. Teachers collaboratively inquire into their use of AfL practices 3. Focus on day-to-day practice in teachers' own classrooms 4. School/district leaders understand AfL at deep level and instantiate it through accountability and support 5. External facilitation by AfL experts
Hallam, S., Kirton, A., Pfeffers, J., Robertson, P. and Stobart, G. (2004). Assessment is for learning: Development (AifL) programme. Evaluation of project 1: Support for professional practice in formative assessment.	Case studies of schools participating in the AifL Support for professional practice in formative assessment	Scotland	Approx. 32 case study schools and approx. 32 comparator schools	Primary, secondary and 1 special school	Evaluation that aimed to consider the extent to which the project was perceived to have changed practices in the classroom, improved pupil learning, motivation and behaviour, improved attainment, influenced change in teachers' beliefs and attitudes, changed teachers' understanding of the assessment process, enhanced the school climate to promote a positive learning environment, and changed parental interest and involvement in their child's education.	1. Teachers understand and commit to AfL to improve student learning 2. Teachers collaboratively inquire into their use of AfL practices 4. School/district leaders understand AfL at deep level and instantiate it through accountability and support 5. External facilitation by AfL experts 6. Regular interactions over time between teachers within and across schools to learn, plan, discuss, evaluate 7. Classroom and school AfL practices aligned with macro-level assessment policies

(continued)

Table 48.1 Empirical studies investigating where assessment for learning has been successfully sustained (Continued)

Author/s and title	Design	Country	N	Scope	Description of Study	Themes that sustained AfL
Hansen, D., Anderson, C., Munger, L. and Chizek, M. (2013). All Aboard! In One Iowa District, All Teachers and Principals Are on the Same Journey.	Not stated	US	1 school district	1 preschool, 3 elementary schools, 2 middle schools and 1 high school	A team of facilitators, using methods specifically designed for assessment for learning, worked with principals and teachers, honing participants' skills to lead and engage in collaborative teams.	4. School/district leaders understand AfL at deep level and instantiate it through accountability and support 5. External facilitation by AfL experts 6. Regular interactions over time between teachers within and across schools to learn, plan, discuss, evaluate 7. Classroom and school AfL practices aligned with macro-level assessment policies
Hargreaves, E. (2013). Assessment for learning and Teacher Learning Communities: UK teachers' experiences.	Qualitative interviews and observations	UK	4 schools	Secondary	This article explores how participants experience the actual functioning of teacher Learning Communities. Teacher Learning Communities' benefits were compromised specifically: where they were imposed on teachers; where they were not accommodated sufficiently within other school commitments; where leaders were too directive; where meeting formats were adhered to inflexibly; and where practice was emphasized at the expense of theories.	2. Teachers collaboratively inquire into their use of AfL practices 3. Focus on day-to-day practice in teachers' own classrooms 5. External facilitation by AfL experts
Hill, M.F. (2011). 'Getting traction': enablers and barriers to implementing Assessment for Learning in secondary schools.	Qualitative case study	New Zealand	3 schools	Secondary	Enablers of effective assessment for learning practices in large secondary schools: principal as 'conductor' of change; senior staff/ management team involvement; alignment with assessment for qualifications; cross-curricular teacher learning about assessment for learning; embedding assessment for learning as part of school culture; tailored facilitation.	2. Teachers collaboratively inquire into their use of AfL practices 3. Focus on day-to-day practice in teachers' own classrooms 4. School/district leaders understand AfL at deep level and instantiate it through accountability and support 5. External facilitation by AfL experts 6. Regular interactions over time between teachers within and across schools to learn, plan, discuss, evaluate

Reference	Method	Country	Sample	Level	Findings	
Hollingworth, L. (2012). Why leadership matters: empowering teachers to implement formative assessment.	Case study, interviews and observations	US	1 school	Secondary	The principal served as a catalyst for building teacher knowledge and implementation of formative assessment practices. The success of the change initiative hinged on relationships between teachers and school leaders. Without question, the professional learning communities could not exist without administrative support of innovation and change: specifically, time to meet, money to support new curriculum, and training. (p. 377)	3. Focus on day-to-day practice in teachers' own classrooms 4. School/district leaders understand AfL at deep level and instantiate it through accountability and support 6. Regular interactions over time between teachers within and across schools to learn, plan, discuss, evaluate
Hopfenbeck, T., Tolo, A., Florez, T. and El Masri, Y. (2013). Balancing trust and accountability? The assessment for learning programme in Norway. A governing complex education systems case study.	Qualitative interviews	Norway	98 participants	Ministry officials, municipality leaders, principals, teachers, students and professional development facilitators	This country case study explored the implementation of an Assessment for Learning programme in Norwegian schools. Successful implementation was facilitated by clear communication and trust between system levels, municipality and school leaders who understood AfL, learning networks established within and between schools including an online platform.	4. School/district leaders understand AfL at deep level and instantiate it through accountability and support 6. Regular interactions over time between teachers within and across schools to learn, plan, discuss, evaluate 7. Classroom and school AfL practices aligned with macro-level assessment policies
James, M. and McCormick, R. (2009). Teachers learning how to learn.	Quantitative, questionnaires from all staff; Qualitative, interviews with co-ordinators and head teachers	England	40 schools	Secondary, primary, infant schools	The TLRP 'Learning How to Learn in Classrooms, Schools and Networks' project researched how practices were developed by teachers in 40 infant, primary and secondary schools in England. A particular interest was in the conditions within schools and networks that are conducive to implementing and sustaining AfL and LHTL practice. A key factor was the teachers' own engagement in collaborative classroom-focused inquiry; however, to be successful, this needed to be supported by school management and leadership. Strong statistical relationships between school policy, teachers' professional learning and their capacity to promote learning autonomy in their pupils. Teacher learning through networking within their schools, and with other teachers in other schools, was also shown to be important.	1. Teachers understand and commit to AfL to improve student learning 2. Teachers collaboratively inquire into their use of AfL practices 3. Focus on day-to-day practice in teachers' own classrooms 4. School/district leaders understand AfL at deep level and instantiate it through accountability and support 5. External facilitation by AfL experts

(continued)

Table 48.1 Empirical studies investigating where assessment for learning has been successfully sustained (Continued)

Author/s and title	Design	Country	N	Scope	Description of study	Themes that sustained AfL
Moss, C.M., Brookhart, S.M and Long, B.A. (2013). Administrators' roles in helping teachers use formative assessment information.	Qualitative and quantitative observations, researchers' feedback to administrators, researchers' field notes from administrative meetings, surveys, photographic evidence	US	24 school administrators: 11 building principals, 6 assistant principals, 5 instructional coaches and 2 school psychologists.	5 secondary, 7 elementary schools	The researchers conducted an exploratory study using 2 years of data from a large, rural school district to describe administrators' learning as they participated in a professional development project designed to increase their knowledge and leadership of formative assessment.	4. School/district leaders understand AfL at deep level and instantiate it through accountability and support
Patterson, D. and Rolheiser, C. (2004). Creating a culture of change: ten strategies for developing an ethic of teamwork.	Qualitative study	Ontario, Canada	60 participants in 1 school district	Not stated	Qualitative interviews with 60 participants across the school district at the beginning and end of one school year where the entire district had worked to implement AfL. Scores on the Provincial Achievement Tests over this time saw an 11.5% improvement and a further (unspecified improvement in the second year).	2. Teachers collaboratively inquire into their use of AfL practices 3. Focus on day-to-day practice in teachers' own classrooms 4. School/district leaders understand AfL at deep level and instantiate it through accountability and support
Poskitt, J. and Taylor, K. (2008). Sustaining professional development: rhetoric or reality?	Evaluative case study of the implementation of AfL using interviews and document analysis	New Zealand	36 schools	Primary schools	Implementing AfL through professional development with four key outcomes: improve student learning and achievement; shift teachers' knowledge and assessment practice; develop coherence between assessment processes, practices and systems; demonstrate a culture of continuous school improvement.	1. Teachers understand and commit to AfL to improve student learning 2. Teachers collaboratively inquire into their use of AfL practices 3. Focus on day-to-day practice in teachers' own classrooms 4. School/district leaders understand AfL at deep level and instantiate it through accountability and support 7. Classroom and school AfL practices aligned with macro-level assessment policies

Reference	Method	Country	Sample	Summary	Criteria
Smith, K. and Engelsen, K.S. (2013). Developing an assessment for learning (AfL) culture in school: the voice of the principals.	Case study Semi-structured group interview with the two principals who had agreed on an interview agenda in advance	Norway	2 principals	Primary schools	This study 3-year action-oriented development project reflects the voice of school leaders (principals) in a Norwegian school development project focusing on AfL. According to the principals, the teachers are now more conscious about focusing on the students' performance in relation to the tasks, and how the students understand and use assessment to enhance their own learning. The principals had become agenda setters for change.	1. Teachers understand and commit to AfL to improve student learning 3. Focus on day-to-day practice in teachers' own classrooms 4. School/district leaders understand AfL at deep level and instantiate it through accountability and support 6. Regular interactions over time between teachers within and across schools to learn, plan, discuss, evaluate
Wilson, N.S. (2008). Teachers expanding pedagogical content knowledge: learning about formative assessment together.	Case study using study group field notes, classroom observations and interviews	US	5 Grade 6–8 English language arts teachers	Middle school	Explores the development of teacher knowledge and use of AfL through a study group acting as a teacher learning community. The findings indicate that interaction in a study group focused on AfL, where discussions played a key role, was an effective tool in changing the PCK (Pedagogical Content Knowledge) of the participating teachers.	1. Teachers understand and commit to AfL to improve student learning 2. Teachers collaboratively inquire into their use of AfL practices 6. Regular interactions over time between teachers within and across schools to learn, plan, discuss, evaluate
Wylie, E.C., Lyon, C.J and Goe, L. (2009). Teacher professional development focused on formative assessment: changing teachers, changing schools.	Qualitative case study TLC observations, classroom observations, interviews with teachers	US	2 school districts	Elementary and high schools	Study provides insight into the ways in which TLCs support implementing formative assessment. Supportive administration where teachers were encouraged to be formative assessment innovators, the project flourished and teachers beyond the initial cohort became engaged with the work.	2. Teachers collaboratively inquire into their use of AfL practices 3. Focus on day-to-day practice in teachers' own classrooms 4. School/district leaders understand AfL at deep level and instantiate it through accountability and support 5. External facilitation by AfL experts 6. Regular interactions over time between teachers within and across schools to learn, plan, discuss, evaluate

performances and providing themselves and each other with feedback and feed forward.

THEME 3: THE FOCUS OF THE LEARNING COMMUNITY AND PROFESSIONAL DEVELOPMENT IS ON THE DAY-TO-DAY PRACTICE IN TEACHERS' OWN CLASSROOMS

A third feature demarking sustained implementation of assessment for learning was the practice-based nature of the cycles of inquiry carried out by teachers. This was a feature of all 19 studies listed in Table 48.1, but specifically singled out for attention in 11 of them. Condie et al. (2005), in the context of the Scottish Assessment is for Learning Initiative, pointed out that change is more likely and more long-lasting where the teachers could see the changes in the learning in their classrooms as they changed the practices they were using. The teachers therefore saw themselves as the agents of change rather than as an object to be changed. By making the teachers' site of practice the subject of the collaborative learning community, every teacher trying out new practices becomes an active member of the community with something to share; therefore, principled, professional experimentation and shared critical reflection about student responses to classroom innovations is at the heart of sustained AfL (Cooper and Cowie, 2010; Hill, 2011; Poskitt and Taylor, 2008; Smith and Engelsen, 2013).

THEME 4: THE SCHOOL AND/OR DISTRICT LEADERS UNDERSTAND AfL AT A DEEP LEVEL AND INSTANTIATE IT THROUGH ACCOUNTABILITY AND SUPPORT

In order to ensure the professional experimentation noted in theme 3, the leadership at the school and/or district level must be conducive. In short, school/district leaders need to understand AfL at a deep level themselves in order to instantiate it within schools in their jurisdiction (Geddes, 2005; Hollingworth, 2012; Smith and Englesen, 2013). One of Hollingworth's participants emphasizes the role of the district superintendent, the building principal and the leadership team 'as twofold: making administrative changes to support and encourage professional learning communities; and, promoting the ways teachers work (to implement assessment for learning) in their classrooms' (Hollingworth, 2012: 373).

Sixteen of the studies emphasized leadership as crucial to sustaining implementation of learning communities and AfL. Leaders who understood AfL conducted relevant change through ensuring the resources, including expert facilitation, time and funding were available (Hill, 2011; Smith and Engelsen, 2013); building a sense of collective efficacy and capacity to advance all students' learning (Birenbaum et al., 2011); requiring accountability through monitoring achievement and teacher appraisal (top–down) whilst simultaneously providing support for teachers to innovate (bottom–up) (Carless, 2005; Hill, 2011; Patterson and Rolheiser, 2004); and through organizational self-review and improvement through analysis of evidence and targeted action (Moss et al., 2013; Poskitt and Taylor, 2008). In short, leadership of change was the critical 'glue' between the wider initiatives for change and teachers taking up and sustaining the work in the classroom. A lack of these leadership factors was noted when AfL was not sustained (Hargreaves, 2013; Hill, 2011).

THEME 5: AFL EXPERTS ARE INCLUDED IN THE PROFESSIONAL DEVELOPMENT PROCESS

The fifth theme noted explicitly in 10 of the studies was the critical role of external facilitation of change. As Hargreaves expressed it, support from external experts for theoretical and well as practical learning is essential because 'if the site of learning is perceived as the limit of learning, then limited learning is likely to be the outcome' (2013: 339). External expertise was procured in a range of ways, including visits from international experts (Carless, 2005; Hopfenbeck et al., 2013), higher education advisors (Hallam et al., 2004; Hopfenbeck et al., 2013; James and McCormick, 2009) and AfL consultants (Carless, 2005, Geddes, 2005; Poskitt and Taylor, 2008).

THEME 6: THERE ARE REGULAR INTERACTIONS OVER TIME BETWEEN TEACHERS WITHIN AND ACROSS SCHOOLS TO LEARN, PLAN, DISCUSS AND EVALUATE THE USE OF AfL

A feature of nearly all the reports of sustained AfL practice was the fact that teachers and school leaders regularly discussed, debated and interrogated their use of AfL over time. This happened both within and between schools as teachers met to learn through planning new practices, discussing outcomes and evaluating their progress (Cooper and Cowie, 2010; Wilson, 2008; Wylie et al., 2009). Ten of the studies explicitly reported how such sharing within teams, between subject teams in secondary schools, and/or between teachers in different schools, benefited sustainability because participants were able to share new ideas, concrete examples of both successful and unsuccessful practice and draw on each others' expertise.

THEME 7: CLASSROOM AND SCHOOL AfL PRACTICES ARE ALIGNED WITH THE MACRO-LEVEL CULTURE OF LEARNING AND ASSESSMENT AND/ OR THE ROLE OF LARGE-SCALE ASSESSMENTS AND QUALIFICATIONS

The final theme in sustaining these learning communities was alignment in support of AfL across the system within which the teachers operated. Birenbaum et al. (2011) explained that the classroom assessment culture in which AfL is conducted tends to mirror the culture prevailing in the larger context in which it is embedded. For some, particularly in larger countries, this meant alignment within a school district, whilst in smaller countries such as Scotland, Norway and New Zealand, national policies and assessment culture were aligned with the district and school-based AfL innovation. When there had been a sustained attempt to implement AfL nationally in all three of these smaller countries, the signs were that change was happening on a large scale and that AfL was, to varying levels, becoming the norm. The evidence for this in Scotland and Norway mainly came though systematic evaluation reports (see Table 48.1) and the New Zealand evidence included an OECD system evaluation (Nusche et al., 2012), in addition to the New Zealand studies reported in Table 48.1. This finding is consistent with the Fullan (2005) and Carless (2005) arguments that a tri-level framework of factors is necessary for sustaining change, such as AfL, within an education system, but it also indicates that the size of the jurisdiction makes a considerable difference. Furthermore, in these three small countries there is no high-stakes testing below about 14 years of age.

HOW LEARNING COMMUNITIES WERE INTERPRETED IN THE STUDIES WHERE AfL WAS SUSTAINED

The studies listed in Table 48.1 were not always clear about how learning communities were constituted within the reported innovation. Although some were explicit about how the group was constituted and the nature of the work carried out in the learning community (for example, Cooper and Cowie, 2010; Hansen et al., 2013), many used terms to suggest learning communities, such as professional learning communities or teacher learning communities, without explicitly describing the nature of these. Reading across the studies it was possible to gain an understanding of how these learning communities were interpreted and functioned and it is to this that the chapter now turns.

Assessment for learning communities had been established almost always by teachers working in groups of about two to six. At times, these communities were initiated by the teachers themselves (Cooper and Cowie, 2010), at others by leaders at the school level (Hill, 2011) and, most often in these studies, by districts and school systems (Condie et al., 2005; Hallam et al., 2004; Hopfenbeck et al., 2013; James and McCormick, 2009). In each learning community groups of teachers met regularly, informally and formally, with a sense of collective efficacy regarding catering for students' learning needs. There was an unrelenting focus in these communities on advancing the learning of all students (see, for example, Hansen et al., 2013). Hargreaves (2013: 342) argues from her work that in contrast to a '"one size fits all" approach…both teachers and learners need to be continually questioning the potential advantages and disadvantages of different approaches and that this argumentation holds the promise of effecting valuable learning'. This challenging focus (Brodie, 2013) is required to sustain AfL practice, to counter difficulties that arise in implementation and to evaluate the progress and achievement of the students as the innovation proceeds (Hallam et al., 2004; Hill, 2011).

Understanding AfL was a central concern of the learning communities in these studies. Essential to this was that theoretical understanding of learning, teaching and assessment was as crucial to knowing how to enact the practices of AfL as knowing some assessment for learning strategies (Hargreaves, 2013). Developing this professional knowledge was central to the work of these learning communities (James and McCormick, 2009). In general, teachers worked to develop this practical professional knowledge and understanding by engaging in small-scale research

or inquiry projects that engaged learners, and gave the teachers a sense of ownership and involvement whilst at the same time building trust, an essential ingredient in learning communities (Brodie, 2013). As Hargreaves explained, 'teachers made commitments to their colleagues to try something out and return to them later to tell them what happened' (2013: 340). As in AfL with students, it is important that everyone's voice is heard, respected and valued. In one learning community, the 'students were invited to feedback to the Teacher Learning Community about how useful they found teacher marking: and then their recommendations were acted on' (Hargreaves, 2013: 342).

In some instances these AfL communities grew and thrived because of the passion and commitment of just a few enthusiast teachers who sometimes worked against the odds to establish and maintain this work (Cooper and Cowie, 2010; Wylie et al., 2009). Working in this way, teachers saw themselves as agents of change.

When learning communities work well, they are often peer- (rather than management-) led (Cooper and Cowie, 2010; Hargreaves, 2013; Hill, 2011). Hargreaves argues that when teachers volunteer to join, learning communities sustained change better than those imposed on teachers. Hill (2011) noted that in each of the three secondary schools where AfL was successfully operating, teachers had chosen whom to work with and how to work within the guidelines leaders provided. In this way trust was offered by management and built between teachers. Furthermore, in at least three studies in secondary schools, AfL had been successfully sustained when the learning communities were trans-disciplinary (Cooper and Cowie, 2010; Hill, 2011; James and McCormick, 2009). This grouping stimulated cross-fertilization of ideas and enabled networks to grow rather than perpetuating subject balkanisation. Between-school networks were also a feature of sustaining AfL within district and countrywide initiatives (Birenbaum et al., 2011; Condie et al., 2005; Hallam et al., 2004; Hill, 2011; Patterson and Rolheiser, 2004). James and McCormick (2009: 982) concluded that 'networking through face-to-face meetings of various kinds builds the social capital (ideas and practices) but the networks should involve a wide variety of links to enable all schools and teachers to take part'.

CONCLUSIONS: GROWING AND SUSTAINING ASSESSMENT FOR LEARNING COMMUNITIES

As the review of the literature in this chapter confirms, AfL communities, suitably encouraged and supported, can be sustained and become a normal feature of school and classroom practice. The evidence supports Fullan's (2005) and Carless's (2005) contention that a tri-level culture of assessment in support of learning can both stimulate and sustain a system in which teachers work together and with their students to implement AfL as briefly described in this article. Clearly, within professional learning communities teachers need to understand and commit to AfL in practice and focus on day-to-day practice in their own classrooms as they learn to implement AfL supported by facilitators with AfL expertise. Furthermore, having school and district leaders who understand AfL at a deep level and consistently reinforce its use through accountability and support assists in sustaining such learning communities. Collaborative inquiry about the use and development of AfL within and across schools also plays a part in successfully embedding it.

As outlined earlier in this chapter, many barriers and challenges exist to successfully embedding AfL. When the themes described in this chapter do not exist or are partially implemented, AfL can fail to be sustained. For example, when the societal context for assessment is not aligned with an AfL culture, it can be very difficult to establish such learning communities (Hargreaves, 2013). Several of the studies in this review (for example,

Condie et al., 2005; Hargreaves, 2013; Hill, 2011) emphasized the importance of a combination of such 'top–down' and 'bottom–up' alignment. Although these consistencies were most apparent in the policies of small countries such as Norway, Scotland and New Zealand, Hansen et al. (2013), Moss et al., (2013) and Patterson and Rolheiser (2004) all demonstrated how district-wide implementation of AfL can be sustained when district administrators support schools and teachers to use AfL practices. This chapter has demonstrated, however, that with the appropriate supports in place, AfL communities are possible and viable for learners, teachers, schools and school systems.

ACKNOWLEDGEMENT

I wish to thank Nike Franke for the work she did to search the literature and find many of the studies used in this chapter. I also wish to acknowledge Susan Ng for her assistance in the preparation of the chapter.

REFERENCES

Absolum, M., Flockton, L., Hattie, J., Hipkins, R. and Reid, I. (2009) *Directions for Assessment in New Zealand (DANZ): Developing Students' Assessment Capabilities.* Wellington, NZ: Ministry of Education.

Assessment Reform Group (1999) *Assessment for Learning: Beyond the 'Black Box'.* Cambridge: University of Cambridge School of Education.

Assessment Reform Group (2002) *Assessment for Learning: 10 Principles.* Available from http://methodenpool.uni-koeln.de/benotung/ assessment_basis.pdf (accessed 15 July 2015).

Bennett, R.E. (2011) 'Formative assessment: a critical review', *Assessment in Education: Principles, Policy & Practice*, 18(1): 5–25.

Birenbaum, M., Kimron, H. and Shilton, H. (2011) 'Nested contexts that shape assessment for learning: School-based professional learning community and classroom culture', *Studies in Educational Evaluation, 37*: 35–48.

Black, P. and Wiliam, D. (1998) 'Assessment and classroom learning', *Assessment in Education: Principles, Policy and Practice*, 5(1): 7–74.

Black, P., Harrison, C., Lee, C., Marshall, B. and Wiliam, D. (2003) *Assessment for Learning: Putting it into Practice*. Maidenhead, UK: Open University Press.

Booth, B., Hill, M.F. and Dixon, H. (2014) 'The assessment capable teacher: are we all on the same page?', *Assessment Matters, 6:* 137–57.

Brodie, K. (2013) 'The power of professional learning communities', *Education as Change*, 17(1): 5–18.

Carless, D. (2005) 'Prospects for the implementation of assessment for learning', *Assessment in Education: Principles, Policy and Practice*, 12(1): 39–54.

Condie, R., Livingstone, K. and Seagraves, L. (2005) *Evaluation of the Assessment is for Learning Programme: Final Report and Appendices*. The Quality of Education Centre, University of Strathclyde. Available from www.scotland.gov.uk/Resource/Doc/47121/0020476.pdf (accessed 10 December 2014).

Cooper, B. and Cowie, B. (2010) 'Collaborative research for assessment for learning', *Teaching and Teacher Education*, 26(4): 979–86.

DeLuca, C., Luu, K., Sun, Y. and Klinger, D. (2012) 'Assessment for learning in the classroom: barriers to implementation and possibilities for teacher professional learning', *Assessment Matters, 4:* 5–29.

Dixon, H. (2008) 'Feedback for learning: deconstructing teachers' conceptions and use of feedback', unpublished doctoral thesis, University of Auckland, New Zealand.

Earl, L.M. (2013) *Assessment as Learning: Using Classroom Assessment to Maximise Student Learning*. Thousand Oaks, CA: Corwin.

Elwood, J. and Klenowski, V. (2002) 'Creating communities of shared practice: the challenges of assessment use in teaching and learning', *Assessment and Evaluation in Higher Education,* 27(3): 243–56.

Fullan, M. (2005) 'Professional learning communities writ large', in R. DuFour, R.E. Eaker and R.B. DuFour (eds.), *On Common Ground*. Bloomington, IN: National Education Service. pp. 209–24.

Geddes, S. (2005) 'Helping teachers develop formative assessment strategies', *New Zealand Journal of Teachers' Work*, 2(1): 49–54.

Hallam, S., Kirton, A., Pfeffers, J., Robertson, P. and Stobart, G. (2004) *Assessment is for Learning: Development Programme. Evaluation of Project 1: Support for Professional Practice in Formative Assessment. Final Report*. Edinburgh: SEED, SQA, LT Scotland. Available from http://www.scotland.gov.uk/library5/education/ep1aldps-00.asp (accessed 10 December 2014).

Hansen, D., Anderson, C., Munger, L. and Chizek, M. (2013) 'All aboard! In one Iowa district, all teachers and principals are on the same journey', *Journal of Staff Development*, 34(2): 18–20.

Hargreaves, E. (2005) 'Assessment for learning? Thinking outside the (black) box', *Cambridge Journal of Education*, 35(2): 213–24.

Hargreaves, E. (2013) 'Assessment for Learning and Teacher Learning Communities: UK teachers' experiences', *Teaching Education*, 24(3): 327–44.

Hill, M.F. (2000) 'Remapping the assessment landscape: Primary teachers reconstructing the assessment landscape in self-managing schools', unpublished doctoral thesis, University of Waikato, Hamilton, New Zealand.

Hill, M.F. (2011) '"Getting traction": enablers and barriers to implementing assessment for learning in secondary schools', *Assessment in Education: Principles, Policy and Practice*, 18(4): 347–64.

Hollingworth, L. (2012) 'Why leadership matters: empowering teachers to implement formative assessment', *Journal of Educational Administration*, 50(3): 365–79.

Hopfenbeck, T., Tolo, A., Florez, T. and El Masri, Y. (2013) *Balancing Trust and Accountability? The Assessment for Learning Programme in Norway. A Governing Complex Education Systems Case Study*. Paris: OECD. Available from http://www.oecd.org/edu/ceri/Norwegian%20GCES%20case%20study%20OECD.pdf (accessed 10 December 2014).

Hord, S. (1997) *Professional Learning Communities: Communities of Continuous Inquiry and Improvement*. Austin, TX: Southwest Educational Development Laboratory.

James, M. and McCormick, R. (2009) 'Teachers learning how to learn', *Teaching and Teacher Education*, 25(7): 973–82.

Katz, S., Earl, L. and Ben Jaafar, S. (2009) *Building and Connecting Learning Communities: The Power of Networks for School Improvement.* Thousand Oaks, CA: Corwin.

Marshall, B. and Drummond, M.J. (2006) 'How teachers engage with assessment for learning: lessons from the classroom', *Research Papers in Education,* 21(2): 133–49.

Ministry of Education (2011) *Ministry of Education Position Paper: Assessment [Schooling Sector].* Wellington, NZ: Learning Media.

Moss, C.M., Brookhart, S.M. and Long, B.A. (2013) 'Administrators' roles in helping teachers use formative assessment information', *Applied Measurement in Education,* 26(3): 205–18.

Nusche, D., Laveault, D., MacBeath, J. and Santiago, P. (2012) *OECD Reviews of Evaluation and Assessment in Education: New Zealand 2011.* Paris: OECD. Available from http://dx.doi.org/10.1787/9789264116917-en (accessed 10 December 2014).

Patterson, D. and Rolheiser, C. (2004) 'Creating a culture of change: ten strategies for developing an ethic of teamwork', *National Staff Development Council,* 25(2): 1–4.

Perrenoud, P. (1998) 'From formative evaluation to a controlled regulation of learning processes: towards a wider conceptual field', *Assessment in Education: Principles, Policy and Practice,* 5(1): 85–102.

Popham, W.J. (2008) 'Classroom assessment: staying instructionally afloat in an ocean of accountability', in C.A. Dwyer (ed.), *The Future of Assessment: Shaping Teaching and Learning.* New York, NY: Lawrence Erlbaum. pp. 263–78.

Poskitt, J. and Taylor, K. (2008) 'Sustaining professional development: rhetoric or reality?', *New Zealand Journal of Educational Studies,* 43(1): 21.

Priestly, M., Biesta, G.J.J. and Robinson, S. (2012) 'Understanding teacher agency: the importance of relationships', paper presented at the Annual Meeting of the American Educational Research Association, Vancouver, Canada, 13–17 April.

Sadler, D. (1989) 'Formative assessment and the design of instructional systems', *Instructional Science,* 18: 119–44.

Shepard, L.A. (2000) 'The role of assessment in a learning culture', *Educational Researcher,* 29(7): 4–14.

Shulman, L.S. (1997) 'Disciplines of inquiry in education: an overview', in R.M. Jaeger (ed.), *Complementary Methods for Researcher in Education.* Washington, DC: American Research Association. pp. 3–20.

Shute, V.J. (2008) 'Focus on formative feedback', *Review of Educational Research,* 78(1): 153–89.

Smith, K. and Engelsen, K.S. (2013) 'Developing an assessment for learning (AfL) culture in school: the voice of the principals', *International Journal of Leadership in Education,* 16(1): 106–25.

Stoll, L. and Seashore Louis, K. (2008) *Professional Learning Communities: Divergence, Depth and Dilemmas.* Maidenhead, UK: Open University Press and McGraw Hill Education.

Thompson, M. and Wiliam, D. (2008) 'Tight but loose: a conceptual framework for scaling up school reforms', in E.C. Wylie (ed.), *Tight but loose: Scaling up teacher professional development in diverse contexts.* Ewing, NJ: ETS. pp. 1–44.

Timperley, H., Wilson, A., Barrar, H. and Fung, I. (2007) *Teacher Professional Learning and Development: Best Evidence Synthesis Iteration [BES].* Wellington, NZ: Ministry of Education.

Wilson, N.S. (2008) 'Teachers expanding pedagogical content knowledge: learning about formative assessment together', *Journal of In-Service Education,* 34(3): 283–98.

Wylie, E.C., Lyon, C.J. and Goe, L. (2009) *Teacher Professional Development Focused on Formative Assessment: Changing Teachers, Changing Schools.* Princeton, NJ: Educational Testing Service.

49

Curriculum Reform in Testing and Accountability Contexts

Val Klenowski and Merilyn Carter

INTRODUCTION

Recent international educational developments have important implications for the skills and understandings in curriculum and assessment that teachers develop, both in pre-service and in practice. Global developments in curriculum and assessment reform require teachers to utilise a network of knowledges and develop a repertoire of assessment skills and understandings. In a context of testing, accountability and auditing, data analysis skills are increasingly required to examine pedagogic practices for the development of intervention teaching and learning strategies to improve learning outcomes for all students (Marsh, 2009). However, too often the data are used predominantly for accountability purposes that serve at national levels as a catalyst for measurement, comparison and allocation of funding (Lingard and Sellar, 2013).

With increased accountability demands brought about by global competitiveness and programs for international measurement of educational attainment, there has also emerged an increase in the use of testing, which in some countries has become the dominant form of assessment. For example in Australia, national testing of students in Years 3, 5, 7 and 9 began in 2008 under the National Australia Program – Literacy and Numeracy (NAPLAN). The results from this program for each school are published on the MySchool website (www.myschool.edu.au), increasing the competitive nature of the testing and intensifying the demands on teachers and schools. In particular, there has been a shift in the enacted curriculum in Australia to a focus on literacy and numeracy because the curriculum is tested.

In China, the *gaokao* or university entrance exam has become an extreme focal point for 9 million students who take this exam annually. The 'super high school' has emerged, which is run along semi-military lines as described by the students:

> I wake up at 5.30 every morning and am required to be out of the dorm by 5.45. I grab my books and go to gather at the track. After jogging ends,

all classes are required to run up the stairs to their morning study sessions. At 6.38, the more than 80 students in my class all vacate the classroom in a matter of seconds (of course there are a seven or eight who don't go to eat), just so they can get breakfast, since we have to be back in class before 7 to begin independent study. If we leave the classroom later than this, with being stuck in the crowded hall for 5 minutes, standing in line for 5 minutes, and 7 minutes to get there and back, we have at least 3 minutes for breakfast. I've been living at Hengshui for three months, and now I understand what human purgatory is. (Education News, China, 2013)

What becomes apparent from a consideration of such schools is that what seems to matter most is the achievement of goals regardless of the means for achieving them. Important curriculum aims of learning how to learn, futures-oriented skills, creativity as well as equity issues can be lost in such examination-driven contexts.

In this chapter we describe and critically analyse how such global trends in education have led to unintended consequences in terms of curriculum and assessment reform, of which teachers, principals, policy officers, and the public may be unaware. We focus on a case study in Australia of the introduction of the first Australian curriculum. In particular, we examine how this move to a national curriculum, together with major national and global testing, have led to issues related to teachers' varying interpretations of learning. In this case, it relates to the across-the-curriculum capability of numeracy and the limited understanding and preparation for this level of curriculum and assessment change.

BACKGROUND

In the global education community policy agents and agencies, such as the Organisation for Economic Co-operation and Development (OECD), can influence education policy development and implementation at international and national levels. The values of current policies, and the reframing of education in economic terms, have typically resulted in education policies that emphasize the production of human capital to ensure international economic competitiveness.

International programs such as the Programme of International Student Assessment (PISA) and Trends in International Maths and Science Study (TIMSS) have been largely responsible for stimulating such competition and educational change. PISA has been used to rank OECD and non-OECD countries using a measure of academic achievement of 15-year-old students in mathematics, science and reading. It is administered every 3 years and, as articulated in a letter to Andreas Schleicher, the OECD's director of PISA, '...results are anxiously awaited by governments, education ministers, and the editorial boards of newspapers, and are cited authoritatively in countless policy reports...' (http://www.globalpolicyjournal.com/blog/05/05/2014/open-letter-andreas-schleicher-oecd-paris).

Governments eager for this information and in response to perceived declining scores have implemented changes to curriculum and assessment practices. For instance, responses to what has been described as the 'PISA shock' include centralized curriculum development and examination-dominated policy. The impact of international programs on curriculum and policy development includes major standards-driven change. For example in Germany, soon after the publication of the OECD annual report in 2000, the national standards-based curriculum was introduced (Klenowski and Wyatt-Smith, 2014: 11). Similarly other systems responded by reviewing their education systems to improve standards and their rankings. Countries such as New Zealand, Canada, the US and Australia have all introduced standards-based reforms. New Zealand adopted National Standards for literacy and numeracy that involves schools making and reporting judgments about the reading, writing and mathematics achievement of children up to Year 8 (the end of primary school) and in Canada, classroom assessment standards aimed at the improvement of assessment practice of K-12 education have been formulated.

For some time, international comparative analyses of student achievement results have been used globally, such as in Germany and Denmark where reaction was rapid (Goldstein and Thomas, 2008). Politically it is argued that examination-dominated policy is needed to maintain success in a world of economic competition (White, 2014). This is particularly evident in England. The same is true in Australia where the focus is on the national testing of NAPLAN, a measure that is used to assess how well every school in the country has performed, with results published so that anyone can compare any school with other 'like' schools. Such measures have become powerful tool for governments, federal and state/territory, to focus on schools that are underperforming and apply pressure for improvement. However, for education systems to be so reliant on just one measure of performance for determining success is limiting and inadequate.

For countries that have implemented curriculum and assessment reforms in such a context of competition, audit and accountability there have been some unintended consequences. These consequences have occurred consistently over time, with remarkable similarities between countries. For instance, Harlen and Deakin-Crick (2010) in a systematic review of research of the impact of testing found that there were negative consequences on student motivation for learning, which in the longer term could be detrimental to future learning. The findings of the review included insights into how the introduction of national tests brought an increase in the use of other tests (Clarke et al., 2000) and that extrinsic motivation associated with tests led to superficial rather than sustained and substantive learning (Crooks, 1988). Other identified problems included test anxiety and its effects on learning (McDonald, 2001) and how high-stakes testing comes to influence what is taught and learned and does not have a positive effect on teaching and learning in the classroom

(Madaus and Clarke, 1999). It was also found that in schools where there were higher numbers of African–American and Latino students, the focus was on activities designed to raise test scores with the consequence of a move away from quality curriculum resources towards test-preparation materials (McNeil and Valenzuela, 1998).

Further, the review identified how external testing also narrows the curriculum and has a limiting effect on teaching methods (Johnston and McClune, 2000), with an emphasis on teaching aligning with the content of the tests (Reay and Wiliam, 1999) and less attention to subjects related to creativity and personal and social development (Gordon and Reese, 1997; Leonard and Davey, 2001). Direct teaching on how to pass the tests was also identified as seriously undermining the breadth and depth of the learning and impacting on the validity of the tests (Harlen and Deakin Crick, 2010. Interestingly a study by Pollard et al. (2000) revealed that after national testing in England, students came to view assessment as wholly summative in contrast to their earlier view prior to the tests when they saw assessment as supportive of their learning.

Such unintended consequences of high stakes testing continue to be documented, such as 'the uses and abuses of testing' (Stobart, 2008) and how testing corrupts schools (Nichols and Berliner, 2007). The intensification of government policy interest in externally mandated testing and the sanctions attached to test scores continue to impact on equity initiatives (Darling-Hammond, 2010). In Australia the approach to accountability through a predominance of testing has led to similar developments. There exists 'pressure on principals to improve their test results at all costs', the emergence of 'commercial products' to assist students to pass the tests (Klenowski and Wyatt-Smith, 2012: 71) and perverse practices to improve test results, such as encouraging those students who may not perform well on the test to stay away from school on the day of the tests.

TESTING

Global rankings have helped to escalate standardized testing with the emergence of a greater reliance on quantitative measures. The 3-year assessment cycle of programs, such as PISA, has created an unrealistic expectation that improvement can be achieved in this time frame (http://www.globalpolicyjournal.com/blog/05/05/2014/open-letter-andreas-schleicher-oecd-paris), and yet research has clearly indicated that substantive change takes longer – at least 4–5 years (Elmore, 2004; Fullan, 1992). As a consequence of second order, uses of assessment data (O'Neill, 2013) for the development of rankings, quick solutions or short-term fixes have been designed to improve a school's position.

The following discussion of national testing in Australia with a particular focus on the subject of numeracy (also called quantitative literacy or mathematical literacy) illustrates how these reforms have led to a narrowing of the curriculum, a rise in testing with a focus on results, a growth in quick fix approaches to teaching and learning, and a reduction in the trust of teacher assessment. These findings derive from research conducted in the state of Queensland, which has underperformed in comparison with the majority of other states. This case illustrates how unintended consequences of curriculum reform arise particularly in relation to cross-curricular numeracy.

Cross-curricular approaches to curriculum present a number of challenges (Hayes, 2010). In the case of numeracy, problems emerged in Australia for a number of reasons. First, there is a historical association of numeracy with competence in basic arithmetic, which is particularly prevalent amongst non-educators. Second, in some schools numeracy is the term used for a curriculum program in remedial mathematics, and third there exists confusion between mathematics and numeracy given the increased reference to primary and lower secondary school mathematics courses as 'numeracy'. The production of curriculum support materials for the teaching of numeracy that closely resemble mathematics teaching resources and the inaccurate labelling of the national tests (NAPLAN) as numeracy (Carter, 2014) are also identified reasons for the difficulties encountered.

Narrowing of the Curriculum

It has been established that if important decisions are presumed to be related to the results of standardized tests, then schools will focus on the test content, with a resulting 'narrowing of the curriculum' (Boston, 2009). Curriculum change that follows can range from exclusion of skills that are not assessed in the tests, such as project and practical work, investigations and performances (Collins et al., 2010), to a reduction of teaching, financial and timetable resources devoted to subjects that are not tested (Boston, 2009; Boyle and Bragg, 2006; Jones et al., 1999; McNeil and Valenzuela, 2001; Nathan, 2008; Nichols and Berliner, 2007). The reduction in resources devoted to other learning areas inevitably has consequences for the knowledge and skills that students learn and for their development as well-rounded individuals (Boston, 2009).

In Queensland, some secondary schools have responded to the NAPLAN improvement agenda by suspending their teaching of the English and/or mathematics curriculum for weeks at a time to prepare for NAPLAN testing (Carter, 2014). Others have timetabled courses for one or more lessons each week, often called 'literacy and numeracy', aimed at remediating students assessed as deficit in the areas tested by NAPLAN. Such courses take time that was previously allocated for study of elective subjects in technical and performance-based areas and languages (Carter, 2014).

A survey of nearly 8000 Australian teachers (Dulfer et al., 2012) found that approximately 50 per cent engaged in NAPLAN test preparation at least three times in the fortnight before the tests, with a further third practising more than six times. Almost 50 per cent also indicated that some form of NAPLAN practice was conducted at least weekly in the five months before the tests. Approximately 80 per cent of teachers agreed that they had prepared students by teaching to the test and that their teaching practice had changed to emphasize the areas assessed by NAPLAN testing. Three-quarters of teachers believed that NAPLAN is impacting on the way in which schools view the curriculum, with literacy and numeracy elevated in importance. The study reported that 'it seems likely, therefore, that through regular test practice, or a focus on specific skills needed for the NAPLAN, the tests may be impacting on the breadth of curriculum that Australian students experience' (Dulfer et al., 2012: 27). Another study (Thompson and Harbaugh, 2013) found that teachers are either choosing or being instructed to teach to the test, resulting in less time being spent on other curriculum areas.

Rise in Testing

NAPLAN test results for every Australian state and territory are published each year. In the first year of NAPLAN testing, Queensland schools were judged to be below the Australian average, creating a 'political furore' (Lingard and Sellar, 2013). The Queensland Government commissioned a report into the reasons for the poor performance. The recommendations advocated reactive and short-term approaches, such as the rehearsing of past test papers and literacy and numeracy tests for pre-service teachers (Masters, 2009). These practices are underpinned by behaviourist assumptions about learning and have been criticized as 'repeating the mistakes of the past' (Klenowski, 2010: 12). A persistent concern about the preparation for standardized testing has been excessive test practice.

With the advent of national testing in Australia, all levels of government now use NAPLAN results as the dominant measure of student achievement and teacher and school efficacy. In other words, this national test has become high stakes for governments and for schools. The emphasis on this one test has occurred without systematic state and regional-level curriculum assistance and advice. This has required schools to develop their own approaches to the testing, with varying degrees of success. Responsive curriculum and pedagogies that are rigorous and appropriate to the school context take time to develop (Comber and Nixon, 2009). The increasing production of commercially available materials that have not necessarily been quality assured has encouraged teachers and schools to adopt these readily available resources. In the absence of nationally developed, quality curriculum support advice and materials, the use of these questionable resources for test preparation has increased. Studies have identified how quick fix programs have been adopted and resulted in less coherent school programs (Luke et al., 2013). Consequently such practices have tended to skew test results and focused learning on only that which is relevant to the test (Luke et al., 2013).

The emphasis on the improvement of NAPLAN results and the requirement to set targets has continued the practice of quick fix approaches (Luke et al., 2013: 413). As Queensland students have continued to underperform in comparison to the majority of their interstate counterparts, the political imperative to improve NAPLAN scores has intensified. Continual NAPLAN improvement is now a target for all Queensland government schools (DETE, 2012; Hardy, 2014; Kaesehagen et al., 2012). Given the norm-referenced nature of NAPLAN test scoring, the target appears to be unachievable (Darling-Hammond, 2007). The trade union representing teachers and principals in Queensland state schools (Ryan, 2009) and some submissions to two Australian Senate inquiries (Australian Senate, 2010, 2013) attest to the considerable pressure for improvement that has been placed on some Queensland government schools, their principals and teachers.

Focus on Results

The rise of testing and the dependence on results in Australia is evident with the emergence of quick fix programs such as a Queensland program promoted as the Great Results Guarantee (Queensland Government, 2014). On 31 January 2014, the Queensland Government announced additional annual funding for government schools, of a total of AUD$131 million. Although the additional funding was welcomed by schools, it was conditional on a commitment from each school that every student will either '…achieve the national minimum standard for literacy and numeracy for their year level [the lowest satisfactory outcome of NAPLAN testing] or have an evidence-based plan…in place to address their specific learning needs' (DETE, 2014: 2).

The search for quick solutions has become more widespread with programs that focus on improvement of test results without sufficient attention to the means for achieving them. The Queensland Great Results Guarantee program established an expectation of improvement in the short-term. Its focus was on '…ensuring there is a safety net to capture the students who are falling below the National Minimum Standards for literacy and numeracy. It is also about preventing our high performing students sliding backwards and making sure that they continue to achieve *better results*' (Queensland Government, 2014, emphasis added).

Schools and teachers have consequently adopted short-term strategies, such as test-and-drill, that focus on improving test scores at the expense of sustained learning of the curriculum. Expectations of improved test results are reasonable if and when the targets are achievable; however, the pressure becomes inappropriate when there are implied sanctions, such as probable impact on future employment. Failure to achieve consistent test improvements can be due to the result of many factors, including normalized test scoring systems and variations between cohorts of students, rather than due to the actions of school managers or teachers.

It is possible for schools to use assessment data such as NAPLAN results in a way that directs pedagogical change with a specific focus on an identified priority, such as the improvement of writing. However, to use assessment data to fulfil a formative function in generating useful feedback on curriculum and teaching development for enhanced student learning requires support and professional development of teachers and school leaders at the local level.

Data Use

NAPLAN testing in Australia in 2008 exemplifies how a national approach to testing emphasizing the measurement and reporting of results neglects the important need for teacher support in the analysis, interpretation and use of test data. Sustaining and maintaining sufficient data support has become an important challenge for educational systems (Marsh, 2009). In particular how to use the data from the system has been neglected. For example, in the Australian case study (Carter, 2014) it was not clear that teachers had sufficient knowledge of the strengths and limitations of the different sources of information about student performance (Klenowski, 2013; Koyama, 2011; Luna and Livingstone Turner, 2001). Student achievement data in all forms was generally regarded as both valid and reliable, with little acknowledgement of the probabilistic nature of the data (Wu, 2010a, 2010b). This led to concerns about decisions based on that information.

In 2014 in Queensland, the Education Queensland Curriculum Assessment Authority, (QCAA) Act made explicit the authority's functions relating to testing with the inclusion of the implementation of procedures to administer common national tests. With this change in emphasis in terms of the functions of QCAA, it was recognised that there was a need to provide schools with timely data to inform teaching and learning programs. Consequently, QCAA provided schools with their NAPLAN test results at least a month earlier than in previous years. This occurred because earlier achievement data distribution would allow for more formative use of summative data; however, teachers need support in how to interpret and use such data, and this type of professional development has not been forthcoming.

What has been striking regarding the changes to the responsibilities of QCAA has been the shift in focus to testing and national tests. Previously, Queensland was seen as an international beacon for externally moderated teacher-based assessment; however, the responsibility and support for such practice has been reduced. The emphasis on national testing and the introduction of an externally assessed test at the senior secondary level have resulted in a shift in the functions of the QCAA towards professional development support for examination and testing practices. The support for teacher assessment and moderation has diminished. Deterioration in the trust of teachers' judgment and a greater reliance on test results is dominating.

Trust in Teachers' Judgments

With increased testing comes a reduction of trust in teachers' judgments – this is extremely important, particularly given the use in Queensland of the externally moderated teacher-based assessment system and recent recommendations to move away from this system. The belief that tests and examinations and the associated data are the only objective and reliable representations of student achievement becomes accepted by the public. Ironically, when standards-driven reforms are initiated, teacher judgment remains fundamental, and yet research conducted in this current context remains limited (Klenowski, 2013). The adoption of a standards-driven approach to curriculum requires responsive changes to pedagogy and assessment. To design, develop and enact these pedagogic and assessment changes require support, not only of resources, but also professional development. Too often systems neglect the

implications of such major changes, and expectations of teachers and schools become unrealistic with insufficient time given for the development and enactment of the changes. The teacher's role, we maintain, remains central to both curriculum and assessment development and yet it seems that it is too often neglected in terms of the resources, professional development and support needs identified and addressed. The resources that teachers need in a standards-referenced curriculum are not just explicit statements of standards but exemplars of the standard required. They need greater awareness about the use of standards in their pedagogy and support for the development of their judgments through moderation and opportunities to discuss their judgments (Klenowski and Wyatt-Smith, 2014).

CURRICULUM REFORM

The states and territories in Australia have constitutional responsibility for curriculum and have historically independently created their own curricula. When the Australian Curriculum Assessment and Reporting Authority (ACARA), which had responsibility for the progressive implementation of National Curriculum and Achievement Standards, introduced the curriculum in 2012 (ACARA, 2014) the inconsistencies that emerged came as no surprise. This was the first time that a national curriculum had been developed in Australia and it had to be endorsed by the eight states and territories. Curriculum content for the Foundation to Year 10 levels for English, mathematics, science, history and geography was endorsed first. By 2014, other curricula for the arts, health and physical education, technologies, civics and citizenship, and economics and business had been developed but had not yet been fully endorsed by all states and territories. Languages other than English, was the last learning area to be developed. The development of a senior (Years 11 and 12) curriculum followed.

With the introduction of national testing, what became apparent was a lack of alignment between the NAPLAN test content and skills with the then-Queensland curriculum. What also became evident was that some states such as New South Wales, in relation to the subject of mathematics at secondary level, were approximately a year ahead in the teaching of content and skills compared to other states, including Queensland. The identification of this gap in the Queensland curriculum prompted Queensland to become one of the first to adopt the new Australian Curriculum in English, mathematics and science (ACARA, 2014) in all year levels, in 2012. This curriculum change was significant, resulting in an immediate increase in the levels of content and skills demanded of most students.

The Australian Curriculum at the time also included the introduction of seven general capabilities that incorporated knowledge, skills, behaviours and dispositions that, together with curriculum content in each learning area, are intended to '…assist students to live and work successfully in the twenty-first century' and to '…become successful learners, confident and creative individuals, and active and informed citizens' (n.p.). These capabilities included literacy, numeracy, information and communication technology capability, critical and creative thinking, personal and social capability, ethical understanding and intercultural understanding (ACARA, 2014a).

At the same time the Queensland Government also adopted the goal of improvement in school literacy and numeracy standards (Hardy, 2014). With changes to curriculum and also the introduction of standards to replace the existing outcomes-based curriculum, the demands on teachers and schools in terms of pedagogy and assessment were considerable. The time frame for the implementation for this change and the transitional arrangements in terms of the development of appropriate support materials and resources to assist teachers and schools were insufficient.

Numeracy

The implementation of the general capability of numeracy illustrates how, in a competitive testing environment, curriculum reform can suffer from a lack of time for preparation and implementation, and limited teacher and school support in terms of advice, resources and guidance. ACARA defined numeracy as 'the knowledge and skills to use mathematics confidently across all learning areas at schools and in their lives more broadly. Numeracy involves students recognising and understanding the role of mathematics in the world and having the dispositions and capacities to use mathematical knowledge and skills purposefully' (ACARA, 2014b: n.p.).

The rationale for the introduction of the numeracy capability drew on recent international and national research, such as the emphasis both on mathematics as a distinct area of study and numeracy as an across-the-curriculum competency as stated in the *National Numeracy Review Report* (Commonwealth of Australia, 2008). Schools were left to interpret how they would implement this across-the-curriculum competency with statements such as, 'In order to develop the ability to communicate numeric information effectively, students should engage in learning that involves using mathematics in the context of other disciplines. This requires a cross-curriculum commitment and is not just the responsibility of the Mathematics Department (Miller, 2010)' (ACARA, 2014b: n.p.). In this Australian curriculum reform context, the educational meaning of numeracy reflected a change from proficiency in basic arithmetic to a conceptualisation that highlights ability and disposition to apply mathematics in other subject areas and in life (Goos, 2007). Such changes in meaning and uses of the term numeracy have inevitably led to some uncertainty resulting in issues and tensions for schools.

The introduction of a national numeracy test together with a national curriculum meant teachers were required to rethink their pedagogy and curriculum. Advice to schools regarding how to implement these changes was limited, and each school interpreted and taught numeracy in a range of ways given their particular context and understanding. Varying approaches to the implementation of the across-the-curriculum initiative of numeracy emerged (Carter, 2014) as a consequence of the lack of direction and support from the central authority. Further, the research (Carter, 2014) found that some schools saw numeracy as the responsibility of the mathematics department in contrast to the curriculum expectation that it should be a shared responsibility across the various learning areas. Tensions arose when, for example, the Head of Mathematics has taken the position that to improve results in NAPLAN it is imperative that numeracy be taught in other learning areas: '…teaching the numeracy skills, numeracy topics well in maths or science or SOSE [Studies of Society and Environment] or whatever subject, Phys Ed [Physical Education] these kinds of things is [sic] going to improve their NAPLAN, is [sic] going to improve their numeracy skills…' (Carter, 2014: 269).

The uncertainty regarding who takes responsibility for the teaching of numeracy became more evident as schools prepared for the national testing program. Here the Year 7–9 Mathematics Coordinator, from the same school as the Head of Mathematics, asserts 'I'm not numeracy. I'm just mathematics'(Carter, 2014: 269). This statement is understandable if numeracy is seen as the application of mathematics to other learning areas. If numeracy and mathematics are different, then the question for schools becomes who takes responsibility for the across-the-curriculum capability (Carter, 2014: 269). It becomes a complex issue, as the Mathematics Coordinator in Carter's study explains:

…we've been trying to let other teachers know. It's a very hard thing to have other HoDs [Heads of Department] understand that numeracy isn't maths and vice versa. And that it's embedded in the curriculum. It's a little easier for them to understand that literacy isn't English because everyone

reads in their subject. But to be able to get them to do numeracy specifically in their assessment is very difficult. I think it lends itself only to specific units that they do and maybe they do it without realising it like in design technology, they do a lot of measuring, and things like that, and graphics. Yeah. It's not something that I think they have really grasped as their responsibility as well. It's a bit of a battle to get that. (Carter, 2014: 270)

The implications of such confusion and uncertainty in relation to responsibility for teaching numeracy and preparing for NAPLAN testing were predictable. The Head of Mathematics thought that the numeracy and mathematics were different and that all subjects shared responsibility for numeracy, and he therefore did not see that he had a special responsibility for NAPLAN numeracy testing:

I guess when I'm thinking NAPLAN, I'm thinking the numeracy component of it too. But I'm not specifically thinking that numeracy and mathematics aren't the same thing. So I'm more conscious… for our [Mathematics] teachers to get our students to be able to use mathematics and use skills like estimation and thinking skills and from that is going to come numeracy skills that maths is going to apply. As far as other faculties go, I would hope that they're going to do their bit as far as numeracy skills are embedded in their course, for example if it is SOSE or something like that, that they use scale to be able to read a map, use scale to be able to find the distance along the road, those sorts of things. (Carter, 2014: 271)

Without clear guidelines and preparation, the teaching of subjects such as these across-the-curriculum capabilities could be neglected. The history of cross curricular literacy and numeracy has not been positive with the identification of concerns such as the 'lack of rigour' and the possibility of students not learning the 'fundamental skills in the key subjects' (Hayes, 2010: 384). The short time frames for implementation and development that have been given are also adding to confusion and misunderstanding. In 2014, with a change of government both at national and state levels, major educational change occurred with a review of the Australian Curriculum, which included within its scope: '…the soundness of the general capabilities and achievement standards in terms of the extent to which they have been linked to curriculum content in this learning area' (Australian Government, 2014: n.p.).

The competitive global testing environment has led to international comparisons of the standards achieved by Australian students compared to the top performing nations, such as Singapore and Finland. From such comparisons the mathematics program in the Australian curriculum was made more demanding than the state and territory curricula, which had been replaced. More recently, the review of the Australian Curriculum by the Australian Government has been conducted to:

> ...ensure Australia was performing well in the international context as measured by tests such as Trends in International Mathematics and Science Study (TIMSS), Programme for International Student Assessment (PISA) and Progress in International Reading Literacy Study (PIRLS) was also an important part of the motivation for the Review. (Australian Government, 2014: n.p.)

International comparisons of achievement data have led to national testing and unrealistic and unrelenting curriculum expectations of teachers and schools.

DISCUSSION

In this chapter, we set out to explore recent curriculum and assessment reforms and some of the unintended consequences that have been identified through research in the context of global and national testing through an illustrative case of Australia. As has been suggested the impact of international testing has been profound, with countries such as Australia, Germany, England, Canada, New Zealand and the US implementing considerable curriculum and assessment reforms in response.

What has also been presented is the contrary nature of the unintended consequences, given the limited consideration of how teachers and principals at the local professional level of the school interpret and understand the changed curriculum or assessment policies. For example, in the Australian case, with the introduction of major curriculum reform of the cross-curriculum general capability of numeracy, there was insufficient understanding about how to embed this capability in all learning areas.

The concept of numeracy was understood differently amongst school leaders and teachers. This is best explained from a social-constructivist perspective, which acknowledges that constructions of meaning are influenced by varying training, experiences and interactions with teaching colleagues. What is disappointing and frustrating is that these inconsistencies in interpretation were predictable from both historical and sociocultural perspectives. The various constructions of numeracy have resulted in a lack of clarity about the responsibility for this cross-curriculum capability in some schools. This case of major curriculum change in numeracy has also highlighted how, in contexts of audit and accountability, raising teachers' awareness and developing their skills in curriculum reform can be neglected. The implication for policy and practice is that greater attention needs to be given to the development of a common understanding of the specific curriculum reform informed by accepted definitions and models. Such changes require greater persistence and commitment from the political centre to the local professional level, in addition to time and resources.

In contexts of major curriculum and assessment reform it is also apparent that different approaches to national testing, teaching and learning will occur. We have highlighted how there has been an escalation of standardized testing for global testing, with a greater reliance on quantitative measures and summative results. The emphasis on accountability and auditing has resulted in further perverse unintended consequences (Lingard and Sellar, 2013) with increased testing at national and local levels, a rise in the focus on results and the emergence of quick fix approaches to teaching and learning. As identified by Bennett (2011: 19) 'the content, format and design of the accountability test' will limit the effectiveness of formative and teacher assessment. We have noted how there has been a reduction in the acceptance and support for school-based assessment and teacher judgment.

In the illustrative case presented in this chapter, the NAPLAN tests currently do not align with the Australian curriculum intent of cross-curriculum numeracy and have, therefore, confused teachers and resulted in the adoption of strategies and approaches aimed at improving student achievement scores. Such add-on test preparation methods focus on the tests (for example, the decontextualised practice of tests in similar formats for entire lessons or for weeks), and teaching the curriculum is a secondary consideration with the diversion of resources from the usual teaching and learning of curriculum-related activities. This test preparation has been challenged on ethical grounds for developing a narrow range of skills and encouraging superficial and rote learning (Black, 1998; Hardison and Sackett, 2008; Mehrens et al., 1998; Miyasaka, 2000; Popham, 2013). A more effective and ethical alternative that has been identified is embedded test preparation, which gives primacy to the development of curriculum knowledge and skills, and with test preparation occurring in the context of the curriculum as opportunities arise (Carter, 2014). However, the pressures of accountability testing drive many teachers to only consider add-on approaches.

We have found that the provision of effective professional development and teaching resources to support an embedded approach to preparation for the summative tests can assist teachers in the use of more effective practices that minimise the use of add-on methods. The implication for central agencies when implementing curriculum and assessment reform is to provide more guidance and support to schools and teachers in acceptable methods of test preparation regularly and prominently. This would include helpful guidelines and examples of how teachers might teach using embedded approaches and incorporating test preparation into their classroom routines. High quality pedagogical resources to support an embedded approach and to assist teachers in developing their own strategies are also needed. Although teachers require professional development in practical strategies for how to embed student preparation for summative testing into their pedagogy, support from school leaders will also be required (Carter, 2014).

The use of student achievement data for diagnostic purposes and the importance of this skill have been identified. The benefits for teachers and schools from the timely provision of test data concerning every child should not be underestimated (Carter, 2014; Spina, Klenowski and Harris, under review). The value of NAPLAN achievement data has been recognised by ACARA (2014) in the move to online assessment and the reduction of time for providing feedback on student performance to students, teachers and parents. The Queensland Curriculum and Assessment Authority understands the importance of this data for schools and teachers and in 2014 provided feedback to schools regarding the students' results much earlier than in previous years (Queensland Governement, n.d).

Multiple sources of data used in cycles of question-driven inquiry are the most resourceful responses to data when used by leaders and teachers. One significant response to data by school leaders is to create a culture of inquiry where assessment evidence is used to enable and drive school improvement to promote equity and inclusion (Ainscow, 2010; Darling-Hammond et al., 2009; Klenowski and Wyatt-Smith, 2014; Peck and McDonald, 2014). However, we agree with others (Petit, 2010; Pierce et al., 2013; Pierce et al., 2014; Schnellert et al., 2008) that teachers currently have a limited capacity to analyse and interpret student achievement data (Spina, Klenowski and Harris, under review). Teachers and school leaders have access to more data than ever before; however, they have limited time, support and skills to make sense of the growing number of data sets in meaningful ways. Although support and professional development may be provided, it will also require willingness on the part of the teachers to consider and apply new pedagogical strategies related to the implementation of assessment and curriculum reforms.

Teacher cooperation could be enhanced by their involvement in decisions about curriculum change and standardized testing. In the Australian context, the changes have not been managed in an inclusive way, with politicians having had a far greater say than practising teachers. It suggests a distrust of and a dissatisfaction with teachers by policymakers (Black and Wiliam, 2005; Luna and Livingstone Turner, 2001; O'Neill, 2013; Smith and Fey, 2000). Educators have been reduced to the status of an interest group, rather than a source of expert advice.

CONCLUSION

In raising the stakes of national tests, such as in Queensland where the government in January 2014 announced additional funding for government schools contingent on short-term improvements in students' literacy and numeracy outcomes (DETE, 2014), the impact on schools, teaching and students has been predictable. There has been increased time and money devoted to preparation for the summative tests, a focus on practice tests, teaching and learning only that which will be tested, and a reduction in the use of teacher assessment and judgment. Whilst education policy persists in adopting quick-fix strategies and ignoring research-informed findings concerning the impact of these approaches, the important issues relating to equity and the disadvantaged will not be addressed.

In some countries such as England there has been some recognition of how current examination and assessment systems are 'outdated and archaic' (Owen, 2014: n.p.) and a greater questioning of 'who needs examinations? (White, 2014). We argue that

what is needed in contexts of curriculum and assessment reform is more recognition and attention at the system level of how we might change the accountability tests so that they are more coherent with what we know about the importance of teacher assessment and school-based curriculum development.

REFERENCES

Ainscow, M. (2010) 'Achieving excellence and equity: reflections on the development of practices in one local district over 10 years', *School Effectiveness and School Improvement,* 21(1): 75–91.

Australian Curriculum Assessment and Reporting Authority (ACARA) (2014a) *General Capabilities.* Available from http://www.acara.edu.au/curriculum/general_capabilities.html (accessed 14 June 2014).

Australian Curriculum Assessment and Reporting Authority (ACARA) (2014b) *The Australian Curriculum v 6.0.* 18 February. Available from http://www.australiancurriculum.edu.au (accessed 14 June 2014).

Australian Government (2014) *Review of the Australian Curriculum – Final Report.* Available from https://docs.education.gov.au/documents/review-australian-curriculum-final-report (accessed 1 April 2015).

Australian Senate (2010) *Administration and reporting of NAPLAN testing.* Canberra: Parliament of Australia.

Australian Senate (2013) *Effectiveness of the National Assessment Program – Literacy and Numeracy: Interim Report.* Available from http://www.aph.gov.au/Senate/committee/eet_ctte/naplan/submissions.htm (accessed 21 December 2013).

Bennett, R. (2011) 'Formative assessment: a critical review', *Assessment in Education: Principles, Policy and Practice,* 18(1): 5–25.

Black, P. J. (1998) *Testing: Friend or Foe? The Theory and Practice of Assessment and Testing.* London: Falmer Press.

Black, P. J. and Wiliam. D. (2005) 'Lessons from around the world: how policies, politics and cultures constrain and afford assessment practices', *Curriculum Journal,* 16(2): 249–61. doi: 10.1080/09585170500136218.

Boston, K. (2009) 'League tables', *Teacher: The National Education Magazine,* 205: 54.

Boyle, B. and Bragg, J. (2006) 'A curriculum without foundation', *British Educational Research Journal,* 32(4): 569–82.

Carter, M. (2014) '*A multiple case study of NAPLAN numeracy testing of Year 9 students in three Queensland secondary schools*', Doctor of Philosophy, monograph, Queensland University of Technology, Brisbane.

Clarke, M., Madaus, G. F., Horn, C. J. and Ramos M. A. (2000) 'Retrospective on educational testing and assessment in the 20th century', *Journal of Curriculum Studies,* 32(2): 159–81.

Collins, S., Reiss, M. and Stobart, G. (2010) 'What happens when high-stakes testing stops? Teachers' perceptions of the impact of compulsory national testing in science of 11-year-olds in England and its abolition in Wales', *Assessment in Education: Principles, Policy and Practice,* 17(3): 273–286. doi: 10.1080/0969594x.2010.496205

Comber, B. and Nixon, H. (2009) 'Teachers' work and pedagogy in an era of accountability', *Discourse: Studies in the Cultural Politics of Education,* 30(3): 333–45.

Commonwealth of Australia (2008) *National Numeracy Review Report.* Available from https://www.coag.gov.au/sites/default/files/national_numeracy_review.pdf (accessed 15 June 2014).

Crooks, T. (1988) 'The impact of classroom evaluation practices on students', *Review of Educational Research,* 58: 438–81.

Darling-Hammond, L. (2007) 'Race, inequality and educational accountability: the irony of "No Child Left Behind"', *Race, Ethnicity and Education,* 10(3): 245–60. doi: 10.1080/13613320701503207.

Darling-Hammond, L. (2010) *The Flat World and Education: How America's Commitment to Equity Will Determine Our Future.* New York, NY: Teachers' College Record.

Darling-Hammond, L., Adree, A., Richardson, N. and Orphanos, S. (2009) *Professional Learning in the Learning Profession: A Status Report on Teacher Development in the United States and Abroad.* Washington, DC: National Staff Development Council.

DETE (2012) *United in Our Pursuit of Excellence: Agenda for Improvement 2012–2016.* Brisbane, Qld: Queensland Government.

Available from http://education.qld.gov.au/corporate/about/pdfs/united-in-our-pursuit-of-excellence.pdf (accessed 2 February 2015).

DETE (2014) *Great Results Guarantee.* Brisbane, Qld: Queensland Government. Available from http://education.qld.gov.au/schools/grants/resources/great-results-guarantee.pdf (accessed 2 February 2015).

Dulfer, N., Polesel, J. and Rice, S. (2012) *The Impacts Of High Stakes Testing On Schools, Students And Their Families: An Educator's Perspective. The Experience of Education.* Sydney, NSW: Whitlam Institute, University of Western Sydney.

Education News, China (2013) 'Military-like super school in Hebei worries educators', *Education New, China.* Available from http://ednewschina.com/?p=723

Elmore, R. (2004). *School Reform from the Inside Out: Policy, Practice and Performance.* Cambridge, MA: Harvard Education Press.

Fullan, M.G. (1992) *Successful School Improvement: The Implementation Perspective and Beyond.* Bristol, PA: Open University Press.

Goldstein, H. and Thomas, S. M. (2008) 'Reflections on the international comparative surveys debate', *Assessment in Education: Principles, Policy and Practice,* 15(3): 215–22.

Goos, M. (2007) 'Developing numeracy in the learning areas (middle years)', paper presented at the South Australian Literacy and Numeracy Expo, Adelaide, Australia. [August 2007]

Gordon, S. and Reese, M. (1997) 'High stakes testing: worth the price?', *Journal of School Leadership,* 7: 345–68.

Hardison, C. M. and Sackett, P. R. (2008) 'Use of writing samples on standardized tests: Susceptibility to rule-based coaching and the resulting effects on score improvement', *Applied Measurement in Education,* 21(3): 227–252.

Hardy, I. (2014) 'A logic of appropriation: enacting national testing (NAPLAN) in Australia', *Journal of Education Policy,* 29(1): 1–18. doi: 10.1080/02680939.2013.782425

Harlen, W. and Deakin-Crick, R. (2010) 'Testing and motivation for learning', *Assessment in Education: Principles, Policy and Practice,* 10(2): 169–207.

Hayes, D. (2010) 'The seductive charms of a cross-curricular approach', *Education 3–13:*

International Journal of Primary, Elementary and Early Years Education, 38(4): 381–7.

Johnston, J. and McClune, W. (2000) 'Selection project Sel 5.1: pupil motivation and attitudes – self-esteem, locus of control, learning disposition and the impact of selection on teaching and learning', in *The Effects of the Selective System of Secondary Education in Northern Ireland: Research Papers Volume II.* Bangor, Northern Ireland: Department of Education.

Jones, M. G., Jones, B. D., Hardin, B., Chapman, L., Yarbrough, T. and Davis, M. (1999) 'The impact of high-stakes testing on teachers and students in North Carolina', *Phi Delta Kappan,* 81(3): 199–203.

Kaesehagen, C., Klenowski, V., Funnell, R. and Tobias, S. (2012) 'Where did I lose you? Accessing the literacy demands of assessment', *Primary and Middle Years Educator,* 10(2): 3–11.

Klenowski, V. (2010) 'Are Australian assessment reforms fit for purpose? Lessons from home and abroad', *Queensland Teachers Union Professional Magazine,* 25: 10–15.

Klenowski, V. (2013) 'Towards fairer assessment', *Australian Educational Researcher.* doi: 10.1007/s13384-013-0132-x.

Klenowski, V. and Wyatt-Smith, C. (2012) 'The impact of high stakes testing', *Assessment in Education: Principles, Policy and Practice,* 19(1): 65–79.

Klenowski, V. and Wyatt-Smith, C. (2014) *Assessment for Education: Standards, Judgement and Moderation.* London: Sage Publications.

Koyama, J. P. (2011) 'Generating, comparing, manipulating, categorizing: reporting, and sometimes fabricating data to comply with No Child Left Behind mandates', *Journal of Education Policy,* 26(5): 701–20. doi: 10.1080/02680939.2011.587542.

Leonard, M. and Davey, C. (2001) *Thoughts on the 11 Plus.* Belfast, Northern Ireland: Save the Children Fund.

Lingard, B. and Sellar, S. (2013) '"Catalyst data": perverse systemic effects of audit and accountability in Australian schooling', *Journal of Education Policy,* 28(5): 634–56.

Luke, A., Cazden, C., Coopes, R., Klenowski, V., Ladwig, J., Lester, J., MacDonald, S., Phillips, J., Shield, P., Spina, N., Theroux, P., Tones, M., Villegas, M. and Woods, A., (2013) *A Summative Evaluation of the Stronger Smarter Learning Communities Project.* March 2013 Report, Vol. 1. Brisbane: Queensland University of Technology.

Luna, C. and Livingstone Turner, C. (2001) 'The impact of the MCAS: Teachers talk about high-stakes testing', *English Journal* 91 (1):79.

Madaus, G. and Clarke, M. (1999) 'The adverse impact of high stakes testing on minority students: evidence from 100 years of test data', paper presented at the High Stakes K–12 Testing Conference, Harvard University, 4 December 1998. Paper revised May 1999.

Marsh, C. (2009) *Key Concepts for Understanding Curriculum.* London: Routledge.

Masters, G. N. (2009) *A Shared Challenge: Improving Literacy, Numeracy and Science Learning in Queensland Primary Schools.* Sydney, NSW: Australian Council for Education. Sydney, NSW: Australian Council for Education Research.

McDonald, A. (2001) 'The prevalence and effects of test anxiety in school children', *Educational Psychology,* 21, 89–101.

McNeil, L. and Valenzuela, A. (1998) 'The harmful effects of the TAAS system of testing in Texas: beneath the accountability rhetoric', paper presented at the High Stakes K-12 Testing Conference, Harvard University, 4 December 1998.

McNeil, L. and Valenzuela, A. (2001) 'The harmful impact of the TAAS system of testing in Texas: beneath the accountability rhetoric', in M. Kornhaber and G. Orfield (eds.), *Raising Standards or Raising Barriers? Inequality and High Stakes Testing in Public Education.* New York, NY: Century Foundation. pp. 127–50.

Mehrens, W. A., Popham, J. W. and Ryan, J. M. (1998) 'How to prepare students for performance assessments', *Educational Measurement: Issues and Practice,* 17(1): 18–22.

Miyasaka, J. R. (2000) 'A framework for evaluating the validity of test preparation practices', paper presented at the Annual Meeting of the American Educational Research Association, New Orleans. April 24–28.

Nathan, L. (2008) 'What's been lost in the bubbles', *Educational Leadership,* 66(2): 52–5.

Nichols, S. L. and Berliner, D. C. (2007) *Collateral Damage: How High-Stakes Testing*

Corrupts America's Schools. Cambridge, MA: Harvard Education Books.

O'Neill, O. (2013) 'Intelligent accountability in education', *Oxford Review of Education,* 39(1): 4–16. doi: 10.1080/03054985.2013.764761.

Owen, J. (2014) 'Exam system is "outdated and archaic" says Eton headmaster Tony Little', *Independent.* Available from http://www.independent.co.uk/news/education/education-news/exam-system-is-archaic-says-eton-headmaster-tony-little-9647651.html (accessed 15 March 2015).

Peck, C. and McDonald, M. A. (2014) 'What is a culture of evidence? How do you get one? And... should you want one?', *Teachers College Record,* 116(3): 1–27.

Petit, P. (2010) 'From data-informed to data-led? School leadership within the context of external testing', *Leading and Managing,* 16(2): 90–107.

Pierce, R., Chick, H. and Gordon, I. (2013) 'Teachers' perceptions of the factors influencing their engagement with statistical reports on student achievement data', *Australian Journal of Education,* 57(3): 237–55. doi: 10.1177/0004944113496176.

Pierce, R., Chick, H., Watson, J., Les, M. and Dalton, M. (2014) 'A statistical literacy hierarchy for interpreting educational system data', *Australian Journal of Education.* 58(2): 195–217. doi: 10.1177/0004944114530067.

Pollard, A., Triggs, P., Broadfoot, P., McNess, E. and Osborn, M. (2000) *What Pupils Say: changing policy and practice in primary education.* London: Continuum.

Popham, W. J. (2013) *Classroom Assessment: What Teachers Need to Know.* 7th edn. Upper Saddle River, NJ: Pearson.

Queensland Government (n.d.) Queensland Curriculum and Assessment Authority NAPLAN portal. Available from https://naplan.qcaa.qld.edu.au/naplan/ (accessed 15 August 2015).

Queensland Government (2014) *Great Results Guarantee.* Available from www.education.qld.gov.au/resultsguarantee (accessed 2 February 2015).

Reay, D. and Wiliam, D. (1999) '"I'll be a nothing": structure, agency and the construction of identity through assessment', *British Educational Research Journal,* 25: 343–54.

Ryan, S. (2009) 'EQ bungling causes NAPLAN fiasco', *Queensland Teachers' Journal,* 32: 7.

Schnellert, L. M., Butler, D. L and Higginson, S. K. (2008) 'Co-constructors of data, co-constructors of meaning: teacher professional development in an age of accountability', *Teaching and Teacher Education,* 24(3): 725–50. doi: http://dx.doi.org/10.1016/j.tate.2007.04.001.

Smith, M. and Fey. P. (2000) 'Validity and accountability in high-stakes testing', *Journal of Teacher Education,* 51(5): 334–44. doi: 10.1177/0022487100051005002.

Spina, N., Klenowski, V. and Harris, J. (under review) 'Moving knowledge around: educational leaders respond to student achievement data', *New Directions in Evaluation.*

Stobart, G. (2008) *Testing Times: The Uses and Abuses of Assessment.* London: Routledge.

Thompson, G. and Harbaugh, A. G. (2013) 'A preliminary analysis of teacher perceptions of the effects of NAPLAN on pedagogy and curriculum', *The Australian Association for Research in Education.* Available from http://link.springer.com/article/10.1007/s13384-013-0093-0 (accessed 21 August 2014).

White, J. (2014) *Who Needs Examinations? A Story of Climbing Ladders and Dodging Snakes.* London: Institute of Education Press.

Wu, M. (2010a) 'The inappropriate use of NAPLAN data', *Professional Voice,* 8(1): 21–6.

Wu, M. (2010b) 'Measurement, sampling, and equating errors in large-scale assessments', *Educational Measurement: Issues and Practice,* 29(4): 15–27.

50

Professional Standards and the Assessment Work of Teachers

Claire Maree Wyatt-Smith and Anne Looney

STANDARDS FOR TEACHERS AND TEACHING

Prescriptions intended to govern teachers' classroom practice, general demeanour and behaviour at school and beyond the classroom have existed in the developed world since teachers were first employed and paid. As discussed in this chapter, the details of the prescriptions vary, even considerably, across contexts and over time. However, they all represent historical, cultural constructs of 'the good teacher' and, as such, they have meaning and influence in the contexts of their origins and in the prevailing valuations of teachers' work. Some earlier formulations are likely to appear unfamiliar, even humorous. Statements about bringing coal to school, about dress, about company-keeping and the avoidance of barbershops and pool halls abound in many lists dating back several generations (for example, Bial, 1999: 29) that point to the restrictions placed on male and female teachers and also to the importance of the moral character of the teacher in the community.

Although concerns have moved on from barbershops and pool halls, the focus on the classroom practice of teachers has intensified in recent times. One manifestation of this attention has been the generation and dissemination of codified representations of teachers' work. These codes, often expressed as standards, have become part of contemporary education policy landscapes. Nomenclature varies. In this chapter the terms 'codes' and 'standards' are used interchangeably, as they are across the literature and the official statutory publications. The Republic of Ireland has a *Code of Professional Conduct* (Teaching Council, 2012), although the code is presented online under a tab labelled Professional Standards. Introducing the code, the Teaching Council website explains that the code 'sets out the standards of professional knowledge, skill, competence and conduct which are expected of registered teachers. The standards are underpinned by four core values – respect, care, integrity and trust, and reflect the complexity of teaching' (Teaching Council, 2012). Australia has *Professional Standards for Teachers* (Australian Institute for Teaching and School Leadership (AITSL), 2011), which according to the AITSL website 'make explicit the elements of high quality teaching'. The Department for Education in England has produced *Teachers' Standards* (2011), which 'set the minimum requirements for teachers practice and conduct', and Scotland's *Standards for Registration* were produced by its General Teaching Council (2012), along with further standards for career development and school leadership. The General Teaching Council in Scotland describes the registration standards as 'benchmarks of competence', but distinguishes between these and the other standards, which, amongst other things, provide a 'framework for evaluation and reflection'. Both *Graduating Teacher Standards* (2007) and *Registered Teacher Criteria* (2013) have been published by the New Zealand Teachers Council. These criteria are described as the 'essential knowledge and capabilities required for quality teaching in New Zealand'. The General Teaching Council of Northern Ireland agreed a set of 27 *Professional Competences* (2007) to 'make explicit the attributes, skills and knowledge that teachers as professionals should possess and exemplify'. Notably, this Council has a caveat that 'rejects a restricted view of teaching competences' being 'mindful that teaching is both an intellectual and practical activity with important emotional and creative dimensions' (GTCNI, 2007: 5).

Typically, such national representations also reflect particular perspectives on teachers and their work, and each has been shaped by particular policy and cultural contexts, mentioned earlier. National articulations also reflect particular understandings of teaching and of the nature and purpose of standards and their function for the profession and the public. Inevitably, these understandings are, in turn, informed by the wider education policy context; however, all reflect and

are informed by the new global attention to teachers and their work.

Responses to the emergence of national standards and codes of practice have ranged from the relatively positive (Darling-Hammond, 1996; Sergiovanni and Starrat, 2002), to the cautious (Sachs, 2003; Kleinhenz and Ingvarson, 2007), to the critical (Clarke and Moore, 2013; Conway and Murphy, 2013). There has been criticism of the hyper-rationality of the language in which standards as codes are expressed; the detailed mapping of teacher work is seen as a sign of mistrust and an attempt at control and at squeezing out the idiosyncratic, leading to what has been called a 'teaching by numbers effect' (Clarke and Moore, 2013: 490).

But even this strong criticism is tempered by recognition that the codes developed in the early decades of the twenty-first century have a number of advantages. They offer increased transparency for pre-service teacher candidates. They provide explicit and public articulations of professional practice that might otherwise remain intuitive and are reliant on private or unstated personal standards. Such standards may well be the benign product of personal educational histories, or ethical and pastoral imperatives, or even fictional representations of teachers and their work, but they can also be poorly informed, based on limited life experience, and at times, questionable. Codes and standards also provide a common professional language for teachers and other education professionals and a public and accessible statement of the complexity and difficulty of teachers' work (Clarke and Moore, 2013). Connell concluded:

> The Standards may also help protect education against abuses of the 'charismatic' image of the good teacher where politicians in search of publicity throw untrained youngsters into very difficult teaching situations on the Hollywood principle that natural talent will triumph in the last reel. (2009: 220)

Hargreaves and Lo (2000) provided an overview of the history of the relationship between public attention and expectation and the teaching profession, and some useful background to the codification of that relationship in legal or quasi-legal forms. They traced the origins of these codified expectations back to the emergence of mass schooling carrying with it the burden of great expectations:

> Schools and teachers have been expected to save children from poverty and destitution; to rebuild nationhood in the aftermath of war; to develop universal literacy as a platform for economic survival; to create skilled workers even when there is no demand for them; to develop tolerance amongst children in nations where adults are divided by religious and ethnic conflict; to cultivate democratic sentiments in societies that bear the scars of totalitarianism; to keep developed nations economically competitive and help developing ones become so. (Hargreaves and Lo, 2000: 168–69)

The 1950s and 1960s were something of a golden age for teachers and teaching (Whitty, 2006). Post-war demographics gave rise to a call for more teachers, which in turn gave teachers a platform to bargain for better salaries and conditions. Teaching became a graduate-based profession and the field of education emerged as an intellectual discipline in its own right. A good teacher brought more than fuel to school; they brought independent thought, disciplinary knowledge and a high degree of professional autonomy (Connell, 2009).

Of note, school systems in the developing world and the teachers who staffed them experienced quite a different trajectory by comparison. As Hargreaves and Lo (2000: 169) observed, such systems faced different challenges, inherited different post-war legacies and 'had a disproportionately tiny share of the world's wealth with which to address them'. In the last decade considerable progress has been made in the professionalisation of the teaching workforce in the developing world, with the support of international organisations such as UNESCO (Adote-Bah Advotevi, 2013). This chapter will focus on the nature and function of professional standards in the developed world.

The beginning of the 1970s brought an end to the developed world's optimistic assumptions about education. The oil crisis, the recession that followed, and the collapse of post-war welfare structures contributed to a re-casting of the place of education, and of teachers, in society. Education stopped being the solution, and began to be perceived as a problem for shrinking economies and falling populations, especially Western economies with increasing youth unemployment (Connell, 2009). The emergence of new testing technologies nurtured the appetite for authorities to measure the scale of that 'problem', and the emergence of comparative tests in mathematics added to anxieties that some countries were racing ahead whilst others were languishing behind (Madaus and O'Dywer, 1999; Shimahara, 1997).

Developments in the academy added further to the pessimism around education. As criticism of post-war social democracy gathered pace, sociological research showed that neither education nor the welfare state had remedied social inequalities. Public choice and neo-liberal theories and critiques became increasingly popular and, with them, a growing suspicion of professions as anti-competitive monopolies (Hargreaves and Lo, 2000; Whitty, 2006; Connell, 2009).

The increasing criticism of post-war democracies and the emergence of neo-liberal and public choice theories had consequences for most areas of public life. Schools and teachers were particularly attractive targets for academic and public scrutiny. Schools, where teachers work, and universities, where teachers learn, are generally agencies of the state, making teachers and their work and preparation particularly vulnerable to the influences and forces of globalization (Tatto, 2006). Connell (2009) noted a further significant development in the academy that contributed to an intense focus on teachers and their work at that time, namely the application of multivariate analysis to educational research and the isolation of 'effectiveness' factors in teacher practice.

The consequence of these global, state and academic shifts was an extensive reorganisation of schools, greater control by others (usually the state, but not always) over the work of teachers and greater accountability by teachers for their work. In 2002, the Organisation for Economic Co-operation and Development (OECD) announced a major project on teacher quality, which led to the publication of the 2005 report *Teachers Matter* and its call for quality teaching for all delivered by 'competent' teachers:

> As the most significant and costly resource in schools, teachers are central to school improvement efforts. Improving the efficiency and equity of schooling depends, in large measure, on ensuring that competent people want to work as teachers, that their teaching is of high quality, and that all students have access to high quality teaching. (OECD, 2005: 1)

Early in the new millennium this explicit and widespread linking of 'quality' with 'competence' acted as a powerful catalyst for work at national and state level that sought to make explicit the elements of quality teaching through an 'imposing new apparatus of certification and regulation for teachers' (Connell, 2009: 214) that focused on 'competence'.

COMPETENCE, QUALITY AND GUILD KNOWLEDGE

The concept of competence first emerged from vocational and apprenticeship training when distinct skills were 'extracted' from occupational practice and used as the basis for modular training courses (Winterton et al., 2006; Connell, 2009). This connection between 'quality' and 'competence' seems relatively benign and the aspirations for high quality teaching seem laudable; however, the relationship between 'high quality teaching' and 'improving the efficiency and equity' of schooling, as suggested by the OECD (2005), has proven seductive for policymakers and others seeking to understand and solve long-standing and, in many cases, growing gaps in achievement between richer and poorer students. Spurred by meta-analyses examining variables that impact student outcomes,

policymakers have focused on quality teachers and teaching as the educational Holy Grail for achievement gaps, particularly those associated with social and economic factors. In one such analysis in New Zealand, for example, Alton-Lee concluded:

> Quality teaching is identified as a key influence on high quality outcomes for diverse students. The evidence reveals that up to 59% of variance between student performance is attributable to differences between teacher and classes, while up to almost 21%, but generally less, is attributable to school level variables. (Alton-Lee, 2003: 2)

The work of consultants such as McKinsey (Mourshed et al., 2010) and others, has given rise to a new 'taxonomy of teaching' (O'Neill and Adams, 2014: 1), which has seen the word teaching 'spot-welded in policy texts to the word quality' (O'Neill and Adams, 2014: 2). Moreover, this combination has evolved into what some have called 'a dangerous proxy concept in the sense that it acts as a cover for any and every political agenda in publicly funded education that aims to further circumscribe teacher autonomy' (O'Neill and Adams, 2014: 2). In developments in Australia, the quality agenda has extended to the reported need for 'developing structures and approaches that ensure widespread use of successful teaching practices to make best practice, common practice' (Dinham, Ingvarson and Kleinshenz, 2008). This move signals some interest in standardising teaching practice, a point revisited later.

This 'new taxonomy of teaching' (O'Neill and Adams, 2014: 1) is in marked contrast to other views of teachers' work. The concept of 'guild' serves as a useful juxtaposition. In a discussion of conceptions of teacher knowledge, Shulman (1986) outlined three types of propositional knowledge in teaching arising from the three major sources of knowledge about teaching: 'disciplined empirical or philosophical inquiry, practical experience and moral or ethical reasoning' (Shulman, 1986: 11). Notably, he also referred to the role of 'remembrances of teaching past' as a source of inspiration for teachers. He asserted that the complexity of teachers' work resists standardisation, and even widely held and applied rules cannot obviate the need for professional judgement to be called into play. This judgement he suggested 'is the hallmark of any learned profession' (Shulman, 1986: 13). For Shulman, it is the idiosyncratic nature of teachers' work and its resistance to standardisation that distinguishes teaching from craft work and forms the basis of the identity of teaching as a profession:

> What distinguishes mere craft from profession is the indeterminacy of rules when applied to particular cases. The professional holds knowledge, not only of how – the capacity for skilled performance – but of what and why. The teacher is not only a master of procedure but also of content and rationale, and capable of explaining why something is done. The teacher is capable of reflection leading to self-knowledge, the metacognitive awareness that distinguishes draftsman from architect, bookkeeper from auditor. (Shulman, 1986: 13)

This identity defines what Shulman called the 'broader academic guild of professional teachers' (1986: 14).

Sadler (1989) used the concept of guild more narrowly, focusing on the 'guild knowledge' that teachers draw on to make sound qualitative judgements in their assessment work. Like Shulman, however, he saw this guild knowledge as complex, and informed by personal and professional histories and experiences. In developing this notion of guild knowledge associated with connoisseurship and expert judgement, Sadler recognised the difficulty and necessity of making this kind of knowledge public, noting that 'how to draw the concept of excellence out of the heads of teachers, give it some external formulation, and make it available to the learner is a non-trivial problem' (Sadler, 1989: 127).

The examples of national standards and codes for teachers introduced earlier in this chapter, and further discussed later, claim to solve that problem of making public what is held as 'guild' knowledge. According to, Kleinhenz and Ingvarson (2007), 'the ability to define and apply standards is the main avenue by which professions demonstrate their credentials as a profession' (2007: v). Our starting proposition is that professional standards function to convey to the community in the broadest sense the knowledges, skills, capabilities and values that the profession accepts, names and 'owns' for itself. In short, the standards come to serve as a public formulation of guild knowledge. They define and in so doing, bring forth what may otherwise be the unstated, although accepted, expectations of the guild of practitioners.

A related proposition is that standards themselves do not constitute professional knowledge; they are a formulation of what the guild of practitioners as recognised experts accept as valued in practice. In this way, standards are understood as historical and cultural constructs, reflective of the times in which they are formulated. Standards typically written as qualitative statements necessarily remain 'fuzzy' in that the terms used to formulate the standard remain open to interpretation and re-interpretation. In short, standards can and should be expected to change to reflect changes and improvements in practice and the generation of new ways of 'knowing', 'doing' and 'being' as valued by the profession; however, this function can be overshadowed by the role of standards in the 'measurement' as well as the articulation of quality. This measurement function can appear benign when presented as an opportunity for teachers to present evidence of their work. Kleinhenz and Ingvarson (2007: 6) suggest that 'one of the hallmarks of a profession is its demonstrated capacity to define and measure quality performance'. This claim that measurement is a 'hallmark' is not uncontested – neither of the medical or the judicial codes discussed in the next section refers to the need to measure. Hargreaves and Goodson (1996: 21) do not refer to it in their discussion of the many different models of professionalism relevant to teaching, nor in the 'seven principles of postmodern professionalism' they propose as the most relevant for teaching. Stephen Ball in his influential paper on the impact of globalisation and new public management on teachers and their work presents a less than positive view of measurement. With its rhetorical title, 'The teacher's soul and the terrors of performativity', the piece juxtaposed the passion and commitment of the teacher with the new requirements to measure performance against externally imposed indicators and noted that teachers were required 'to set aside beliefs and commitments and live a life of calculation' (Ball, 2003: 215).

STANDARDS FOR OTHER GUILDS

Such a 'life of calculation' is not envisaged in the preface to the guide to judicial conduct in Australia, which includes the following extract from Thomas (1997):

> Citizens cannot be sure that they or their fortunes will not some day depend on our judgement. They will not wish such power to be reposed in anyone whose honesty, ability or personal standards are questionable. It is necessary for the continuity of the system of law as we know it, that there be standards of conduct, both in and out of court, which are designed to maintain confidence in those expectations... (Council of Chief Justices of Australia, 2007: ix)

Similarly, the General Medical Council (2013) in the UK opens its guidance, *Good Medical Practice*, by directly addressing members of the medical profession on the issue of public trust: 'Patients must be able to trust doctors with their lives and health. To justify that trust you must show respect for human life and make sure your practice meets the standards expected of you...' (General Medical Council, 2013: 2). Thus, professional standards, whether for education, for the judiciary or for medicine, appear to be located 'between' the members of the profession and the wider public as a formal recognition of, response to, and assurance of public trust. In short, they provide formulations of professional practice that are at the heart of a contract of trust between the professional and the community.

Instead of attempting to describe quality medical practice, the focus in the medical standards is on 'good' medical practice, even on the 'good doctor' (as in the case of the UK code). Competence is rooted in explicitly moral purpose:

> Patients need good doctors. Good doctors make the care of their patients their first concern: they are competent, keep their knowledge and skills up to date, establish and maintain good relationships with patients and colleagues, are honest and trustworthy, and act with integrity and within the law. (General Medical Council, 2013: 7)

A second striking difference arises from the relationship between the professional and the standards. The standards for judges and doctors make clear that ultimate responsibility for professional judgement rests with the professional. Meeting the standards is not a proxy for professional judgement. In both fields, in line with the conceptions of Shulman and Sadler, the standards state that situations will arise beyond the compass of the standards or, in the case of judicial codes, when 'the overall interest of justice require a departure from the propositions as literally stated in the guide' (Judiciary of England and Wales, 2013: 8). 'Nothing', according to the Australian code for good medical practice, 'can replace the insight and professional judgement of good doctors' (Medical Board of Australia, 2014: 4). Contemporary standards or codes for teaching afford the professional no such latitude.

STANDARDS AND THE CONSTRUCTION OF TEACHER IDENTITY

The concept of teacher identity has been explored in a variety of very different ways, including perspectives on the multiple re-inventions that teachers undergo in the course of their professional lives (Hargreaves and Goodson, 1996; Mitchell and Weber, 1999); narratives that teachers create to explain themselves and their work (Connelly and Clandinin,

Figure 50.1   Contextual factors and their relationship in the construction of teacher identity

Source: Based on Mockler, 2011.

1999); metaphors that guide and inform how teachers see themselves in relation to their students and professional settings (Leavy, McSorley and Bote, 2007; and responses to structural or political changes in education that reframe or change how teachers are understood and understand themselves (Mockler, 2011).

Most interpretations adopt a socio-cultural stance towards the concept of identity. That is, it is framed and reframed over a career and mediated by the contexts in which teachers work and live. Most interpretations also agree that it is unstable and shifts over time as a result of a range of external contextual and internal factors (Beijaard et al., 2004; Day et al., 2006). Mockler (2011: 9) usefully grouped the contextual factors under three headings: personal experience, professional context and external political and cultural context (see Figure 50.1).

Although these contextual factors are not mutually exclusive, each has its own particular focus. Personal experience includes biography and personal and social history, but for teachers it also includes influential personal experience of teachers, teaching

and schooling in the formative years, the 'remembrance of teaching past' to use Shulman's (1986) phrase. The professional context comprises those factors that shape the classroom work of teachers – curriculum, pedagogy, assessment, school climate, culture and organisation, collegial relationships and engagement with reform. Related to this is Mockler's third set of factors, the political and cultural which includes media commentary and debates about education and teachers and their work, which in turn reflects the degree of public trust and confidence in teachers and in the teaching profession more generally. Mockler suggested that these all contribute to teacher identity at any particular moment in time.

Interestingly, Mockler located teacher standards in the social and political contexts that shape teacher identity, but commented that the codes tend to privilege particular facets of teacher identity, specifically the 'function' of teachers (what they 'do'), rather than consideration of teacher 'identity' (associated with who teachers 'are') (2011: 525). The apparent assumption is that the former is easy to see, codify and measure. It is this mix of identity and function that is played out in debates about 'effective' teaching, and this mix between 'being' and 'doing' also represents an unresolved tension in the professional codes or standards for teachers.

Of note, the balance between 'being' and 'doing' is somewhat different in the codes for the medical and judicial professions. The codes for teaching are written in the third person; those for medicine make direct address to the members of the profession and are written in the second person. The consequent difference in tone is remarkable. For example, codes for medicine and for teaching both reference the importance of continually updating professional knowledge. Australian teachers are expected to 'demonstrate an understanding of the rationale for continued professional learning and the implications for improved student learning' (AITSL, 2011: 16). Doctors are addressed directly using the second person: 'Good medical practice involves keeping *your* knowledge and skills up to date' and 'participating regularly in activities that maintain and further develop *your* knowledge, skills and performance' (Medical Board of Australia, 2014: 20, emphasis added). As an illustrative counterpoint, in Scotland the third person is used: teachers should 'adopt an enquiring approach to *their* professional practice and engage in professional enquiry and professional dialogue' (General Teaching Council for Scotland, 2012a: 19, emphasis added). Doctors in Scotland and Australia are addressed directly: 'You must keep up to date, and follow the law, our guidance, and other regulations relevant to your work' (General Medical Council, 2014: 6). The use of the strong term 'must' signals responsibility and expected action – responsibility for following or adhering to various regulations external to the medical profession including the law, and action to maintain currency. In this way, the medical profession is characterised by explicit reference to other professions so that professional practice involves knowledge and awareness that goes beyond the

boundaries of their own practice. Typically, this professional interconnectedness is not a feature in the codes for teaching. Although the Australian standards for teachers aspire to articulate the elements of 'high quality teaching' and those developed for Scotland reference the professional values and commitment associated with 'being a teacher', the phrase 'good teacher' is notably absent. In contrast, the actual phrase 'good doctor' appears in the medical codes. Who doctors 'are' and what they 'do' are connected in these codes: the expectation of ethical practice, for example, connects with the individual doctor's agency in, and responsibility for, updating knowledge and skills in their practice. The same emphasis is not evident in the teaching codes.

Beijaard et al. (2004) highlighted the importance of the values and emotions underpinning teacher identity. They believe that in any analysis or discussion of identity, place should be given to the question of how it 'feels' to be a teacher in the school system at any point in time. It is suggested that such emotion becomes particularly significant at times of educational reform (Hargreaves, 2003, Hargreaves and Fullan, 1998), but tends to be under-researched. Day et al. (2006) also noted that insufficient attention is paid to emotional factors in the discussion of teacher identity. In their review of the theme of personal and professional identities, they pointed to the important tension between the 'structures' within which teachers work and which exert influence on that work, and the 'agency' of teachers, which they described as the ability to pursue valued goals. Both are significant in the construction of teacher identity, and 'emotions are the necessary link between the social structures in which teachers work and the ways they act' (Day et al., 2006: 613) and interact with others, including students, parents and the wider community.

Of the sets of standards currently in use, those developed for Australia and Scotland are particularly noteworthy for their focus not only on requirements for initial registration, but also on pathways for career development. In Scotland, these are expressed in two separate codes produced by the General Teaching Council – the *Standard for Registration* (General Teaching Council Scotland, 2012a) and the *Standard for Career-Long Professional Learning* (General Teaching Council Scotland, 2012b).The first code has two categories, one for provisional registration and one for full registration. In Australia, a unified set of national standards – *Australian Professional Standards for Teachers* – has been produced by the AITSL (2011). These show progression across various career stages from 'graduate' through to 'proficient' to 'highly accomplished' and 'lead'.

The Australian standards are framed by an introduction that describes the standards as 'an outline of what teachers should know and be able to do' (AITSL, 2011). The 'three domains of teaching' into which the standards are grouped are also introduced: professional knowledge, professional practice and professional engagement. Professional engagement refers to professional learning and relationships with parents, colleagues and the wider community.

The Scottish standards also frame the standards with an introduction that positions the standards as 'the gateway to the profession and the benchmark of teacher competence for all teachers' (General Teaching Council, 2012a: 2). This 'clear and concise description of the professional qualities and capabilities fully registered teachers are expected to maintain and enhance through their careers' is also presented in three groups. Although these are broadly aligned with the Australian categories of professional knowledge, practice and engagement, there is a marked difference in emphasis. The Scottish standards place 'professional values and personal commitment' as 'the heart' of teaching, and they are listed first:

> Professional values are at the core of the Professional Standards. The educational experiences of all our learners are shaped by the values and dispositions of all those who work to educate them. Values are complex and the ideal by which we shape our practice as professionals. (General Teaching Council, 2012a: 5)

In contrast, and of note for the later analysis on assessment, neither 'values' nor 'dispositions' appear in the Australian standards. This observation is consistent with the point made earlier regarding the values and dispositions tied to *identity*, on the one hand, and *role*, on the other. The caveat in the introduction to the code for Northern Ireland makes specific reference to the emotional dimension of teaching, but presents it as beyond or outside the competences presented in the code itself (General Teaching Council for Northern Ireland, 2007: 13).

ASSESSMENT IN CODES AND STANDARDS – THE CASES OF AUSTRALIA AND SCOTLAND

Assessment as a category of teacher work appears in two forms in the Australian standards. First, along with curriculum and reporting, assessment is listed as one of the resources used by teachers to 'design learning sequences and lesson plans (AITSL, 2011: 12). Second, it appears as a standalone standard, which states that teachers 'assess, provide feedback and report on student learning' (AITSL, 2011: 16). This standard provides a detailed breakdown of the actions required of teachers, including demonstrating understanding of the purpose of feedback to students; demonstrating understanding of social moderation and its application to support consistent and comparable judgements of student learning; and demonstrating 'the capacity to interpret student assessment data to evaluate student learning and modify teaching practice' (AITSL, 2011: 17). Teachers should also be able to demonstrate a range of strategies for reporting to students and parents and understand the purpose of accurate record keeping.

Assessment appears twice in the Scottish standards. The first reference is to assessment embedded in the teaching process. The second reference is explicit and more developed.

As part of professional knowledge and understanding, teachers are expected to 'know and understand how to apply the principles of assessment, recording and reporting as an integral part of the teaching process', (General Teaching Council for Scotland, 2012a: 9) as well as having

> extensive knowledge and a secure understanding of the principles of assessment, methods of recording assessment information, the use of assessment in reviewing progress, in improving teaching and learning, identifying next steps and the need to produce clear, informed and sensitive reports. (General Teaching Council for Scotland, 2012a: 9)

In the more detailed standard specifically referencing assessment, explicit connections are made between the assessment work of teachers and student learning, and with external audiences such as parents and awarding bodies such as examination authorities. The requirement for teachers to design assessment strategies 'appropriate to the needs of all learners' (General Teaching Council Scotland, 2012a: 17) is included, and reference is made to 'dialogue with learners about their progress and targets' (2012a: 18). Of special interest is the understanding of assessment as inclusive practice (with reference to the needs of all learners) and that student voice matters because teachers and students share dialogue about learning progress.

Using this initial comparative analysis of the requirements for teachers' assessment work, a number of common factors emerge, some of which are unique to each set of standards. Teachers in both Australia and Scotland require knowledge about assessment, as well as an understanding of assessment, and the skills to apply such knowledge and understanding in classrooms with students, particularly in giving feedback to students on their learning. Teachers in both jurisdictions have to be able to report assessment results outside the classroom to parents (both) and awarding bodies (Scotland), and both standards make an explicit reference to using assessment results to review and improve teaching. Only Australian teachers

Table 50.1 Teachers' assessment work in Scotland and Australia standards

Teachers assessment work	Australia	Scotland
Knowledge about assessment	Yes	Yes
Understanding of assessment	Yes	Yes
Skills in assessment	Yes	Yes
Feedback to learners	Yes	Yes
Use feedback to review/improve teaching	Yes	Yes
Dialogue with learners	No	Yes
Understanding of moderation	Yes	No
Consistent and comparable judgement	Yes	No
Assessing diverse learners	No	Yes
Report results of assessment to parents and beyond	Yes	Yes

have to understand social moderation processes and arrive at consistent and comparable judgements to meet the requirements of their standards. Only Scottish teachers have to 'dialogue' with learners about progress and deploy their assessment knowledge, understanding and skills to meet the needs of diverse learners as required by theirs. A summary of the analysis of teacher assessment work in the standards for Scotland and Australia is provided in Table 50.1.

The categories constructed from this initial analysis were used in a review of the assessment work in the codes and standards from a number of other English-speaking jurisdictions (see Table 50.2). The year in which the relevant codes were published is also included and the analysis is restricted to the graduate level teacher.

In addition to the codes and standards published in English, an 11-country audit of 'teacher competency standards' (Seameo Innotech Regional Education Program, 2010) produced for the Southeast Asian Ministers of Education Organisation was also considered. The review identified five common domains within the teaching standards reviewed. Similar to those from the English-speaking or bilingual contexts, professional knowledge and skills were identified in the teaching standards across the region, together with

Table 50.2 Teachers' assessment work in other standards

Teachers' assessment work	New Zealand	Ireland	Northern Ireland	England	Ontario	Wales
	2009	2012	2007	2011	2000	2011
Knowledge about assessment	No	No	Yes	Yes	No	No
Understanding of assessment	No	No	No	Yes	No	No
Skills in assessment	Yes	Yes	Yes	No	Yes	Yes
Feedback to learners	Yes	Yes	Yes	Yes	Yes	Yes
Use feedback to review/improve teaching	Yes	No	Yes	Yes	No	Yes
Dialogue with learners	No	Yes	Yes	No	No	Yes
Understanding of moderation	No	No	No	No	No	Yes
Consistent and comparable judgement	No	No	No	No	No	No
Assessing diverse learners	No	Yes	No	No	Yes	Yes
Report results of assessment to parents and beyond	Yes	No	Yes	No	Yes	Yes

professional development and lifelong learning. Of note, two other domains that were not common to most of the others (although strongly referenced in Scotland and Ireland) were the domains of 'personal characteristics' and 'professional/personal ethical standards and values' which, according to the report 'refers to sound and ethical standards of ethics and morality resulting in teachers being good role models in the school and community' (Seameo Innotech Regional Education Program, 2010: 2). The review generated a generic competency framework for the region that included 'facilitating learning', 'developing higher order thinking-skills', and 'assessing and evaluating learner performance' (p. 3).

CONNECTING TEACHER IDENTITY, PRACTICE AND VALUES

In all the codes and standards reviewed, assessment constitutes a significant part of teachers' work, as expected. Across the examples considered, it should be noted that assessment 'skills' are accorded greater emphasis than both knowledge and understanding. For Ryan and Bourke (2012), this reflects the inevitable focus on actions and behaviours associated with the credentials of the codes and standards, rather than emotions and intellectuality, such as deep thinking and reflection.

Feedback to learners is referenced in all the codes and standards, but not all include a reference to using the evidence generated by assessment to review or improve teaching. Only in Australia is there reference to the 'quality' of assessment; teachers need to be able to conduct consistent and comparable assessments. As shown in the table above, three of the codes make specific reference to some form of dialogue with learners, thus moving beyond a linear view of feedback as a form of messaging from teacher to learner towards the more complex exchanges that can give rise to greater self-direction in student learning (Sadler, 1989). However, such exchanges depend on more than assessment knowledge and skills. James and Pedder (2006) noted in a study of teachers' classroom assessment practices that:

> There is a danger that the importance of this values dimension is underplayed and that assessment for learning becomes caricatured as merely another set of unexamined classroom strategies that teachers can use off the shelf, across all contexts and without reference to educational values or beliefs. (2006: 110–11)

They argued that teachers' beliefs and values provide the necessary reason to act, and that any consideration of assessment should include both practice and values. Indeed, they also suggested that failure to consider teacher values, and failure to afford teachers an opportunity to consider their own educational values, will lead to assessment for learning (the focus of their study) being seen as a set of strategies and techniques to be added to the teaching repertoire. To use the categories of Mockler's (2011) model of teacher identity discussed earlier, James and Pedder's (2006) analysis would suggest that the personal lives of teachers, their educational histories and experience of assessment is as important in the consideration of their assessment work as assessment knowledge and skills, and that 'teachers' values and the moral dimension of their practice that these values express, needs to be acknowledged in a discourse that goes beyond instrumental questions of method' (James and Pedder, 2006: 131). In their study involving 558 teachers in England, they found that teachers experienced the greatest tension between values and practice when it came to promotion of learning autonomy, which teachers believed to be a key strategy in helping students to improve the quality of their learning. Thus, a gap was identified between their moral purpose and emotional commitment to teaching, and the assessment practice required of them by the policy context in which they worked.

The work of Ryan and Bourke (2012) who undertook analysis of the English and Australian codes using the concept of reflexivity and the realist social theory of Margaret Archer (1995) is relevant to this discussion. Their analysis identified differences between the English and Australian codes. They suggested that the Australian standards have a problem/solution orientation with compelling references throughout to improving, but they do not attempt to define the problem or present evidence of it. By contrast, England's standards present a strong advancement and progression rhetoric, and draw heavily upon an assumption that career advancement is the goal of every teacher. For Ryan and Bourke, both codes share little concern for the moral, attitudinal or emotional aspects of teaching and 'little acknowledgement of the complex, subjective and objective influences in teachers' work' (Ryan and Bourke, 2012: 420). The limitations of this for assessment are particularly acute. All the codes and standards reviewed signal that teachers' assessment work is important for student learning. However, the complex dimensions of that work described by Ryan and Bourke, are not recognised. Although this gap appears in the professional standards, there is growing interest in the concept of teachers' assessment literacy and its relationship to teacher identity.

ASSESSMENT LITERACY AND IDENTITY

The concept of assessment literacy was first introduced by Stiggins (1991) writing in the context of the US. Stiggins suggested that assessment literacy involved understanding how to produce good achievement data on both large-scale and classroom tests, and the ability to interrogate and critique the tests or assessment approaches used and the data produced. He referred to the 'built-in alarms' (Stiggins, 1991: 535), which alert those who are assessment literate, that go off 'when an assessment target is unclear, when an assessment method misses the target, when a sample of performance is inadequate, when extraneous factors are creeping into the data, and when the results are simply not meaningful to them' (Stiggins, 1991: 535). He also emphasized that knowing that there is a problem is not enough – those who are literate will demand or make changes when that alarm goes off.

Some years later, Stiggins noted positive trends in the field, including the articulation of the assessment competencies for teachers developed jointly by the National Council on Measurement in Education, and American Federation of Teachers, and the National Education Association (Stiggins, 1995).

However, he also noted barriers to assessment literacy, and of particular interest to our discussion are those arising from what he labels 'fear of assessment and evaluation' (Stiggins, 1995: 243).

> For most practicing educators, this fear of assessment has been cultivated over many years as a direct result of many levels of unpleasant assessment experiences. The foundation was laid in during our youth, when our own teachers often left us wondering what would be on the test and how to prepare for it. In our youth, assessment was frequently used to gain compliance rather than to promote improvement. (Stiggins, 1995: 243)

These 'negative emotions', Stiggins suggested, did not stop at school, but could continue into teacher preparation where courses in assessment and measurement may add a further 'layer of negative associations'. He went on to claim that the final layer in the US context is the relentless focus on standardised test scores that reflect only a small part of what is taught in classrooms, leaving teachers 'feeling victimised by assessment once again' (Stiggins, 1995: 243).

A number of years, later Popham (2009) also addressed this question of assessment literacy, noting that teachers continue to know little about assessment mainly because of the lack of courses in assessment in teacher education. He suggested that assessment literacy was needed to inform the assessment decisions teachers need to make, and to challenge the high stakes accountability tests that abound in education in the US. Although he acknowledged that, for some teachers, 'test is a four letter word' (Popham, 2009: 4), he does not address the issues of fear or anxiety raised by Stiggins. By 2011, Popham had come to define assessment literacy as 'an individual's understandings of the fundamental assessment concepts and procedures deemed likely to influence educational decisions' (2011: 267).

The point of interest is that for Stiggins, assessment literacy necessarily extends to the emotion, affective and the moral. For Popham, on the other hand, priority is given to the cognitive aspects of assessment work.

The connecting of these perspectives serves to illustrate the challenge inherent in professional standards in how they recognise and reconcile these dimensions in the representation of teacher assessment identity.

PROFESSIONAL STANDARDS AND ASSESSMENT PRACTICE

Revisiting 'Guild Knowledge'

Three main findings emerge from the preceding discussion of standards for teachers and teaching. First is the prevalence of standards and their salience across countries, jurisdictions and related policy contexts. Although the specific characteristics or features of quality that constitute the standards vary, collectively they function as formulations of professional practice to make valued aspects of teacher work explicit and available for scrutiny. The variation in the standards can be understood as reflecting the contexts in which they have their origins. Further, all standards are produce of a particular time and context and so reflect decisions about what to include and exclude at a particular point in time. As such, they are understood to be susceptible to change. They also capture public attitudes to teachers and their work.

Second, a related finding is that the teaching standards as official statements of expectations are sites where different formulations of 'the good teacher' and 'good teaching' jostle and compete with one another, although the term good teacher does not appear. By contrast, in the standards for medical practice there is explicit reference made to the good doctor. Further, the language for both the medical and judicial codes give agency to the members of these professions through the choice of syntax and mode of address. This was in marked contrast to the language used in the teacher codes, which largely served to obscure the person of the teacher and their values and beliefs.

Third, it is our contention that the codes collectively fall short in representing the complexity of teachers' assessment work and their roles as assessors, even though this work is of increasing priority in education policy making. Further, there is an already strong and growing field of research into the concept of teachers' assessment literacy, with some writers representing teachers' assessment work as complex and multidimensional, going beyond a focus on the assessment work of teachers to the identities that teachers take on. Looking at the representation of teachers' assessment work across a range of standards has highlighted their limitations in addressing the task of making the complexity and the emotional aspects of teachers' work explicit for teachers and the general public. Our analysis of some examples of medical and judicial codes has shown that such representations are possible and have been afforded to other professions. Extending these kinds of representations to the work of teachers remains a challenge.

In recognising the scale of this challenge, we propose that standards are best understood as dynamic and responsive to the challenges of emerging practice and insights of research, as discussed in this chapter. This duality is the essence of guild knowledge. Accordingly, standards in how they are formulated and applied should extend to 'intellectual resources' such as the knowledge and skills that competent teachers need, the recognition of 'experiential resources' that teachers accrue from their histories inside and outside schooling, and 'personal resources' that include dispositions and values. This rich mix is consistent with the proper valuing of teaching as a profession with responsibility for preparing young people to use existing knowledge, generate new knowledge and lead fulfilling lives. Finally, in light of the developing use the codes as a basis for teacher evaluation and other performance measures tied to remuneration, there is a pressing and urgent need to claim overtly the codes for the guild and, in so doing, represent both what teachers 'do' *and* who they 'are'.

REFERENCES

Adote-Bah Advotevi, J. (2013) *Developing Teachers Qualifications Frameworks*. Dakar: UNESCO.

Alton-Lee, A. (2003) *Quality teaching for diverse students in schooling: Best Evidence Synthesis Iteration (BES)*. Ministry of Education: Wellington, New Zealand.

Archer, M.S. (1995) *Realist Social Theory; The Morphogenetic Approach*. Cambridge: Cambridge University Press.

Australian Institute for Teaching and School Leadership (AITSL) (2011) *Professional Standards for Teachers*. Melbourne: Author. Available from http://www.aitsl.edu.au/australian-professional-standards-for-teachers (accessed 16 July 2015).

Ball, S. J. (2003) 'The teacher's soul and the terrors of performativity', *Journal of Education Policy*, 18(2): 215–28.

Beijaard, D., Meijer, P. C. and Verloop, N. (2004) 'Reconsidering research on teachers' professional identity', *Teaching and Teacher Education*, 20(2): 107–28.

Bial, R., (1999) *One Room School*. Boston, MA: Houghton Mifflin.

Clarke, M. and Moore, A. (2013) 'Professional standards, teacher identities and an ethics of singularity', *Cambridge Journal of Education*, 43(4): 487–500.

Connell, R. (2009) 'Good teachers on dangerous ground: towards a new view of teacher quality and professionalism', *Critical Studies in Education*, 50(3): 213–29.

Connelly, F. M. and Clandinin, D. J. (1999) *Shaping a Professional Identity: Stories of Education Practice*. London: Althouse Press.

Conway, P. F. and Murphy, R. (2013) 'A rising tide meets a perfect storm: new accountabilities in teaching and teacher education in Ireland', *Irish Educational Studies*, 32(1): 11–36.

Council of Chief Justices of Australia (2007) *Guide to Judicial Conduct (Second Edition)*. Melbourne: Institute of Judicial Administration Incorporated. Available from http://www.supremecourt.wa.gov.au/_files/GuidetoJudicialConduct(2ndEd).pdf (accessed 16 July 2015).

Darling-Hammond, L. (1996) 'The quiet revolution: rethinking teacher development', *Educational Leadership*, 53(6): 4–10.

Day, C., Kington, A., Stobart, G. and Sammons, P. (2006) 'The personal and professional selves of teachers: stable and unstable identities', *British Educational Research Journal*, 32(4): 601–16.

Department for Education (2011) *Teachers' Standards*. London: Author. Available from https://www.gov.uk/government/publications/teachers-standards

Dinham, S., Ingvarson, L. and Kleinhenz, E. (2008) 'Investing in Teacher Quality: Doing What Matters Most' in Business Council of Australia, *Teaching Talent: The Best Teachers for Australia's Classroom*. Melbourne: Author. pp. 5–49 Available from http://research.acer.edu.au/teaching_standards/12/ (accessed 16 July 2015).

General Medical Council (2013) *Good Medical Practice*. London: Author. Available from http://www.gmc-uk.org/guidance/good_medical_practice.asp (accessed 1 July 2015).

General Teaching Council for Northern Ireland (2007) *Professional Competences*. Belfast: Author. Available from http://www.gtcni.org.uk//index.cfm/area/information/page/ProfStandard (accessed 16 July 2015).

General Teaching Council for Scotland (2012a) The *Standards for Registration: mandatory requirements for registrations with the General Teaching Council, Scotland*. Edinburgh: Author: Available from http://www.gtcs.org.uk/standards/standards.aspx (accessed 16 July 2015).

General Teaching Council for Scotland, (2012b) The *Standard for Career-Long Professional Learning: supporting the development of teacher professional learning*. Edinburgh: Author. Available from http://www.gtcs.org.uk/web/FILES/the-standards/standard-for-career-long-professional-learning-1212.pdf (accessed 16 July 2015).

Hargreaves, A. (2003) *Teaching in the Knowledge Society. Education in the Age of Insecurity*. New York: Teachers College Press.

Hargreaves, A., and Fullan, M. (1998) *What's Worth Fighting for Out There*. New York: Teachers College Press.

Hargreaves, A. and Goodson, I. (1996) 'Teachers' professional lives: aspirations and actualities', in I. Goodson and A. Hargreaves (eds.), *Teachers' Professional Lives*. London: Falmer Press. pp. 1–27.

Hargreaves, A. and Lo, L. N. (2000) 'The paradoxical profession: teaching at the turn of the century', *Prospects*, 30(2): 167–80.

James, M. and Pedder, D. (2006) 'Beyond method: assessment and learning practices and values', *Curriculum Journal*, 17(2): 109–38.

Judiciary of England and Wales (2013) *Guide to Judical Conduct*. Available from https://www.judiciary.gov.uk/wp-(content/uploads/JCO/Documents/Guidance/judicial_conduct_2013.pdf (accessed 16 July 2015).

Kleinhenz, E. and Ingvarson, L. (2007) *Standards for Teaching: Theoretical Underpinnings and Applications*. Melbourne: Australian Council for Educational Research. Available from http://research.acer.edu.au/cgi/viewcontent.cgi?article=1000&context=teaching_standards (accessed 16 July 2015).

Leavy, A. M., McSorly, F. A. and Bote, L. A. (2007) 'An examination of what metaphor construction reveals about the evolution of pre-service teachers beliefs about teaching and learning', *Teaching and Teacher Education*, 23(7): 1217–33.

Madaus, G. F. and O'Dwyer, L. M. (1999) 'A short history of performance assessment', *Phi Delta Kappan*, 80(9): 688–95.

Medical Board of Australia (2014) *Good Medical Practice: a Code of Conduct for Doctors in Australia*. Available at http://www.medicalboard.gov.au/Codes-Guidelines-Policies/Code-of-conduct.aspx (accessed 16 July 2015).

Mitchell, C. and Weber, S. (1999) *Reinventing Ourselves as Teachers: Beyond Nostalgia*. London: Falmer Press.

Mockler, N. (2011) 'Beyond "what works": understanding teacher identity as a practical and political tool', *Teachers and Teaching*, 17(5): 517–28.

Mourshed, M., Chijioke, C. and Barber, M. (2010) *How the world's most improved school systems keep getting better*. McKinsey and Company. Available from http://mckinseyonsociety.com/downloads/reports/Education/How-the-Worlds-Most-Improved-School-Systems-Keep-Getting-Better_Download-version_Final.pdf (accessed 16 July 2015).

New Zealand Teachers Council (2007) *Graduating Teacher Standards*. Wellington: Author: Available from http://www.teacherscouncil.govt.nz/content/graduating-teacher-standards-poster-english-pdf-616kb (accessed 16 July 2015).

New Zealand Teachers Council (2013) *Registered Teacher Criteria*. Wellington: Author. Available from http://www.teacherscouncil.govt.nz/content/registered-teacher-criteria-english (accessed 16 July 2015).

O'Neill, J. and Adams, P. (2014) 'The future of teacher professionalism and professionality in teaching', *New Zealand Journal of Teachers' Work*, 11(1): 1–2.

Ontario College of Teachers, (2000). *Professional Standards*. Toronto: Author. Retreived from http://www.oct.ca/public/professional-standards (accessed 16 July 2015).

Organisation for Economic Co-operation and Development (OECD) (2005) *Teachers Matter. Attracting, Developing and Retaining Effective Teachers*. Paris. Author. Available from http://www.oecd.org/education/school/34990905.pdf (accessed 16 July 2015).

Popham, J. (2009) 'Assessment literacy for teachers: faddish or fundamental?', *Theory Into Practice*, 48(1): 4–11.

Popham, W. J. (2011) *Transformative Assessment in Action: An Inside Look at Applying the Process*. Alexandria, VA: ASCD.

Ryan, M. and Bourke, T. (2012) 'The teacher as reflexive professional: making visible the excluded discourse in teacher standards', *Discourse: Studies in the Cultural Politics of Education*. 34(3): 411–23. doi: 10.1080/01596306.2012.717193.

Sachs, J. (2003) 'Teacher Professional Standards: Controlling or developing teaching?' *Teachers and Teaching*, 9(2), 175–186.

Sadler, D. R. (1989) 'Formative assessment and the design of instructional systems', *Instructional Science*, 18(2): 119–44.

Seameo Innotech Regional Education Program (2010) *Teaching Competency Standards in Southeast Asian Countries*. Quezon City, Phillipines: Author. Available from http://www.seameo.org/_files/SEAMEO_Teaching_Competency_Standards-WTD.pdf (accessed 16 July 2015).

Sergiovanni, T. J. and Starratt, R. J. (2002). *Supervision: A redefinition*. New York: McGraw Hill.

Shimahara, K. (1997) 'Japanese lessons for educational reform', in A. Hargeaves and R. Evans (eds.), *Beyond Educational Reform*. Buckingham, UK: Open University Press. pp. 94–104.

Shulman, L. (1986) 'Those who understand: knowledge growth in teaching', *Educational Researcher*, 15(2): 4–14.

Stiggins, R. (1991) 'Assessment literacy', *Phi Delta Kappan*, 72(7): 534–39.

Stiggins, R. (1995) 'Assessment literacy for the 21st century', *Phi Delta Kappan*, 77(3): 238–45.

Tatto, M. T. (2006) 'Education reform and the global regulation of teachers' education, development and work: a cross-cultural analysis', *International Journal of Educational Research*, 45(4–5): 231–41. doi: 10.1016/j.ijer.2007.02.003.

Teaching Council (2012) *Code of Professional Conduct for Teachers*. Maynooth, Ireland: Author. Available from http://www.teaching-council.ie/professional-standards/code-of-professional-conduct-for-teachers.1425.html (accessed 16 July 2015).

Thomas, J. (1997) *Judicial Ethics in Australia* (2nd ed.). Sydney: LBC Information Services.

Welsh Government (2011) *Revised Professional Standards for Education Practitioners in Wales*. Cardiff: Author. Available from http://learning.wales.gov.uk/docs/learningwales/publications/140630-revised-professional-standards-en.pdf (accessed 16 July 2015).

Whitty, G. (2006) 'Teacher professonalism in a new era', paper presented at the Annual Lecture of the General Teaching Council Northern Ireland. Belfast, March 2006. Available from http://www.gtcni.org.uk/publications/uploads/document/annual%20lecture%20paper.pdf (accessed 16 July 2015).

Winterton, J., Delamere-LeDeist, F. and Stringfellow, E. (2006) *Typology of Knowledge, Skills and Competences*. Luxembourg: CEDEFOP. Available from http://www.cedefop.europa.eu/en/Files/3048_EN.PDF (accessed 16 July 2015).

51

Curriculum in the Twenty-First Century and the Future of Examinations

Jo-Anne Baird and Therese N. Hopfenbeck

INTRODUCTION

When children go through the school gate for the first time, parents think about how they will cope and what their experiences will be like. Foremost in parents' minds is the social experience of schooling, but also the learning journey that those children will make. Most of them in developed societies will gain powerful skills of reading, writing and arithmetic in the first few years, and these will be building blocks for the rest of their lifelong learning journeys. Schooling is also a hugely socialising force and will shape pupils' interactions with one another and how they see themselves. The last thing on parents' minds on that first day at the school gate is how these youngsters will perform in their examinations. Yet for over three decades, researchers have been documenting the dominance of assessment over teaching and learning experiences in many settings internationally (Frederiksen and Collins, 1989; Madaus, Russell and Higgins, 2009; Nuttall, 1987).

As we discuss later, international forces are increasingly influencing national examinations. With the rise in power of assessments to shape educational experiences and their stakes, we do not see a respondent increase in teachers' professional development and assessment literacy (Popham, 2011). Over the past three decades, the centralisation of curriculum (Bishop, 1971; Pring et al., 2009: 190; Tattersall, 2007) and assessment has meant that professional engagement with these matters is largely external to the school. Assessment is primarily something imposed from outside, with which teachers and students must comply (see, for example, Bradbury, 2011).

Schools must submit to assessment requirements because they are embedded in a range of devices imposed by governments (Higham and Yeomans, 2010). Examination results are tied into the following levers and controls in a range of countries: school funding regulations, inspections, league tables, teacher performance reviews and salaries. At an extreme, teachers deliver detailed, sched-uled, daily lesson plans that follow an exter-nal curriculum and are designed to meet the external assessment targets set by various government agencies. What happens in the classroom when a child enters on her first day at school is part of this bigger picture.

Assessment data have assumed impor-tance because of their use in so many of these systems. Newton (2007) described 18 different ways in which assessment data are used. We might well question whether all of these are good uses of the data, but the fact is that they *are* used in these ways. For exam-ple, assessment of pupils is not sensitive to the quality of teaching that they receive (Popham, 2007). Some examination ques-tions test materials that the children learn outside school. If you have never encoun-tered an avocado, arithmetic questions about avocados are more difficult to understand. Nobody would object to learning outside of school, but the use of pupil examina-tion results to evaluate teachers does then become questionable.

Nonetheless, we have long observed that numbers assume a life of their own, with peo-ple neglecting to consider what generated the numbers; what they were intended to show in the first place. And so it is with assessment data. Hanson (1993, 2000) noted that assess-ment results are not the learning themselves – they are signifiers of that learning. These signifiers can go on to assume greater impor-tance than the thing itself. Money is one such example and we have seen the complex sys-tems that have been set up around that sig-nifier – and the disastrous consequences for the 2008 world economy due to the lack of transparency about how the figures were generated. So, too, we see that examination results are used in systems as a signifier with multiple, powerful indices that are distanced from the learning itself. Their meaning is altered in this process. Few people using the data at such a distance understand the content of the curriculum or assessments underlying the data, let alone the capacity of the data to act as a valid signifier in their systems. For

example, test score data might be used to indicate a nation's level of 'literacy', 'com-petency' or 'skill'. These terms can mean a variety of things to the people interpreting them and without an understanding of the test content and process it would be all too easy to draw erroneous conclusions. For exam-ple, the International Adult Literacy Survey (IALS) published in 1997 (Organisation for Economic Co-operation and Development (OECD), 1997) showed that three-quarters of the French population had low levels of lit-eracy, which would make everyday reading a problem (such as understanding the newspa-per or a payslip). Blum et al. (2001) re-tested French adults with a Swiss version of the test and found that they did much better. The low scores were in part due to problems with the translation of the questions, which misled the test-takers. Further, there are questions about how international tests define literacy, as they typically test reading and not writing, speak-ing or listening.

For example, in England, using league tables (which rank schools by examina-tion outcomes) to choose a school for your child has a number of problems, not least of which is that by the time your child takes the examinations that were used to compose the league table, the school performance is likely to have change dramatically (Leckie and Goldstein, 2009). Worse still, once the socioeconomic group of the student intake is taken into account, there are few signifi-cant differences between schools' examina-tion outcomes (Goldstein, 1997). Also, in many countries, the use of private tutors is so prevalent (European Commission, 2011) that the school's examination scores also reflect the teaching conducted outside it. Thus, there are concerns that league tables[1] are an unstable indicator of learning oppor-tunity, which is to some extent outside the control of school.

League tables fit into a bigger pattern – bigger than the world of education. New public management (Hood, 1989) is the notion that the public sector can be man-aged similarly to private organisations and that market forces can be operationalised to produce more efficient systems. In turn, new public management is underpinned by neoliberal hegemony. This worldview is characterised by the notion that markets are self-organising, efficient and liberating, which is a naïvely false and outdated view of economics (Birch and Mykhnenko, 2009). Notwithstanding, these ideas are the foundational, organising principles for so much of how modern society operates, even if some foresee the end of this era (Birch and Mykhnenko, 2009). Politicians seek to shrink the role of the state under neoliberal policies and produce explanations for life chances that rest with the individual rather than at a societal level.

And so it is in this context that educational assessment has risen to power. Neoliberal, new public management has also seen the privatisation of many aspects of society over which governments previously had control. With the assumption of the importance of assessment and the lack of government influence over other areas, political interest in assessment has also risen. In this chapter, we outline five of the challenges that we foresee for curriculum and assessment in the next few decades. Many technical assessment challenges could have formed the basis of this chapter, such as validity, reliability, fairness, assessment models, standard-setting practices or theories for predictions of task difficulty. However, to focus on these aspects would have been to divert attention from the broader picture. The danger is that because we practice assessment *within* the five challenges that we outline, we do not see how they impact upon curriculum and assessment, and, blind to them, we will not be able to evaluate and tackle them. The challenges that we outline are at once philosophical and political, as well as educational. What counts as learning, who decides this, and the effects of these decisions, connect the challenges thematically. These five challenges need to be tackled for the production of assessment systems that support valuable learning, rather than undermine it.

THE CHALLENGES

Challenge 1 – Crisis of Knowledge

Knowledge is at our fingertips with information technology, so memorisation and recital of facts are no longer as important or impressive as they would have been in times gone by, whether of a poem, mathematical proof or the periodic table. Basic skills and content knowledge are still important to understand the world around us, but this is no longer enough. A statement made by President Obama summarised this aspect of the crisis of knowledge that the world is facing:

> I am calling on our nation's Governors and state education chiefs to develop standards and assessments that don't simply measure whether students can fill in a bubble on a test, but whether they possess 21st century skills like problem-solving and critical thinking, entrepreneurship and creativity. (10 March, 2009)

The rapidly changing world demands from us the abilities to apply, synthesise and organise knowledge, to know how to learn new knowledge for the rest of our lives and to adapt this to unanticipated situations. Furthermore, it is vital to be able to judge the quality of the knowledge presented and to be critical of the sources behind it. Can we really trust the knowledge source? Do we have education systems that produce independent, critical thinkers?

Valuable learning in fifteenth-century Europe was demonstrated by the ability to read and understand religious texts, but nowadays the Church and Bible have far less influence on what is seen as knowledge in contemporary Europe. In the modern day, we witness debates in countries such as England regarding syllabus content and what should have a prominent role. One illustrative example is the reaction to the former Secretary of State for Education Michael Gove's changes to the English curriculum for 16-year-olds in 2013. The syllabus, published on the Department of Education's (DfE) website, reads as follows:

Students should study a range of high quality, intellectually challenging, and substantial whole texts in detail. These must include: at least one play by Shakespeare; at least one 19th-century novel; a selection of poetry since 1789, including representative Romantic poetry; and fiction or drama from the British Isles from 1914 onwards. All works should have been originally written in English. (DfE, 2013).

As a result, some English exam boards decided to leave out American literature such as John Steinbeck's *Of Mice and Men*, Arthur Miller's play *The Crucible* and Harper Lee's *To Kill a Mockingbird*, literature which cohorts of 16-year-old pupils of English had been reading for years. Several researchers and media commentators warned about the consequences of such curriculum changes (Kennedy, 2014), but the Secretary of State made it clear that the new guidelines did not leave out any particular classics because examiners would be able to add any extra works of literature that they wanted to teach. But, in practice, little room would remain for any twentieth-century writing from outside the UK.

The broader changes in England have been described as a curriculum for compliance, encouraging more memorisation and rote learning (Young, 2012). This is often presented as a 'back to basics' curriculum and seen negatively. However, moving away from teaching the basics will have negative consequences for minority ethnic and lower socio-economic status groups, since it limits their access to powerful resources (Rata, 2012). In summary, conceptual knowledge is important, but it should no longer constitute the entire curriculum.

The English example illustrates a challenge in the field of education, where what counts as knowledge is highly influenced by politics. Unlike other sciences, such as medicine and law, education is more vulnerable as a field to power struggles, with different agents competing to define what counts as valuable learning regardless of their own educational background or expertise. Furthermore, education is highly influenced by different policies in countries around the world. In some countries, girls are not offered the same education as boys, or are given no education at all (see, for example, Shabaya and Konadu-Agyemang, 2004). Equally, politics influences what can be taught in school, for example leaving out evolution theory from science (*New York Times*, 2001), history books that are coloured by the leading regime in the country (Pinar, 2013), or what methods should be used in teaching.

Over the past twenty years, there has been an increasing focus upon what are known as higher order thinking skills, or 21st century skills. Although different frameworks have been developed, such as *Partnership for 21st Century Skills* (P21)[2], *Assessment and Teaching of 21st Century Skills* (ATC21S)[3], *New Millennium Learners*, and *Defining and Selecting of Key Competencies* (DeSeCo)[4], there is a gap between the policy intentions and practice. Few empirical studies demonstrate how these skills are used in practice in the classroom (Voogt and Roblin, 2012).

Thus, the crisis of knowledge runs deep, as there are political battles over what should be taught in schools and what counts as valuable learning. At the heart of this crisis of knowledge is the definition of generic thinking skills, which is theoretical and philosophical. Moreover, the crisis of knowledge is ultimately a matter of practice because what teachers and students focus upon in classrooms is key to changing what students learn.

Challenge 2 – Spiraling Reforms

Given the crisis of knowledge challenge, it is not surprising that governments the world over worry about whether their children are learning the right kinds of thing, in the right ways, to the right standard. This has led to curricular and examination reforms in many countries (Berry and Adamson, 2011) that seek to address the crisis of knowledge challenge. These political responses have, in turn, created new challenges.

In most countries, the electoral cycle is shorter than that required to plan a reform, let alone implement and evaluate it (Baird and Lee-Kelley, 2009). As political structures vary, this is not the case in every setting and we should expect to see different reform life-cycles in China, Singapore and Hong Kong to those in Europe or the US. Equally, when there is broad political consensus over a reform, we might expect it to have more longevity, such as the Curriculum for Excellence reforms in Scotland (Priestley and Humes, 2010). Many writers acknowledge frenetic reform activities (for example, Ball et al., 2012). We illustrate the issues with reference to the '14–19 Centre Research Study' (CReSt, Baird et al., 2011) conducted with 52 schools in England and return to the broader themes later.

Reforms keep educational systems busy managing changes. They chew up a great deal of resources in staff time, costs for textbooks, software developments, training courses, policy documents and so on. They need to be worth this investment, and yet there is repeated questioning of the quality of curricula and assessments in line with different values. Headteachers interviewed for the CReSt study were engaging with a broad range of educational reforms from funding arrangements, through the school leaving age being raised, to the requirement for partnership working between educational institutions and the revision of national assessments. The modern way of managing reform in many Western societies involves:

> … a top-down approach to governance, which relies on unelected arm's length agencies, policy-steering mechanisms and institutional autonomy to shape the organisational landscape and 14–19 provision. (Pring et al., 2009: 169)

We return to some of these governance issues in the next section on the pervasive performativity challenge. For now, suffice to say that headteachers are corralled into behaving in line with policy through funding and inspection systems, performance-related pay and so on. Despite this, headteachers in the CReSt study demonstrated their strategic leadership by carefully questioning the extent to which they would engage with specific policies.

Although central governments view policy through a top–down agenda, it has long been recognised that policy is not always implemented fully – and sometimes not at all (for example, Bowe et al., 1992).

Six policy tests were gleaned from the interviews with headteachers, which articulated how headteachers decided the extent to which they would incorporate policies in the strategies for their schools and colleges (see Figure 51.1). Headteachers questioned whether the policies were relevant and in the best interests of their students. As there was so much policy activity, experienced headteachers knew that not all of the policies would last, and they carefully considered each in this knowledge. The long-term sustainability of the policy upon the institution was considered, as well as the fit (or clash) with other policies. Interestingly, the similarity of current policies to other policies was often discussed. Headteachers evaluated current policies alongside previous ones to unpick whether there were benefits or drawbacks, as they might have invested a great deal in previous, flawed policies or be disappointed by revisionist policies.

Naturally, too, there were power issues associated with policies, and headteachers considered whether they needed to comply with them due to legal or other pressures. Other literature has cast schools as being at the mercy of policy (Lumby, 2002), as being change-resistant (Hargreaves, 2005) or as actively transforming policies as they integrate them into their practices (Ball et al., 2012). However, the CReSt study provided evidence of the strategic, rational choices that headteachers make when faced with the barrage of policy reforms directed at them by central government. This is cheering because without such leadership, the teachers and students in schools would be caught up in the waves of reform activity to an even greater extent than they are now (Day and Smethem, 2009).

Reforms are politically driven in many contexts. Further, we observe cycles of reform in which themes are revisited with policy 'solutions' that appear to tackle at

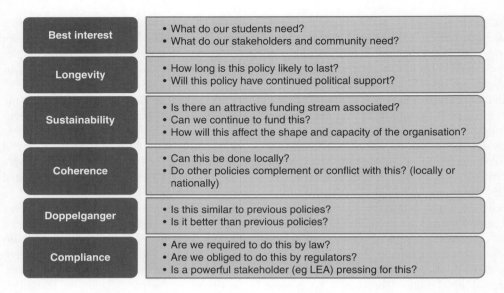

Figure 51.1   Policy tests – how headteachers decide the extent to incorporate policies in their strategies

least similar problems. An example of this in England would be the functional skills tests, designed to address weak literacy and numeracy of a worryingly high minority of school leavers. This new test followed Key Skills, Basic Skills and Core Skills initiatives. Experience of reforms and their lack of impact, or the lack of consensus regarding a positive impact, disenfranchises educators. Not only do reform cycles like this court demotivation of the teaching profession, they waste resources, especially when the opportunity cost of a better use of those resources is considered.

Challenge 3 – Globalisation

Countries used to develop their national education system taking into consideration their own culture, local context and history. Contemporary economics and globalisation have shifted the focus to education systems that aim to develop global citizens, and where international benchmarking is a legitimate activity (Kamens, 2013). Giddens' classic definition of globalisation is as follows:

> …the intensification of worldwide social relations which link distant localities in such a way that local happenings are shaped by events occurring many miles away and vice-versa. This is a dialectical process because such local happenings may move in an observed direction from the very distanciated relations that shaped them. Local transformation is as much a part of globalization as the lateral extension of social connections across time and space. (Giddens, 1990: 64)

In the field of assessment, the development of international large-scale assessment studies such as TIMSS (Trends in International Mathematics and Science Study), PIRLS (Progress in International Reading Literacy Study) and PISA (Programme for International Student Assessment) have signalled the increase in competitive global education systems. Policymakers around the world now respond to a nation's results on international tests, in comparison with others. In particular, PISA has had a major influence, becoming the 'sine qua non of education policy-making in Europe' (Grek, 2012: 243). In England, this was evident in 2010, when the then Secretary of State for Education, Michael Gove commented upon England's

PISA results, indicating that the results of the international tests tell us that the solutions to higher standards and more equality for education in England lie abroad:

> Today's PISA report underlines the urgent need to reform our school system. We need to learn from the best-performing countries. Other regions and nations have succeeded in closing the gap and in raising attainment for all students at the same time. They have made opportunity more equal, democratised access to knowledge and placed an uncompromising emphasis on higher standards all at the same time. These regions and nations – from Alberta to Singapore, Finland to Hong Kong, Harlem to South Korea should be our inspiration. (DfE, 2010)

The international tests have drawn education into competition in the knowledge economy. Issues regarding standards and what counts as valuable learning are now discussed amongst policymakers as well as researchers. International testing has also led to 'policy borrowing' where countries adapt ideas from afar to their local context (Phillips, 2004). There has also been 'travelling' policy (Jones and Alexiadou, 2001), which is 'globalizing trends in pursuit of successful competition in the new knowledge economy… (and) supra and transnational agency activity, as well as common agendas' (Ozga and Jones, 2006: 1–2). Very often the perceived answer for raising standards has been standardised testing, accountability measures and national standards, as seen in US and England (Au, 2007).

Kamens (2013) claimed that national societies are increasingly perceived as open systems as globalisation has intensified. Previously, focus upon individual countries was perceived positively – it was acknowledged, for example, that France would educate students to be citizens of France, in their tradition of Cartesian logic and philosophy, with the ideal of the rational citizen and detached from religion. The new way, following globalisation and the rise of supranational organisations, such as the World Bank, UNESCO, United Nations, European Union and the OECD, is that all countries now educate their students for 'the world' society, and the OECD is seen as the 'unelected world ministry of education' (Meyer, cited in Kamens, 2013: 123).

A notable exception is Finland, which is a high-performing country that counters global trends on curriculum and assessment reforms, national tests and inspections. It continues to be a country with state-funded schools for all students, no national tests and no official league tables. According to the Finnish scholar Pasi Sahlberg, this is the Finnish way: the Finnish dream of education is that it is made in Finland, owned by the Finnish and not rented (Sahlberg, 2011: 7). However, Finland is still party to this globalisation in another way because there has been a huge volume of educational tourism to Finland to find out how they do so well in the international test league tables.

Nonetheless, the globalisation of education has created an international market for edu-businesses that deliver curriculum and assessment packages to countries that are eager to offer mass education for all, purportedly in support of the Millennium Development Goals (Ball, 2009, 2012). Over the past thirty years or so globalisation has been neoliberal, with markets promoted over the state and regulation and individual advancement or self-interest over the collective good and common well-being (Ball, 2012: 2). In such systems, the individual will be responsible for their own 'self-capitalising', and critics such as Ball (2012) suggest that it is the beginning of the end of education in its welfare form. One of the concerns regarding globalisation is how international tests, such as PISA, influence national education systems and national capacities to construct curricula and assessment and to self-evaluate. The process of globalisation shifts the power to do these things to the supranational agencies, meaning that there is less trust and less investment in professional capacity at the national, local level. Indeed, professionals are governed through target setting, which leads to our next challenge.

Challenge 4 – Pervasive Performativity

We noted in the introduction to this chapter how assessment data have risen to power as part of the neoliberal hegemony and the governing of people and institutions through data (Ozga, 2012). Power (1997) outlined how the notion of audit was extended into our thinking about how professionals and institutions must be governed. With a combination of constant target setting and auditing, professionals are on treadmills of somebody else's making (Peck, 2002). No longer are governments responsible for the delivery of state systems – in the 'hollow state' (Rhodes, 1997), the public sector has shrunk and it provides fewer services directly. Instead, agencies have been set up to perform audits of professionals and institutions.

Thus, the kinds of targets set really matter because rational actors within such systems will seek to find ways of meeting those targets efficiently. Goodhart's Law (1975) comes into play, which states that 'When a measure becomes a target, it ceases to be a good measure.' Translated into educational achievement targets, professionals and institutions are driven by the system to maximise achievement scores efficiently. Production of higher scores in tests can then replace the original learning aims, resulting in students being drilled for examination performances to the detriment of deep and broad understanding (Au, 2007; Darling-Hammond, 2010; Madaus et al., 2009). In a survey of teachers in England, one-third of the respondents considered that the target-driven regime they were working under could compromise their professional integrity. One teacher (Richardson, 2012) commented to the BBC on the survey results as follows:

> In some cases I end up virtually rewriting my students' homework to match the marking criteria, rather than teach them my subject, French. I do this because there is simply not time to do both!

Maximising efficiency in these systems is known as performativity (Lyotard, 1984), involving performance to meet targets without necessarily a good alignment between professional beliefs and goals and those of the system. An institutional level, a school might choose particular qualifications due to the currency they have in league tables, rather than their educational benefits for pupils (Baird et al., 2011). This performativity culture has had a number of adverse, unintended consequences, as the numbers produced from assessment systems have taken on a life of their own, supposedly signifying student learning, teacher performance and school effectiveness at a stroke (Ball, 2003; Hanson, 2000).

With attention drawn to these indicators, the government and their many agencies can point to the shortcomings of the education system without delegating responsibility for fixing the problems. Professionals within the system are therefore caught in a bind because it is hard to argue against transparent accounting mechanisms in a blanket fashion. Further, the agenda is rarely upon analysing the problems or their solutions. Public debates about the quality of our education systems therefore assume a scapegoating narrative, with teachers being blamed for poor educational results (Holland, 2013; Thrupp, 2009). With the increase in accountability systems and their associated transparency, we might anticipate more trust within our education systems, but the opposite is true (O'Neill, 2005). Professionals within these systems, in this case teachers, become disengaged and alienated because the systems do not reflect their local priorities, needs and values. They undermine human capacity (McNeil, 1988; Shepard, 2000) because the targets are set and monitored externally and do not require professionals to think strategically or deeply for themselves about what the targets should be in their context. Indeed, in large part due to the bureaucracy around meeting the targets, they actively discourage professional engagement with pedagogical considerations that could have a real and lasting impact upon the very thing that is of interest here: learning. In England, where the performativity project has reached a mature phase, teachers might even swallow the targets whole as the only acceptable way of running a school (Clapham, 2014).

The challenge of performativity will be intensified by advances in technology. Some educational institutions already think it is acceptable to monitor their teachers using videos in the classroom (Warnick, 2008). With CCTV cameras watching our movements in so many areas of our lives, this is a small step from the broader societal changes. Further, the internet has brought great leaps in how we are able to search and manage large volumes of, perhaps diverse, data. Learning analytics (Siemens, 2013), in which these large volumes of data can be crunched to produce summaries, flags or indices, is an active research area. Some propose to collect a wide range of data about students from current systems and put them to use for assessment purposes. For example, one might wish to predict who is likely to fail or drop out of a course on the basis of general patterns of student behaviour (Eynon, 2013). In the future, that information could be used to set student targets and reminders, or even to select students for a course in the first place. Learning could be surveilled and the data aggregated to tell us how good the teachers are and which countries have the best education systems.

Challenge 5 – Rising Educational Standards or Grade Inflation?

Educational outcomes are rising in many countries. The proportion of people in tertiary education rose by 3 per cent per year between 2000 and 2012 in OECD countries (OECD, 2014). Taking England as an example, we see that the proportion of students graduating with good degrees (upper second or first class) was 50 per cent in 1999, but just over two-thirds by 2013 (Higher Education Statistics Agency (HESA), 2000, 2014). In 1951, when the A-level school-leaving examinations were first introduced, there were 37,000 candidates and

approximately 8 per cent were awarded a grade A. By 2011, the entry figure was ten times this level and the grade A rate had gone up to 26 per cent. In 1986, just under a quarter of students who took the national examinations at age 16 achieved five passes at grade C or above (Bolton, 2012). By 2014, over half of 16-year-olds in England achieved five good passes, including English and maths (DfE, 2015). All of this is good news if these figures are interpreted as things getting better, but there are differing positions on this. For some, the rise in outcomes indicates *falling* standards, arguing that as the standards for a degree or an examination grade, have been reduced, to produce higher outcomes without the requisite educational achievements.

Those who equate rising outcomes as, at least in part, falling standards, often use the term 'grade inflation'. This is not a technical, assessment term. In 84 publications using the term in scientific journals, only 56 presented research (Oleinik, 2009). In contrast, 989 articles in newspapers and magazines discussed grade inflation between 1993 and 2009 (Oleinik, 2009). The term appears to have been coined[5] in a 1975 *Science* Editorial by Amitai Etzioni where the concern focused upon increases in grades in tertiary education in the US. The term is borrowed from economics, and it is useful to reflect upon the analogy that is created in its use. Inflation is an increase in prices.[6] It makes no sense to compare this directly with educational outcomes because 'price' does not have a direct analogy; all metaphors have limitations in their explanatory power. However, the use of this metaphor appeals to the listener in two senses. Users of the metaphor might not always be aware of these two senses, though Etzioni's Editorial is consistent with what follows.

The first – falling pound – metaphor is the analogy with the value of money being lowered by inflation – you can buy less tomorrow with a pound than you can today. Thus, the idea is that students who gain a particular level of skills cost more in grades now than they did in the past; we give them higher grades than we would have done before. The value of grades has been weakened.

Quantitative easing[7] is a technique in which governments print more money to tackle the economic circumstances. The second – quantitative easing – sense of the grade inflation analogy is that, even if people had the same level of skills as in the past, there are just too many of them with the grades. This causes problems for the selective use of grades for jobs and higher education. This sense of the inflation analogy conjures scenes of people needing wheelbarrows of money to buy a loaf of bread in countries where rampant inflation took hold, such as in Zimbabwe in 2007 (Hanke and Krus, 2012).

Underlying these two senses (falling pound and quantitative easing) are conceptually different views of education and standard setting. Individuals need not subscribe entirely to one or the other camp, even if the approaches are conceptually distinct. In the falling pound metaphor, our interest is in the knowledge and skills that candidates have, which aligns best with criterion referencing approaches to standard setting. In this worldview, standards are defined by the knowledge and skills that are demonstrated in the assessment. Theoretically, then, all students – or no students – might pass an examination with this approach to standard setting. In the quantitative easing metaphor, interest is drawn to the number of candidates with the grades. This approach aligns to norm-referenced approaches to standard setting to a greater extent. In norm referencing, a fixed proportion of students are awarded the grades in the examination, no matter the knowledge and skills demonstrated. In practice, most standard-setting systems use a combination of these two views to set standards (Cizek and Bunch, 2007).

When standards are attacked, the argument typically jumps from one conceptual worldview to the other, apparently without the speakers recognising that the argument has lost clarity. This matters because we need a firm approach to defining whether standards have risen or if we have grade inflation. If grades are to hold their value, putting pegs in the ground regarding how educational standards are measured and monitored is a big challenge for the future. This goes back to Challenge 1 – the crisis of knowledge – because the lack of consensus on what counts as valuable learning means that there is a constant shift in curricula and assessment content. What students know and can do today is not the same as yesteryear.

DISCUSSION

Conceptual, theoretical and power dimensions of what counts as valuable learning run through this chapter. In the first challenge, we discussed the crisis of knowledge and the political disputes that can arise because of the lack of consensus regarding curricula and assessments. Education is not recognised as a discipline by some (Pietig, 1984) and it is clear that non-specialists commonly regard themselves as 'experts by experience' to use a term that has been adopted in healthcare. That is, people believe they have expertise to bring to decisions on curricula and assessment because they have been recipients of education. This must be partly true, but the question is what role this kind of expertise should play. Equally, there are questions regarding the role of politicians. Discussions about the quality of curricula and assessments often play out in the media too, which can be a powerful force for shaping public opinion.

In each of these fora (politics, media, laypeople), the rules of engagement with respect to treatment of information sources and the way in which arguments are put differ. For example, the media seek to create interest in a story by dramatising issues with oppositional ideas. An example is the treatment of global warming. Watching news broadcasts on global warming, it appears that equally pitted experts simply disagree about the evidence for global warming, but in fact there is consensus amongst scientists that global warming is happening (Oreskes, 2004). Agreement does not make for a good media story and journalists also have ethical responsibilities to show a range of voices. Neither of these considerations makes for good science. Given different agendas and ways of knowing, we can anticipate different positions from stakeholder groups regarding curricula and assessment.

Additionally, it is clear that there is no one group in charge of the future of curricula and assessment. Politicians and policymakers might frequently reform these areas of public life, but as we argued in this chapter, teachers have strategic ways of engaging with these policies that affect the extent of their implementation in practice. The damaging effects of endless reform cycles – Challenge 2 – surely need to be recognised and ways out of these downward spirals should be constructed. Due to the 'hollow state', there are fewer structures in society to put the brakes on zealous politicians or policymakers in many countries. However, not all countries are suffering from spiraling reform cycles to the same extent. Some cultures, such as Scandinavian societies, trust teachers and researchers to a larger extent, placing the responsibility upon them to improve the education system (Hopfenbeck et al., 2015). Cross-political party consensus would also seem to be a prerequisite for stability in curricula and assessment (Telhaug, 2006).

Above, there was an implication that education is a scientific discipline. How science itself is defined and whether educational research is based upon scientific principles are also sources of controversy (Shulman, 1999). Our point here is not that there are interesting philosophical differences in methodology used by educational researchers, but that ways of knowing differ. At the edges, this blurs distinctions between academic research and work conducted by think tanks or consultants (such as KPMG or OECD) because the research methods used might be similar, but their purposes, audiences and levels of independence differ. Universities have become increasingly commercial spaces, such that academics conduct consultancy work as well as traditional academic research. Without clear boundaries, it is harder to unpick the evidential basis for claims made. Questions of quality and the trustworthiness of sources of information are endemic.

Let us look at a short case study to illustrate the issues. Capitalising upon technology, curricula can be delivered to students through Massive Open Online Courses (MOOCs). Claims for MOOCs have been manifold: that universities will no longer be needed, that they will produce deeper learning, build global communities, motivate disenfranchised students and develop new methods of pedagogy (Breslow et al., 2013). Online podcasts and other materials are useful educational resources and will surely play a larger part in the future of curricula and assessment; however, the claims made for MOOCs have not come to fruition. Indeed, only 10 per cent of enrolled students typically complete MOOCs (Breslow et al., 2013). Interaction between students and teachers, as well as meaningful, face-to-face discussion between students, and multiple ways of looking at difficult concepts have long been known to foster learning. Learning is not simply online exposure to ideas. The crisis of knowledge and lack of trust in traditional sources of expertise create a situation in which superficially attractive arguments can gain attention and funding. Neoliberalism has created a space for edu-business, including consultancies, to make claims and create markets. Evaluating the claims through careful research takes time, but scholarship is needed if we are to make real gains with curricula and assessment in the twenty-first century. More work is needed on criteria for evaluating claims in education.

The above challenges accumulate, forming a shared unease that children are going to be disadvantaged in a global jobs market. There are concerns that standards of education are ever in decline and other countries are out-performing our own on international tests. But education is not economics and the relationship between them is not simple

(Wolf, 2002). Better models of ways to construct and modify curricula and how they interact with learning are needed to short-cut the fretting about standards and the endless policy reforms. Unless the relationship between curricula assessment and learning is given more attention, the future will be a world of busy fools, striving for targets that divert attention and energy from deep learning. Amidst this future is the prospect of increased surveillance of our behaviour, in the name of assessment. The extent to which this will bring about educational good needs careful consideration.

CONCLUSION

A big question for the twenty-first century is whether there will be a world curriculum. Globalisation and the impact of international tests mean that the world is a smaller place and work has already started on spelling out the common curricula in particular areas, such as mathematics, reading, science, citizenship, problem-solving and now global competence. In 2018, PISA will include a test of 'global competence', which will indicate the extent to which a country's 15-year-olds have the knowledge and skills to work and interact with others internationally. To score well on global competence, knowledge of other cultures and certain attitudes such as curiosity and openness are needed. As such, the OECD is setting a new way for countries to compete – on the extent to which they have what must surely be an elite group of children who will grow up as globe-trotting knowledge workers. The relationship between socioeconomic status and global competence scores is likely to be high. We predict an interesting political dynamic in relation to this test because of its close relationship with neoliberal politics. Some countries might not take part because they do not necessarily want to grow a nation of knowledge workers of this kind, preferring instead to value local culture to a larger extent. The

relationships between local and global contexts and cultures can still form part of the curriculum where nations choose to focus more upon local culture.

Research has documented the 'steering at a distance' and 'governing by numbers', which we see through international tests and supranational institutions (Ozga, 2012). Further, policy solutions are borrowed by one country from another, with external experts and agendas holding sway over the local. However, policies are not adopted wholesale by countries; instead, they are adapted to the local context, albeit using the same language as the source policy (Carvalho, 2012: 183). The supranational is uninterested in the local, in what matters to people's lives in communities and in nation building. We predict more tension in the relationship between the supranational curricula and assessment and the local in the twenty-first century as educators formulate views about what the supranational does and does not offer them for progress in education.

How is a rational actor to behave in a world with these challenges? Education professionals cannot ignore them because they impinge upon them directly; for many upon their very livelihoods, with test outcomes used in accountability mechanisms. Control of the curriculum and assessment can be exercised in a highly undemocratic manner (Kelly, 2009), which makes it very difficult for individuals to have influence. Neither will a sanguine approach see educationalists through entirely, as the goalposts are constantly changing. You can try to play the game, but the rules will change after the game has started. At the root of these changes are different political views on what counts as knowledge and the purpose of education.

Many educationalists will see advantages in accountability systems as they improve transparency and are intended to provide feedback that will improve performance. Some will favour outcome-based accountability systems, whilst others might argue for process-based systems. After all, test outcomes are not produced by teaching alone and therefore there could be more emphasis upon the quality of teaching and other school processes in accountability mechanisms. However, some see these arguments as an excuse to stitch up the system in favour of the professionals within it. In research on management accountability systems, it has been shown that those who favour process-based accountability are more likely to lean to the left politically and those who favour outcome-based accountability are more likely to be towards the right of the political spectrum (Tetlock, 2011). There are deep, complex value systems underpinning our beliefs about accountability systems that determine our response to the tension between overly trusting professionals at one extreme versus Stalinist control at the other. Finding a happy balance between these is theoretically possible, but in practice there will be disagreements about whether this has been reached (Tetlock, 2011: 701–2).

Returning to the teacher and the classroom setting, we know that good teaching requires reflective practitioners (Schön, 1988) who can think for themselves. Automatons, delivering training programmes devised elsewhere are increasingly defunct with advances in technology. Therefore, education systems must foster, not undermine, reflective teaching practices, in which teachers can adapt to the reality of the contexts in which they work. Teacher professional engagement with the design of curriculum and assessment systems and their operation is essential to teacher development and to the quality of those systems (Stobart, 2008). Some countries readily recognise these issues and have policy formation practices that engage teachers, others use superficial public consultation to masquerade as being open and a third group do not even go to the lengths of pretending to be open.

The central message of this chapter is that if we want highly professional teachers and a good quality education system, we can anticipate serious debate, but also institutional resistance to teachers' questioning of existing (and changing) curricula and examinations. The alternative path is to accept curricula and examination targets set in some distant place, which change regularly, keep teachers busy and undermine professional teaching capacity and confidence in the education system. Certainly, it is hard to see how this alternative will improve matters, although it might be less expensive than policies addressing educational processes, such as professional development programmes. Weakened state education systems become less attractive in this scenario, and those who can, will send their children to private schools, which might not be under the same controls. If we want a high standard of education for all in society, private schooling is not the answer because it breeds higher levels of inequality, which in turn breeds social problems rather than solutions (Piketty, 2014; Ravitch, 2013; Sahlberg, 2011; Wilkinson and Pickett, 2009). Left to their own devices, the five challenges raised in this chapter conspire against good state education. Most of the problems we have identified derive from neoliberal hegemony. Thus, the challenge for those of us who value good state education is to overcome the potentially insidious effects of these challenges.

NOTES

1 Some league table systems adjust for the intake of schools, but this does not make them more stable indicators over time.
2 See http://www.p21.org/our-work/p21-framework (accessed 15 July 2015).
3 See http://www.atc21s.org/ (accessed 15 July 2015).
4 See http://www.deseco.admin.ch/ (accessed 15 July 2015).
5 Electronic search conducted on 28 November 2014 using the Oxford University SOLO search engine. http://libguides.bodleian.ox.ac.uk/content.php?pid=228044&sid=2357096 (accessed 15 July 2015).
6 See http://lexicon.ft.com/Term?term=inflation (accessed 15 July 2015).
7 See http://lexicon.ft.com/Term?term=quantitative-easing (accessed 15 July 2015).

REFERENCES

Au, W. (2007) 'High-stakes testing and curricular control: a qualitative metasynthesis', *Educational Researcher*, 36: 258–67. doi:10.3102/0013189X07306523.

Baird, J. and Lee-Kelley, L. (2009) 'The dearth of managerialism in implementation of national examinations policy', *Journal of Education Policy*, 24(1): 55–81. doi:10.1080/02680930802382938.

Baird, J., Elwood, J., Duffy, G., Feiler, A., O'Boyle, A., Rose, J., Stobart, G. and McWhirter A. (2011) *14–19 Centre Research Study: Educational Reforms in Schools and Colleges in England Annual Report*. London: Qualifications and Curriculum Development Agency. Available from http://oucea.education.ox.ac.uk/wordpress/wp-content/uploads/2013/04/CReSt-Annual-Report-Final-whole.pdf (accessed 15 July 2015).

Ball, S.J. (2003) 'The teacher's soul and the terrors of performativity', *Journal of Education Policy*, 18(2): 215–28. doi:10.1080/0268093022000043065.

Ball, S.J. (2009) 'Privatising education, privatising education policy, privatising educational research: network governance and the "competition state"', *Journal of Education Policy*, 24(1): 83–99.

Ball, S.J. (2012) *Global Education Inc. New Policy Networks and the Neo-Liberal Imaginery*. Abingdon, UK: Routledge.

Ball, S.J., Maguire, M. and Braun, A. (2012) *How Schools Do Policy: Policy Enactments in Secondary Schools*. Abingdon, UK: Routledge.

Berry, R. and Adamson, B. (eds.) (2011) *Assessment Reform in Education: Policy and Practice. Education in the Asia-Pacific Region: Issues, Concerns and Prospects,* Vol. 14. Springer Dordrecht: Springer.

Birch, K. and Mykhnenko, V. (2009) 'Varieties of neoliberalism? Restructuring in large industrially dependent regions across Western and Eastern Europe', *Journal of Economic Geography*, 9: 355–80. doi:10.1093/jeg/lbn058.

Birch, K. and Mykhnenko, V. (2010) *The Rise and Fall of Neoliberalism: The Collapse of an Economic Order?* London: Zed Books.

Bishop, A.S. (1971) *The Rise of a Central Authority for English Education*. Cambridge: Cambridge University Press.

Blum, A., Goldstein, H. and Guerin-Pace, F. (2001) 'International Adult Literacy Survey (IALS): an analysis of the international comparisons of adult literacy', *Assessment in Education: Principles, Policy and Practice*, 8(2): 225–46. doi: 10.1080/09695940123977.

Bolton, P. (2012) *Education: Historical Statistics*. Standard Note: SN/SG/4252. London, House of Commons Library.

Bowe, R., Ball, S.J. and Gold, A. (1992) *Reforming Education and Changing Schools*. London: Routledge.

Bradbury, A. (2011) 'Rethinking assessment and inequality: the production of disparities in attainment in early years education', *Journal of Education Policy*, 26(5): 655–76.

Breslow, L., Pritchard, D.E., DeBoer, J., Stump, G.S., Ho, A.D. and Seaton, D.T. (2013) 'Studying learning in the worldwide classroom. Research into edX's first MOOC', *Research and Practice in Assessment*, 8 (March): 13–25.

Carvalho, L.M. (2012) 'The fabrications and travels of a knowledge-policy instrument', *European Educational Research Journal*, 11(2): 172–88.

Cizek, G.J and Bunch, M.B. (2007) *Standard Setting: A Guide to Establishing and Evaluating Performance Standards on Tests*. Thousand Oaks, CA: Sage Publications.

Clapham, A. (2014) 'Post-fabrication and putting on a show: examining the impact of short notice inspections', *British Educational Research Journal*. 41(4): 613–28. doi: 10.1002/berj.3159.

Darling-Hammond, L. (2010) *The Flat World and Education: How America's Commitment to Equity Will Determine Our Future*. New York: Teachers College Press.

Day, C. and Smethem, L. (2009) 'The effects of reform: have teachers really lost their sense of professionalism?', *Journal of Educational Change*, 10(2–3): 141–57. doi:10.1007/s10833-009-9110-5.

Department for Education (DfE) (2010) *Major International Study Shows England's 15-year-olds Performing Poorly in Mathematics, Science and Reading*. Available from www.gov.uk/government/news/major-international-study-shows-englands-15-year-olds-performing-poorly-in-mathematics-science-and-reading (accessed 15 July 2015)/

Department for Education (DfE) (2013) *English Literature: GCSE Subject Content and*

Assessment Objectives. Available from https://www.gov.uk/government/uploads/system/uploads/attachment_data/file/254498/GCSE_English_literature.pdf (accessed 15 July 2015).

Department for Education (DfE) (2015) *Revised GCSE and equivalents results in England, 2013 to 2014.* Statistical First Release. SFR 02/2015. Available from https://www.gov.uk/government/uploads/system/uploads/attachment_data/file/406314/SFR_02_2015-revised_GCSE_and_equivalents.pdf. (accessed 15 July 2015).

Etzioni, A. (1975) 'Reports on increasing grade inflation in higher education in the United States and offers and suggestions for curbing the phenomenon', *Science,* 190 (4210): 101.

European Commission (2011) *The Challenge of Shadow Education: Private Tutoring and its Implications for Policy Makers in the European Union. An Independent Report Prepared for the European Commission by the NESSE Network of Experts.* Available from http://bookshop.europa.eu/en/the-challenge-of-shadow-education-pbNC3011077/ (accessed 15 July 2015).

Eynon, R. (2013) 'The rise of Big Data: what does it mean for education, technology, and media research?', *Learning, Media and Technology,* 38: 237–40. doi: 10.1080/17439884.2013.771783.

Frederiksen, J.R and Collins, A. (1989) 'A systems approach to educational testing', *Educational Researcher,* 18(9): 27–32.

Giddens, A. (1990) *The Consequences of Modernity.* Stanford, CA: Stanford University Press.

Goldstein, H. (1997) 'Methods in school effectiveness research', *School Effectiveness and School Improvement,* 8(4): 369–95. doi:10.1080/0924345970080401

Goodhart, C.A.E. (1975). 'Problems of Monetary Management: The U.K. Experience'. Papers in Monetary Economics (Reserve Bank of Australia) I.

Grek. S. (2012) 'What PISA knows and can do: studying the role of national actors in the making of PISA', *European Educational Research Journal,* 11(2): 243–54.

Hanke, S.H. and Krus, N.E., 'World Hyperinflations' (August 15, 2012). Cato Institute Working Paper. Available at SSRN: http://ssrn.com/abstract=2226980 or http://dx.doi.org/10.2139/ssrn.2226980. (accessed 15 July 2015.)

Hanson, F.A (1993) *Testing Testing. Social Consequences of the Examined Life.* Oakland, CA: University of California Press.

Hanson, F.A. (2000) 'How tests create what they are intended to measure', in A. Filer (ed.), *Assessment. Social Practice and Social Product.* London, Routledge. pp. 67–81.

Hargreaves, A. (2005) 'Educational change takes ages: life, career and generational factors in teachers' emotional responses to educational change', *Teaching and Teacher Education,* 21(8): 967–83. doi:10.1016/j.tate.2005.06.007.

Higham, J. and Yeomans, D. (2010) 'Working together? Partnership approaches to 14–19 education in England', *British Educational Research Journal,* 36(3): 379–401.

Higher Education Statistics Agency (HESA) (2000) 'Qualifications Obtained by and Examination Results of Higher Education Students at Higher Education Institutions in the United Kingdom for the Academic Year 1998/99'. Available from http://www.hesa.ac.uk/content/view/934/161/. (accessed 15 July 2015.)

Higher Education Statistics Agency (HESA) (2014) 'Higher Education Student Enrolments and Qualifications Obtained at Higher Education Institutions in the United Kingdom for the Academic Year 2012/13'. Available from https://www.hesa.ac.uk/pr/3103-statistical-first-release-197 (accessed 15 July 2015.)

Holland, J. (2013) 'Teachers make handy scapegoats, but spiralling inequality is really what ails our education system', *SCOPE Stanford Center for Opportunity Policy in Education.* Available from https://edpolicy.stanford.edu/news/articles/743 (accessed 15 July 2015).

Hood, C. (1989) 'Public administration and public policy: intellectual', *Australian Journal of Public Administration,* 48(4): 13.

Hopfenbeck, T.N., Florez, M.T. and Tolo, A. (2015) 'Balancing tensions in educational policy reforms: large-scale implementation of assessment for learning in Norway', *Assessment in Education, Principles, Policy and Practice,* 22(1): 44–60.

Jones, K. and Alexiadou, N. (2001) 'Travelling Policy: Local Spaces', paper in The Global and the National: Reflections on the Experience of Three European States' paper presented at the European Conference on Educational Research, Lille, 5–8 September.

Kamens, D.H. (2013) 'Globalization and the emergence of an audit culture: PISA and the search for "best practices" and magic bullets,' in H.D. Meyer and A. Benavot (eds.), *PISA, Power and Policy: The Emergence of Global Educational Governance*. Oxford: Symposium Books. pp. 117–40.

Kelly, A.V. (2009) *The Curriculum: Theory and Practice*. 6th edn. London: Sage Publications.

Kennedy, M. (2014) 'To Kill a Mockingbird and Of Mice and Men axed as Gove orders more Brit Lit'. *The Guardian*, 25 May 2014. Available from http://www.theguardian.com/education/2014/may/25/mockingbird-mice-and-men-axed-michael-gove-gcse. (accessed 15 July 2015.)

Leckie, G. and Goldstein, H. (2009) 'The limitations of using school league tables to inform school choice', *Journal of the Royal Statistical Society: Series A (Statistics in Society)*, 172(4): 835–51 doi:10.1111/j.1467-985X.2009.00597.

Lumby, J. (2002) 'Vision and Strategic planning', in T. Bush and L. Bell (eds.), *The Principles and Practice of Management*. London: Sage Publications. pp. 86–100.

Lyotard, J.-F. (1984) *The Postmodern Condition: A Report on Knowledge (Theory and History of Literature)*. Vol. 10. Manchester, UK: Manchester University Press.

Madaus, G.F., Russell, M.K. and Higgins, J. (2009) *The Paradoxes of High Stakes Testing: How they Affect Students, their Parents, Teachers, Principals, Schools, and Society*. Charlotte, NC: Information Age Publishing.

McNeil, L.M. (1988) *Contradictions of Control: School Structure and School Knowledge*. New York, NY: Routledge.

Newton, P.E. (2007) 'Clarifying the purposes of educational assessment', *Assessment in Education*, 14(2): 149–70.

New York Times (2001) 'Alabama Retains Disclaimer on Evolution'. *New York Times*, 10 November 2001. Available from http://www.nytimes.com/2001/11/10/us/alabama-retains-disclaimer-on-evolution.html. (accessed 15 July 2015).

Nuttall, D.L. (1987) 'The validity of assessments', *European Journal of Psychology of Education*, 2(2): 109–18.

President Barack Obama (2009) 'Remarks to the United States Hispanic Chamber of Commerce.' 10 March. Public Papers of the Presidents of the United States. Book 1 – January 20 to June 30, 2009.

Oleinik, A. (2009) 'Does education corrupt? Theories of grade inflation', *Educational Research Review*, 4, 156–164.

O'Neill, O. (2005) *Assessment, Public Accountability and Trust*. Available from http://www.cambridgeassessment.org.uk (accessed 25 May 2007).

Oreskes, N. (2004) 'Beyond the ivory tower: the scientific consensus on climate change', *Science*, 306(5702): 1686. doi: 10.1126/science.1103618.

Organisation for Economic Co-operation and Development (OECD) (1997) *Literacy Skills for the Knowledge Society*. Paris: Organisation for Economic Co-operation and Development.

Organisation for Economic Co-operation and Development (OECD) (2014) *Education at a Glance 2014: OECD Indicators*. Paris: Organisation for Economic Co-operation and Development. Available from http://dx.doi.org/10.1787/eag-2014-en (accessed 15 July 2015).

Ozga, J. (2012) 'Introduction: assessing PISA', *European Educational Research Journal*, 11(2): 166–71.

Ozga, J. and Jones, R. (2006) 'Travelling and embedded policy: the case of knowledge transfer', *Journal of Education Policy*, 21: 1–17.

Peck, J. (2002) 'Political economies of scale: fast policy, interscalar relations, and neoliberal workfare', *Economic Geography*, 78(3): 331–60.

Phillips, D. (2004) 'Toward a theory of policy attraction in education', in G. Steiner-Khamsi (ed.), *The Global Politics of Educational Borrowing and Lending*. New York, NY: Teachers College, Columbia University. pp. 54–67.

Piketty, T. (2014) *Captial in the Twenty-First Century*. Cambridge, MA: Harvard University Press.

Pietig, J. (1984) 'Is education a discipline?', *The Educational Forum*, 48(3): 365–72. doi: 10.1080/00131728409335915.

Pinar, W.F. (ed.) (2013) *Curriculum: Toward New Identities*. New York, NY: Routledge.

Popham, W.J. (2007) 'Instructional sensitivity of tests: accountability's dire drawback', *Phi Delta Kappan*, 89(2): 146–50.

Popham, W.J. (2011) 'Assessment literacy overlooked: a teacher educator's confession', *The Teacher Educator*, 46(4): 265–73. doi: 10.1080/08878730.2011.605048.

Power, M. (1997) *The Audit Society: Rituals of Verification*. Oxford: Oxford University Press.

Priestley, M. and Humes, W. (2010) 'The development of Scotland's Curriculum for Excellence: amnesia and déjà vu', *Oxford Review of Education*, 36(3): 345–61. doi: 10.1080/03054980903518951.

Pring, R., Hayward, G., Hodgson, A., Johnson, J., Keep, E., Oancea, A., Rees, G., Spours, K. and Wilde, S. (2009) *Education for All: The Future of Education and Training for 14–19 Year Olds*. London: Routledge.

Rata, E. (2012) 'The politics of knowledge in education', *British Educational Research Journal*, 38(1): 103–24.

Ravitch, D. (2013) *Reign of Error: The Hoax of the Privatization Movement and the Danger to America's Public Schools*. New York, NY: Alfred. A. Knopf.

Rhodes, R.A.W. (1997) *Understanding Governance*. Buckingham, UK: Open University Press.

Richardson, H. (2012) 'Exam pressure 'undermining teacher's integrity'. *BBC,* 2 April 2012. Available from http://www.bbc.co.uk/news/education-17564311 (accessed 15 July 2015).

Sahlberg, P. (2011) *Finnish Lessons: What Can the World Learn from Educational Change in Finland?* New York, NY: Teacher College Press.

Schön, D.A. (1988) 'From technical rationality to reflection-in-action', in J. Dowie and A. Elstein (eds.), *Professional Judgment: A Reader in Clinical Decision Making*. Cambridge: Cambridge University Press.

Shabaya, J. and Konadu-Agyemang, K. (2004) 'Unequal access, unequal participation: some spatial and socio-economic dimensions of the gender gap in education in Africa with special reference to Ghana, Zimbabwe and Kenya', *Compare: A Journal of Comparative and International Education*, 34(4): 395–424.

Shepard, L.A. (2000) 'The role of assessment in a learning culture', *Educational Researcher*, 29(7): 4–14.

Shulman, L.S. (1999) 'Taking learning seriously', *Change: The Magazine of Higher Learning*, 31(4): 10–17. doi: 10.1080/00091389909602695.

Siemens, G. (2013) 'Learning analytics: the emergence of a discipline', *American Behavioral Scientist*, 57: 1380–400. doi:10.1177/0002764213498851.

Stobart, G. (2008) *Testing Times: The Uses and Abuses of Assessment*. Abingdon, UK: Routledge.

Tattersall, K. (2007) 'A brief history of policies, practices and issues relating to comparability', in P. Newton, J. Baird, H. Goldstein, H. Patrick and P. Tymms (eds.), *Techniques for Monitoring the Comparability of Examination Standards*. London: Qualifications and Curriculum Authority. Chapter 2. Available at: http://webarchive.nationalarchives.gov.uk/+/www.ofqual.gov.uk/83.aspx (accessed 15 July 2015).

Telhaug, A.O. (2006) 'The Nordic model in education: education as a part of the political system in the last 50 years', *Scandinavian Journal of Educational Research*, 50(3): 245–83.

Tetlock, P.E. (2011) 'Vying for rhetorical high ground in accountability debates: it is easy to look down on those who look soft on', *Administration and Society*, 43(6): 693–703.

Thrupp, M. (2009) 'Teachers, social contexts and the politics of blame', *QTU Professional Magazine,* 24: 6–12.

Voogt, J. and N. Roblin (2012) 'A comparative analysis of international frameworks for 21st century competences: implications for national curriculum policies', *Journal of Curriculum Studies*, 44(3): 299–321.

Warnick, B.R. (2008) 'Surveillance cameras in schools: an ethical analysis', *Harvard Educational Review*, 77(3): 317–43.

Wilkinson, R. and Pickett, K. (2009) *The Spirit Level: Why More Equal Societies Almost Always Do Better*. London: Allen Lane.

Wolf, A. (2002) *Does Education Matter? Myths About Education and Economic Growth*. London: Penguin.

Young, M. (2012) 'The return to subjects: a sociological perspective on the UK Coalition government's approach to the 14–19 curriculum', *The Curriculum Journal*, 22(2): 265–78.

52

Student Assessment and its Relationship with Curriculum, Teaching and Learning in the Twenty-First Century

Deborah Nusche

INTRODUCTION

National learning goals in many OECD school systems have been revised to emphasise the development of complex, cross-curricular competencies in addition to specific knowledge and skills. Despite this general trend, there are pronounced differences in the degree to which countries formulate concrete expectations for student performance to guide classroom practice. Research has revealed challenges in ensuring that curriculum, standards, teaching and assessment are consistent. Although there is a strong ambition to focus school systems increasingly on the development of complex competencies, national frameworks for student assessment are rarely aligned to such ambitions – both central and teacher-based assessments typically focus on a more narrow range of knowledge and skills. Following a review of country practices, this chapter concludes with a range of suggestions and examples for introducing broader assessments to match countries' twenty-first-century learning goals.

This chapter is based on the results of the OECD Review on Evaluation and Assessment Frameworks for Improving School Outcomes, a comprehensive international study of evaluation and assessment policies across 29 school systems. The chapter draws from evidence generated by 25 national background reports prepared by participating countries, 15 country-specific review reports drafted by international review teams (released as a publication series, *OECD Reviews of Evaluation and Assessment in Education*), the Review's final synthesis report *Synergies for Better Learning* (OECD, 2013a) and several related research papers (all available on the project's website at www.oecd.org/edu/evaluation-policy). The Review was conducted between 2009 and 2013 with the objective to provide analysis and policy advice to countries on how evaluation and assessment can be embedded within a consistent framework to support improvements in teaching and learning. Unless otherwise indicated, all information on country practices is drawn from OECD (2013).

Following this introduction, this chapter is organised in four main sections. Section one describes common trends across OECD countries in defining national goals for student learning in the twenty-first century. Section two analyses the degree to which different countries specify concrete expectations for student performance in national curricula and standards. Section three reviews how such learning goals and standards are reflected in assessment policy and practice internationally, and section four discusses a number of ways to ensure better coherence between valued learning goals and student assessment approaches.

DEFINING KEY COMPETENCIES FOR THE TWENTY-FIRST CENTURY

Over the past years, OECD school systems have been undergoing profound changes. Research has added to and in some cases radically changed conceptions of teaching, learning and assessment. Schools and teachers are increasingly being asked to move away from traditional educational approaches focusing primarily on knowledge transmission. The national learning goals in many OECD school systems have been revised accordingly to emphasize the development of complex competencies rather than a narrow focus on specific knowledge and skills. Most OECD curricula now feature a list of key competencies that the school system should seek to promote across all subjects and year levels.

In Europe, with the Recommendation on Key Competences in 2006, all EU member states agreed on a framework of eight 'key competencies' that are seen as necessary for personal fulfilment and development, active citizenship, social inclusion and employment (European Commission, 2011a). These include competencies in communication, mathematics, science and technology as well as learning to learn, social and civic competencies, sense of initiative, entrepreneurship

and cultural awareness and expression. The European Framework highlights that these competencies are underpinned by process dimensions, such as critical thinking, creativity, problem solving and decision taking (European Commission, 2011b; 2012). The European focus on key competencies is reflected across national learning goals in Europe, with most EU member states reporting that they have already changed their primary and secondary school curricula to incorporate elements of the key competencies or even the complete framework (OECD, 2013a).

Similar trends can be observed beyond Europe. The United Nations Educational, Scientific and Cultural Organisation (UNESCO) has been promoting a focus on 'life skills', which it defines as including competencies, such as critical thinking, creativity, ability to organise, social and communication skills, adaptability, problem solving, ability to co-operate on a democratic basis, that are needed for actively shaping a peaceful future (Singh, 2003). The terminology of life skills has been included in several national curricula. In Mexico, for example, the curriculum for basic education was reformed in 2011 around five 'competencies for life' as promoted by UNESCO: lifelong learning; information management; management of situations; coexistence; and life in society (Santiago et al., 2012a).

In the US, the terms most commonly used are that of 'twenty-first-century skills' or 'twenty-first-century competencies'. These were defined by Binkley et al. (2010) as including (1) ways of thinking (creativity, innovation, critical thinking, problem solving, decision making, learning to learn, metacognition); (2) ways of working (communication, collaboration); (3) tools for working (information literacy, ICT literacy); and (3) living in the world (local and global citizenship, life and career, personal and social responsibility). According to the Partnership for 21st Century Skills (P21), the focus on twenty-first-century skills has been incorporated into the educational systems of at least

19 states in the US (see www.p21.org). In Canada, all jurisdictions have, to a varying degree, reshaped curriculum from a focus on knowledge to a focus on performance, with a new emphasis on problem solving and cognitive application of knowledge using higher-level skills beyond recall and comprehension (Fournier and Mildon, forthcoming).

In Australia, the Melbourne Declaration on Educational Goals for Young Australians, released in December 2008, and agreed to by all education ministers through the Ministerial Council on Education, Employment, Training and Youth Affairs (MCEETYA, 2008) sets the overarching goal that all young Australians become successful learners, confident and creative individuals and active and informed citizens (Santiago et al., 2011). Before the introduction of the Australian Curriculum (which includes a set of General Capabilities encompassing the knowledge, skills, behaviours and dispositions that, together with curriculum content in each learning area, will assist students to live and work successfully in the twenty-first century), individual Australian states had already done much pioneering development of broader competency standards and frameworks.

The New Zealand Curriculum, revised in 2007, is organised around five key competencies: (1) thinking; (2) using language, symbols and text; (3) managing self; (4) relating to others and (5) participating and contributing. The curriculum highlights that:

> people use these competencies to live, learn, work and contribute as active members of their communities. More complex than skills, the competencies draw also on knowledge, attitudes, and values in ways that lead to action. They are not separate or stand-alone. They are the key to learning in every area. (See www.nzcurriculum.tki.org.nz)

Across the OECD, several public and private actors are increasingly investing in research and development regarding the teaching and assessment of key competencies. One example is the Assessment and Teaching of 21st Century Skills (ATC21s) project at the University of Melbourne, Australia, which is sponsored by private companies Cisco, Intel and Microsoft, and governed by an executive board comprising ministries of education, academics and industry leaders from a range of countries (www.atc21s.org).

Although the definitions of key competencies vary considerably across countries, they reflect a similar ambition: overcoming traditional educational approaches focusing primarily on knowledge transmission and acquisition of basic skills. The aim of many recent curriculum reforms is to promote a broader model of learning that comprises a complex integration of knowledge, skills, attitudes and action in order to carry out a task successfully in real-life contexts. Such key competencies, or 'twenty-first-century skills', typically include dimensions such as critical thinking, creativity, problem-solving, communication, ICT literacy, as well as collaborative, social and citizen skills (OECD, 2013a).

An important similarity of most definitions of key competencies is a shared focus on 'learning for life', 'lifelong learning' or 'learning to learn'. Although they emphasize different elements, these terms are clear in suggesting that what is learned must have relevance beyond school (Lucas and Claxton, 2009). This responds to a concern that school settings sometimes tend to promote a narrow set of cognitive skills and attitudes that have limited relevance outside the classroom, such as taking accurate handwritten notes, remembering detailed information acquired months or years ago and sitting still for long periods of the day. Although these may be essential 'school skills', they are insufficient to equip students for active participation in society and the world of work in the future (Lucas and Claxton, 2009).

In particular, the exponential increase in the availability of information has made it less important for learners to be able to recall and reproduce facts, and made it more important to develop competencies to synthesise, transform and apply learning in real-world situations, think creatively and critically, collaborate with others, communicate effectively and adapt to rapidly developing environments. Hence, although numeric, verbal and scientific literacy will remain important building blocks of education, more generic and transversal competencies are becoming increasingly important (European Commission, 2011a; 2012).

DIFFERENT APPROACHES TO CURRICULUM DEVELOPMENT

Despite a general trend towards including so-called twenty-first-century competencies as key learning goals across OECD school systems, there are pronounced differences in the degree to which countries specify concrete expectations for student performance to guide teaching, learning and assessment across schools. Information on expected learning outcomes and developments are typically expressed in national curricula and educational standards.

National curricula generally describe overarching learning objectives for the school system and explain the underlying values and culture that should shape teaching and learning. Countries take different approaches to how they design curricula, and although some set out the teaching content, methods, materials and assessment criteria to be applied in different subjects and year levels, others establish broad guidelines, leaving room for local authorities and schools to decide upon more specific goals, content and methods.

It is common for OECD countries to have system-wide curriculum frameworks that set objectives for student learning, but the degree of prescription varies widely between countries. Detailed central curricula can act as a legal trigger to promote valued learning content and bring specific pedagogical approaches within the reach of all schools and teachers, but they may not respond equally well to different local and school contexts (Elmore and Sykes, 1992; Westbury, 2007; Kärkkäinen, 2012). More decentralised curricula, on the other hand, allow schools and teachers to experiment and develop curriculum innovations that are relevant to local contexts and may spread through horizontal

networks of schools (Elmore and Sykes, 1992; Elmore, 1996; Darling-Hammond, 1998; Marsh and Willis; 2007; Kärkkäinen, 2012).

Several school systems have adopted participatory approaches to developing curricula where the central level education authority provides the core of overarching objectives, whereas the more specific goals and curriculum content and assessment criteria are developed at the local and/or school level. This is the case, for example, in the Flemish Community of Belgium, the Czech Republic, Denmark, Finland, Norway and the Slovak Republic. Such curricular autonomy is intended to provide space for local interpretation and adaptation of goals. It is also expected to help strengthen local ownership of the teaching programme.

Although keeping curricula open allows for teachers' professional judgements and innovations in the classroom, such a decentralised approach may also lead to a lack of clarity regarding the specific goals to be achieved by all students in different subjects and year levels. There are often large variations in schools' capacity and expertise to implement effective local curricula and assessment approaches. This may lead to a lack of equivalence and fairness in educational opportunities for students across a given school system. In the absence of clear and specific system-wide objectives, teachers may find it difficult to develop concrete lesson plans, learning goals and assessment strategies that are in line with national expectations.

The introduction of more detailed national standards (or expectations or benchmarks or competency goals) for what should be taught, learned and assessed in schools has been debated and tried to varying extents in many countries over the last quarter century. Educational standards refer to descriptions of what students should know (content standards) and be able to do (performance standards) at different stages of the learning process. In some countries, standards are only available for the core subjects, such as literacy and mathematics, whereas in other countries they exist for a broad range of subjects. The standards may be set out in a separate document, or may be embedded in the curriculum.

Central standards are intended to provide consistency and coherence, especially in contexts where there is a high degree of local autonomy regarding the development of curricula, teaching programmes and assessment. Although it may appear straightforward to create statements of expected learning and levels of proficiency, experiences in different school systems have shown that it is not an easy task to identify clear and agreed standards and criteria (Looney, 2011; Nusche et al., 2011).

Research has revealed challenges in ensuring that the curriculum, standards, teaching and assessment are consistent (Looney, 2011). The core logic of standards-based systems rests upon the alignment of these key elements. If the assessments do not match the curriculum and the standards, then assessment results have little value in judging how well students are learning. This, in turn, will make it difficult to diagnose and respond to student or school needs. Policy therefore needs to give considerable attention to sound strategies that assess student performance in relation to the curriculum and standards.

Aligning Assessment Approaches to Twenty-First-Century Curricula

As expectations of what students should achieve have changed with the focus on twenty-first-century competencies, there has been parallel reflection in research and policy development on how to best design assessment approaches that can actually measure such broader competencies. This is important because the scope of student assessment, especially when it has high stakes for teachers and students, can strongly influence the scope of teaching and learning.

Although assessment is primarily intended to measure the progress and outcomes of learning, it also has effects on the learning process itself (Somerset, 1996). Several authors have described this influence of assessment on teaching and learning as the 'backwash effect' of student assessment (Alderson and Wall, 1993; Somerset, 1996; Baartman et al., 2006). This close interrelationship makes assessment an important tool to signal and clarify the key goals that students are expected to achieve; however, if assessment only covers a small fraction of the valued curriculum goals, then the impact of assessment on teaching and learning can be restrictive (Harlen, 2007).

Given the well known 'backwash effect' of assessment, curriculum innovations are more likely to be to be translated into changes in teaching and learning if they are accompanied by related innovations in assessment (Cizek, 1997). This means that for assessment to be meaningful, it must be well aligned to the type of learning that is valued. For example, factual knowledge tests are well suited to assess the outcomes of traditional teaching approaches based on rote learning and knowledge transfer. But such tests are less adequate when it comes to assessing complex competencies (Biggs, 1996; 1999).

A great deal of the assessment research in recent years has focused on innovative and 'authentic' forms of assessment that would be able to capture the type of learning that is valued in today's societies. These alternative forms of assessment are most commonly referred to as performance-based assessment. They may include open-ended tasks such as oral presentations, essays, experiments, projects, presentations, collaborative tasks, real-life cases, problem-solving assignments and portfolios. The main characteristic of performance assessments is that they assess a range of integrated knowledge and skills by asking students to perform a task rather than to provide a correct answer. As such, they are more effective at capturing more complex achievements than closed-ended formats (Looney, 2011).

However, although there is a strong ambition to focus school systems increasingly on the development of complex competencies, the OECD Reviews of Evaluation and

Assessment in 15 school systems found that national frameworks for student assessment were typically lagging behind such competency-based curricula. The curriculum might be competency-based, but the assessment system may not adequately capture many of the key objectives of the curriculum. Where this is the case, the assessment system can become a 'hidden curriculum' encouraging a narrower approach to teaching and learning.

Although no directly comparable information is available regarding the scope of student assessment across countries, this section brings together information collected on the scope and format of assessment across the 29 school systems participating in the OECD Review.

Central Assessments and Examinations

It is generally expected that all subjects are given some attention in teacher-based assessment, but standardised assessments and examinations – where they exist – tend to focus on a few priority subjects. The subjects assessed in central examinations vary across school systems, but the subjects most frequently assessed across OECD countries are the language of instruction and mathematics.

As is typical for standardised assessment, the vast majority of school systems use written formats for their central assessments and examinations. Table 52.1 presents an overview of testing formats used in 2012 in national assessments of mathematics and the language of instruction that did not have formal consequences for students. Findings are for countries that participated in the *OECD Review on Evaluation and Assessment Frameworks for Improving School Outcomes*. The table shows the most common format in the first column and the least common format in the final column. It clearly shows that multiple-choice tests are by far the most frequently used assessment format. Closed-format short-answer questions (for example, yes/no; true/false; selecting a word; providing

the result to a calculation) and open-ended writing tasks/open calculations are also frequently applied. Many countries use a mix of these three formats. Only a few countries use oral questions or require students to perform oral presentations as part of such national assessments. The use of performance tasks is also very limited.

The limited use of these formats in central assessments with no stakes for students might be explained by the fact that such assessments serve primarily for monitoring and comparing student results across regions and schools and the purpose is to obtain highly reliable and easily comparable scores. The administration and scoring of multiple-choice and closed-format short-answer questions is also less costly and time-intensive than other assessment formats.

In standardised central examinations that do have formal consequences for individual students, the most frequently used assessment formats are open-ended written tasks. Multiple-choice items are also frequently used, especially in examinations in the language of instruction. A few school systems also use closed-ended short-answer formats (for more information, see OECD, 2013a). In many countries, however, these centrally designed standardised components are complemented by non-standardised parts of the examinations that are locally designed and marked. As there are limits to what any centrally administered standardised assessment can assess, it is often expected that the assessment of a broader range of skills and competencies happens in such local assessments.

In recent years, the potential of information and communication technologies (ICT) to influence and shape assessment approaches has been increasingly recognised across OECD countries. Developments in ICT have opened new avenues for the assessment of complex competencies. Technology-enhanced learning environments can provide tools and systems that recreate learning situations requiring complex thinking, problem-solving and collaboration strategies and thus allow for the assessment of

Table 52.1 Testing formats used in national assessments (2012)

	ISCED* level	Multiple choice	Closed-format short-answer questions	Open-ended writing tasks/ calculations	Performing a task	Oral questions and answers	Oral presentation
Austria	1; 2	Yes	Yes	Yes	No	Yes	Yes
Australia	1; 2	Yes	Yes	Yes	No	No	No
Belgium (French Community)	1[1]; 2; 3	Yes	Yes	Yes	Yes	No	No
Belgium (Flemish Community)[1]	1; 2; 3	Yes	Yes	No	Yes	No	No
Canada	2	Yes	Yes	Yes	No	No	No
Chile	1; 2; 3	Yes	No	Yes	No	No	No
Czech Republic	1; 2	Yes	Yes	No	No	No	No
Denmark[1,2]	1; 2	Yes	Yes	No	No	No	No
Estonia	1	Yes	Yes	Yes	No	No	No
Finland[1]	1; 2	Yes	Yes	ISCED 2 only	No	No	ISCED 2 only
France	1; 2	Yes	Yes	Yes	No	No	No
Hungary	1[1]; 2; 3	Yes	Yes	No	No	No	No
Iceland	1; 2	Yes	No	ISCED 2 only	ISCED 1 only	ISCED 2 only	No
Ireland	1	Yes	Yes	No	No	No	No
Israel[3]	1; 2	Yes	Yes	Yes	No	No	No
Italy	1; 2; 3	Yes	Yes	Yes	No	No	No
Korea	1; 2; 3	Yes	Yes	No	No	No	No
Luxembourg	1; 2	Yes	No	No	ISCED 1 only	ISCED 1 only	No
Mexico (sample)	1; 2	Yes	Yes	Yes	No	No	No
Mexico (full)	1; 2; 3	Yes	No	No	No	No	No
Netherlands[1]	1; 2; 3	Yes	No	Yes	No	No	No
New Zealand[1]	1; 2	Yes	Yes	Yes	Yes	Yes	No
Norway	1; 2	Yes	Yes	No	No	No	No
Poland	1	Yes	No	Yes	No	No	No
Portugal	1	Yes	Yes	Yes	No	No	No
Slovak Republic[4]	2	Yes	Yes	No	No	No	No
Slovenia	1; 2	Yes	No	Yes	No	No	No
Spain[5]	1; 2	Yes	Yes	Yes	No	No	No
Sweden	1; 2; 3	Yes	Yes	Yes	ISCED 1 only	Yes	Yes
Total number of systems using this format		28	22	18	7	6	3

[1] National assessments are not compulsory.

[2] Matching items are also used which require students to match pictures/drawings with words.

[3] The statistical data for Israel are supplied by and under the responsibility of the relevant Israeli authorities.

The use of such data by the OECD is without prejudice to the status of the Golan Heights, East Jerusalem and Israeli settlements in the West Bank under the terms of international law.

[4] National assessments are being developed for ISCED 1 also.

[5] Last administered in 2010 and currently under development.

*The International Standard Classification of Education (ISCED) is a statistical framework for organising information on education maintained by the United Nations Educational, Scientific and Cultural Organisation (UNESCO). ISCED 1 refers to primary education, ISCED 2 refers to lower secondary education and ISCED 3 refers to upper secondary education.

Source: OECD, 2013a.

such competencies (European Commission, 2011a). Innovative computer-based assessments may now score student performances on complex cognitive tasks, such as how students go about problem solving, or open-ended performances such as written essays, or student collaboration on constructed response formats (Mislevy et al., 2001).

Binkley et al. (2010) describe two key strategies regarding the use of ICT in assessment. First, the 'migratory' strategy refers to the use of ICT to deliver traditional assessment formats more effectively and efficiently. Second, the 'transformative' strategy refers to the use of ICT to change how competencies are assessed and develop formats that facilitate the assessment of competencies that have been difficult to capture with traditional assessment formats (Ripley, 2009; Binkley et al., 2010; European Commission, 2011a).

Information collected from school systems participating in the OECD Review indicates that the use of ICT for assessment has not yet become common practice internationally. In the few systems where technology is used for standardised central assessments or examinations, it is mostly done in a 'migratory' perspective. Technology is most typically used for data management purposes, such as data sheet scanning, inputting marks or results management, whilst assessments remain paper-based, and some countries use computer-based uniform technology for the actual administration of central assessments (for more information, see OECD, 2013a).

The limited use of performance-based tasks in large-scale assessments may be explained by a combination of concerns about reliability, resources and timing. There are challenges related to creating reliable measures of complex competencies, such as problem solving, creativity and collaboration. Performance-based assessments tend to have lower comparability of results than standardised paper-and-pencil assessments. Research in some countries has shown that higher-order thinking skills are context and situation specific, that is it is difficult to generalise from hands-on performance-based

tasks to make judgements about student competencies (Shavelson et al., 1990; Linn et al., 1991). The use of closed-ended paper-and-pencil tests is often motivated by the need for objectivity, fairness and impartiality in assessment, especially where high stakes are attached. Performance-based assessments are also more costly and time-consuming to implement on a large scale, in particular when they require one-to-one assessment situations.

Teacher-Based Assessment

Although standardised assessments will always be limited to measuring a selected subset of curriculum goals, the assessment of more complex competencies is generally expected to happen in classroom assessment where teachers can use richer and more in-depth assessment tasks.

In most OECD countries, schools benefit from considerable autonomy in the organisation of internal student assessments. School leaders, together with teachers and sometimes in co-operation with school governing boards or education authorities, are typically in charge of establishing school policies for student assessment. In the OECD's Programme for International Student Assessment (PISA) in 2012, 47 per cent of 15-year-old students across OECD countries were in schools whose principals reported that the school alone had the main responsibility for establishing student assessment policies, and 41 per cent of students were in schools where the school, together with the regional and/or national education authority or school governing board, had considerable responsibility for student assessment policies (OECD, 2013b).

Most OECD countries have long-standing traditions of teacher-developed assessment and rely strongly on teachers' professional judgements in assessment. Teachers are generally expected to take responsibility for different functions of assessment, including diagnostic, formative and summative. Although teachers tend to have the exclusive responsibility for summative assessment in primary education, their assessment approaches are typically complemented by regionally or nationally implemented standardised examinations at the secondary level. The distribution of responsibilities tends to be organised in a way that teachers assess and report on student performance in relation to the full range of curriculum goals, whilst standardised examinations and assessments assess a particular subset of learning goals in specific year levels.

However, although teacher-based assessment provides opportunities for diverse and innovative assessment approaches covering the full range of curriculum goals, studies from different countries indicate that teachers do not necessarily use such approaches. In fact, the validity of teacher-based assessment depends to a large extent on the assessment opportunities provided by individual teachers. It is difficult to ensure that all teachers indeed use the potential of internal assessment to cover the full range of goals specified in the curriculum (Harlen, 2007). Several reviews of research on teacher-based assessment note that teacher-made assessments are often no more diverse or innovative than external assessments, encouraging rote learning and recall of fragmented knowledge rather than critical thinking and deeper learning (for example, Crooks, 1988; Black, 1993; Black and Wiliam, 1998; Harlen, 2007).

There are a number of challenges for teachers to assess the key competencies outlined in many curricula. First, there is often a lack of clarity on how to translate competency aims into concrete teaching and assessment activities. Competency goals are often stated in a general way with little guidance regarding what exactly teachers are expected to change in their teaching and assessment. Second, the transversal nature of competencies – they tend to involve several subjects or go beyond school subjects altogether – makes it challenging for teachers to see who should be responsible for assessing them and how to fit them within particular subjects or disciplines. Third, the high visibility of standardised assessments may put pressure on teachers to adapt their own assessment to the format used in national tests. Teachers may be tempted to narrow their teaching and assessment in order to best prepare their students for closed-ended national tests, to the detriment of richer more performance-based approaches (Lucas and Claxton, 2009; European Commission, 2011b, Pepper, 2011).

Broadening Assessment to Match Twenty-First-Century Curricula

Across OECD curricula, there is a shared ambition to move school systems beyond pedagogical approaches focusing on knowledge transmission and to promote a broader model of learning that includes competencies to synthesise, transform and apply learning in real-world situations. Current paper-and-pencil tests with their limited item formats will not be able to appropriately assess these skills, either for formative or for summative purposes. There will therefore be a need to develop the expertise, technical capacity and support to design, develop, deliver and evaluate more complex assessments. Some of these assessments will be integrated with instruction and take place in settings using ICT, with access to the Internet, in closed micro-worlds, or in game-like environments. This section explores a range of potential directions for policy and practice that might help achieve better alignment between competency-based curricula and assessment approaches, both large-scale and classroom-based.

Developing Learning Progressions

As curricular statements of broad competency goals often remain vague and provide little guidance for pedagogy, professionals in schools could benefit from support in translating competency goals into concrete lesson plans, teaching units and assessment approaches. Specific learning progressions, describing how students typically move through learning in each subject area, can help to clarify national curriculum goals for teachers. Research-based learning progressions can provide a picture from beginning learning to expertise and help provide teachers, parents and other stakeholders with concrete images of what to expect in student learning, with direct links to the final learning objectives and reference levels. Such learning progressions can provide a clear conceptual basis for a coherent assessment framework, along with assessment tools that are aligned to different stages in the progressions (Nusche et al., 2011).

Teachers can use these learning progressions as roadmaps to identify the set of skills and bodies of enabling knowledge that students must master on the way to becoming competent in the more complex and multifaceted learning objectives defined for the end of primary and secondary education. School systems can also facilitate the development of assessment criteria for rating different aspects of performance and exemplars illustrating student performance at different levels of proficiency. These can be used to define what constitutes adequate, good and excellent work in relation to broader competency goals. They can also support professionals in clarifying quality definitions and making accurate judgements about student performance and progress in different curriculum areas (Nusche et al., 2011).

Such materials can be promoted as voluntary resources that teachers use as signposts in their assessment. They can help raise aspirations and communicate a focus on excellence and continuous improvement. Such guidance could help teachers design their instructional plans and classroom assessment strategies in alignment with national objectives and progressions. Teachers could also be encouraged to share and co-construct intermediate learning goals and assessment criteria with students so that they understand different levels of expected learning and performance. Such common work on goals and criteria can promote both student learning and reflective teaching practice (Andrade, 2005; Jonsson and Svingby, 2007).

Support and Incentives for Teachers

It is also important to expand teachers' assessment expertise in directions that will facilitate the introduction of the new forms

of assessment demanded by new curricular goals. One approach is to support small-scale innovation projects that will lead to pilot administrations of innovative assessments. Such projects could involve partnerships between assessment researchers and groups of schools where the pilots would take place. Ideally, some of the educators in these schools would participate in the research and development effort, and not simply serve as proctors during administration. Initially, such assessments could generate data for formative purposes and be embedded in instruction. For example, in science classes, pedagogy centred on micro-worlds and other kinds of simulations could incorporate tasks that require higher order critical thinking, collaboration and effective communication, which are all twenty-first-century skills. Such tasks would challenge both students and teachers, and yield new types of data that could serve as a focus for professional development (Nusche et al., 2014).

The success of such initiatives depends, in part, on the existence of networks of educators that can facilitate collaboration and dissemination of new approaches and best practices in assessment (as well as other aspects of pedagogy and didactics). Professional learning opportunities where teachers can discuss and collaborate in assessing actual student products can further contribute to their understanding of broader assessment practices. In addition, school systems could consider strategies for accommodating and even rewarding schools' innovative assessment practices, especially if there is reasonable evidence that they are supporting student learning. For example, inspectorates or external review bodies can favourably recognise schools instituting programmes of professional development that highlight improved assessment practice as a key target (Nusche et al., 2014).

Developing Test Banks

Furthermore, innovative assessment formats can also be developed centrally to complement teacher-made assessments. Due to concerns about reliability and resources, 'performance-based' or 'authentic' assessments are often challenging to implement on a large scale and in a standardised way. Alternatively, school systems can opt for developing test banks for teachers, which can provide a range of innovative assessment tools for teachers to draw from when their students are ready. Such test banks provide an excellent opportunity to promote innovative assessment tools that have proven successful elsewhere. They can offer a map of assessment items suitable to assess the key areas and competencies outlined in the curriculum.

Assessing Broader Learning Goals through Sample-Based Assessments

Another option is to implement innovative assessments that cover larger parts of the curriculum on a sample basis. Sample-based assessments that are applied to a representative proportion of the student cohort allow the assessment of a broader range of curriculum content at relatively low cost, whilst at the same time avoiding distortions deriving from potential 'teaching to the test'. Such assessments may be organised in cycles, assessing a different curriculum area each year and not assessing all students on the same tasks, thus allowing the assessment of a wider range of content without overburdening individual students.

Although the purpose of such sample-based assessment typically is to monitor the school system, they can still be beneficial for individual teachers and students when they receive their results. The tasks of previous years may also be made available for teachers to use in their formative classroom assessment. Where teachers are centrally employed and trained to correct such sample-based assessments, this can constitute a valuable professional learning experience that will also help them in their classroom teaching and assessment practice.

Building on Innovative Approaches Developed in Particular Education Sectors

In many countries, there are some education sectors that have a longer tradition than others in using innovative assessment approaches. Often, there is a stronger tradition in the vocational education and training (VET) sector than in general education programmes to include innovative assessment approaches that may take place in practical and authentic work situations and are connected to real-life challenges that graduates may encounter in the workplace (Santiago et al., 2012a, 2012b).

Sometimes there is also greater attention paid to assessing authentic performances in special needs education, second chance education programmes or special programmes for migrant students. In designing assessment approaches for general education programmes, it would be important to pay close attention to innovative assessments developed in other programmes and learn from approaches that have proven successful and could be integrated and/or adapted. Policymakers should promote communication and collaboration regarding the assessment of competencies across education sectors and programmes, so that mutual learning can be facilitated. Exploratory projects can build the expertise needed when versions of these assessments are eventually brought to scale.

Using ICT to Develop Sophisticated Assessment Instruments

Increasingly sophisticated ICT programmes that score open-ended performances, measure students' reasoning processes, examine how students go about thinking through problems and even provide feedback to students have been developed in some settings. Although it has always been possible for teachers or external assessors to perform these functions, ICT offers the possibility for large-scale and more cost-effective assessment of complex skills (Mislevy et al., 2001; Looney, 2009).

The systematic use of ICT to transform central assessment systems is still limited, and many public and private actors are increasingly investing in research and development in this area. Several innovations in assessment around the world are taking advantage of recent advances in ICT. Increasingly sophisticated ICT programmes are now able to score 'open-ended performances', such as essays. These programmes typically use natural-language processing and information retrieval technologies to detect textual features of essays, for example variety in use of syntax, quality of content and organisation of ideas (Looney, 2009). These ICT models are still in the relatively early stages of development, and although they may facilitate scoring of large-scale assessments, they cannot replace human raters. Further studies are also needed to determine the validity and reliability of different automated essay scoring tools (Wang and Brown, 2007, cited in Looney, 2009).

Technology-based assessments may also incorporate simulation, interactivity and constructed response formats. For example, students may use the multimedia functions of ICT to show how they would perform a science experiment or other problem-solving tasks. Some assessments require students to use and judge information on the Internet or to develop concept maps using online tools to show their understanding of processes. The student's map is scored by comparing it against an expert's map (Bennett, 2001; Looney, 2009). There are also examples of web-based peer assessment and collaborative problem solving, for example students can send information and documents to each other and work on tasks together using ICT (Binkley et al., 2010).

Developments in ICT are relevant not only for standardised assessments, but they can also influence regular assessment practices in the classroom, for example there has been increased interest in using digital portfolios (or e-portfolios) across countries (McFarlane, 2003; Binkley et al., 2010; Pepper, 2011). Although portfolios have been used in many countries for some time, the use of digital tools allows collecting information on student progress in a broader range of formats, including text with hyperlinks, video, audio and simulations. Digital portfolios also make it easier for teachers to comment on assignments and track student progress. Students' own work with the digital portfolios can enhance their skills in learning to learn, ICT literacy and self-monitoring (Binkley et al., 2010; Pepper, 2011).

CONCLUSION

This chapter aimed to disentangle the complex relationships between curriculum, pedagogy and assessment and shed some light on the degree to which these elements are coherent in different school systems. Coherence between curriculum, pedagogy and assessment can help increase the focus on valued learning goals across school systems and support effective teaching and learning. Conversely, a lack of alignment between valued learning goals and student assessment frameworks will send conflicting signals to teachers and students, with potentially detrimental effects on teaching and learning.

This chapter's review of country practices and relevant literature indicates that both central assessments and teachers' classroom-based assessments often lag behind countries' ambitions to support cross-curricular learning preparing students for life and work in the mid-twenty-first century. At the same time, there is increasing emphasis in research and practice on developing more complex assessments that can support such broader learning goals. This chapter suggests several ways for policymakers and practitioners to support broader assessment practices. These include developing learning progressions to provide a clear conceptual basis for broader assessment approaches, supporting teachers in developing expertise in this area, developing test banks and sample-based assessments to assess broader learning goals and using ICT to create sophisticated assessment instruments.

ACKNOWLEDGEMENTS

The work presented in this chapter is based on research and policy analysis conducted as part of the OECD Review on Evaluation and Assessment Frameworks for Improving School Outcomes and greatly benefited from my collaboration with colleagues at the OECD, in particular Paulo Santiago, Claire Shewbridge and Thomas Radinger. The opinions expressed and arguments employed in this chapter are those of the author and do not necessarily reflect the official views of the OECD or of the governments of its member countries.

REFERENCES

Alderson, C. and D. Wall (1993) 'Does wash-back exist?', *Applied Linguistics*, 14: 115–29.

Andrade, H. (2005) 'Teaching with rubrics: the good, the bad, and the ugly', *College Teaching*, 53(1): 27–30.

Baartman, L.K.J., T.J. Bastiaens, P.A. Kirschner, C.P.M. Van der Vleuten (2006) 'The wheel of competency assessment: presenting quality criteria for competency assessment programs', *Studies in Educational Evaluation*, 32: 153–70.

Bennett, R.E. (2001) 'How the Internet will help large-scale assessment reinvent itself', *Education Policy Analysis*, 9(5): 1–25.

Biggs, J. (1996) 'Enhancing teaching through constructive alignment', *Higher Education*, 32: 347–64.

Biggs, J. (1999) *Teaching for Quality Learning at University*. Buckingham, UK: SRHE and Open University Press.

Binkley, M., Erstad, O., Herman, J., Raizen, S., Ripley M. with Rumble M. (2010) *Draft White Paper 1: Defining 21st Century Skills*. Available from http://atc21s.org/wp-content/uploads/2011/11/1-Defining-21st-Century-Skills.pdf

Black, P. (1993) 'Formative and summative assessments by teachers', *Studies in Science Education*, 21: 49–97.

Black, P. and D. Wiliam (1998) 'Assessment and classroom learning', *Assessment in Education: Principles, Policy and Practice*, 5: 7–74.

Cizek, G.J. (1997) 'Learning, achievement, and assessment: constructs at a crossroads', in G.D. Phye (ed.), *Handbook of Classroom Assessment: Learning, Achievement, and Adjustment*. San Diego, CA: Academic Press. pp. 1–32.

Crooks, T.J. (1988) 'The impact of classroom evaluation practices on students', *Review of Educational Research*, 58: 438–81.

Darling-Hammond, L. (1998) 'Policy and change: getting beyond bureaucracy', in A. Hargreaves, A. Lieberman, M. Fullan and D. Hopkins (eds.), *International Handbook of Educational Change*. Dordrecht, Netherlands: Kluwer Academic Publishers. pp. 642–667.

Elmore, R. (1996) 'Getting to scale with good educational practice', *Harvard Educational Review*, 66(1): 1–26.

Elmore, R. and G. Sykes (1992) 'Curriculum policy', in P.W. Jackson (ed.), *Handbook of Research on Curriculum*. New York, NY: Macmillan.

European Commission (2011a) *Evidence on the Use of ICT for the Assessment of Key Competences*. Brussels: European Commission.

European Commission (2011b) *Assessment of Key Competences: Policy Handbook*. Brussels: European Commission.

European Commission (2012) *Assessment of Key Competences in Initial Education and Training: Policy Guidance, Commission Staff Working Document*. Brussels: European Commission. Available from http://ec.europa.eu/education/news/rethinking/sw371_en.pdf

Fournier, G. and D. Mildon (forthcoming), *OECD Review on Evaluation and Assessment Frameworks for Improving School Outcomes: Country Background Report for Canada*, prepared for The Council of Ministers of Education, Canada (CMEC).

Harlen, W. (2007) 'Criteria for evaluating systems for student assessment', *Studies in Educational Evaluation*, 33: 15–28.

Jonsson, A. and G. Svingby (2007) 'The use of scoring rubrics: reliability, validity and educational consequences', *Educational Research Review*, 2: 130–44.

Kärkkäinen, K. (2012) *Bringing about Curriculum Innovations: Implicit Approaches in the OECD Area*. OECD Education Working Papers, No. 82. Paris: OECD. Available from www.oecd.org/edu/workingpapers

Linn, R.L., Baker, E.L. and Dunbar, S.B. (1991) *Complex, Performance-Based Assessment: Expectations and Validation Criteria*. CSE Technical Report 331.

Looney, J. (2009) *Assessment and Innovation in Education*. OECD Education Working Papers, No. 24. Paris: OECD. Available from www.oecd.org/edu/workingpapers

Looney, J. (2011) *Alignment in Complex Systems: Achieving Balance and Coherence*. OECD Education Working Papers, No. 64. Paris: OECD. Available from www.oecd.org/edu/workingpapers

Lucas, B. and Claxton, G. (2009) *Wider Skills for Learning: What Are they, How Can they Be Cultivated, How Could they Be Measured and Why Are they Important for Innovation?'*, Winchester, UK: Centre for Real-World Learning, University of Winchester.

Marsh, C.J. and Willis, G. (2007) *Curriculum: Alternative Approaches, Ongoing Issues*. Upper Saddle River, NJ: Pearson Education.

McFarlane, A. (2003) 'Editorial. Assessment for the digital age', *Assessment in Education*, 10: 261–6.

Ministerial Council on Education, Employment, Training and Youth Affairs (MCEETYA) (2008) *Melbourne Declaration on Educational Goals for Young Australians*. Canberra: Ministerial Council on Education, Employment, Training and Youth Affairs.

Mislevy, R.J., Steinberg, L.S., Breyer, F.J., Almond, R.G. and Johnson, L. (2001) *Making Sense of Data From Complex Assessments*. Los Angeles, CA: University of California, National Center for Research on Evaluation, Standards, and Student Testing (CRESST).

Nusche, D., Braun, H., Halász, G. and Santiago, P. (2014) *OECD Reviews of Evaluation and Assessment in Education: Netherlands*. Paris: OECD. Available from www.oecd.org/edu/evaluationpolicy

Nusche, D., Earl, L., Maxwell, W. and Shewbridge, C. (2011) *OECD Reviews of Evaluation and Assessment in Education: Norway*. Available from www.oecd.org/edu/evaluationpolicy

Organisation for Economic Co-operation and Development (OECD) (n.d.) *OECD Review on Evaluation and Assessment Frameworks for Improving School Outcomes*. Paris: OECD. Available from www.oecd.org/edu/evaluationpolicy

Organisation for Economic Co-operation and Development (OECD) (2013a) *Synergies for Better Learning: An International Perspective on Evaluation and Assessment*. Paris: OECD. Available from http://www.oecd.org/edu/school/synergies-for-better-learning.htm

Organisation for Economic Co-operation and Development (OECD) (2013b) *PISA 2012 Results: What Makes Schools Successful? Resources, Policies and Practices*. Vol. IV. Paris: OECD.

Pepper, D. (2011) 'Assessing key competences across the curriculum – and Europe', *European Journal of Education*, 46(3): 335–353.

Ripley, M. (2009) 'Transformational computer-based testing', in F. Scheuermann and J. Björnsson (eds.), *The Transition to Computer-Based Assessment: New Approaches to Skills Assessment and Implications for Large-scale Testing*. Luxembourg: Office for Official Publications of the European Communities. pp. 92–98.

Santiago, P., Donaldson, G., Herman, J. and Shewbridge, C. (2011) *OECD Reviews of Evaluation and Assessment in Education: Australia*. Paris: OECD. Available from www.oecd.org/edu/evaluationpolicy

Santiago, P., McGregor, I., Nusche, D., Ravela, P. and Toledo, D. (2012a) *OECD Reviews of Evaluation and Assessment in Education: Mexico*. Paris: OECD. Available from www.oecd.org/edu/evaluationpolicy

Santiago, P., Donaldson, G., Looney, A. and Nusche, D. (2012b) *OECD Reviews of Evaluation and Assessment in Education: Portugal*. Paris: OECD. Available from www.oecd.org/edu/evaluationpolicy

Shavelson, R.J., Baxter, G.P. and Pine, J. (1990) 'What alternative assessments look like in science', paper presented at the Office of Educational Research and Improvement Conference: The Promise and Peril of Alternative Assessment, Washington, DC, October 1990.

Singh, M. (2003) 'Understanding life skills', background Paper prepared for the Education for All Global Monitoring Report 2003/4 *Gender and Education for All: The Leap to Equality*. Hamburg: UNESCO Institute for Education. Available from http://unesdoc.unesco.org/images/0014/001469/146963e.pdf

Somerset, A. (1996) 'Examinations and educational quality', in A. Little and A. Wolf, *Assessment in Transition, Learning Monitoring and Selection in International Perspective*. Oxford: Pergamon, Elsevier Science. pp. 263–284.

Wang, J. and M.S. Brown (2007) 'Automated essay scoring versus human scoring: a comparative study', *The Journal of Technology, Learning, and Assessment*, 6(2): 310–325.

Westbury, I. (2007) 'Making curricula: why do states make curricula, and how?' in M. Connelly, M.F. He and J.A. Phillion (eds.), *Handbook of Curriculum and Instruction*, Thousand Oaks, CA: Sage Publications. pp. 45–65.

53

National Assessment and Intelligent Accountability

Sandra Johnson

INTRODUCTION

The accountability drive that has been inexorably increasing over decades around the world has arguably been stimulated and fuelled by the cross-national assessment activities of the International Association for the Evaluation of Educational Achievement (IEA) with its Trends in Mathematics and Science Study (TIMSS) and Progress in International Reading Literacy Study (PIRLS), and the Organisation for Economic Cooperation and Development (OECD) with its Programme for International Student Assessment (PISA). One impressive result is the mushrooming of national assessment programmes intended to serve monitoring and accountability purposes at system level, and in many cases also at school level. Over the space of a decade, the old scenario, in which only a handful of countries operated their own locally-targeted system-monitoring programmes, has been supplanted by a present reality in which large numbers of countries have newly launched national assessment programmes, resulting in a wide variety of purposes and models (Eurydice, 2009; INCA, 2012; Rey, 2010).

But what is 'national assessment'? What is 'intelligent' accountability? How can national assessment programmes potentially serve intelligent accountability? And why is this potential not always realised? These questions are the focus of this chapter.

National Assessment

National assessment can be defined as any system of assessment in which every student in the school population at a given stage, or every student in a randomly selected sample of that population, is assessed in such a way that dependable inferences about population attainment in some subject domain or subdomain can be drawn. The former model is technically census-based assessment, also known as 'exhaustive' or 'cohort' assessment, whilst the alternative model is sample-based assessment.

The history of national assessment is relatively short and is intertwined with that of the international survey programmes, which by their nature comprise multiple national attainment surveys. The initial emergence of national assessment, in the US in the late 1960s followed by the UK in the 1970s, was arguably triggered by the first survey activity of the IEA in the early 1960s, which focused on the attainment of 10- and 14-year-olds in a variety of subjects. The IEA was founded by a small group of leading school effectiveness researchers, whose hope was that looking across borders would provide richer information with which to explore the issue of school impact on student achievement (Husen and Postlethwaite, 1996) by introducing greater heterogeneity into educational provision than is typically found in one country alone (Purves, 1991).

The IEA had no political motivation in its early survey activity. However, its research focus inevitably meant that national attainment outcomes were being incidentally exposed in survey reports (Peaker, 1975). This will have whetted the appetite of national policymakers for further outcomes information for their own systems, along with continually updated information about their standing internationally. But the IEA was not in a position in those early days to guarantee further subject surveys, least of all on a regular basis. In response, some countries took steps to develop assessment systems of their own to provide them with regular national outcomes information.

The US was the first country to introduce a formal national assessment programme when it launched its National Assessment of Educational Progress (NAEP) in 1969/1970 (Jones, 1996; Pellegrino, 2014). The UK followed closely behind, launching its Assessment of Performance Unit (APU) survey programmes in England, Wales and Northern Ireland in the late 1970s (Foxman et al., 1991; Johnson, 1989), modelled to a great extent on NAEP. Scotland followed by launching its Assessment of Achievement Programme (AAP) in the mid-1980s (Condie

et al., 2003), modelled to some extent on England's APU. Meanwhile, in the early 1970s, Ireland carried out attainment surveys periodically in a variety of subjects (Shiel et al., 2014), but because performance change over time was not a priority prior to 2009, the grade levels at which surveys took place varied each time. In the mid-1980s, the Netherlands launched its Periodic National Assessment programme (*Peridodiek Peilings Onderzoek,* PPON), which, like NAEP, continues to this day (Scheerens et al., 2012). New Zealand's National Education Monitoring Programme (NEMP) was launched in the mid-1990s and was unique in its focus on reporting performance at item/task-level only, for the benefit of the teaching profession rather than policymakers (Crooks and Flockton, 1993).

In these sample-based programmes, with rare exceptions, assessment took place towards the end of a school year, the attainment information often being complemented by questionnaire-based 'background' information, for example about students' learning attitudes, interests and environments. Achievement results were not reported in any of these programmes at school or individual student level.

France took a different direction when it launched a programme of 'diagnostic' national assessment in the late 1980s (Bonnet, 1997; Trosseille and Rocher, 2015). This was exhaustive assessment, intended primarily to provide information for school inspectors and receiving teachers about the strengths and weaknesses of students as they started a new school year, so that appropriate teaching programmes might be planned for that year. Like NEMP, there was no overt political motivation behind this programme. The purpose was simply to support teaching and learning, and in this way to quality assure system effectiveness.

Intelligent Accountability

The term 'intelligent accountability' was coined by O'Neill (2013) in the context of the draconian accountability environment that continues to prevail in England. Intelligent accountability essentially has to do with validity, fairness, transparency, trust and sustainability.

In an attainment monitoring application, validity has to do with the appropriateness both of the subject or subject domain being assessed and of the assessment tools used to measure attainment. This is appropriateness in terms of the inferences to be drawn about system effectiveness on the basis of the resulting attainment data (consequential validity). A narrow reading test would generally not be agreed to be a valid tool from which to arrive at comparative statements about the effectiveness of different schools, or of a single educational system over time, in terms of developing students' 'language ability'. A combination of numeracy and literacy attainment results at the end of primary schooling might not be a valid basis for statements about relative between-school achievement in chemistry at age 15, or even in mathematics at that age.

Validity also has to do with the adequacy of any explicit or implicit student sampling. The attainment results of a self-selected, or otherwise potentially biased, sample of students would not be a valid basis for inferences about the attainment of an entire national, or even within-school, student population. National qualifications data, for example, are often not valid for system-level evaluation because of non-representation arising both from general self-selection (not every student in the age population choosing to study for qualifications) and from further self-selection where optional subject choices are available (given issues to do with the likely non-comparability of grading standards across subjects). O'Neill (2013) effectively illustrates the issues in a comprehensive critical overview of practice in England.

Item and task sampling is relevant, too, whether the sampling is implicit or explicit. Administering the same short reading test to every student in all primary schools throughout a country in an annual attainment survey will arguably produce less generalizable

attainment results than administering more items in several such tests using matrix sampling (where the different tests are randomly allocated to different students). Assessment validity is compromised when the subject domain is not fully represented.

Fairness is an aspect of assessment validity in the sense that any degree of non-validity in general accountability model design will have implications for fair comparisons amongst students, teachers and schools – this is not to forget the essential requirement for technical reliability in assessment.

Transparency is an essential prerequisite of an 'intelligent' accountability system if stakeholder buy-in and trust is to be ensured. It is essential that assessment results are understandable to all concerned and accountability implications immediately clear. Neither mean test scores nor 'scaled' scores are user-friendly in this sense, which is why the international survey programmes report proportions of students in various 'performance bands' or 'levels of achievement', to which are attached short verbal descriptions of the demonstrated abilities and skills concerned.

Finally, for sustainability, an intelligent accountability system is one that is manageable in terms in particular of assessment workload in schools.

National Assessment Serving Intelligent Accountability

To illustrate the potential value of national assessment in intelligent accountability, along with the effects that politicians have had – and will continue to have – on such programmes and on their actual value as accountability tools, it might be instructive to consider some of the more salient experiences of a subset of the countries previously mentioned that have the longest histories of national assessment to date.

The selected subset comprises the US, England, Scotland and France. The US's NAEP, the world's earliest-established, longest-running and still surviving national assessment programme, has over its lifetime been subject to many political pressures to change. In response, it has expanded its activities, but also succeeded in retaining an accountability function at system level only. In contrast with the US, England's system evaluation history is a particularly chequered one. It has been characterised by continuing political interference, with the current system now serving a draconian school-level accountability function. Scotland is interesting in the way that it has up to now resisted pressures to provide information of value in school-level accountability, choosing quite a different path from the one England is pursuing. France is included for its continued resistance to international trends, along with its cultural attachment to informing teachers about student learning in the expectation that they will know how to react for the better, rather than admonishing schools for their 'unsatisfactory' achievement.

NATIONAL ASSESSMENT IN THE US

1970s: The First Decade

NAEP was originally planned to monitor the achievement of students aged 9, 13 and 17 and young adults (this latter intention never materialised) in different subject areas (Pellegrino, 2014). The first surveys in 1969/1970 were in science, citizenship and writing. Performance reporting would be for the national population at each age and for demographic subgroups within this, including gender. In response to the concerns of state and local leaders about the possible introduction of a national curriculum, and pressure for accountability, the programme was designed to report at national level and not by state, district or school.

From its inception, NAEP has used matrix sampling in order to limit the number of test items and tasks put before individual students, whilst maximising the number administered in the survey as a whole. This is to ensure assessment validity through broad curriculum coverage without rendering assessment unmanageable in schools and unacceptable for students. Initially, performance was reported item-by-item, task-by-task, with some items and tasks released for exemplification and others retained securely for re-use in later surveys in order to monitor change over time.

Item-by-item reporting, however, although interesting for teachers and educational researchers, is not particularly useful for policymakers. Policymakers need summative information, particularly for evaluating educational initiatives aimed at improving population or subgroup attainment generally. Moreover, NAEP reported on the basis of age not grade, and again this was a problem when it came to using the information in educational policy making.

1980s: The NAEP Redesign

NAEP is one of the best illustrations of the reality that, in order to survive, national assessment programmes must remain responsive to policy pressures. A redesign in the 1980s was such a response. In 1984, responsibility for NAEP development and administration moved from the Education Commission of the States to the Educational Testing Service, and many procedural changes were introduced at that point. These included a new dual focus on age and grade, a reporting model newly based on subjects rather than on individual items and tasks, an increase in the use of multiple-choice items and the adoption of item response theory (IRT) for response modelling and analysis (Messick et al., 1983). However, the adoption of IRT, with its strong assumptions about item invariance, quickly resulted in implausible trend results for reading (between 1984 and 1986), leading to the often-quoted message, 'When measuring change, do not change the measure' (Beaton, 1990: 165). The measure clearly had to change, however, because of the intention to continue with IRT in the future.

In order to monitor the effectiveness of numerous state-level reforms, driven by the report *A Nation at Risk* (National Commission on Excellence in Education, 1983), NAEP also began to come under pressure in the late 1980s/early 1990s to provide state-level and even district-level results in addition to national results, a move that would begin to newly assign to the programme an overt system-level accountability role beyond that of the national system. An important reporting change that was made at this time in the interests of user interpretability was the introduction of 'levels of achievement', with labels 'basic', 'proficient' and 'advanced'. These levels, to which individual students are assigned before aggregated distributions are produced, are determined on the basis of achieved scaled scores. Their validity has come under severe scrutiny in formal NAEP evaluations and elsewhere (Buckendahl et al., 2009; Pellegrino, 2014).

1990s: Trend NAEP and Main NAEP

Another inevitable pressure that NAEP experienced after some years in operation was to change its subject assessment focus to reflect a changing curriculum. Such pressure could have resulted in abandonment of the original NAEP model, with a complete loss of trend data from that point on. Instead, resistance resulted in a decision to run two NAEP programmes in parallel in the future: Trend NAEP and Main NAEP.

Trend NAEP follows the original NAEP design and, as its name suggests, is responsible for continuing to document change over time in a selected set of subject areas at the original ages of 9, 13 and 17 using items already used in previous NAEP surveys. The subject areas were reading, writing, mathematics and science. In practice, writing assessment was dropped because of lack of reliability and science was also eventually

dropped because the original content coverage (the science assessment framework) had become outdated. As a result, trend data over the past four decades is available for reading and mathematics only (National Center for Educational Statistics, 2013).

Main NAEP, in contrast, is designed to measure not what students 'know and can do', as in Trend NAEP, but rather to reflect contemporary thinking about what students 'should know and be able to do' in a range of subject areas, with the assessment frameworks revised periodically to maintain currency, for example to embrace interactive digital teaching. There are two component programmes here: National NAEP and State NAEP. The first is based on nationally representative samples of students in grades 4, 8 and 12, and assesses achievement in a range of subject areas: mathematics and reading are assessed every 2 years, science and writing are assessed every 4 years, with other subjects assessed periodically, including the arts, civics, economics, geography, technology and engineering literacy, and US history. State NAEP is based on representative state samples of students in the same grades as National NAEP, and assesses achievement in reading, writing, mathematics and science, in participating states.

2000s Onwards: A Mandatory State-Level Assessment Role

State participation was voluntary during the 1990s – it became mandatory in 2001 following the introduction of the No Child Left Behind Act. NAEP has consequently evolved from a programme that furnished national-level attainment information only, of value to federal politicians and policymakers, to a programme that now also provides state-level attainment information (in the same graphical 'league table' form as PISA country comparisons) for use by state as well as federal authorities. NAEP is not involved, however, in school-level attainment reporting – it leaves school-level accountability with the associated performance incentives and penalties (teachers' pay linked to their students' performance) to the states themselves through their own state-wide exhaustive testing programmes (Hout and Elliott, 2011).

NATIONAL ASSESSMENT IN ENGLAND

1950s Through 1970s: Standardised Testing

England's earliest attempts to monitor population attainment focused on 'reading ability' at age 11 (the end of primary schooling) and age 15 (then the end of compulsory secondary schooling). Sample-based surveys were conducted periodically from 1948 to the late 1970s, based on repeated administration of two standardized sentence completion tests. Reported attainment initially rose slightly, but then began to fall away (Kellaghan and Madaus, 1982; Start and Wells, 1972), triggering debate about how real the attainment changes might be and what could be done to redress the situation should the decline be genuine. The tests inevitably came in for criticism that focused on decreasing relevance (outdated vocabulary items) and fundamental validity (could sentence completion be an acceptable vehicle for assessing 'reading comprehension'?). Concern was compounded by the fact that important attainment ceiling effects were apparent at both ages tested.

In response to this experience, the Government set up a Committee of Inquiry to look into all aspects of the teaching of English in schools, not just reading. In their influential 'Bullock Report', the Committee outlined what it considered would be a more effective alternative methodology for attainment monitoring (Department of Education and Science, 1975, Chapter 3). The central pivot of their proposed new strategy would be a dynamic question bank, from within which questions would be selected to create monitoring instruments that would be responsive to developments in the curriculum, and which would allow comparable assessments of performance over time.

1980s: The APU

Modelled in some respects on NAEP, the APU survey programmes came into being in England, Wales and Northern Ireland in the late 1970s (Newton, 2008). Sample-based surveys were carried out in English language (not reading alone), mathematics and science – with foreign language and design and technology surveys appearing later as one-off exercises. Like the reading surveys that preceded them, the new surveys focused on 11-year-olds and 15-year-olds, with 13-year-olds included for science because this was the last opportunity to assess population attainment before students made their optional science subject choices in preparation for national qualifications. Surveys began on an annual cycle, with an intention to move to a 3-year cycle after 5 years.

Matrix sampling was adopted for the administration of relatively large numbers of items and tasks in surveys, whilst keeping the testing load low for individual students. In addition, both students and teachers were invited to complete questionnaires to provide information about the learning environment, with which to contextualise the attainment results, potentially enhancing their policy value.

Interestingly, system monitoring was not initially an explicit programme objective – the 'identification of underachievement' was, even though the meaning of the term 'underachievement' had never been clarified. The label 'underachievement' implicitly presupposes that the achievement level concerned should be higher, and might be improved through policy initiatives. But how to recognise underachievement? Following extensive debate, it was agreed that 'relatively low achievement' would be the programme focus (for example, of one gender compared with the other, or of particular regions of the country), with no particular accountability implications.

It was widely acknowledged that much of the materials development work of the APU teams was ground-breaking and that the impact on teaching was positive and considerable. In addition to full survey reports, several feedback booklets for teachers were produced on a variety of topics, including practical assessment in science, understanding decimals, and assessing speaking and listening. Frontiers were also pushed on the technical side (for overviews of the APU experience and comprehensive lists of APU publications, see Foxman et al., 1991; Johnson, 1989).

Late 1980s: A Growing Thirst for School-Level Accountability

Whatever the strengths and weaknesses of the APU programme as a whole, it is fair to say that the Conservative politicians that rose to power as a result of a change of government soon after the programme was launched were not enamoured of it.

Although the programme reported attainment at the level of items and tasks, as well as at the level of subject subdomains, such as 'reading' and 'oracy' in English language, none reported attainment at the level of whole subjects in a 'user-friendly' rapidly digestible form, which politicians newly craved. It would have been possible to provide descriptive 'levels of achievement' of the sort introduced by Main NAEP in the US, or 'proficiency levels' as used for reporting purposes in PISA, but no time was allowed for this development before the programme was abandoned.

Manageability also became a problem. It could, and should, have been anticipated that once three subject programmes were underway annually, as they were during the early 1980s, with a total of 7 age-related subject surveys in operation in each school year, school participation, which was voluntary, would be affected detrimentally. Indeed, at one point teachers threatened to boycott the testing.

Arguably, though, it was the APU's designed impotence as a tool for school-level accountability that led to its eventual demise.

Late 1980s: Introduction of a National Curriculum and Associated National Assessment

In response to its disillusionment with the APU, in 1987 Margaret Thatcher's Conservative Government took steps to introduce a national curriculum, along with an associated school-level assessment programme. The National Curriculum Task Group on Assessment and Testing (TGAT) was under severe pressure to deliver, and submitted its final report to the government after just 6 months of work (TGAT, 1988). The Government acted quickly. The APU survey programmes were summarily ended and the 1988 Education Reform Act – a national curriculum for students aged 5 to 16, with a few differences in coverage from one country to another (Johnson, 2012) – was introduced into England and Wales, along with accompanying statutory assessment arrangements for cohort assessment. Northern Ireland followed suit under the Education Reform (Northern Ireland) Order 1989, again with some differences in the adopted national curriculum.

National curriculum assessment (NCA) was to take place at the end of each of three key stages in schooling: key stage 1 (age 7), key stage 2 (end of primary school, age 11) and key stage 3 (lower secondary school, age 14). System monitoring remained a principal purpose. But two further principal purposes were added: first, the provision of student-level attainment information for the benefit of students, teachers and parents/carers; and second, aggregated student attainment data for use in school self-evaluation and external school accountability.

The main features of the TGAT assessment recommendations were the introduction of a flexible 10-level progression framework spanning numerous broadly defined 'attainment targets' described in the form of 'statements of attainment' (SoAs) that would serve as references for teacher assessment. To support teachers when arriving at summative level judgements, 'standard assessment tasks' (SATs) would be provided for classroom use. These were the tasks that former APU team members and others soon found themselves developing.

This early NCA model was doomed to failure from the start. For what exactly were teachers expected to do under this new system in terms of student assessment? 'Too much' was the answer. So much too much that the system soon cracked (see Sainsbury (1994) for an interesting account). Here, in brief, is why.

The progression framework was in principle a criterion-referenced framework, the SoAs being the criteria against which level attainment would be judged. Teachers were expected to assess each of their students against each statement of attainment, and come to decisions about appropriate levels in each of a range of subjects. One immediate problem was that the number of attainment targets was large in some subjects, and there were multiple statements of attainment against each level within each of these. Between English, mathematics and science alone there were hundreds of SoAs. The requirement to assess all of them left teachers with a predictably impossible job to do, and eventually they rebelled. Manageability, or, rather unmanageability, ultimately led to the abandonment of this particular model of national assessment, although issues of assessment reliability and whole-cohort interpretability also contributed. This was very clearly a non-intelligent accountability model.

The politicians' response was to introduce into all three countries a regime of exhaustive national testing at the end of the three key stages, complemented by a simplified 8-level framework for teacher assessment, using 'best fit' descriptors. 'National assessment moved away from teachers' control and was transformed into written examinations in

English, mathematics and science…taken by an entire year group simultaneously' (Isaacs, 2010: 323). One interesting national difference worthy of note is that there was no plan to introduce the same national test system into Northern Ireland at the end of key stage 2, given that the 11+ examination, a nationally administered grammar school selection device, was still in operation in that country at the time and was set to continue indefinitely. In fact, the statutory 11+ examination was abandoned in 2008, leaving a political vacuum, within which 'a non-statutory, unregulated and private transfer system operates without evaluation or scrutiny' at this point (Elwood, 2013: 211).

Further problems ensued and in 1993, in response to a threatened teacher boycott of the planned testing that year, the government set up a review of the curriculum and its assessment (Dearing, 1993). As a result, testing was dropped for key stage 1, so that only teacher assessment remained, and although tests continued to feature at key stages 2 and 3, these were shorter than before (with new implications for 'intelligent' accountability) and were, from then on, externally marked.

Mid-1990s: the Introduction of School League Tables

It was in 1996 that test results and teacher assessments at key stages 2 and 3 began to be used to produce school 'league tables' (teacher assessments were dropped from the performance tables in 1999, only to be reintroduced in 2010). With the introduction of league tables, system-level accountability was now officially extended to school-level accountability, with the steadily increasing use of NCA results to admonish schools for 'poor' performance, and even to close schools considered to be 'failing' (both practices continue, and indeed are reinforced).

In 2002, the NCA was supplemented by the introduction of a teacher-assessed Early Years Foundation Stage (EYFS) profile for 3–5-year-olds, thus extending the monitored age range downwards from 7-year-olds to 3-year-olds.

From the mid-2000s onwards, Wales and Northern Ireland broke away from the pattern for England, abandoning testing and introducing teacher assessment in its place – decisions that have brought their own problems in terms of data dependability (Johnson, 2013). In the meantime, England continued along its now well-established testing path, punctuated by further curriculum reviews, a review of cumulated NCA experience, and consequent changes to NCA (see Department for Education (2014) for a detailed timeline of changes). In particular, in response to the NCA review report (Expert Group on Assessment, 2009), testing at key stage 3 was abandoned, and cohort testing at key stage 2 in science was replaced with sample-based testing (a quarter of the sampled schools failed to take part in the first round of sample-based testing in 2010, the final annual survey taking place in 2012). In a separate development, a statutory phonics check for all 6-year-olds in state-funded schools was introduced in England in 2012 (see Bradbury (2014) for reflections on the accountability motivation for the phonics check, and for the EYFS profile mentioned earlier).

In 2014, a new national curriculum was introduced, and from 2016 the assessment of English, mathematics and science will take a new form. In particular, achievement levels have been abandoned. In their place, individual students will achieve one IRT-based scaled score as a result of key stage 1 testing and a second as a result of key stage 2 testing, with the difference in scores indicating the extent of progression relative to the average for all students with the same key stage 1 score. In principle, this 'value added' model takes account of the differential intakes of schools and provides more valid comparisons of school effectiveness. Teacher assessment will also be included using new performance descriptors.

In addition to system-level monitoring, school-level accountability remains an assessment purpose for English and mathematics, which will involve cohort-testing as before, although not for science, for which surveys will continue to be sample-based on a new 2-year cycle.

Following extensive stakeholder consultation (Lynch et al., 2015), a new initiative – 'reception baseline assessment' – is to see the introduction of *formal* assessment of basic skills in literacy, reading and cognition at age 4. The programme, for launch in September 2016, replaces the EYFS profile. The Government's motivation for introducing assessment at the start of the primary reception year is to improve how primary schools' progress is measured. How intelligent this new model of 'value-added' national assessment proves to be in practice remains to be seen.

NATIONAL ASSESSMENT IN SCOTLAND

1950s to 1980s: Standardised Testing

Like England, Scotland, which has independent control of its educational system, has a long history of attainment monitoring, with primary sector surveys (Scottish Scholastic Survey) of the attainment of 10-year-olds in English and arithmetic having been conducted as far back as 1953 and repeated in 1963 using standardised tests. The evidence from the surveys was that attainment had improved in both areas in the intervening period (Scottish Council for Research in Education, 1968). An inactivity gap of 15 years followed after which, in 1978 and 1981, two national surveys of reading were again carried out (Neville, 1988), this time at ages 9 and 12, thus extending coverage to the lower secondary school.

Mid-1980s: Sample-Based National Assessment

In the mid-1980s Scotland followed England by introducing a sample-based system-monitoring programme. This was the Assessment of Achievement Programme (AAP), which was to focus on the attainments of 9-year-olds (mid-primary), 12-year-olds (end of primary school) and 14-year-olds (lower secondary school) in English, mathematics and science (Condie et al., 2003).

Initially, like early NAEP in the US, the AAP reported estimated population and subgroup performance item-by-item. But as the programme rolled along through the late 1980s and early 1990s, a national 5–14 curriculum was introduced into the country along with associated 6-level attainment progression frameworks for most school subjects. Unlike England in the late 1980s, Scotland did not at this point introduce statutory assessment, and neither did it abandon the AAP. Instead, the AAP was adapted, so that the surveys eventually reported with reference to the same 5–14 curriculum attainment levels that teachers were themselves now using in the classroom (Munro, 2003).

There was no statutory obligation on schools to have teachers assess their students against the 5–14 progressive level framework at any stage of schooling, nor to submit these assessments to other bodies. Nevertheless, the adoption of the 5–14 assessment framework was widespread and the submission of teachers' assessments to local authorities and central government became almost universal throughout the 1990s and early 2000s. In aggregated form, the data were used for school evaluation purposes by local authorities and the school inspectorate, with feedback to schools taking the form of advice for improvement, along with suggested improvement targets – no league tables were published. Judgements were aggregated nationally for the 'National Audit' and were used by the Scottish Government for system monitoring, alongside other relevant system information, including AAP results.

Mid-2000s: Extension to Local Authority System Assessment

Following a national consultation on assessment in the early 2000s, the National Audit was discontinued and the AAP was replaced, or, rather, enlarged and rebranded. Its successor, the Scottish Survey of Achievement (SSA) was launched in 2005 and was given the broader remit to assess and report attainment in key subjects at local education authority level, as well as nationally (Hutchinson and Young, 2011). By this time, the AAP had changed its focus from ages 9, 12 and 14 to ages 8, 10, 12 and 14 to increase the policy value of statements about age-related attainment progression. Each year there was, in principle, a focus on one of four curriculum areas – English Language, Social Subjects, Science and Mathematics – with some practically-based core skills assessed annually, although less formally (for example, ICT, 'working with others', problem solving). In practice, the assessment of literacy and numeracy predominated, with science benefitting from just one single survey in the SSA's 5-year life span.

Wherever possible, attainment continued to be reported with reference to the 5–14 assessment framework. Interestingly, unlike the AAP, the SSA also gathered teachers' judgements of the 5–14 attainment levels of those students who had been sampled for survey participation. This permitted a direct comparison of teacher judgements and test-based classifications, with interesting results that would support the inference that dependable system-level monitoring could not be based on teacher assessment (Johnson and Munro, 2008). To continue to provide a learning context against which to reflect on the attainment findings, students and teachers were invited to complete background questionnaires if they had participated in the survey.

One insurmountable issue that arose for the SSA in relation to authority-level reporting concerned school workload. Scotland is a small country, with around 60,000 school students in an age group, and as many as 32 different local education authorities of varying population sizes were operating at the time. In order to provide sufficient numbers of students for testing, high proportions of secondary schools were being selected for authority participation in many cases, with high numbers of students selected from within each school. In the smaller authorities, exhaustive testing was the order of the day. Should the programme have continued longer than it did the burden on the school system would have become intolerable, particularly as international surveys were also taking place from time to time.

There were two other reasons for abandoning the extended remit. First, high numbers of sampled students in each survey school rendered any attempt to manage practically-based assessment even more problematic than it had been previously, and practical assessment had always featured in the surveys, albeit more informally than the written testing. Second, dependable school-level attainment estimates were in principle newly available, given the high numbers of students now tested in many schools. The Scottish Government came under increasing pressure from the schools inspectorate to make these data available for use in school-level monitoring. However, the SSA, like the AAP before it, had never been intended to provide data at the level of individual schools or students, and policymakers at the time had no desire to change this situation.

With these issues in mind, the final survey in the SSA's short lifespan, carried out in 2009, reverted to national reporting only. The SSA could have continued on this basis, were it not for the fact that the 5–14 curriculum was replaced towards the end of the decade by the Curriculum for Excellence (CfE), and policymakers and others assumed (one could argue wrongly) that a new curriculum, or, rather, a new form of curriculum delivery, 'necessarily' implied the need for a new attainment monitoring programme.

2010s: A Reversion to National System Monitoring Only, and Narrower Scope

As its name implies, the new survey programme, the Scottish Survey of Literacy and Numeracy (SSLN), focuses on the assessment of literacy and numeracy, in alternate years (Spencer, 2013). The programme was launched with a first survey of numeracy skills in 2011, with attainment reported at ages 9, 12 and 14 (note the reversion from ages 8 and 10 – as in the SSA – to age 9 as in the earlier AAP) using achievement levels established by judgemental standard setting in the absence of any form of CfE attainment framework that the programme might have made useful reference to.

The reduction in the subject coverage of the new programme can be justified in terms of international trends, but it might also be considered a convenient opportunity for science to be dropped, given that national 5–14 attainment, as estimated in the AAP and the SSA, had routinely fallen well short of official government attainment targets at all ages assessed. The degree of 'intelligence' in the system-monitoring model was consequently reduced.

An interesting decision to change the procedure for selecting the national samples of students for assessment at each school stage was that school sampling would no longer be practised. All schools were to be invited to take part in SSLN surveys. But within each participating primary school just two students would be randomly selected for testing in each relevant age group, and even within secondary schools the student sample sizes would be modest (at a maximum of 12). There were two principal reasons for this change. First, small in-school student samples would facilitate practical assessment, and this was a particularly important desire in light of the skills emphasis in the CfE. Second, with only two students tested at each relevant age in each primary school, and a maximum of 12 in each secondary school, there could no longer be pressure from the inspectorate or other bodies to make data available for school-level comparisons. System-level evaluation would remain the function of the programme.

Perhaps predictably, however, the designed inability of the SSLN to offer school-level attainment results soon became perceived by politicians and policymakers as a weakness rather than a strength. A ministerial announcement in September 2015 finally signalled its imminent demise (The Scottish Government, 2015). In its place will be an exhaustive programme of 'standardized testing' of reading, writing and numeracy, planned for introduction into the Scottish school system from 2017.

NATIONAL ASSESSMENT IN FRANCE

Late 1980s to Mid-2000s: 'Diagnostic' National Assessment

What particularly distinguishes France from the other countries described earlier is the 'diagnostic' survey programme that ran from the late 1980s to the mid-2000s (Trosseille and Rocher, 2015). Between 1987 and 2007 every child in the country took the same tests in literacy (French) and numeracy at the beginning of their fourth year in primary school (age 8) and at the beginning of their first year in the *collège*, or lower secondary school (age 11). The schools inspectorate determined what the assessment should focus on each year, depending on their current areas of concern (fractions, dictation, writing, or whatever).

The timing of assessment, at the beginning rather than at the end of a school year, was of benefit to receiving class teachers, who personally marked the tests and, on the advice of the school inspectors, used the results in their child-centred programme planning for the coming year. For teachers, a secondary benefit of the timing was that there was no personal accountability threat associated with the testing as there inevitably is when testing takes place at the end of a school year. For both reasons, teachers, including headteachers, appreciated the value of the testing for helping to ensure system effectiveness. Professional buy-in was high.

Although aggregated results were produced at regional and national level, this particular assessment programme could not serve the function of system monitoring in any direct sense because its assessment focus was not fixed (the inspectors decided what was assessed each time), and yet there were multiple growing pressures to monitor the system. First, there were what policymakers considered on the basis of misleading league table positions to be poor performances in PISA (but which in reality were average for the OECD on the basis of mean scaled scores). The second influence was the introduction in 2006 of a national curriculum (*Le socle commun*) into the school system. A third source of pressure was the emergence of a new national programme of administration accountability. In response, the diagnostic survey programme was abandoned and replaced with a new 'accountability programme' (Jeantheau and Johnson, 2012), partially modelled on the NCA in England. The new monitoring programme was ushered in towards the end of the decade.

Late 2000s: The New 'Accountability' Programme

Exhaustive assessment continued, with all students in an age group taking the same tests in literacy and in numeracy, as before, and with class teachers marking their own students' scripts. Crucially, however, the timing of the assessment was modified: testing was moved from the beginning of the school year to the end of the previous school year (actually to the end of the second year and to the middle of the final year of primary school). Teachers in schools that were randomly selected as part of a representative national subsample were required to key their results into a supplied database for the purpose of transmission to central government.

In general, the results from the new programme had much less value for teachers and schools than in the past, and teachers were aware that they could be held accountable for their students' performances. Even though the government repeatedly stated that it had no intention of reporting results by school, and in fact no schools were identified in the web-based results reported each year, the exhaustive testing meant that this possibility always remained an option. The accountability threat was ever-present.

There was vociferous dissent among practitioners and other stakeholders about the programme design change (Education Commission, 2011; Jeantheau and Johnson, 2012). Criticisms focused on a variety of issues. Unsurprisingly, these included the timing of the testing, which obviated any possibility of providing useable diagnostic feedback for teachers, and which also rendered the validity of the test results dubious as measures of learning over any meaningful period of schooling. The 'unsuitable' nature of the test items, the majority of which were multiple-choice with binary scoring, also invited criticism, as did the limited representation of the curriculum in the tests. Payment to teachers for marking, and for keying test results for transmission to authorities and government, was another point of contention.

After 3 years or so of experience under the new system, and despite the continued absence of any sign that school league tables might be introduced, the dissent continued and boycotts threatened. Introducing partial credit in marking and moving the mid-year testing to the end of the school year failed to placate the critics. In response, the Government drew up plans to replace the existing programme with one that would monitor science and technology as well as reading and numeracy, with each subject assessed on a 3-year survey cycle rather than all subjects each year. There would also be changes to the timing of assessment: surveys would take place at the end of the second year in the primary school (one year earlier than before), and at the beginning and end of the lower secondary school (MEN-DEPP, 2014). The new programme never materialised, however. A change of Government in 2012 led to a political decision to abandon this form of system monitoring as 'inappropriate' – a reaction, perhaps, to the volume of criticism of the existing programme, with its

fluid objectives and acknowledged technical weaknesses (Trosseille and Rocher, 2015). A final annual survey was run under the old programme in 2013, for the benefit of teachers and parents only, with voluntary school participation.

Early 2000s Onwards: Broader Curriculum Monitoring Develops

Meanwhile, a programme of sample-based subject assessment that began in 2003 continues. Known as CEDRE (*Le cycle des évaluations disciplinaires réalisées sur échantillons*), the programme assesses achievement at the end of primary school and at the end of the lower secondary school in several curriculum subjects or subject groups, each on a 6-year cycle: French; mathematics; modern languages; civics, history and geography; and experimental science. The majority of test items are multiple-choice, IRT is the technical methodology used for data analysis, and an ambition for the programme is to move to computer-based assessment as soon as feasible. Details of this and other continuing forms of system monitoring in France, including occasional longitudinal surveys and panel studies, are offered by Trosseille and Rocher (2015).

CONCLUSION

National assessment design is a challenging activity, whether the data to be furnished by surveys is for system description and monitoring only, or for explicit use in accountability at some level (Greaney and Kellaghan, 2008; Kellaghan, et al., 2009). In particular, to serve purposes of quality research – system description and monitoring – and of 'intelligent' accountability, the attainment measures produced in national assessment must be meaningful, relevant and dependable. The degree to which these properties will be achieved will depend on what, in principle, is being assessed (for example, 'reading', 'problem-solving skills'), how the assessment is carried out (written tests, teacher judgement, observer-completed rubrics, etc.), what degree of population and subgroup representativeness is achieved in sampling (for example, age-group representation for students, domain representation for items/tasks, population representation for markers and raters) and how attainment results are reported (mean domain scores, mean scaled scores, percentage distributions across performance levels). In addition, the assessment process itself must be manageable in terms of teacher workload and general burden on schools, the findings must be readily interpretable and widely accepted as valid and fair, and use of the findings by politicians and policymakers must be to support rather than to sanction.

Narrowly defined standardized tests, whose results might be meaningful to teachers as a result of test familiarity, have little curriculum relevance in system monitoring terms, and little if any consequential validity for use in accountability. Attainment results produced by sentence completion or arithmetic tests are of limited value as indicators of population performance in reading comprehension or numeracy more broadly defined. In turn, performances in written tests of reading comprehension or of numeracy will have limited value as indicators of population performance in language or mathematics more generally. The assessment of 'science knowledge and understanding' does not necessarily tell us anything about how well developed students' 'science literacy' is, and vice versa.

When subjects like history, geography and music do not feature in national assessment, none of the outcomes information for subjects that do feature will be relevant. Subjects included in the survey might also attract more attention in teaching, to the detriment of those not included. Despite the greater challenges in terms of logistics, cost and reliability, some countries do attempt to cover a broader range of curriculum subjects in their large-scale assessment, for example the US (with Main NAEP), Sweden, Belgium (Flanders) – and

France once again after its unhappy flirtation with the English cohort assessment model. Nevertheless, the growing emphasis on literacy and numeracy in national assessment worldwide must be of some concern, in terms of 'intelligent accountability'.

Attainment reporting is another issue. Mean domain scores are interpretable only to the extent that they enable comparisons between subgroups and over time. In themselves they are not appealing to policymakers because national targets based on mean scores are practically impossible to set. Greater problems arise when attainment is reported in terms of mean scaled scores, particularly when (IRT) scales are artificially elongated and impossible for the non-technical stakeholder to relate to reality. This is why performance bands, or levels of achievement, carry such appeal, given their reification in short performance descriptors. Such bands, however, are typically defined on the basis of standard setting procedures in which appropriate cut scores are identified through judgemental reviews of test items, with verbal performance descriptors similarly based on scrutiny of 'borderline' items. Different reviewers will have different opinions about where the score boundaries should be placed, and yet reliability information is rarely furnished to support the cut score decisions finally made. NAEP uses performance bands in reporting, as do the international survey programmes and growing numbers of other national assessment programmes. Validating cut score decisions for this purpose, as has been carried out in NAEP, is essential if intelligent accountability is to be properly supported. Similar comments are relevant when borderline items, sometimes few in number, are subjectively reviewed to produce seductively plausible performance descriptors.

Administering numerous individual items and tasks, including performance assessments, in surveys, and reporting attainment on an illustrative subset, might in principle be more useful for teachers than summative reporting, with a potentially positive impact on teaching and learning. But such reporting is understandably of little value or interest to policymakers, as NAEP in the US, the APU in England, and the AAP in Scotland discovered. In this regard, it is perhaps astonishing that New Zealand's NEMP, despite its high quality standards and effective dissemination to schools, continued with this approach for as long as it did until it eventually and inevitably succumbed to the growing international pressure for system accountability programmes of value to policymakers above all other stakeholders (Smaill, 2013).

In terms of appropriateness for system monitoring, programmes that employ matrix sampling to administer large numbers of items and tasks to students, reporting summative results at domain or subdomain levels in addition to item-level performance results, arguably offer the highest utility value, both for policymakers and practitioners. NAEP, the APU and Scotland's SSA are examples.

Manageability pressure on schools and class teachers can be an issue that threatens even an otherwise intelligent accountability model. As noted earlier, both the APU and the SSA became unmanageable, operating as they were with annual surveys at multiple stages in the school system and in different curriculum subjects in relatively small countries. The testing burden on schools became intolerable in both cases, and, along with other factors, led to the demise of both programmes. NAEP was untouched by this problem in the very much larger US.

The most compelling weakness that led to the abandonment of the APU, however, was not manageability, cost, quality or relevance. It was a shift in political priorities that the APU could not respond to, brought about by a change of government after the programme had been in operation for several years. This was the desire to extend assessment and reporting to embrace school-level attainment results for accountability purposes. Schooling in the US is the responsibility of state authorities and not federal government, and NAEP therefore escaped this pressure, as it had escaped school burden issues, and the states themselves put

in place their own incentive-based school accountability systems (teacher pay linked to student attainment). Ironically, despite the cost and logistics involved in exhaustive student testing and the demoralising effect that incentive-based accountability has on teachers, few, if any, benefits have been reported in terms of increased state system effectiveness in the intervening two decades (Hout and Elliott, 2011).

Although there are no visible benefits associated with accountability-driven cohort testing, there are important losses. In particular, in order to have direct comparisons of school-level attainment, such programmes typically administer the same set of items/tasks to all students in all schools in any survey, packaged in one or more short tests to avoid overburdening individual students. Compared with the matrix sampling models used in sample-based surveys, fewer items and tasks are administered each time – and fewer items overall implies reduced curriculum coverage. This, in turn, reduces the validity of the attainment results as indicators of subject achievement, and therefore the validity of their use in system accountability, nationally, regionally, locally or at school level. It also means that a very much longer time period is needed before large pools of items become available that could be used as resources for positive curriculum impact through focused analyses and reports.

As mentioned earlier, one of the biggest impacts that the international surveys have had on education systems worldwide is the recent and rapid expansion of national assessment programmes, with many countries newly benefiting from the availability of this valuable policy tool. Programmes are relatively new, and it remains to be seen how well they will perform and, in particular, how effectively they will respond to policy pressures for change in the future. The lessons learned from the extensive national assessment experience of those few countries considered here should be of value to programme designers and managers as they attempt to anticipate and meet new policy demands.

REFERENCES

Beaton, A.E. (1990) 'Introduction', in A.E. Beaton and R. Zwick (eds.), *The Effect of Changes in the National Assessment: Disentangling the NAEP 1985–86 Reading Anomaly.* Report No. 17-TR-21. Princeton, NJ: Educational Testing Service, National Assessment of Educational Progress. pp. 1–14.

Bonnet, G. (1997) 'Country profile from France', *Assessment in Education: Principles, Policy and Practice*, 4: 295–306.

Bradbury, A. (2014) '"Slimmed down" assessment or increased accountability? Teachers, elections and UK government assessment policy', *Oxford Review of Education*, 40: 610–27.

Buckendahl, C.W., Plake, B.S. and Davis, S.L. (2009) 'Conducting a lifecycle audit of the National Assessment of Educational Progress', *Applied Measurement in Education*, 22: 321–38.

Condie, R., Robertson, I.J. and Napuk, A. (2003) 'The Assessment of Achievement Programme', in T.G.K. Bryce, and W.M. Humes (eds.), *Scottish Education.* Edinburgh: Edinburgh University Press. pp. 766–76.

Crooks, T.J. and Flockton, L.C. (1993) *The Design and Implementation of National Monitoring of Educational Outcomes in New Zealand Primary Schools.* Dunedin, New Zealand: Higher Education Development Centre.

Dearing, R. (1993) *The National Curriculum and its Assessment: Final Report.* London: School Curriculum and Assessment Authority.

Department for Education (2014) *Quality and Methodology Information: Attainment in Primary Schools in England.* London: Department for Education.

Department of Education and Science (1975) *A Language for Life: The Bullock Report.* London: HMSO.

Education Commission (2011) *Les indicateurs relatifs aux acquis des élèves: bilan des résultats de l'école – 2011.* Paris: Haut Conseil de l'Education.

Elwood, J. (2013) 'Educational assessment policy and practice: a matter of ethics', *Assessment in Education: Principles, Policy & Practice,* 20: 205–20.

Eurydice (2009) *National Testing of Pupils in Europe: Objectives, Organisation and Use of Results.* Brussels: Education, Audiovisual and Culture Executive Agency.

Expert Group on Assessment (2009) *Report of the Expert Group on Assessment.* London: Department for Children, Schools and Families.

Foxman, D., Hutchison, D. and Bloomfield, B. (1991) *The APU Experience 1977–1990.* London: Schools Examination and Assessment Council.

Greaney, V. and Kellaghan, T. (2008) *Assessing National Achievement Levels in Education. Volume 1.* Washington, DC: The World Bank.

Hout, M. and Elliott, S.W. (eds.) (2011) *Incentives and Test-Based Accountability in Education.* Washington, DC: The National Academies Press.

Husen, T. and Postlethwaite, T.N. (1996) 'A brief history of the International Association for the Evaluation of Educational Achievement (IEA)', *Assessment in Education: Principles, Policy & Practice,* 3: 129–42.

Hutchinson, C. and Young, M. (2011) 'Assessment for learning in the accountability era: Empirical evidence from Scotland', *Studies in Educational Evaluation*, 37: 62–70.

INCA (2012) *National Assessment and Public Examination Arrangements.* International Review of Curriculum and Assessment Frameworks Internet Archive. Table 9.

Isaacs, T. (2010) 'Educational assessment in England', *Assessment in Education: Principles, Policy & Practice*, 17: 315–34.

Jeantheau, J.-P. and Johnson, S. (2012) 'Quels objectifs pour les évaluations nationales en France?', Proceedings of the Annual Conference of the Association pour le Développement des Méthodes de l'Evaluation en Education (ADMEE), 11–13 January, Luxembourg.

Johnson, S. (1989) *Monitoring Science Performance: The APU Experience.* A Technical Report on Programme Development Experience. London: HMSO.

Johnson, S. (2012) *Assessing Learning in the Primary Classroom.* London: Routledge.

Johnson, S. (2013) 'On the reliability of high-stakes teacher assessment', *Research Papers in Education*, 28: 91–105.

Johnson, S. and Munro, L. (2008) 'Teacher judgement and test results: should teachers and tests agree?', paper presented at the Annual Conference of the Association for

Educational Assessment – Europe, 6–8 November, Hissar, Bulgaria.

Jones, L.V. (1996) 'A history of the National Assessment of Educational Progress and some questions about its future', *Educational Researcher*, 25: 1–8.

Kellaghan, T. and Madaus, G.F. (1982) 'Trends in educational standards in Great Britain and Ireland', in G.R. Austin, and H. Jarber (eds.), *The Rise and Fall of National Test Scores*. New York, NY: Academic Press.

Kellaghan, T., Greaney, V. and Murray, T.S. (2009) *Using the Results of a National Assessment of Educational Achievement*. Washington, DC: The World Bank.

Lynch, S., Bamford, H. and Sims, D. (2015) *Reception Baseline Research: Views of Teachers, School Leaders, Parents and Carers*. London: Department for Education.

MEN-DEPP (2014) *Programme d'activité. Direction de l'évaluation, de la prospective et de la performance*. Circular no. 2014-013 du 5-2-2014. Paris: Ministry of Education.

Messick, S., Beaton, A. and Lord, F. (1983) *National Assessment of Educational Progress Reconsidered: A New Design for a New Era*. Princeton, NJ: National Assessment of Educational Progress.

Munro, L. (2003) 'National testing and national assessments', in T.G.K. Bryce, and W.M. Humes (eds.), *Scottish Education: Post-Devolution*. Edinburgh: Edinburgh University Press. pp. 746–55.

National Center for Educational Statistics (2013) *The Nation's Report Card: Trends in Academic Progress 2012 (NCES 2013 456)*. Washington, DC: Institute of Education Sciences, US Department of Education.

National Commission on Excellence in Education (1983) *A Nation at Risk: the Imperative for Educational Reform*. Washington, DC: US Department of Education.

Neville, M. (1988) *Assessing and teaching language: Literacy and oracy in schools*. Basingstoke, UK: Macmillan.

Newton, P.E. (2008) *Monitoring National Attainment Standards*. London: Office for Qualifications and Examinations Regulation.

O'Neill, O. (2013) 'Intelligent accountability in education', *Oxford Review of Education*, 39: 4–16.

Peaker, G.F. (1975) *An Empirical Study of Education in Twenty-One Countries: A Technical Report*. New York, NY: Wiley.

Pellegrino, J.W. (2014) *National Assessment of Educational Progress*. Available from http://education.stateuniversity.com/pages/1767/Assessment-NATIONAL-ASSESSMENT-EDUCATIONAL-PROGRESS.html (accessed 6 August 2015).

Purves, A.C. (1991) 'Brief history of IEA', in W.A. Hayes (ed.), *Activities, Institutions and People. IEA Guidebook 1991*. The Hague: The International Association for the Evaluation of Educational Achievement. pp. 34–48.

Rey, O. (2010) 'The use of external assessments and the impact on educational systems', in S.M. Stoney (ed.), *Beyond Lisbon 2010: Perspectives from Research and Development for Education Policy in Europe*. (CIDREE Yearbook 2010). Slough, UK: National Foundation for Education Research. pp. 137–58.

Sainsbury, M. (1994) 'The structure of National Curriculum Assessment', in D. Hutchison, and I. Schagen (eds.), *How Reliable is National Curriculum Assessment?* Slough, UK: National Foundation for Education Research. pp. 1–10.

Scheerens, J., Ehren, M., Sleegers, P. and de Leeuw, R. (2012). *OECD Review on Evaluation and Assessment Frameworks for Improving School Outcomes. Country Background Report for the Netherlands*. Paris: OECD.

Scottish Council for Research in Education (1968) *Rising Standards in Scottish Primary Schools 1953–1963*. London: University of London Press.

The Scottish Government (2015) *Creating a Smarter Scotland. A Draft National Improvement Framework for Scottish Education*. Edinburgh: Scottish Government.

Shiel, G., Kavanagh, L. and Millar, D. (2014) *The 2014 National Assessments of English Reading and Mathematics. Volume 1: Performance Report*. Dublin: Educational Research Centre.

Smaill, E. (2013) 'Moderating New Zealand's national standards: teacher learning and assessment outcomes', *Assessment in Education: Principles, Policy & Practice*, 20: 250–65.

Spencer, E. (2013) 'National assessments: improving learning and teaching through national monitoring?', in T.G.K. Bryce, W.M. Humes, D. Gillies and A. Kennedy (eds.), *Education in Scotland*. Edinburgh: Edinburgh University Press.

Start, K.B. and Wells, B.K. (1972) *The Trend in Reading Standards*. Slough, UK: National Foundation for Educational Research.

TGAT (1988) *National curriculum: Report of the Task Group on Assessment and Testing.* London: Department of Education and Science.

TGAT (1988) *National curriculum. Report of the Task Group on Assessment and Testing.* London: Department of Education and Science.

Trosseille, B. and Rocher, T. (2015). 'Les évaluations standardisées des élèves: perspective historique', *Education et Formations*, 86-87: 15-36.

PART VI

The Curriculum and Educational Policy

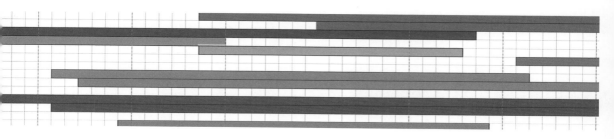

54

Economic Impact of Education: Evidence and Relevance

Kristinn Hermannsson

INTRODUCTION

The application of economic analysis to various aspects of education dates back at least to the work of Adam Smith[1] who recognised the skills of the population[2] as one of the manifestations of an economy's capital stock. The modern literature on the economics of education as a special sub-field spans approximately half a century (De Meulemeester and Diebolt, 2004), stretching back to Schultz (1961) who argued for public intervention to facilitate human capital accumulation, and Becker (1964) who presented a model of investment in human capital analogous to investment in physical capital. Since then the field has grown to include a huge literature encompassing broad topics including the role of education in influencing economy-wide outcomes, such as in economic growth and development; labour market outcomes and the functioning of school systems and individual institutions.[3] How much of a role, if any, that economic perspectives should have

in shaping education policy is beyond this chapter to resolve; however, there is significant evidence to suggest that education policy will always have economic implications, whether intended or not.

The economics of education is not a unified body of knowledge, but rather one that is spread across time and several sub-disciplines of economics. For this overview I shall build on McMahon's taxonomy of identifying impacts along the two dimensions of private/public and market/non-market. The main emphasis is on the labour market impacts of qualifications. This is by far the most widely researched aspect of the economic impact of education. I examine how this translates into a macroeconomic impact in the context of human capital and signalling theories. Furthermore, the chapter examines the wider economic impacts of education, such as through impacts on health, crime and household production. Where appropriate I shall highlight tensions between popular perception and the evidence base and point out areas for further research.

As is common in applied research, the evidence base on the economic impact of education falls short of some of the detailed requirements of the decisions facing policy-makers. Empirical evidence relies primarily on observational data, which for causal inference requires more elaborate identification strategies such as natural experiments. Furthermore, the level of detail is often limited by the nature of the data collected and statistical power. For instance, information on the association between the level of qualifications and labour market outcomes are available for most countries. Digging deeper, however, into subject of study, type of education institutions attended, or regional or socioeconomic variation, the evidence rapidly becomes more difficult to obtain. The aim of this chapter is to offer an accessible introduction to empirical work on the economic impact of education.

Before digging into the actual evidence, it is useful to clarify what is meant when referring to economic impact. I shall briefly define two concepts that typically lurk in the background of any discussion of the economic implications of policy: National Accounting and its result the Gross Domestic Product (GDP), and also Cost Benefit Analysis (CBA).

HOW DO WE DEFINE 'THE ECONOMY'?

It is frequently asserted in public-policy discourse that a particular course of events would be good or bad for the economy. Sometimes the direction and/or magnitude of this impact is contested, but despite the definitive article, this reference to 'the economy' is rarely clarified. Does it refer to a conceptual notion of the economy, a particular metric such as GDP or employment, or perhaps to the interests of a particular subpopulation such as rentiers or wage earners? Furthermore, is the definition restricted to market-based activity, which can be clearly attributed a monetary value or does it also account

for a wider range of impacts, such as on leisure, home-production or the environment?

A clear delimitation of some of these boundaries is still a work in progress (for a comprehensive discussion, see Stiglitz et al., 2010); however, two yardsticks are often applied in the evaluation of the economic merits of public policy. One is the contribution of policy to macroeconomic aggregates (GDP, Gross National Product (GNP), etc.) as defined by national accounting; the other is the sum of total costs and total benefits as articulated in CBA.

Modern national accounting took hold in the 1940s and has evolved through successive revisions of the United Nations System of National Accounts, although the precursors date back to the seventeenth century.[4] In a nutshell, the national accounts count the amount of output, income and expenditures of households, government and businesses for a particular place over a particular period at market prices. One of the results of this exercise are frequently referenced macroeconomic aggregates. Gross Domestic Product or GDP (expenditure view) is defined as the total market value of all final goods and services produced within an economy.[5] GDP (income view) can also be defined as the total factor incomes (wages and other value added) generated in the economy.[6]

From the definition of GDP, the limitations of the concept are clear. It is a measure based on aggregate market activity and has little to offer on non-market issues or the composition of the aggregate. As Okun (1971: 133) highlights, the 'beauty of the present practice is that no sensible person could seriously mistake the GNP for [a measure of social welfare]'; however, an increase in GDP or GNP is often interpreted as a proxy for much broader advancement. A comprehensive review of these issues is presented in Stiglitz et al., (2010), which bring together a discussion of the 'classical' measurement issues associated with GDP and GNP, in addition to environmental issues and the more philosophical issue defining and measuring quality of life.

As useful as national accounting principles are when applied to their intended domain, these clearly omit important aspects of what is sought after in public policy. Public services are counted in GDP at their input costs, not their output value. This can provide a very misleading target for establishing policy priorities because the most expensive policy would contribute the most to GDP.[7] Economic benefits of education, such as a skilled workforce, impact through contributing to the activity of all the sectors in the economy.[8]

Arguably the most prevalent approach for establishing the economic merits of policy is CBA. CBA is widely used to derive an estimate of the social net-benefit of public projects by enumerating and evaluating the total social costs and total social benefits. To this end, a range of methods and rules are applied.

CBA is a bottom–up approach that includes identifying the relevant costs and benefits (including externalities), assigning each a monetary value and applying an appropriate discount rate to derive a present value of future cost and benefit streams.[9] As with any method in applied economics, each of these steps requires careful consideration and should not be treated as a mechanical exercise. Costs and benefits have to be identified so there is neither under- nor over-attribution of costs or benefits to the activity being evaluated. Various techniques are used to assign prices depending on circumstance and available information, and no single discount rate is universally appropriate or accepted. Sensitivity analyses, however, can be applied around critical parameters to produce a range of plausible outcomes. One of the benefits of CBA is that it is a well-established approach with well-known qualities and limitations. If done in a transparent way, users should be reasonably able to draw their own judgements as to the validity of assessment for the valuation of individual components and adjust their interpretation of conclusions accordingly.

CBA approaches are outlined in the policy manuals of various governments and international organisations, for example, the UK's Green Book on Appraisal and Evaluation in Central Government (HM Treasury, 2003).[10] Often in practice, simplified routines are adopted for CBA that are sanctioned by convention in the field of application; however at a more general level the methods involved raise some significant theoretical and practical challenges (for a comprehensive discussion, see Layard and Glaister, 1994).

Typically it is straightforward to estimate the cost of education on the basis of accounting data; however, as we shall see, valuing the benefits is more challenging.

ECONOMIC IMPACTS OF EDUCATION: AN OVERVIEW

Education policy impacts the economy through a wide range of channels. These vary in terms of their salience, clarity and depth of understanding. In its simplest incarnation, education can be viewed as any other production sector, where education institutions purchase inputs and pay wages. Similarly students can be treated like tourists, affecting the economy through consumption expenditures. This is particularly relevant for higher education where students are mobile, concentrated in a few student centres and are sometimes a source of significant export earnings, as in the UK case.[11] These are referred to as demand-side or expenditure effects.[12]

More fundamentally, qualified individuals directly stimulate the productive capacity (supply-side) of the economy through the skills they offer in the workplace, but also through a range of indirect effects. Furthermore, many of the benefits of education are non-pecuniary. In order to classify these supply-side and wider impacts, I follow McMahon's (2009) classification along two axes: private or public and market or non-market. This results in four categories (see Table 54.1): private market benefits, private non-market benefits, external market benefits and external non-market benefits.

Table 54.1   Classification of returns to education

		Who benefits?	
		Private	External
Type of benefit	Market	Higher wages Higher employment Lower unemployment	Higher productivity of other workers (productivity spillovers) Higher Total Factor Productivity (TFP) due to knowledge spillovers
	Non-market	Better own health Longer life expectancy Improvement in happiness	Lower crime Democratisation Civic society

Source: Hermannsson et al. (2012).

Private market benefits of education are the labour market benefits enjoyed by individuals as a result of their level of education. They manifest themselves in higher earnings and lower unemployment rates, relative to less qualified individuals. Similarly, private non-market impacts of education are the benefits enjoyed by individuals outside the labour market that are directly attributable to their level of education. These include positive effects on health, longevity, happiness and many other benefits. These effects are strongly correlated with income and other attributes, which make it challenging to identify the specific contributions of education.

External impacts of education (or externalities) refer to benefits enjoyed by wider society as a result of the level of education of the general population. These externalities can be manifested in terms of higher wages and higher profits and are reflected in GDP per capita; however, they are not 'internalised' by particular qualified individuals and are enjoyed by other agents in the economy. Examples include the higher productivity and wages of non-graduates generated by working with graduates and the education system's (typically focusing on HEIs) contribution to R&D and innovation (of a public good nature).

Similarly, external non-market impacts improve quality of life, but are not necessarily directly translatable into pecuniary benefits. Examples would include any education-induced reduction in crime levels, improvements in public health, democratisation or political stability. These are non-monetary benefits

that are captured at a social level as an indirect impact of the level of education in the community. They are not captured in measures of economic output but may improve other development indicators. This category would include education's contributions to various types of social advancement, such as the quality of culture or the rule of law as reflected in quality of life metrics, for example happiness scales (independent of the effects of income on the same metrics to avoid double counting).

It is apparent that accurately attributing these effects to their source is challenging. Often outcomes are difficult to measure, random assignment is usually not possible and there are various confounding factors that need to be taken into consideration. However, it is worthwhile attempting to clarify this inherently messy situation because the alternative of assuming that these effects simply do not exist could lead to under-investment in education, which is harmful to society.

LABOUR MARKET BENEFITS OF EDUCATION FOR INDIVIDUALS (PRIVATE-MARKET IMPACTS)

An extensive literature documents the labour market benefits of education (typically referred to as the returns to education) at various levels of schooling, in different countries, at different times. Sometimes the results are further disaggregated by characteristics such as gender, discipline and social background.

These studies reveal a clear correlation between education and income, and provide rich information about the nature of this relationship. Due to an obvious inability to conduct controlled experiments in the field, verifying the causality between education and income has proven difficult. More recently a wealth of papers has been published utilising advanced statistical approaches, that is instrument variables, controlling for fixed effects (using samples of twins) and natural experiments to clarify the issue.

Numerous reviews of the microeconomic literature on returns to education have been published, for example Dickson and Harmon (2011), Checchi (2006), Blundell et al. (2005), Psacharopoulos and Patrinos (2002, 2004), Harmon and Walker (2003) and Krueger and Lindahl (2001). These estimates are obtained through regression analysis of cross-sectional data, such as those available for the UK in the Family Expenditure Survey, the General Household Survey and the Labour Force Survey (Blundell et al., 2005). An earning function (see Mincer, 1974) is fitted where indicators for formal education, labour market experience and individual characteristics are used to explain wage income.

These studies find higher returns to education in lower income countries where education levels are generally lower. This is seen as consistent with the notion of diminishing returns to education, with the return to education falling as the average education levels rise. However, as discussed later, the dynamism of these diminishing returns is more complex than a simple analysis of increasing supply within a comparative static framework because it is not only the supply of education that can change but also the demand for it.

UK-regions, but a wealth of evidence is available for other countries (for an overview, see Psacharopoulos and Patrinos, 2002, 2004).

A key result, repeatedly found in studies of this kind is that qualifications increase the likelihood of employment and more qualified workers generally earn higher wages. For example, Walker and Zhu (2007a, 2007b) pool 10 years of data from the Labour Force Surveys in 1996–2005 to construct a large enough sample to estimate wage premia by qualification level at a regional level within Great Britain. Their broad findings are in line with other work in the field. For men and women, they find the value of qualifications broadly similar across Great Britain. To demonstrate the stylised findings I shall focus on results for Scotland.

Walker and Zhu (2007a, 2007b) find strong wage premia effects for both vocational and academic qualifications.[13] These are detailed in Table 54.2. Overall, the academic qualifications yield higher wage premia, but what is also noteworthy is how the structure of the wage premium by levels of qualification differs between vocational and academic qualifications. The marginal effect of low-level vocational qualifications is modest compared to low-level academic qualifications, and the additional wage premia gained by postgraduate study is modest. From a human capital perspective, these findings may not be surprising if the amount of schooling behind these education levels is examined. For example, a Level 4 undergraduate degree typically takes four academic years to complete, whereas a common duration for masters degrees is 12 months[14] and the wage premia earned per effective duration of study (and therefore also the return to education) is broadly similar between Level 4 and Level 5.

Returns to Education in the UK

A large body of statistical work examines the labour market benefits of education in high-income countries. In the remainder of this section I shall focus on the UK and

Returns to Education by Subject

A perennial question is whether the returns to education differ between subjects. Strong views on this can be found in popular perception, but a rigorous quantitative confirmation

Table 54.2   Hourly wage premium of vocational and academic qualifications in Scotland

Vocational wage premium	Male	Male (cumulative)	Female	Female (cumulative)
None	Base	Base	Base	Base
Level 1	9%	9%	11%	11%
Level 2	7%	16%	9%	20%
Level 3	19%	35%	9%	29%
Level 4	17%	52%	23%	52%
Above level 4	30%	82%	29%	81%
Academic wage premium	Male	Male (cumulative)	Female	Female (cumulative)
None	Base	Base	Base	Base
Level 1	17%	17%	18%	18%
Level 2	12%	29%	12%	30%
Level 3	19%	48%	13%	43%
Level 4	31%	79%	34%	77%
Above level 4	12%	91%	13%	90%

Source: Walker and Zhu (2007b).

of differing returns to subjects is harder to provide. The key limitation for statistical estimates is the size of the samples available. Blundell and Deardren (2000) report some individual subject findings for higher education graduates in the UK based on the National Child Development Survey, which tracks a cohort of people born in 1958. For most subjects, differences were found to be insignificant. For men a significant negative effect was found for biology, chemistry, environmental sciences and geography. The returns are calculated based on comparing the earnings of university graduates with the earnings of those with sufficient qualifications to enter university. A weak return therefore reflects the relatively weak earnings power of a particular subject, but are also influenced by the earning power of non-graduates. For women, the

pattern is somewhat different because they were found to earn higher returns in education, economics, accountancy and law and the 'other social sciences' category. To control for the quality of the student intake into the subjects, they included A-Level results in their regressions. Inclusion of this variable did not alter the results qualitatively.

O'Leary and Sloane (2005) analyse returns to higher education degree subjects. To obtain a sufficiently large sample for this breakdown they pool observations from the Labour Force Survey from 1994 to 2002. For men with undergraduate degrees, they find the lowest wage premium accrues to holders of arts degrees, –2.5 per cent compared to those who have completed two A-Levels,[15] based on an earnings index where earnings of Arts degree holders (including performance arts) were

Table 54.3   Examples of SVQ/NVQ Levels

SVQ/NVQ level	Academic qualification	Vocations qualification
5	PhD, Masters degree	PGCE, non-masters postgraduate qualifications
4	Undergraduate degree	HNC/HND
3	2+ A-levels/3+ Highers	OND, ONC
2	5+ GCSEs at A–C, O Grades, Credit Standard Grade	GSVQ/NVQ intermediate, RSA diploma
1	<5 GCSE, General Standard Grade	BTEC, SCOTVEC first or general certificate

Source: Walker and Zhu (2007b).

fixed at 100 the highest wage premia accrue to accountancy, medicine, engineering and maths and computing (with an earnings index in excess of 130). Next in line (130>125) are law, business and finance and education, followed by geography and architecture (125>120). Lower wage premia (120>110) are earned in nursing, biology, psychology, other social sciences, English, history and languages. Interestingly, no subject falls in the range between 100 and 110, implying there is a significant jump in wage premia from holding an Arts degree to the next tier above.

A different pattern emerges for women. Compared to those who have completed two A-Levels, women earn significant wage premia on Arts degrees (19.29 per cent). Again, based on an earnings index where holders of Arts degrees are set at 100, fewer of the subjects were found to earn a statistically significant wage premia compared to an arts degree. Statistically significant differences for the biggest wage premium for women are in accountancy (137). The next tier (130>120) is composed of medicine, law and education. Many subjects fall in the range between 120 and 110, including nursing, maths and computing, engineering, architecture and business and financial studies. In the range closest to arts (110>100) we find sciences, sociology, economics and English.

O'Leary and Sloan (2005) base the disaggregation of the subjects on what was feasible with the available data, with popular fields allowing more disaggregation because of larger samples. In their regressions, they include a control for the quality of the student intake.[16] This affects the final ranking of the subjects, where a wage premium is reduced if a subject has a relatively high quality student intake, but inflated (in relative terms) if the student intake is of a relatively low quality.

Walker and Zhu (2011) revisited this issue and find limited variation across subjects for women, but a more pronounced effect for men, where law, economics and management offer the best financial outcome. Degree class has large effects in all subjects, suggesting the possibility of large returns to effort. Similarly, postgraduate study has large effects, independently of first-degree class. Chevalier (2011) argues that an overlooked aspect with regards to the economic pay-off from subject choice is the distribution of earnings around the mean. Graduates in some subjects exhibit earnings that are relatively tightly clustered around the mean, for example education and subjects allied to medicine where most graduates enter relatively centralised labour markets with formal pay scales. Conversely, for other subjects, outcomes are much more widely dispersed, making the subject choice more risky from an investment point of view.

Interpreting the Statistical Association Between Education and Earnings

Although the correlation between earnings and education is a well-established fact, the presence of correlation is not sufficient to establish causality. There are two main theoretical perspectives on this subject. First, the human capital school has its origins in the works of Mincer (1958), Schultz (1961) and Becker (1964) and this tradition maintains that education is an investment in human capital, which in turn increases the productivity of workers. Second, an alternative perspective is that of the signalling school, which stems from the works of Arrow (1973), Spence (1973) and Stiglitz (1975). In the most extreme version of this theory, education has no impact on productivity, but simply reveals (signals) innate ability to employers.

Signalling and Screening

An often-raised concern is that education may have a value in the labour market, not because of the positive effects of formal education upon productivity but for spurious reasons. It is particularly stressed that education may act as a signal of ability or other characteristics that employers value but cannot easily observe. In the extreme case, these abilities are unaffected by education altogether. That is to

Table 54.4   Index number of returns to narrow first-degree subjects for men and women, based on several waves of the Labour Force Survey (1994Q1–2002Q4)[1, 2, 3]

	Men				Women			
	n	index no	SE	rank	n	index no	SE	rank
Medicine and related	336	132.06+	0.0474	5	597	127.52+	0.0305	2
Nursing	25	114.39+	0.0358	20	220	113.93+	0.0301	9
Sciences	1327	125.22+	0.0335	12	696	106.13+	0.0261	17
Biology	130	115.87+	0.0482	18	188	101.6	0.0356	22
Psychology	125	118.66+	0.0454	17	303	101.98	0.0262	21
Geography	298	123.42+	0.0477	13	261	104.34	0.0398	19
Maths and computing	975	137.23+	0.031	3	346	118.10+	0.037	7
Engineering and technology	650	131.85+	0.0313	6	97	113.54+	0.0556	12
Civil engineering	411	129.25+	0.0325	7	24	113.7	0.095	11
Mechanical engineering	524	133.71+	0.0339	4	19	113.84+	0.0286	10
Electrical engineering	682	140.73+	0.0313	2	28	119.04+	0.0233	5
Architecture and related	410	120.97+	0.0288	15	83	118.70+	0.037	6
Social sciences	132	114.20+	0.0451	21	286	113.45+	0.0313	13
Sociology	126	110.83+	0.0394	24	269	106.50+	0.0292	16
Politics	118	115.70+	0.0477	19	72	99.09	0.0508	25
Law	315	128.04+	0.041	9	302	123.97+	0.0372	3
Business and financial studies	827	126.53+	0.0266	11	691	114.34+	0.0234	8
Economics	430	128.57+	0.0445	8	110	109.68++	0.0508	14
Accountancy	193	142.15+	0.047	1	95	137.12+	0.0504	1
Arts	804	100	n.a.	25	1091	100	n.a.	24
English	213	110.84+	0.0423	23	468	106.65+	0.0322	15
History	306	111.69+	0.041	22	318	110.95	0.0365	23
Languages	110	119.22+	0.054	16	291	103.3	0.0386	20
Education	490	126.73+	0.0316	10	1283	122.40+	0.0223	4
Combined	2529	122.41+	0.0241	14	3135	105.58+	0.0187	18

Notes

[1] *All* returns are measured relative to an arts degree (base = 100).

[2] Return to an arts degree relative to 2+ A-levels is –3.25% (men) and 19.29% (women).

[3] +, statistically significant difference in returns at 95% confidence interval; ++, statistically significant difference in returns at 90% confidence level.

Source: O'Leary and Sloane (2005: 82–3, Tables 7 and 8).

say, education signals but does not contribute to the workers' inherent productivity. As noted by Harmon and Walker (2003), there is a fundamental difficulty in unravelling the extent to which education is a signal of existing productivity or truly enhancing productivity. This is because both human capital and signalling theories suggest that there is a positive correlation between earnings and education, but for very different reasons.

Brown and Sessions (2004) refer to the theory proclaiming that education 'signals' or 'screens' intrinsic productivity as the 'sorting' hypothesis. Signalling and screening refer to two related genres of models that describe this process from opposite starting points. Signalling models (Arrow, 1973; Spence, 1973) describe the process from the point of view of the employee obtaining a signal to enhance his labour market performance. Screening models turn the sequence around to have employers screening the labour market by setting a required signal their applicants need to obtain (Stiglitz, 1975).

These models[17] draw on the theoretical work on asymmetric information and market imperfections, where often a single transaction takes place between the buyer and the seller and therefore asymmetric information can be used to the sellers advantage;[18] however, an employment relationship is continuous and firms can revise their employment and wage decisions. Even if firms are paying their wages purely on the basis of credentials in the short term, over time they gather their own information about the employee and can change wages, through redundancy or promotion; therefore, over longer time horizons employers should correct for a potential initial effect of signalling. Indeed, examples of signalling models with employer learning can be found in contemporary work, for example Lange and Topel (2006). For a review of empirical evidence, including studies allowing for learning, see Brown and Sessions (2004).

Spence (1973) gives a dynamic description of how signalling might work in that observed labour quality feeds into the value assigned to education signals in the labour market (see Figure 54.1). Over time, the signal is not static but reflects recent observations of actual labour productivity by education level. A scenario where qualified workers are overpaid relative to their actual productivity can only occur under quite restrictive assumptions. The quality of new graduates entering the labour force has to be worse than in previous periods and the informational feedback sluggish enough not to adjust the wage premium assigned to a particular education level based on new observations of productivity. Needless to say, such overpayment relative to productivity cannot persist indefinitely – sooner or later market participants will discover that the quality of new graduate entrants is not the same as before and adjust the wage premia assigned to the education signals accordingly.

As summarised by Harmon and Walker (2003),[19] there are various ways of finessing the problem of estimating empirically the extent of signalling in the labour market. One of the ways suggested is to compare the wages of the employed and self-employed.[20] This is predicated on the assumption that education has no value as a signal for the self-employed because individuals know their own productivity and therefore do not need to signal it to themselves. Harmon and Walker (2003) argue, based on British Household Panel Survey data, that the rates of return to education are quite comparable between the two groups, implying that

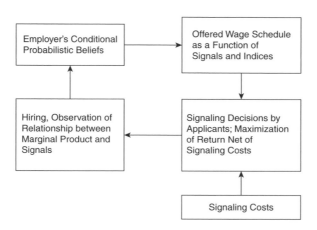

Figure 54.1   Informational feedback in the job market

Source: Spence, 1973: 359, Figure 1.

the signalling component is quite small. A weakness of this approach, however, is that self-employment is not random and that individuals with specific and often unobservable characteristics choose to be self-employed. Another approach is to directly include ability measures in the regressions. This, however, requires that the ability measures are 'uncontaminated' by the effects of education or they will select its productivity enhancing effects, and that ability measures reflect ability to make money rather than ability in an IQ sense. As Harmon and Walker (2003: 134) point out, it 'seems unlikely that any ability measure would be able to satisfy both of these requirements exactly'. Harmon and Walker (2003: 149–150) conclude that it is possible that the returns to education reflect innate ability signalled by credentials; however, they find that the effect is small because the inclusion of ability measures lowers the return to schooling by less than one percentage point.

As of yet, there is not a widespread consensus on how best to reconcile human capital and signalling theories as explanations of graduate wage premia; however, most well informed readers of both theories will conclude that these are not incompatible. Brown and Sessions (2004: 94) argue that it is a misinterpretation of sorting (signalling and screening) that education only signals productivity and cannot cause it; however, a clear dichotomy is a useful modelling expediency. As Brown and Sessions (2004: 94) point out, the 'pioneering theoretical work of Spence (1973), Arrow (1973) and Stiglitz (1975) only abstracted from an augmenting role for education to clarify their analysis'. Indeed as Arrow (1973) states, he did not believe education was unproductive; rather, that this assumption was adopted because the extreme view made the modelling process easier. Conversely, there is not a basis to reject signalling altogether. The current state of the academic debate about the value of education is not about seeing education as productivity enhancing or as just a signal, but to narrow the range for which education may

have a true treatment effect on worker productivity, as reflected in wages (apart from any wider impacts of course).

Does Education Drive Earnings or Vice-Versa?

The correlation between education and wages has also been scrutinised from a more purely empirical point of view. An obvious weakness of the link drawn between education and earnings is that it cannot be verified by means of a controlled experiment where randomly selected individuals would be given different education treatments and their labour market outcomes subsequently compared; instead, we have to rely on analyses of actual observations. It is therefore not clear *ex ante* whether the causality runs from education to earnings or the other way around, that is, individuals with better earning capabilities seek out more education.

Various adjustments to the basic analysis of cross-sectional labour market data have been used to identify bias in estimates of the rates of return to education. These include adjustment for the anticipated growth in earnings, mortality, unemployment, taxes and innate ability. Authors of various recent surveys (Bonjour et al., 2003; Checchi, 2006; Krueger and Lindhahl, 2001; Psacharopoulos and Patrinos, 2004) have pointed out, following Card (1999), that the application of a range of adjustments has led to the conclusion that the counteracting biases effectively cancel so that the end result is a net benefit almost equal to the unadjusted one. The use of unadjusted returns has therefore become prevalent. In his survey, Checchi (2006) identifies three types of weaknesses of the estimated returns to education that could bias the results: omitted variables, measurement error and heterogeneity of returns in the population.

The case of omitted variables can apply when the researcher is unable to control for characteristics that might raise earnings independently of education, such as family background or individual ability. 'A typical example is unobservable ability: more talented persons achieve more education because it is easier for them to do so, and at the same time they are more productive when working' (Checchi, 2006: 201). The sign of the bias is ambiguous. It could be positive because more intelligent and disciplined people also perform better as students, thus achieving longer schooling; however, the bias could also be negative if better endowed individuals face a higher opportunity cost of schooling and therefore leave education earlier. Further ambiguity arises as parents may take decisions on educational investment. They may do so on the basis of efficiency where more is invested in abler individuals producing a positive bias. Conversely, they may be driven by equity considerations where more is invested in less able individuals to compensate for their shortcomings, resulting in a negative bias.[21]

Measurement errors are a second source of bias. It has been observed that self-reported schooling is not completely accurate and that the measurement errors do not cancel out because the least educated cannot under-report and the most educated cannot over-report. 'Research in the U.S. over the past three decades has concluded that the reliability of self-reported schooling is 85–90 percent (Angrist and Krueger (1999, Table 9)), implying that the downward bias is on the order of 10–15 percent – enough to offset a modest upward ability bias' (Card, 2001: 1135).

The third source of bias stems from the heterogeneity of the coefficient to be estimated in the population. Card (1995) points to two potential sources of the heterogeneity: ability bias and cost bias. The first is driven by the fact that differences in abilities result in differences in productivity so that more able individuals can expect a higher payback for any level of education achieved. The second originates from financial market imperfections, where people of different family backgrounds face different marginal cost in acquiring education, so that poor families face higher cost.

The consequence of both distortions is that the subset of the population with low educational attainment will be composed of individuals with lower returns (less able) and by individuals facing higher costs (poorer backgrounds). Since the underlying model implies that each individual will optimally select the amount of education that will equate his/her expected returns to his/her marginal cost, the population estimate of the return on education will depend on sub-group composition. If the group of less able individuals prevails, I observe a positive correlation between education and error component ε in the wage function, and therefore the OLS estimate will be upwardly biased. Otherwise when the group of individuals from poorer families prevails, the opposite situation will occur, and I will observe a downward bias. (Checchi, 2006: 202–3).

One way to dealing with this issue is to analyse returns to education in samples of twins. Twins share biological and social backgrounds, and analysing variation within twin-pairs controls for the fixed effects of genetics and the home, which is seen as (at least partial) controls for individual ability bias. As McMahon (2009: 332) points out, there is 'wide agreement that identical twins studies offer probably the best basis for estimating the pure returns to education since they provide highly controlled conditions for the identical abilities and family backgrounds of monozygotic twins'.

McMahon (2009) summarises US studies utilising within twin-pairs differences in earnings and education to estimate 'net-ability bias' in estimates of return to education. He points out these studies have found evidence of significant ability bias, but that these are partially offset by a downward biased measurement error. Early studies found a wide range of estimates for net ability bias, but McMahon (2009) argues that in more recent studies, with larger samples and methodological advancement, estimates have converged on a more narrow range from 0.9 per cent to 13.7 per cent.[22] Perhaps the most prominent twin study based on data from UK twins is by Bonjour et al. (2003), who corroborate findings of previous authors that there is indeed an upwards ability bias in estimates for returns to education, but that this is offset by a downwards bias caused by measurement error. They conclude that these roughly cancel out.

Skill Biased Technical Change and the Return to Education Over Time

In cross-sectional comparisons, institutional features of the labour market affect wage premia. Over time, however, it is not only the relative supply of workers at different skill levels (for example, graduates) that determines wage premia, but also demand. Demand for skilled labour has been gradually increasing – a fact typically attributed to technical change.[23] Goldin and Katz (2007) use estimates of supply and demand for graduate labour to investigate the level of the graduate wage premium in the US over the 90-year period from 1915 to 2005.[24] They find that the graduate wage premium (compared to those with high school qualifications) was at a similar value (around 65 per cent) at the beginning of the period as the end, albeit with significant intermittent fluctuations. Two troughs can be identified: around 1950 when it fell close to 30 per cent and in 1980 when it fell slightly below 40 per cent.[25]

Acemoglu (2002) reviews evidence and theoretical perspectives on the links between technical change and skills premia in the labour market, drawing on economic

history to argue that technological change can be skill-biased (increasing the need for skilled labour) but can also be skill-replacing (decreasing the need for skills). Although evidence from the US in the twentieth century suggests that technological change has been skill-biased, counterexamples are found in nineteenth-century Britain where industrialization made highly skilled artisans redundant because they were substituted by low-skill factory workers. He argues that this dual nature of technological change can be understood if it is recognised that the development and use of technology responds to profit incentives. In circumstances where it is profitable to develop and implement technologies that complement low-skill workers, technological change will tend to be skills-replacing; however, when technological advances requiring high-skill operators are more profitable, technological change will tend to be skill-biased.

I suggest that the early nineteenth century was characterized by skill-replacing developments because the increased supply of unskilled workers in the English cities (resulting from migration from rural areas and from Ireland) made the introduction

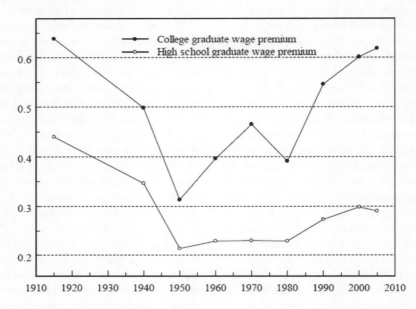

Figure 54.2   US college and high school graduate wage premiums 1915 to 2005

Source: Goldin and Katz (2007: 32, Figure 1)

of these technologies profitable. In contrast, the twentieth century has been characterized by skill-biased technical change because the rapid increase in the supply of skilled workers has induced the development of skill-complementary technologies (Acemoglu, 2002: 9).

Furthermore, Acemoglu (2002) argues that the acceleration of skill-biased technical change is likely to have been a response to the increased supply of skilled workers, which made skill-intensive production methods more competitive. This point, however, does not have to imply that the overall rate of technical change has increased, but rather that the types of technologies being developed has shifted.

In addition to technical change, wage premia attributed to qualifications have been affected by other factors, such as changes in labour market structure (that is, union power), changes in firm organisation and increasing trade between high-skill and low-skill countries. McMahon (2009) points out that the rise in the wage premium of high-skill workers in the US since 1980 can partially be explained by negative real-term growth in the wages of unskilled labour. He attributes this fact to a relative abundance of unskilled labour, partly because of an effective increase in the supply of unskilled labour through increased integration of developing countries in the World economy. Furthermore, he suggests that automation has replaced many low-skill jobs and therefore reduced the demand for uneducated workers. Acemoglu (2002) suggests that all these factors have amplified the effect of technical change upon the graduate wage premium and are likely causes for the real wage decline of low skill workers observed in the US.

Historical data reflect the average outcomes of all people with a particular level of qualification. More recently, labour market researchers have begun focusing on the variability within those averages. Walker and Zhu (2008) point out that at a UK level, although the average return to higher education has remained stable, the distribution has widened with increased participation, where higher ability people are earning more than the average and lower ability people are falling further behind the average. They argue that this might be the joint effect of increasing demand for skilled workers and growing heterogeneity in student intake of higher education. They argue that strong candidates (high unobserved abilities) are earning a greater wage premium than people of similar abilities in previous generations; however, the number of graduates with relatively lesser abilities has increased and these individuals are earning below average wage premia. Some work argues for falling wage premia (see, for example, McGuinness and Bennett, 2005), but the overall effects are modest.

WIDER IMPACTS OF EDUCATION

Most of the academic effort hitherto has focused on the more direct impacts of education for the economy, in particular institutional demand-side impacts and private returns to education; however, these only constitute a part of the overall impact of education for the economy. As outlined in Table 54.1 each effect within the overall impacts can be attributed to one of four quadrangles. So far, only the first of these has been discussed, the private market impacts. I shall now provide a brief overview of the three remaining fields of impact: private non-market benefits and external benefits – market and non-market.

In relation to the labour market impacts surveyed in the previous section of this chapter, where much has been published over several decades, systematic analysis of the wider impacts of education is underdeveloped. There is a substantial literature analysing specific, often quite narrow effects; however, this evidence base is fragmented. McMahon (2004, 2009: Chapter 4) summarises the relevant existing literature and uses it to estimate the economic impact of wider effects of education. Haveman and Wolfe (1984) and Oreopolous and Salvanes (2011) provide a review of the non-pecuniary impacts of education accruing to individuals. The Department for Business Innovation and Skills (BIS) also summarises the evidence relating to the wider benefits of higher education (2011: Chapter 3).

McMahon (2004, 2009) argues that the economic contribution of these wider impacts can be significant, but measurement problems make them difficult to pin down. Many of these impacts only reveal themselves with long time lags and there is an inherent difficulty in disentangling the impact of education per se from the impact of other developments. For example, education increases income and socioeconomic advancement, but rising income also has a beneficial impact on many socioeconomic metrics. Determining causation is therefore difficult because it is attributing outcomes to particular actions or developments. Many of these effects are particularly relevant for developing countries (for example, birth rates, political stability, rule of law), but potentially very significant benefits can be reaped by developed economies as well, such as through educations' impacts on health and crime rates.

Private Non-Market Benefits

Private non-market benefits are the various non-monetary benefits that accrue to a particular educated individual. Probably the most important of these is improved own health, but a range of effects have been explored in the literature, including longevity, child health, child education, husband's health, fertility, happiness, consumption and saving, job and location amenities, lifelong learning and consumption benefits (for an overview, see Oreopoulos and Salvanes, 2011 and McMahon, 2009: Chapter 4). These effects are strongly correlated with income, which is typically controlled for.

A number of studies show statistical association between children's educational attainment and that of their parents (see BIS (2011: Chapter 5) for a summary of some of the UK evidence; and Wolfe and Haveman (2001) for

international summary). What mechanism might explain this transmission? It is highly likely that selection issues play a role in the statistics. That is to say that unobservable characteristics that facilitate success in education attainment also facilitate success in parenting; however, there may be additional transmission channels, for example Bynner et al. (2003) point out that graduate parents read more to their children and own more books than non-graduates. Other channels include income – because income is correlated with more education, higher income can be used to purchase goods and experiences that enhance childhood development; however, as Oreopolous and Salvanes (2011) point out, conditioning on income does not eliminate these effects. The study by BIS (2011: 57) concludes that there is 'no clear-cut evidence as to what underlies the parenting results'.

McMahon (2009) details methods and sources for a range of non-market private benefits (including only studies that have income and education in the equation, allowing income-equivalent benefits to be computed). He estimates that in the case of higher education, the non-market benefits to the individual are 122 per cent of the earnings increase. This is huge, with obvious implications for the incentive for individuals to invest in higher education provided they have access to the relevant information.

Public Benefits of Education

Education is associated with a number of public benefits. Some are clearly market-based and are likely to be picked up in national accounting, others are non-pecuniary and likely to impact the economy through much more indirect channels.

Perhaps the most obvious market-based public benefits of education are productivity externalities (Battu et al., 2003; Heurman, 2011; Moretti, 2004). More indirectly, there are externalities that feed back to economic growth, especially over longer time horizons, for example effects that arise through more investment in physical capital, more invest-ment in education, adoption of technology, improved R&D and innovation and slower population (particularly relevant for less developed economies, see Kravdal, 2002).

Public non-market benefits of education are non-monetary benefits that are captured at a social level as an indirect impact of the level of education in the community. These are not captured in measures of economic output but may improve other development indicators. This category includes education's contri-butions to various types of social advance-ment, such as public health (Feinstein et al., 2006), strengthening of civic institutions and social engagement (Campbell, 2006), lower crime rates (Machin et al., 2011) and envi-ronmental effects (Appiah and McMahon, 2002). McMahon (2004: 218, Table 6.1) lists 13 examples of effects that contribute to non-market aspects of economic devel-opment, many of which are seen as particu-larly relevant at earlier stages of economic development.

There is a small but growing literature on the crime-reducing effect of education (Haveman and Wolfe, 1984; Lochner, 2004; Lochner and Moretti, 2001; Machin et al., 2011). These authors identify several factors that explain the negative relationship between the level of education and criminal activity. First, education increases opportunity cost of criminal activity by increasing the returns from legal work and increasing the cost of potential incarceration. Second, time spent in education reduces time available for partici-pation in criminal activity. Third, education may reduce the chances of involvement in criminal activity by increasing patience and risk aversion.

Machin et al. (2011) estimate a causal edu-cation impact on crime, exploiting, as a nat-ural experiment, the rise in the compulsory school-leaving age from 15 to 16 in England and Wales in 1972. This law generated a dis-continuity in the average age of people leav-ing school and the proportion of men aged 18–40 born between 1950 and 1965 with no qualification. Simultaneously, the authors

observe a drop in the conviction rates for men leaving school after the school-leaving reform. Similarly, Lochner (2004) found that education reduces criminal behaviour and estimated that the social value of this was equivalent to between 14 and 26 per cent of the private return to schooling.

Overall Magnitude of Wider Impacts

To estimate the impact of wider benefits of education, cross-country macro-regressions can be used; however, these are limited in that they include various controls for devel-opment indicators that are themselves influ-enced by education (for example, political stability, fixed-effect dummies) and therefore pick up some of the educational benefits. Furthermore, if these include time dummies or are conducted over a short-time horizon, many of the effects will not be picked up because they occur with long time lags of at least 10 to 20 years. These highly controlled regressions risk underestimating the wider impacts of education. If these controls are relaxed, researchers potentially overstate the impacts because education starts to pick up the beneficial impacts of other closely related socioeconomic developments. Researchers have attempted to engage with this problem by applying different specifications in which each has its potential positive or negative biases. These recent studies have provided a range of results that give an indication of a plausible magnitude of the wider impacts of education.

McMahon (2004) combines a variety of estimates for the social rate of return to edu-cation, as found in macroeconometric stud-ies, and broad findings for private rates of return to provide a possible range for the magnitude of the wider impacts of education (Table 54.5). Based on recent literature, he argues that a plausible social rate of return of education may vary from approximately 10 per cent to 30 per cent. The lower bound implies the returns to education are almost

Table 54.5   Estimates of social returns to education in the OECD countries

	Conventional monetary social rates of return (A1+B1)	Non-market private returns (A2+B2)	Non-market education externalities (B-3)	Total social rates of return (includes non-monetary)
Primary	8.5	6.8	2.5	17.8
Secondary	9.4	7.5	2.8	19.7
Higher	8.5	6.8	2.5	17.8

Source: McMahon (2004: 244, Table 6.5).

solely based on private market returns with limited or no wider impacts. The result is based on tightly controlled static regressions, which McMahon (2004) argues fail to attribute wider impacts to education, and therefore understate education's impact. The upper bound is based on dynamic, more loosely controlled specifications, which he conversely argues is probably overstated because the lack of controls means that the education variable picks up effects from other economic developments. Drawing on a number of empirical studies and simulations he presents 'educated guesses' by economic development and education level.

These estimates reveal that the typically unmeasured impacts of education are at least as big as the frequently estimated private returns to education; however, most of these wider impacts are, in fact, non-market benefits accruing to the educated individual. The externalities, although significant, are relatively small. In relation to education levels, their economic impacts seem to be broadly of the same order of magnitude, which implies that expansion of education at any level will have a high social rate of return.[26]

CONCLUSION

Available evidence on the economic impact of education is broad-brush in nature and shaped by the availability of data. Aspects of education that have been tracked in large-scale secondary data sets, such as labour market outcomes, have been thoroughly researched. Much less is known about how particular details shape outcomes.

Repeated cross-sectional analysis across the world reveals that formal qualifications provide positive wage premia and increase the likelihood of being in employment. In the UK, each increment of attainment, as captured in the National Vocational Qualifications scale, provides a positive benefit on average, although the impact of some of these is quite small.

A sizeable literature has grown around how to interpret these cross-sectional observations. There is the obvious problem of ability bias that occurs as more gifted students self-select into education, thereby inflating perceived wage premia; however, there are also counteracting biases through measurement issues and cost-bias, which pushes gifted students out of education. Through careful analysis of natural experiments and twin-studies a consensus has emerged that qualifications provide a treatment effect and are not simply a reflection of selection or a signal of underlying ability. However, several authors have argued that around 10–15 per cent of the effect could be spurious.

There is growing interest in moving beyond such broad aggregate measures and looking in more depth at different sub-groups. This is particularly urgent because in recent years the dispersion of outcomes for highly skilled workers has increased.

There is much less understanding of the magnitude of the wider benefits of education, but it is clear that education provides multiple benefits in addition to its labour market impact. Education is associated with various non-monetary benefits, such as success in marital and family life, happiness, health and longevity; however, the private non-market effects are also closely associated with, for example, income, making the relationship difficult to disentangle. Furthermore, education is associated with a number of public benefits, such as innovation, public health and reduced crime rates. The challenge is to disentangle the role of education from other socioeconomic causes.

The strength of using large-scale social surveys to conduct research into the economic impact of education is that these can often produce robust results; however, the outputs from such analysis are disappointingly aggregate for many policymakers. In the day-to-day decision, the issues are often quite nuanced, such as cutting a particular programme to fund another one or vice versa. There is still much work to be done utilising large social surveys, but also leveraging a wealth of administrative data. Future policy analysis is most likely to benefit from enhanced efforts to collaborate through mixed methods, combining the scaffolding of statistical analysis with the rich impression of case studies and observations.

ACKNOWLEDGEMENT

I am indebted to my co-authors, Katerina Lisenkova, Kim Swales, Patrizio Lecca and Peter McGregor, both directly for their contributions to the work cited in this chapter, but even more so for a number of stimulating conversations on this topic through the years. Furthermore, I acknowledge the guidance of two anonymous referees and the editors of this Handbook.

NOTES

1   De Meulemeester and Diebolt (2004) suggest early precedents can be found in the work of William Petty but that Smith was clearly the first to articulate the concept of human capital.
2   'The acquired and useful abilities of all the inhabitants or members of the society. The acquisition of such talents, by the maintenance of the acquirer during his education, study, or apprenticeship, always costs a real expense, which is a capital fixed and realized, as it were, in his person. Those talents, as they make a part of his fortune, so do they likewise of that of the society to which he belongs' (Smith, 1776, book II, ch.1, para. 17).
3   See, for example, Johnes and Johnes (2004) for an overview of different strands of education economics.
4   As Bos (1992) points out, the impetus for articulating the amount of economic activity was provided by the needs of England and France to levy taxes in order to pay for war and other activities of the state.
5   The small qualification of 'final' is important in this context as by this GDP cancels out the double counting that occurs where the output of a sector is used as an intermediate input as products and services move between producers in the supply chain.
6   A closely related concept is the GNP, which adjusts GDP for net payments abroad. GNP therefore represents only activity attributable to the citizens of a particular country (whether home or abroad), whereas GPD includes economic activity within a particular place, whether attributable to domestic or foreign subjects.
7   However, such boosts to economic activity can be important, particularly in a local context, and they no doubt play a role in the overall policy setting. See, for instance, Hermannsson et al. (2014) for an analysis of the contribution of higher education to the GDP of Scotland.
8   To capture these effects research have used simulation models to estimate the impact of education outputs on the macro economy. Hermannsson et al. (2014) estimate the contribution of skilled labour from higher education in Scotland and Hermannsson, Lecca and Swales (2014) estimate the contribution of a single graduation cohort from Scottish Further Education Colleges. Giesecke and Madden (2006) estimate the economy wide contribution of university research in Australia.
9   CBA draws close parallels with investment appraisal in that the objective is to establish what outlays are recouped over a particular time horizon. However, CBA allows for non-pecuniary benefits and costs as opposed to a sole focus on cash flow, as is the case in conventional investment appraisal.
10   For details see: https://www.gov.uk/government/publications/the-green-book-appraisal-and-evaluation-in-central-governent
11   In 2013, The Department for Business Innovation and Skills (BIS) announced a strategy to further increase the export of education services from the UK: https://www.gov.uk/government/news/new-push-to-grow-uks-175-billion-education-exports-industry

12 This literature has a long tradition. For an overview, see Florax (1992) and Siegfried et al. (2007). The methods of these studies are revisited by Hermannsson et al. (2013, 2014) who allow for the influence of public funding constraints and compare the impacts of different institutions.

13 For vocational qualifications, they use standard classification from 'Level 1' (lowest) to 'Above level 4' (highest) as found in the National Vocational Qualifications (NVQ). Although an official equivalent ranking does not exist for academic qualifications, labour market researchers have established conventions for equivalent ranking of academic qualifications.

14 Presumably respondents with masters degrees dominate the sample because the PhD graduates are less common.

15 The negative wage premia for men's Arts degrees is striking because it suggests that these individuals might have been better off in monetary terms from entering the labour market after completing secondary school; however, the converse applies to women with arts degrees who earn positive wage premia.

16 Leslie's degree acceptance quality variable, see O'Leary and Sloan (2005: 77).

17 I shall not elaborate on the models here, but shall refer interested readers to Brown and Sessions (2004) and Checchi (2006).

18 See Ackerlof (1970).

19 For a further review of empirical evidence on sorting hypotheses, see Brown and Sessions (2004).

20 Some studies compare returns to education in the public and private sectors, but these have been found less credible. See Harmon and Walker (2003: 134).

21 For details, see Checchi (2006: 201–2).

22 These are percentage (not percentage points) deviations, and so if a graduate wage premia of say 50 per cent were to be revised downwards, it would become 49.55 per cent (50/1.009) or 43.97 per cent (50/1.137) for the lower and upper bounds, respectively.

23 For a review, see Machin (2004) and Acemoglu (2002).

24 Some metrics examine even longer periods from 1890 to 2005.

25 Goldin and Katz (2007) argue that these are not fully explained by the simple supply and demand framework, but are influenced by institutional features of the labour market, such as strong unionisation in the 1940s and inflation in the 1970s eroding the real value of graduate wages relative to lower skilled workers on indexed contracts. The growth in the graduate wage premium after the 1980s was driven by a slowdown in graduate attainment growth and weaker bargaining position of lower skilled workers.

26 McMahon (2004) makes similar estimates for developing countries where social returns are sometimes twice as large, in particular for primary education.

REFERENCES

Acemoglu, D. (2002) 'Technical change, inequality, and the labour market', *Journal of Economic Literature*, 40(1): 7–72.

Ackerlof, G.A. (1970) 'The market for "lemons": quality uncertainty and the market mechanism', *Quarterly Journal of Economics*, 84(3): 488–500.

Angrist, J.D. and Krueger, A.B. (1999) 'Empirical strategies in labour economics', in Card, D. and Ashenfelter, O. (eds.), *Handbook of Labour Economics*. Vol. 3A. New York, NY: North Holland. pp. 1277–1366.

Appiah, E.N. and McMahon, W. (2002) 'The social outcomes of education and feedbacks on growth in Africa', *Journal of Development Studies*, 38(4): 27–68.

Arrow, K. (1973) 'Higher education as a filter', *Journal of Public Economics*, 2(3): 193–216.

Battu, H., Belfield, C.R. and Sloane, P.J. (2003) 'Human capital spillovers within the workplace: Evidence for Great Britain', *Oxford Bulletin of Economics and Statistics*, 65(5): 575–94.

Becker, G. (1964) *Human Capital*. Chicago, IL: University of Chicago Press.

Blundell, R. and Deardren, L. (2000) 'The returns to higher education in Britain: evidence from a British cohort', *Economic Journal*, 110(461): F82–99.

Blundell, R., Deardren, L. and Sianesi, B. (2005) 'Measuring the returns to education', in S. Machin and A. Vignoles (eds.), *What's the Good of Education: The Economics of Education in the UK*. Princeton, NJ: Princeton University Press. pp. 117–145.

Bonjour, D., Cherkas, L.F., Haskel, J.E., Hawkes, D.D. and Spector, T.D. (2003) 'Returns to education: evidence from UK twins', *American Economic Review*, 93(5): 1799–812.

Bos, F. (1992) 'The history of national accounting', Statistics Netherlands National Accounts Occasional Paper No. 48. The Hague, the Netherlands: Statistics Netherlands.

Brown, S. and Sessions, J. (2004) 'Signalling and screening', in G. Johnes and J. Johnes (eds.), *International Handbook on the Economics of Education*. Cheltenham, UK: Edward Elgar. pp. 58–100.

Bynner, J., Dolton, P., Fenstein, L., Makepeace, G., Malmberg, L. and Woods, L. (2003) *Revisiting the Benefits of Higher Education*. Report by the Bedford Group for Lifecourse and Statistical Studies, Institute of Education.

Campbell, D.E. (2006) 'What is education's impact on civic and social engagement?', in R. Desjardins and T. Schuller (eds.), *Measuring the Effects of Education on Health and Civic Engagement: Proceedings of the Copenhagen Symposium*. Paris: OECD. Available from http://www.oecd.org/education/innovation-education/37425694.pdf (accessed 7 August 2015).

Card, D. (1995) 'Using Geographic Variation in College Proximity to Estimate the Return to Schooling', National Bureau of Economic Research, Working Paper 4483.

Card, D. (1999) 'The causal effect of education on earnings', in D. Card and O. Ashenfelter, (eds.), *Handbook of Labor Economics*. Vol. 3. Amsterdam: Elsevier. pp. 1801–1863.

Card, D. (2001) 'Estimating the return to schooling: progress on some persistent econometric problems', *Econometrica,* 69(5): 1127–60.

Checchi, D. (2006) *The Economics of Education: Human Capital, Family Background and Inequality.* Cambridge: Cambridge University Press.

Chevalier, A. (2011) 'Subject choice and earnings of UK graduates', *Economics of Education Review,* 30(6): 1187–201.

De Muelemeester, J.L. and Diebolt, C. (2004) 'The economics of education: unkept promises?', *Brussels Economics Review,* 47(3/4): 303–320.

Department for Business Innovation and Skills (BIS) (2011) 'Supporting Analysis for the Higher Education White Paper', BIS Economics Paper No. 14.

Dickson, M. and Harmon, C. (2011) 'Economic returns to education: what we know, what we don't know, and where we are going – some brief pointers', *Economics of Education Review,* 30(6): 1118–22.

Feinstein, L., Sabates, R., Anderson, T.M., Sorhaindo, A. and Hammond, C. (2006) 'What are the effects of education on health?', in R. Desjardins and T. Schuller (eds.), *Measuring the Effects of Education on Health and Civic Engagement: Proceedings of the Copenhagen Symposium.* Paris: OECD. Available from http://www.oecd.org/edu/innovation-education/37437718.pdf (accessed 7 August 2015).

Florax, R.J.G.M. (1992) *The University: A Regional Booster?* Aldershot, UK: Avebury.

Giesecke, J.A. and Madden, J.R. (2006) 'CGE evaluation of a university's effects on a regional economy: an integrated assessment of expenditure and knowledge impacts', *Review of Urban and Regional Development Studies,* 18(3): 229–51.

Goldin, C. and Katz, L. (2007) 'The Race between Education and Technology: The Evolution of US Educational Wage Differentials, 1890 to 2005', National Bureau for Economic Research (NBER) Working Paper 12984. Available from http://www.nber.org/papers/w12984.pdf (accessed 7 August 2015).

Harmon, C. and Walker, I. (2003) 'The returns to education: microeconomics', *Journal of Economic Surveys,* 17(2): 115–53.

Haveman, R. and Wolfe, B. (1984) 'Schooling and economic wellbeing: the role of non-market effects', *Journal of Human Resources,* 19(3): 377–407.

Her Majesty's Treasury (2003) *The Green Book: Appraisal and Evaluation in Central Government.* London: TSO. Available from https://www.gov.uk/government/publications/the-green-book-appraisal-and-evaluation-in-central-governent (accessed 7 August 2015).

Hermannsson, K., Lecca, P., Lisenkova, K., McGregor, P. and Swales, K. (2012) 'The System-wide Impacts of the Social and Private Non-market Benefits of Higher Education', Discussion Paper 12-04, University of Strathclyde Business School, Department of Economics.

Hermannsson, K., Lecca, P., Lisenkova, K., McGregor, P. and Swales, K. (2014) 'The importance of graduates for the Scottish economy: a "micro-to-macro" approach', *Environment and Planning A,* 46(2): 471–87.

Hermannsson, K., Lecca, P. and Swales, K. (2014) 'How much does a single graduation cohort from further education colleges contribute to an open regional economy?' Working Paper 14–04, University of Strathclyde Business School, Glasgow, UK.

Hermannsson, K., Lisenkova, K., McGregor, P.G. and Swales, J.K. (2013) 'The expenditure impacts of individual higher education institutions and their students on the Scottish economy under a regional government budget constraint: homogeneity or heterogeneity?', *Environment and Planning A*, 45: 710–27.

Hermannsson, K., Lisenkova, K., McGregor, P.G. and Swales, J.K. (2014) '"Policy skepticism" and the impact of Scottish higher education institutions (HEIs) on their host region: accounting for regional budget constraints under devolution', *Regional Studies*, 48(2), 400–17.

Heurman, D. (2011) 'Human capital externalities in Western Germany', *Spatial Economic Analysis*, 6(2): 139–66.

Johnes, G. and Johnes, J. (2004) *International Handbook on the Economics of Education*. Cheltenham, UK: Edward Elgar.

Kravdal, Ø. (2002) 'Education and fertility in sub-Saharan Africa: individual and community effects', *Demography*, 39(2): 233–50.

Krueger, A.B. and Lindahl, M. (2001) 'Education for growth: why and for whom?', *Journal of Economic Literature*, 39(4): 1101–36.

Lange, F. and Topel, R. (2006) 'The social value of education and human capital', in E. Hanushek and F. Welch (eds.), *Handbook of Education Economics*. Vol. 1. Amsterdam: North-Holland. pp. 459–509.

Layard, R. and Glaister, S. (eds.) (1994) *Cost Benefit Analysis*. Cambridge: Cambridge University Press.

Lochner, L. (2004) 'Education, work, and crime: a human capital approach', *International Economic Review*, 45(3): 811–43.

Lochner, L. and Moretti, E. (2001) *The Effect of Education on Crime: Evidence from Prison Inmates, Arrests, and Self-Reports*. Report No. w8605. Cambridge, MA: National Bureau of Economic Research.

Machin, S. (2004) 'Skill-biased technical change and educational outcomes', in G. Johnes and J. Johnes (eds.), *International Handbook on the Economics of Education*. Cheltenham, UK: Edward Elgar. pp. 189–211.

Machin, S., Marie, O. and Vujic, S. (2011) 'The crime reducing effect of education', *Economic Journal*, 121: 463–84.

McGuinness, S. and Bennett, J. (2005) 'Intra and inter-generational changes in the returns to schooling 1991–2002', Economic Research Institute of Northern Ireland Working Paper Series No. 6.

McMahon, W.W. (2004) 'The social and external benefits of education', in G. Johnes and J. Johnes (eds.), *International Handbook on the Economics of Education*. Cheltenham, UK: Edward Elgar. pp. 211–259.

McMahon, W.W. (2009) *Higher Learning, Greater Good: The Private and Social Benefits of Higher Education*. Baltimore, MD: Johns Hopkins University Press.

Mincer, J. (1958) 'Investment in human capital and personal income distribution', *Journal of Political Economy*, 281–302.

Mincer, J. (1974) *Schooling, Experience and Earnings*. New York, NY: National Bureau of Economic Research. Available from http://papers.nber.org/books/minc74-1 (accessed 7 August 2015).

Moretti, E. (2004) 'Workers' education, spillovers and productivity: evidence from plant-level production functions', *American Economic Review*, 94(3): 656–90.

Okun, A.M. (1971) 'Social welfare has no price tag', *Survey of Current Business*, 51(7 Part II): 129–33.

O'Leary, N. and Sloane, P. (2005) 'The return to a university education in Great Britain', *National Institute Economic Review*, 193(1): 75–89.

Oreopoulos, P. and Salvanes, K.G. (2011) 'Priceless: the nonpecuniary benefits of schooling', *Journal of Economic Perspectives*, 25(1): 159–84.

Psacharopoulos, G. and Patrinos, H.A. (2002) 'Returns to investment in education: a further education'. Policy Research Working Paper: WPS 2881. Washington, DC: The World Bank, Latin America and the Caribbean Region, Education Sector Unit.

Psacharopoulos, G. and Patrinos, H.A. (2004) 'Human capital and rates of return', in G. Johnes and J. Johnes (eds.). *International Handbook on the Economics of Education*. Cheltenham, UK: Edward Elgar. pp. 1–57.

Schultz, T. (1961) 'Investing in human capital', *American Economic Review*, 51(1): 1–17.

Siegfried, J.J., Sanderson, A.R. and McHenry, P. (2007) 'The economic impact of colleges and universities', *Economics of Education Review*, 26: 546–58.

Smith, A. (1776) *An Inquiry into the Nature and Causes of the Wealth of Nations*. E. Cannan (ed.) London: Methuen and Co.

1904. Library of Economics and Liberty [online]. Available from http://www.econlib.org/library/Smith/smWN6.html (accessed 14 December 2010).

Spence, M. (1973) 'Job market signaling', *Quarterly Journal of Economics*, 87(3): 355–74.

Stiglitz, J.E. (1975) 'The theory of "screening", education, and the distribution of income', *American Economic Review,* 56(3): 283–300.

Stiglitz, J.E., Sen, A. and Fitoussi, J.P. (2010) *Report by the Commission on the Measurement of Economic Performance and Social Progress.* Paris: Commission on the Measurement of Economic Performance and Social Progress.

Walker, I. and Zhu, Y. (2007a) *The Labour Market Effects of Qualifications: Technical Report.* Futureskills Scotland – Research Series. Available from http://www.scotland.gov.uk/Resource/Doc/919/0065442.pdf (accessed 7 August 2015).

Walker, I. and Zhu, Y. (2007b) *The Labour Market Effects of Qualifications: Summary Report.* Futureskills Scotland – Research Series. Available from http://www.scotland.gov.uk/Resource/Doc/919/0065443.pdf (accessed 7 August 2015).

Walker, I. and Zhu, Y. (2008) 'The college wage premium and the expansion of higher education in the UK', *Scandinavian Journal of Economics,* 110(4): 695–709.

Walker, I. and Zhu, Y. (2011) 'Differences by degree: evidence of the net financial rates of return to undergraduate study for England and Wales', *Economics of Education Review,* 30(6): 1177–186.

Wolfe, B. and Haveman, R.H. (2001) *Accounting for the Social and Non-Market Benefit of Education.* Madison, WI: Institute for Research on Poverty, University of Wisconsin-Madison.

55

Public and Private Boundaries in Curriculum and Educational Policy

Vera Peroni

INTRODUCTION

This chapter discusses the changes that have been taking place in the relationship between public and private in this period of capitalism, with redefinitions of the role of the state,[1] and their implications for the democratization of education, which is materialized in educational and curricular issues in all education spheres, from the design of national educational policies to changes in the curriculum in the classrooms. The boundaries between public and private have been shifting during the current crisis of capitalism at a time when the strategies to overcome the crisis – neoliberalism, globalization, production restructuring and the Third Way – are redefining the role of the state, particularly with regards to social policy. In this chapter, we will focus on changes that have occurred in education, specifically how the private sector has come to define the curriculum in public schools, the knowledge to be taught, how it should be taught and how it should be assessed.

It is important to point out that, from our theoretical–methodological perspective, educational policy is not determined simply by social and economic changes, but is a constituent part of those changes, and the state, as well as capital, should be regarded as a relationship and process. Hence, we understand that the state is an important part of the movement of correlation of forces of subjects[2] situated in a specific historical and geographical context.[3] State and civil society are therefore pervaded by correlations of forces of different social classes and different types of societal projects. It is worth mentioning that our studies focus on the market-based civil society, where the private is linked to the market. We analyze the privatization of the public, within the logic of the market, and its implications for the democratization of education (Peroni, 2013a).

In this sense, there is no opposition between state and civil society because we live in a class society where civil society and the state are pervaded by market interests. After all, as Wood (2014) points out, the economic power of capital cannot exist without the support of extra-economic forces, and the extra-economic forces are today, as before, primarily those of the state.It is also important to point out that the relationship between public and private did not begin in this particular period of capitalism; historically, the dividing line between public and private has always been blurred in Brazil. The democratization of public education, therefore, still has a long way to go, and we raise questions about the implications of the mercantilization of the public in this process.

The concept of democracy upon which our analysis is based is the non-separation between the economic and the political, with social rights materialized in the form of social policies (Wood, 2003) and the collectivization of decision-making (Vieira, 1998) where policies are elaborated through critical and auto-critical social practices during the process of their development (Mészáros, 2002). In other words, democracy is not an abstraction – it is the materialization of rights in the form of policies that are collectively constructed through auto-critical social practices (Peroni, 2013a).

When we debate the relationship between public and private in education, our main focus is the curriculum, the production and appropriation of knowledge; hence, we ask 'what knowledge'? Who decides what to teach and how to teach? We agree with Apple's approach (Apple, 1995), which offers a good summary of the discussion presented in this chapter.

> The curriculum is never simply a neutral assemblage of knowledge, somehow appearing in the texts and lessons of a nation. It is always part of a *selective tradition*, someone's selection, some group's vision of legitimate knowledge. It is produced out of the cultural, political and economic conflicts, tensions and compromises that organize and disorganize a people. (Apple, 1995: 153)

Goodson (2007) also warns about the power relations linked to the curriculum:

> Over the years, the alliance between prescription and power has been carefully nurtured so that the curriculum becomes a device to reproduce existing power relations in society. The children of powerful, resourceful parents enjoy curriculum inclusion and the less advantaged suffer from curriculum exclusion. (Goodson, 2007: 246)

In our studies, we have observed that the private takes the reins of educational policies and defines the curriculum, the production and appropriation of knowledge, as pointed out by Young (2014):

> In developing an argument about what we might mean by the idea of curriculum, I borrow an idea from a recent article by my colleague David Scott (Scott and Hargreaves, 2014). His starting point is not curriculum as such but learning as the most basic human activity. What makes human learning human, he argues, is that it is an epistemic activity, in other words, it is involved in producing knowledge. (Young, 2014: 198)

Also on the conception of curriculum, Miller (2014) makes a critique of 'a technical-rational conception of "curriculum" only as pre-determined "content" into active processes of "understanding curriculum"' (Miller, 2014: 2043) and she highlights the interaction between curriculum, learning and teaching. In the partnerships examined, we observed that the conception of curriculum that the private brings to schools is a set of predetermined contents. We will present the testimony of a teacher, who says that she was not allowed to make any changes to the lesson plans, which came ready-made by the school. This teacher also tells us that there was intense monitoring through assessments in order to evaluate the progress of that prescriptive curriculum proposition.

Pacheco and Paraskeva (1999) highlight the importance of 'decisions in the practices of curriculum conception, development and assessment, with curriculum understood as a continuum that includes both the intentions, or theoretical aspect, and the reality, or practical aspect, so that it becomes a formative project within a concrete time and space' (Pacheco and Paraskeva, 1999: 8).

Hypólito (2010) warns us about the implications of this privatization process for the autonomy of teachers. Thus, we return to the important question raised by Miller (2014) and Pacheco and Paraskeva (1999) about who decides the school curriculum:

> …there is not much space for increased autonomy. What has been happening is that the control over the social and political objectives of education – the decisions about curriculum and programs, about what and how to teach – have been increasingly transferred from teachers to the control of managers, politicians and wider economic interests. (Hypólito, 2010: 1345)

Hypólito criticizes the mercantilization of teaching and its effects on education:

> …the regulatory state has been efficient redefining its educational and curricular policies, submitting education and schools to the market, both through the mercantilization of pedagogical materials and teaching methods, with significant effects for teacher education and the formation of consumers – teachers and students – achieving success in the constitution of teaching identities who are coadjuvants in the neoliberal and conservative agenda. (Hypólito, 2010: 1353)

In relation to the mercantilization of teaching materials, we give an example in this chapter of how it occurs in Brazil through the network of businesses gathered in the movement *Todos pela Educação* [All for Education], which sells teaching materials to the Ministry of Education.

Apple and Mead (2015) question the results of the process of education privatization in terms of quality improvements:

> If research supported the assertion that funding private school vouchers resulted in better outcomes for children, such a risk to the public school system might be justified. However, research has clearly demonstrated that children in voucher programs do no better, and often worse, than their peers educated in the public system. It is false to assert that competition between schools will improve outcomes. The state has now invested millions of dollars in an experiment that did not bear fruit. (http://host.madison.com/wsj/news/opinion/column/guest/michael-apple-and-julie-mead-don-t-privatize-strong-public/article_2e448fd4-3e5a-54ca-b20e-7739049d269a.html)

Another important issue regarding the curriculum discussed in the chapter is the debate on the relation between curriculum and the world of work. According to Tonet (2012):

> In the past decades, with the information revolution, the world of work has changed dramatically. A new productive model has been installed – a process that is still under way – which is characterized by an ever greater incorporation of science and technology into production, by flexibility, by decentralization, by the need for a very fast turnover of products and by a production designed to meet a more individualized demand. (Tonet, 2012: 13)

Tonet (2012) highlights how these changes relate to curriculum:

> …workers must learn to think, to solve new and unpredicted problems; they need to have a versatile education, i.e., a kind of training that allows them to move between different jobs, since stability is no longer part of this new form of production. (Tonet, 2012: 13)

Tonet also criticizes naturalized assumptions, for example that the mercantile character of society is something that is part of its own nature and that the essential function of education is to prepare individuals for the market place (Tonet, 2012: 14).

For Goodson (2007), the prescriptive curriculum is not adequate to the changes in the world of work:

> In the new era of flexible work organisation, workers face unpredictable and constantly changing assignments….Long-established and prescribed courses of study therefore become a handicap for the new flexible work order. Curriculum as prescription might provide residual patterns of social reproduction, but its increasing economic disfunctionality calls its continuity into question by powerful economic interests and global pressures….'Prospective planning' of learning, curriculum as prescription, is then colossally inappropriate to the flexible work order – in this analysis it is doomed and will require rapid replacement by new forms of learning organisation. (Goodson, 2007: 248)

Many questions arise from this debate, including should knowledge be instrumental to society's economic project in the sense of preparation for work? Is the curriculum proposed by private institutions linked to the logic of the market appropriate to a knowledge that is adequate to the changes in the world of work? Or does it prepare only a few to work as a team, to be creative, to be problem solvers, whilst the majority are left with a prescriptive curriculum that is inadequate to the changes taking place not only in the world of work, but also in the life of society.

Work is an important dimension of human formation, although it is not the only one. The conceptions of work and the world of work are therefore also in dispute when we discuss curriculum. We would like to highlight that not even the conception that capital itself proposes is being discussed, as was promised in the partnerships.

In our studies, we observed that in the public schools targeted by private partnerships, the curriculum proposed is standardized, replicable, basic and more appropriate to a bygone Fordist era than to the current period of capitalism of flexible accumulation. Despite a discourse that argues that the private should define the content of education because it is linked to a market-based conception of quality and an economic development project that needs education as a tool to train adequate labor, it is not what we have seen in our investigation. In this chapter we discuss how the private has been determining the direction of public education and, more specifically, the curriculum through three examples, which were part of our research.

We observed several forms of privatization of the public: through changes of ownership, with the transference of ownership from the state to non-profit or for-profit third sector organizations or to the private sector; through partnerships between public institutions and for-profit or non-profit private institutions, where the private defines the public; or through organizations that remain in state hands but follow the logic of the market, mainly through the reorganization of the management processes and the redefinition of the content of educational policy.

This chapter presents three examples based on research that analyze how this process is materializing in basic education: in the relation between the *Movimento Todos Pela Educação* [All for Education Movement]

and the Brazilian Ministry of Education's Technologies Guide, and also the partnerships between two private institutes and public schools – the Instituto Ayrton Senna (IAS) with primary and lower secondary schools, and the Instituto Unibanco, with upper secondary schools.

We understand that the changes in the boundaries between public and private are part of the redefinition of the role of the state, which is a consequence of the profound crisis the world is going through today. This discussion is taken up in the following section.

THE REDEFINITIONS OF THE ROLE OF THE STATE

We understand the redefinitions of the role of the state as part of the social and economic changes taking place in this particular period[4] of structural crisis of capitalism, where the contradictions have deepened. For Mészáros (2011: 2), 'the crisis of capital we are experiencing is an all-embracing structural crisis'. In the same sense, Antunes (1999) points out that the crises of Fordism and Keynesianism was the phenomenic expression of the more complex, critical situation of the downward trend in profit rates. Brenner (2008) agrees on the depth of the crisis and the fact that it is rooted in falling profit rates. Brenner also highlights that the 'weakness of underlying capital accumulation and the meltdown of the banking system is what's made the downward slide so intractable for policymakers and its potential for disaster so serious' (Brenner, 2008: 1). He warns that those paying the 'bill' for the crisis are states and workers, as exploitation has already increased, with longer working hours and lower pay, and states are getting into debt to finance the crisis (Peroni, 2013a).

The state has historically been called upon to control or regulate the contradictions of capital and the capital/labor relation. Currently, despite the minimal state propounded by neoliberals, the state is being called upon to 'rescue' the productive and financial capital at a moment of great crisis. Paradoxically, it is considered 'guilty of the crisis' by neoliberal theory (Peroni, 2013b).

Although in the post-war period the strategies of the state were mainly Fordism/Keynesianism in the central countries and developmentalism in the peripheral countries, in the current period the main strategies are neoliberalism, production restructuring, globalization, and the Third Way. Another theoretical assumption in the analysis of the process of the redefinition of the role of the state is that the fiscal crisis is part of a broader crisis of capitalism, and not its cause, as diagnosed by neoliberalism and accepted by the Third Way.

The role of the state regarding social policies has changed as the neoliberal diagnosis offered two prescriptions: to rationalize resources and to take power away from institutions because democratic institutions are subject to the pressures and demands of the population and are also considered unproductive by the logic of the market. The responsibility for the execution of social policies must therefore be transferred to society – for neoliberals through privatization (the market) and for the Third Way through the third sector (Peroni, 2013a).

Buchanan et al. (1984), who were neoliberal theoreticians, consider contemporary democratic institutions irresponsible and the remedial action they prescribe are constitutional measures to contain government, placing the control tools outside representative institutions based on the principle that political controls are inferior to market controls. In our research into public–private partnerships, we observed that this has been one of the justifications used by private institutions to enter partnerships, for example in the case of Instituto Ayrton Senna,[5] where the basic assumption is that public education is in trouble and that it must 'save it':

> Instituto Ayrton Senna's programs are *educational solutions that help tackle the main problems of public education* in Brazil. And they contemplate three large areas: formal education, complementary education and education and technology....

Implemented at large scale, with pre-defined strategies and targets, the programs are systematically monitored and evaluated, with the aim of achieving a single goal: the success of students at school.[6] (emphasis added)

It is interesting to point out that the institute works on the formulation of policies and on the conception, monitoring and assessment of the education provided by the partnered public education networks. In the justification of its activities, it cites quality of education and takes on tasks that should be the state's responsibility within public education policy.

This 'savior' viewpoint, according to which the market-based private sector should ensure the quality of public education, is not the isolated view of one institute, but is embedded in a logic that naturalizes this participation because it is grounded on the neoliberal assumption that it is not capitalism that is in crisis, but the state. According to this conception, the strategy is to reform the state or to minimize its actions in order to overcome the crisis. It is the market that should remedy the failures of the state and, therefore, the logic of the market must prevail within the state so it can become more efficient and productive.

For neoliberal thought, there is a tension between individual freedom and democracy. According to Hayek (1983), the maximization of freedom resides in protecting the market as something necessary and sufficient for the existence of freedom. The market must therefore be protected against the state and the tyranny of the majority, and Hayek warns that if the state is influenced or vulnerable to the influence of the masses, the two dangers merge.

According to that theory, through the vote, citizens decide about goods that are not theirs, generating a conflict with the owners because it is seen as a form of distribution of wealth. Hayek (1983) denounces that democracy is guilty of plundering the property of others and because it is impossible to totally suppress democracy (the vote, political parties) in many cases, the effort is directed at depleting its power.

For Hayek (1983), unlimited democracy leads to planned economy, which is one step away from totalitarianism. He warns against the perils of unlimited democracy: 'a democracy may well yield totalitarian powers, and it is at least conceivable that a totalitarian government may act on liberal principles. Liberalism is thus incompatible with unlimited democracy' (Hayek, 1983: 143).

The Public Choice Theory makes an economic analysis of politics. Public Choice's starting point is that the economy and politics of a country are inseparable. The key idea is that all human actions in every dimension are rooted in an exchange, in vested interests – that is both an assumption and a prescription, in the sense that every relationship is modeled on an exchange (Buchanan et al., 1984). We have seen this prescription materialize in education in different ways, either through outside influence in a process that Ball and Junemann (2012) call exogenous privatization, or within the public sector through endogenous privatization.

Ball and Olmedo (2013) makes a critical analysis of the presence of 'other' subjects linked to the market that take on a leading role in the definition of educational policies, which used to be the responsibility of the state, and emphasizes that governmental organizations have also been working with market-based parameters (competition, choice, and performance-related funding). New voices and interests are represented in the political process and new nodes of power and influence are built and strengthened (Ball, 2013: 177).

In this sense, Sacristan (1998) highlights the importance of public discussion of the curriculum in a country in a democratic process:

I believe that, in a democracy, the publicly discussed and agreed upon intervention of the state in the curriculum in order to establish some rules of the game at the service of public interest may be preferable to a curriculum determined by multinational corporations, as it is already starting to happen in other contexts, or by private publishing companies producing textbooks. (Sacristan, 1998: 97)

Sacristan (1998) makes an important warning about the need to democratically define the curriculum, and we stress that the very concept of democracy is under discussion. In our view, the participation of subjects connected to the market in discussions about curricular issues is not accidental, but part of an assumption defended by Public Choice, according to which democracy and state regulation are detrimental to the functioning of the free market. It is therefore necessary to set constitutional limits on current democratic institutions: eliminating the vote, which would be more difficult, or restricting the impact of the vote through privatization and deregulation, leading to the dismantling of the state (Buchanan et al., 1984).

The Third Way,[7] the present social democracy, offers the same diagnosis, that is, that the crisis is in the state, and it proposes that social policy should be transferred to civil society through partnerships with the third sector. In this sense, the conception of democracy as the non-separation between the economic and the political (Wood, 2003), and as social rights materialized in universal policies, is replaced by another idea of democracy, according to which the participation of society means, in many cases, taking responsibility for the execution of social policies, rather than participating in decision-making and social control.

Robertson and Verger (2012) also cite questions about democracy in the debate on the relationship between public and private: 'partnerships and regulatory networks tend to reduce democracy to negotiation within civil society between extremely unequal actors' (Robertson and Verger, 2012: 1138).

The non-governmental character assumed by the third sector, which implies that it is not subject to institutional control, points to an important issue as these organizations have ever increasing power. In whose name do these organizations operate? As they are often directly connected to international agencies, who are they accountable to? What are their ethical judgment standards? Who judges their actions? In case they have legitimacy, who grants it?

Ball stresses the importance of this sector, which he calls new philanthropy. 'What is "new" in "new philanthropy" is the direct relationship between "giving" and the "outcomes" of the direct involvement of givers in the philanthropic actions and policy communities' (Ball and Olmedo, 2013: 33). The authors point out that the changes in traditional philanthropy happened in a three-stage move from palliative giving (traditional philanthropy or 'philanthropy 1.0') to developmental ('philanthropy 2.0') and, finally, to 'profitable' giving, constituting what has been termed as 'philanthropy 3.0' (Ball and Olmedo, 2013: 33–34). It is important to mention that we understand networks as subjects (individual and collective) in relationships[8] as a class project.

We present an example of the influence of the market as private businesses sell educational technologies[9] to Brazilian public schools through a federal government program,[10] which designs technical and/or financial assistance actions that can be requested by municipalities in their respective plans, as well as sub-actions executed by the municipalities themselves. There are four dimensions divided into indicators and areas. Dimension 1 covers education management; dimension 2, the education and training of teachers and school service and support staff; dimension 3, teaching practice and assessment; and dimension 4, physical infrastructure and teaching aids.

The offer is implemented through the Technologies Guide (BRASIL, 2011), which is provided to schools so that they can decide according to the problems diagnosed in their plans. We question whether the 'basket of products' offered is actually suited to the needs of the schools or whether the schools have to adapt to what is offered to them if they need any type of government help to solve their problems. It is important to highlight that these actions address the more relevant issues of education, such as teachers' education, teaching practice and assessment, which are defining aspects of the Brazilian educational policy. However, the state promotes partnerships with private institutions in the most important areas of the plan, as shown in Table 55.1.

Among the Guide's categories, we draw attention to teaching–learning, which shows a predominance of technologies developed outside the Ministry of Education. Sacristan (1998) warns about the importance of who decides the content of public education:

I think that discussing the existence or absence of control over the curriculum is pointless, as it seems unthinkable that this control would not exist, given the close ties that the school system has with the social system … the problem lies in establishing who exerts control and through what mechanisms (Sacristan, 1998: 97)

According to Bernardi et al. (2014) the same subjects of the corporate movement *Todos*

Table 55.1   Educational Technologies Guide 2009 and 2011/2012

Item	Category	Technology developed by MEC		Technology developed outside MEC		Total	
		2009	2011	2009	2011	2009	2011
1	Education management	09	11	06	07	15	18
2	Teaching–learning	04	09	51	51	55	60
3	Training of education professionals	10	12	14	15	24	22
4	Inclusive education	06	11	01	01	07	12
5	Educational portals	04	05	02	11	16	16
6	Diversity and young people – and adult education	10	17	07	11	17	28
7	Children's education	–	–	–	08	–	08
8	TOTAL	43	65	91	104	134	169

Sources: Technologies Guide (BRASIL, 2009: e 2011/2012) and Rossi et al. (2013).

pela Educação act as agents and representatives at the public sector, that is, the Ministry of Education, thereby becoming clients of the state when they offer their recommendations or their products in the Technologies Guide. Bernardi et al. (2014) present[11] the governance council and the institutions, as in Figure 55.1.

This connection between the *Todos pela Educação* movement and the products offered in the Technologies Guide refers us to the connection that Ball and Junemann (2012) and Rhodes (1996) call 'steering' and 'rowing' (execution) in network analysis. In this case, entrepreneurs act in the steering and in the rowing because they strongly influence

national policies and are also present in the classroom through the sale of their educational products. Robertson et al. (2012) highlights this as the influence of the private sector in all instances of education: 'PPPs have enabled their rapid advance, so that the private sector is now deeply embedded in the heart of the state's education services at all levels, from policy and research work to delivering learning in classrooms' (Robertson et al., 2012: 1149). There is also what Ball designates as philanthropy 3.0, when so-called non-profit organizations obtain profit through the sales of products to public education networks and schools. Another issue that deserves attention is the relationship between public and private

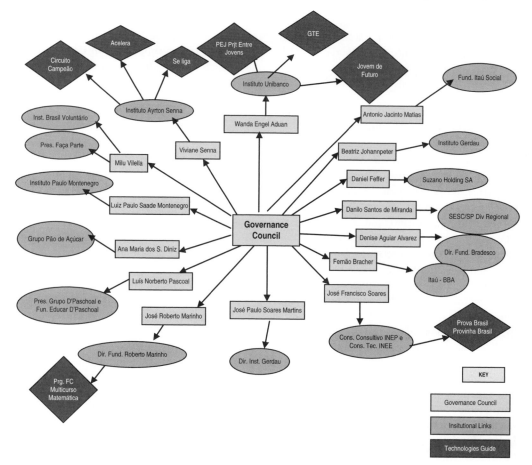

Figure 55.1   Individual and collective subjects and their relationships with the Technologies Guide

Source: Technologies Guide (BRASIL, 2009: e 2011/2012) and Movement All for Education Governance Council (Bernardi et al., 2014)

within the "Plano de Desenvolvimento da Educação" (BRASIL, 2007)[12], through which the federal government is more present than before in the history of Brazilian education, whilst is also entering partnerships with the private sector in strategic areas of education that promote the logic of the market within public schools.

Besides the participation of the policy networks, as in the example of the *Movimento Todos pela Educação*, which influences educational policy, we have observed other forms of privatization of the public. We were able to observe this in two research studies that examined partnerships between public education networks and private institutions. The first study looked at the partnerships between basic education schools (up to 9th grade) and IAS. The second study examined Instituto Unibanco and its partnerships with secondary schools.

INSTITUTO AYRTON SENNA

This section is based on the nationwide research study 'Analysis of the consequences of partnerships between Brazilian municipalities and the Ayrton Senna Institute (IAS) for education' (Adrião and Peroni, 2010). The study aimed to capture the specific consequences of the partnerships between IAS and public school networks. Due to the extreme inequality and diversity existing between the different Brazilian regions and municipalities, the study selected one municipality from each region to conduct ten case studies. The main research sources were interviews with secretaries of education, principals, teachers, teaching coordinators and coordinators of the programs during the partnership. We also analyzed information from institutional documents produced by IAS or by the private institutions involved in the implementation of the programs, as well as documents drawn by municipal governments. Local teams conducted documentary research; changes in the municipalities' education

laws; types of teachers' employment and remuneration; and organization of the municipal education networks (enrolment, management policies, curriculum policies, assessment results, etc.). The research methodology used in the schools consisted of semi-structured interviews and observation (Adrião and Peroni, 2010).

IAS is a non-profit, non-governmental organization founded in November 1994, which has partnerships with municipal, state and federal public education networks. We should point out that IAS has been expanding its actions and consequent prominence in the definition of educational policies, with its participation in the Technologies Guide, discussed earlier. As the institute declares: 'currently, the programs *Se Liga* [Tune in], *Acelera Brasil* [Speed up, Brazil] and *Circuito Campeão* [Champion Circuit] have been accredited by the Ministry of Education as support tools to the public education systems for the promotion of the quality of education'.[13]

To start with, IAS offered complementary programs in the opposite shift to school hours and only in remedial classes, but it eventually came to influence educational policy as a whole, from curriculum and lessons through to the management of education networks and schools, as we will demonstrate later. The IAS realized that in order for the changes to be substantial, it would not suffice to act only on specific issues, but rather that it should act on education as a whole. It is now involved in planning, monitoring and assessing public education systems through the *Rede Vencer* [Winning Network], an IAS project that aims to improve the learning of public school students and articulate knowledges from different social technologies developed and implemented by the Institute. Those technologies involve the [AY1]mainstreaming of students through the programs *Se Liga* and *Acelera Brasil*. The *Se Liga* program is concerned with literacy for students lagging behind and *Acelera Brasil* is designed to speed up the learning of students who are behind. The program *Circuito Campeão* deals with literacy in the regular grades of primary school through managing the first 4 years, and the program *Gestão Nota 10* [Grade A Management] addresses school management and the municipal departments of education.

It is important to know the objectives of *Rede Vencer* in order to analyze the IAS's conception of education, curriculum and assessment:

(1) To institutionalize **managerial practices** in the schools' daily routine, which can substitute the "culture of failure" by the "culture of success";
(2) To establish the planning of teaching practices based on assessments of the teaching–learning process;
(3) To train teams from the departments of education and the schools to enable them to perform their functions with a **focus on outcomes and targets**, assuming the respective responsibilities for the **learning outcomes** of every student; and,
(4) To generate opportunities for the professional development of the school staff so as to enable the generation of knowledge, **especially in the areas of reading, writing and mathematics**, the foundations of learning in every area of human knowledge. (Adrião and Peroni, 2010: 319, emphasis added)

IAS links learning to school management. In its view, schools must have a strictly monitored managerial administration, with standardized activities through pre-set lessons and a routine. The focus should be on mathematics and Portuguese, which are the activities assessed through national tests. The IAS sees learning as a product that is measured by test results and pre-established targets and the material is strongly prescriptive:

In the *Circuito Campeão* program, which deals with literacy, the lesson plans are sent to IAS by the municipal coordinator from the first to the last day of the school year, in December, and the schools must inform the themes, the abilities and skills that will be developed on each day of the school year. The advance lesson plans are done in advance for the year's 200 school days. When teachers make their plans, they must follow the steps that the Circuito Campeão program denominates 'routine'. (Caetano, 2013: 207)

In the program *Gestão Nota 10*, the data (grades, assessments, attendance sheets, targets achieved) are collected by teachers who conduct the individual monitoring of students, and then pass the information on to the principal. The principal then makes a consolidated report on the data, analyzing them in order to check whether the students have achieved the set targets. The material is sent to the Municipal Education Department, which produces another consolidated report on the municipal schools. That material is finally sent to IAS through the *Sistema Instituto Ayrton Senna de Informação – SIASI* (Ayrton Senna Institute's Information System), which, according to the results, sends specific material to the schools and education networks. Indicators of success, diagnoses of the educational reality, monitoring reports, interventions, processes and results therefore dictate the technical work to be done.

The IAS relates quality control to the products of the assessments and the strict control over teachers' work, which is measurable in SIASI's virtual platform. Young (2014) alerts to the dangers of an assessment-driven curriculum:

My view is that if outcomes or competences or more broadly assessment drives the curriculum, it will be unable to provide access to knowledge; knowledge is about being able to envisage alternatives whether in literature or chemistry; it can never be outcomes, skills or assessments led. (Michael Young, 2014: 195)

Another important aspect in relation to curriculum is the IAS's work through the *Programa Circuito Campeão* (PCC), which deals with the period of literacy learning, working exclusively with the mother tongue (in this case Portuguese) and Mathematics, which are the disciplines that are assessed through national tests, as Caetano's (2013) studies demonstrate.

The monitoring of the teachers' work is done through weekly visits by the supervisor and the participation of teachers in biweekly meetings for assessment, exchange of experiences and shared planning with other teachers. The training courses are provided through distance learning. There is daily collection of information on students' and teachers' attendance, student dropout, records of supervisors' visits, teachers' participation in the quarterly meetings and even on the number of books read by students. This constant monitoring significantly limits teachers' autonomy.

A school principal mentions the competition that is stimulated between schools and between classes in the same school:

> … you had to send the flipcharts and the competition it generated was not very nice. So much so, that the Department of Education stopped it. They used to name the school, to show this or that school and its place as 1st, 2nd, 3rd, last place…. And then there were the tests, the institute designed the tests, the external assessments, to check the level of the students. We used to apply them, and then the results of the tests came, and also the place. (Principal from Municipality B)[14]

Another aspect addressed by the teacher was the assessments – carried out by IAS itself. We understand that assessments are done partly in order to have control over the program, however, they are also done because of the IAS's view that testing induces quality and that people will work harder if they are constantly monitored. Moreover, the fact that the tests come ready-made from IAS is another controversial aspect because the debate on the assessment of the learning process has evolved significantly, and tests are no longer considered the only or the most adequate form of assessment:

> …in April and September, we had to apply tests that came ready-made from the institute. My 1st graders had to do 5 pages of Portuguese and 5 pages of Mathematics….but never, at any moment, was the educational material ever discussed, and neither were any alternatives to improve the results of the assessment. (Teacher 1 from Municipality B)[15]

Another controversial aspect is the set lessons:

> …there was a list of planned contents that we had to observe strictly, so, when the supervisor entered the classroom, he checked what school-day number it was, what the sub-project and the class

were. On that day, you had to work on that theme and it had to be during that pre-defined period.

And heaven forbid if you did not do it correctly. (Teacher 1 from Municipality B)[16]

Just as the assessments are a way of monitoring teachers' work, the set lessons originate from the idea that teachers are incapable of planning their tasks and therefore should receive everything prepared for them, as Viviane Senna, the IAS President, explains:

> The materials are highly structured in order to ensure that even an inexperienced teacher, or one who is insufficiently prepared – as is the case of many teachers in Brazil – is able to offer students a quality program, with a high degree of student participation in the class, in the school and in the community. (Senna, 2000: 146)

As Senna puts it, the content is 'highly structured', which we see as a step backwards in terms of the autonomy of schools and teachers, and thus in the process of democratization of education. We agree with Young's (2014) critique about teachers being told what they should teach:

> No teacher wants solutions from curriculum theory – in the sense of "being told what to teach." That is technicism and undermines teachers. However, like any profession, teachers would be isolated and lose whatever authority they have without curriculum guidelines and principles derived from curriculum theory. In other words, teachers need curriculum theory to affirm their professional authority. (Young, 2014: 195)

During our study, we noticed that IAS had no interest in establishing a dialog with the school community. We emphasize that the changes introduced by IAS are not exclusively technical because they also interfere in the curriculum, conceptions and goals in what we have designated, in our latest studies[17] (Peroni, 2013), as the 'content of education'. The material provided by IAS is highly structured, as declared by the President of the IAE, Viviane Senna. We observed in our nationwide field research, which covered ten Brazilian states with very different characteristics, that the material is standardized and the same material is used for indigenous schools in the Amazon region and also for schools in urban municipalities in São Paulo or Rio Grande do Sul. That seems to be at odds with the neoliberal discourse on quality of education to meet the demands of the market because the demands of current capitalism for the restructuring of production require flexible workers who are able to think for themselves and work in teams, and that is the exact opposite of what IAS is offering their partner schools and networks.

The study of this partnership raises questions, such as what are the consequences for a democratic definition of curriculum when IAS determines how and what will be taught, and when it monitors every action of the municipality, thereby removing a great deal of its autonomy? What happens to the participation of different educational segments in educational decisions? What leads the public education system to seek this type of partnership?

As a consequence of this type of partnership, social control and the collectivization of decisions, which are such crucial factors in the construction of democracy in Brazil, eventually give way to external control by a private institution, which determines the content of public education policies from legislation and the organization of the educational system through to daily educational practices. The process of construction of democratic management is therefore thwarted, with IAS determining what is to be done at every level, from the head of the state's Department of Education to teachers and students.

INSTITUTO UNIBANCO

The Instituto Unibanco was founded in 1982, initially to promote the bank's social investments and initiatives.[18] It expanded its activities in formal education in 2003 when President Lula came to power and Brazilian society expected educational policies that

had greater regard for the working class. Instituto Unibanco's goal was for its technologies to become public policy, and in 2007 it conceived and implemented the *Projeto Jovem de Futuro – PJF* [Youth with a Future Project], which was experimentally implemented in secondary schools. In 2011, PJF had its technology validated and expanded for large-scale implementation in partnership with the Ministry of Education, within the program *Ensino Médio Inovador* [Innovative Secondary Education]. The partnership was denominated ProEMI/JF.

ProEMI is a governmental program created through a process of correlation of forces, with a conception of curriculum – which was different from that which had been developing in the country – was connected to abilities and skills. The program *Ensino Médio Inovador* was created 'with the aim of supporting and enhancing the development of innovative curricular propositions in non-technical secondary schools' (Portaria 971/09 art. 1, BRASIL, 2009). The document presents a definition of curriculum that supports its proposition:

> The curriculum, in all its actions and dimensions, should be designed in order to guarantee the students' right to learning and development through actions and activities that contemplate, from this perspective of curricular integration, the acquisition of knowledge, the development of experiences and the promotion of actions that materialize into a holistic human education, fostering students' capacity for critical reflection and autonomy. (BRASIL, MEC, 2014: 8–9).

We have also observed that ProEMI has the aim of fostering emancipatory methodologies and offers conditions for public systems and schools to build democratically debated curricular propositions. According to ProEMI's guiding document, 'The construction of the *Projeto de Redesenho Curricular – PRC* [Curriculum Redesign Project] will take place in a collective and participatory manner, contemplating actions that correspond to the reality of schools and students' (BRASIL, MEC, 2014: 14).

However, the federal government, which enabled the construction of a participatory and democratic curricular policy for secondary schools, made an agreement with the Instituto Unibanco, opening the possibility for the states' public education systems to establish partnerships for the implementation of ProEMI. Instead of being a democratic and collective construction in schools, the curricular proposition should therefore occur through a standardized management and assessment system, which, in Instituto Unibanco's view, is the way to improve students' learning.

> For the program *Jovem de Futuro*, efficient and participative management focused on positive learning outcomes can decisively influence the quality of education offered by schools. From that perspective, as well as encouraging the redesign of schools' curricula, guided and funded by the Ministry of Education, ProEMI/JF also seeks to enhance school management, focusing on the improvement of teaching results. (Instituto Unibanco, 2013: 11)

As we have seen, ProEMI's proposition focuses on the curriculum, whilst Instituto Unibanco, through the PJF, presents a proposition that sees school management as inductive to students' learning. The PJF is based on the perception that the problem lies in the management of the schools, which is deemed inefficient and ineffective, and it proposes the *Gestão Escolar para Resultados – GEpR* [Results-based School Management]. This system adopts information systems for monitoring, control and assessment, and uses communication programs to ensure broader community commitment to the actions of the school, aiming at improving students' outcomes.[19]

The GEpR concept is based on the assumption that 'any organization', particularly public interest ones, must have technically and socially qualified management (Instituto Unibanco, 2014: 4, emphasis added). In the Instituto Unibanco's view, the school management has no specificities and can adopt the management perspective of 'any organization'.

Results-based management is done in schools through the construction of a Plan of Action 'based on planning, execution, monitoring and assessment activities that constitute a continuous cyclic process, with constant feedback. Therefore we call it "Management Circuit"' (Instituto Unibanco, 2014: 10). According to one of the Instituto Unibanco's documents, the results expected are:

1 *From students.* R1: Students with developed skills and abilities in Portuguese and Mathematics. R2: Students with high attendance rates.
2 *From teachers.* R3: Teachers with high attendance rates. R4: Improved teaching practices.
3 *From management.* R5: Results-based school management. R6: Improved school infrastructure.

The Plan of Action is designed to guarantee the expected outcomes and, if the school does not achieve them, it suffers financial sanctions, as shown in Figure 55.2.

It is clear that the performance-related payments are seen as an incentive, fitting perfectly with the logic of the market. When the representative of Instituto Unibanco comes to deprived schools, with very low-paid teachers and socially disadvantaged students, it encounters very little resistance. That raises the question of whether this is a form of privatization of public schools and buying educational policies and principles.

In order to control the actions of the PJF, Instituto Unibanco developed an online platform to manage school projects and distance education. It is currently formed by the *Sistema de Gestão de Projetos* – SGP [Project Management System] and by the *Ambiente Virtual de Aprendizagem* – AVA [Virtual Learning Environment]. This control system is very similar to SIASI.

Another highlight is the training of teachers and managers in results-based management. In order to participate in the PJF, teachers and managers attend a training course lasting approximately 120 hours, offered during the 3 years of the project. It is important to highlight that the course is intended for the staff from schools and from the Department of Education, who are at the center of the decisions about the definition and development of policies. At the schools, the participants are

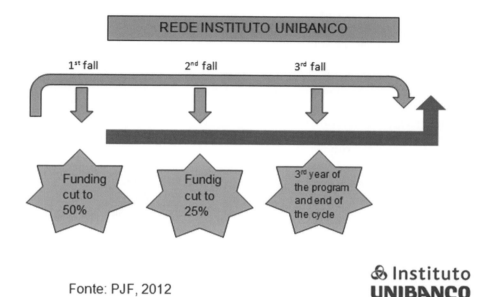

Figure 55.2   Results-based sanctions policy

Source: ProEMI/Jovem de Futuro Apresentação do Jovem de Futuro Ceará (slides), Peroni and Caetano (2014).

the principal, the teaching coordinator and a teacher, and in the state's Department of Education, the participants are the supervisors and technicians responsible for monitoring the schools.

A further important issue is that the school's council, one of the essential pillars of democratic management, loses its significance because another council, which is linked to the project, is constituted at the school. According to one of Instituto Unibanco's documents, the 'role of the managing group, alongside with the school's principal, is to plan and coordinate the elaboration of the Plan of Action, to implement and execute the ProEMI/JF, making the necessary decisions to guarantee its success'. (Instituto Unibanco, 2013: 50)

We would like to point out that the PJF uses standardized programs for the different Brazilian states and strict control and monitoring of results, as we have seen in other programs, such as those of IAS.

We agree with Alferes and Mainardes (2014) when they say that the 'silence of the government with regards to the design of a common curriculum defined nationally or locally (for one public school network), has been facilitating the interference of private organizations through advisory services on the adoption of teaching materials, workbooks or literacy methods' (Alferes and Mainardes, 2014: 253). They also highlight the consequences that the partnerships have on students' learning (which we illustrate with the examples in this chapter): 'In many public school networks, a significant portion of public funds is destined to the purchase of these materials and advisory services, which results are debatable from the point of view of guaranteeing the appropriation of knowledge by all students' (Alferes and Mainardes, 2014: 253). In Brazil, we do not have a national curriculum, only curricular guidelines. This is a controversial topic and it generates heated debates at national level about the increasing presence of the commercial private sector in public education. A democratically debated national curriculum can help to prevent it being defined only by national assessments, textbooks and private companies in partnerships with public schools. In this sense, we agree with Alferes and Mainardes (2014) in that 'the definition of a common curriculum and the publication of complementary materials are strategies that can instrumentalize public school networks to effectively improve the quality of education without transferring funds to private organizations' (2014: 253).

In this chapter, we present one example of private corporate networks influencing the direction of educational policies, entering the classroom and influencing the curriculum through the sale of technologies to public schools; and two examples of partnerships between private institutes and public primary and secondary schools. These examples involve forms of relations between the public and private in education in Brazil; however, this process is also taking place internationally and in different ways, as shown by the studies of Robertson et al. (2012); Ball (2012, 2013); Ball and Olmedo (2013); Ball and Junemann (2012) and Gewirtz and Ball (2011).

CONCLUSION

In this chapter we have presented elements for the debate on how redefinitions of the role of the state are reorganizing the boundaries between public and private and materializing in different ways in public primary and secondary education, as well as their implications for the process of democratization of education. We emphasize that, in Brazil today, the guarantee of access to public education is being expanded, which we consider a step forward in this process; however, we are also seeing an increasing presence of the private sector defining public education. The state remains responsible for access and is even increasing the number of places in public schools, but the educational 'content' (teaching, curriculum, assessment) is

increasingly determined by institutions that introduce the logic of the market, with the justification that they are contributing to improving the quality of public schools.

In our research, we analyzed different forms of relationship between public and private in basic education. We attempted to analyze more specifically how the private interferes in the public through partnerships in which the ownership remains public, but the private institution interferes in the content of education, introducing an individualistic and competitive business logic. That logic focuses on results at the expense of the democratic process, which is grounded on collectivist principles and focused on the construction of democratic values.

The partnerships are one of the ways to gain direct access to schools and classrooms, and to define and control what will be taught and how. In the examples given, we observed that the content is highly prescriptive. In the partnerships with the IAS, we saw that the lesson plans came ready-made for every school day and that SIASI [Ayrton Senna Information System] exercised strict monitoring to check whether the targets set by the IAS were being met. For IAS, learning and curriculum are linked with schools' management.

In secondary education, an attempt at a democratic process in the definition of the curriculum has been under way but, with the partnership, the focus was shifted from curriculum to management. It was also shifted to outcome-based management based on business management principles. This shift from curriculum to management is part and parcel of the neoliberal diagnosis discussed in the beginning of this chapter. According to this diagnosis, the current crisis is because of poor public sector management and, therefore, business-style management would solve it. This diagnosis is based on the assumption that learning is a product, and it can be measured and use managing devices to allow an 'outcome' that meets the targets. If we return to the conception of curriculum at the start of this chapter, which argues that curriculum is connected with knowledge production (Miller,

2014; Young, 2014), this knowledge is not neutral (Apple, 1995; Goodson, 2007) but connected to power relations in the construction of different types of social processes. The conception of learning as a measurable, highly prescriptive, standardized and replicable product (or in other words, the same for all) is part of a market-based vision where everything is a product and everything, including knowledge, subjects and social processes, has an exchange value. In this sense, we question the reason why public education networks seek partnerships with private institutions, and miss the possibility to collectively discuss a curriculum connected with a knowledge production process and a societal project. The curriculum – the teaching proposition of the school – is bought as if they were buying notebooks, pencils or any other product.

We agree with Miller (2014) on the importance of theoretical discussions about curriculum, to 'shift the current and excessive obsession of test producers and assessment gurus with "certainty", regarding curriculum merely as "preternined, packed, fixed, unchangeable and testable knowledge"'. (Miller, 2014: 2051). In the sense of 'who and what "counts" in education' (Miller, 2014: 2051).

It is also interesting to point out that the institutes we analyzed work on the definition of policies, on their conception, and on monitoring and evaluating education in the partner public education networks. In the justification for their activities, they cite quality of education, and they take on tasks that ought to be the responsibility of the state regarding public education policies. The methods used are standardized and replicable, which are contradictory to the production restructuring programs of capital itself, which propose educating workers who are creative and able to respond quickly to demands and to think for themselves and work in a team.

The Instituto Unibanco has a peculiarity that causes us great concern – it funds schools and, therefore, many public schools join its programs in order to receive financial resources. The schools therefore have to subscribe to the Institute's targets, which influence every aspect of education – from the school's council through to the syllabus – and because they apply the assessment tests, the schools that do not achieve the set targets have their funding cut. We question whether this is a case of 'buying public schools', many of which are in a precarious state due to the lack of investment in educational policies that occurred in Brazil, particularly in the 1990s.

Another issue we have looked into, which is connected with the role of the state, is the importance of the global networks for the definition of education. With new actors that have come to exert powerful influence on educational policies, such as philanthropic organizations and global networks, the responsibilities are getting increasingly diluted with regards to the responsibility for the provision of the right to education. We emphasize that we understand networks as subjects (individual or collective) in relationship, situated in a historical and geographic context (Harvey, 2005) and pervaded by class objectives. The networks can either be tools for increased participation or for control and influence. In this sense, the central issue is that networks should not replace government in the execution of social rights or in the public debate about the content of education, or in a conception of teaching, curriculum and assessment that is connected to the debate about the role of knowledge in a fairer and more democratic societal project.

We understand that the private commercial sector, whether or not organized in networks, is not an abstraction, but rather it is formed and operated by individual and collective subjects in a class project – and these subjects are part of a historic offensive of capital, with the specificities of this particular period of capitalism.

The relations between public and private refer to the redefinitions of the role of the state, and here we agree with Wood (2014: 18) in that '…the state is more essential than ever to capital even, or especially, in its global form'. He also points out that 'global capitalism is what it is not because it is global, but, above all, because it is capitalist' (Wood, 2014:24). The problems associated with globalization 'are not simply because the economy is "global", or because global corporations are uniquely vicious, or even because they are exceptionally powerful…globalization is the result, not the cause' (Wood, 2014: 24). In this sense, 'even the most benign or responsible of global corporations can escape the compulsions of capital, but must follow the laws of the market in order to survive' (Wood, 2014: 24), and hence 'the problem is not this or that corporation, nor this or that international agency, but the capitalist system itself ' (Wood, 2014: 25).

Finally, in accordance with the concept of democracy adopted in this chapter, that is, the collectivization of decisions (Vieira, 1998), social rights materialized in policies (Wood, 2003), and the elaboration of policies through critical and auto-critical social practices in the course of their development (Mészáros, 2002), we emphasize that the different forms of relationship between public and private, materialized in educational policies, have significant implications for the democratization of education.

ACKNOWLEDGEMENT

Text translated by Lisa Gertum Becker.

NOTES

1   State is understood as historical, concrete, class state, and, in this sense, maximum state for the capital because in the process of correlation of forces, it is the capital that has hegemony.
2   Individual and collective subjects as in Thompson's conception (1981).
3   Historical and geographical context as in Harvey's conception (2005).
4   Particularly as in Lukács's (1978) conception: 'The movement from singular to universal and vice-versa is always mediated by the particular; it is a real intermediary member, both in the objective reality and in the thinking that reflects it in an approximately adequate way' (Lukács, 1978: 112).

5   On the issue of partnerships between the public basic education systems and the Ayrton Senna Institute, see the research report by Adrião and Peroni (2010).
6   See http://senna.globo.com/institutoayrtonsenna/ programas/programas_educacao_formal.asp (accessed 2 February 2014).
7   The Third Way is presented by Giddens (2001) as an alternative to neoliberalism and to old-style social democracy.
8   Subjects and relations as in Thompson's conception (1981).
9   According to the Ministry of Education (BRASIL, 2009), educational technologies are the teaching practices, methods or techniques accompanied by instrumental devices, equipment or tools, including those already being used by school systems or institutions, which represent a potential positive impact in the improvement of public basic education, to be employed as support tools to the educational systems and learning-teaching processes developed in the classroom.
10 See Farenzena (2012).
11 Table 55.1 presents only the direct offer of technologies. There is also a series of support mechanisms and partnerships between the subjects.
12 Development Program for Education
13 See http://senna.globo.com/institutoayrtonsenna/ (accessed 13 September 2010).
14 Head of the Department of Education of municipality B [Interview] (2007) Interview given to Juliana Lumertz and Daniela Dinis on 11 September 2007 at the Municipal Department of Education, Research Files, Porto Alegre.
15 Teaching Coordinator at municipality B [Interview] (2007) Interview given to Vera Maria Vidal Peroni; Daniela Diniz Dahm; Daniela de Oliveira Pires on 1 August 2007 at the Municipal Department of Education, Research Files, Porto Alegre.
16 Teaching Coordinator at municipality A [Interview] (2006) Interview given to Vera Maria Vidal Peroni; Juliana Selau Lumertz on 30 May 2006 at the Municipal Department of Education, Research Files, Porto Alegre.
17 Peroni and Adrião, 2007; Adrião and Peroni, 2010; Peroni, 2013
18 In 2008, it formed the conglomerate Itaú Unibanco.
19 See http://www.portalinstitutounibanco.org.br/ index.php?option=com_content&view=article&id=10&Itemid=8 (accessed 21 May 2014).

REFERENCES

Adrião, T. and Peroni, V. (2010) *Análise das consequências de parcerias firmadas entre municípios brasileiros e a Fundação Ayrton*

Senna para a oferta educacional. Relatório de pesquisa. Campinas, Unicamp. Available in: http://www.ufrgs.br/faced/peroni/docs/INSTITUTO%20AYRTON%20SENNA%20RELATORIO.pdf. (accesed 2 March 2015).

Alferes, M. and Mainardes, J. (2014) Um currículo nacional para os anos iniciais? Análise preliminar do documento 'Elementos conceituais e metodológicos para definição dos direitos de aprendizagem e desenvolvimento do ciclo de alfabetização (1°, 2° e 3° anos) do Ensino Fundamental'. *Currículo sem Fronteiras*, 14(1): 243–59.

Antunes, R. (1999) *Os Sentidos do Trabalho: Ensaios sobre a afirmação e a negação do trabalho.* São Paulo: Boitempo editorial.

Apple, M. (1995) *Volver a pensar la educación Política, educación y sociedad.* Madrid: Ediciones Morata.

Apple, M. and Mead, J. (2015) 'Grading Wisconsin's education options. Don't privatize our public school system', *Wisconsin State Journal,* 03/22/2015, Available in: http://host.madison.com/wsj/news/opinion/column/guest/michael-apple-and-julie-mead-don-t-privatize-strong-public/article_2e448fd4-3e5a-54ca-b20e-7739049d269a.html)

Ball, S. (2012) *Global education INC: New policy networks and the neo-liberal imaginary.* London: Routledge.

Ball, S. and Junemann, C. (2012) *Networks, new governance and education.* Bristol, UK: Policy Press.

Ball, S. and Olmedo. A. (2013) 'A "nova" filantropia, o capitalismo social e as redes de políticas globais em educação', in V. Peroni (org.), *Redefinições das fronteiras entre o público e o privado*: implicações para a democratização da educação. Brasília: Liber Livro. pp. 33–47.

Ball. S. (2013) 'Novos estados, nova governança e nova política educacional', in M. Apple, S. Ball and L.A. Gandin, (eds.), *Sociologia da Educação análise internacional.* Porto Alegre: Penso.

Bernardi, L., Uczak L. and Rossi, A. (2014) Do Movimento Todos pela Educação ao Plano de Ações Articuladas e Guia de Tecnologias: empresários interlocutores e clientes do Estado. Paper . Seminário de Pesquisa em Educação da Região Sul. Available in: http://xanpedsul.faed.udesc.br/arq_pdf/596-0.pdf

BRASIL (2007) Decreto n° 6.094, de 24 abril de 2007. Dispõe sobre a implementação do Plano de Metas Compromisso Todos pela Educação, pela União Federal, em regime de colaboração com Municípios, Distrito Federal e Estados, e a participação das famílias e da comunidade, mediante programas e ações de assistência técnica e financeira, visando a mobilização social pela melhoria da qualidade da educação básica.

BRASIL (2009) Aviso de Chamamento Público MEC/SEB/SECAD/SEED/SEESP N°. 1/2009. Préqualificação de Tecnologias que Promovam a Qualidade da Educação Básica. Publicado no D.O.U. Seção 3, pág. 41/42/43/44, de 21/05/2009

BRASIL, MEC. (2011) Guia de Tecnologias Educacionais 2011/12/organização COGETEC. Brasília: Ministério da Educação, Secretaria de Educação Básica. p. 196.

BRASIL, MEC. (2014) Programa ensino médio inovador: documento orientador Brasília, DF: MEC. Available in: http://portal.mec.gov.br (accessed 5 October 2014).

Brenner, R. O (2008) Princípio de uma crise devastadora. Available in: http://www.carta-maior.com.br/templates/ (accessed 10 July 2008).

Buchanan, J., McCormick, R. and Tollison, R. (1984) *El analisis economico de lo politico*: *lecturas sobre la teoria de la elección publica.* Madrid: Instituto de Estudios Economicos.

Caetano M. R. (2013) Relações entre o Público e o Privado: A gestão pedagógica da educação no Programa Circuito Campeão do Instituto Ayrton Senna (2007–2010), Porto Alegre: UFRGS, 2013. 303 f. *Tese (Doutorado em Educação)* – Programa de Pós Graduação em Educação, Faculdade de Educação: Universidade Federal do Rio Grande do Sul, Porto Alegre.

Farenzena, N. (org) (2012) *Implementação de planos de ações articuladas municipais: uma avaliação em quatro estados brasileiros.* Pelotas: Editora UFPel.

Giddens, A. (2001) *A Terceira Via: reflexões sobre o impasse político atual e o futuro da social-democracia.* Rio de Janeiro: Record.

Gewirtz, S. and Ball, S. (2011) 'Do modelo de gestão do "Bem Estar Social" ao "novo gerencialismo" mudanças discursivas sobre gestão escolar no Mercado educacional', in S. Ball and J. Mainardes (org.), *Políticas educacionais questões e dilemas.* São Paulo: Cortez editora. pp.193–221.

Goodson, I. (2007) 'Currículo, narrativa e o futuro social', *Revista Brasileira de Educação,* 12(35): 241–252.

Hayek, F. (1983) *O caminho da servidão*. Rio de Janeiro: Livraria O Globo.

Harvey, D. (2005) *O neoliberalismo história e implicações*. São Paulo: Loyola.

Hypólito, A.M. (2010) 'Políticas curriculares, Estado e regulação', *Educação e Sociedade, Campinas,* 31(113): 1337–54.

Instituto Unibanco. (2013) *Relatório de Atividades 2013*. Available in: http://www.institutounibanco.org.br/relatorio (accessed 30 December 2014).

Lukács, G. (1978) *Introdução a uma estética marxista*. Rio de Janeiro: Civilização Brasileira.

Mészáros, I. (2002) *Para além do Capital*. São Paulo: Boitempo Editorial, Campinas: Editora da UNICAMP.

Mészáros, I. (2011) *Crise estrutural necessita de mudança estrutural*. Conferência de abertura do II Encontro de São Lázaro. Salvador: UFBA.

Miller, J. (2014) Teorização do currículo como antídoto contra/na cultura da testagem. *Revista e-Currículum,* São Paulo, 12(3): 2043–63.

Pacheco, J. and Paraskeva, J. (1999) As tomadas de decisão na contextualização curricular *Cadernos de Educação FaE/UFPe1*, Pelotas, 13: 7–18.

Peroni, V. and Adrião, T. (org.) (2007) *Programa Dinheiro Direto na Escola: uma proposta de redefinição do papel do Estado na educação?* Instituto Nacional de Estudos e Pesquisas Educacionais Anísio Teixeira, Brasília.

Peroni, V. (org) (2013a) *Redefinições das fronteiras entre o público e o privado: implicações para a democratização da educação.* Brasília: Liber Livro.

Peroni, V. (2013b) As Relações entre o Público e o Privado nas Políticas Educacionais no Contexto da Terceira Via. *Currículo sem Fronteiras* Privatização da educação no contexto da(s) 'Terceira(s) Via(s)': uma caracterização em análise. 13(2): 234–255.

Peroni V. and Caetano, R. (2014) Relações entre o público e o privado na educação: Projeto Jovem de Futuro do Instituto Unibanco. Trabalho apresentado na ANPAE Sudeste.

Rhodes, R.A.W (1996) 'The new governance: governing without government', *Political Studies,* XLIV: 65.

Robertson, S., Mundy, K., Verger, A. and Menashy, F. (2012) *Public–private Partnerships in Education: New Actors and Modes of Governance in a Globalizing World.* London: Edward Elgar.

Robertson, S. and Verger, A. (2012) 'A origem das parcerias público-privada na governança global da educação', *Educação & Sociedade.,* 33(121): 1133–56.

Rossi, A., Bernardi, L. and Uczak, L. (2013) 'Relação público-privada no Programa de desenvolvimento da educação: uma análise do Plano de Ações articuladas', in V. Peroni (org.), *Redefinições das fronteiras entre o público e o privado: implicações para a democratização da educação.* Brasília: Liber Livro. pp. 198–219.

Sacristan, G. (1998) 'Reformas educativas y reformas del curriculo', in M. Warde (org.), Novas políticas educacionais: críticas e perspectivas. São Paulo: Programa de estudos Pós-graduados em Educação: História e Filosofia da educação da Pontifícia Universidade Católica de São Paulo. pp. 5–26.

Senna, V. (2000) O Programa Acelera Brasil. In: *Em aberto.* vol.17, n.71. Brasília: Ministério da Educação/Instituto Nacional de Pesquisa Educacionais. pp. 145–148.

Thompson, E.P. (1981) *A miséria da teoria ou um planetário de erros*. Rio de Janeiro: Zahar.

Tonet, I. (2012) *Educação contra o capital*. São Paulo: Instituto Lukács.

Vieira, E. (1998) 'O Estado e a sociedade civil perante o ECA e a LOAS', *Serviço Social & Sociedade,* São Paulo, 56: 9–23.

Wood, E.M. (2003) *Democracia contra o capitalismo a renovação do materialismo histórico*. São Paulo: Boitempo Editorial.

Wood, E. (2014) *O Império do capital*. São Paulo: Boitempo.

Young, M. (2014) 'Teoria do currículo: o que é e por que é importante', *Cadernos de Pesquisa,* 44(151): 190–202.

56

International Assessments of Student Learning Outcomes

Andreas Schleicher

Following a brief introduction to the history of international assessments, this chapter sets out the potential that international assessments offer for educational policy and practice, as well as some of the challenges they face in providing valid, comparable and reliable evidence.

INTRODUCTION

Parents, students, and those who teach and run educational administrations seek good information on how well their education systems prepare students for life. Most countries monitor students' learning in order to provide answers to this question (Organisation for Economic Co-operation and Development (OECD), 2013a). Comparative international assessments can extend and enrich the national picture by providing a larger context within which to interpret national performance. In a global context, where the yardsticks for educational improvement are no longer national standards alone but increasingly the best

performing education systems internationally, that perspective is gaining prominence.

Although efforts to compare education systems internationally can be traced back to the early nineteenth century (for example, Jullien, 1817), the discourse on international comparisons of learning outcomes started to emerge during the 1950s and 1960s. In 1958, an expert group led by William Douglas Wall, including prominent researchers such as Benjamin Bloom, Robert Thorndike, Arthur Wellesley Foshay, Arnold Anderson, Gaston Mialaret and Torsten Husen, met under the auspices of UNESCO's International Institute of Education in Hamburg to launch a feasibility study to compare student performance internationally. The feasibility study involved 12,000 13-year-olds in 12 countries and its results were published in 1962 (Foshay et al., 1962). The International Association for the Evaluation of Educational Achievement (IEA) emerged out of this collaboration, which then conducted a series of international assessments (see Table 56.1). The most prominent regular surveys conducted by the IEA are now the

Table 56.1 International assessments conducted by the IEA

	Study	Data collection	Target population	Coverage
1960	Pilot Study	1960	13 years	Mathematics, science, reading, geography, non-verbal abilities
	First International Mathematics Study (FIMS)	1964	13 years and last year of upper secondary education	Mathematics
1970	The Six Subject Survey	1970–71	10 years, 14 years and last year of upper secondary education	Reading comprehension Literature First International Science Study English as a Foreign Language French as a Foreign Language Civic Education
1980	Second International Mathematics Study (SIMS)	1980–82	13 years and last year of upper secondary education	
	Classroom Environment Study	1982–83	9 and 15 years	Instructional methods in mathematics, science and history
	Second International Science Study (SISS)	1983–84	10 years, 14 years and last year of upper secondary education	Science
	Written Composition	1985	10 years, 14–16 years and last year of upper secondary education	Writing
	Computers in Education (COMPED)	1989 and 1992	10 and 13 years	Availability and use of computers and technology
	Pre-primary project	1986–94 1989–2003 1993–2003	Longitudinal study following children from 4–7 years	Quality of early childhood provision
1990	Reading Literacy Study (RLS)	1990–91	9 and 14 years	Reading comprehension
	Third International Mathematics and Science Study (TIMSS 1995)	1994–95	9 and 13 years and last year of upper secondary education	Mathematics and science
	Civic Education Study (CIVED)	1996–97 1999–2000	14 years and 16–18 years	Civic education
	Second Information Technology in Education Study Module 1 (SITES-M1)	1998–99		Availability and use of technology
	Third International Mathematics and Science Study Repeat (TIMSS-R 1999)	1998–99	9 and 13 years and last year of upper secondary education	Mathematics and science
2000	Progress in International Reading Literacy Study 2001 (PIRLS)	2001	9 years	Reading comprehension
	Trends in Mathematics and Science Study 2003 (TIMSS 2003)	2002–3	9 and 14 years	Mathematics and science
	(In progress) Progress in International Reading Literacy Study 2006 (PIRLS 2006)	2005–6	9 years	Reading comprehension
	(In progress) Second Information on Technology in Education Study 2006 (SITES 2006)	2006		Availability and use of technology
	(In progress) Teacher Education and Development Study – Mathematics TEDS-M 2008	2007–8		Teacher training
	(In progress) Trends in International Mathematics and Science Study 2007 – TIMSS 2007	2006–7	9 and 13 years	Mathematics and science
	(In progress) TIMSS Advanced 2008	2007–8	Last year of upper secondary education	Mathematics and physics
	(In progress) International Civic and Citizenship Education Study (ICCS 2009)	2008–9	13 years	Civic education

Source: Siniscalco (2007).

4-yearly Trends in Mathematics and Science Study (TIMSS) and the 5-yearly Progress in Reading Literacy Study (PIRLS).

In 1988 the Education Testing Service in the US conducted the International Assessment of Educational Progress (IAEP) (LaPointe et al., 1989) and a follow-up study in 1991 (Lapointe et al., 1992).

The latest generation of international assessments has been developed by the OECD as part of the Programme for International Student Assessment (PISA). PISA surveys have been conducted every 3 years since 2000 in key content areas such as reading, mathematics and science, but they also cover cross-curricular domains such as problem-solving as well as a range of non-cognitive outcomes. PISA provides the assessment with the widest geographic coverage.

Country participation in international achievement studies grew steadily over the years. By the late 1990s all OECD countries had participated in an international study (Table 56.2).

Research Frameworks of International Assessments

OECD and IEA assessments seek to contextualise measures of student learning outcomes with background information collected from students, school principals, and sometimes teachers and parents in order to interpret the observed variation in learning outcomes between students, classrooms, schools and education systems. To facilitate this, they operate with research frameworks that provide data at up to four levels of the education system, namely:

- The education system as a whole;
- The educational institutions and providers of educational services;
- The classrooms or instructional setting; and
- The learners themselves (see Table 56.3).

The research frameworks address different classes of research questions:

- A first class relates to comparing learning outcomes at each of the four levels.
- The second class provides information on the policy levers or circumstances that shape the outputs and outcomes at each level of the education system. This includes, for example, measures of attitudes and behaviours at the level of students, measures of student learning and teacher working conditions and human and material resources at the level of instructional settings and institutions, and measures of structures and resource allocation policies and practices at the level of the education system. These policy levers and contexts typically have antecedents – factors that define or constrain policy, which are represented in a third class of research areas.
- The third class which, for example, provides information on the socio-economic context of students, schools or systems is particularly important in an international comparative context because it allows 'like with like' comparisons,

Table 56.2 OECD country participation in international achievement studies (2012)

Study first joined	First-time participants
1963–67 First International Mathematics Study (FIMS)	Australia, Belgium, Finland, France, Germany (FRG), Japan, Netherlands, Sweden, UK (England and Scotland), US
1968–72 First International Science Study (FISS)	Hungary, Italy, New Zealand
1977–81 Second International Mathematics Study (SIMS)	Canada (British Columbia and Ontario), Luxembourg, UK (Wales)
1982–86 Second International Science Study (SISS)	Canada (other provinces), Korea, Norway, Poland
1993–97 Third International Mathematics and Science Study (TIMSS 1995)	Austria, Czech Republic, Denmark, Greece, Iceland, Ireland, Mexico, Portugal, Slovak Republic, Spain, Switzerland
1997–2001 Third International Mathematics and Science Study Repeat (TIMSS-R 1999)	Chile, Turkey
Programme for International Student Assessment (PISA)	All 34 OECD countries

Source: OECD (2013).

Table 56.3   Research frameworks for international assessments

	(1) Education and learning outputs and outcomes	(2) Policy levers and contexts shaping educational outcomes	(3) Antecedents or constraints that contextualise policy
(I) Individual participants in education and learning	(1.I) The quality and distribution of individual educational outcomes	(2.I) Individual attitudes, engagement, and behaviour	(3.I) Background characteristics of the individual learners
(II) Instructional settings	(1.II) The quality of instructional delivery	(2.II) Curriculum, pedagogy and learning practices and classroom climate	(3.II) Student learning conditions and teacher working conditions
(III) Providers of educational services	(1.III) The output of educational institutions and institutional performance	(2.III) School environment and organisation	(3.III) Characteristics of the service providers and their communities
(IV) The education system as a whole	(1.IV) The overall performance of the education system	(2.IV) System-wide institutional settings, resource allocations and policies	(3.IV) The national educational, social, economic and demographic contexts

for example comparisons of schools that have a similar socio-economic intake or countries that operate under similar socio-economic conditions.

Each of the cells in Table 56.3 resulting from cross-classifying these above two dimensions (horizontal axis and the vertical axis) can then be used to address a variety of research issues from different perspectives relating, for example, to the quality of educational outcomes and educational provision; to issues of equality of educational outcomes and equity in educational opportunities; or to the adequacy, effectiveness and efficiency of resource management (see Table 56.3).

THE POTENTIAL OF INTERNATIONAL ASSESSMENTS FOR POLICY AND PRACTICE

The design and conduct of international assessments was originally motivated by research objectives. More recently, governments have also begun to attribute growing importance to international assessments and have, for example, invested considerable resources into the development and implementation of PISA. This interest derives from several considerations:

- By describing student performance in the countries with the highest or most rapidly improving assessment results, international assessments can reveal what is possible in education.

- Although international assessments alone cannot identify cause-and-effect relationships between inputs, processes and educational outcomes, they can shed light on key features in which education systems show similarities and differences.
- International assessments are also increasingly used to set policy targets in terms of measurable goals achieved by other systems and to establish trajectories for reform.
- International assessments can assist with gauging the pace of educational progress and help review the reality of educational delivery at the frontline.
- Last but not least, international assessments can support the political economy of educational reform, which is a major issue in education where any pay-off to reform almost inevitably accrues to successive governments if not generations.

Some of these issues are examined more closely in the remainder of this section.

Revealing What is Possible in Education and Identifying Factors that Contribute to Educational Success

Although it is sometimes argued that weighing the pig does not make it fatter, diagnosing underweight can be an important first step towards therapy. Increased public awareness of student performance through international comparisons has, in some countries, also created an important political momentum and engaged educational stakeholders, including teacher or/and employer organisations, in support of policy reform.

In Germany, for example, equity in learning opportunities across schools had often been taken for granted because significant efforts were devoted to ensuring that schools are adequately and equitably resourced. The PISA 2000 results, however, revealed large socio-economic disparities in educational outcomes between schools. Further analyses that separated equity-related issues between those that relate to the socio-economic heterogeneity within schools and those that relate to socio-economic segregation through the school system, suggested that German students from more privileged social backgrounds are directed into the more prestigious academic schools that yield superior educational outcomes, whilst students from less privileged social backgrounds are directed into less prestigious vocational schools that yield poorer educational outcomes, even where their performance on the PISA assessment was similar. This raised the spectre that the German education system was reinforcing rather than moderating socio-economic background factors. Such results, and the ensuing public debate, inspired a wide range of equity-related reform efforts in Germany, some of which have been transformational in nature. These include giving early childhood education, which had hitherto been considered largely an aspect of social welfare, an educational orientation and better institutionalising early-childhood provision; establishing national educational standards for schools in a country where regional and local autonomy had long been the overriding paradigm; or enhancing the support for disadvantaged students, such as students with a migration background.

For many educators and experts in Germany, the socio-economic disparities that PISA revealed were unsurprising; however, it was often taken for granted and outside the scope of public policy that disadvantaged children would fare less well in school. The fact that PISA revealed how the impact of socio-economic background on students and school performance varied considerably across countries, and that other countries appeared to moderate socio-economic disparities much more effectively, showed that improvement was possible and provided the momentum for changing public policy. For example, significant investments were made into expanding access to early childhood education and care, to enhance learning opportunities for disadvantaged students through full-day schooling, and to focus on improved education for children with an immigrant background. Interestingly, the PISA results in subsequent years showed significant improvements in learning outcomes, particularly among socio-economically disadvantaged groups, as well as amongst students with an immigrant background (see Klieme et al., 2010; OECD, 2013b).

Showing that strong educational performance as well as educational improvement are possible seems to be two of the most prominent uses of international assessments. Whether in Asia (like in Japan, Korea, Shanghai or Singapore), in Europe (like in Finland or in the Netherlands) or in North America (like in Canada), many countries display strong overall performance in international assessments and, equally important, some of these countries also show that poor performance in school does not automatically follow from a disadvantaged socio-economic background. Last, but not least, some countries show that success can become a consistent and predictable educational outcome: In Finland, for example, the performance variation between schools amounted in 2012 to only 5 per cent of students' overall performance variation. Parents can therefore rely on high and consistent performance standards in whatever school they choose to enrol their children. Considerable research has been invested into the features of these education systems. In some countries, governments have used knowledge provided by PISA as a starting point for a peer review to study policies and practices in countries operating under similar context that achieve better results. Obviously, learning outcomes also reflect features of social and economic policies that extend well beyond the education system, such that it is often difficult to discern effective educational policies and practices.

International assessments have at times raised awareness that led to a public debate about education, with citizens recognising that their countries educational performance will not simply need to match average performance, but that they will need to do better if their children want to justify above-average wages.

Putting National Targets into a Broader Perspective

International assessments can also play an important role in putting national performance targets into perspective. Educators are often faced with the following dilemma: if, at the national level, the percentage of students achieving good exam scores in school increases, some will claim that the school system has improved. Others, however, will claim that standards must have been lowered, and behind the suspicion that better results reflect lowered standards is often a belief that overall performance in education cannot be raised. International assessments frame those perceptions in a wider perspective by allowing schools and education systems to look at themselves in the mirror of the performance of schools and education systems in other countries. Some countries have actively embraced this perspective and systematically related national performance to international assessments, for example, by embedding components of the PISA or TIMSS assessments into their national assessments.

Assessing the Pace of Change in Educational Improvement

A third important aspect is that international comparisons provide a frame of reference to assess the pace of change in educational development. Although a national framework allows progress to be assessed in absolute terms, an internationally comparative perspective allows an assessment of whether that progress matches the pace of change observed elsewhere.

A Tool for the Political Economy of Reform

International assessments can also support the political economy of reform. For example, in the 2007 Mexican national survey of parents 77 per cent of parents interviewed reported that the quality of educational services provided by their children's school was good or very good. However, in OECD's PISA 2006 assessment, roughly half of the Mexican 15-year-olds who were enrolled in school performed at or below the lowest level of proficiency established by PISA (IFIE-ALDUCIN, 2007; OECD, 2007). There may be many reasons for such a discrepancy between perceived educational quality and performance on international assessments. For example, this may be partly because the educational services that Mexican children receive are significantly enhanced over the quality of schooling that their parents experienced. However, the point here is that justifying the investment of public resources into areas for which there seems no public demand poses difficult challenges for the political economy of reform. One response by the Mexican presidential office has been to include a 'PISA performance target' in the Mexican plan for educational reform that served to highlight the gap between national performance and international standards. It was associated with a reform trajectory and delivery chain of support systems, incentive structures and also improved access to professional development to assist school leaders and teachers in meeting the target. Brazil has taken a similar route, providing each secondary school with information on the level of progress that is needed to perform at the OECD average performance level on PISA by 2021.

Japan is one of the best performing education systems on the various international assessments. However, PISA revealed that although students tended to do very well on tasks that require reproducing subject matter content, they did much worse on open-ended constructed tasks requiring them to demonstrate their capacity to extrapolate from what they know and apply their knowledge in novel settings. Conveying that to parents and a general public who are used to certain types of tests poses a challenge for the political economy of reform too. The policy response in Japan has been to incorporate 'PISA-type' open-constructed tasks into the national assessment, with the aim that skills that are considered important become valued in the education system. Similarly, Korea has recently incorporated advanced PISA-type literacy tasks in its university entrance examinations in order to enhance excellence in the capacity of its students to access, manage, integrate and evaluate written material. In both countries, these changes represent transformational change that would have been much harder to imagine without the challenges revealed by PISA.

DESIGN ISSUES AND CHALLENGES FOR INTERNATIONAL ASSESSMENTS

The design of international assessments of learning outcomes needs to fulfil different, and sometimes competing demands:

- International assessments need to ensure that their outcomes are valid across cultural, national and linguistic boundaries and that the target populations from which the samples in the participating countries are drawn are comparable.
- They need to offer added value to what can be accomplished through national analysis.
- Although international assessments need to be as comparable as possible, they also need to be country-specific in order to adequately capture historical, systemic and cultural variation amongst countries.

- The resultant measures need to be as simple as possible to be widely understood, whilst remaining as complex as necessary to reflect multi-faceted educational realities.
- Although there is a general desire to keep any set performance measures as small as possible, it needs to be large enough to be useful for research and policy across countries that face different educational challenges. Some of the design issues involved in meeting and balancing these various demands are laid out in the remainder of this section.

Cross-Country Validity and Comparability in the Assessment Instruments

International assessments necessarily are limited in their scope. This is because:

- There is no international agreement on what fundamental competencies students in a particular grade or at a particular age should possess;
- An assessment can only capture a selection of competencies because student response time will always be limited; and
- Various methodological constraints limit the nature of competencies that are currently amenable to large-scale assessment, international assessments necessarily are limited in their scope.

International assessments have made considerable progress towards assessing knowledge and skills in content areas such as mathematics, reading, science and problem solving; however, they have not yet been able to evaluate, for example, social and emotional dimensions of competencies, which are of increasing importance, such as the capacity of students to relate well to others, to manage and resolve conflicts, or to respect and appreciate different values, beliefs or cultures. Similarly, they provide only very crude self-reported measures of intrapersonal dimensions of competencies, which are of increasing importance because individuals need to be able to constantly adjust to their right place in an increasingly complex world.

Even in established content areas, internationally comparative measurement poses major challenges. Countries vary widely in their intended, implemented and achieved curricula. Inevitably, international assessments need to strike a balance between narrowing the focus to what is common across the different curricula of school systems, on the one hand, and capturing a wide enough range of competencies to reflect the content domains to be assessed adequately, on the other. Leaning towards the former, as has been the tendency for the assessments of the IEA, ensures that what is being tested internationally reflects what is being taught nationally. This is an important aspect of fairness, but it risks that the assessment reflects just the lowest common denominator of national curricula and lacks important aspects of curricula that are not taught in all countries as well as the content validity that is required to faithfully represent the relevant subject area. Leaning towards the latter, as is the case for the PISA assessments, enhances content validity but risks that students are being confronted with assessment material they may not have been taught.

In whatever way the various international assessments have struck these balances, they have tried to build them through a carefully designed interactive process between the agencies developing the assessment instruments, various international expert groups working under the auspices of the respective organisations, and national experts charged with the development and implementation of the surveys in their countries. Often, a panel of international experts, in close consultation with participating countries, led to the identification of the range of knowledge and skills in the respective assessment domains that were considered to be crucial for a student's capacity to fully participate in and contribute to a successful modern society. A description of the assessment domains was created called the assessment framework, which was used by participating countries and other test development professionals who contributed to assessment materials. This framework typically involved:

- The development of a working definition for the assessment area and a description of the assumptions that underlies this definition;

- An evaluation of how to organise the set of tasks constructed in order to report to policymakers and researchers on performance in each assessment area among 15-year-old students in participating countries;
- The identification of a set of key characteristics to be taken into account when assessment tasks were constructed for international use;
- The operationalisation of the set of key characteristics to be used in test construction, with definitions based on existing literature and the experience of other large-scale assessments;
- The validation of the variables, and assessment of the contribution that each made to the understanding of task difficulty in participating countries; and
- The preparation of an interpretative scheme for the results.

In the case of PISA, for example, the assessment is defined through three interrelated dimensions, namely the knowledge or structure of knowledge that students need to acquire (for example, familiarity with scientific concepts); competencies that students need to apply (for example, carrying out a particular scientific process); and the contexts in which students encounter scientific problems and the relevant knowledge and skills that are applied (for example, making decisions in relation to personal life, understanding world affairs).

The use of an international framework limits the ability of international assessments to give a comprehensive overview of any one national system (Bialecki et al., 2002; Ofqual, 2008). International assessments may also not come at optimum times to monitor extensive system reform or innovation (Green and Oates, 2009; Ofqual, 2008).

Once the assessment framework is established and agreed upon, which tends to be the most challenging aspect of an international assessment, assessment items are developed to reflect the intentions of the frameworks and they need to be carefully piloted before final assessment instruments can be established. To some extent, the question to what extent the tasks in international assessments are comparable across countries can be answered empirically. Analyses of this were first undertaken for the IEA Trends in Mathematics and Science Study (Beaton et al., 1996). The authors compared the percentage of correct answers in each country according to the international assessment as a whole, with the percentage correct in each country for the items stated by the country that address its curriculum in mathematics. Singapore, for example, had 144 out of 162 items that were stated to be covered by the Singaporean curriculum. The percentage of items correct on the whole test and on the items covered in the curriculum was 79 in both cases. Singapore also scored between 79 and 81 per cent correct on the items that other countries considered covered in their own curricula. These ranged from 76 items in Greece to 162 items in the US. For most countries, the results were similarly consistent, suggesting that the composition of the tests had no major impact on the relative standing of countries in the international comparisons. Such analyses have also been conducted for PISA, which yielded similar results.

International assessments pay close attention to reflecting the national, cultural and linguistic variety among participating countries. OECD's PISA assessments employ the most sophisticated and rigorous process to this end. The agency charged with the development of the instruments uses professional test item development teams in several different countries. In addition to the items developed by these teams, the assessment material contributed by participating countries is carefully evaluated and matched against the framework. Furthermore, each item included in the assessment pool is rated by each country for:

- Potential cultural, gender or other bias;
- Relevance to the students to be assessed in school and non-school contexts; and
- Familiarity and level of interest.

Another important aspect concerns the nature and form of the assessment, as reflected in the task and item types. Although multiple-choice tasks are the most cost-effective way to assess knowledge and skills, and have therefore dominated earlier international assessments, they have important limitations in assessing more complex skills, particularly those that require students not just to recall but to produce knowledge. Moreover, because the nature of assessment tasks, and in particular student familiarity with multiple-choice tasks, varies considerably across countries, heavy reliance on any single item type, such as multiple-choice tasks, can be an important source of response bias. The PISA assessments have tried to address this through employing a broad range of assessment tasks, with a large share of the questions requiring students to construct their own responses. Another way to improve the nature of the assessments task is by either providing a brief answer (short-response questions) or by constructing a longer response (open-constructed response questions), allowing for the possibility of divergent individual responses and an assessment of students' justification of their viewpoints. Partial credit is given for partly correct or less complex answers, with questions assessed by trained specialists using detailed scoring guides that give direction on the codes to assign to various responses. Open-ended assessment tasks, however, raise other challenges, in particular the need to ensure inter-rater reliability in the results. For PISA, sub-samples of the assessment booklets are coded independently by four coders and examined by the international contractor. In order to examine the consistency of this coding process in more detail within each country and to estimate the magnitude of the variance components associated with the use of coders, an inter-coder reliability study on the sub-sample of assessment booklets is carried out and homogeneity analysis is applied to the national sets of multiple coding. Similarly, at the between-country level, an international coding review is implemented to check the consistency of application of response coding standards across all participating countries, with the objective to estimate potential bias (either leniency or harshness) in the coding standards applied in participating countries.

In order to cover the intended broad range of content whilst meeting the limits of individual assessment time, most modern international assessments are now using multiple test forms that are distributed amongst students in a systematic manner. These test forms typically have a common set of test items that can be used to link the results.

Ensuring that international assessments are comparable across countries is one thing, but the more important challenges actually relate to their external validity, which involves verifying that the assessments measure what they set out to measure.

A shortcoming of international assessments is their lack of a longitudinal component. As OECD's review of Evaluation and Assessment framework notes, their cross-sectional nature (that is, one measurement at one point in time) means that it is not possible to measure student progress for a given student cohort (for example, Egelund, 2008; Goldstein and Thomas, 2008; OECD, 2001, 2013b). This also calls for caution on using such correlational data to infer causal relationships. International assessment results cannot provide definitive evidence on performance variations, but can raise important questions to be investigated by further research (Goldstein and Thomas, 2008; McGaw, 2008). Caution should be taken in interpreting results due to the 'often narrow focus of comparative data and the consequential risk of misinterpretation' (Tamassia and Adams, 2009).

However, it is possible to provide some insights on the extent to which the knowledge and skills that are being assessed are predictive for future outcomes in adulthood. Used in conjunction with the results from PISA, data from the Survey of Adult Skills (a product of the OECD Programme for the International Assessment of Adult Competencies, or PIAAC) provides some insights into whether countries with high

mean performance in PISA maintain their lead later or whether countries' performance tend to converge once students leave compulsory education. In general, there is a positive relationship between performance in PISA and the corresponding age group's performance in the Survey of Adult Skills (OECD 2013c). Countries that had high, middling or low mean scores in a given wave of PISA also tended to have high mean, middling or low mean scores for the corresponding age group in the adult survey. For example, in 2000, 15-year-olds in Finland, Japan, Korea and Sweden performed above average; 12 years later, 26–28-year-olds in these countries also performed above average in the Survey of Adult Skills. Similarly, Austria, Germany, Italy, Poland and Spain performed below average in PISA 2000 and did again in the adult survey for the corresponding age group. It is noteworthy that no country has higher-than-expected performance in the adult survey, suggesting that it may be particularly hard for countries to catch up when young people leave school with a poor set of skills. The findings of this analysis should not be taken as implying that performance at the age of 15 represents destiny at the individual level. The results concern the mean performance of an age cohort. Within a given age group, the rate of learning gain in literacy or numeracy from the age of 15 may differ considerably amongst the individual members of that group. In fact, in Canada and Denmark, the same students who sat the PISA test in 2000 were retested at later ages, and results suggest that there is a high degree of variability in achievement growth after the age of 15. In Canada, for example, students who had sat the PISA 2000 assessment were retested using the PISA instruments in 2009, when they were 24. Results indicated that over time, skills levels amongst individuals converge, but that students who showed an early performance disadvantage did not overcome it by the time they were 24. In Denmark, students who had participated in PISA in 2000 also participated in the Survey of Adult Skills in 2011–12. Although many students maintained their relative ranking in the two assessments, around one-quarter performed relatively better in the adult survey than in PISA, and another quarter performed relatively worse.

Comparability of the Target Populations

Even if the assessment instruments are valid and reliable, meaningful comparisons can only be made if the target populations being assessed are also comparable. International assessments therefore need to use great care when:

- Defining comparable target populations;
- Ensuring that they are exhaustively covered with minimal and well-defined population exclusions; and
- Ensuring that the sampled students do participate in the assessment.

In relation to defining target populations, important trade-offs need to be made between international comparability, on the one hand, and relating the target populations to national institutional structures on the other. Differences between countries in the nature and extent of pre-primary education and care, the age of entry to formal schooling and the institutional structure of educational systems do not allow the establishment of internationally comparable grade levels of schooling. Consequently, international comparisons of educational performance typically define their populations with reference to a target age group. International assessments of the IEA have defined these target groups on the basis of the grade level that provides maximum coverage of a particular age cohort (such as the grade in which most 13-year-olds are enrolled). The advantage of this is that a grade level can be easily interpreted within the national institutional structure and provides a cost-effective way towards assessment, with minimal disruption of the school day. However, a disadvantage is that slight variations in the age distribution of students across grade levels often lead to the selection of different target grades in different countries, or between education systems within countries, raising serious questions about the comparability of results across, and at times within, countries. In addition, because not all students of the desired age are usually represented in grade-based samples, there may be a more serious potential bias in the results if the unrepresented students are typically enrolled in the next higher grade in some countries and the next lower grade in others. This excludes students with potentially higher levels of performance in the former countries and students with potentially lower levels of performance in the latter. To address these problems, the assessments of the OECD use an age-based definition for their target populations – one that is not tied to the institutional structures of national education systems. For example, PISA assesses students who were aged between 15 years and 3 (complete) months and 16 years and 2 (complete) months at the beginning of the assessment period and who were enrolled in an educational institution, regardless of the grade levels or type of institution in which they were enrolled, and regardless of whether they were in full-time or part-time education. The disadvantages of this age-based approach are that this is costly, the assessment process becomes more disruptive and it is more difficult to relate the results of individual students to teachers and classrooms.

The accuracy of any survey results also depends on the quality of the information on which national samples are based, as well as on the sampling procedures. For PISA, advanced quality standards, procedures, instruments and verification mechanisms have been developed that ensure the national samples yield comparable data and the results could be compared with confidence (OECD, 2014). Data from countries not meeting the international PISA sampling standards have been excluded from international comparisons.

Comparability in Survey Implementation

Finally, well-designed international assessments need to be well implemented to yield reliable results. The process begins with ensuring consistent quality and linguistic equivalence of the assessment instruments across countries. PISA, which provides the most advanced procedures to this end, seeks to achieve this through providing countries with equivalent source versions of the assessment instruments in English and French and requiring countries (other than those assessing students in English and French) to prepare and consolidate two independent translations using both source versions. Precise translation and adaptation guidelines are supplied, also including instructions for the selection and training of the translators. For each country, the translation and format of the assessment instruments (including test materials, marking guides, questionnaires and manuals) are verified by expert translators (whose mother tongue is the language of instruction in the country concerned and who is knowledgeable about education systems) appointed by agency charged with the development of the assessment instruments before they are used.

The assessments are then implemented through standardised procedures. Comprehensive manuals typically explain the implementation of the survey, including precise instructions for the work of school co-ordinators and scripts for test administrators for use during the assessment sessions. Proposed adaptations to survey procedures, or proposed modifications to the assessment session script, are reviewed internationally before they are employed at a national level. In the case of PISA, specially designated quality monitors visited all national centres to review data-collection procedures and school quality. Monitors from the international agency visited a sample of 15 schools during the assessment. Marking procedures are designed to ensure consistent and accurate application of the internationally agreed marking guides.

International validation studies have been carried out to ascertain inter-rater reliability as well as similar rater harshness across countries (OECD, 2014).

IMPACT

The OECD review of Evaluation and Assessment systems describes a shift to an increased focus on outcomes and attributes this, in part, to a growing prominence of both national and international standardised assessment results in national policy and public debate. In countries such as Austria, Denmark and Luxembourg, where there is no established tradition of monitoring outcomes of the education system, this shift is widely recognised as a result of the impact of PISA. For example, in Austria various studies have documented how the influence of international assessments (as part of system evaluation) has seen the introduction of education standards, the establishment of a specific agency to undertake evaluation and assessment and the development of national assessments. This pattern is mirrored in Denmark and Luxembourg. Several research studies have discussed the impact of international assessments on national policy making and the use of different results to argue positions by different stakeholders (for example, see Carvalho and Costa, 2009 for an overview; Delvaux and Mangez, 2008; Grek, 2009; Gür et al., 2011; Rautalin and Alasuutari, 2007). The PISA Governing Board has gained some further insight into this (see Box 56.1).

CONCLUSIONS

In a globalised world, the yardsticks for success in education are no longer national goals or standards alone, but increasingly the performance of the most successful education systems internationally. International assessments can be powerful instruments for educational

Box 56.1   The impact of PISA on national policy making

In 2007, the PISA Governing Board commissioned a study to evaluate the impact of PISA results in participating countries (Hopkins et al., 2008). The study collected feedback through standardised questionnaires sent to policymakers, local government officials, school leaders, parents, researchers and media in 43 countries (548 questionnaires were returned), as well as to the PISA Governing Board members and representatives from the business community and labour organisations. This was complemented by case studies in Canada, Hong Kong–China, Norway, Poland and Spain.

Results showed that PISA results are mainly used by policymakers, followed by local authority officials and school leaders; PISA is used to monitor and evaluate both performance and equity of the education system and has a high level of credibility and influence; countries and stakeholder groups increasingly value the skills assessed in PISA and promote these within their systems; the influence of PISA on both national and local policy formation is increasing, but has less impact on the school and classroom levels; PISA had made an impact on policy in all countries studied, but more so in countries with relatively low performance on the test, where many policy initiatives had been introduced directly as a consequence of PISA; and also the level of awareness among stakeholders varied across countries, but there was greater awareness in systems where policymakers and the media place more emphasis on results and generally in countries where average performance was lower. However, the study suggests that the media play the most important role in countries without comprehensive strategies for the dissemination of PISA results, which is likely to have a negative impact. PISA results were found to influence policies on curriculum revision, alignment of curriculum with assessment and instruction and accountability, for example with some countries introducing national testing and others refining their accountability frameworks. The study also identified an emerging trend of countries aligning their assessment systems more closely with PISA and that there were some unexpected impacts, including increased confidence in the education system, high levels of debate among stakeholders and a focus on regional differences and exploring reasons behind these.

In 2011, a short survey was administered to members of the PISA Governing Board to gain more insight into the impact of PISA and to explore to what extent PISA results were being used to evaluate and improve education system performance (Breakspear, 2012). Policymakers reported that PISA results were influencing policy to some degree in the majority of countries, regardless of their average performance on the test. The survey also revealed that PISA was being embedded in national policies to varying extent and in varying forms, through curriculum standards, assessment practices or performance targets.

Source: OECD (2013c).

research, policy and practice by allowing education systems to look at themselves in comparison to intended, implemented and achieved policies elsewhere. They can show what is possible in education, in terms of quality, equity and efficiency in educational services, and they can foster better understanding of how different education systems address similar problems. Most importantly, by providing an opportunity for policymakers and practitioners to look beyond the experiences evident in their own systems and thus to reflect on some of the paradigms and beliefs underlying these, they hold out the promise to facilitate educational improvement. As this chapter has shown, designing and implementing valid and reliable international assessments poses major challenges, including defining the criteria for

success in ways that are both comparable across countries whilst remaining meaningful at national levels, establishing comparable target populations and carrying out the surveys under strictly standardised conditions. However, more recently, international assessments have made significant strides towards this end.

Some contend that international benchmarking encourages an undesirable process of degrading cultural and educational diversity amongst institutions and education systems, but the opposite can be argued as well: in the dark, all institutions and education systems look the same and it is comparative benchmarking that can shed light on differences on which reform efforts can then capitalise upon. Who took notice of how Finland, Canada, Japan or

Shanghai ran their education systems before PISA revealed the success of these education systems, in terms of the quality, equity and coherence of learning outcomes?

Of course, international assessments have their pitfalls: policymakers tend to use them selectively, often in support of existing policies rather than as an instrument to challenge them and to explore alternatives. Moreover, highlighting specific features of educational performance may detract attention from other features that are equally important, thus potentially influencing individual, institutional or systemic behaviour in ineffective or even undesirable ways. This can be like the drunken driver who looks for his car key under a street lantern and, when questioned whether he lost it there, responds no, but that it was the only place where he could see. This risk of undesirable consequences of inadequately defined performance benchmarks is real because teachers and policymakers are led to focus their work on those issues that performance benchmarks value and are put into the spotlight of the public debate.

As OECD's review of evaluation and assessment policies notes, measures of education system performance should therefore aim to be broad enough to capture the whole range of student learning objectives. It is not always possible to devise assessments across all the objectives of the education system and, therefore, it needs to be recognised that policy making at the system level needs to be informed by high quality data and evidence, but not driven by the availability of such information. Qualitative studies, as well as secondary analysis of the available measures and indicators, are essential information to take into account in policy development and implementation.

Ways to ensure that international assessments are of high quality include ensuring systematic collection to agreed definitions of existing information at different levels in the system; promoting data quality improvement; undertaking research to shed light on some of the 'gaps' where systematic collection is too costly/not feasible; and developing a long-term strategy to improve measurement tools for future information needs.

Although the development of international assessments is fraught with difficulties and their comparability remains open to challenges, cultural differences among individuals, institutions and systems should not suffice as a justification to reject their use, given that the success of individuals and nations increasingly depends upon their global competitiveness.

REFERENCES

Beaton, A.E., Mullis, I.V.S., Martin, M.O., Gonzales, E.J., Kelly, D.L. and Smith, T.A. (1996). *Mathematics Achievement in the Middle School Years*. Chestnut Hill, MA: Center for the Study of Testing, Evaluation, and Educational Policy, Boston College.

Bialecki, I., Johnson, S. and Thorpe, G. (2002) 'Preparing for national monitoring in Poland', *Assessment in Education: Principles, Policy and Practice*, 9(2): 221–36.

Breakspear, S. (2012) 'The policy impact of PISA: An exploration of the normative effects of international benchmarking in school system performance', OECD Education Working Papers, No. 71. Paris: OECD. Available from www.oecd.org/edu/workingpapers (accessed 7 August 2015).

Carvalho, L.M. and Costa, E. (2009) *Production of OECD's Programme for International Student Assessment (PISA), KNOWandPOL Orientation 3 Supra-National Instruments WP11*. Knowledge and Policy in Education and Health Sectors.

Delvaux, B. and Mangez, E. (2008) *Towards a Sociology of the Knowledge–Policy Relation: Literature Review, Integrative Report, September 2008*. Knowledge and Policy in Education and Health Sectors.

Egelund, N. (2008) 'The value of international comparative studies of achievement – a Danish perspective', *Assessment in Education: Principles, Policy & Practice*, 15(3): 245–51.

Foshay, A.W., Thorndike, R.L., Hotyat, F., Pidgeon, D.A. and Walker, D.A. (1962) *Educational Achievement of Thirteen-Year-Olds in Twelve Countries*. Hamburg: UNESCO Institute for Education.

Goldstein, H. and Thomas, S. (2008) 'Reflections on the international comparative surveys debate', *Assessment in Education: Principles, Policy & Practice*, 15(3): 215–22.

Green, S. and Oates, T. (2009) 'Considering alternatives to national assessment arrangement in England: possibilities and opportunities', *Educational Research*, 51(2): 229–45.

Grek, S. (2009) 'Governing by numbers: the PISA effect in Europe', *Journal of Education Policy*, 24(1): 23–37.

Gür, B.S., Çelik, Z. and Özoglu, M. (2011) 'Policy options for Turkey: a critique of the interpretation and utilisation of PISA results in Turkey', *Journal of Education Policy*, 27(1): 1–21.

Hopkins, D., Pennock, D., Ritzen, J. (2008) *Evaluation of the Policy Impact of PISA*. Paris: OECD.

IFIE-ALDUCIN (2007) *Mexican National Survey to Parents Regarding the Quality of Basic Education*. Mexico City: International Forum for Investor Education.

Jullien, M.A. (1817) Esquisse et vues préliminaires d'un ouvrage sur l'éducation comparée, Paris: L. Colas.

Klieme, E., Artelt, C., Hartig, J. and Jude, N. (2010) *PISA 2009. Bilanz nach einem Jahrzehnt*. Münster, Germany: Waxmann.

LaPointe, A.E., Mead, N.A. and Phillips, G.W. (1989) *A World of Differences: An International Assessment of Mathematics and Science*. Princeton, NJ: Educational Testing Service.

LaPointe, A.E., Mead, N.A. and Askew, J.M. (1992) *The International Assessment of Educational Progress Report*. Princeton, NJ: Educational Testing Service.

McGaw, B. (2008) 'The role of the OECD in international comparative studies of achievement', *Assessment in Education: Principles, Policy & Practice*, 15(3): 223–43.

Ofqual (2008) *The Regulation of Examinations and Qualifications: An International Study*. London: Office of the Qualifications and Examinations Regulator. Available from http://inca.org.uk/ofqual-08-3736_regulation_of_examinations_and_qualifications.pdf (accessed 7 August 2015).

Organisation for Economic Co-operation and Development (OECD) (2001) *Knowledge and Skills for Life – First Results from PISA 2000*. Paris: OECD.

Organisation for Economic Co-operation and Development (OECD) (2004) *Reviews of National Policies for Education – Denmark: Lessons from PISA 2000*. Paris: OECD.

Organisation for Economic Co-operation and Development (OECD) (2007) *Reviews of National Policies for Education: Quality and Equity of Schooling in Scotland*. Paris: OECD.

Organisation for Economic Co-operation and Development (OECD) (2008) *Education at a Glance – OECD Indicators 2007*. Paris: OECD.

Organisation for Economic Co-operation and Development (OECD) (2013a) *Synergies for Better Learning: An International Perspective on Evaluation and Assessment*. Paris: OECD.

Organisation for Economic Co-operation and Development (OECD) (2013b) *PISA 2012 Results*. Paris: OECD.

Organisation for Economic Co-operation and Development (OECD) (2013c) *OECD Skills Outlook 2013*. Paris: OECD.

Organisation for Economic Co-operation and Development (OECD) (2014) *PISA 2012 Technical Report*. Paris: OECD.

Organisation for Economic Co-operation and Development (OECD) and Statistics Canada (2000) *Literacy Skills for the Information Age*. Paris: OECD, Ottawa: Statistics Canada.

Rautalin, M. and Alasuutari, P. (2007) 'The curse of success: the impact of OECD's Programme for International Student Assessment on the discourses of the teaching profession in Finland', *European Educational Research Journal*, 6(4): 348–63.

Siniscalco, M.T. (2007) 'PISA e le valutazioni internazionali dei risultati della scuola', in M.T. Siniscalco, R. Bolletta, M. Mayer and S. Pozio (eds.), *Le Valutazioni Internazionali e la Scuola Italiana*. Bologna, Italy: Zanichelli. pp. ??.

Tamassia, C. and Adams, R. (2009) 'International assessments and indicators – how will assessments and performance indicators improve educational policies and practices in a globalised society?', in K. Ryan (ed.), *The SAGE International Handbook of Educational Evaluation*. Thousand Oaks, CA: Sage Publications. pp. 213–230.

57

Comparison and Countries

Esther Care and Bruce Beswick

INTRODUCTION

Comparison studies in education are undertaken with the presumption that we can identify, and thereafter select, an optimal set of resources that are associated with desired learning outcomes. This approach assumes commonality at one or both of the ends of the predictive pathway, either of the desired learning outcomes, or the probability that identified resources are both accessible and able to be combined. There are different approaches to comparative education, and in this chapter we review a number of these in order to arrive at a conclusion concerning the reasonableness of this proposition.

In 2000, a special issue of the journal *Comparative Education* offered an overview of the field and looked ahead to the challenges it faced in the twenty-first century. In the introduction to that issue, Michael Crossley and Peter Jarvis (2000) noted that the year 2000 marked the 100th anniversary of Sir Michael Sadler's Guildford address, 'How far can we learn anything of practical

value from the study of foreign systems of education?' (Bereday, 1964). As Crossley and Jarvis noted, Sadler's address represented, for many, the foundations of 'the socio-cultural, interpretive dimension of the field' (Crossley & Jarvis, 2000: 262) and the millennial issue of *Comparative Education* acknowledged and addressed the significance of the 'Sadlerian canon'. However, as Edmund King's article in that issue (King, 2000) pointed out, another approach to comparative education was initiated in the second half of the twentieth century by the International Association for the Evaluation of Educational Achievement (IEA), which began international comparative testing in 1966 after conducting a pilot study of 12 countries from 1959 to 1961. The IEA's research represented a genuine departure from previous comparative studies because it was the first to use the same objective cognitive tests in more than one country (Plomp, 1992). Initially, according to King (2000), with the aim of minimising cultural differences, the organisation chose mathematics as its assessment subject, but in later years its range of assessments expanded to include the mother tongue, science, foreign language learning and civic knowledge. Home backgrounds and related factors were also documented. As King remarked of the IEA assessments, their 'detailed and meticulously scrutinised data about school learning and teaching have given plenty for the world (and comparativists) to reflect on' (King, 2000: 273). But, as King also noted, some well-known centres of comparative education played little part in the early work of the IEA, and some professional comparativists 'would have nothing to do with it' (2000: 273). King explains the rift that developed between the IEA and other comparativists:

> Most of the IEA's initial leaders were experts in psychometric or sociometric methods or curriculum studies, rather than alerted to the contextual emphases now usual in comparative education. Consequently, perhaps, a major overall criticism might be that IEA studies have been mainly about within-school questions or the impact of *calculable* outside factors on them. The subtle cultural ecology or inner dynamics of the learning process and its possible follow-up lacked sufficient attention. (2000: 273)

Since the appearance of international large-scale assessments on the scene of comparative education, and despite the Sadlerian tradition, the opportunity afforded by this large-scale approach has not been superseded by any viable alternatives. Notwithstanding this reality, the approach is flawed. In this chapter, we identify the most simple and implicit model behind comparative studies – that there are inputs and outcomes. We focus attention on curriculum as an input and large-scale assessment studies as indicators of outcomes. In addition, we focus on the classroom as the least distal influence on students. We show how each of these indicators varies and argue that this variation can deny attempts to identify predictive relationships within country, and confound attempts to identify common predictive relationships across countries.

The focus in this discussion is on the use of comparative data to inform questions of optimal combinations of inputs to ensure optimal outcomes. In the dynamic twenty-first century, agreement concerning those optimal outcomes is in a state of flux – at least at the global level. As education systems become more aware of each other's characteristics, there is a tension between adoption of the values and goals espoused by international organisations, such as the OECD or UNESCO, and the adoption of values and goals that are peculiar to each nation. Another complicating factor is that national values and goals are not static but move in response to internal and external factors. Education systems tend to be reactive and responsive to national agendas, rather than being proactive.

The outcome of this dynamic is that clarity around what constitutes desirable outcomes is lacking and is also typically out of sync with the current state of inputs. Against this dynamic, the data presented in comparative studies feed the assumption that inputs and outcomes can be measured in the same moment of time with an assumption of a predictive pathway. Experts will be aware of the complexities inherent in collecting and analysing data and drawing appropriate conclusions, but the difficulties inherent in communicating these complexities challenge useful documentation and dissemination of the information. The search for simplicity may be the confounding variable in the use of comparative data.

The introduction of large-scale assessments has provided a set of tools that increase focus on educational outcomes, and have been presumed to facilitate the process of cross-country comparisons. In so doing, assessment results may have deflected attention away from the quality of the educational endeavours designed by countries to inform their particular world views, their values and their aspirations. When discussing the ways in which large-scale assessments can be misused, Clarke (2002: 7) notes the existence of 'curricula or teaching practices that were never designed to achieve the goals of the global curriculum on which such studies appear predicated'. An inherent danger in large-scale comparative studies is that they will not measure the achievement of the different curricular goals of the participating countries.

In summary, despite the ongoing development of large-scale assessments, agreement on desirable outcomes has not been achieved and predictability from inputs has not been established. If a single factor underlies and unites these two observations, it may be that local culture determines what is desired and how it is achieved. In other words, cultural differences between countries are expressed in different goals and values and in different educational outcomes, leaving large-scale comparative studies with some problematic challenges.

INTERNATIONAL LARGE-SCALE ASSESSMENT

Assessment of student learning outcomes has multiple functions. At the broadest level, assessment results inform policy and teaching. Countries may wish for an external set of criteria by which they can evaluate educational quality, and which will be presumed to contribute to and predict economic outcomes. Specifically, they may wish to identify how their students are progressing against other countries in order to benchmark within and over time to establish justification for curriculum reform, or for expenditure decisions. For policymakers, assessment results may provide information about products of their education systems and student learning that can inform workforce planning (Upsing et al., 2011). The purpose for the establishment of large-scale assessment programs is frequently cited as interest in comparable information about skills of particular groups, and how these skills relate to social and economic outcomes.

Proponents of the value of international assessments cite their benefits as allowing for decomposition of variation in performance across student, school and system levels, and that in relationship to these, the influence of input and process factors can be identified. The aim is to generalise findings for the purpose of explanation and prediction, which in turn inform planning. Additional 'advantages' of these studies are listed by Hanushek and Woessman (2010), such as their capacity to exploit identified variation between countries for analysis, increased statistical power, the standardisation of the data collection and sampling processes, and the capacity to identify systematic heterogeneity in effects across countries.

Three international testing programs are currently pre-eminent. The Programme for International Student Assessment (PISA) has tested mathematics, science and reading performance of 15-year-olds on a 3-year cycle since 2000, with the addition of other constructs over time; the Trends in International Mathematics and Science Study (TIMSS) has tested mathematics and science performance of eighth grade students on a 4-year cycle since 1995; and the Progress in International Reading Literacy Study (PIRLS) has tested primary school reading performance on a 5-year cycle since 2001. PISA was developed to evaluate performance of school systems in Organisation for Economic Co-operation and Development (OECD) countries. It was designed to measure applied knowledge and skills, at some variance with the IEA's TIMSS, which, although developed by international panels, relates to common elements of curriculum across countries. Despite this self-conscious difference in targeting, common variance between the two sets of data at country levels has been shown to be 0.75, and greater in like-discipline areas.

Lesser known are large-scale assessment programs implemented by regional consortia, such as the Southern and Eastern Africa Consortium for Monitoring Education Quality (SACMEQ), sponsored by UNESCO and announced in 1995. Both OECD (Bloem, 2013) and UNESCO's Learning Metrics Task Force have called attention to the lack of outcomes measurement in, and the appropriateness for, less developed countries. Initiatives such as OECD's PISA for Development and

UNICEF's Southeast Asia Primary Learning Metric project are taking into account dissatisfaction with the 'big three' assessment programs – PISA, TIMSS and PIRLS – in an effort to develop comparative student assessments that are more attuned to regional local conditions. Such initiatives are testament to the limitations of international large-scale assessment projects in informing different countries about associations between inputs, processes and outcomes. In this chapter, we explore the theoretical justifications for this shift to localisation in comparative studies.

There is no doubt that information derived from large-scale assessments can be valuable in many ways (Engel and Frizzell, 2015). For example, in the SACMEQ project it is regularly shown that the goals of the intended curriculum far exceed the performance levels of the students as measured in the achieved curriculum. Textbooks translate the intended curriculum into activities for the classroom, and teachers are held accountable for delivering those particular subjects as intended. Although in South Africa, Botswana, Namibia and several other countries, the typical performance of Grade 6 students is at least 3 years behind the intended curriculum in the levels expected of them, textbooks, teaching materials and teaching strategies maintain a focus on the intended curriculum, rather than targeting the point at which students are able to engage and learn. It may be that some systems are unwilling to target instruction at the zone of proximal development (ZPD) because of a public perception of inadequate educational standards. The validity of the approach's measurements is not in question; it is the subsequent use of the emanating information that may be subject to criticism. Although there are clear benefits to individual countries in participating in large-scale assessment, the capacity of countries to act on comparative outcomes varies. Notwithstanding, large-scale assessment can act as a trigger for a more profound pedagogical change (Beller, 2013) as well as political change.

Temporal issues exist in two ways. The task of interpreting large-scale assessment results in the context of the inputs (that is, the education system and the student and teacher demographics) presents one such issue. Collection of input and output data in the same time period makes an assumption about the longevity and stability of both, which is typically not merited. We discuss the reasons for this later. The second temporal issue concerns the functions to which these data are applied. The first function is the use of the data to identify the current state – a benchmarking approach. The second function is the use of data to drive change. Assessment for the current state may inform policy; assessment for change informs learning and teaching. The nature of the data for these purposes has typically differed. Now we are seeing efforts to use one assessment approach to inform both functions (Care et al., 2014). Whether this is possible without requiring compromises that will diminish the functionality of the assessment for either or both purposes remains to be established.

RECOGNITION OF CULTURAL DIFFERENCES IN LARGE-SCALE ASSESSMENTS

In his account of the IEA's approach to its research, then chairman Tjeerd Plomp (1992) emphasized the organisation's reluctance to report the raw scores of its testing. This was to avoid its studies being interpreted and publicised as an education 'Olympics' or 'horse-race' (1992: 282, 285) and to recognise the differences between education systems that make such simple comparisons misleading. One way in which the IEA sought to avoid such comparisons was by using a measure it called Opportunity to Learn (OTL) (Plomp, 1992: 282), which asks whether the content required for answering an item was actually taught to the students being tested. At the most basic level, this can result in different 'cognitive yields' in different countries. In one study, for example, raw scores in science achievement for 13-year-olds in Thailand and the US were the same (IEA, 1988) but only one-third of Thai 13-year-olds were in school in the year the test was administered. The IEA's aim was to assess the whole population of 13-year-olds in each country, and so the cognitive yield for Thailand fell dramatically when the number of 13-year-olds out of school was taken into account. Of course, this reveals nothing about the structure of the education systems in Thailand or the US, or about differences in the ways they achieve the same level of accomplishment amongst those students who do attend their schools. Plomp (1992) was cognisant of this and provided a list of other factors that may contribute to level of achievement:

- The effects of the curriculum and the organization of schools and classrooms on learning;
- The relationship between achievement and attitudes;
- The effects of certain subject matter practices, such as laboratory work in science, time spent in class, and composition teaching in the mother tongue;
- Different educational practices; and
- The attainment of special groups.

What is noticeable about these factors is that, for the most part, they are measurable or, to use King's (2000) term, 'calculable' inputs, and Plomp (1992) was open about the purpose for which the organisation studies them: 'The (IEA) collects the sort of data policymakers can use as a basis for decision-making to improve education' (1992: 279). If these factors are linked to performance, they will be able to inform education policy because they are not only measurable but, largely, controllable. With the exception of 'attitudes', they are parts of the education system in which practical measures can be implemented; however, it is possible that other factors are of equal or greater importance in educational achievement. Betts (1999), for example, notes a law of diminishing returns in educational resourcing. Beyond a certain level already achieved in most developed countries, improvements in teacher salaries and teacher–student ratios

have had little impact on student performance. Coleman et al. (1966) found that the most important determinants of student performance were family background and student's peer groups – two factors over which governments and school administrators have little or no control.

Others have emphasized broader contributors to educational outcomes that are even less likely to come under the purview of governments and administrators. Kandel (1933) emphasized the importance of 'intangible, impalpable, spiritual and cultural forces which underlie an education system' (1933: xix) and Clarke (2002: 8) wrote of 'strange, invisible, and unquestioned routines and rituals' of school systems. These unspoken, assumed or unconscious factors may have an impact on learning outcomes but, precisely because they are intangible or invisible, they may not be measurable or controllable. Plomp (1992), in his role as IEA chairman, did not deny the significance of cultural factors in education. He noted the potential effect, for example, of the importance placed by a culture on the learning of a second language. Arguing that OTL can be used to carry out 'nuanced comparisons which tell why students do poorly on tests or test items' (1992: 282), he asked whether it would be fair to compare second language acquisition in a country that provides many opportunities for students to practise their language skills with one that provides few similar opportunities. 'Perhaps', he observed, 'scores should be adjusted automatically for opportunity to learn' (1992: 283).

PISA, administered by the OECD, attempts to reduce cultural bias in the following way:

All PISA participants are invited to submit questions to the international contractors; in addition, the international contractors write some questions. The questions are reviewed by the international contractors and by participants and are carefully checked for cultural bias. Only those questions that are unanimously approved are used in PISA. Further, before the real test there is a trial run in all participants. If any test questions prove to have been too easy or too hard in certain countries/economies, they are dropped from the real test in all countries and economies. (OECD, n.d.)

This may seem a thorough way of ensuring cultural neutrality, but because it allows the inclusion of only those questions that are acceptable to all participating countries, it also ensures, *ipso facto*, that any educational achievements that are not shared by all participating countries will not be tested. A participating country may have a particular educational strength, or a number of strengths, that remain untested by PISA. Indeed, particular strengths may be shared by a number of participating countries and remain untested because they are not shared by all countries.

INPUT–OUTCOME

Despite some recognition of the challenges raised by cultural differences, large-scale assessments have persisted with an input–outcome model of evaluation, which is most easily understood through the lens of an economic model. The model adopts some specific measures of achievement as the outcome and estimates the relative importance of a number of inputs to that outcome. As we are beginning to see, however, the application of this approach (for example, Betts, 1999) has demonstrated that the model is not sufficient to explain differences in student achievement outcomes.

Interactive effects between economic resourcing, education quality, specific classroom tools and pedagogies and student characteristics (Fuller and Clarke, 1994; Hanushek, 1995) serve to show that a simple input–outcome model will not invariably deliver the same outcomes. Sometimes referred to as a 'logic model' when depicted visually and for the purposes of clarifying connections between what is planned and what is achieved, such a model may be used to view connections conceptually or empirically. Wyatt Knowlton and Phillips (2013) distinguish between 'theory of change' models and 'program logic' models, with the latter including specific details of resources and inputs of activities, outputs and impacts.

Moving beyond this approach to evaluation, Stufflebeam (2000) incorporates a context parameter, which is of particular relevance to the application of an input–outcome approach to curriculum comparison.

Fuller and Clarke (1994) argue persuasively for a heightened acknowledgement of context or culture. They differentiate between two approaches, one held by 'policy mechanics' and one by 'classroom culturalists'. Although applied at classroom level, this distinction is also a useful one for analysis of education system comparison approaches. Fuller and Clarke see the policy mechanics as focused on instructional inputs, uniform teaching practices and on the links of these with achievement. Criticism of the policy mechanics' approach is based on lack of evidence to demonstrate that particular pedagogical behaviours, for example, lead ubiquitously to cognitive gains. Among the input factors, Fuller and Clarke (1994) identify school spending; specific school factors, such as class size and teaching tools; teacher attributes, such as length of education and salary level; classroom pedagogy and organisation, such as instructional time and frequency of homework; and school management, such as inspection visits and student streaming. Fuller and Clarke (1994) point out that this approach has failed (across large numbers of studies) to specify the conditions under which some factors are more likely than others to influence achievement. School effects vary across region, across subject areas and across classrooms. This leads to an argument for greater accounting of localisation factors or contextual differences. Hanushek (1995) concludes from meta-analyses of over 100 studies that the effectiveness of particular inputs varies across developed and developing countries, and that resourcing does not reliably lead to improvements in student outcomes. The policy mechanics' approach therefore appears to fail where the classroom culturalists' approach might succeed. But culture is not created in the classroom – teachers operate within a culture that exists at a broader level and that changes along with the developing goals and values of its people.

CURRICULA

Curricula are a means to an end. They are linked to society's social and economic needs, and are therefore naturally dynamic, although primarily responsive. The implementation of curricula is dependent on national education frameworks. These include resourcing, assessment and reporting, philosophical approaches to teaching and learning, and statements of goals and values. These components are interdependent. Changes in any one component will affect others and full-scale change must take all into account.

As noted by the European Centre for the Development of Vocational Training (CEDEFOP, 2012) in their report concerning design and delivery of outcome-oriented curricula, curriculum statements specifying learning outcomes influence the teaching and learning process. The level of detail in the statements has implications for pedagogy and for assessment. For example, CEDEFOP found that curricula that focus on outcomes statements promoted learner-centred pedagogies because outcomes are measures of student learning. Notwithstanding, it should be noted that how outcomes statements are written presumably influences the degree to which pedagogy will be teacher- or student-centred. These interdependencies make the identification of specific predictors of student outcomes more complex. Although the outcomes orientation in curriculum design has been driven by economic factors – countries seeking to enhance skills relevant to their national agendas – these are naturally linked with their social and political values.

This complex and dynamic mix of influences means that adequacy of education at any given point is difficult to explain in terms of identifiable contributing factors. What is measured at a particular point in time cannot be explained by concurrent education endeavours, given continual reforms (see Shuayb and O'Donnell (2008) for examples). As goals and values shift, and different governments have control of education systems, outcomes can become disconnected from goals. As we have seen, education is a long process, and it is the accumulation of learning over time that is measured on any one occasion. To explain student learning outcomes in a given year by reference only to the education system in that year is to overlook the cumulative effect of previous years, and this has implications for comparisons between nations. Since student assessment can occur at different phases of each nation's implementation of change, contributing factors across different nations may not be commensurate at any given time.

CURRICULUM COMPARISON

There has been an increasing number of cross-national educational comparison studies performed since the mid 1990s. Although there are no methodological approaches unique to the field, there are some preferred approaches (Heyneman, 2004), and although even these have their limitations, they can be used as a foundation on which to build better forms of comparison. Promising methods of curriculum comparison have been outlined by the IEA and by Brimer and Griffin (1985) who reported on the Hong Kong findings of SIMS. The IEA outlines its method within its final study reports (for example, Kennedy et al., 2007; Mullis et al., 2009). The method considers curriculum as 'intended', that is, 'reflected in official documents articulating national policies and societal visions, educational planning and official or politically sanctioned for education objectives' (Houang and Schmidt, 2008: 3). Approached in this way, comparisons most appropriately rest on the formal curriculum of each educational system as released by the respective governments. This approach provides the facility for comparing different curricula by organising their content and structure in relation to one another. Under this method, comparison of content and skills within subject areas can be completed through a comprehensive audit of curricula, and topics and skills can be cross-referenced. Methods of this kind result in comparison matrices, where information is organised by grade level and then by the sequence in which content occurs across grade levels. The matrices provide the data for analysis of thematic similarities and differences across constituencies emerging from the information. There are, of course, challenges in implementing this approach, including obtaining access to the raw data – the actual curricula. Curriculum structures also vary widely and analysis is not always straightforward. In many cases, the language in which the curriculum is written acts as an additional barrier, as do slightly different meanings attributed to translated terms.

Nevertheless, a localisation approach to curriculum comparisons, where differences in the goals of curricula are taken into account, can focus on school outcomes linked through social-economic goals to national goals and values. From this outcomes perspective, it is necessary to go back through a curriculum to identify the degree to which its specific grade level and subject level goals, and the detail of the curricular materials, are consistent with over-arching national goals and values. The way that we construe knowledge aims, objectives and learning outcomes must influence many aspects of education practice: pedagogy; subject-based teaching; knowledge, skill, and disposition orientation; knowledge framing in the classroom; progression and pacing; relations between teacher and learner; relations between types of learners; spatial and temporal arrangements; formative assessment and feedback processes; and criteria for evaluation. These are essential components, not least because a curriculum is an intended program of learning – that is, a set of prescriptions. This approach also informs how to identify the curriculum paths of comparator countries consistent with their particular national goals. The comparison of one national curriculum with another must be undertaken with recognition of the similarities and differences between different nations' objectives and values, and the implications these have for curricula, rather than being undertaken with focus only on the curriculum itself.

The method for identifying congruence across the components of this process is described in Figure 57.1. As can be seen, the socio-economic outcomes are predicted (in part) from a process that originates in the development of the curriculum and the degree to which it is explicit concerning subject outcomes, leading to graduate and post-secondary outcomes. Figure 57.1 depicts a flow of processes delivering outcomes. It is clear that a country's economic outcomes that are dependent on human capital rely on how that human capital is managed and developed. The primary conduit for this development is through population-wide education. This model implies that the specific learning goals of a curriculum will be evaluated in terms of their intended links with graduate outcomes. This contextual evaluation provides a framework within which each country's curriculum can be seen to cohere with intended national education outcomes.

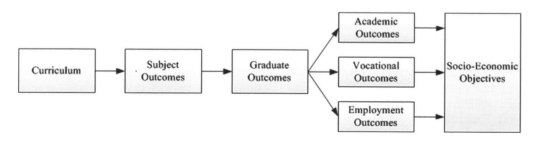

Figure 57.1   Curriculum pathway to outcomes

Source: Care (2011)

NEW PERSPECTIVES ON THE USES OF LARGE-SCALE ASSESSMENTS FOR COMPARISON

The need to account for influences on outcomes that are not easily collected at large scale has informed the recent work of Klieme (2013) and Zuzovsky (2013). Klieme (2013) differentiates between the interests of policymakers and researchers with the view that the former are interested in indicators of the functioning, productivity and equity of education, and the latter are interested in factors that influence effectiveness and data that provide a resource with which to investigate scientific (research) questions. He draws attention to the temporal issue raised earlier in this discussion – to the cumulative nature of learning (or yield) that informs large-scale assessment results, rather than immediate year or class-level outcomes. The issue is that assessment results do not reflect the most recent year or specific curriculum context in which the tested students have been studying. For the assessment to reveal salient input factors, they would need to be identified some years before the performance is measured.

Klieme (2013) argues that student learning outcomes are the unique product of pedagogical interventions that take prior learning into account, and the effects of these interventions cannot be estimated from cross-sectional data. Intrinsic to this argument is the notion of localisation of the education process, which is a challenge to the validity or usefulness of comparison studies. Notwithstanding, Klieme (2013) allows for the utility of an interplay between large-scale assessment and what he terms 'effectiveness research'. He refers to the Context-Input-Process-Outcome (CIPO) model, which informed early design of large-scale assessment initiatives, as an opportunity to create more sophisticated designs for integrating the two interest groups and their activities. The purpose of comparative education studies is to identify what works and what does not.

Klieme's (2013: 123–124) summary of the challenges to educational effectiveness research includes:

- The adaptive nature of education and its processes, which translates to a dynamic paradigm in which outputs may merge into inputs or have reciprocal effects;
- The complex nature of mediating effects on performance due to student, class and school level variables;
- The differential influence of factors within different contexts; and
- The weakness of distal effects such that individual learning activities have more impact than classroom or school characteristics.

Each of these issues is central to comparison studies of education, quite independently of the particular challenges posed by analysis of cross-country data acquired through large-scale assessment.

Reflecting Fuller and Clarke's (1994) thesis of variability of outcomes across different countries, Zuzovsky (2013: 3) takes the perspective that in 'facing an educational reality in which variability exceeds similarity', the early intentions of large-scale assessments to identify strengths and weaknesses of educational practices in an input–output model, which might lead to a comprehensive educational theory, cannot be realised. In fact, research since 2005 has attempted to describe systematic patterns of input and output, following factors such as the implemented and achieved curricula, student background, classrooms and actual test item responses. The identification of region as an explanatory factor also reached its most ludicrous point, with an argument for broad areas such as Europe, Asia, and America providing useful distinctions. We know from studies of pedagogy and classrooms globally that such gross groupings obscure important differences. The work of Clarke and colleagues (2006), for example, demonstrates striking differences in pedagogical practices in classrooms within regions.

THE SALIENCE OF THE CLASSROOM

Clarke et al. (2006: 1) have provided evidence of how 'culturally-situated are the practices of classrooms around the world'. Starting from a different ground – the classroom – these researchers analysed in detail the presence and frequency of practices. They noted that similar classroom practices are enacted globally, but differ in frequency and in co-occurrence. As with large-scale testing, Clarke and colleagues (2006) looked for patterns across cultures but emphasized the lack of evaluative judgement in their work. In addition they drew attention to the 'homogenization of…curriculum' (2006: 4), which is to some extent an outcome of large-scale assessment initiatives. The view that curriculum is socially constructed is an important aspect of this approach, and one that is pivotal to critical analysis of the adequacy of large-scale assessments in evaluating educational outcomes across different national education systems. Clarke and colleagues (for example, 2006) have found differences across and within countries in curriculum, its organisation and delivery, and pedagogical practices, leading them to conclude that the interconnections between and amongst them, rather than mere frequency or nature, are the salient factors that might describe comparative educational systems.

In literature focused on pedagogy, Western educational pedagogical practices have often been characterised as 'student-centred', and Asian classrooms have been typified as 'teacher-centred'. These terms have been used to reflect a dichotomous and mutually exclusive set of practices between the two settings. Research in each setting (see Fang and Gopinathan, 2009) has confirmed the value of practices associated with Western classrooms whilst acknowledging that students in the Asian settings have been highly successful in international achievement studies. However, Clarke and colleagues believe that classroom practices across international settings have been misrepresented by the use of this dichotomy.

Clarke and Seah (2005) examined communication and discourse in instruction and learning from three perspectives: teacher–class, teacher–student and student–student interactions. Lessons were videotaped in mathematics classrooms of competent teachers in four major cities (Shanghai, Hong Kong, Melbourne, San Diego). Teacher and student post-lesson interviews, in which participants were asked to share classroom activities and their learning, were also analysed. Findings revealed differences within and across teacher practices in these four cities.

In Shanghai, teachers were observed to provide scaffolding to students for mathematical problem solutions, with a clear devolution of responsibility over time from teacher to students, which resulted in students teaching each other alternative problem-solving strategies. In Hong Kong, students did not appear to be given similar opportunities to contribute or communicate in lessons – teachers provided explicit instruction and guidance for every step of problem solving. In Melbourne, there were several patterns of differences between teachers. In San Diego, teacher questioning was obvious in introducing mathematical rules and concepts to students after they had described their problem-solving attempts. Findings reflected the authors' views that there were differences in responsibility for knowledge generation in the classrooms observed; however, variation existed within and across typical 'Western' and 'Asian' teacher practices. This was confirmed in a later study by Clarke et al. (2010), who found that assumptions that there would be similarities in practice in classrooms that were culturally similar (for example, Asian versus Western cities) were unfounded. In addition, differences in practices of teachers in Seoul, Shanghai, Hong Kong and Tokyo showed that there is difficulty characterising the 'Asian classroom'.

Taking these research studies into consideration, Clarke and colleagues question the usefulness of large-scale assessment programs in terms of their capacity to inform cross-cultural comparisons. Equally the researchers question the usefulness of self-report measures from teachers, given that teachers are embedded in their own cultural context and will bring to their judgements local interpretations that can nullify comparability. Clarke's use of videotaping classrooms is argued to offer a form of documentation that denies subjective judgements and is capable of presenting data that permit legitimate comparisons.

Zuzovsky (2013) also noted the variability in instructional practices within cultural and geographic groups and turned to an alternative method of identifying criteria that might help to make sense of the interactions of inputs, student learning outcomes and cultural phenomena. Zuzovsky grouped countries according to the actual achievement levels of students, following Postlethwaite and Ross (1992), in order to identify factors that discriminated between the groups. Putting aside resourcing inputs, Zuzovsky concentrated on interaction effects between types of instructional practices and membership of three achievement groups: low, medium and high achieving. Her focus was on identifying which practices worked with which group(s), and so her approach takes a step forward from the descriptive approach of the work of Clarke and colleagues. The identification of achievement groups rested on the mathematics and science TIMSS scales, and each group comprised 15–17 countries from the 2007 study. This grouping defies the developed versus developing dichotomy, or the regional classifications. The research question that framed the work concerned the relationships between frequency of specific instructional practices and learning outcomes across the three groups of countries. The nature of the TIMSS sampling design is such that a full class constitutes school-level data. Zuzovsky found that effectiveness of particular practices varied across the low and high achieving groups; in other words, a practice does not have an inherent quality for the good – it varies according to the context in which it is enacted. For example, certain instructional practices associated with developing computational skills (for example, memorising formulas and procedures) were associated more positively with learning outcomes for low achieving than high achieving groups, whilst others (for example, beginning homework in class) were associated with negative outcomes for low achieving, with little effect for high achieving groups. Zuzovsky's innovative approach highlights the potential of large-scale assessment studies to inform country-specific needs, and also the understanding of the characteristics – and influence – of classroom practice.

THE VALIDITY OF CONSTRUCTS

As we noted at the outset, the use of large-scale assessments for comparisons of education systems and effectiveness across countries presumes that there is constancy of either predictive or predicted factors. For this reason, particularly when relying on the student learning outcomes as the criteria, clarity about what these represent is paramount. Typically, literacy, mathematics, science and, more recently, problem solving, have been the selected skill areas for large-scale student assessment. The creation of test blueprints against descriptions of these skills with subsequent item development should ensure that what is being assessed is indeed what is of interest. The degree to which each country's understanding of these skillsets is met by their curriculum is not clear. This is not a question of the validity of the assessment, but of the alignment of the assessment construct with what is valued and taught in country curricula. The large-scale assessment programs have well-documented methods of ensuring validity of their measures in the sense that the underpinning construct is the focus.

Literacy and numeracy are examples of skills domains that are relatively well accepted globally, although there may be differences in understandings about how these develop and their definition. That such skills domains are adopted for large-scale studies underwrites the relative robustness of this understanding; however, despite strong commonalities across many continents in the understanding of these skills, they are taught and demonstrated in many different ways. Notwithstanding the commonality, the differences can have substantial impact for assessment of student learning outcomes because of their encapsulation in local curricula. Although core skills that can be equally responded to by students may exist, this cannot be taken to imply that students are learning in environments that treat these skills equally or value these skills in the same way. The links between national goals and values with curriculum, discussed earlier, have a backwards-mapping effect on curriculum development. What is valued by the country will flavour how even core skills are perceived, taught and learnt. This flavour is embodied in national curriculum frameworks.

THE LOCALISATION OF EDUCATION

Comparative studies tend to assume that input, process or output factors will be common across the participating units. Globalisation provides a facility for greater commonality by virtue of mere information dissemination. Globalisation of values is increasingly pushed by international organisations such as OECD, UNESCO and UNICEF. In the context of the precepts promulgated by these organisations, specific initiatives such as the Millennium Development Goals (MDGs) imply a growing agreement between nations on goals and values. Endorsement of these initiatives requires critical review within countries of their goals and values. Constructivist paradigms view knowledge as being actively built up by the individual and within learning situations. If we accept this premise then it

should be equally true that a curriculum system established by a country will actively build a unique knowledge infrastructure. Equally, the context and unique learning environment will strongly influence student learning outcomes. To apply an international global assessment standard to such unique situations is irrational.

Behind every syllabus there are certain fundamental principles and consideration of curriculum elements – a curriculum code – that directs the manner in which formal documents, teaching materials and assessment practices are combined to make up the curriculum (Lundgren, 1979). Accordingly, school subjects, as written curricula, reflect societal, sociological and philosophical factors (Sivesind and Karseth, 2014). In terms of localisation, therefore, the starting point is national goals and values. These vary, sometimes radically, across countries and can be presumed to imbue what may be seen as similar school subjects with very different characteristics. These differences, in turn, will have an impact on how students will engage with test items designed to measure agreed constructs of interest.

CURRICULUM DIFFERENCES BETWEEN AND WITHIN COUNTRIES

A challenge for international comparative studies is the accommodation of different educational missions or goals, not only in the different countries but also in the different periods of each country's history. What is valued in each country and in each period finds expression in different curricula, and yet large-scale international assessments set out to measure the same student outcomes across these different curricula. Perhaps the most inflammatory expression of this problem is that of Thorsten (2000: 71), who described the TIMSS assessments as '41 bureaucratic gazes, all linked to the seduction of one global economic curriculum'. The point is that what is valued in each curriculum influences the teaching of even the core skills that are typically assessed in international comparisons. Differences in curriculum and national values within country, and across country, are presented in the following examples.

The Philippines

The variability of educational values not only across countries but also across time is illustrated by the example of the Philippines. In the Spanish period of the Philippines' history (1556–1898) the main objective of schools was religious education. This was followed by a period of rule by the US (1898–1942), under which Philippine schools taught English language and American history and prepared the best-performing students for roles in US government offices. During the Japanese occupation (1942–45), the principal aim of education in the Philippines was proclaimed as the promulgation of the 'New Order' within East Asia. Notably, each occupying force attempted to embed its language in the country, using education as a medium. From this, the impact of social and political context on curriculum itself, as well as the cultural context for the use of language, can be seen clearly. Criticisms of the system in 1949 included its academic flavour – considered inappropriate for a population not destined to reach the end of secondary education, let alone university entry – and recommendations included the development of an understanding and appreciation of Filipino traditions and ideas in line with the nation's new-found independence in 1946, as well as an emphasis on practical economy-related skills. With the implementation of the K-12 Basic Reform Agenda in 2013, the Philippines now espouses curriculum relevance (to context), proficiency in mother tongue, integrated and seamless learning, orientation to the future, and nurturing 'the holistically developed Filipino' (Care, 2011; Okabe, 2013), a very different set of values from those of its Spanish and American periods.

Where such huge change is underway, the justifiable attribution of educational outcomes to inputs cannot take place for at least a full 10–12-year education delivery of a particular curriculum, and this may be a conservative estimate. In order to roll out the education reform, curriculum rewriting is just one step. The training of teachers to focus on new goals of the education system, on understanding and application rather than content coverage, is another. Introducing three additional years of education, and providing the trained teacher resource is yet another, as is the provision of material resources, such as classrooms and classroom facilities. The country currently has more than 655,000 teachers, with an estimated one-third of these certified to teach, and almost 24 million children enrolled in Kindergarten through to Grade 10. It is estimated that an additional 80,000+ teachers will be required to staff the two senior years of secondary school. The conditions under which the reforms are being implemented will no longer exist in a decade, and educational outcomes will be a function of these changing times, not of the status quo, either now or in that decade's time.

It is clear from this example that we cannot measure educational achievement as though it is invariant across different historical periods. It seems reasonable, therefore, to question whether we can measure educational achievement as though it is invariant across different geographic or national contexts. Even in the same subject areas, curricula in different countries can have different aims and produce different achievement outcomes. In the Philippines, for example, under the new K-12 curriculum, the subjects of Geology and Meteorology have a strong focus on local conditions in that country. From Grade 7 through to Grade 9, the Geology curriculum is focused on the Ring of Fire – the area of volcanic and earthquake activity that borders the Pacific Ocean and creates volatile geological conditions in the Philippines (Department of Education (DepEd), 2013). The Meteorology curriculum for Grades 7 and 8 has a similar focus on local conditions. Students are taught about the Inter-Tropical Convergence Zone, which directly affects weather in the Philippines, and about monsoons and typhoons. This focus on addressing local conditions or problems is also evident in the curriculum's Conceptual Framework for the entire discipline of Science, which is notable for its opening reference to 'applications of scientific knowledge that may have social, health, or environmental impacts' (DepEd, 2013: 2). Although the framework acknowledges the wider role of science as a global discipline, it returns regularly to the theme of science as 'relevant and useful', closing with a reference to its 'application to real-life situations' (DepEd, 2013: 2).

Australia

In contrast to the Philippines, the goals of the Australian education system do not make reference to any specifically national character, despite explicit recognition of the country's indigenous children. The Melbourne Declaration on Educational Goals for Young Australians (Ministerial Council for Education, Early Childhood Development and Youth Affairs (MCEECDYA), 2008) expressed two overarching goals:

- Goal 1: Australian schooling promotes equity and excellence.
- Goal 2: All young Australians become successful learners, confident and creative individuals, and active and informed citizens.

When this declaration was followed by *The National Education Agreement* (Council of Australian Governments (COAG), 2009), the stated goals became more explicitly international than national. They included a commitment 'to ensure that all Australian school students acquire the knowledge and skills to participate effectively in society and employment in a globalised economy' (COAG, 2009: 1) and they identified the following outcomes:

- All children are engaged in, and benefiting from, schooling.
- Young people are meeting basic literacy and numeracy standards, and overall levels of literacy and numeracy achievement are improving.

- Australian students excel by international standards.
- Schooling promotes social inclusion and reduces the education disadvantage of children, especially Indigenous children.
- Young people make a successful transition from school to work and further study. (COAG, 2009: 1)

Taking into consideration Australia's less recent transition from colonialism, its educational goals are understandably less nationalistic than those of the Philippines and more focused on the place of its citizens in a globalised and internationally competitive world. In the Australian curriculum, an emphasis on global twenty-first-century skills is reflected in the 'General Capabilities' (Australian Curriculum, Assessment and Reporting Authority (ACARA), 2013). There are seven of these: Literacy; Numeracy; Information and Communication Technology (ICT) Capability; Critical and Creative Thinking; Personal and Social Capability; Ethical Understanding; and Intercultural Understanding (ACARA, 2013: 3). These are designed to address Goal 2 of the Melbourne Declaration, as illustrated in Figure 57.2. Teachers are expected to teach these General Capabilities explicitly within their subject specialisations (Howes, 2012). The place of the capabilities is highlighted within curriculum year-level content for subjects so that teachers can relatively easily recognise opportunities to develop the skills in their students.

A similar level of difference is revealed by a comparison of the Australian and Philippine Science curricula. The Australian Science curriculum acknowledges the practical uses of science but explicitly states that, 'in addition to its practical applications, learning science is a valuable pursuit in its own right' (ACARA, 2015: 3). The overview of the Science curriculum refers to 'the joy of scientific discovery' and 'natural curiosity about the world', emphasizing the discipline of science as a 'collaborative and creative human endeavour' that seeks to explain the world, 'exploring the unknown' and 'investigating

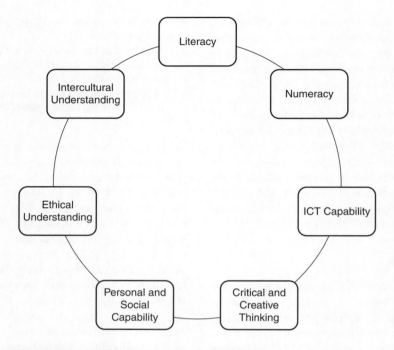

Figure 57.2   General capabilities in the Australian curriculum

Source: http://www.australiancurriculum.edu.au/generalcapabilities/overview/general-capabilities-in-the-australian-curriculum (accessed 15 March 2015).

universal mysteries' (ACARA, 2015: 3). The language of the Australian curriculum is more towards the pure than the applied end of the science spectrum, emphasizing free inquiry over practical application, and notably also making reference to the possibility of students participating 'if they so wish, in science-related careers' (ACARA, 2015: 3). Nevertheless, in its descriptions of specific subject areas, a local Australian focus becomes discernible in the curriculum. In Years 7 and 8, students in Earth and Space Sciences are taught about renewable and non-renewable resources, with specific reference to water and mineral deposits (ACARA, 2012). Australia is a drought-prone country with vast mineral resources that play a significant role in its economy. Although Australian students learn about science as a pure research endeavour, they are also taught about its practical applications in specifically Australian settings.

It is clear that there are significant differences in what is valued by these countries' education systems, and these differences impact on curriculum, teaching and learning. Although there are common core competencies, their acquisition by students will occur within idiosyncratic cultural contexts. Large-scale assessment may be designed such that no bias exists in items across populations, but how the competencies are taught and learned will vary. These variations may be significant for the countries and highly valued, but not reflected in outcome measures that are comparable between countries.

CONCLUSION

The difficulties that comparative studies encounter are clear. The large-scale assessment approach is primarily an identification of comparative outcomes, and the pre-selection of specific resourcing factors, which are thought to influence these outcomes. The curriculum comparison approach encounters difficulties in terms of access to comparable data. The localisation of education systems similarly establishes difficulties in comparison due to differences in goals, values and their embodiment in education systems.

It is noteworthy that much of the comparative work that seeks to explain student learning outcomes rests on instructional practices, rather than on curriculum itself. The delivery is given priority over content. This implies that the delivery is assumed to be the troublemaker, and that the curriculum is an accurate representation of national goals and values and therefore does not require analytic attention. This possibility would ensure that for each country one part of the predictive model – the curriculum – would be assumed to be a constant.

What is valued by a country permeates its curriculum and its education system. Current approaches to educational comparisons indicate awareness that there are few constants available to enable analysis within simple inputs–outcomes models. It is tempting to conclude that current state has not moved beyond Sadler's 1900 perception: 'in studying foreign systems of education we should not forget that the things outside the schools matter even more than the things inside the schools, and govern and interpret the things inside' (Bereday, 1964: 312). That one kind of education might suit all nations is obviously incorrect. The cultural neutrality claimed as characteristic of large-scale assessments does not obviate the fact that although there may be sufficient commonality between countries to measure the same construct, that construct will have different valence in each country by virtue of its unique cultural perspective and the way this permeates its education system.

REFERENCES

Australian Curriculum, Assessment and Reporting Authority (ACARA) (2012) *The Australian Curriculum: Science Scope and Sequence. Year 5 to Year 10*. Sydney: ACARA.

Australian Curriculum, Assessment and Reporting Authority (ACARA) (2013) *General Capabilities in the Australian Currciulum*. Sydney: ACARA.

Australian Curriculum, Assessment and Reporting Authority (ACARA) (2015) *The Australian Curriculum: Science*. Version 7.4. 30 March 2015. Sydney: ACARA.

Beller (2013) 'Technologies in large-scale assessments: new directions, challenges, and opportunities', in M. von Davier, E. Gonzalez, I. Kirsch and K. Yamamoto (eds.) *The Role of International Large-Scale Assessments: Perspectives from Technology, Economy and Educational Research*. Dordrecht, Netherlands: Springer. pp. 25–45.

Bereday, G. Z. F. (1964) 'Sir Michael Sadler's "Study of Foreign Systems of Education"', *Comparative Education Review*, 7(3): 307–14.

Betts, J. R. (1999) *Returns to Quality of Education*. Economics of Education Series 1. Washington, DC: World Bank.

Bloem, S. (2013) 'PISA in low and middle income countries', *OECD Education Working Papers*, 93, OECD Publishing: http://dx.doi.org/10.1787/5k41tm2gx2vd-en

Brimer, A. and Griffin, P. (1985) *Mathematics Achievement in Hong Kong Secondary Schools: A Report on the Conduct in Hong Kong of the Second International Mathematics Study within the International Association for the Evaluation of Educational Achievement*. Hong Kong: Center of Asian Studies.

Care, E. (2011) *Curriculum Comparison Study for the Philippines Basic Education Sector*. National Library of Australia. Available from http://catalogue.nla.gov.au/Record/5632358 (accessed 15 March 2015).

Care, E., Griffin, P., Zhang, Z. and Hutchinson, D. (2014) 'Large-scale testing and its contribution to learning', in C. Wyatt-Smith, V. Klenowski, and P. Colbert (eds.), *Designing Assessment for Quality Learning*. Dordrecht, Netherlands: Springer. pp. 55–71.

Clarke, D. J. (2002) '*Developments in international comparative research in mathematics education: problematising cultural explanations*', in S. L. Y. Yam and S. Y. S. Lau (eds.), ICMI Comparative Study Conference 2002: Pre-Conference Proceedings, Hong Kong: University of Hong Kong. p. 7–16.

Clarke, D. J. and Seah, L. H. (2005) 'Studying the distribution of responsibility for the generation of knowledge in mathematics classrooms in Hong Kong, Melbourne, San Diego and Shanghai', *Proceedings of the 29th Conference of the International Group for the Psychology of Mathematics Education, 2*: 257–64. Melbourne: PME.

Clarke, D. J., Emanuelsson, J., Jablonka, E., and Mok, I. A. C. (eds.) (2006) *Making Connections: Comparing Mathematics Classrooms around the World*. Rotterdam: Sense Publishers.

Clarke, D. J., Xu, L. H. and Wan, M. (2010) 'Student speech as an instructional priority: Mathematics classrooms in seven culturally-differentiated cities', *Procedia Social and Behavioural Sciences*, 2: 3811–17.

Coleman, J., Campbell, E., Hobson, C., McPartland, J., Mood., A. Weinfeld, F., and York, R. (1966) *Equality of Educational Opportunity*. Washington, DC: Office of Education, U.S. Department of Health, Education and Welfare.

Council of Australian Governments (COAG) (2009) *The National Education Agreement*. Commonwealth of Australia.

Crossley, M. and Jarvis, P. (2000) 'Introduction: Continuity, challenge and change in comparative and international education', *Comparative Education* 36(3): 261–265.

Department of Education (DepEd) (2013) *K to 12 Science Curriculum Guide 2013*. Manila, Republic of the Philippines: DepEd.

Engel, L. C. and Frizzell, M. O. (2015) 'Competitive comparison and PISA bragging rights: sub-national uses of the OECD's PISA in Canada and the USA', *Studies in the Cultural Politics of Education*, 36(5): 1–18.

European Centre for the Development of Vocational Training (CEDEFOP) (2012) *Curriculum Reform in Europe: The Impact of Learning Outcomes*. Luxembourg: Publications Office of the European Union.

Fang, Y. and Gopinathan, S. (2009) 'Teaching in schools in eastern and western contexts', in L. J. Saha and A. G. Dworkin (eds.) *The New International Handbook for Teachers and Teaching*. New York: Springer: 557–572.

Fuller, B. and Clarke, P. (1994) 'Raising school effects while ignoring culture? Local conditions and the influence of classroom tools, rules and pedagogy', *Review of Educational Research*, 64(1): 119–57.

Hanushek, E. A. (1995) 'Interpreting recent research on schooling in developing countries', *The World Bank Research Observer*, 10(2): 227–46.

Hanushek, E. A. and Woessman, L. (2010) 'The economics of international differences in educational achievement', NBER Working Papers 15949. Cambridge, MA: National Bureau of Economic Research.

Heyneman, S. (2004) 'The use of cross-national comparisons for local education policy', *Curriculum Inquiry* 34(3): 345–352.

Houang, R. T. and Schmidt, W. H. (2008) *TIMSS International Curriculum Analysis and Measuring Educational Opportunities*. Amsterdam: International Association for the Evaluation of Educational Achievement.

Howes, D. (2012) 'AusVELS: A principled and pragmatic curriculum framework', Primarily English, 1(2): 3–10.

Kandel, I. (1933) *Comparative Education*. Boston: Houghton Mifflin.

Kennedy, A. M., Mullis, I. V. S., Martin, M. O. and Trong, K. (eds.) (2007) *PIRLS 2006 Encyclopedia: A Guide to Reading Education in the Forty PIRLS 2006 Countries*. Chestnut Hill, MA: TIMSS & PIRLS International Study Center, Boston College.

King, E. (2000) 'A century of evolution in comparative studies', *Comparative Education* 36(3): 267–277.

Klieme, E. (2013) 'The role of large-scale assessment in research on educational effectiveness and school development', in M. von Davier, E. Gonzalez, I. Kirsch, and K. Yamamoto (eds.), *The Role of International Large-Scale Assessments: Perspectives from Technology, Economy, and Educational Research*. Dordrecht, Netherlands: Springer. pp. 115–147.

Lundgren, U. (1979) 'Background: the conceptual framework', in U. Lundgren and S. Pettersson (eds.) *Code, Context and Curriculum Processes*, Stockholm: CWK Gleerup. pp. 5–35.

Ministerial Council for Education, Early Childhood Development and Youth Affairs (MCEECDYA) (2008) *The Melbourne Declaration on Educational Goals for Young Australians*. Commonwealth of Australia.

Mullis, I.V.S., Martin, M.O., Ruddock, G.J., O'Sullivan, C.Y. and Preuschoff, C. (2009) *TIMSS 2011 Assessment Frameworks*. Chestnut Hill, MA: Boston College.

Okabe, M. (2013) 'Where does Philippine education go? The "K to 12" program and reform of Philippine Basic Education', Institute of Developing Economies Discussion Paper No 425. Available from http://www.ide.go.jp/English/Publish/Download/Dp/pdf/425.pdf (accessed 15 March 2015).

Organisation for Economic Co-operation and Development (OECD) (n.d.) *PISA FAQ: Background and Basics.* Available from http://www.oecd.org/pisa/aboutpisa/pisafaq.htm (accessed 15 March 2015).

Plomp, T. (1992) Conceptualizing a comparative educational research framework, *Prospects* 22(3): 278-288.

Postlethwaite, T. N. and Ross, K. N. (1992) *Effective Schools In Reading: Implications for Educational Planners.* The Hague, Netherlands: International Association for the Evaluation of Educational Achievement.

Shuayb, M. and O'Donnell, S. (2008) *Aims and Values in Primary Education: England and other Countries. The Primary Review.* Slough, UK: National Foundation for Educational Research.

Sivesind, K. and Karseth, B. (2014) 'Curriculum theory and research in Norway: traditions, trends, and topics', in W. F. Pinar (ed.), *International Handbook of Curriculum Research.* Abingdon, UK: Routledge. pp. 362–75.

Stufflebeam, D. (2000) 'The CIPP model for evaluation', in G. Madaus and T. Kellaghan (eds.), *Evaluation in Education and Human Services.* Dordrecht, Netherlands: Springer. pp. 279–317.

Thorsten, M. (2000) 'Once upon a TIMSS: American and Japanese narrations of the Third International Mathematics and Science Study', *Education and Society,* 18(3): 45–76.

Upsing, B., Gissler, G., Goldhammer, F., Rolke, H. and Ferrari, A. (2011) 'Localisation in international large-scale assessments of competencies: challenges and solutions', *International Journal of Localisation,* 10(1): 44–57.

Wyatt Knowlton, L. and Phillips, C. (2013) *The Logic Model Guidebook.* London: Sage Publications.

Zuzovsky, R. (2013) 'What works where? The relationship between instructional variables and schools' mean scores in mathematics and science in low-, medium-, and high achieving countries', *Large scale Assessments in Education,* 1(2): 1–19.

58

Effects of Globalised Assessment on Local Curricula: What Japanese Teachers Face and How They Challenge It

Shinya Takekawa

INTRODUCTION

The educational systems of Japan and other East Asian countries have been modified by their centralised governments with a view to achieve rapid modernisation. Further, these educational systems focus on preparing students to pass competitive entrance examinations for high schools and universities, and classroom teaching is based on intensive cramming. In Japan, there has been a powerful centralised system of control over the class curriculum. The curriculum guideline for Japan's national curriculum, which is deemed to be legally binding, regulates the screening of textbooks, thereby determining a school curriculum and controlling what should be taught in every classroom. Japan's curriculum policy focuses on curriculum content, and on how to ensure that teachers comply with such content.

However, such a characteristic of education in East Asia as described is currently showing signs of change. There is a shift towards new priorities embodied by buzzwords such as 'globalisation', 'equity and quality', 'market', 'decentralisation', 'literacy', and 'competency'. One obvious factor behind this shift is the socio-political transition brought about by globalisation; however, education in East Asia is influenced, both directly and indirectly, by educational policies and the project of performance indicators that are designed to globalise education, for example the Organisation for Economic Co-operation and Development's (OECD) Programme for International Student Assessment (PISA).

Ulrich Beck (1992) mentioned 'risk society' and 'individualisation' as the key themes in globalisation. In a globalised society, the role played by the modern nation state is changing; it is no longer in charge of determining everything about education. It is expected to establish rules that regulate the actions of people participating in the market. Individuals, by contrast, are expected to take measures on their own against risks from unseen power.

The OECD's educational policy, discussed later in this chapter, is not to advance a form of globalisation based purely on the principle of marketisation, but rather to demand individuals a functionalism that meets certain global standards (Matsushita, 2014). Education systems and teaching practices have adapted to globalisation in varying degrees depending on the political context of each country, but, generally, risks that warrant an individualised response are currently being imposed on teachers, students and parents. This chapter analyses how this transnational phenomenon has manifested in current Japanese education and, in doing so, identifies the practical challenges concerning planning curriculum and pedagogy. It also looks at examples of classroom teaching in Japan with the objective of identifying a fundamental framework for educational practices that can address these challenges.

The first section examines the PISA survey's influence on Japanese curriculum policy and curricula. The response in Japan to the PISA focused entirely on its rankings, with no consideration of other factors, and PISA became a pretext for introducing standardised testing. This response has thus resulted in the controlling of schools and teachers through an accountability system, and to the impoverishment of classroom teaching. The chapter explores the OECD's conception of 'key competencies', PISA's conception of literacy and the Assessment and Teaching of 21st Century Skills (ATC21s) project's conception of twenty-first-century skills. It also critically analyses the competency model, which forms the backdrop to these concepts, whilst referring to Beck's concept of a 'risk society' and how it 'individualises' risk. The final section explores case studies of teaching practices in Japan in order to identify a theoretical and practical framework for a critical teaching practice that emphasizes curriculum content research. The purpose of such a framework is to provide an alternative to the competency and literacy model that portrays a set of resources and competencies required by individuals in a globalised world.

CURRICULUM REFORM IN JAPAN: AFTER THE INTRODUCTION OF PISA

A Typically Japanese Reception – and Misreading – of PISA

Since the beginning of PISA, education in Japan has been showing signs of change. Specifically, there has been a rapid shift in the way that curricula are controlled. Traditionally, curricula were controlled through regulating teaching content; however, teachers' performance is currently governed through a Plan-Do-Check-Action (PDCA) cycle centred around testing and accountability (Kodama, 2013). In addition, local governments and schools, rather than the central government, have proactively implemented this PDCA cycle-based management system. Amidst the proliferation of the discourse of 'teachers' autonomy' and 'bringing out the uniqueness of regions and schools', teachers are actually becoming increasingly apolitical towards the politics of the curriculum and pedagogy they partake in. Teachers, local governments and schools, which have traditionally resisted systems of state control, are now voluntarily furthering the politics of globalisation and nationalism. Is there really no alternative to this situation? This chapter begins by outlining the conditions regarding Japan's curriculum and the testing system after the introduction of PISA.

The so-called PISA shock was not a reaction to the results of the PISA 2000 survey, but rather to Japan's rankings having declined further in the PISA 2003 survey, and which have continued to decline in successive surveys. Certain conservative politicians, education researchers and sectors of the media have directed public attention squarely upon the decline in rankings despite the PISA survey results having revealed a more serious concern – a gap of socio-economic background in literacy results. The public focus on the decline in rankings sparked a further wave of criticism against child-centred and problem-solving teaching, which has already been the target of much criticism in the past, and it accelerated a change in direction towards the learning of basic skills. Concurrently, Japan's response policy to the PISA literacy survey emphasized linguistic competency. Accordingly, in 2006 an expert working group from the Ministry of Education, Culture, Sports, Science and Technology (MEXT) presented a learning model (MEXT, 2006); however, this model differs considerably in nature from PISA's definition of literacy in the following ways.

First, the PISA literacy conception has been depoliticised. PISA is based on the OECD's Definition and Selection of Competencies (DeSeCo) project, which examines the competencies that ought to be mastered by individuals in the globalised society of the twenty-first century, and it only measures a part of three categories of key competencies, namely 'using tools interactively', 'interacting in homogeneous groups', and 'acting autonomously'. The DeSeCo project was conceived within a social democratic political context – the so-called Third Way (Giddens, 1998) – and this context is reflected in the PISA literacy concept (Rychen and Salganik, 2003). The OECD (1999: 20) defines 'reading literacy' as 'understanding, using, and reflecting on written texts, in order to achieve one's goals, to develop one's knowledge and potential, and to participate in society', and it therefore views the purpose of literacy as raising 'constructive, concerned and reflective citizens'. The strategy of PISA in Japan's educational policy removed the social democratic politics from the concept of PISA literacy.

Second, this depoliticised conception of literacy has resulted in a skills-based approach to teaching reading. The following is an example of a classroom teaching model presented to teachers by the National Institute for Educational Policy Research (NIER, 2011: 2).

- Aim: to foster *effective reading* of newspaper articles in order to obtain the information required.
- Learning task: students read newspapers, compare them and report their findings on *the editing style of the newspapers and the writing style in the articles.*

Step 1

- Discuss how newspapers focus on society, economics, politics, education, culture, sports, and so on.
- Provide a learning task in which students comparatively read two newspapers edited for elementary school students and report the findings, and then prepare a study plan accordingly.

Step 2

- Students read similar articles that appear in both newspapers, and then compare the articles in terms of the content of the headline, as well as that of the lead (introductory passage) and main text, and the quantity and structure of the text.
- Students form groups, allocate the common articles in the two newspapers, and compare their findings using worksheets.
- In groups, students summarise their thoughts on the readability of the articles in terms of their content and structure, and the opinions and bias of the articles' authors.

Step 3

- Students report to each other and then summarise their findings and opinions on the editing style of the newspapers and the writing style in the articles.

Although this classroom teaching model teaches students about how language is used in daily life, the learning objective of 'read effectively' becomes replaced by general skills for extracting necessary information (that is, students are instructed to focus on 'the editing style of the newspapers and the writing style in the articles'), and the decoding of the sociocultural/political contexts in the text are dismissed. In this way, the act of reading, which should be situated and comprehensive, is converted into fragmented skills and the students end up being taught 'packaged' reading skills that are geared towards the acquisition of the various competencies. In Japan, therefore, the PISA literacy concept has been segmented into basic learning such as vocabulary and arithmetic on the one hand and decontextualised and depoliticised learning skills on the other, and it has permeated into classrooms in such form. The driving force behind this permeation is the national test, which was launched in 2007.

From PISA to National Test and a Reform of National Curriculum

The misreading of PISA has invited a more severe crisis. Since 2007, an annual nationwide survey of scholastic ability has been conducted on sixth-grade students of elementary school and third-grade students of junior high school. The 2015 survey targeted 1,104,000 elementary students and 1,122,000 junior high students (MEXT, 2015). This survey imitates the PISA survey in that it covers language literacy and numeracy (it has also covered science since 2012), and it tests student competencies, not only on basic skills but also on logical thinking. However, unlike PISA, the survey has separate questions for basic skills (Test A) and logical thinking (Test B), and this has led to the stratification or tiering of learning, which is discussed later.

The average test scores (for Tests A and B) in each prefecture are published, and the prefectures are ranked accordingly. Regarding the scores for local body and each school, the local boards of education are notified of the scores for all schools under their jurisdiction, whereas each school are notified only of their respective scores. MEXT initially adopted a cautious approach towards the publication of results at a local-, government- and school-level over concerns pertaining to the ranking of different schools, but in 2013 it signalled its willingness to allow such publications, provided that the boards of education and schools consented. As revealed in a questionnaire survey, the boards of education and schools expressed concern that certain schools and students may be stigmatised because of their scores, and as a result few local bodies have actually

publicised the test results (MEXT, 2013). The current stated aim of this national test is not to create league tables, such as in England, or to scrap schools that fail to meet certain standards, as in the US No Child Left Behind Act, MEXT states that it is not a test, but rather a 'survey' of students' learning and their learning background, and that it is conducted in order to raise educational standards. However, it essentially compels schools and teachers to voluntarily and actively conduct classes that are standardised according to the national curriculum guidelines. This fact is evidenced in the close linkage between the content of the test and that of the national curriculum guidelines published in 2008, one year after the test was launched.

It has been indicated that in the PISA surveys, Japanese students are particularly weak in the competencies of reflecting and evaluating text (NIER, 2002). In order to inculcate such components of literacy, the national curriculum guidelines state that the curriculum should be based on two principles: full mastery of basic skills and utilisation of such knowledge. Basic skills would henceforth be assessed in Test A, with utilisation learning in Test B. Herein exists the inverted relationship between educational content and assessment. Normally, the content and approach of assessments are configured according to the particular content to be assessed, but in this case, the assessment content is prepared in advance and educational content is devised afterwards to correspond to the assessment. In order to improve the test scores, schools and teachers are therefore expected to adhere all the more closely to the curriculum guidelines. The use of this test as a means of controlling the curriculum is addressed in greater detail, focusing on the issues associated with the two principles of basic skill and its utilisation in the national curriculum.

The issues with these two principles are twofold: they trivialise the concept of literacy and impoverish learning. Literacy is a socially, politically and economically situated practice and it is a holistic competency; however, in Japan's national curriculum, literacy is interpreted as a set comprising basic knowledge and thinking skills. This interpretation has, amidst the fixation on assessments through national tests, fostered the attitude in schools that teaching should focus chiefly on the mastery of basic knowledge. One educational research company in Japan surveyed elementary and junior high school teachers about how they put emphasis on 'mastery' of basic knowledge or 'utilisation' in their class following the revision of the national curriculum guidelines (Benesse, 2010).

According to the survey, 79.4 per cent of elementary teachers and 77.0 per cent of junior high teachers are putting their emphasis on 'mastery' of basic knowledge. On the other hand, teaching 'utilisation' of knowledge remains 43.9 per cent in elementary and 47.4 per cent in junior high teachers. It was evident that both elementary and junior high school teachers predominantly focus on basic knowledge mastery, and one may conclude that they consider mastery and utilisation learning to be two separate stages of learning. Furthermore, this survey examined the type of pedagogy the teachers adopt for their teaching. It shows that schools with lower scholastic achievements tend to emphasize learning, whereas those with higher scholastic achievements tend to extend their focus to include utilisation learning. In order to master basic knowledge, repetitive drills and rote memorisation tend to be dominant. This trivialisation of the literacy concept and the understanding of mastery and utilisation as two separate tiers of learning push students into a negative cycle, particularly those with a lower scholastic achievement. Schools with low scholastic achievements feel under pressure to improve their test scores, and they attempt to remedy their situation by focusing intensively on basic knowledge. However, by implementing such a teaching with no real life context, students become even more demotivated and disinterested in learning.

MEXT has asserted that the new national curriculum was devised in view of the PISA literacy standards, and it also claims that the guidelines aim to deliver education in accordance with global standards. Koyasu (2008) argues that such dichotomous/tiered learning leads to a pitfall where students end up cram-learning basic knowledge and a fixed set of skills, and fail to acquire either satisfactorily. Koyasu also argues that such learning further widens the disparity in literacy between social classes. Japan's cram-learning, which typifies the learning style of East Asia, is, to use Paulo Freire's terminology, 'banking education' (Freire, 1996). Although it is important to maintain a critical attitude towards the political and economical background in which the PISA's literacy concept was formed (that is, responding to globalisation), the concept does have the potential to shift Japan's traditional learning style towards critical reading and thinking practices. However, the style of education currently being undertaken by Japan is banking education geared towards a globalised world. Particularly notable is that this style of education is not only being advanced by the central government, it is also being developed through teacher performance under the test-accountability system. The standardized tests and the control of the curriculum are discussed next.

Control of the Curriculum Through PDCA

The beginning of the curriculum guidelines clearly states that each school is responsible for organising its curriculum (MEXT, 2008); however, the education system in Japan has hitherto imposed a system of unitary control over what teachers can teach (that is, through the screening of textbooks), which is based on the legal enforceability of the national curriculum guidelines. Curricula and teachers are therefore currently controlled in a multidimensional way through standardized testing. Shimizu (2014) aptly terms this situation the 'test regime'. Under this condition, the raising of scores in standardized tests becomes the ultimate goal, and in order to achieve this objective at all costs, there is a general mobilisation of politicians, central and regional education bureaucrats, principals, teachers and parents/guardians (a mobilisation that leaves children behind).

According to Matsushita (2012), the fact that the national test in Japan is an exhaustive survey signifies not that it is designed to ascertain the scholastic levels of students, as mentioned in MEXT's official statement of purpose, but that it is designed to permeate a test-accountability system based on the PDCA cycle amongst each board of education and school. Although the test results of specific schools are not published, the results are published at the prefectural level, and this is conducted for a purpose: the function of the nationwide standardized test is to have teachers and schools assume responsibility over managing educational objectives and content. The power that is operating here is relatively different from Foucault's (1995) concept of disciplinary power. Foucault envisaged a form of power that manages individuals by instilling norms in them, provided that such individuals possess shared values (Foucault, 1995). This type of power applies to power structures that developed in the modernisation process against the backdrop of a grand narrative. For example, physical discipline has been embodied by schools in various aspects against a backdrop of social values, including 'social mobility based on academic credentials' and 'if you work hard, you will be rewarded'. However, Azuma and Osawa (2003) argue that this power has now shifted into a more subtle form, namely 'environmental governance'. A plurality of values is embraced with 'environmental governance', and individuals appear to act as they choose, but in reality, those in power are pulling the strings at the individual level and determining the extent of freedom allocated to each person (Azuma and Osawa, 2003). This model of power can explain power structures in a society where not everyone partakes in the grand narrative. Thus, for the nationwide standardized test, teachers, parents and children all know that the test does not guarantee an improvement in student's learning or their future position in society. Moreover, individual students are not informed of their test results; however, the data are used to govern teachers and the curriculum.

We now examine a number of phenomena related to the nationwide standardized test that confirms the reality of this situation – one in which individuals act voluntarily, but lack awareness of the power politics that are subtly steering their decisions. Consider, for example, the changes to school objectives following the introduction of the national test. Table 58.1 shows the results of a survey on the changes in objectives upheld by schools in two time points: 2002, when the national curriculum guidelines were emphasizing problem-solving learning; and 2010, the year after the introduction of the nationwide standardized test and the accompanying revision to the national curriculum guidelines (the revision that resulted in the current guidelines). The results revealed that words such as 'improvement of learning and literacy' and 'learning habits' were being incorporated into school objectives to a greater extent in 2010. It is possible to infer from these results that, under the test-accountability system, schools have started viewing improvements of test score as the ultimate goal.

Table 58.1 Shifting goal of local schools after national standardized test

Year	2002 (%)	2010 (%)	Difference (%)
Self-learning	59.8	53.9	−5.9
Improvement of learning and literacy	20.7	41.8	+21.1
Improvement of basic lifestyle	20.9	34.1	+13.2
Establishing learning habits	8.4	27.7	+19.3
Social norm and rule	13.7	22.9	+9.2

Source: Adapted from Benesse (2010)

The incorporation of learning improvement into objectives was not brought about through MEXT's direct control. According to the environmental governance framework, those in power have fostered an environment in which schools and teachers feel compelled to perform. This condition is achieved through the objective-evaluation system based on the PDCA cycle.

Walter A. Shewhart and Edwards Deming propagated the PDCA cycle in post-war US as a quality control method. It is currently incorporated in control systems such as ISO9000 and ISO14001. This quality control system for corporations has been transplanted directly into schools to serve as a teaching quality assurance system.

In Japan, the power to determine 'quality' objectives under the objective-evaluation system is possessed entirely by the government. In 2006, the Basic Act on Education (a law that determines the constitutional position of education) was revised, and part of this revision included the designation of specific competencies that ought to be targeted. Accordingly, the subordinate legislation (the School Education Act) stipulated target competencies for each stage of school education, competencies that are decontextualised. Also incorporated into the legislation was the duty to improve school management with a view to achieving such targets. This revision represented a big change to a legislative framework. The national government could now have decision-making powers over the general purpose of education, as well as in internal matters such as objective-setting and curriculum content. From a practical aspect, in 2006 MEXT issued guidelines for school assessments that required schools to assess and improve their educational activities continually through the PDCA cycle (MEXT, 2010), including a section on 'educational curriculum and learning guidance' that listed the scores in the national test as one of the performance indicators.

In relation to this situation, Nakajima (2007: 30) indicated that the PDCA cycle, as it is used in Japan, comprises the following four steps: (1) the central government determines the objectives to be achieved in compulsory education; (2) local boards of education and schools are tasked with meeting these targets; (3) the national government assesses the extent to which the objectives are being met; and (4) based on this assessment, the state encourages local communities and schools to improve as necessary. Nakajima argued that by having hegemony over the 'check' and 'action' steps, the objective-evaluation system serves to control school education in a unitary manner. Thus, whilst trumpeting local autonomy and devolution to schools, in reality, the test-accountability system conditions schools and teachers to 'voluntarily' accept an excessive burden.

Under this system of spontaneous subjugation, what challenges do teachers face? One challenge is that in order to raise rankings on the nationwide standardized test, teachers are compelled to advance intensive test preps under the direction of the prefectural board of education. Test preps are conducted more in communities and schools that are ranked low on the national test and involve, for example, having students repeat past test questions.

Learning standards are also set at the local government level, and each local government implements its own scholastic tests to measure the extent to which these standards are being attained. These standards and tests are modelled after the national test, and in this sense, they are clearly designed to improve scores in the nationwide survey.

The ideology that underlines this situation is 'performativity', a results-oriented approach. Stephen Ball (2006) pointed out that performativity is the situation where we are operating within a baffling array of figures, performance indicators, comparisons and competitions. In the name of accountability, the outcomes of students' educational activities from kindergarten to higher education are quantified and assessed. In this climate of performativity, what was originally a means for assessing educational content has become the end in itself, with educational activities currently being designed to fulfil all assessment criteria. The adverse effects of this inversion penetrate every part of education. In Japan, the objective-evaluation system has fostered a management-led school culture, with a decline in democratic collegiality and professional autonomy. In the classroom, teaching is becoming 'manualised', students are streamed according to their achievement level, and the attempts to improve students' learning levels in this manner certainly lead to a diminished student interest in learning. Teachers must spend copious amounts of time and energy in test preps, and they feel powerless in planning a curriculum on their own.

PISA has therefore impacted school education in Japan substantially under a conception of literacy that differs from its original conception. Educational reform has sparked a crisis and delivered a fatal blow to the classroom teaching practice of each teacher. Although it was originally a policy performance indicator, PISA has become a national standard of learning and objectives, and, in turn, a local indicator that assesses schools and teachers under a curriculum–test–evaluation system.

This chapter has discussed how PISA, which was launched in a globalised context, has been transmuted into Japanese national and local contexts. Although the manner of Japan's reception of PISA reflects a certain kind of politics, one cannot ignore that problems are inherent in PISA itself, as well as in the competency model upon which PISA is based. The issue concerns PISA defining competencies of the globalised world as 'quantifiable' and 'partial', and then grading the particular strength of each competency. The following section critically analyses PISA and the competency model that has been proposed for a globalised world.

A CRITIQUE OF GLOBAL COMPETENCIES

There has already been a considerable amount of criticism against PISA. These critiques can be divided broadly into two categories.

The first criticises how PISA provides only the measurable rankings of competencies in each country, and how this prompts countries to devise quick-fix measures to boost their rankings. A critique of this category that gained considerable attention was in the 'Open Letter to Andreas Schleicher', composed by a group of educational researchers known worldwide and published in *The Guardian* in May 2014 (*The Guardian*, 2014). The letter criticised PISA for contributing to an increased reliance on standardised testing and quantitative measures and causing, with its 3-year assessment cycle, a shift in attention to short-term fixes designed to help the country improve its rankings, ultimately leading to more 'vendor'-made lessons, less autonomy for teachers and the impoverishment of classroom teaching. The letter labels the situation 'educational colonialism' – and this situation, as described in the letter, matches the circumstances described in this chapter for Japan.

The second criticism levied against PISA concerns the model of economic globalisation and competency upon which it is based. Economic globalisation and the accompanying changes in social structure are obviously altering the labour model. The new realities of the labour model will be arguably reflected in school education in the form of the competency model. PISA is predicated on key competencies proposed by the OECD-sponsored DeSeCo project, and DeSeCo stipulated key competencies that should be mastered by individuals so that they may lead full lives in a globalised world and contribute to society (Rychen and Salganik, 2003). These key competencies comprise three categories: (1) using tools interactively; (2) interacting in heterogeneous groups; and (3) acting autonomously. Each category contains three subcategories (see Table 58.2). PISA is designed to measure part of the first key competency – using tools interactively. Collaborative problem solving competency was added from the 2015 survey onwards, and there is a plan to expand the range of the PISA survey to cover the second key competency – interacting in heterogeneous groups.

Table 58.2   Key competencies (DeSeCo) and twenty-first century skills (ATC21s)

	Key competencies	21st century skills
For the world	Using tool interactively • Use language, symbols and texts interactively • Use knowledge and information interactively • Use technology interactively	Ways of thinking • Creativity and innovation • Critical thinking, problem-solving, decision-making • Learning to learn, metacognition (knowledge about cognitive process) Tools for working • Information and literacy • ICT literacy
For other	Interacting in heterogeneous group • Relate well to others • Co-operate, work in teams • Manage and resolve conflicts	Ways of working • Communication • Collaboration (teamwork)
For self	Acting autonomously • Act within the big picture • Form and conduct life plans and personal projects • Defend and assert rights, interest, limits and needs	Ways of living in the world • Citizenship – local and global • Life and career • Professional and social responsibility, including cultural awareness and competence

Source: Adapted from Rychen and Salganik (2003) and Griffin, McGaw and Care (2011).

The term 'competency' has traditionally been used in business management studies, but when DeSeCo uses the term 'key competency', it is not only the economic aspects. Although the competencies upheld as essential for individual and social achievement include 'economic positions and resources' and 'economic productivity', it also includes 'democratic processes', 'solidarity and social cohesion', 'human rights and peace', 'equity, equality, and absence of discrimination', and 'ecological sustainability', and these competencies encompass political, social, cultural and biological values (Rychen and Salganik, 2003). However, Matsushita (2014) argues that PISA has such an influence over countries worldwide because the logic of 'magnet economy' behind PISA. For example, the OECD report (2011) that analysed the educational policies of countries that achieved top PISA rankings cites that these policies have focused on competition over the quality of human resources in a global-scale labour market. Further, the principle of economic growth in a globalised economy has had a major bearing on the definition of key competencies as well as on PISA's literacy concept. As evidence for this claim, OECD Education

and Skills Director, Andreas Schleicher, projected that if the US improved its PISA scores by 25 points over the next 20 years, there would be a gain of US$41 trillion in the US economy (OECD, 2011). It is possible to interpret the incorporation of these political, social and cultural values as representing a response to a situation where such issues must be cleared in order to advance global economic development.

Likewise, the institution that proposed the model of competencies in a globalised economy was the ATC21s project, which was sponsored by Microsoft, Intel and Cisco Systems, and assigned a key role to the University of Melbourne, Australia. The ATC21s project defined ten core twenty-first-century skills, which were sorted into four categories: (1) Ways of Thinking; (2) Ways of Working; (3) Tools for Working; and (4) Living in the World (Griffin et al., 2011). The ATC21s framework is notable because it provides a model of specific skills for the actual workplace as opposed to general skills, differentiating it from the key competencies (see Table 58.2). By being so specific, the model stands out as a framework for skills expected of company workers, such as creativity, innovation, collaboration and problem solving.

Iwakawa (2005) argues that although the PISA literacy concept measures competencies that promote citizenship and social participation, one should be aware of how PISA displays concern for a system of global competition and the quantity and quality of human capital within such a system. It is reasonable to suppose that, irrespective of how globalised economies become, the majority of children will lead working and civic lives in their country of birth. When determining what skills should be aimed by public education and what content it should teach, policymakers should not be caught up entirely in the dominant neoliberal conception of economic globalisation.

This chapter now elaborates on the two main criticisms of PISA by exploring two key problem areas: how standardised testing is silent in relation to research on educational content in the curriculum, and 'the individualisation of risk' as a perspective that links standardised testing with the global competencies model.

Lack of Educational Content, Disregard for the Value of Knowledge

PISA has dramatically transformed the curriculum policies of participating countries. Although PISA and the DeSeCo's key competencies upon which it is based clarify necessary competencies, there is no mention of what knowledge should be taught; and instead PISA emphasises performance – what students should be able to do, rather than what they should know.

Knowledge is therefore viewed in the same way as a skill, and regarded as a means to master competencies. According to Bernstein (1996: 87), this represents 'a fundamental break in the relation between the knower and what is known' and 'knowledge is separated from inwardness, from commitments, from personal dedication, from the deep structure

of the self'. Thus, knowledge is no longer regarded as a dynamic framework by which we can understand the world and form relationships with it.

Moreover, when curricula are being configured, the emphasis is on competency rather than on knowledge, meaning that the relationship between knowledge and power is no longer considered. The relationship between knowledge and power is lost because listing a set of competencies on the basis that they are essential for a globalised society creates the illusion that everyone is equally capable of mastering them. Bernstein's (1975) ideas offers an insight – he analysed pedagogies in Britain using a theoretical framework that divided pedagogies into visible and invisible pedagogies, and concluded that the latter, which would seem at first to be democratic, actually serve to reproduce social class inequality in learning. During the 1990s, Bernstein (1996) developed his theoretical framework into a 'performance model' and 'competence model'. He then criticised the competence model on the basis that it assumes 'a universal democracy of acquisition. All are inherently competent and all possess common procedures' and then combines with 'a tendency to embrace populism' to end up 'abstracting the individual from the analysis of distribution of power and principles of control which selectively specialise modes of acquisition and realisations' (Bernstein, 1996: 56). Kodama (2013) argues that a competence-based curriculum is responsible for shifting attention away from the question of what knowledge to teach in schools, thereby inculcating the view that 'anyone can do it if they try hard enough'.

The danger with curricula devoid of a perspective on knowledge as educational content is that they can result in abstracted competency/skill-based learning. Such learning is particularly harmful for students on the socioeconomic peripheries because although competencies and skills may at first seem abstract and value-neutral, their acquisition is dependent on the learner's cultural habits and the continuity/discontinuity (of the competencies) with the individual's socio-economic environment. In other words, for students in a certain socioeconomic class, seemingly abstract competencies and skills are continuous with the abilities that the student has cultivated in his/her family home, and they therefore function as meaningful competencies. When competency-based standardised tests, such as PISA, are emphasized, the importance of explicit knowledge in curriculum making is downplayed, which, in turn, leads to a wider gap in competency belied by the slogan of learning improvement.

Risk Society and Individualisation

Another issue with standardised tests such as PISA is the individualisation of risk. Standardised testing and economic globalisation both operate on the principle of the individualisation of risk. I now discuss this problem with reference to Beck's theory of the risk society, mentioned at the beginning of the chapter.

Beck (1992) made two main claims, the first of which is that the present society is a society of increased 'risk' from forces that are uncontrollable and unknowable. Although modernity has increased wealth by controlling nature scientifically, the price of society's maturation is a dramatic increase in risks. Thus, society, Beck argues, has now morphed into a risk society, where the production and distribution of risks become the social point of contention. We live in a society that bears risks in exchange for wealth. Moreover, these risks are not constrained by national borders. As examples such as nuclear waste and terrorism clearly show, the people who produce risks are not necessarily those who take them on. According to Beck, a 'risk society' is a society in which everyone is equally exposed to risks.

As Beck believes, risks are unknowable (to laypeople), and we must therefore rely on the judgment of experts – scientific knowledge – to determine where the risks lie and how serious they are. However, scientific understanding is itself highly contentious, and many risks are assessed differently (for example, consider the debate over the safety of nuclear power generation in Japan following the 11 March 2011 earthquake and tsunami).

Beck's (1992) second main claim concerns the way a risk society addresses risk – by individualising it. This argument is predicated on the view that the unit of social life is no longer class or family, but the individual. Risk falls directly on individuals without being mediated by intermediary organisations, and these individuals are responsible for taking appropriate measures by themselves. This situation does not emerge because individuals actively take on risks themselves, but rather because there are fewer social capacities for risk to be distributed to. When a society becomes a risk society, the process of decision-making is entrusted to individuals. Beck (1994: 7) describes this situation as 'people are not being "released" from feudal and religious-transcendental certainties into the world of industrial society, but rather from industrial society into the turbulence of the global risk society. They are being expected to live with a broad variety of different, mutually contradictory, global and personal risks'.

There are arguments against Beck, which call into question whether the globalisation of society has really heralded the retreat of intermediary organisations (that mediate risk) and the individualisation of risk (Lauder et al., 2006). However, even if these counter-arguments are considered, by placing individualised risk management at the core of social analysis, Beck's theory has undoubtedly raised important questions in relation to education.

When viewed through the prism of risk, a system such as PISA can be understood as one that produces risks that must be borne by individual teachers and individual students. Specifically, there are countries that take on the risks of PISA and others that do not. Japan is clearly among the latter. In Japan, PISA, the curricula and tests that are standardised by national and local governments, and the teaching processes designed around them have become a system that justifies the socio-economic class-based gap amongst students. PISA and other standardised tests are merely one type of social system, but they ascribe a shape and scale to individuals' 'competencies', consequently individualising the risk of reproducing low achievement.

This system has also produced risks that must be borne by teachers. Teachers have been robbed of the essential question that concerns their expertise and autonomous decision-making – the question of what to teach – and in return they have been lumbered with the risk of being responsible for the outcomes of their teaching (that is, the scholastic level of the children they have taught). Here, again, this risk is produced socially, whereas the risk-response is individualised.

How can we sever the linkage between standardized test and accountability systems and the individualisation of risk? We must wield the language of systems and the language of practice. The next section examines a counter strategy for the case of Japan.

A CRITICAL TURN IN THE STUDY OF CURRICULUM CONTENT

Standardised testing increases the individualised risks to be faced by teachers and students. In a world where the global, national and local levels all operate on the same principles, standardised testing doubles and triples the risk to teachers and students. This section explores teaching practices in Japan that use a bottom–up approach and derives from these case studies the counter principles of teaching practice that can provide an alternative to the present situations.

The first step to challenging the assumption that standardisation is essential in a globalised world, and the belief that standardised testing is essential to develop global competencies, is to be aware of the inconsistencies of globalisation and standardisation. Beck (2000) presented the three concepts of 'globalisation', 'globality', and 'globalism', and

argued that comprehending the difference between globalism, on the one hand, and globalisation and globality on the other, is key to challenging the orthodoxy of the prevailing ideology associated with globalisation, the ideology that Beck identifies as globalism. By globalism, Beck is referring to the globalised rule of neoliberal ideology, an ideology based purely on the market economy principle. Globalisation and globalism tend to be used as interchangeable terms. To help differentiate the terms, Beck (2000) defines the historical and social phenomenon of globalisation in terms of its multidimensional, pluralistic and spontaneous aspects. He states the following:

> *Globalization* lays the stress upon a transnational process, in the dimensions we have considered
>
> 1 It refers to intensification of transnational spaces, events, problems, conflict and biographies.
> 2 This tendency – contrary to everything the word 'global' suggest – should not be understood either as linear or as 'total' or 'all-encompassing'. Rather, it should be thought of as only *contingent* and *dialectical* – as *glocal*. This will become clearer if the conceptual figure of 'inclusive distinction or opposition' is employed as the underlying principle of biography, identity and organization.
> 3 It then becomes necessary to consider the *degree, density* and *extent* of globalization/localization in the various dimensions. Thus, the manifestation of glocalization can and must be *empirically* investigated. (Beck, 2000: 87–88, emphasis original)

Beck argues that globalisation as a process is headed towards globality as a state of existence, and he defines globality as a multidimensional, pluralistic, spontaneous and political outcome.

Beck does not regard neoliberal globalism as a given and unavoidable process. Although globalisation is a historical and social reality, there is no reason to respond to it with globalism. According to Beck's view, globalisation cannot mean the predominance of a singular orthodoxy such as this. An important question when considering education systems is how to construct multidimensional, spontaneous and political spaces.

The same principle must be applied when developing educational practice. In the face of standardised learning criteria and teaching styles, the fundamental principle is to determine how to create pluralistic teaching and learning.

One concrete/specific approach that is essential for converting this fundamental principle into teaching practice is the 'precautionary approach', which refers to the belief that measures against risk must be taken, even if scientific understanding is insufficient. The *Rio Declaration on Environment and Development* made at the 1992 UN Conference on Environment and Development (UNCED) in Rio de Janeiro states the following:

> In order to protect the environment, the precautionary approach shall be widely applied by States according to their capabilities. Where there are threats of serious or irreversible damage, lack of full scientific certainty shall not be used as a reason for postponing cost-effective measures to prevent environmental degradation. (United Nations, 1992: n.p.)

Predicated on the relativism, pluralism and fallibility of science, this statement declares the principle that precautionary measures against individualised risks should be taken at a societal level. The antithesis of this principle is the preventive approach. Although the term itself is uncommon, it refers to the belief that measures should be taken only in cases where the cause–effect relationship of risks and their occurrence has been scientifically proven. The same concept is embodied in Japan's Product Liability Act, which declares manufacturers to be legally exempt (from liability for damaged goods, and so on) if they have taken measures against proven risks.

This preventive approach was dealt a decisive blow by the tsunami and Fukushima Daiichi nuclear power plant disaster following the Great East Japan Earthquake of 11 March 2011. This chapter will not go into detail, but the disaster can be regarded as a consequence of Japan advancing its nuclear energy policy and disaster-preparedness policy based on the preventive approach, allowing state-sanctioned science to be the driving force and excluding numerous scientific opinions that had already raised many cautions. In view of the sheer number of victims it produced – 15,889 individuals perished and 2,597 still missing (as of November 2014) – the disaster has forced Japanese society as a whole, including the entirety of public education, to confront issues that must be generalised and universalised. It is not enough to merely provide teaching regarding the risks of nuclear energy and natural disasters – the question is how schools should teach students about the relationship between knowledge and the world. This issue cannot be managed with packaged classroom teaching focused purely on achieving the targeted competencies and skills. It is essential to have a perspective on knowledge, its plurality and the politics that can make it a reality. This paper now introduces two case studies of teaching practice that provide clues in this respect, and it derives from these case studies a framework of curriculum research with a view to achieving a shift from a standardised curriculum towards pluralist and political education.

The first case study is the disaster-preparedness curriculum of Kamaishi, a city that was devastated in the Great East Japan Earthquake, and yet protected the lives of 99.8 per cent of its 3,000 students through swift evacuation action. The saving of so many lives has been dubbed 'the Miracle of Kamaishi'; however, rather than being a miracle, this accomplishment was due to risk education. In other words, schools collaborated with the local community to ensure the teaching, learning and mastery of a plurality of disaster-preparedness thinking and action skills.

According to a report by the headmistress of Kamaishi Elementary School, the school executed a disaster-preparedness curriculum in the following four levels:

1 Tsunami hazard mapmaking;
2 Evacuation trainings in anticipation of a tsunami striking when students are walking home from school;

3 Tsunami disaster-preparedness lesson; and
4 The importance of the old saying of *tsunami-tendenko*. (Kato, 2013: 25–27)

Regarding hazard mapmaking (Level 1), schools had parents join students in investigating the routes between the school and homes to identify potentially dangerous points as well as evacuation sites. The information was shared and then incorporated into a large map, which was then posted on a wall that students would often pass to ensure it would become a familiar sight. Evacuation trainings (Level 2) were conducted to prepare students for an earthquake/tsunami disaster that strikes during their walk home from school or whilst playing outside the school. These trainings were conducted with the participation of local residents. When the 11 March earthquake struck, one elementary school student who was fishing at sea at the time initially rushed to an evacuation centre near the shore, but then, deciding that the location was too dangerous, ran to another evacuation centre 1 km inland. This action saved the student's life. Regarding Level 3, teaching units on disaster preparedness were prepared and implemented systematically under the direction of Professor Toshitaka Katada, a disaster social-engineering expert at Gunma University.

Katada (2012) highlighted the following three key points of disaster-preparedness teaching:

1 Do not place too much faith in 'assumptions'.
2 When disaster strikes, do everything you can.
3 Take the initiative in evacuating.

The first key point is undoubtedly based on the precautionary approach. The disaster-preparedness education in Kamaishi included informing students about the forecasted figures for the amount of inundation based on data from a tsunami that hit Kamaishi in the past, but the students were instructed not to trust the forecasts blindly. The students were also taught not to wait until the announcement to evacuate, but to take the initiative and flee. Such teaching was not only based

on Katada's ideas, it also incorporated the old saying in Kamaishi and throughout the Tohoku coastal region, namely *tsunami-tenko*. *Tsunami-tenko* is the maxim that, in the event of a tsunami, individuals should flee separately to higher ground and it is based on the accumulated wisdom of the region. Thus, the so-called Kamaishi Miracle was achieved by virtue of the fact that, although scientific assumptions were set as the premise, disaster knowledge was pluralised through personal judgments and local knowledge. In fact, one first-grade elementary school student who had undergone such education made a personal judgment not to stay at the designated evacuation centre, but to head instead for higher ground. The student had to endure two nights on his own as a result, but had the wherewithal to calmly await the arrival of his parents.

Kamaishi's disaster-preparedness curriculum comprises the following four areas (Table 58.3): 'Understanding earthquakes and tsunami', 'Understanding the measures to take', 'Considering how tsunamis will damage the local community' and 'Learning from past experience' (Kamaishi-shi Board of Education et al., 2010). In addition, the educational content as a whole has been reorganised from a disaster-preparedness perspective by selecting learning units related to earthquakes and tsunami within each grade and subject. For example, in the sixth-grade elementary mathematics class, one learning unit is entitled, 'Expressing speed'. As part of this learning unit, students indicate the speed of a tsunami in metres per second, and they then consider how many seconds it would take the tsunami to reach their home. Likewise, in the sixth-grade elementary science class, there is a learning unit entitled, 'formation and change of the land'. As part of this learning unit, students learn about the mechanisms of earthquakes, their destructive force, the danger of tsunami that can sometimes follow earthquakes, how to prepare and respond to earthquakes in the middle of scientific experimentation.

There are guidelines on disaster-preparedness teaching issued by national government;

Table 58.3   The framework of disaster-preparedness curriculum in Kamaishi

Content		Primary 1–2[1,2]	Primary 3–4[1,2]	Primary 5–6[1,2]	Junior High 1–3[1,2]
I. Understanding the earthquake and tsunami	A. To know the mechanism of seismic tsunami		SA (1)	SA (1)	SC (1)
	B. To know the characteristic of tsunami	PE and SA (1) MT	SA (1)		
	C. To know the need of evacuation	SA (1)			
	D. To understand various characteristics of the tsunami			SA (1) SA (1)	
	E. To understand the characteristic of the shaking of the earthquake				SC (1)
II. Understanding the measures to take	A. To know the method to protect the body from an earthquake		SA (1)		
	B. To understand the way of evacuation from a tsunami		SA (1)	SA (1)	
	C. To know the place of evacuation around the school and the home	LES (1) LES (1)	SS (2)	IS (1)	
	D. To think about various ways of evacuation				SS (1) SS (3)
	E. To think about the action after evacuation				SA (2) SA (1)
	F. To consider psychology of those who cannot evacuate				IS or SA (1)
III. Considering how tsunamis will damage the local community	A. To know the past tsunami damage in the area		SA (1)	IS (1–3)	
	B. To think about the measures to protect the area from a tsunami		SA (1)	IS (1) SA (1)	
IV. Learning from past experience	A. To hear the story from a person who experienced tsunami and earthquake		SA (1)		
	B. Tsunami-Tendenko			SA (1)	
	C. To think about responsibility to hand down				ME (1)

Notes

1 SA: Special Activity; PE: Physical Education; MT: Mathematic; SC: Science; LES: Life Environmental Studies; SS: Social Studies; IS: Integrated Studies; ME: Moral Education.

2 Parenthesis shows the hours of the lesson.

Source: Kamaishi-shi Board of Education et al (2010: 11)

however, amidst an extremely centralised system of national control, the same by-the-book principles are followed even through the process of transforming the guidelines content into concrete measures at a pre-fectural level. In this context, Kamaishi's disaster-preparedness curriculum is crucial for reorganising and pluralising the guidelines content at the local level. This reorganisation and pluralisation resulted in activities that saved the lives of 99.8 per cent of students.

The Kamaishi case is an example of a curriculum that includes learning content on social risks themselves. Teaching students that social risks are themselves contentious in terms of the measures (risk-response measures) and their assessment, promotes the pluralisation and politicisation of knowledge. If such a curriculum has the potential to further develop learning content on social risks, what about other subjects?

I have argued in this chapter that standardised testing, by simplifying the teaching process, individualises the risks associated with developing students' competency. In brief, in measuring students against the standards, the endpoint is whether one 'can or cannot'. However, there have been attempts to create alternative classroom teaching, a teaching practice that can cater to the 'non-comprehension' of students who 'cannot'. A former elementary school teacher in Japan, Etsuko Watanabe developed her own teaching practice based on the essential aspect of classroom teaching content, namely the question of what to teach. Let us consider her mathematics class for third-grade elementary school students as a case study.

In Japanese elementary schools, students study multiplication in the second grade and then start learning division from the third grade. In Watanabe's class, two students named Hiroshi and Mari were struggling to grasp multiplication. It was natural to assume that Hiroshi and Mari would struggle with the concept of division with remainders. In response to such a situation, most teachers would drill these students on the times table; however, Watanabe recognised that the learning content was arranged in a systematic manner, and as such, could not necessarily cater to the student's way of understanding, and so she decided to develop a style of classroom teaching that aligned with the students' respective thinking process. Watanabe handed Hiroshi and Mari cups and marbles and the students then speculated their thinking by manipulating these tools (concrete operation). As a result, Hiroshi reached the understanding that 'division means dividing a number into equal parts'.

According to Lev Vygotsky (1978), these students were practicing operational thinking through the manipulation of external tools. For Hiroshi, this had significance for learning in that the external tools (the cup and the marbles) had been converted into internal tools of the mind. However, the significance of this tool-facilitated thinking did not stop with Hiroshi and Mari. Those students who could translate mathematical word problems into mathematical expressions adeptly before proceeding to solve them, could independently review their answers through the mediation of the operational thinking that Hiroshi and Mari practiced, and this led to a renewed understanding of the meaning of division. It can be claimed that Hiroshi and the other students in the class had attained, what Lev Vygotsky (1978) refers to, as the 'zone of proximal development'.

Watanabe's success story could certainly not have occurred through standardised teaching. In Watanabe's class, multiple perspectives on the meaning of division were given recognition and this facilitated unlearning. This result was achieved because Watanabe understood that the mathematical content to be taught in this learning unit should be 'division means dividing a number into equal parts' and also because the process by which students obtain this cognition was pluralised. By developing a class that helps students develop a plurality of understandings, rather than being concerned for whether the student will ultimately provide the singular correct answer, Watanabe ensured that the risk of having difficulty in learning would not become an individualised risk. Further, this case demonstrates that if being robbed of the question of 'what to teach' generates risks for teachers, then reclaiming this question generates plurality in teaching and learning.

CONCLUSION: UNLEARNING THE CURRICULUM

This chapter analysed the present situation of education in Japan to determine the impact of standardised testing, such as PISA, upon school curricula and classroom teaching. Standardised testing leads to standardised curricula and classroom teaching that is designed around the test, thereby leading to risks being imposed on teachers and students alike. Amidst this present trend in curriculum policy and teaching practice, there are also examples of curricula and classroom teaching that incorporate a bottom–up approach. This chapter examined such cases and clarified the fundamental principles upon which they are based. These examples revealed that an important principle is for teachers to manifest plurality in teaching and learning and, to this end, to assume ownership over the question of 'what to teach'.

The discussion revealed the importance of changing the approach to curriculum inquiry and teaching methods. According to Koyasu (2013), in curriculum research it was traditionally acceptable to simply ascertain the officially recognised achievements of science or to provide teaching based on the latest outcomes of scientific research at the podium. However, in a risk society, there is a need to proactively explore research and the findings that can clarify and challenge commonly accepted theories (Koyasu, 2013). Koyasu's claim echoes the teaching practice case studies presented in this chapter. To make such curriculum inquiry a reality, teachers must 'unlearn' the curriculum. According to Gayatri Spivak (1988), learning or gaining knowledge is a privilege, but it simultaneously signifies that the person has not gained other knowledge. To 'unlearn' in this context means to recognise that with one's privilege (knowledge), there is also much loss (ignorance of alternative knowledge), and then to deconstruct one's knowledge in order to open the opportunities for alternative knowledge; Spivak, 1988; Landry and MacLean, 1996). To unlearn does not mean to cease learning or to forget everything that one has learnt; instead, it involves focusing on the knowledge one was prevented from learning through the process of learning what one does know, and then redrawing the boundaries of one's knowledge accordingly.

In Japan, there is currently an ongoing discussion over the forthcoming changes to the national curriculum, and the new curriculum is anticipated to be based on the competency model. At the same time, extremely powerful nationalistic controls are being exerted over teaching from the kindergarten to university levels. In December 2013, MEXT unveiled an action plan to revise the textbook screening system under which textbook screening, which has already been shown to be highly problematic, would be further reformed along nationalist lines. The new guidelines require textbook publishers to ensure that their textbooks offer 'balanced' teaching content if no views have been established on the subject matter in academia, or if the government has an official position on such subject matter (MEXT, 2013). Although it may seem that these guidelines are promoting balanced content, under the system of textbook screening, textbook publishers are effectively compelled to present the official view of the government and leave out multiple alternative views. This will lead to students being taught only the official government line on content such as the territorial disputes with neighbouring countries or the portrayal of Japan's role in World War II. In addition to standardisation, school curricula in Japan are being exposed to the risks of nationalism.

This chapter focused on bottom–up approaches taken at a school and individual teacher level; however, it is also important to expand the scope of research to include an analysis of educational policy as the politics of teaching practice, or policymaking for teaching. It is hoped that these issues will be addressed in the future.

REFERENCES

Azuma, H. and Osawa, M. (2003) *Jiyu wo kangaeru: 9.11 ikou no gendai sisou*. Tokyo: NHK Syuppan.

Ball, S.J. (2006) 'Performativities and fabrications in the education economy: towards the performative society', in H. Lauder, P. Brown, J.-A. Dillabough and A.H. Halsey (eds.), *Education, Globalization, and Social Change*. New York, NY: Oxford University Press. pp. 692–701.

Beck, U. (1992) *Risk Society: Towards a New Modernity*. [Trans M. Ritter]. Los Angeles, CA: Sage Publications.

Beck, U. (1994) 'The reinvention of politics: towards a theory of reflexive modernization', in U. Beck, A. Giddens and S. Lash (eds.), *Reflexive Modernization: Politics, Tradition and Aesthetics in the Modern Social Order*. Cambridge, UK: Polity Press. pp. 1–55.

Beck, U. (2000) *What is Globalization?* [Trans P. Camiller]. Cambridge, UK: Polity Press.

Benesse Kyouiku Sougo Kenkyujo (2010) *Dai 5 kai gakusyu sido kihon chousa shogakko chugakko ban*. Available from http://berd.benesse.jp/shotouchutou/research/detail1.php?id=3243 (accessed 7 August 2015).

Bernstein, B. (1975) *Class, Codes and Control 3: Towards a Theory of Educational Transmissions*. London: Routledge & Kegan Paul.

Bernstein, B. (1996) *Pedagogy, Symbolic Control, and Identity: Theory, Research, Critique*. London: Taylor & Francis.

Foucault, M. (1995) *Discipline and Punish: the Birth of the Prison*. 2nd Vintage Books edn. [Trans A. Sheridan]. New York, NY: Random House.

Freire, P. (1996) *Pedagogy of the Oppressed*. [Trans M. A. Ramos]. New York, NY: Continuum.

Giddens, A. (1998) *The Third Way: The Renewal of Social Democracy*. Cambridge, UK: Polity Press.

Griffin, P., McGaw, B. and Care, E. (eds.) (2011) *Assessment and Teaching of 21st Century Skills*. Dordrecht. Netherlands: Springer.

Iwakawa, N. (2005) ' Kyouiku niokeru chikara no datsukochiku: Jiko jitsugen kara outokanosei e', in Y. Kudomi and T. Tanaka (eds.). *Kibo wo tsumugu gakuryoku*. Tokyo: Akashi Shoten. pp. 220–247.

Kamaishi-shi Board of Education, Kamaishi-shi bousaika and Gunma daigaku saigai syakai-kogaku kenkyushitsu (2010) *Kamaishi-shi tsunami bousai kyoiku no tame no tebiki*. Available from http://dsel.ce.gunma-u.ac.jp/kamaishi_tool/doc/manual_full.pdf (accessed 7 August 2015).

Katada, T. (2012) *Hito ga shinanai bousai*. Tokyo: Syueisya.

Kato, K. (2013) 'Otsunami wo ikinuita kodomo-dachi no kiseki de wa nai Kamaishi no kiseki', in Zenkoku koritsu gakko kyoto-kai (eds.), *Gakkou unei*, 619: 24–27.

Kodama, S. (2013) *Gakuryoku gensou*. Tokyo: Chikuma Shobo.

Koyasu, J. (2008) 'Kuruma no ryourin towa nani ka: kakujitsu na shutoku to katsuyou no mondaiten', in T. Takeuchi (ed.), *Gakushu shidouyouryou wo yomu shiten*. Tokyo: Hakutaku sha. pp. 27–38.

Koyasu, J. (2013) *Risk syakai no jyugyou zukuri*. Tokyo: Hakutakusya.

Landry, D. and MacLean, G. (eds.) (1996) *The Spivak Reader: Selected Works of Gayati Chakravorty Spivak*. New York, NY: Routledge.

Lauder, H., Brown, P., Dillabough, J.-A. and Halsey, A.H. (eds.) (2006) 'Introduction: the prospects for education: individualization, globalization, and social change', in H. Lauder, P. Brown, J.-A. Dillabough and A.H. Halsey (eds.), *Education, Globalization, and Social Change*. New York, NY: Oxford University Press. pp. 1–70.

Matsushita, K. (2012) 'Gakkou wa naze konnanimo hyouka mamire nanoka: kyouiku no global ka no hatashita yakuwari', in Group Didaktika (eds.), *Kyoushi ni narukoto kyoushi de ari tsuzukeru koto*. Tokyo: Keisou shobou, pp. 23–45.

Matsushita, K. (2014) 'The taming of PISA literacy: global functional literacy and national educational content', *The Japanese Journal of Educational Research*, 81(2): 150–63.

Ministry of Education, Culture, Sports, Science & Technology (MEXT) (2006) *Dokkai ryoku koujyou ni kansuru shidou shiryo*. Tokyo: Touyou kan shuppan sha.

Ministry of Education, Culture, Sports, Science & Technology (MEXT) (2008) *Shogakkou gakusyu shido-yoryo*. Tokyo: Tokyo Shoseki.

Ministry of Education, Culture, Sports, Science & Technology (MEXT) (2010) *Gakkou hyouka gaidorain*. Available from http://www.mext.go.jp/a_menu/shotou/gakko-hyoka/index.htm (accessed 7 August 2015).

Ministry of Education, Culture, Sports, Science & Technology (MEXT) (2013) *Zenkoku gakuryoku gakusyu jyoukyou chousa no kekka kohyou no toriatsukai ni kansuru anketo*. Available from http://www.mext.go.jp/b_menu/shingi/chousa/shotou/098/shiryo/__icsFiles/

afieldfile/2013/10/21/1340623_1_1.pdf (accessed 7 August 2015).

Ministry of Education, Culture, Sports, Science & Technology (MEXT) (2013) *Kyokasho kaikaku jikko plan*. Available from http://www.mext.go.jp/b_menu/houdou/25/11/__icsFiles/afieldfile/2013/11/15/1341515_01.pdf (accessed 7 August 2015).

Ministry of Education, Culture, Sports, Science & Technology (MEXT) (2015) *Heisei 27nendo zenkoku gakuryoku gakusyujyokyo chosa no sankakosu tonitsuite*. Available from http://www.mext.go.jp/a_menu/shotou/gakuryoku-chousa/zenkoku/__icsFiles/afieldfile/2015/04/17/1356677_1_1.pdf (accessed 7 August 2015).

Nakajima, T. (2007) 'Kyouiku kihonhou kaisei gono shin jiyu shugi kyouiku: PDCA saikuru ni housetsu sareru kyouiku genba', in Kyouiku kagku kenkyu kai (eds.) *Kyouiku, No. 739*, Tokyo: Kokudo sha. pp. 27–32.

National Institute for Educational Policy Research (NIER) (2002) *Ikirutame no chishiki to gino (knowledge and skills for life): OECD seito no gakusyutoutatsudo chosa (PISA)*. Tokyo: Gyosei.

National Institute for Educational Policy Research (NIER) (2011) *Heisei 23 nendo shougakkou kokugo no chousa mondai wo fumaeta jugyou aidea rei*. Available from http://www.nier.go.jp/11chousa/23_sho_koku_jugyourei.pdf (accessed 7 August 2015).

Organisation for Economic Co-operation and Development (OECD) (1999) *Measuring Student Knowledge and Skills: A New Framework for Assessment*. Paris, OECD. Available from http://www.oecd.org/edu/school/programmeforinternational studentassessmentpisa/33693997.pdf (accessed 7 August 2015).

Organisation for Economic Co-operation and Development (OECD) (2011) *Lessons from PISA for the United States: Strong Performers and Successful Reformers in Education*. Paris: OECD. Available from http://dx.doi.org/10.1787/9789264096660-en (accessed 7 August 2015).

Rychen, D.S. and Salganik, L.H. (eds.) (2003) *Key Competencies for a Successful Life and a Well-Functioning Society*. Cambridge, MA: Hogrefe & Huber.

Shimizu, K. (2014) ' "Gakuryoku testo kekka" no syakaiteki haikei', in Kyoiku Kagaku Kenkyu kai (eds.), *Kyouiku*, No. 825. Tokyo: Kokudo sha. pp. 57–64.

Spivak, G. (1988) 'Can the subaltern speak?', in C. Nelson and L. Grossberg (eds.), *Marxism and the Interpretation of Culture*. Urbana and Chicago, IL: Board of Trustees of the University of Illinois. pp. 271–316.

The Guardian (2014) 'OECD and PISA tests are damaging education worldwide – academics', *The Guardian*, 6 May. Available from http://www.theguardian.com/education/2014/may/06/oecd-pisa-tests-damaging-education-academics (accessed 7 August 2015).

United Nations (1992) *Report on the United Nations Conference on Environment and Development*. Available from http://www.un.org/documents/ga/conf151/aconf15126-1annex1.htm (accessed 7 August 2015).

Vygotsky, L. S. (1978) *Mind in Society: Development of Higher Psychological Processes*. Cambridge, MA: Harvard University Press.

59

The Ebb and Flow of Curricular Autonomy: Balance Between Local Freedom and National Prescription in Curricula

Claire Sinnema

CURRICULAR AUTONOMY

The purpose of this chapter is to problematize the notion of curricular autonomy, and in particular the autonomy that national curricula afford to those implementing teaching and learning programmes in local settings. It is important to do so because national curricula are constantly changing, and their balance between prescription and autonomy is a source of much debate in policy and public contexts. That debate draws on divergent perspectives about the benefits and risks of curricular autonomy and often leads to changes in the degree of prescription in national curricula – similar to the ebb and flow of the tide, there are constant fluctuations in curricular autonomy over time and it is high in some places whilst low in others. My intention in this chapter is to contribute to debates about curricular autonomy by proposing two frameworks – the first framework of curricular autonomy encompasses elements both within and beyond a documented curriculum. The utility of the framework is

demonstrated through applying it to the comparison of curricula in two contrasting contexts – England and New Zealand. The balance between prescription and autonomy in those two cases is quite different, leading me to propose a second framework that captures the relationship between system conditions and considerations of appropriate balance between national prescription and local freedom in national curricula.

Tides of Curricular Autonomy

Characteristic of educational policy in many jurisdictions in recent times is an emphasis on curricular autonomy, or at least moves toward increased curricular autonomy compared to previous curricula. Although the degree of autonomy and the elements of the curriculum it relates to vary from place to place, and systems offering low levels of curricular autonomy remain fairly common across OECD countries, 'the most common configuration is the one that gives schools the freedom to make curricular decisions' (OECD, 2011a: 45). That increase in school-level authority to make decisions about curriculum content has been noted in relation to the curricula of Scotland and New Zealand (Sinnema and Aitken, 2013) and of Finland, Japan, Brazil and parts of China and Canada (OECD, 2011a). Curriculum – and I refer here specifically to the planned curriculum – is increasingly deemed to be not only the concern of policymakers, but also the concern of practitioners based in schools, including school leaders and teachers. Schools are asked to address the challenges inherent in designing and implementing a local curriculum in a manner that also ensures they give effect to a national curriculum. Those challenges are strongly impacted by the degree and nature of autonomy in the national curriculum.

Although there is evidence of increasing curricular autonomy in many jurisdictions, the pattern internationally is mixed. Describing the current pattern across nations with regard to curricula (and their autonomy) is complex, given those curricula are in a constant state of change – at any given time, countries are often either embarking on, in the midst of, or responding to curriculum review processes of some sort. Central issues that are typically addressed in those reviews are about alternatives in what a revised curriculum should emphasize: autonomy versus prescription; reduced versus expanded curriculum content; local versus national priorities; and knowledge versus competencies. In some countries, New Zealand and Scotland for example, curriculum change has led to increased local decision making, greater autonomy for schools, reduced content prescribed at a national level and emphasis on competencies and capabilities. The tide of curricula autonomy in those countries might be described as high (with high freedom for teachers). In England and Australia, by contrast, the tide has been going out – with tightening of national control, prescription and regulation over curriculum, with expanding curriculum content and a more explicit emphasis on core knowledge.

The analogy of tides and curricular autonomy works in at least two ways. First, like tides, levels of curricular autonomy are different in different places at the same time. Although the issues that national curriculum reviews often respond to are sometimes quite similar in different contexts (the need for improved teaching quality, higher student achievement, schooling improvement and greater education system equity, for example), some systems take the autonomy route, whilst others the prescription route. That contrast is evident currently in the curricula of New Zealand and England. Second, like tides, levels of curricula autonomy are constantly changing. A national curriculum that is highly prescriptive at one point in time is often reported to be much less so at a subsequent point in time, and vice versa. These changes in the nature of curricula are influenced by policymakers' perceptions of the problems that policymakers seek to address in the design, or re-design, of a national curriculum. During curriculum developments in New Zealand in the mid-2000s, for example, over-crowding in the curriculum of the preceding decade was considered a problem (Le Métais, 2002). That problem was emphasized in calls to revise the curriculum and strengthen its role as a lever for improving student achievement. The revised curriculum of 2007 sought to address the over-crowding problem by significantly reducing prescription. In addition a great deal of emphasis was given, in the national curriculum itself, to the importance of schools designing a locally relevant curriculum to give effect to broad curriculum requirements. Not long after, the efforts to put a national curriculum in place in Australia began. In that context a key problem being addressed in the developments was a lack of consistency across the country, given the absence of a national curriculum. Curriculum development in Australia sought to ensure that sufficient content was outlined in the curriculum to ensure national consistency – a notable change for a country that previously did not have a national curriculum. Recent critiques of the new curriculum, however, claim that it is overcrowded and content heavy, and that depth has been compromised for breadth. Those concerns have been substantiated in a review of the Australian curriculum and accepted by policymakers as needing to be addressed:

> In announcing the Review of the Australian Curriculum, we already knew that many stakeholders had been critical of the overcrowding of the Australian Curriculum and the content being excessive, unduly rigid and prescriptive in many of the learning areas. The findings of the Review of the Australian Curriculum have confirmed that this is a real concern. (Department of Education, 2014a: 6)

One might reasonably predict that the outgoing tide in Australia is on the turn, and the tide of curricular autonomy will come back in (to at least some extent), just as it has in many jurisdictions following critique of an overcrowded curriculum. South Korea is an example where that was the case. Criticisms suggested that the heavily packed content knowledge of curriculum subjects caused students to become overwhelmed. Those criticisms led to a new curriculum in 2009 designed to both reduce academic workload for students and enhance school-based curricular autonomy (Hong and Youngs, 2014).

Situating Curricular Autonomy

Given the recent attention to curricular autonomy in policy, research and practice, it is important to also situate the concept from a theoretical point of view. In this section I outline a definition of curricular autonomy, as it is referred to in this chapter, and discuss how levels of autonomy in national curricula are strongly related to the ideologies and associated curriculum theories that inform curriculum policies.

Curricular autonomy is used here as a broad term to encompass the approaches to curriculum variously described in the literature over recent decades in ways that emphasize different aspects of autonomy. Some perspectives on autonomy emphasize the 'person' or role

that holds autonomy, for example 'teachers as curriculum makers' (Craig and Ross, 2008) or 'teacher agency in curriculum making' (Leander and Osborne, 2008; Priestley et al., 2012). Others emphasize the 'location' of the autonomy, for example 'school-based curriculum development' (Prideaux, 1993; Priestley et al., 2014; Skilbeck, 1984; Xu and Wong, 2011), school-based curriculum innovation (Darling-Hammond, 1998; Fullan, 2007) or 'local curriculum control' (Tyree, 1993). Some of the literature emphasizes not so much the person or location of the autonomy, but the 'nature' of the autonomy, for example 'professional autonomy' (Honig and Rainey, 2012; Kasher, 2005), 'freedom' (Cunningham, 2002), 'flexibility' (Nir and Eyal, 2008), 'accountable autonomy' (MacKinnon, 2011) or 'curriculum decision making' (Johnston, 1995). Despite the variations in terminology, these perspectives all have relevance to the issue of balance between national and local curricula. Furthermore, the salience of these various notions of autonomy depends greatly on the curriculum ideologies that govern the decisions of curriculum designers and policymakers. There are varying degrees of compatibility with regard to curricular autonomy within the four curriculum ideologies outlined by Schiro (2013) – scholar academic, social efficiency, learner-centred and social reconstruction.

A learner-centred ideology (Schiro, 2013) is entirely compatible with the notions of curricular autonomy. Underpinned by the image of ideal schooling put forward by Dewey and Dewey (1915), the theory of learner-centred education is that people have the right to determine what they will learn. The curriculum, under this ideology, does not require rigidly organized content, but rather opportunities for activity and experience (often referred to as project work) that is flexible and responsive to students' needs and interests.

The emphasis for teaching and learning under a learner-centred ideology is on learners having first-hand experience with reality in ways that are developmentally appropriate in order to grow, learn and construct meaning – value is placed on rich and authentic social and physical activity inside and outside the classroom. This ideology positions children as having the right to make decisions about their own learning, and does not predetermine the knowledge they will learn. The starting point of education, from a curriculum point of view, is the immediate interests of the student (Rugg and Shumaker, 1928), along with their needs and concerns (Weber, 1971).

A social-efficiency ideology (Schiro, 2013) is compatible with the notion of curricular autonomy but to a lesser extent than the learner-centred one – it treats preparation for adulthood as the ultimate goal of education, and focuses on shaping the behaviour of students towards pre-determined behavioural objectives. It is compatible with the notion of curricular autonomy because there is a degree of flexibility and recognition of a need for adjustments in response to particular students. As Schiro puts it, 'the job of teaching is to fit the student to the curriculum and fit the curriculum to the student … The curriculum developer designs curriculum for a standard student; the teacher makes adjustments for particular students' (2013: 86).

A scholar-academic ideology (Schiro, 2013) is more likely than the others to be considered incompatible with the notion of curricular autonomy. Given that this ideology foregrounds the perspective of academic disciplines and views the induction of a child into an academic discipline as the goal of a curriculum (Schiro, 2013), there is little room for autonomy, particularly with regard to curriculum content. A scholar-academic ideology is most compatible with a curriculum that is prescriptive because ensuring curriculum knowledge and content excludes any concerns other than those embodied within the discipline itself almost certainly requires prescription. Under this ideology 'all curriculum content should be drawn from the disciplines' and, furthermore, 'only knowledge contained in the disciplines is appropriate to the curriculum' (Phenix, 1962: 57–8, emphasis added).

There is, therefore, no value placed on local decision making about content in response to students' needs or interests, and therefore little place for curricular autonomy in that regard.

The fourth ideology described by Schiro (2013) is also compatible with the notion of curricular autonomy. The social reconstructionist ideology views curriculum from a social perspective, and assumes that the deep social structures involved in societal problems can be addressed through attending to the hidden curriculum that contributes to them. Curricula, when social reconstructionist in nature, are relevant to students' lives, with topics often derived from the concerns of students themselves. Notions of what is worthwhile, including curriculum content, are derived from the subjective reality of individuals. In order to meet the goals of a social reconstruction ideology, such as responding to social crisis, a social reconstructionist curriculum aspires for students who are 'motivated to understand the nature of society, envision a better society, and act to reconstruct society' (Schiro, 2013: 165–6). The purpose of addressing societal issues and inequities through connecting with students, therefore, is slightly different to the more individual purpose of connecting with students' needs and interests under the learner-centred ideology. But both suggest the relevance of a degree of curricular autonomy.

A FRAMEWORK FOR EXAMINING CURRICULAR AUTONOMY

Consideration of curricular autonomy in national curricula is a complex business because messages about autonomy in the curriculum literature and descriptions regarding prescription and autonomy in curricula themselves can be mixed or contradictory. Furthermore, those coming from different perspectives can make quite opposite claims about the curricular autonomy of the very same curriculum. This is because autonomy is a relative concept. A curriculum might be considered 'very prescriptive' if it is more so than the previous one, if it is more so than curricula in other places, or even if it is more so than an individual thinks it ought to be. In an effort to begin addressing that complexity, I propose a framework for examining curricular autonomy (see Table 59.1) that seeks to provide a common basis for describing curricular autonomy. The framework refers to both within-curriculum dimensions and beyond-curriculum dimensions – it prompts attention to what the curriculum itself indicates about curricular autonomy and also to the system dimensions that influence how that autonomy can be realized in practice.

Within-Curriculum Dimensions of Curricular Autonomy

The within-curriculum section of the framework deals both with aspects of curricula (content or competency/skill outcomes and processes) and the degrees of prescription in those aspects (broad prescription across schooling, broad prescription at particular curriculum levels and specific prescription at particular curriculum levels). The degrees of prescription are suggested as an indicator for autonomy – higher prescription signals lower autonomy, whilst less prescription signals higher autonomy. This approach (focused on identifying indicators of prescription rather than indicators of autonomy) was taken because it was deemed more useful to identify what can be seen (prescription) rather than what cannot be seen (because that which is not detailed might be considered open to local interpretation). The prescription as a proxy for autonomy approach also makes sense given that even prescription-heavy curricula make claims about curricular freedom, autonomy or flexibility. In Australia, for example, the curriculum that has led to

Table 59.1   Curricular autonomy framework

Curriculum aspects	Within curriculum dimensions of autonomy			System dimensions of autonomy	
	High autonomy	*Moderate autonomy*	*Low autonomy*	*High autonomy*	*Low autonomy*
	Broad prescription across schooling	**Broad prescription at particular curriculum levels**	**Specific prescription at particular curriculum levels**	**Low influence system elements**	**High influence system elements**
Content outcomes	Broad areas of content and concepts of subjects/ learning areas	Broad areas of content and concepts of subjects/learning areas	Specific areas of content and concepts of subjects/learning areas, including conceptual understandings or topics	System elements have low influence on curriculum content outcomes in practice	System elements have high influence on curriculum content outcomes in practice
Competency/ skill outcomes	Broad competencies and skills to be developed	Broad competencies and skills to be developed	Specific competencies and skills to be developed in relation to specific areas of content	System elements have low influence on curriculum competency/ skill outcomes in practice	System elements have high influence on curriculum competency/ skill outcomes in practice
Teaching processes	Broad teaching approaches	Broad teaching approaches	Specific teaching strategies, activities, experiences, resources	System elements have high influence on teaching processes in practice	System elements have high influence on teaching processes in practice

criticism of being content-prescription heavy is also claimed to have been developed using criteria for a quality curriculum such as 'The curriculum is flexible enough that it can accommodate the reality of student, teacher and school diversity' (Australian Curriculum, Assessment and Reporting Authority (ACARA), 2014: 6). It is apparent that claims made specifically about autonomy in a curriculum cannot be relied upon as indicators of actual curricular autonomy. The extent to which those claims can be realized depends largely upon what else a curriculum requires. A curriculum that promotes autonomy alongside prescription of just 'broad' objectives, or 'broad' guidelines for content will allow more autonomy to be realized in practice than a curriculum that also promotes autonomy but alongside the prescription of 'detailed' objectives and 'required' content.

In some places, the rhetoric of policymakers is used to signal a turn in the tide toward autonomy when key features of the curriculum policy work against that turn. The England National Curriculum in place in 2014, for example, speaks of teachers having freedom to shape the curriculum to their pupils' needs. Although it sets out a core of essential knowledge, and not the knowledge required across all areas of learning (hence the argument for describing it as allowing teachers freedom), what it sets out in those core areas is very much more prescriptive than in other places. In the England National Curriculum, although there is the appearance of some flexibility, limits on that espoused flexibility are clear:

> Schools are, however, only required to teach the relevant programme of study by the end of the key stage. Within each key stage, schools therefore have the flexibility to introduce content earlier or later than set out in the programme of study. In addition, schools can introduce key stage content during an earlier key stage if appropriate. (Department for Education, 2013a: 6)

In other words, there is flexibility only in the timing of implementation of highly prescriptive curriculum content. Furthermore, the appearance of flexibility signalled by the term 'guidance' is somewhat misleading because clarifications about the 'statutory guidance' make clear that it is not so much presented to guide, but rather to ensure, as a statutory requirement, that 'Schools and local authorities are required by law to follow the statutory guidance that applies to them. These publications reflect the current legal position' (Department for Education, 2014a: para 1). The language of compulsion is prevalent in the programmes of study that comprise the 'statutory guidance'. In those programmes of study there are statements about what schools 'must start teaching', and what 'must be taught', with a signal that only examples provided between square brackets or explicitly labelled non-statutory are not required by law (Department for Education, 2013a).

Beyond-Curriculum Dimensions of Curricular Autonomy: The Influence of System Elements

The extent to which aspirations for curricular autonomy can be achieved is also influenced by the educational context beyond the curriculum itself. The approach taken and expectations set out in other system elements inevitably create conditions for implementation. Those conditions may influence curriculum in ways that either promote or constrain curricular autonomy in practice. Examples include the approach to assessment, national testing, inspection and evaluation in schools and teaching processes promoted in professional learning opportunities and resources. In some jurisdictions, there is a paradox at play – autonomy on the one hand and constraint on the other. As Glatter (2012: 564) puts it in reference to the system in England, 'a paradox of the current position is that despite the persistent and growing emphasis on autonomy most school practitioners consider themselves significantly constrained by government requirements'. The government requirement for inspection in Scotland

See OECD-designed LFE

alongside a curriculum that gives a great deal of freedom to teachers is one such example of supposed autonomy being constrained – as MacKinnon notes, 'school inspection with its basis in specifications and fixed measures conflicts with the formative agenda of the incoming curriculum, causing a barrier to its creative realisation in schools' (MacKinnon, 2011: 89). This paradox, which is widespread in OECD countries at least, is seen when there are simultaneous initiatives to decentralize curriculum and centralize for learning (Looney, 2011). In the education systems of more than half of the OECD education systems, Kärkkäinen (2012) reports, there are criterion-referenced test-based national examinations and/or assessments for all lower-secondary school students, which limit the extent to which schools can exercise the freedom they ostensibly have for innovation and curriculum decision making.

Trade-Offs in Curricular Decisions

The changing patterns of curricular autonomy internationally indicate the trade-offs that are made in curriculum design decisions in different contexts. Those decisions depend on the weight given to perceived benefits and risks when considered in relation to the issues of particular educational contexts. A perceived benefit of enhancing teacher efficacy, for example, might be given weight in a time of teacher contract negotiations. Similarly, the risk of increasing variability in teacher practice and outcomes might have weight for those determining autonomy levels when results of global assessments point to a pattern of underachievement. The question of balance between national prescription and local autonomy cannot be considered without attention to context. Just as a balanced diet looks different for individuals with different health conditions and medical issues, so does a balanced curriculum looks different for educational systems with varying conditions and issues. Benefits and risks to consider in examining balance are elaborated next.

The Benefits of Curricular Autonomy

Calls for curricular autonomy, and claims about its benefits, are by no means new. As long ago as 1925 there was talk in the literature of the warrant for local curriculum making. As Bobbitt (1925) explained,

> educational plans will not be properly appreciated and understood if they are merely taken over from some outside source. Those responsible for the work come to realize the nature and intent of the plans through formulating them. Local curriculum-making, therefore, should be the method of arriving at the curriculum for any community. (1925: 654)

This claim, like many others since, focuses on the benefit of practitioners being heavily involved in curriculum design, which is evident when they come to implement the curriculum – the ownership argument (Bakah et al., 2012; Brennan, 2011; Huizinga et al., 2014; Johansen, 1967). A lack of ownership of the curriculum in the Australian context, for example, has been attributed to a curriculum development process that failed to engage well with professional associations and teachers (Australian Government, 2014).

An alternative argument about participation in curriculum design leading to better implementation is the argument that autonomy creates space for innovation (Fullan, 2007). In other words it broadens the scope of implementation possibilities beyond those that a prescriptive curriculum might include. Space for innovation is argued by some to be desirable because practitioners can develop local solutions for local problems in ways that are responsive to their students' particular needs. Furthermore, responses developed through local experimentation can subsequently benefit those in other schools – horizontal spread.

There is also a professional identity and satisfaction argument for practitioner participation in curriculum design – this argument suggests that not only does participation in the process make implementation more likely, but it also gives practitioners greater satisfaction and a stronger sense of professional identity as they go about that implementation (Howells, 2003). When teachers are free of central regulation and able to make decisions about what they teach as well as how they teach, they have better morale and enjoy their work more. But that argument is a contested one. The logic is not entirely supported in empirical studies of curriculum design and implementation, including a study of curriculum control and teachers' perceptions of autonomy and satisfaction by Archbald and Porter (1994). In response to the contention that 'large-scale testing, prescriptive curriculum guides, and textbook adoption regulations are antithetic to teacher professionalism' (Archbald and Porter, 1994: 31), they compared the ratings of 195 teachers from districts in the US categorized as high, medium or low control. In the high control districts there were detailed curriculum guides (which prescribed units, topics and lesson ideas), the requirement to adopt a single set textbook and district-wide tests for courses. In the low control districts, by contrast, curriculum guides were completely voluntary and non-prescriptive (without details or connection to set textbooks), leaving much room for interpretation. Results from teachers' ratings on two empowerment scales (self-efficacy and job satisfaction) were ambiguous. Differences between the ratings of teachers in the three control categories on the self-efficacy scale were not statistically significantly different. On the satisfaction scale, ratings were statistically significantly different only between the low and medium groups, but not between the low and high control group.

Archbald and Porter's (1994) findings did not support the contention that greater control would lead to reduced satisfaction. They also found that higher control policies, despite what one might expect, did not lead teachers to report higher levels of control over instruction – 'despite prescribed textbooks, specific course content guidelines, and required district tests for each course, teachers reported high levels of control over instruction' (Archbald and Porter, 1994: 35).

The authors suggested that teachers continued to have control over when and how to follow the policies, and the predisposition to teach prescribed topics explained that finding. Similar findings were reported in a more recent study of teachers in Florida by Pearson and Moomaw (2005). They found that 'as curriculum autonomy increased on-the-job stress decreased, but there was little association between curriculum autonomy and job satisfaction' (2005: 47).

Other claims about the benefits of autonomy go beyond just those relating to teachers. There are suggestions that improved student achievement and schooling improvement also result from greater curricular freedom for teachers and schools. As Honig and Rainey (2012) explain in relation to reform in the US, 'autonomous schools' and 'empowerment schools' initiatives are based on assumptions about the influence of autonomy:

> "autonomy" – generally defined in policy designs as authority over key decisions about school improvement – will enable schools to develop and implement approaches to teaching and learning that better build on their strengths and address the needs of their students than if policy makers or others outside schools made those decisions. In turn, such initiatives will leverage improvements in student learning. (Honig and Rainey, 2012: 466)

There are those, however, who consider claims about the benefits of curricular autonomy to be at best not compelling and at worst outweighed by significant risks.

Risks in Curricular Autonomy

There are a number of perceived risks of curricula creating space for or having emphasis on local decision-making. Those risks focus on both teachers (what they are capable of and how they regard autonomy) and also on students (in particular, their curriculum entitlement and entitlement to equity).

First, a risk of greater curriculum autonomy is that teachers' desire for autonomy might not be matched by their capacity and expertise. This risk does not seek to downplay the capacity and expertise teachers have for teaching, but rather to highlight the quite different expertise required to meet the demands of the task of designing curricula. If it is true that teachers lack both the design expertise (Huizinga et al., 2014; Nir and Eyal, 2008) and the capacity to develop a curriculum at school level (Priestley et al., 2014), then cautions laid out by Archbald and Porter (1994) should be heeded. They cautioned that one cannot assume, as those promoting greater discretion for local actors do, that 'in the absence of central curriculum control policies, local actors would make different and better content and pedagogical decisions leading to improved student achievement' (Archbald and Porter, 1994: 21). This issue highlights the debate between those who see teachers as lacking capability, and those who view teachers as capable curriculum makers, who are knowing and knowledgeable about such matters and the appropriate people to be designing curricula (Clandinin and Connelly, 1992; Craig, 2006; Craig and Ross, 2008; Schwab, 1969, 2013).

There are limits to the capacity of even the most capable of teachers and this has important implications for the expectations (or autonomy) placed on teachers for curriculum design. Drawing on the example of the 1997 New Zealand Social Studies Curriculum, Aitken (2005) explains how the 'discretionary space' (Hlebowitsh, 2005) afforded teachers in that curriculum meant that teachers were left with an impossible task – impossible from a cognitive load perspective because it required them to deal with the integration of more elements than is actually possible. Those elements included a subject aim, five conceptual strands, two achievement aims for each strand, two achievement objectives per strand achievement aim, three to four indicators per achievement objective, three processes with one achievement aim, an achievement objective per process and 206 indicators per process achievement objective, five perspectives, five settings and 19 aspects of essential learning about New Zealand society. The task of considering, simultaneously, all of the required elements and also the number of interacting elements

meant the cognitive load required for the task was excessively high and beyond the working memory capacity of any individual (Sweller, 1994). Although it is possible for curriculum design features to reduce the associated extraneous cognitive load (the load arising from how a task is represented), when the intrinsic load of the task itself is excessive, as is likely for those seeking to make sense of and implement permissive curricula, the load is simply too high. When curricula are not designed in ways that address such issues, there is the risk of confusion, contradiction and uncertainty being perpetuated about the status of a curriculum (Aitken, 2005). A permissiveness curriculum, combined with excessive intrinsic load and insufficient attention to design features for reducing extraneous cognitive load might be considered a recipe for implementation failure. That failure implicates curriculum designers rather than teachers.

A second frequently mentioned risk is focused not so much on the capability of teachers or the relevance of curriculum design work to their role, but on their response to such demands. Although the Pearson and Moomaw (2005) study described earlier found that greater curriculum autonomy was associated with lower levels of teacher stress, for some this autonomy brings with it a burden that is unwelcome. That seems to be so across different contexts – in New Zealand, for example, where new-found freedom for curriculum decision-making was considered by teachers to be both a blessing and a burden (Sinnema, 2011) and in China where greater freedom followed the previously tightly prescribed curriculum prescription. As Xu and Wong (2011) explain, curriculum reforms gave teachers a new role beyond their previous role as passive curriculum implementers – the role of curriculum developers. That role, however, was not well received:

> Ironically enough, this top–down honorable invitation has not yet been welcomed by teachers....the policy has not been kindly accepted by teachers and schools in many places as expected in the process of implementation. On the contrary, not only do many teachers and schools refuse the

offer, but they also regard it as an extra burden that they have been trying to undertake or even to escape. (Xu and Wong, 2011: 47)

The third risk is one focused not so much on teachers, as the first two risks are, but on students – the risk of jeopardizing the curriculum entitlement that a prescriptive national curriculum ensures for students. A curriculum entitlement refers to a legislated statement of what all students are entitled to have access to and, therefore, expectation for curriculum provision. It is prominent in most national curriculum policies. Although the specifics of the entitlement varies, the underpinning principle of entitlement and positioning of equity as central to it, is common across countries. For example, this was established in the national curriculum of the 1980s in England:

Pupils should be entitled to the same opportunities wherever they go to school...ensuring that all pupils, regardless of sex, ethnic origin and geographical location have access to broadly the same good and relevant curriculum and programmes of study which include the key content, skills and processes which they need to learn and which ensure that the content and teaching of the various elements of the national curriculum bring out their relevance to and links with pupils' own experiences and their practical applications and continuing value to adult and working life. (Department of Education and Science, 1987: paras 7, 8)

A similar notion of entitlement is evident in the more recent curriculum in Scotland, despite the form of that curriculum being quite different to that in England:

All children and young people in Scotland have an entitlement to a curriculum which will support them in developing their values and beliefs and enable them to: develop knowledge and understanding of society, the world and Scotland's place in it. (Scottish Government, 2008: 14)

Although the notion of an entitlement is widely accepted, the nature of the knowledge students are entitled to is somewhat contested – there are those who argue for the inclusion of everyday knowledge serving instrumental purposes, whilst others argue

that what matters is access for all to powerful knowledge (Rata, 2011; Young and Muller, 2010), the knowledge of the disciplines that takes young people beyond their own experience. The risk of high levels of autonomy in curricula is that such powerful knowledge cannot be ensured from a policy point of view. Students are at the mercy of individual schools or teachers regarding the knowledge they encounter, and equity is threatened. As Sabar and Mathias (2003) report, there are questions about whether greater curricular autonomy in Israel supports social solidarity, integration and equal opportunity for all, or whether it perpetuates gaps, division and disparity between cultures and social groups.

A final risk, as perceived by some, is that of reduced regulation of evidence-informed practice, be that in the form of scaling up exemplary interventions (McDonald et al., 2006) or using syntheses of evidence for educational improvement (Alton-Lee, 2011). There are strong arguments for the view that reducing the potential influence of such evidence is undesirable. Although it is possible for a prescriptive national curriculum policy to embed the learning from research evidence in the requirements it sets out, a less prescriptive curriculum might be seen as leaving to chance the influence of significant research findings. That argument could be unwarranted where there is local capacity for and commitment to engaging with research because schools could ensure their curriculum and implementation responds to research of most relevance to that setting, in a way that would not be possible if greater central control is in place.

The appropriateness of best methods approaches, when applied to education, is not, it should be noted, universally accepted. There are those who raise questions about its logic on the basis that 'identifying a general set of best methods that holds for particularized teaching problems and teaching contexts is dubious at best and arguably impossible' (Hlebowitsh, 2012: 3). However, when combined with a requirement for inquiry-oriented practice alongside engagement with research, as in the teaching as inquiry model of the New Zealand curriculum, that risk is largely mitigated. In that curriculum model it is made clear that the general explanations about best practice do not hold, but rather increase the likelihood (not certainty) of effective teaching, and should inform (not determine) decisions that are subject to practitioner inquiry in their own context (Sinnema and Aitken, 2011, 2012, 2014).

APPLICATION OF THE CURRICULAR AUTONOMY FRAMEWORK

This section explores the use of the curricular autonomy framework introduced earlier to compare two contrasting curriculum cases – the New Zealand Curriculum and the England National Curriculum. It demonstrates how the framework can form the basis of a curricular autonomy profile that indicates the degree of prescription of content outcomes, competency/skill outcomes and teaching processes.

The England National Curriculum

The profile in Table 59.2 for the England National Curriculum is explained by drawing on examples from the History, Science and English programme of study.

Prescription of content outcomes

The History programme of study (Department for Education, 2013b) is a particularly relevant example for considering the prescription of content outcomes given persistent controversies and debates over time regarding the prescription of historical content knowledge – debates about what should be prescribed and, furthermore, whose version of the past should be represented in that prescription (Harris and Burn, 2011). In the 2013 programme of study there is broad prescription of content across schooling for History (cell A1 in Table 59.2). It outlines, for example, that the purpose of history education is to 'help pupils gain a coherent knowledge and understanding of Britain's past and that of the wider world. It should inspire pupils' curiosity to know more about the past' (Department for Education, 2013b: 1) and aims include that all pupils 'know and understand the history of these islands as a coherent, chronological narrative, from the earliest times to the present day: how people's lives have shaped this nation and how Britain has influenced and been influenced by the wider world' (Department for Education, 2013b: 1) and 'know and understand significant aspects of the history of the wider world: the nature of ancient civilisations; the expansion and dissolution of empires; characteristic features of past non-European societies; achievements and follies of mankind' (Department for Education, 2013b: 1). There is also broad prescription of content at particular

Table 59.2 Applying the curricular autonomy framework

Aspect of prescription	England National Curriculum			The New Zealand Curriculum		
	1. Broad prescription across schooling	2. Broad prescription at particular curriculum levels	3. Specific prescription at particular curriculum levels	1. Broad prescription across schooling	2. Broad prescription at particular curriculum levels	3. Specific prescription at particular curriculum levels
A. Content outcomes	*	*	*	*		
B. Competency/ skill outcomes	*	*	*	*		
C. Teaching processes	*	*	*			

curriculum levels (see cell A2 in Table 59.2). In History, at key stage 2, for example, 'pupils should continue to develop a chronologically secure knowledge and understanding of British, local and world history, establishing clear narratives within and across the periods they study' (Department for Education, 2013b: 3). That prescription goes even further by setting out specific topics required at particular levels (cell A3 in Table 59.2). At key stage 2 in History, the list of what students should be taught includes changes in Britain from the Stone Age to the Iron Age; Britain's settlement by Anglo-Saxons and Scots; the achievements of the earliest civilizations (an overview of where and when the first civilizations appeared and an in-depth study of one of the following: Ancient Sumer, The Indus Valley, Ancient Egypt, or The Shang Dynasty of Ancient China); and Ancient Greece (a study of Greek life and achievements and their influence on the Western world as well as a local history study).

Prescription of Competency/Skill Outcomes

There is prescription of competencies and skills in the England National Curriculum in broad terms across schooling (cell B1 in Table 59.2) and at particular curriculum levels (cell B2 in Table 59.2). In History it is prescribed that students will 'understand the methods of historical enquiry, including how evidence is used rigorously to make historical claims, and discern how and why contrasting arguments and interpretations of the past have been constructed' (Department for Education, 2013b: 1). In addition, there are similar prescriptions for competency outcomes at particular key stages.

Prescription of Process

In England some broad teaching processes that should apply across schooling are prescribed (cell C1 in Table 59.2). The Science programme, for example, states 'teachers should ensure that pupils build secure foundations by using discussion to probe and remedy their misconceptions' (Department

for Education, 2013c: 4). There are also statements prescribing broad prescription of teaching processes at particular curriculum levels (cell C2 in Table 59.2). In the English programme of study, this is seen through the requirement to use a systematic phonics programme for students still struggling at Year 2 to decode and spell (Department for Education, 2013a).

The New Zealand Curriculum

The profile in Table 59.2 for the New Zealand National Curriculum is explained by drawing on examples from the Social Sciences learning area (used as the example because it parallels the History one outlined earlier) and from more general sections of the policy.

Prescription of Content Outcomes

In New Zealand the most recent national curriculum drastically reduced the extent to which content outcomes were prescribed. In the curricula of the 1990s, detailed sets of numerous achievement objectives were outlined at each of seven levels for each aim of each strand in each curriculum area. This resulted in many hundreds of achievement objectives to be addressed by teachers. The 2007 curriculum, in contrast, sets out short statements (just one or two pages) for each learning area that prescribe, broadly, the compulsory content. They state what the learning area is about, the rationale for studying it and an explanation of how it is structured (including the broad strands within the learning area). Although achievement objectives are still provided, they are not compulsory and have the status of guidance only – schools are free to use them as is, but are encouraged to select from them and develop their own.

The curriculum statement for Social Sciences (Ministry of Education, 2007a) for example, like those for other learning areas, prescribes the broad content required across schooling for that learning area (cell A1 in Table 59.2). It signals, for example, that the social sciences are about 'how societies work and how people can participate as critical, active, informed, and responsible citizens. Contexts are drawn from the past, present, and future and from places within and beyond New Zealand' (Ministry of Education, 2007a: 30). It also signals the overarching purpose of the learning area throughout schooling (including to better understand, participate in and contribute to the local, national and global communities in which they live and work) and a general statement of what students learn about (people, places, cultures, histories, and the economic world, within and beyond New Zealand), as well as the conceptual strands that should be addressed (identity, culture and organisation; place and environment; continuity and change; and the economic world). The broadness of what is prescribed can be seen, for example, in the aim for the place and environment strand – 'students learn about how people perceive, represent, interpret, and interact with places and environments. They come to understand the relationships that exist between people and the environment' (Ministry of Education, 2007b: 30). The nature of the perceptions, representations, interpretations and interactions and the conceptual understandings relating to those are left for teachers to determine, and the contexts used – the particular places and environments and people(s) of focus – are also left to teachers. Importantly, the freedoms signalled by the broadness of the curriculum prescription is somewhat constrained when beyond-curriculum elements are taken into account. National standards for reading, writing and mathematics in Years 1–8 developed shortly after the curriculum policy itself are much more specific in signalling priority outcomes for each curriculum level – specificity that was welcomed by some but criticized by others for, amongst other issues, removing the freedoms promised in the curriculum.

Prescription of Competency/Skill Outcomes

Five key competencies are prescribed in the New Zealand Curriculum (Ministry of Education, 2007b). These capabilities for living and lifelong learning are thinking; using language, symbols, and texts; managing self; relating to others; and participating and contributing. They are explained to be 'more complex than skills' because they 'draw on knowledge, attitudes, and values in a way that lead to action' (Ministry of Education, 2007b: 12). They are considered key to learning in the learning areas, and broad statements about each are outlined that apply across schooling. Skill outcomes are referred to in the learning area statements particular to certain learning areas (social inquiry in the social sciences, for example), and these also apply across schooling – there are no similar prescriptions for competencies or skills that apply to specific levels of the curriculum.

Prescription of Process

The New Zealand Curriculum emphasizes process through a prominently positioned section on effective pedagogy. It sets out broad statements of pedagogical approaches for which there is evidence of positive impacts on student learning. These suggest teachers should create a supportive learning environment, encourage reflective thought and action, enhance the relevance of new learning, facilitate shared learning, make connections to prior learning and experience, and provide sufficient opportunities to learn. It also sets out a model of effective pedagogy – teaching as inquiry, which requires three kinds of inquiry: focusing inquiry, teaching inquiry and learning inquiry (Sinnema and Aitken, 2011; Sinnema, Sewell, and Milligan, 2011). The focusing inquiry requires attention to the priorities for students given curriculum requirements, community expectations and, most importantly, the learning needs, interests and experiences of the learner. The teaching inquiry requires attention to outcomes-linked research evidence and also practitioner experience to inform decisions about teaching strategies. The learning inquiry requires teachers to systematically examine the impact of teaching actions on student outcomes and experience, and the relationship between the teaching and students' learning. This falls outside the sections of the curriculum document that are officially required, but its prominence in curriculum implementation support, professional learning initiatives and resources for school leaders and teachers gave it much the same status as other elements of the curriculum that were officially prescribed.

Balance Between National Prescription and Local Autonomy in Curriculum

Curriculum policymakers in countries seeking to address similar educational issues respond quite differently, from a curriculum point of view, when their profiles of autonomy are compared. Notions of balance vary from place to place and over time. The question of

balance in the degree of national prescription and local autonomy in a curriculum is not a normative one (what degree of prescription versus autonomy ought a national curriculum have?), but a contextual one, given the educational context of a particular system at a particular point in time (what degree of prescription versus autonomy in a curriculum could be justified and in relation to which curriculum elements?). Aspects of an educational context of particular relevance to that question are outlined in Figure 59.1.

Those designing curricula need to be attentive in their decision-making about autonomy within the curriculum to the dimensions beyond the curriculum that will enable or constrain that autonomy (as outlined in Table 59.1 – the curricular autonomy framework). They also need to consider balance with regard to system conditions, including the accountability context (such as assessment

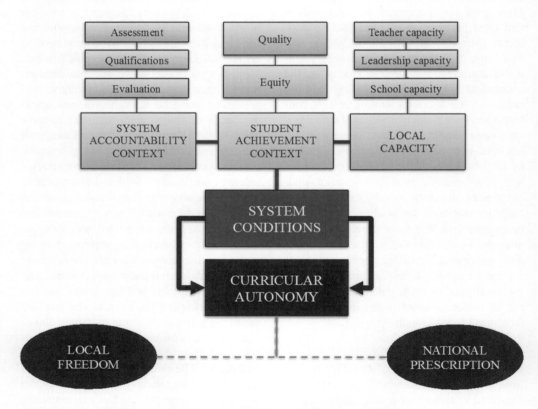

Figure 59.1   Balance in curricular autonomy: the role of system conditions

systems, qualifications frameworks and approaches to school principal and teacher evaluation), the student achievement context (including both the quality of achievement and equity of achievement across a system) and local capacity (the capacity of teachers, school leaders and schools to design and give effect to a curriculum).

Achieving appropriate balance between local freedom and national prescription requires policymakers, researchers, curriculum designers and practitioners to engage in a process of dialogue about all the system conditions that have implications for curricular autonomy. Such a process is likely to improve the quality of implementation as well as the quality of the curriculum itself (by quality I refer to the suitability of a curriculum for a given context at a given time). The appropriate weight to give to the various system conditions when making curricular autonomy decisions will vary from place to place and at different times. More weight should be given, arguably, to local capacity in contexts where there is widespread low capacity alongside low levels of system equity in student achievement. In that context an argument could reasonably be made for increased prescription. Slightly less weight might be given to local capacity where there is extremely high leadership capacity alongside low, but an improving teacher capacity and tight alignment between assessment frameworks and the curriculum itself. In that context an argument could reasonably be made for increased autonomy.

Without consideration of system conditions there is the potential for a lack of coherence in the policies practitioners are expected to give effect to. A lack of coherence will lead to competing pressures that increase the challenge of implementation. One potential pressure is a combination of flexibility for teachers to determine relevant local outcomes, whilst simultaneously having accountability for different outcomes determined nationally. Another is the pressure to deal effectively with both national and local achievement issues – tighter prescription risks supporting national student achievement priorities at the expense of local ones, whilst looser prescription risks the opposite. Furthermore, without attention to local capacity, practitioners will face one of two challenges: either the challenge of dealing with local freedom for curriculum decisions for which there is insufficient capacity or the frustration of curricular constraint that is inappropriate given the level of professional capacity and expertise at the local level.

The call for dialogue about and responsiveness to system conditions positions curriculum design itself as a behaviour that is derived from the theory of action of the curriculum designer. Theories of action all have the same form, 'in situation S, if you want to achieve consequence C, do A' (Argyris and Schön, 1974: 5). Applied to curriculum, the adequacy of the theory depends, at least in part, on the scope and rigorousness of the consideration given to the situation. There is a risk that curriculum designers, when persuaded by firmly held curriculum ideologies, will focus on the final part of a theory of action ('if you want to achieve consequence C, do A), without adequate consideration of relevant system conditions. It is the task of those leading the curriculum revision work to engage with, critique and integrate the multiple theories that inform an overall theory of use – these include but are not limited to theories about curriculum (Schiro, 2013), theories of professionalism (Pratte and Rury, 1988), and theories about the current system context with regard to accountability, achievement and capacity.

Curricular autonomy, when intelligently combined with accountability, has been associated with better student performance. The OECD reported that 'the greater the number of schools that have the responsibility to define and elaborate their curricula and assessments, the better the performance of the entire school system, even after accounting for national income' (OECD, 2011b: 2). That finding has important implications for questions of autonomy in national curriculum revisions, but it should not be assumed, as the policy borrowing literature warns, that the association between curricular autonomy and better student performance will hold across different contexts. Context, as Philipps and Ochs (2003: 457) explain, has complex significance, given 'the "embeddedness" of aspects of educational approaches and provision in the locally prevailing cultural and other conditions'.

The suggestion that 'intelligent' combination of autonomy and accountability might contribute to better outcomes for students requires systematic analysis of the current curricular autonomy profile and of the current system conditions. Identifying the current curricular autonomy profile of a national curriculum will deepen understandings about what changes to that profile will mean for those implementing a curriculum policy. Identifying system conditions will provide insight into the constraints on action – the limitations and affordances of system elements that influence the likelihood of a curriculum, be it a flexible or prescriptive one, being implemented in accordance with its intentions.

REFERENCES

Aitken, G. (2005) 'Curriculum Design in New Zealand Social Studies: Learning from the Past', EdD doctoral thesis, The University of Auckland, Auckland, New Zealand. Available from https://researchspace.auckland.ac.nz/handle/2292/22856 (accessed 2 October 2014).

Alton-Lee, A. (2011) '(Using) evidence for educational improvement', Cambridge Journal of Education, 3: 303–29. doi: 10.1080/0305764X.2011.607150.

Archbald, D.A. and Porter, A.C. (1994) 'Curriculum control and teachers' perceptions of autonomy and satisfaction', Educational Evaluation and Policy Analysis, 16(1): 21–39. doi: 10.3102/01623737016001021.

Argyris, C. and Schön, D. (1974) Theory in Practice: Increasing Professional Effectiveness. New York, NY: Jossey-Bass.

Australian Curriculum, Assessment and Reporting Authority (ACARA) (2014) 'Review of the Australian Curriculum: A Statement by the Australian Curriculum, Assessment and Reporting Authority. Available from http://www.acara.edu.au/verve/_resources/STATEMENT_Review_of_the_Australian_Curriculum_20140324.pdf (accessed 29 September 2014).

Australian Government (2014) Review of the Australian Curriculum. Available from https://docs.education.gov.au/documents/review-australian-curriculum-final-report (accessed 29 September 2014).

Bakah, M.A.B., Voogt, J.M. and Pieters, J.M. (2012) 'Advancing perspectives of sustainability and large-scale implementation of design teams in Ghana's polytechnics: issues and opportunities', International Journal of Educational Development, 32: 787–96.

Bobbitt, F. (1925) 'Difficulties to be met in local curriculum-making', The Elementary School Journal, 25(9): 653. doi: 10.1086/455785.

Brennan, M. (2011) 'National curriculum: a political–educational tangle', Australian Journal of Education, 55(3): 259–80. doi: 10.1177/000494411105500307.

Clandinin, D.J. and Connelly, F.M. (1992) 'Teacher as curriculum maker', in P. W. Jackson (ed.), Handbook of Curriculum. New York, NY: Macmillan. pp. 363–401.

Craig, C.J. (2006) 'Why is dissemination so difficult? The nature of teacher knowledge and the spread of curriculum reform', American Educational Research Journal, 43(2): 257–93. doi: 10.3102/00028312043002257.

Craig, C.J. and Ross, V. (2008) 'Cultivating the image of teachers as curriculum makers', in M.F. Connelly, M.F. He and J. Phillion (eds.), The Sage Handbook of Curriculum and Instruction. Thousand Oaks, CA: Sage Publications. pp. 282–306.

Cunningham, P. (2002) 'Progressivism, decentralisation and recentralisation: local education authorities and the primary curriculum, 1902–2002', Oxford Review of Education, 28(2/3): 217–33. doi: 10.1080/03054980220143388.

Darling-Hammond, L. (1998) 'Policy and change: getting beyond bureaucracy', in A. Hargreaves, A. Lieberman, M. Fullan and D. Hopkins (eds.), International Handbook of Educational Change, Part 1. Dordrecht, Netherlands: Kluwer Academic Publishers. pp. 642–67.

Department for Education (2013a) English Programmes of Study: Key Stages 1 and 2.

National Curriculum in England. London: Crown Publishing.

Department for Education (2013b) *History Programmes of Study: Key Stages 1 and 2. National Curriculum in England*. London: Crown Publishing

Department for Education (2013c) *Science Programmes of Study: Key Stages 1 and 2. National Curriculum in England*. London: Crown Publishing.

Department for Education (2014a) *The Department for Education's Statutory Guidance Publications for Schools and Local Authorities*. Available from https://www.gov.uk/government/collections/statutory-guidance-schools (accessed 29 September 2014).

Department of Education (2014b) *Review of the Australian Curriculum: Initial Australian Government Response*. Australian Government. Available from http://docs.education.gov.au/system/files/doc/other/initial_australian_government_response_final_0.pdf (accessed 29 September 2014).

Department of Education and Science (1987) *The National Curriculum 5–16. A Consultation Document*. London: HMSO.

Dewey, E. and Dewey, J. (1915) *Schools of Tomorrow*. New York, NY: E.P. Dutton.

Fullan, M. (2007) *The New Meaning of Educational Change*. New York, NY: Teachers College Press.

Glatter, R. (2012) 'Persistent preoccupations: the rise and rise of school autonomy and accountability in England', *Educational Management Administration and Leadership*, 40(5): 559–75. doi: 10.1177/1741143212451171.

Harris, R. and Burn, K. (2011) 'Curriculum theory, curriculum policy and the problem of ill-disciplined thinking', *Journal of Education Policy*, 26(2): 245–61. doi: 10.1080/02680939.2010.498902.

Hlebowitsh, P. (2005) *Designing the School Curriculum*. Boston, MA: Pearson Education.

Hlebowitsh, P. (2012) 'When best practices aren't: a Schwabian perspective on teaching', *Journal of Curriculum Studies*, 44(1): 1–12. doi: 10.1080/00220272.2011.637184.

Hong, W.-P. and Youngs, P. (2014) 'Why are teachers afraid of curricular autonomy? Contradictory effects of the new national curriculum in South Korea', *Asia-Pacific Journal of Education*, 1–14. doi: 10.1080/02188791.2014.959471.

Honig, M.I. and Rainey, L.R. (2012) 'Autonomy and school improvement: what do we know and where do we go from here?', *Educational Policy*, 26(3): 465–95. doi: 10.1177/0895904811417590.

Howells, H. (2003) 'Teacher professionalism and curriculum power: a cautionary tale', *English in Australia*, 136: 27–39.

Huizinga, T., Handelzalts, A., Nieveen, N. and Voogt, J.M. (2014) 'Teacher involvement in curriculum design: need for support to enhance teachers' design expertise', *Journal of Curriculum Studies*, 46(1): 33–57. doi: 10.1080/00220272.2013.834077.

Johansen, J.H. (1967) 'The relationships between teachers' perceptions of influence in local curriculum decision-making and curriculum implementation', *The Journal of Educational Research*, 61(2): 81–3.

Johnston, S. (1995) 'Curriculum decision making at the school level: is it just a case of teachers learning to act like administrators?', *Journal of Curriculum and Supervision*, 10(2): 136–54.

Kärkkäinen, K. (2012) *Bringing about Curriculum Innovations: Implicit Approaches in the OECD Area*. Paris: OECD.

Kasher, A. (2005) 'Professional ethics and collective professional autonomy: a conceptual analysis', *Ethical Perspectives*, 12(1): 67–97.

Leander, K.M. and Osborne, M.D. (2008) 'Complex positioning: teachers as agents of curricular and pedagogical reform', *Journal of Curriculum Studies*, 40(1): 23–46.

Le Métais, J. (2002) *New Zealand Stocktake: An International Critique*. Wellington, New Zealand: The Ministry of Education.

Looney, J. (2011) 'Alignment in complex education systems: achieving balance and coherence', OECD Education Working Papers, No. 64. Paris: OECD.

MacKinnon, N. (2011) 'The urgent need for new approaches in school evaluation to enable Scotland's curriculum for excellence', *Educational Assessment, Evaluation and Accountability*, 23(1): 89–106. doi: 10.1007/s11092-011-9116-4.

McDonald, S.-K., Keesler, V.A., Kauffman, N.J. and Schneider, B. (2006) 'Scaling-up exemplary interventions', *Educational Researcher*, 35(3): 15–24. doi: 10.2307/3700103.

Ministry of Education (2007a) *Social Sciences in the New Zealand Curriculum*. Wellington,

New Zealand: New Zealand Government Available from http://nzcurriculum.tki.org.nz/The-New-Zealand-Curriculum/Learning-areas/Social-sciences (accessed 30 September 2014).

Ministry of Education (2007b) *The New Zealand Curriculum*. Wellington, New Zealand: Learning Media.

Nir, A.E. and Eyal, O. (2008) 'Setting a national curriculum: bridging the gap between professionalism and politics', in J.N. Casey and R.E. Upton (eds.), *Educational Curricula: Development and Evaluation*. New York, NY: Nova Science Publishers. pp. 235–51.

Organisation for Economic Co-operation and Development (OECD) (2011a) *Lessons from PISA for the United States, Strong Performers and Successful Reformers in Education*. Paris: OECD.

Organisation for Economic Co-operation and Development (OECD) (2011b) *School Autonomy and Accountability: Are They Related to Student Performance? PISA in Focus*. Paris: OECD.

Pearson, L.C. and Moomaw, W. (2005) 'The relationship between teacher autonomy and stress, work satisfaction, empowerment, and professionalism', *Educational Research Quarterly,* 29(1): 37–53.

Phenix, P.H. (ed.) (1962) *The Disciplines as Curriculum Content*. New York, NY: Teachers College Press.

Phillips, D. and Ochs, K. (2003) 'Processes of policy borrowing in education: some explanatory and analytical devices', *Comparative Education,* 39(4): 451–61. doi: 10.1080/0305006032000162020.

Pratte, R. and Rury, J.L. (1988) 'Professionalism, autonomy, and teachers', *Educational Policy,* 2(1): 71–89. doi: 10.1177/0895904888002001005.

Prideaux, D. (1993) 'School-based curriculum development: partial, paradoxical and piecemeal', *Journal of Curriculum Studies,* 25(2): 169–78. doi: 10.1080/0022027930250206.

Priestley, M., Edwards, R., Priestley, A. and Miller, K. (2012) 'Teacher agency in curriculum making: agents of change and spaces for manoeuvre', *Curriculum Inquiry,* 43(2): 191–214.

Priestley, M., Minty, S. and Eager, M. (2014) 'School-based curriculum development in Scotland: curriculum policy and enactment',

Pedagogy, Culture and Society, 22(2): 189–211. doi: 10.1080/14681366.2013.812137.

Rata, E. (2011) 'The politics of knowledge in education', *British Educational Research Journal,* 38(1): 103–24. doi: 10.1080/01411926.2011.615388.

Rugg, H.O. and Shumaker, A. (1928) *The Child-Centered School*. New York, NY: World Book.

Sabar, N. and Mathias, Y. (2003) 'Curriculum planning at the threshold of the third millennium: The Israeli case', in W.F. Pinar (ed.), *International Handbook of Curriculum Research*. Hillsdale, NJ: Lawrence Erlbaum Associates. pp. 381–400.

Schiro, M. (2013) *Curriculum Theory: Conflicting Visions and Enduring Concerns*. 2nd edn. Thousand Oaks, CA: Sage Publications.

Schwab, J.J. (1969) 'The practical: a language for curriculum', *School Review,* 78: 1–24.

Schwab, J.J. (2013) 'The practical: a language for curriculum', *Journal of Curriculum Studies,* 45(5): 591–621. doi: 10.1080/00220272.2013.809152.

Scottish Government (2008) *Curriculum for Excellence – Building the Curriculum 3: A Framework for Learning And Teaching*. Edinburgh: Scottish Government.

Sinnema, C. (2011) *Monitoring and Evaluating Curriculum Implementation: Final Evaluation Report on the Implementation of the New Zealand Curriculum 2008–2009*. Wellington: The Ministry of Education.

Sinnema, C. and Aitken, G. (2011) 'Teaching as inquiry in the New Zealand curriculum: origins and implementation', in J. Parr, H. Hedges and S. May (eds.), *Changing Trajectories of Teaching and Learning*. Wellington: New Zealand Council for Education Research. pp. 29–48.

Sinnema, C. and Aitken, G. (2012) *Effective Pedagogy in Social Sciences. Educational Practice Series*. Vol. 23. Geneva: International Bureau of Education.

Sinnema, C. and Aitken, G. (2013) 'Emerging international trends in curriculum', in M. Priestley and G.J.J. Biesta (eds.), *Reinventing the Curriculum: New Trends in Curriculum Policy and Practice*. London: Bloomsbury Academic. pp. 141–163.

Sinnema, C. and Aitken, G. (2014) 'Teachers' use of research to improve practice: why should we, how could we?', in A. St George,

S. Brown and J. O'Neill (eds.), *Facing the Big Questions in Teaching.* 2nd edn. Melbourne, Australia: Cengage. pp. 146–53.

Sinnema, C., Sewell, A. and Milligan, A. (2011) 'Evidence-informed collaborative inquiry for improving teaching and learning', *Asia-Pacific Journal of Teacher Education,* 39(3): 247–61. doi: 10.1080/1359866X.2011.597050.

Skilbeck, M. (1984) *School-Based Curriculum Development.* London: Harper and Row.

Sweller, J. (1994) 'Cognitive load theory, learning difficulty, and instructional design', *Learning and Instruction,* 4(4): 295–312. doi: 10.1016/0959-4752(94)90003-5.

Tyree, J.A.K. (1993) 'Examining the evidence: have states reduced local control of curriculum?', *Educational Evaluation and Policy Analysis,* 15(1): 34–50.

Weber, L. (1971) *The English Infant School and Informal Education.* Englewood Cliffs, NJ: Prentice Hall.

Xu, Y. and Wong, H. (2011) 'School-based curriculum development in China: policy analysis, theoretical controversy, and practical exploration', *Chinese Education and Society,* 4: 44–63. doi: 10.2753/CED1061-1932440403.

Young, M. and Muller, J. (2010) 'Three educational scenarios for the future: lessons from the sociology of knowledge', *European Journal of Education,* 45(1): 11–27. doi: 10.1111/j.1465-3435.2009.01413.x.

60

National Standards in Policy and Practice

Michael Moore, Don Zancanella
and JuliAnna Ávila

One noteworthy characteristic of educational policy in the late twentieth and early twenty-first century is the interconnectedness of its various parts. Curriculum is linked to technology, funding is linked to local, national, and even international politics, and the testing of 8-year-olds in Kansas may well be discussed in relation to college graduation or to the performance of children in Singapore or Finland. This interconnectedness means that the role of standards in today's schools cannot be fully understood without a consideration of the political and policy environment in which standards are embedded or without addressing their linkage to other educational processes, projects, and debates.

As we write from inside the US context, we find ourselves in the midst of what might be called the era of standards. After a period when efforts by the federal government to use testing as a means of prodding schools to adopt various reforms (from changes in teacher licensure to changes in how reading is taught), a set of quasi-national standards,

the Common Core State Standards, have taken center-stage in the world of education policy and reform. Almost every day, news outlets, from the *New York Times* to CNN to Fox News feature items about school standards alongside items about conflict in the Middle East or the release of the newest model of the iPhone.

Unfortunately (at least for the authors of pieces such as this), the term 'standards' raises a number of definitional problems. It can mean 'academic standards', which is often translated as 'what students should know and be able to do' at the end of particular course of instruction. However, in some instances, the term 'outcomes' is used for this same purpose. In the non-US context, 'educational standards' also may refer to a range of 'measurable indicators' related to such things as class size and teacher qualifications. To further complicate matters the distinction between 'standards' and 'curriculum' is not always clear. In the US, the relationship between these two terms has been of considerable interest because of the tradition of 'local control' and the resistance to a 'national' curriculum. In other countries, connecting and combining standards and curriculum seems generally unproblematic. In this chapter, we use the term 'standards' to mean 'academic standards', that is, measurable statements about what students should learn from a particular course of study. Whenever the term is used in a different way, we will mark the difference and explain.

Although discussions about education in other countries may not be quite so dominated by standards as they are at present in the US, the increase in interest in international assessments such as PISA (Programme for International Student Assessment) and TIMSS (Trends in International Mathematics and Science Study) has invariably increased interest in what schools teach. Indeed, in many contexts the word 'standards' cannot be used without following it with 'and testing'. Therefore, as long as the globalization of education continues, the interest from policymakers, educators, and the public in measuring what students know and are able to do will spawn additional interest in what schools and school systems are attempting to teach. Interest, that is, in standards.

In this chapter, we approach this large and complex issue from four directions: (1) the history of school standards as an idea in the US, with special attention to how it appeared in the popular press and public discourse; (2) the nature of debates about school standards in two countries other than the US (Italy and Australia); (3) the role of money, business, and the 'new philanthropies' in policy-making related to standards; and (4) the impact of standards on practice.

STANDARDS IN US POPULAR PRESS AS REFLECTION OF PUBLIC DISCOURSE

The debate from points along the political spectrum over implementation of Common Core State Standards in the US populates headlines in newspapers, blogs and newsletters from professional education organizations; however, public debate over educational standards has not always maintained such a high profile – prior to the early 1980s, US newspapers rarely mentioned educational standards. The publication of *A Nation at Risk* in 1983 under then-Secretary T.H. Bell marked the official beginning of standards becoming part of the national dialogue, as far as the popular press was concerned.

Bell organized a commission 'to address what he termed "the widespread public perception that something is seriously remiss in our educational system"' (Fiske, 1983). Excerpts from the report, quoted in the *Washington Post* state:

> We recommend that schools, colleges and universities adopt more rigorous and measurable standards...Standardized tests of achievement (not to be confused with aptitude tests) should be administered at major transition points from one level of schooling to another and particularly from high school to college to work. The purpose of these tests would be to: (a) certify the student's credentials; (b) identify the need for remedial intervention; and (c) identify the opportunity for advanced or accelerated work. The tests should be administered as part of a nationwide (but not federal) system of state and local standardized tests. (National Commission on Excellence in Education, 1983).

The very title of the article, 'Rising tide of mediocrity threatens our very future as a nation' signifies a panicked tone, which conveys the idea that we might well have taken our eyes off of the tide for too long with catastrophic results if we do not correct this, and soon. Not surprisingly, 1983 marks the start of more frequent public discussion about education standards, and from the mid-1980s onward, articles dealing with education standards number in the thousands, a presence that continues today.

As is the case today, debates about education standards taking place 30 years ago were also accompanied by discussions of other, namely the power struggle between the national government, states and local districts. In 1978, there was even mention of the creation of national standards as 'proposals have been advanced to create new national education standards and otherwise involve the federal government more deeply in local classrooms' (Jencks, 1978). This tension was perhaps captured by the tenure of T.H. Bell, described in another article from the *Washington Post* (Aplin-Brownlee, 1984) as being 'charged with carrying out President Reagan's campaign promise to abolish the Department of Education'. Aplin-Brownlee (1984) argues that, '[i]nstead, Bell raised the department's profile, defined the state of education and established a leadership role for the federal government in education, even as the administration urged more state and local control'.

Although *A Nation at Risk* was published in April of 1983 and carried the subtitle of being *An Open Letter to the American People*, individual states would respond on behalf of its citizens. In August of that same year, Balz reported that

> ...state governments have taken the message of a string of recent reports decrying what the National Commission on Education Excellence called 'a rising tide of mediocrity' in American education and are now leading the drive to find solutions... The connection between education and economic vitality was a central part of the opening session of the National Governors Association meeting here today, as the governors unanimously approved a resolution calling for stepped-up emphasis on educational improvements and the creation of partnerships – especially with business – to carry out those changes. (Balz, 1983)

Two days later, also in the *Washington Post*, Broder (1983), who had conducted interviews at the National Governor's Association, stated that while states wanted to be proactive, '[n]one of the governors believes the federal government should abandon its role in education'.

In December of the following year, the *New York Times* reported that a 'fundamental change' and 'fundamental shift' had occurred:

> Hundreds of new laws enacted to improve the quality of elementary and secondary schools are giving states around the country increased control over public education. State legislatures and

boards of education have been paying more of the cost of public education than local school districts for five years and are extending their influence over teaching and learning...others fear that 'writing curriculum on the floor of the legislature' is unworkable and will undermine the longstanding tradition of local control of public schools...But the growing movement for educational change in the 1980's has dramatically intensified the trend toward state control, extending it for the first time into curriculum and related areas... (Fiske, 1984)

In this same article, Fiske proceeded to quote Michael Timpane, past president of Teachers College, who 'suggested that the heightened interest in education at the state level had brought "new actors" into educational policy-making' including 'corporate leaders and other private individuals' resulting in 'a broader constituency of leadership' (Timpane cited in Fiske, 1984).

During this time, the popular press narrowed its focus even further to profile an individual teacher, and the concern that non-educators and politicians would exert control over curricula, as mentioned in Friske's 1984 *New York Times* article, was also echoed in Battiata's (1984) 'Structure, demands tie instructors' hands' article in the *Washington Post*. In this piece, Battiata profiled eighth-grade teacher Gail Palmer in the context of 'everyone from President Reagan to the local PTA agoniz[ing] over the state of the nation's public schools'. In a scenario that would likely sound familiar to many current educators, Palmer's reality was

> a crowded classroom, in which the conflicting interests and influence of parents, politicians, administrators and educational experts converge. She must contend with increasing administrative demands on her time, with meddling in what and how she teaches, with low pay, and with a feeling that school has become somehow less central in the lives of the children she must educate...'You're supposed to be performing minor miracles [she says], and if you're going to do it the right way, there's not a whole lot of time to chat'. (Battiata, 1984)

The impossibility of trying to orchestrate 'minor miracles' whilst on a non-negotiable schedule set by those who do not regularly spend time in classrooms (or do not trust teachers to make curricular decisions) is a situation that has not changed enough in 30 years. In fact, it harkens back to the 'scientific management' approach that would characterize American education beginning in the early 1900s, when standardization would be used 'as a means of efficient operation similar to the expanding US industrialization of the time' (Au, 2011: 15).

This profile of educator Gail Palmer personalized the standardization debate (counter to an impersonal 'scientific' or industrial focus), despite maintaining that 'much of the responsibility for declining educational standards rests with the way public schools are structured and with demands on students that are outside a teacher's sphere of influence' (Battiata, 1984). The teacher's sphere, and the standards that come along with it, would be irrevocably widened after 1983, as Wixson, Dutro, and Athan (2003) describe:

> Since *A Nation at Risk* mobilized the nation around education, many stakeholders have become involved in curricular reform. As business leaders, politicians, and the general public have joined educators in thinking about what students should know and be able to do in subject areas, competing values and ideas have increasingly come into play, as have the practical issues involved in implementing standards. (2003: 103)

If recent issues of *Education Week* are a current reflection of public dialogue about standards, then the stakeholders are largely unhappy. Not only are educators questioning the content and implementation of Common Core State Standards, but the public has also expressed 'stiff opposition' (Camera, 2014). Now that we are a few years into the execution of CCSS, the practical issues that Wixson et al. (2003) referred to are (perhaps?) more contentious than in decades past; however, the philosophical as well as pragmatic tensions that have come to define the national discussion of standards is not confined to the US.

INTERNATIONAL TRENDS

As American scholars, our previous work focused on the new Common Core State Standards, and yet we're quite aware that such standards are but one aspect of a much broader international movement in educational policy and practice. Typical elements of this movement include a shift in policy actors, from governmental and professional to philanthropic and private; an increase in the use of quantitative data for decision-making purposes; and a shift from public ownership of various aspects of education to private ownership. Each country that has taken up this agenda has approached it in a somewhat different way, but in virtually all cases, reforms have been linked to the 'measuring of student performance in relation to a set of standards'. The measurements are then used to determine the success of whatever policies or practices have been adopted. In view of reformers, once academic standards are in place and once tests are in place to determine how students are performing against those standards, any number of different programs and practices can be evaluated for effectiveness.

Luke (2011) describes the current international wave of reform as:

> In board rooms and in staff rooms there is a new common sense: that standards will enable equity, that this is about self-evident 'basics', that teachers and professors will perform better if there are stronger merit incentives and performance benchmarks, that to catch up with country or system X in the competitive production of human capital requires we must adopt a hardnosed approach to outcomes,…that parents or communities…must be able to access transparent information to enable market choices of educational goods and services. (2011: 372).

Luke is critiquing these shifts, but those who favor them and who see them as the future of education, describe them in a similar way. In the words of Rupert Murdoch (2011), founder and chairman of the multinational news and publishing conglomerate Newscorp:

> With common standards and a competitive market, we can deliver a first-class education to any child, from any background, in any classroom…I don't pretend to be an expert on academic standards. But as a business leader, I do know something about how common standards unlock

investments and unleash innovation. With those standards in place, investors are willing to take bigger risks because there are bigger rewards. (Murdoch, 2011).

As both Luke and Murdoch indicate, the link between standards and tests is the lynchpin of the current wave of educational reform. It is standards and the accompanying tests that will 'prove' that the reforms work. Although it is beyond the scope of this chapter to provide a comprehensive survey of how school reform is playing out around the world, the brief case studies of Italy and Australia that follow show that the US is not alone in its current focus on standards and testing.

Italy

According to Grimaldi and Serpieri (2013: 444) 'the perceived imperatives of global competiveness have been increasingly used as rationale for a project to modernise [the Italian] education field'. At the core of this project has been an emphasis on accountability. Overall, reforms aim to 'change the regime of practice that regulates the conduct of schools and educational professionals, redrawing it according to a new business-like ethos'. (2013: 455). This ethos involves, among other things, 'reproducing zero-sum games and [the] winner-loser logic of the market'; encouraging the abandonment of qualitative and internal criteria of evaluation so that they may be replaced with 'externally-driven measurable indicators' to judge both individuals and the entire organization; and 'importing into the education field the private-sector rule stating that which is not measured is not valued' (2013: 455).

As in the US, these changes have been promoted not by educational professionals but by private businesses and, especially, by new philanthropies. Although reforms had been underway since about 1997 (Grimaldi and Serpieri, 2013), the financial crisis that began in 2007 gave reformers new impetus. In August 2011, Jean-Claude Trichet

(President of the European Central Bank from 2003–2011) and Mario Draghi (President of the European Central Bank after November 2011) sent President of Italy Silvio Berlusconi a letter calling for 'the adoption and diffusion of performance indicators in health, justice, and schooling' (Landri, 2014). According to Landri,

> The letter reassures its readers and, in particular, financial markets, that in the next school year: a) schools would be more 'accountable' (the Italian text uses exactly the English term 'accountability') through the INVALSI testing (standardised assessment tests at the national level) and that policies will be devised to restructure those schools with low performances; and b) teachers would work longer hours although they will compete for merit-based awards...and thus start a new system of selection and recruitment to improve the school system's overall efficiency. (2014: 29).

Teachers and other professional educators have resisted these changes, but 'the logic of calculability seems to have partially succeeded in colonising the education field, establishing data on student performance... as the only reliable device to formulate a "realist" and "objective" judgment on the functioning of the education system, its organisations and professional communities' (Serpieri, 2012, cited in Grimaldi and Serpieri, 2013: 460).

As we have suggested, in the present context, academic standards are nearly always embedded in a web of educational reforms and to speak of them without reference to the other elements in those webs obscures their function. This interconnectedness between standards and other elements of education reform tends to be especially clear in countries such as Italy, where standards have been viewed as part of a 'package' of accountability policies. Grimaldi and Serpieri therefore refer to the recent wave of reform as 'the making of education as a domain calculability' (2013: 460). Citing Ball, Landri writes that 'the use of data and performance indicators, in particular, favours the development of a regime of performativity; a regime of governance where the measurement, comparison and judgment of performances is a mechanism to promote competitiveness and also solicit the ongoing improvement of educational and orginisational school outcomes' (Ball, 1998, cited in Landri, 2014: 27).

Australia

In 2007, the new Labor government in Australia proposed its own set of reforms. They included 'a national curriculum that focused on the basics, a one-laptop-per-child policy, and expanded testing and accountability system' (Luke, 2011: 372). By 2012, the implementation of these reforms had resulted in a national curriculum, national standards for teachers, national standardized testing, a National Assessment Program – Literacy and Numeracy (NAPLAN), and a 'My School' website, created so that the performance of individual schools could be compared to one another (Allard and Doecke, 2014: 44). The testing focuses on 'meeting targets' with the accompanying political rhetoric of goals, measures, and consequences for substandard performance (Hogan, 2012: 5). For example, a 2012 report on an interview with then-prime minister Julia Gillard, published in *The Australian*, states that, 'Ms Gillard told *The Australian* that Labor could demonstrate its reform program was "making a difference" and delivering real improvements, but the figures showed other nations were also lifting school standards, with the average Australian 15-year-old students as much as six months behind an equivalent student in leading nations' (Franklin, 2012).

As in the No Child Left Behind legislation in the US, the Australian reforms are part of 'a bi-partisan federal education policy, with both Liberal and Labor Governments progressively implementing a series of reforms that have led to increasing regulation of teachers' work' (Allard and Doecke, 2014: 44), and, as in the US, the pressure on school to raise student achievement as measured against the standards is intense.

In October 2014, the Business Council of Australia urged that 'federal schools funding should be conditional on the states requiring primary students to meet minimum literacy and numeracy standards before entering high school' (Maher, 2014).

In a study of the impact of standards-based reform on the experiences of early career teachers in Australia, Allard and Doecke discuss one secondary school English teacher, Marie, who finds herself in a 'world of standards-based reforms…[which] effectively discounts the knowledge that she brings to her work' (2014: 50). Because of high stakes tests, she must place a priority on 'learning outcomes crudely organized around constructions of cognitive development, unanchored within any robust understanding of the principles of inquiry that constitute each curriculum area' (2014: 50). Thus she must work 'against the grain' and raise 'disturbing questions about where her professional knowledge sits within the heavily regulated policy environment in which she is teaching' (2014: 50).[1, 2]

THE ROLE OF MONEY, BUSINESS, AND NEW PHILANTHROPIES IN STANDARDS-BASED REFORM

Investment in standards-based reform internationally is a result of the new markets opened to provide standards assessments, teacher development, assessment preparation, and especially technology, whether it's iPads with Microsoft software for every child in India or new infrastructure for schools or online remedial programs. For example, although corporate foundation interest in American public schooling might seem like a recent development, it actually goes back to the early 1900s when the Rockefeller, Ford and Carnegie foundations sought to influence educational policy (Gatto, 2000). The Rockefeller Foundation financed the John Dewey-organized Progressive Education Association at Columbia Teachers College, which sought to politically influence public schools. It is interesting to note that a century ago the government had a much smaller impact on education, as well as on welfare and health (Reckhow, 2013). Philanthropists today find themselves competing with local, state, and federal in education politics. With less free reign, investors are clearly more 'results-oriented' in their giving (Scott, 2009).

There were an estimated 50,000 corporate foundations by 1990 (Gatto, 2000) and since 2000 national advocacy funding has risen more than 23 percent (Reckhow and Snyder, 2014). The authors note:

> …increasing grant-making directed toward national research and advocacy suggests efforts to inject new perspectives including charter school advocacy, into national education policy debates. In this regard philanthropists' attempts to cultivate challengers to traditional school operations coincide with the amplification of new voices in national education politics. (Reckhow and Snyder, 2014: 193)

Foundations led by Eli and Edythe Broad, Flora Hewlitt, Michael and Susan Dell, Fisher, and Bill and Melinda Gates have mounted a massive effort to privatize and run public education like businesses especially for low-income and minority children (and this is based, at least partially, on the assumption that those who have been highly successful in business will therefore be equally successful in education policy and reform). The belief is that private sector solutions will work better than previous public efforts. These schools are the most cashed-starved and are more than willing to take money that comes with many attached strings. The privatization of educational services leading up to the era of No Child Left Behind was primarily for non-instructional services. Whitty and Power (2000) offer that the term privatization should be replaced with the term marketization because previously state-run educational programming, such as assessment, remediation, teacher development, have increasingly become privatized. The proliferation of non-profit organizations especially in

urban settings is not new but has certainly grown. Complicit in this model is the Obama/Duncan administration as seen in the education section of the American Reinvestment and Recovery Act (ARRA), Race to the Top and Investing in Innovation Fund grants (Bulkley and Burch, 2011).

Examples of non-profits organizations involved in the education sector include Teach for America and its iterations in other countries (Teach for India), which are backed by McKinsey & Company, Goldman Sachs, and the Ashoka Foundation, amongst others (Ball, 2012). Through a school improvement framework, these non-profits situated in high urban and poor rural settings offer alternatives to traditional teacher training programs and have garnered widespread publicity and funding and have slowly begun transforming traditional schools and settings. These same non-profits and foundations have begun to exert political influence through charter organizations like KIPP, National Alliance for Public Charter Schools, Democrats for Education Reform, and many others. Policy pressure is not only at the national level, but also at state and local levels. Ball refers to it as '…the increasingly complex and opaque crossings, blurrings, interweavings, or hybridities, that constitute and animate this neoliberal landscape of enterprise' (2012: 89).

Pearson is an example of bridging the gap between the non-profit foundations and for-profit enterprises. In 2011, Pearson hired Sir Michael Barber from McKinsey & Company as their Chief Education Advisor. Through Pearson's publishing, assessment (Pearson won the PARRC [Partnership for Assessment of Readiness for College and careers] assessment contract), curriculum development products, technical infrastructure (partnered with Microsoft), professional development materials, remediation materials, and its training of evaluators 'contributes to what cultural knowledge is most worthwhile and these products have invested with them particular conceptions of educational process and organization' (Ball, 2012: 127).

Curiously, the initial rollout of the Common Core State Standards was not met with much opposition. The rollout seemed remarkably bi-partisan in the same way that No Child Left Behind was heralded as a bi-partisan effort; however, opposition to the Common Core State Standards has slowly and steadily mounted, but with no clear partisan distinction. As No Child Left Behind folded its tent heralded by defunding the Reading First Act, many states and school districts felt relief from having to determine Annual Yearly Progress.

Slowly, opposition started with the anti-testing crowd in several states who feared that curriculum would continue to be test controlled. Opposition also emerged from both the conservative right and teacher unions, concerned that Race to the Top federal money meant federal intervention in the standards movement. Curiously, these groups still contained a number of influential politicians, including former Florida Governor Jeb Bush who continued to argue for the Common Core State Standards. Rather than the debate being played out nationally, it has become a state issue, with several states opting out of the Common Core State Standards and/or opting out of their previous commitments to the assessment consortiums. The real Common Core State Standards battlegrounds are now in gubernatorial and state superintendent races as a premier campaign issue.

At a 2009 Grant Makers for Education conference, Secretary of Education, Arne Duncan, said, 'We are on the cusp of a new era of innovation and entrepreneurship in education that was almost unimaginable a decade ago. I am convinced that every problem in education has been solved before, somewhere – and often with philanthropic support' (US Department of Education, 2009). In his address announcing his Investment in Innovation (i3) Fund, Secretary Duncan asked teachers, students, administrators, school boards, community organizations and other traditional stakeholders to move over because he had just opened the door for

foundations to have a seat at the table (US Department of Education, 2011). The federal government has no business telling foundations how to spend their money; however, government transparency in decision-making can point the way to where foundation money would be the most appreciated. By outlining his department's goals and providing an assessment as to how philanthropic foundations can support these goals, Secretary Duncan skirted the edges of federal intrusion into education.

The US spends about US$500 billion per year on K-12 public schooling. According to the Foundation Center (http://foundation center.org/), the leading source of information on philanthropy worldwide, philanthropic giving to transform public education has reached about US$8 billion annually (only religious organizations receive more). Of the many private non-profit givers, the big three funders who appear to have the most influence are the Bill & Melinda Gates Foundation, The Eli and Edythe Broad Foundation, and the Walton Family Foundation. Although their reasons for giving might be different, they still appear to be like-minded when it comes to 'choice, competition, deregulation, accountability, and data-based decision-making' (Barkan, 2011: 49). Coincidentally, so does Secretary Duncan with Race to the Top funding. Basically, the big three want to close down low performing schools, increase charters, implement vouchers, evaluate teachers based on student test scores, award merit pay based on these same test scores, and increase the stakes in high stakes testing. However, not considered are the data on charter school performance compared with public schools, the data on value-added measures to assess teaching performance, data on test scores measuring student ability, data on class size, and data on the effects of poverty on schooling.

Teachers, administrators, school boards, mayors, legislators and governors are accountable for their decisions either to elected boards or to voters. Non-profit foundations are not accountable and immune from outside control. Additionally, gross changes in campaign finance laws have allowed for-profit and non-profit organizations unprecedented access in influencing public policy.

THE IMPACT OF STANDARDS ON PRACTICE

Reviewing the chronology of standards-based reform has been an emotional roller coaster ride. The standards-based reform in the educational landscape continues to change – beginning with *A Nation at Risk* (1983) and including the 1989 Charlottesville Education Summit; the 1994 Goals 2000: Educate America Act; 2002's No Child Left Behind Act, through 2009 with the approval of 48 states adopting the Common Core State Standards, to 2014 with three states removing themselves from the Common Core and a number of states reviewing their own involvement. What started as an altruistic bi-partisan national effort is now a fractured, acrimonious political quagmire. In 1989, then Arkansas Governor, Bill Clinton, said at the Charlottesville Summit:

> This is the first time a President and Governor have ever stood before the American people and said: 'Not only are we going to set national performance goals, which are ambitious, not only are we going to develop strategies to achieve them, but we stand here before you and tell you we expect to be held personally accountable for the progress we make in moving this country to a brighter future. (Fiske,1989: n.p.)

However, the only group that now seems to have been held accountable has been teachers. No Child Left Behind's Reading First Act had virtually no effect on practice (Manzo, 2008). The effect of the current Striving Readers Act, which targets at-risk middle and high school students, is unknown. Implementation of the untested Common Core State Standards across states has been wildly unsystematic and leaves school districts to fend for themselves.

Evidence from the National Assessment of Educational Progress (NAEP) indicates that the sharp focus on assessment and teacher accountability has had no impact on student performance (Brandenberg, 2014), has had widespread testing scandals, and the creation and growth of grassroots organizations, such as the Badass Teachers, suggest that they have also had a deleterious effect on teaching (Strauss, 2013). The proliferation of educational start-ups, non-profit, and for-profit philanthropic educational involvement, all promising silver bullet solutions for schools and assessment consortiums providing assessments and materials, have led to curricula driven by commercial programs. Professional national content organizations noticeably have not endorsed the Common Core State Standards, and offer tepid and cautious support for teachers.

Up to this point, our focus has been on standards as policy instruments; however, we would be remiss if we did not touch on the standards themselves. The Common Core State Standards (Common Core States Standards Initiative, n.d.) identify three key instructional shifts: (1) regular practice with complex texts and their academic language; (2) reading, writing, and speaking 'grounded in evidence from texts', both literary and informational; and (3) building knowledge through content-rich non-fiction. These instructional shifts and how they have been presented to teachers appear at odds with research that supports socially constructed collaboration amongst the teacher, students, and the curriculum.

Consider, for example, the implication of how the English Language Arts & Literacy RI9-10.9 state standard ('Analyze seminal US documents of historical and literary significance (for example, Washington's Farewell Address, The Gettysburg Address, Roosevelt's four freedoms speech, King's 'Letter from Birmingham Jail') including how they address related themes and concepts') should be taught. First, although these are indicated as examples, our history with state standards and recommended texts tells us that these 'examples' actually become the texts that teachers use. Considering that the PARRC and Smarter Balanced assessors have also read the standards, it is no mental jump to think these iconic texts 'might be in the test'. Teachers would have to supplement this list if they wanted women and authors of color represented. Additionally, these listed iconic texts exist in social, cultural, and political contexts; however, what is tested becomes the curriculum and how it is taught depends on how the questions are framed. Add in Text Complexity and a whole new impact on practice emerges. Fisher and Frey (2014: 237) wrote: 'Here we define text complexity as a set of quantitative and qualitative attributes that collectively describe the features of a text. Text difficulty – how hard a given text is for a particular reader – forms a subset of the attributes of text complexity'. The authors then seem to use the terms 'critical thinking' and 'deep thinking' interchangeably. Martinez and McGee (2000) defined 'deep thinking' as 'seeing more than one perspective, searching out a variety of interpretations, and finding compelling connections among and between perspectives, interpretations, and self (2000: 166). Qualitative attributes, critical thinking, and deep thinking can be confusing for teachers who have a variety of ability levels in the same classroom. When classrooms contain students who are reading at or above grade levels alongside students who must have these texts read to them, we wonder how much of any student thinking gets done.

In short, there is a great deal to debate within the standards themselves – how they present school subjects, their implied vision of teaching and learning, their research base (or lack thereof), their theoretical base (or lack thereof), and their relationship to tests; however, those debates never took place. In a sense, they were turned over to the private sector to sort out. The result has been that implementing the standards in practice is currently a free-for-all. There are two types of markets that the Common Core State Standards impose on language arts curricula. The first is characterized by a set of rules imposed on the game. These rules inform states how to compete for federal monies, philanthropic dollars,

and rules for conducting business. The second market 'pits established and startup profit and nonprofit businesses against one another in order to supply states and schools with the commodities and services to make CCSS work (Shannon, 2014: 267.) This second market – think Pearson, McGraw Hill and the like – become the engine that drives, instruction, teacher development, and especially assessment.

We began this chapter with an attempt to situate standards from four distinct, but complimentary directions: (1) the history of school standards as an idea in the US, with special attention to how they appeared in the popular press and public discourse; (2) the nature of debates about school standards in two countries other than the US (Italy and Australia); (3) the role of money, business, and the 'new philanthropies' in policy-making related to standards; and (4) how the standards are shaping teaching and learning.

Taking a brief historical vantage point by reviewing the inclusion and visibility of standards in the popular press of the US reveals a shift in public discourse: the public began to converse about standards with a new frequency and entitlement. Public education is fundamentally public, but the public is not represented or empowered equally, and the tensions that are an inextricable part of public discourse are not unique to the US. As we discussed, the conceptions of standards in both Italy and Australia illustrate the point that the movement to evaluate the efficacy of standards by measuring student performance is not restricted to the US. We transitioned into an examination of the recent impact of business on the implementation of standards-based reform and concluded with a snapshot of the complications involved in putting the standards into practice.

We have attempted to scratch the thin veneer of altruism that disguises standards-based reform; however, once scratched, political agendas, national posturing, profiteering, corporate interests, among others, become all too apparent. There is little to no control of the direction of the standards beast. Internationally, the same scenario appears to be playing out in the same way. It is our hope that questioning and contextualizing will lead to a critical and thoughtful approach to the adoption and implementation of standards in the US and beyond.

NOTES

1   At this point it's important to note that the words used to describe various aspects of educational reform change from country to country and even from researcher to researcher. For instance, in the US we have tended to use the term 'standards' for statements of what students should 'know and be able to do' at the end of particular course of instruction. In the earlier remarks, the term 'measureable indicators' is used instead. In other instances, the comparable term is 'outcomes'. In the non-US context, 'educational standards' also may refer to a range of 'measurable indicators' related to such things as class size and teacher qualifications (see Landri, 2014: 26).
2   In the US context, the distinction between 'standards' and 'curriculum' has been of considerable interest because of the tradition of 'local control' and the resistance to a 'national' curriculum.

REFERENCES

Allard, A. and Doecke, B. (2014) 'Professional knowledge and standards-based reforms: Learning from the experiences of early career teachers', *English Teaching: Practice and Critique,* 13(1): 39–54.

Aplin-Brownlee, V. (1984) School study was high point, Bell says; brought in to abolish education department, the secretary built it up. *Washington Post.* November 9. Available from http://www.lexisnexis.com.librarylink.uncc.edu/hottopics/lnacademic/?shr=t&sfi=AC01NBSimplSrch (accessed 4 August 2014).

Au, W. (2011) 'Teaching under the new Taylorism: high-stakes testing and the standardization of the 21st century curriculum', *Journal of Curriculum Studies,* 43(1): 25–45. doi: 10.1080/00220272.2010.521261.

Ball, S.J. (1998) 'Big policies/small world: an introduction to international perspectives in education policy', *Comparative Education,* 34(2): 119–30.

Ball, S.J. (2012) *Global Education Inc: New Policy Networks and the Neo-Liberal Imaginary.* London: Routledge.

Balz, D. (1983) State governments leading the drive to upgrade education. *Washington Post.* August 1. Available from http://www.lexisnexis.com.librarylink.uncc.edu/hottopics/lnacademic/?shr=t&sfi=AC01NBSimplSrch (accessed 7 August 2014).

Barkan, J. (2011)' Got dough? How billionaires Rule Our Schools', *Dissent,* Winter, https://www.dissentmagazine.org/article/got-dough-how-billionaires-rule-our-schools.

Battiata, M. (1984) Structure, demands tie instructors' hands. *Washington Post.* February 26. Available from http://www.lexisnexis.com.librarylink.uncc.edu/hottopics/lnacademic/?shr=t&sfi=AC01NBSimplSrch (accessed 7 August 2014).

Brandenberg, G.F. (2014) Just how flat ARE those 12th grade NAEP scores? GFBrandenberg's Blog. May 8. Available from https://gfbrandenburg.wordpress.com/2014/05/08/just-how-flat-are-those-12th-grade-naep-scores/ (Accessed 5 December 2014).

Broder, D.S. (1983) Tackling education. *Washington Post.* August 3. Available from http://www.lexisnexis.com.librarylink.uncc.edu/hottopics/lnacademic/?shr=t&sfi=AC01NBSimplSrch (accessed 12 August 2014).

Bulkley, K.E. and Burch, P. (2011) 'The changing nature of private engagement in public education: for-profit an nonprofit organizations and educational reform', *Peabody Journal of Education,* 86: 236–51.

Camera, L. (2014) Polls capture public's sour view of Common Core. *Education Week.* August 26. Available from http://www.edweek.org/ew/articles/2014/08/27/02pdk.h34.html?cmp=ENL-CCO-NEWS1 (accessed 7 August 2014).

Common Core States Standards Initiative (n.d.) *Key Shifts in English Language Arts: Common Core States Standards.* Available from http://www.corestandards.org/other-resources/key-shifts-in-english-language-arts/ (accessed 5 May 2013).

Council of Chief State School Officers and the National Governors Association (2010) *English Language Arts & Literacy in History/*

Social Studies, Science, and Technical Subjects: Appendix A: Research Supporting Key Elements of the Standards. Available from www.corestandards.org/assets/Appendix_A.pdf (accessed 3 Novermber 2012).

Editorial desk (1983) School standards cost money. *New York Times.* August 5. Available from http://www.lexisnexis.com.librarylink.uncc.edu/hottopics/lnacademic/?shr=t&sfi=AC01NBSimplSrch (accessed 12 August 2014).

Fisher, D. and Frey, N. (2014) 'Addressing CCSS anchor standard 10: Text Complexity', *Language Arts*, 91: 236–250.

Fiske, E.B. (1983) Commission on education warns 'tide of mediocrity' imperils US. *New York Times.* April 27. Available from http://www.lexisnexis.com.librarylink.uncc.edu/hottopics/lnacademic/?shr=t&sfi=AC01NBSimplSrch (accessed 12 August 2014).

Fiske, E.B. (1984) States gain wider influence on school policy. *New York Times.* December. Available from http://www.lexisnexis.com.librarylink.uncc.edu/hottopics/lnacademic/?shr=t&sfi=AC01NBSimplSrch (accessed 12 August 2014).

Franklin, M. (2012) We risk losing education race, Julia Gillard warns. *The Australian.* January 24. Available from http://www.theaustralian.com.au/national-affairs/education/we-risk-losing-education-race-julia-gillard-warns/story-fn59nlz9-1226251791091 (accessed 30 November 2014).

Gatto, J. (2000) *The Underground History of American Education.* New York, NY: Odysseus Group.

Grimaldi, E. and Serpieri, R. (2013) 'Privitising education policy-making in Italy: new governance and the reculturing of a welfarist education state', *Education Inquiry*, 4(3): 443–72.

Hogan, A. (2012) 'The changing nature of the Australian education policy field: the rise of edu-business', paper presented at the Joint AARE APERA International Conference, Sydney 2012.

Jencks, C. (1978) The wrong answer for schools is: (b) back to basics; 'back to basics' is the wrong answer; don't go 'back to basics'. *Washington Post.* February 19. Available from http://www.lexisnexis.com.librarylink.uncc.edu/hottopics/lnacademic/?shr=t&sfi=AC01NBSimplSrch (accessed 25 August 2014).

Landri, P. (2014) 'Governing by standards: the fabrication of austerity in the Italian educational system', *Education Inquiry*, 5(1): 25–41.

Luke, A. (2011) 'Generalizing across borders policy and the limits of educational science', *Educational Researcher*, 40(8): 367–77.

Maher, S. (2014) Tie school funds to literacy standards: Business Council. *The Australian.* October 4. Available from: http://www.theaustralian.com.au/national-affairs/education/tie-school-funds-to-literacy-standards-business-council/story-fn59nlz9-1227075799966 (accessed 30 November 2014).

Manzo, K.K. (2008) 'Reading First' research offers no definitive answers. *EdWeek.* June 4. Available from http://www.edweek.org/ew/articles/2008/06/04/39read.h27.html (accessed 15 October 2014).

Martinez, M. and McGee, L. (2000) 'Literature-based reading instruction: past, present and future', *Reading Research Quarterly*, 35: 154–69.

Murdoch, R. (2011) Let's bring classrooms into the 21st century. *The Australian.* October 15. Available from http://www.theaustralian.com.au/media/rupert-murdochs-keynote-address-to-the-foundation-for-excellence-in-education-summit/story-e6frg996-1226166961 384 (accessed 30 November 2014).

National Commission on Excellence in Education (1983) Rising tide of mediocrity threatens our very future as a nation. *Washington Post.* April 27. Available from http://www.lexisnexis.com.librarylink.uncc.edu/hottopics/lnacademic/?shr=t&sfi=AC01NBSimplSrch (accessed 18 August 2014).

National Commission on Excellence in Education (1983) *A Nation at Risk: The Imperative for Educational Reform.* Washington, D.C.: U.S. GPO.

Reckhow, S. (2013) *Follow the Money: How Foundation Dollars Change Public School Politics.* New York: Oxford University Press.

Reckhow, S. and Snyder, J.W. (2014) 'The expanding role of philanthropy in education politics', *Educational Researcher*, 43(4): 186–95.

Scott, J. (2009) 'The politics of venture philanthropy in charter school policy and advocacy', *Educational Policy*, 23(1): 106–136.

Serpieri, R. (2012) *Senza Leadership, La con-struzione del dirigente scolastico.* Milan, Italy: FrancoAngeli.

Shannon, P. (2014) 'With all due respect', *Language Arts,* 91: 267.

Strauss, V. (2013) 'How mad are some teachers? This mad', *Washington Post.* July 12.

US Department of Education (2009) 'Shooting for the moon: a joint venture', *The Education Innovator: Office of Innovation & Improvement,* 7(8): 1–11.

US Department of Education (2011) i3 Projects Receive $18 Million in Matching Funds From Private Sector: Remarks of Secretary Arne Duncan. Available from http://www.ed.gov/news/press-releases/i3-projects-receive-18-million-matching-funds-private-sector (accessed 4 August 2014).

Whitty, G. and Power, S (2000) 'Marketization and privatization in mass education systems', *International Journal of Educational Development,* 20: 93–107.

Wixson, K.K., Dutro, E. and Athan, R.G. (2003) 'The challenge of developing content standards', *Review of Research in Education,* 27: 69–107.

61

Curriculum Development and School Leadership: Unattainable Responsibility or Realistic Ambition?

Ciaran Sugrue

INTRODUCTION

When Thomas Mann (Secretary of the Board of Education, Massachusetts, US), visited schools in Germany, parts of Great Britain and Ireland in the 1840s, he reported thus:

> I do not hesitate to say, that there are many things abroad which we, at home, should do well to imitate; things, some of which are here, as yet, mere matters of speculation and theory, but which, there, have long been in operation, and are now producing a harvest of rich and abundant blessings. (Mann, 1846: 18)

His observations provide evidence of comparison, of policy borrowing, whilst simultaneously providing critical comments levelled at education in Prussia as 'actually producing, a spirit of blind acquiescence to arbitrary power, in things spiritual as well as temporal, as being, … a system of education, adapted to enslave, and not to enfranchise the human mind' (Mann: 1846: 19). More than a century later, a similar transatlantic set of observations were provided on 'progressive' primary

education as documented by US researchers in England (Berlak and Berlak, 1975; Berlak et al., 1976). Attention was drawn to the significance of dilemmas in teaching and reflective practice, whilst the 'big picture' concern was tension between 'progressive' reforms and more traditional approaches to schooling, neatly captured in the phrase: 'how far "back to the basics" to go' (Berlak and Berlak, 1975: 2). Such progressive transplant efforts were heavily criticised (Sugrue, 2010).

Contemporary resonances of these tensions are evident in *Finnish Lessons* for the rest of 'the world', reinforcing the view that policy export or policy borrowing across national boundaries continues (Sahlberg, 2011). More recent, however, is the emergence of powerful international organisations such as International Monetary Fund (IMF), European Central Bank (ECB), European Union (EU), Organisation for Economic Cooperation and Development (OECD), International Association for the Evaluation of Educational Achievement (IEA) to mention but a few. These are the super-tankers on the high seas of policy making. Driven by the powerful winds of globalisation, they circumnavigate the globe and penetrate national, regional and local policy making in a manner never encountered before (Ball, 2012; Lawn and Grek, 2012) with a tendency to become policy imperatives rather than possible options. However, there is growing recognition that 'if curricula are... historically formed within systems of Ideas, research cannot but proceed with historical methods' and that curriculum may be understood 'genealogically' (Thröhler, 2014: 62). For contemporary school leaders, many of whom are in the grip of 'austerity' that has cultivated a fatalistic policy climate of 'more for less' whilst enabling policymakers to promulgate a rhetoric that 'there is no alternative', 'a synchronic comparative stance' is necessary to avoid a fatalistic view when faced with external change forces in order 'to gain emancipatory energy' (Thröhler, 2014: 62). Additionally, in order for school leaders in particular to avoid some of the worst features of policy borrowing and superficial adoption, a rigorous and critical approach becomes a necessity in contexts of 'raging globalisation' (Beck, 2000, 2006, 2013; Smith, 2014; Wallerstein et al., 2013).

Curriculum development, since the emergence of (national) systems of education, is an intensely contested space; a contest that is about much more than test scores (Apple, 2004; Goodson, 1994). Writing in 1918, Bobbitt (1918: v) was explicit about the necessity for a step change in education: 'education is to be called upon to bear a hitherto undreamed-of burden of responsibility; and to undertake unaccustomed labors'. More recently, on the European side of the Atlantic, similar sentiments have been articulated: 'curriculum research and theory must begin by investigating how the curriculum is currently constructed and then produced by teachers in the "differing circumstances in which they are placed"' (Goodson, 1994: 37). Throughout these periods there have been ongoing tensions between those who emphasize content and mastery in contrast to those

who give primacy to experience, motivation, engagement, affective and aesthetic learning (Bruner, 1960/1997; Egan, 1997; Eisner, 1979). Curriculum may therefore be interpreted on a continuum from formal syllabus of a course or programme to the totality of experience, thus 'curriculum is everything a child experiences from the moment he or she wakes up in the morning until the moment at which he or she goes to bed at night' (McDermott, 2013: 19). School leaders, despite more recent policy tendencies towards external prescription, have also enjoyed varying degrees of professional autonomy to exercise professional judgement with regard to the overall focus of curricula, teaching and learning. The increasing tendency towards centrally prescribed, internationally inspired, technical rational, instrumentalisation of curricula is in sharp contrast to what Stenhouse articulated a generation ago in the UK context:

> A curriculum is an attempt to communicate the essential principles and features of an educational proposal in such a form that it is open to critical scrutiny and capable of effective translation into practice. (Stenhouse, 1975: 4, emphasis in original)

Due to the increasing impact of global forces, it is more difficult if not impossible to escape the influence of an unfettered and more triumphalist neo-liberal ideology, particularly during the past three decades. Consequently, the relative autonomy afforded to teachers for constructing curricula has been seriously eroded and heavily circumscribed with variation across jurisdictions. International rhetorics of 'devolution of responsibility and decision-making to the level of the school' have shone a particularly harsh light on the role of school leaders (Pont et al., 2008). In more recent times, therefore, they have been positioned in the eye of this ongoing ideological storm because 'As the key intermediary between the classroom, school and the education system as a whole, effective school leadership is essential to improve its efficiency and equity of schooling' (Pont et al., 2008: 16).

In recent times, and particularly (although not exclusively) in the English-speaking world, the role of the school leader as gatekeeper and conduit for an externally prescribed curriculum has been privileged. Nevertheless, it is necessary also to recognise that the manner in which school leadership has evolved in different jurisdictions has consequences for the role as currently conceived and enacted.

Consideration of school curricula, their underlying principles, content and pedagogies, as well as the manner in which principals are expected to lead school communities are ensnared in a considerable ideological battle that may be more adequately understood by excavating the manner in which underlying considerations infiltrate and occupy discourses on school leadership and curriculum reform. Appropriately undertaken, this task necessitates a 'change over time perspective' whilst acknowledging also the significance of periodisation (Goodson, 2004; Hargreaves and Goodson, 2006).

The embrace of 'leadership' as an alternative term to more traditional labels such as 'principalship' or 'headship' has come about partly as a consequence of a loss of certainty and increasing complexity in terms of the role and responsibility (Sugrue, 2015). Belatedly:

> The education field is finally embracing school leadership as an essential ingredient in reform, worthy of investment in its own right. Facing pressure..., states and districts increasingly are recognizing that successful school reform depends on having principals well prepared to change schools and improve instruction, not just manage buildings and budgets. (Mitgang, 2012: 5)

These changed and changing circumstances 'have made school leadership a priority in education policy agendas across OECD and partner countries' to the possible detriment of curriculum development (Pont et al., 2008: 16).

Against this general backdrop, the next section situates leadership and curriculum reform within these wider ideological struggles by focusing on the distinct language and logic of accountability and responsibility. This framing provides this chapter's analytical lens through which subsequent sections are presented and interrogated. The first of these is a succinct account of the evolution of the field of leadership, highlighting the significance of language and underlying logic throughout. The following section examines the evolution of curriculum during this period, posing the question 'leadership for and of what', and this analysis heralds what Biesta (2010) has labelled the 'learnification' of schooling and teacher–student relationships with profound consequences for education. The chapter's focus then turns to priorities currently being given to the preparation of school leaders and the extent to which 'learnification' of leadership is prioritised. In the final section, the 'zone of proximal distance' is proposed and described as a means of cultivating and sustaining a professionally responsible leadership that embraces curriculum development. The chapter concludes that considerable benefits accrue from contemplating school leadership, leader professional preparation and curriculum development as elements of the same educational script.

REFORMS: LANGUAGE, LOGICS AND IDEOLOGICAL ROOTS OF ACCOUNTABILITY AND RESPONSIBILITY

The language and logic of neo-liberalism is one of deregulation and the roll back of the state; for life to be 'ruled' by market forces (Couldry, 2010/2012). Cloned from the same ideological gene pool, New Public Management (NPM) has become the staple policy discourse of an increasing number of governments, and includes the following megatrends:

> ...to *slow down or reverse government growth* in terms of overt public spending and staffing...shift toward *privatization and quasi-privatization*...the development of *automation*,...and...the development of a more *international* agenda, increasingly

focused on general issues of public management, policy design, decision styles and intergovernmental cooperation. (Hood, 1991: 3, emphasis in original)

Although Hood recognises that NPM is 'ill-defined', he identifies common characteristics that include the disaggregation of the monolithic public sector into cost centres, privatisation of services where possible, competitiveness (quasi-markets), specification of standards, a parsimoniousness characterised by 'more for less' and the application of private sector management norms in the public sector (see Hood, 1991: 4–5). These characteristics are readily evident in the lives and work of teachers internationally, even if more pronounced in some jurisdictions. School leadership and curriculum are perceived very differently when viewed through the lens, language and inherent logic of 'accountability' on the one hand, and professional 'responsibility' on the other (see Solbrekke and Englund, 2011).

To 'profess' carries vocational overtones of responding to a 'calling'; its Latin root – *profiteri* – means to declare publicly. When combined with the Latin root of responsibility – *respondere* – to answer or to offer in return or by way of reciprocation, professional responsibility includes:

> ...a sense of calling to provide service for the benefit of others, to take care of individuals as well as cater for the public welfare....being morally responsible for one's behaviour; to take on important duties while being willing to make independent decisions and being entrusted to do so....It connotes both the personal and moral dimensions of having a commitment to care that includes a combination of control, duties and decisions. (Solbrekke and Sugrue, 2011: 13)

Responsibility therefore 'relies on trust', as well as the professional 'being qualified and willing to handle dilemmas and having the freedom to deliberate on alternative courses of action', which are not always predictable, nor possible to pre-determine their 'outcomes'. Consequently, the exercise of professional responsibility 'goes beyond the limits of accountability and is linked to a sense of

freedom because professionals are *trusted* yet also *committed* to act in the interest of others' (Solbrekke and Englund, 2011: 854). In contrast, the inherent logic of accountability relies on compliance, conformity to a set of predetermined measures or outcomes. Consequently, it is predisposed towards 'control rather than trust and "good services" are guaranteed by means of measuring and accounting instruments rather than relying on professional discretion' (Solbrekke and Englund, 2011: 855). It is possible, therefore, to be accountable without being professionally responsible, and the language and logic of accountability potentially hollows out not only a sense of professional responsibility, but also what is entailed in leading a school community and divining an appropriate curriculum. Such hollowing out is captured succinctly in the following:

> *Efficere* translates...as 'to bring about', to accomplish, to effect. Only in modern times do we separate effectiveness, efficacy and efficiency and our public conversation is consequently fractured – and impoverished (Gross Stein, 2001: 2)

By privileging efficiency and effectiveness, the efficacy of professional responsibility is potentially compromised – whilst purporting to 'speak on behalf of taxpayers and consumers' it pits itself 'against cosy cultures of professional self-regulation' (Power, 1999: 44). Table 61.1 summarises these different languages, their logics and the tensions they create for school leaders, how they perceive their roles and also exercise their responsibilities.

This representation inadequately depicts the force field created by the underlying logics. Nevertheless, the ensuing tension is the terrain in which school leaders are obliged to function. Is professionally responsible leadership, when external control and prescription is pervasive, consigned to the margins by the ensuing 'performativity' culture that further promotes 'managerial accountability'? (Green, 2011).

> Performativity is a technology, a culture and a mode of regulation that employs judgements,

Table 61.1 Language and logic of responsibility and accountability[1]

Responsibility	Accountability
Based in professional mandate	Defined by current governance
Situated judgement	Standardised by contract
Trust	Control
Moral rationale	Economic/legal rationale
Internal evaluation	External auditing
Negotiated standards	Predetermined indicators
Implicit language	Transparent language
Framed by professions	Framed by political goals
Relative autonomy and personally inescapable	Compliance with employers'/politicians' decisions
Proactive	Reactive
Leadership	Management
Citizen	Client/customer
Education	Learning (outcomes)
Public good	Consumer/consumption/choice
Professional collaboration	Competition
Professional judgment	Inspection/league tables

Note

[1] The keywords in both columns above the line are the original list provided by Solbrekke and Englund (2011). The keywords that appear below the line in both columns have been added more specifically to reflect leadership, whilst also indicating the manner in which language reshapes discourses and, in the process, influences the dispositions and actions of learners, teachers and leaders.

Source: Adapted from Solbrekke and Englund (2011: 855).

comparisons and displays as means of incentive, control, attrition and change based on rewards and sanctions (both material and symbolic). The performances (of individual subjects or organizations) serve as measures of productivity or output....The issue of who controls the field of judgement is crucial. (Ball, 2003: 216)

School leadership in particular is at the epicentre of this phenomenon. It is 'one manifestation of a global reworking of the economic, social, moral and political foundations of public service provision and the development of new kinds of responses to social disadvantage' and inequality (Ball, 2012: 15).

Table 61.1 contrasts the major shift in language use whereby responsibilities are being determined increasingly by governments or external bodies, and are informed increasingly by international organisations through rankings of student performance (OECD, 2010b, 2013). Such 'measures' may result in knee-jerk policy responses that restrict curricula through national prescription and attendant funding mechanisms.[1] Such panicked and politically motivated policy decision making casts principals in the role of

conduits for official policy, rather than catalysts for curriculum making.[2] What Table 61.1 encapsulates is the extent to which principals in various jurisdictions and to varying degrees are progressively coerced into working from a prepared script that is dictated remotely, centrally and shaped internationally, several removes from the daily realities for which they are increasingly held accountable rather than being accorded the necessary professional autonomy, trust and support to exercise professionally responsible leadership (Lawn and Grek, 2012).

FROM PRINCIPAL TO LEADER: PERFORMATIVE ACCOUNTABILITY OR PROFESSIONAL RESPONSIBILITY?

Until relatively recently in an Irish context, the principal's responsibility was to 'keep the Register, Daily Report Book and Roll Book accurately, neatly and according to the instructions prescribed by the Minister' (Department of Education, 1965). These minimal administrative duties contrast sharply with a recent study in England and Wales where researchers identified '30 categories' of work undertaken 'in a typical week' (Smithers and Robinson, 2007: 21). Smithers and Robinson (2007) asked a representative sample, which although 'necessarily small for a study based on in-depth interviews…are representative of the population of schools in England and Wales by region, size, type, funding method, age range, and in the case of secondary schools by their specialisation' (Smithers and Robinson, 2007: 15), how the role and responsibilities had changed during their tenure (which ranged from 1 to 22 years), they

> …mentioned 58 things that had been added to their responsibilities or changes with which they had had to cope during their time in post…. Changes in the nature of headship, school organisation, staffing, curriculum and assessment accountability, funding arrangements, responsibility for premises, the social agenda and in society itself immediately came to their minds. (2007: 22)

Interviewees did not indicate that anything had been removed, strongly suggesting intensification. Nevertheless, 'both primary and secondary heads said that it was the people aspects of the job they most enjoyed', whilst 'it was the bureaucracy, external interference and excessive regulation that they liked least' (2007: 21). These tensions are reflected within leadership literature.

Intersecting Literatures and School Leadership Trajectories

Much of the 'what' and the 'why' of leadership have already been documented, albeit from different perspectives. School effectiveness (Teddlie and Reynolds, 2000), which after a period of time and sustained criticism, metamorphosed into effectiveness and improvement (Townsend, 2007). Other perspectives added to this growing literature, such as 'educational change' (Hargreaves et al., 1998, 2010) or school development in a more holistic manner (Day, 2012), whilst others subjected ongoing policy and practice

to analysis through a leadership lens (Leithwood et al., 1996, 2002) or endeavoured to make sense of ongoing school reform through an evaluation aperture (Ryan and Bradley Cousins, 2009). Motivations for undertaking related research are multi-various, including quality, policy, practice and equity to mention but a few (Sammons et al., 1995), driven in part by a reaction to the more pessimistic views that schooling had negligible impact on disadvantaged students (Coleman et al., 1966; Jencks et al., 1972). Subsequent cumulative research evidence indicated that schools indeed make a difference, and such positive influences varied depending on the nature of the school's leadership (Rutter et al., 1979). However, evidence of the positive impact of leadership has fostered further research on various leadership styles, with a tendency to narrowly focus on 'instructional leadership' rather than curriculum development. Styles have been distributed (no pun intended!) across a spectrum from authoritarian to *laissez faire*, with consultative and collaborative emerging as significant, whilst empowering others to varying degrees depending on whether such interactions were 'transactional' or 'transformative' (Leithwood et al., 2002). This literature is largely silent on leaders' curriculum responsibilities, increasingly determined from without the school rather than from within.

This research literature revealed leadership as being shaped by place and time to a significant degree. With a general move away from the 'super' leader (Copland, 2001; Hall, 1996; Reynolds, 2002; Smulyan, 2000), there emerged a more pervasive view that 'heroic' forms of leadership, with an over-reliance on charisma, were neither appropriate nor adequate to the increasingly complex responsibilities (Gronn, 2003). As the pace of change accelerated internationally through the 1990s, leadership literature was being influenced more by business school thinking and private sector norms with a consequent ratcheting up of tension between accountability and responsibility that fostered leadership 'hybrids'(Gronn, 2009). As external policy pressures intensified, the 'cellular' structure of schools' architecture and dominant cultures was superseded by persistent calls for more evidence-based collaboration (Hargreaves, 1994) and such organizational cultural reforms led to more demand for, and awareness of, the necessity for 'teacher leadership' (Lieberman and Miller, 2004). In turn, this cultural shift began to be superseded by 'distributed' leadership (Spillane, 2006), which was rapidly adopted as a policy orthodoxy despite initially lacking supporting evidence (Leithwood, Mascall & Strauss, 2009), whilst this evidentiary lacuna was swiftly being filled by accumulating evidence that distributed leadership 'matters' considerably (Harris, 2008, 2014). Increasingly, in and between various styles of leadership, there was also evidence of the necessity to be adept, flexible, a style switcher, a chameleon (Kets de Vries, 2006). This relative autonomy enjoyed by school leaders and their teaching colleagues in the 1980s that facilitated 'school-based curriculum development' was replaced by increasing external curricular prescription (Skilbeck, 1990, 1998). As Hargreaves (1989: 163) counselled, 'the broad international trend towards more centralized patterns of curriculum development is…placing profound restrictions on the possibilities for teacher development' and leadership trends had become complicit in this asphyxiation.

Legislating Leadership and Curriculum Reform

Without factoring into consideration larger political forces that have been buffeting and re-shaping the educational landscape in significant ways during this period, this account may seem rather tame, innocuous even. In order to illustrate this in a general and trans-Atlantic manner, two pieces of legislation are hugely significant. The first is the Educational Reform Act of 1988 (revised in 1992, and subsequently) in England and Wales, and the second is the No Child Left Behind (NCLB) legislation of the Bush administration in the US in 2001. In the case of the former, it fundamentally altered established norms by prescribing a national curriculum (for the period of compulsory schooling) divided into 'key stages' with national testing to be undertaken at these points. It also facilitated schools in separating from their Local Authorities whereby through Local Management of Schools (LMS) they could opt to be grant-maintained or independent under the rubric of creating a market for schooling and choice for parents. The NCLB Act, signed into law on 8 January 2002, created unprecedented federal intrusion into state responsibility for education to 'drive broad gains in student achievement and to hold states and schools more accountable for student progress' (Education Week, 2004). Similar to its English near relative, there was significant emphasis on testing, and federal funding was tied to schools able to demonstrate 'adequate yearly progress' (AYP) (Lasky, 2012), with serious consequences if targets were not met, similar to England's 'naming and shaming' culture (Bevan and Wilson, 2013). The locus of decision-making, the degree of prescription, the responsibilities of principals and the manner in which they would be held to account, as well as the language in which these reforms were written, fundamentally altered the educational landscape. This general trend has been subsequently extended by the advent of Academies in England, as well as vouchers and Charter schools in the US. More than anything else, these provisions are manifestations of a market logic and the creation of a quasi-market in education of 'edu-business' (see Ball, 2012: 116–36). The next section examines the consequences of these unprecedented legislative policy shifts and their consequences for the curricula of schools and the content of principal preparation programmes.

LEADING CURRICULUM: EXTERNALLY PRESCRIBED 'LEARNING OUTCOMES', SCRIPTED LEADERSHIP

For more than two decades, with schools as 'units of production' in the increasing quasi-market of education shaped by considerations of choice and competition, the spotlight has been focused increasingly on school leader preparation (Walker and Hallinger, 2013), fuelled by considerations of revolving door appointments (particularly in the US, see Renihan, 2012), recruitment and succession (MacBeath et al., 2009). Some have considered this as a 'makeover' that induces conformity and homogenisation rather than creativity and imagination – more management and less leadership – (Gunter and Thomson, 2009), whilst others see the shift in emphasis from education to learning as retrograde (Biesta, 2014). The erosion of trust and the application of market forces to educational services have intensified performativity trends, whilst reducing the spaces and opportunities for the exercise of responsible leadership and the relative autonomy necessary for discretionary judgement, which is a hallmark of curriculum development at the level of the school.

In Table 61.1, learning and education are accorded different logics. Biesta (2014) summarises this distinction and its implications, and although he is not against learning and its significance per se, his point is that learning is distinct from education.

> … the point of education is not that students learn, but that they learn *something*, that they learn it for particular *reasons*, and that they learn it *from someone*. The problem with the language of learning is that it is a language that refers to processes that are 'empty' with regard to content and purpose … a language of education always needs to pay attention to questions of *content*, *purpose* and *relationships*. (Biesta, 2014: 3)

Consequently, there has been a hollowing out of what goes on in schools to the point where, in some instances, schools, as part of a 'makeover' of a more market-sensitive approach to the 'services' they provide, have taken to 'branding' themselves as places of 'learning' rather than teaching, and school leaders are made over into 'lead learner' to avoid perceived negative connotations (Biesta, 2014). Biesta's point is that for learning to be genuinely educative it requires

content, a set of processes as well as a set of relationships. These three purposes of education are 'qualification' (achievement), 'socialisation' (both formal and informal) and 'subjectification', which, along with socialisation, contributes to the 'formation' of the individual whereby the student becomes the subject of education rather than being a mere spectator whilst mastering certain skills. Even if schools become preoccupied with, and overly focused on, 'performance' this narrowing of the curriculum has consequences for socialisation and subjectification – 'which is about the ways in which students can be(come) subjects in their own right and not just remain objects of the desires and directions of others' (Biesta, 2014: 4). I concur with the conclusion that 'the language of learning is unable to provide a sense of direction to the educational process, which is precisely where its deficiency as an educational language lies' (Biesta, 2014: 4).

Hollowing out of education by privileging learning has additional negative consequences because the language of learning is 'an ideology, making what really goes on invisible and inaccessible' (Biesta, 2012: 38). The adoption of 'the empty language of learning to speak about education' frequently results in questions such as 'what is education *for*' or indeed what is the 'good' of education being ignored (Biesta, 2010: 2). Teaching is also diminished when learning becomes the central focus and the role of the teacher is reduced to being 'a guide on the side'. By insisting that teaching and teachers are at the heart of the relationship between teacher and student, it follows that a teacher 'plays a central role in engaging with the question as to what is educationally desirable in each concrete situation, both with regard to the aims and to the '"means" of education' (Biesta, 2012: 39). Such responsibilities are 'a matter of judgement, not a matter of the execution of directives from elsewhere' (Biesta, 2012: 39). This hollowing out of education by a process of 'learnification' replaces 'the normative question of good education with technical and managerial questions about the efficiency and effectiveness of processes, not what these processes are supposed to be for' (Biesta, 2010: 2), a process described as 'policy by numbers' (Lingard et al., 2003) where what counts is test scores ('learning outcomes') – achievement. Critically, when moving beyond the limits of the language of learning, teachers' responsibilities are reasserted because 'teacher's responsibility for making situated judgements about the educational desirability of the means and ends of how education "proceeds" is integral to the role and responsibility' (Biesta, 2012: 40). To emphasize the significance of teaching as part of an educative process, Biesta (2012: 40–2) distinguishes between 'learning from' and 'being taught by' as two phrases that capture significant qualitative differences. Such a relationship requires receptivity on the part of the learner and an openness to being educated. The process of formation includes 'critical self-reflection' as well as 'moral dimensions' (Sutphen and de Lange, 2014). Formation has much in common with 'subjectification' whereby the student, through reflective engagement in the encounter, takes ownership as a subject for 'action and responsibility' (Biesta, 2012: 39). Has learnification of school leaders followed from this hollowing out of education?

The 'Making Over' and Over Again of School Leaders?

The 'makeover' of school leaders has potential to be authentic, and in the manner in which it is used by Gunter and Thomson (2009) – borrowed from popular culture – the 'change' is largely cosmetic, superficial and determined by others, whereby those who endure a makeover are 'bettered', even temporarily, by their betters. In the infotainment world, the more insidious influences of makeover programmes are often hidden from view, and yet 'this mediatised cultural space obscures the reality that the ongoing surveillance practised in reality television programmes '…is increasingly the stuff of a CCTV-ridden "audit society"' (Lyon, 1994; McGrath, 2004; Power, 1999)' (Gunter and

Thomson, 2009: 470). This perspective suggests that leadership has been reduced to a form of surveillance, whereby 'organisations [including schools] must be changed to make them auditable', an endless proliferation of policies and paper trails (Power, 1999: 47). Without trust, more 'technologies of control' are perceived as a necessity, where being held to account becomes a performance, often a negation of the exercise of professional judgement and responsibility. Gunter and Thomson (2009: 471) argue that principals in the English context over the past 20 years have been subjected to 'direct expert control exercised through leadership development to effect permanent changes to the minds and bodies of leaders and through them, their schools'. Given the ubiquitous permeation of the language and logic of accountability in various reforms, to what extent has the makeover or learnification of leadership become an international phenomenon?

The Learnification of School Leader Preparation?

Although evidence is limited, there are 'discernible patterns' (Gunter, 2008) in the English context, and 'many of the issues that continue to bedevil meaningful leadership development exhibit a certain commonality across very different settings' when selected programmes internationally are compared (Walker and Hallinger, 2013: 401). Such influences are evident even in the selection of leadership programmes for review, where those high performing systems – as indicated by Programme for International Student Assessment (PISA) – studies were selected. However, some of the most highly ranked countries in these studies, such as Finland, New Zealand and the Netherlands, do not have 'required pre-service preparation programmes' for principals, and principal preparation in these jurisdictions is therefore not available for analysis (Walker et al., 2013: 409).

At the beginning of the twenty-first century, when programmes in fifteen centres in nine countries were compared, there was considerable debate regarding the advisability of compulsion, as well as the extent of such provisions in terms of time commitment and accessibility in an effort to broaden the leadership talent pool (Bush and Jackson, 2002). There was a discernible tendency towards accreditation of programmes, contributing to a Masters, if not a Masters award. Additional considerations were the necessity to include theoretical perspectives that recognised, however reluctantly in some jurisdictions, that 'all leaders need frames of reference to guide decision-making' because 'theory…provides a valid base for evaluating possible solutions to educational problems' (Bush and Jackson, 2002: 424). When turning their attention to the future direction of leadership preparation, Bush and Jackson cautiously recognised that leadership preparation for all teachers would need consideration and this would require tailoring to principals' and teachers' career stages. They also acknowledged that technology could be harnessed to create virtual learning communities that would support schools as learning organisations, and research and mentoring would also need greater attention (Bush and Jackson, 2002). But these are boundary issues and, although important, say little about the actual formation of the next generation of school leaders.

Selecting compulsory programmes for review on the basis of PISA rankings recognises the prevalence of 'performativity' internationally. Walker et al. (2013) compare programmes in 'Australia, Canada, Hong Kong, Singapore and the USA' (2013: 408), and in the US, where such programmes have existed for several decades, a study in the noughties indicates the increasing homogenisation now being experienced elsewhere – perhaps with a particular US flavour in the wake of NCLB legislation (2001):

- Alignment to 'state and professional standards', an
- Emphasis on 'instructional leadership and school improvement';
- Student-centred learning;
- Formalized mentoring; and
- Site-based internships. (Darling-Hammond et al., 2010: 181–2)

This is evidence of learnification of leadership, which is emphasising the practical, possibly at the expense of theoretical considerations, and these efforts on both sides of the Atlantic have been criticised as being overly 'structuralist–functionalist' (Gronn, 2003). Additionally, the pervasiveness of accountability and NPM is immediately evident in the language used by the researchers to describe these programmes' content and outcomes. Consequently, commentators argue justifiably and consistently with hyping of 'efficiency', to the detriment of efficacy (Gross Stein 2001, above) and Ball's 'technologies of control' (2003) to the extent that homogenisation is evident in increasing external accreditation and prescription of frameworks, content and processes, which is a 'practice' orientation typically involving a placement. Emphasizing 'practice' is often accompanied with a focus on evidence of what works, whereas emphasis on 'training' ignores 'the tension between scientific and democratic control over educational practice and educational research' (Biesta, 2007: 5). Research that favours 'evidence-based education' has a strong preference for 'a technocratic model in which it is assumed that the only relevant research questions are questions about the effectiveness of educational means and techniques, forgetting, amongst other things, that what counts as '"effective" crucially depends on judgments about what is educationally desirable' (Biesta, 2007: 5). From a leadership preparation perspective, if the intent is to improve action rather than test scores, then leadership preparation of all 'must be informed by a critical engagement with the social sciences and philosophy' (Gunter and Ribbins, 2002: 388).

Comparative analysis of five programmes (Walker et al., 2013) provides valuable insights into the structure, content and programme processes, their emphasis on placement and mentoring, as well as their duration, but this does not include the experiences of participants and how they engage with the opportunities. The terms 'curriculum' or 'curriculum developer' do not feature in the analysis of programmes. 'Learning' is much more prevalent, particularly in the description of the New York programme with its 'leadership Performance Standards Matrix', which 'drives content and assessment across 12 dimensions' and programme participants 'must demonstrate competency in each dimension, further delineated by 55 behavioural criteria, which are...defined along a continuum of not meeting, progressing towards and meeting the standard' (Walker et al., 2013: 415). Such detailed specification of learning outcomes has been identified by Green as a management preoccupation with 'explicitness' (see Green, 2011: 139–55). In such circumstances, tacit knowledge and its manifestations through practical judgement and action, are turned into rules thus 'knowing how' gets confused with or conflated into 'knowing that' even 'where efficient practice is the deliberate application of … prescriptions … putting the prescriptions into practice is not identical with…grasping the prescriptions' (Ryle, 2000: 49, cited in Green, 2011: 160). Consistent with the general trend towards homogenisation, Walker et al. (2013: 420–2) conclude that providing a common language of leadership may be conducive to building leadership capacity and increasing the leadership talent pool, whilst programmes that are highly competitive and selective may serve as a disincentive to a more broadly based approach to building leadership capacity. Although attempting to increase access through multiple providers, programmes run the risk of being overly focused on the local. Some suggest that leadership preparation programmes 'must expand the scope of vision of school leaders to include an understanding of education in the global context' and that 'an international or global outlook among citizens of all countries' should be promoted 'as an issue of social justice' (Walker et al., 2013: 417). Although such aspirations are laudable given national and regional policy contexts where test scores predominate, technologies of control seriously circumscribe the dispositions and actions of school leaders and teachers alike, promoting a climate of 'teaching to

the test' (Koretz, 2008; Koretz, 2010; Lasky, 2012). In such circumstances, it is considerably more likely that they 'see professional formational virtue of *responsibleness* as an "add on"' to accountability obligations (Green, 2011: 170), extras that may prove impossible to provide depending on the coercive forces that play out in their particular policy-practice context. Such considerations amidst this pervasive managerialism suggest that there needs to be space for practical wisdom and professional judgement, and that over prescription does violence to the '*personal* in educational life' (Green, 2011: 171). In pursuing a more pivotal role for subjectification of leaders and learners alike in their formation, what potential does the zone of proximal distance have in bringing leadership preparation and curriculum development into generative tension?

DEVELOPING LEADERS OF CURRICULUM: THE GENERATIVE POTENTIAL OF THE ZONE OF PROXIMAL DISTANCE?

The foregoing analysis suggests curricula have become more prescriptive and the standards agendas, through national-international testing regimes of control and accountability, have intensified. In the process, learnification has hollowed out the experiences of learners and leaders. It is timely, therefore, as part of the process of understanding long-wave cycles of reform, to reconnect curriculum development with the professional formation of school leaders – a generative process that begins in and is sustained within the zone of proximal distance.

Recently, I completed a longitudinal life history of school leaders in Ireland (Sugrue, 2015). Its data comprised 60 in-depth life history interviews with sixteen primary school principals at varying career stages over a period of ten years, beginning in 1999–2000 and concluding in 2008.[3] What emerged from this in-depth analysis was the necessity for what I call the zone of proximal distance. In the first instance, it is important to acknowledge Vygotsky's seminal contribution – the 'zone of proximal development' where the tension in the 'zo-ped' between what is previously known and what is being learned requires appropriate scaffolding (Vygotsky, 1978). Similarly, but differently, tension in the zone of proximal distance is between the personal and the professional, between external policy prescriptions and internal beliefs, values and dispositions. This analysis clearly indicates its generative potential for leadership formation (Sugrue, 2015). I argue here that curriculum development and leadership formation are two sides of one coin, and it is as these are encountered within the zone of proximal distance that leadership education rather than learninfication is fostered, the subjectification of leaders and learners accommodated and addressed, their formation sustained. Dealing with such tension has the additional responsibility to reinstate relative professional autonomy as an essential element of the life-blood of leading education, and thus also curriculum development.

The Genesis of the Zone of Proximal Distance

In the Irish context, because principals are appointed for life some may be in the role, often in the same school, for more than three decades, and without systemic provision to enable principals to revert to teaching responsibilities.[4] In the absence of adequate mobility, the study indicates that principals tend towards privileging good 'personal' relationships, with a commitment to 'keeping the peace' and smoothing over actual and potential conflict. In such circumstances, there is a degree of 'intimacy' or 'proximity' whereby 'good' relationships are anchored in the personal, and troubling disagreements are avoided. Such dynamics may play out to the (potential) detriment of more robust professional relationships where a degree of professional 'distance' is necessary to create spaces

and opportunities for principled disagreements and more robust professional conversations. There is evidence of the need for both proximity and distance in such relationships. In order to draw attention to this tension, rather like James Joyce describing his native Dublin as 'lugly' (simultaneously ugly and lovely) (Kearney, 1985), the compound term 'per-fessional' draws attention to the intimacy between the personal and professional, and attendant tension between proximity and distance (Sugrue, 2015). Relationships are critical and there is increasing recognition that in 'building professional capacity or "capital"… collaborative cultures build social capital and…also *professional capital* in a school community' (Hargreaves and Fullan, 2012: 114, emphasis in original). However, 'collaborative or shared leadership is not the same as cosy consensus or unfocused cooperation' (Harris, 2014: 4). Nevertheless, in far too many instances this awareness and recognition does not translate into the actual efforts through professional preparation programmes to build on this reality. This tension is exacerbated in a climate of performativity and external prescription. The zone of proximal distance is therefore generative and intent on building leadership capacity whilst simultaneously moving beyond the unease, distrust and inhibition that are generated by externally driven demands for higher standards from learners and greater 'performance' from leaders and practitioners alike. These tensions are evident in and integral to the force field that constitutes the zone of proximal distance (Figure 61.1).

Maximising space and time within the zone recognises the importance of various competing and conflicting interests whilst also suggesting that finding an appropriate settlement between them is critical to per-fessional integrity, morale and commitment. In this regard, leadership formation is intimately connected to curriculum development. Recognising subjectification as integral to their own formation as professional and leader, they gain insight into the

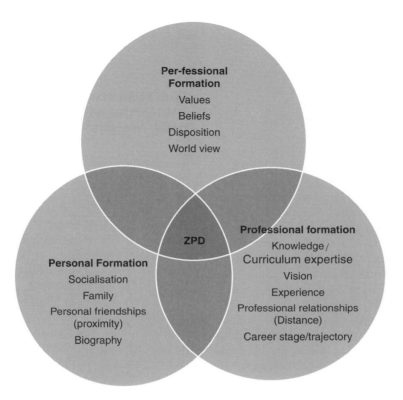

Figure 61.1   Zone of Proximal Distance (ZPD)

responsibility that their engagement with learners encompasses, namely to construct a curriculum that contributes to their formation rather than merely facilitating mastery of particular skills. This new synergy realises that a 'good' education cannot ignore purposes, including the formation of a moral compass for positive and productive citizenship in the knowledge society or participation in the knowledge economy (Hargreaves, 2003).

Leadership Formation: Zone of Proximal Distance

When a premium is placed on personal friendships this inhibits the development of professional relationships and therefore also the trust and robustness necessary for professional growth; communication tends to remain focused on social topics of conversation that largely do not intrude into the professional domain (Sugrue, 2015). In Figure 61.1,

communication is largely confined to the left circle, leaving professional formation mostly undisturbed. However, if external pressures are intensified to a point where survival becomes a major consideration, then it is more difficult, if not impossible, to create productive dissonance or temporary settlement between the personal sense of self and integrity, and also the demands of the role and its responsibilities. When there is insufficient time or space through the zone of proximal distance to process policy demands, there is greater likelihood of a sundering between the personal and the professional when it is no longer possible to hold them in productive tension. In such circumstances, the focus shifts to the circle on the right and it is more challenging to make meaning for the personal (and professional) – in fact it is more likely to induce compliance accompanied by decline in morale and commitment, potentially leading to disillusion and disengagement. It is possible to understand performativity as a similar sundering whereby the professional becomes technical and instrumental and is no longer resonant with values and beliefs. The personal therefore becomes disconnected when generative tension is no longer possible, and a sense of professional responsibility is hollowed out and reduced to a measure of accountability where, over time, meaningfulness gives way to meaninglessness. I am in agreement with the assertion that 'the technical–managerial approach to accountability can in no way be reconciled with an approach in which responsibility is central' (Biesta, 2010: 70). In such circumstances, 'legitimate compromise' (May, 1996) is no longer possible – professionals are compromised, denied the space and opportunity to fashion their own education, and are also compromising the curriculum they enact for their students. This is not an argument that suggests permanent and immutable features of the zone of proximal distance; rather, values, beliefs and dispositions are in dynamic interplay as the engine room where personal and professional are continuously renewed and re-educated, at once cultivating a dynamic disposition that recognises a similarly holistic and internally coherent curriculum as the entitlement of learners.

Evidence from my study and elsewhere (Hargreaves and Shirley, 2012) indicates that there is need for both time and space to be in the zone. In the absence of adequate opportunity for leadership learning and curriculum development, there are limitations to the cultivation of trust and professional relationships. It becomes clearer, however, that it is necessary in and out of school and in considering the building of leadership capacity systemically that the personal and the professional need appropriate and sustained attention. This is not a panacea and although there is evidence that communities of practice and learning communities have potential to facilitate capacity building, they can also become safe havens for complaint in the face of increasing performativity policy demands,

rather than more robust places where learning is advanced and capacity enhanced.

CONCLUSIONS: LEADERSHIP FORMATION AS CURRICULUM DEVELOPMENT

This evidence and argument shows that, to a significant extent, curriculum development has been 'outsourced' and is no longer the professional responsibility of teachers and designated school leaders. Intensification of external prescription, exacerbated by a variety of technologies of control, have conspired, wittingly or otherwise, to increase the learnification of leadership as well as hollowing out curricula. This has short-changed learners and reduced their formation to acquisition of skills whilst largely ignoring their formation through education. Consequently, 'the rising tide of standardized education … and a one-size-fits-all model of measurement is rapidly dissolving our innate power as professional educators to create meaningful life-changing experiences in our classrooms' (McDermott, 2013: 104). Similarly, and simultaneously, Hargreaves et al.'s (2014) *Uplifting Leadership* indicates that 'sustainable success requires a solid footing, as well as a manageable rate of progress and an ability and willingness to ensure that immediate actions are connected to long-term results' (2014: 157). This solid footing and its attendant uplifting professional conversation begins and resides within the zone of proximal distance, where school leadership re-unites with and recognises curriculum development as an attainable responsibility, and where it cultivates the capacity to provide a good education for all.

NOTES

1   It would be instructive in this regard to scrutinise literacy and numeracy policies in various jurisdictions, their genesis in each case, and to evaluate the extent of their impact on the quality of

the curriculum, teaching, learning and leading in these systems.

2   A particularly good example of political policy making is provided in the Irish context when, in 2011, the then Minister for Education and Skills introduced a 'national strategy' for 'literacy and numeracy' in response to a decline in national performance in PISA tests (OECD, 2010a) (see Department of Education and Skills (DES), 2011).

3   For a more detailed account of the methodology and data analysis, see Sugrue (2015: 14–20).

4   This reality is a major legacy issue because teachers and principals are appointed to particular schools, although all are paid by the state. This has major implications for staffing and leadership within school communities.

REFERENCES

Apple, M. (2004) *Ideology and Curriculum.* 3rd edn. Abingdon, UK: Routledge.

Ball, S. (2003) 'The teacher's soul and the terrors of performativity', *Journal of Education Policy,* 18(2): 215–28.

Ball, S. (2012) *Global Education Inc. New Policy Networks and The Neo-Liberal Imaginary.* Abingdon, UK: Routledge.

Beck, U. (2000) *What Is Globalization?* Cambridge: Polity Press.

Beck, U. (2006) *Cosmopolitan Vision.* Cambridge: Polity Press.

Beck, U. (2013) *German Europe.* Cambridge: Polity Press.

Berlak, A. and Berlak, H. (1975) *The Dilemmas of Schooling.* London: Methuen.

Berlak, A., Berlak, H., Tushnet Bagentos, N. and Mikel, E. (1976) Teaching and learning in English primary schools', in M. Hammersley and P. Woods (eds.), *The Process of Schooling.* pp. 86–97. London: Routledge & Kegan Paul.

Bevan, G. and Wilson, D. (2013) 'Does "naming and shaming" work for schools and hospitals? Lessons from a natural experiment following devolution in England and Wales', *Public Money & Management,* 33(4): 245–52.

Biesta, G. (2007) 'Why "what works" won't work: evidence-based practice and the democratic deficit in educational research', *Educational Theory,* 57(1): 1–22.

Biesta, G. (2010) *Good Education In An Age Of Measurement Ethics, Politics, Democracy.* Boulder, CO: Paradigm Publishers.

Biesta, G. (2012) 'Giving teaching back to education: responding to the disappearance of the teacher', *Phenomenology & Practice,* 6(2): 35–49.

Biesta, G. (2014) 'Lead learner or head teacher? Exploring connections between curriculum, leadership and evaluation in an "age of measurement"', paper presented at the Annual Conference of the European Educational Research Association, ECER 2014, Porto, Portugal.

Bobbitt, J. F. (1918) *The Curriculum.* Boston & New York: Houghton Mifflin & Co.

Bruner, J. (1960/1997) *The Process of Education (A Landmark in Educational Theory Now Reassessed by the Author in a New Introduction).* Cambridge, MA: Harvard University Press.

Bush, T. and Jackson, D. (2002) 'A preparation for school leadership', *Educational Management & Administration,* 30(4): 417–29.

Coleman, J.S., Campbell, E., Hobson, E., McPartland, J., Mood, A., Weinfield, F. and York, R. (1966) *Equality of Educational Opportunity.* Washington, DC: US Government Printing Office.

Copland, M.A. (2001) 'The myth of the superprincipal', *Phi Delta Kappan,* 82(7): 528–33.

Couldry, N. (2010/2012) *'Why Voice Matters: Culture and Politics after NeoLiberalism.* Thousand Oaks, CA: Sage Publications.

Darling-Hammond, L., Meyerson, D., LaPointe, M. and Terry Orr, M. (2010) *'Preparing Principals for a Changing World: Lessons From Effective School Leadership Programmes',* San Francisco, CA: Jossey-Bass.

Day, C. (ed.) '(2012) *'The Routledge International Handbook of Teacher and School Development.* London: Routledge.

Department of Education (1965) *The Rules for National Schools.* Dublin, Ireland: Stationery Office.

Department of Education and Skills (DES) (2011) *Literacy and Numeracy for Life and Learning: The National Strategy to Improve Literacy and Numeracy among Children and Young People 2011–2020.* Dublin, Ireland: Department of Education and Skills.

Education Week (2004) *No Child Left Behind.* Available from http://www.edweek.org/ew/issues/no-child-left-behind/ (accessed ??). Please provide access date 11/11/'14

Egan, K. (1997) *The Educated Mind*. Chicago, IL: Chicago University Press.

Eisner, E. (1979) *The Educational Imagination*. New York, NY: Collier Macmillan.

Goodson, I.F. (1994) *Studying Curriculum*. New York, NY: Teachers College, Columbia University.

Goodson, I.F. (2004) 'Change processes and historical periods: an international perspective', in C. Sugrue (ed.), *Curriculum and Ideology: Irish Experiences, International Perspectives*. Dublin, Ireland: Liffey Press. pp. 19–34.

Green, J. (2011) *Education, Professionalism and the Quest for Accountability Hitting the Target but Missing the Point*. London: Routledge.

Gronn, P. (2003) *The New Work of Educational Leaders Changing Leadership Practice in an Era of School Reform*. London: Paul Chapman.

Gronn, P. (2009) 'Hybrid leadership', in K. Leithwood, B. Mascall and T. Strauss (eds.), *Distributed Leadership According to the Evidence*. London: Routledge. pp. 17–40.

Gross Stein, J. (2001) *The Cult of Efficiency*. Toronto: Anansi Press.

Gunter, H. (2008) 'Policy and workforce reform in England', *Educational Management Administration & Leadership,* 36: 253–70.

Gunter, H. and Ribbins, P. (2002) 'Leadership studies in education towards a map of the field', *Educational Management and Administration,* 30(4): 387–416.

Gunter, H. and Thomson, P. (2009) 'The makeover: a new logic in leadership development in England', *Educational Review,* 61(4): 469–83.

Hall, V. (1996) *Dancing on The Ceiling: A Study of Women Managers in Education*. London: Paul Chapman.

Hargreaves, A. (1989) *Curriculum and Assessment Reform* (critical introduction by Ivor Goodson). Milton Keynes: Open University Press.

Hargreaves, A. (1994) *Changing Teachers, Changing Times*. London: Cassell.

Hargreaves, A. (2003) *Teaching in the Knowledge Society*. Buckingham, UK: Open University Press.

Hargreaves, A. and Fullan, M. (2012) *Professional Capital Transforming Teaching in Every School*. New York, NY: Teachers College Press.

Hargreaves, A., and Goodson, I. F. (2006) 'Educational change over time: the sustainability and nonsustainability of three decades of secondary school change and continuity', *Educational Administration Quarterly,* 42(1): 3–41.

Hargreaves, A. and Shirley, D. (2012) *The Global Fourth Way: The Quest for Educational Excellence*. Thousand Oaks, CA: Corwin and Ontario Principals' Council.

Hargreaves, A., Boyle, A. and Harris, A. (2014) *Uplifting Leadership: How Organisations, Teams and Communities Raise Performance*. San Francisco, CA: Jossey-Bass.

Hargreaves, A., Lieberman, A., Fullan, M. and Hopkins, D. (1998) *International Handbook of Educational Change*. Dordrecht, Netherlands: Kluwer.

Hargreaves, A., Lieberman, A., Fullan, M. and Hopkins, D. (2010) *Second International Handbook of Educational Change*. Dordrecht, Netherlands: Springer.

Harris, A. (2008) *Distributed School Leadership Developing Tomorrow's Leaders*. London: Routledge.

Harris, A. (2014) *Distributed Leadership Matters*. Los Angeles, CA: Corwin.

Hood, C. (1991) 'A public management for all seasons', *Public Administration,* 69(Spring): 3–19.

Jencks, C., Smith, M., Acland, H., Bane, M.J., Cohen, D., Gintis, H., Heyns, B., and Michelson, S. (1972) *Inequality: A Reassessment of the Effects of Family and Schooling in America*. New York, NY: Basic Books.

Kearney, R. (1985) *The Irish Mind: Exploring Intellectual Traditions*. Dublin, Ireland: Wolfhound Press.

Kets de Vries, M. (2006) *The Leader on the Couch: A Clinical Approach to Changing People and Organizations*. San Francisco, CA: Jossey-Bass.

Koretz, D. (2008) *Measuring Up What Educational Testing Really Tells Us*. Cambridge, MA: Harvard University Press.

Koretz, D. (2010) 'The validity of score gains on high-stakes tests', in B. McGraw, P.L. Peterson and E. Baker (eds.), *International Encyclopaedia of Education*. 3rd edn., Vol. 4. Oxford: Elsevier. pp. 186–92.

Lasky, S. (2012) 'Warehousing the schoolhouse: impact on teachers' work and lives', in C. Day (ed.), *The Routledge International Handbook of Teacher and School Development*. Abingdon, UK: Routledge. pp. 73–83.

Lawn, M. and Grek, S. (2012) *Europeanizing Education: Governing a New Policy Space*. Oxford: Symposium Books.

Leithwood, K., Chapman, J., Corson, D., Hallinger, P. and Hart, A. (ed.) (1996) *International Handbook of Educational Leadership and Administration*. Dordrecht, Netherlands: Kluwer.

Leithwood, K., Hallinger, P., Furman, K., Riley, K., MacBeath, J., Gronn, P. and Mulford, B. (2002) *Second International Handbook of Educational Leadership and Administration*. Dordrecht, Netherlands: Springer.

Leithwood, K., Mascall, B. and Strauss, T. (eds.) (2009) *Distributed Leadership According to the Evidence*. New York, NY: Routledge.

Lieberman, A. and Miller, L. (2004) *Teacher Leadership*. San Francisco, CA: Jossey-Bass.

Lingard, B., Hayes, D., MIlls, M. and Christie, P. (2003) *Leading Learning: Making Hope Practical In Schools*. Maidenhead, UK: Open University Press.

Lyon, D. (1994) *The Electronic Eye: The Rise of the Surveillance Society*. Minneapolis: University of Minnesota Press.

MacBeath, J., Gronn, P., Opfer, D., Lowden, K., Forde, C., Cowie, M., and O'Brien, J. (2009). *The Recruitment and Retention of Headteachers in Scotland* (Report to the Scottish Government). Edinburgh: The Scottish Government.

Mann, H. (1846) *Report of an Educational Tour in Germany and Parts of Great Britain and Ireland* (with Preface and Notes by W.B. Hodgson). London: Simpkin, Marshall & Company and D. Marples.

May, L. (1996) *The Socially Responsive Self: Social Theory and Professional Ethics*. Chicago, IL: Chicago University Press.

McDermott, M. (2013) *The Left-Handed Curriculum: Creative Experiences for Empowering Teachers*. Charlotte, NC: Information Age Publishing.

McGrath, J. (2004) 'Notes on "What Not To Wear" and post-feminist symbolic violence', *The Sociological Review*, 52(2): 99–109.

Mitgang, L. (2012) *The Making of The Principal: Five Lessons In Leadership Training*. New York, NY: The Wallace Foundation.

Organisation for Economic Co-operation and Development (OECD) (2010a) *PISA 2009 Results: What Students Know and Can Do – Student Performance in Reading, Mathematics and Science*. Vol. 1. Paris: OECD.

Organisation for Economic Co-operation and Development (OECD) (2010b) *PISA 2009 Results: Learning Trends Changes in Student Performance since 2000*. Vol. 5. Paris: OECD.

Organisation for Economic Co-operation and Development (OECD) (2013) *Education at a Glance: 2013 OECD Indicators*. Paris: OECD.

Pont, B., Nusche, D. and Moorman, H. (2008) *Improving School Leadership. Vol. 1: Policy and Practice*. Paris: OECD.

Power, M. (1999) *The Audity Society Rituals of Verification*. Oxford: Oxford University Press.

Renihan, P.J. (2012) 'Leadership succession for tomorrow's schools', *Procedia – Social and Behavioral Sciences*, 55(0): 138–47. doi: http://dx.doi.org/10.1016/j.sbspro.2012.09.487.

Reynolds, C. (ed.) (2002) *Women and School Leadership: International Perspectives*. Albany, NY: State University of New York Press.

Rutter, M., Maughan, B., Mortimore, P. and Ouston, J. (1979) *Fifteen Thousand Hours: Secondary Schools and their Effects on Children*. London: Open Books.

Ryan, K. and Bradley Cousins, J. (2009) *The Sage International Handbook of Educational Evaluation*. Thousand Oaks, CA: Sage Publications.

Ryle, G. (2000) *The Concept of Mind*. London: Penguin Classics.

Sahlberg, P. (2011) *Finnish Lessons: What Can the World Learn from Educational Change in Finland (with a foreword by Andy Hargreaves)*. New York, NY: Teachers' College Press.

Sammons, P., Hillman, J., and Mortimore, P. (1995) *Key Characteristics of Effective Schools: A Review of Schools Effectiveness Research (for the Office of Standards in Education [Ofsted])*. London Institute of Education.

Skilbeck, M. (1990) *Curriculum Reform: An Overview of Trends*. Paris: OECD.

Skilbeck, M. (1998) 'School-Based Curriculum Development', in A. Hargreaves, A. Lieberman, M. Fullan and D. Hopkins (eds.), *International Handbook of Educational Change*. Vol. 1. Dordrecht, Netherlands: Kluwer. pp. 121–44.

Smith, D.G. (2014) 'Wisdom responses to globalization', in W. Pinar (ed.), *International*

Handbook of Curriculum Research. London: Routledge. pp. 45–59.

Smithers, A. and Robinson, P. (2007) *School Headship Present and Future* (produced with the support of the National Union of Teachers). Buckingham, UK: Centre for Education and Employment Research, University of Buckingham.

Smulyan, L. (2000) *Balancing Acts: Women Principals at Work*. New York, NY: State University of New York Press.

Solbrekke, T.D. and Englund, T. (2011) 'Bringing professional responsibility back in?', *Studies in Higher Education,* 36(7): 847–61.

Solbrekke, T.D. and Sugrue, C. (2011) 'Professional responsibility – back to the future', in T. Dyrdal Solbrekke and C. Sugrue (eds.), *Professional Responsibility: New Horizons of Praxis*. London: Routledge. pp. 10–28.

Spillane, J. (2006) *Distributed Leadership*. San Francisco, CA: Jossey-Bass.

Stenhouse, L. (1975) *An Introduction to Curriculum Research and Development*. London: Heinemann.

Sugrue, C. (2010) 'Plowden: progressive education – a 4-decade odyssey?', *Curriculum Inquiry,* 40(1): 105–24.

Sugrue, C. (2015) *Unmasking School Leadership: A Longitudinal Life History of School Leaders*. Dordrecht, Netherlands: Springer.

Sutphen, M. and de Lange, T. (2014) 'What is formation? A conceptual discussion', *Higher Education Research and Development,* 34(2): 411–19.

Teddlie, C. and Reynolds, D. (eds.) (2000) *The International Handbook of School Effectiveness Research*. London: RoutledgeFalmer.

Thröhler, D. (2014) 'International curriculum research', in W. Pinar (ed.), *International Handbook of Curriculum Research*. London: Routledge. pp. 60–6.

Townsend, T. (2007) *International Handbook of School Effectiveness and Improvement*. Dordrecht, Netherlands: Springer.

Vygotsky, L.S. (1978) *Mind in Society*. Cambridge, MA: Harvard University Press.

Walker, A. and Hallinger, P. (2013) 'International perspectives on leader development: definition and design', *Educational Management Administration & Leadership,* 41(4): 401–4.

Walker, A., Bryant, D. and Lee, M. (2013) 'International patterns in principal preparation: commonalities and variations in pre-service programmes', *Educational Management Administration & Leadership,* 41(4): 405–34.

Wallerstein, I., Collins, R., Mann, M., Derlugian, G. and Calhoun, C. (2013) *Does Capitalism Have A Future?* Oxford: Oxford University Press.

62

Teacher Education – Making Connections with Curriculum, Pedagogy and Assessment

Ian Menter

INTRODUCTION

Teacher education has a dual relationship with Bernstein's three message systems of curriculum, pedagogy and evaluation (or assessment) (Bernstein, 1975). The first aspect relates to how teacher education is provided, what are the respective approaches to curriculum, pedagogy and assessment in the way the beginning teachers experience them as learners. In other words what is the teacher education curriculum, how are the students' learning experiences structured and how are the students assessed? But then the second aspect lies within the curriculum component itself – what is it that is taught and learnt in relation to the topics of curriculum, pedagogy and assessment within the teacher education programme?

This distinction may seem to be a somewhat 'precious' point to make but it cannot be assumed that these two elements coincide. For example, a very inclusive pedagogy could notionally be taught in a very non-inclusive manner; or student teachers might be tested in their final exams in their understanding of formative assessment, but yet never have benefitted from formative assessment during the course of their learning. These two aspects are theoretically distinctive.

In this chapter the two aspects of each message system are considered in turn, taking the programmatic element first and then, somewhat more briefly, looking at the approach taken to each of the three topics within the teacher education curriculum. But before discussing these aspects, some scene setting is necessary. It is important to offer an account – albeit brief – of the institutional development of teacher education and to identify some of the enduring issues in teacher education. This is necessary in order for us to get to grips with the more specific concerns around the three message systems later in this chapter. In the interests of concision, the focus is almost entirely on the UK, with particular emphasis on England.

Underlying the whole chapter, however, are two further underlying theoretical themes that must concern us and are amongst the enduring questions in the study of teacher education (Cochran-Smith et al., 2008). First, what is the nature of the relationship between schooling and teacher education? It may well be assumed that teacher education should 'serve' the schooling system – that is, the way in which teachers are prepared should be consistent with the current approaches to curriculum, pedagogy and assessment within the schools. However, it might also be suggested that teacher education could be an important source for change and development within schooling, not least if significant parts of teacher education take place within contexts of 'knowledge production', such as universities. Second, although much of the discussion may be concerned with initial teacher education – sometimes known as pre-service teacher education – we should not forget the important dimensions of later professional learning, through teacher induction, ongoing or continuing professional development and leadership development. This is partly to suggest that it will not be possible for beginning teachers to learn everything a teacher needs to know or be able to do during their initial period of preparation. It is now a widely held view that ongoing development throughout a teacher's career is a prerequisite for a strong education system and this is certainly the view taken in recent reviews of teacher education in the UK (Donaldson, 2011; Furlong, 2015).

THE DEVELOPMENT OF TEACHER EDUCATION

The approaches to teacher education which exist today in the 'developed' world have their origins in a range of traditions, including the tutoring at home of wealthy young people, the provision of religious training both for the clergy and for monks and nuns, but also especially from the second half of the nineteenth century onwards, for the growing numbers of the urban working class. In these settings the religious organisations played a very central part in the early emergence of systematic preparation of teachers. In the schools of the late nineteenth century in England and Scotland, certain pupils were identified as having the potential to become teachers themselves and were trained by their own teachers in the early stages of becoming a teacher (Dent, 1977). Such candidates were called 'pupil teachers'. As Cruickshank (1970) writes in her history of teacher education in Scotland:

> Pupil teachers were in the words of Matthew Arnold the 'drudges' of the profession. Occasionally in the parish schools they attended advanced classes in Latin or mathematics, but in general they were engaged in teaching the whole of the school day. The teachers in charge were required to give them one and a half hours of private instruction, but in fact the practice varied. (1970: 59)

This system became the basis for the development of 'normal schools', where such preparation became a feature of the schools and they were seen as sites for the training and preparation for growing numbers of teachers who, on completion of training, could then be deployed elsewhere. In some cases these normal schools provided the basis for the subsequent creation of teacher training colleges (Cook, 1984). These were still very much religiously driven organisations, with the central ethos being a Christian one and the central knowledge to be conveyed by teachers to pupils being Bible studies. In order to be able to read the Bible, literacy was of course a requirement, and so this was the main early driver for teaching pupils to be able to read, rather than any broader disposition towards literacy for either functional or pleasurable purposes.

The elementary school system developed around the transition from the nineteenth to the twentieth century, and so that by the time of the introduction of the 'Elementary Code' of 1904, all elementary school teachers were expected to be able to meet the purposes of this stage of schooling, which were to:

> ...train the children carefully in habits of observation and clear reasoning, so that they may gain an

intelligent acquaintance with some of the facts and laws of nature; to arouse in them a living interest in the ideals and achievements of mankind, and to bring them to some familiarity with the literature and history of their own country; to give them some power over language as an instrument of thought and expression... (cited by Maclure, 1986: 154)

The idea of a school 'curriculum' only emerged during the twentieth century, at least so far as the publicly funded sector was concerned. Prior to that there were many assumptions about the purposes of schooling, which led to a simple definition of the school syllabus and to the testing of pupils' learning through simple tests and exams. The methods of teaching were also largely taken for granted and were simple techniques of transmission of knowledge using chalkboards, slates, maps, globes and the like. What might now be called 'behaviour management' was largely a matter of strict codes of discipline and accompanying sanctions, including physical punishment, as a means of ensuring compliance by pupils.

Although we are focusing here on developments in England, there were broadly similar developments elsewhere in the Western world with the steady institutionalisation of teacher training and education. In some contexts, model schools were an important element. These were schools that were taken to exemplify good practice in teaching and where trainees could observe and be observed as they developed their own skills. Again many colleges of education had schools attached to them, and in some cases special observation theatres were developed within the college (Robinson, 2004). The 'crit room' at one College of Education in a Victorian building, where the author of the present chapter worked during the 1980s, was a large classroom with a banked semi-circle of seating for students to observe demonstrations of teaching conducted at the centre of the room.

The colleges of education then were initially church-based single-sex institutions scattered across the country, many of them located in beautiful pastoral settings with the trainees living in residence and undertaking their classes during the day and being placed in schools in the area for periods of practical experience. However, during the twentieth century, as local education authorities (committees established by locally elected councils) increasingly became responsible for establishing and maintaining elementary and then primary and secondary schools, so some of these authorities also established colleges of education that were not run by religious organisations but by the local authorities themselves. The early twentieth century – especially after the end of World War I – was also a period when some universities were increasingly becoming directly involved in the preparation of secondary school teachers through establishing Departments of Education and/or supporting Area Training Organisations (ATOs).

The end of the World War II saw a period during which there was such a shortage of teachers that short 'emergency training' routes into teaching were introduced to help to address the shortfall, but with the postwar 'settlement' on education under the auspices of the 1944 Education Act, which introduced secondary education for all, there was a rapid expansion of the training system both in colleges and in universities. The period saw a move towards the introduction of academic awards being associated with teaching qualifications, initially through 'Teaching Certificates' and later during the 1960s the introduction of Bachelor of Education degrees. By the 1970s, The James Report on Teacher Education (Department for Education and Science (DES), 1972) both consolidated the idea of an 'all-graduate' teaching profession and pointed out that teacher education should be a career-long process, with the initial pre-service period being only the precursor to subsequent stages of professional learning.

ISSUES IN TEACHER EDUCATION

Elsewhere in the developed world, similar processes were happening, although the particular institutional arrangements varied considerably and these differences still continue to influence provision to this day. However, as this range of institutionalised approaches to teacher preparation developed during the twentieth century, it became possible to identify a number of common critical themes that were addressed and variously contested and debated. Perhaps the most enduring of these themes is that of the balance in learning between theory and practice. This may seem like a simple distinction, but it has been increasingly recognised as actually being very complex. The issue really does relate closely to how the activity of teaching is understood. As indicated, in the early days of teacher training there were many simple assumptions about what it was to be a teacher. If the task of a teacher was 'simply' to impart knowledge to learners, then the essence of teaching was for the teacher to have the requisite knowledge and to be able to 'transmit' it to the learners – two simple qualities: knowledge and skills of communication. If the knowledge was prescribed, then it was assumed that it could be learnt through a process of study by the intending teacher. As for communication skills, it was assumed that they could best be learnt through a kind of apprenticeship with an experienced teacher, observing and imitating the best practice of experienced mentors. There was, in other words, very little need for any theoretical learning at all, certainly very little need for educational theory. However, as interest in processes of teaching and learning grew during the twentieth century, there were influences from philosophy and psychology in particular, which began to call into question some of these simple assumptions. The philosophers were beginning to question the underlying purposes of education and asking other questions relating to values in society. The psychologists were beginning to question what were the most effective means of learning for children and to examine in some detail how children developed.

This was the beginning of 'educational sciences' or 'educational studies' and for the first time it appeared to indicate that some theoretical study of education might be important for beginning teachers, in order that they could not only 'do' teaching but could also understand how to make improvements to their teaching and to understand why certain approaches might be desirable or indeed better than certain others (Furlong, 2013). In other words, the idea of teachers as decision makers was beginning to take hold.

The tension between theory and practice has, to some extent, become a debate about where student teachers should learn – what should be the balance between 'theoretical' learning in the academy (the College of Education or the University) on the one hand and 'practical' or 'experiential' learning in the school setting on the other. In recent decades, as teacher education has become increasingly politicised, many politicians have developed a populist rhetoric that derides the study of theory and insists that the most important learning is done, as a recent English Secretary of State in England chose to term it, 'on the job' (Department of Education (DfE), 2010).

However, there have also been attempts over many years to bring theory and practice into closer relationship, indeed to integrate these two aspects of beginning teachers' learning. There are few teachers or teacher educators who would deny the critical importance of both aspects of learning, and the challenge really should be to establish not how much of each they should have, but rather to identify the appropriate nature of the relationship between the two. These debates have been informed by a developing understanding of 'workplace learning' (McNamara et al., 2013) and also by the development of ideas around 'clinical practice' in teacher education (Burn and Mutton, 2013). Most such approaches involve beginning teachers not only carrying out some teaching in school but also the gathering of 'data', often observational data, and then analysing it in a way that is informed by theory. A number of teacher education schemes around the world now adopt this kind of integrated learning approach and some involve the concepts of 'theorised practice' and/or 'practical theorising' (see Hagger and McIntyre, 2006).

If the relationship between theory and practice is one major theme, a second one that is very closely related is the nature of the relationship between the school and the higher education setting in contributing to teacher learning. The word that has been deployed to characterise this relationship in many settings is 'partnership'. What is the nature of the partnership between schools and Higher Education Institutions (HEIs) in teacher learning? During much of the twentieth century in teacher education programmes across the world, the two settings were seen as very discrete, each making a distinctive contribution to the student teacher's learning. Programmes were usually led, managed and administered by an HEI, with students spending much of their time studying education, their chosen subject and approaches to pedagogy in that setting. This element was interspersed by relatively short periods of placement – traditionally called 'teaching practice' but more recently 'school experience'. In the US such placements were usually termed 'field experience' or latterly, 'the practicum'. The dominant mode of learning here was observation of teachers and periods of student teaching with the student taking on steadily increasing responsibility in the classroom. The role of the teachers in the school who were supporting the students was usually implicit rather than clearly codified. However, this did begin to change in some parts of the UK in the early 1990s, when government prescribed not only the amount of time that 'trainees' should spend within the school (this had first been a subject for prescription earlier in the 1980s), but also that the HEI provider was required to establish a 'partnership agreement' that would specify a sum of money to be transferred to the school in recognition of the formal support that would be provided by the teachers in the school. This led to the development of much more formal designation of roles within HEI–school partnerships and, perhaps most

significantly, led to school teachers taking on a role in the assessment of the performance of the trainee teacher, and contributing to the decision of whether or not the student should actually qualify as a teacher.

In the 1990s in England teacher education programmes were required to adopt a model of partnership. A major study in that period found that there were different approaches to this, ranging from 'collaborative' or 'integrated' models where the partners could jointly lead the programme, through to 'complementary' models where the distinctive roles of the different partners were clearly defined but did not effectively interact with each other – these tended to be dominated by the HEI partner (Furlong et al., 2000).

However, from the late 1980s onwards, in part because of problems with teacher supply, some 'employment-based routes' were introduced. These routes very often had a reduced role for the HEIs, and now include, in England, programmes such as Teach First, School-Centred Initial Teacher Training (SCITT) and School Direct (Salaried) (Childs and Menter, 2013; Teacher Education Group, 2015).

The concern with assessment, mentioned earlier, was also associated with a third key theme – that of standards in teaching. If student teachers were to be assessed in a consistent and professional manner, what were the criteria against which these judgements should be made? During the 1990s across the UK, we saw the identification of a series of 'competences' that beginning teachers should be able to demonstrate. Latterly these became a list of 'standards' (Mahony and Hextall, 2000) sometimes, as in Scotland, grouped under an overarching Standard, such as the Standard for Initial Teacher Education (Kennedy, 2013). In all UK jurisdictions we saw the creation of a list of observable behaviours, which trainee teachers would need be able to demonstrate in order to achieve their teaching qualification. In most settings now, there is actually a series of Standards designed to relate to each stage of a teacher's development, from initial qualification through to school headship.

The growth of standards was associated with the international concern with 'the quality of teaching', which from the 1980s onwards has increasingly been recognised as perhaps the key factor in ensuring that education systems are themselves of high quality. Sahlberg (2011) has identified the GERM – the Global Education Reform Movement – that has 'infected' education systems around the world and includes 'standardization' as one of its key characteristics, but it also includes 'high-stakes accountability' as another feature and this has certainly been manifest in many Western teacher education systems. At its most extreme it has seen the development of an inspection framework in England, led by the Office for Standards in Education (Ofsted), that threatens teacher education providers with reduced resources or even closure if they are not able to demonstrate their successful compliance with the requirements laid down by government.

These three themes – theory/practice, 'partnership' and standards/accountability – are themes that influence the questions of curriculum, assessment and pedagogy in teacher education, as we shall see in the following sections.

THE TEACHER EDUCATION CURRICULUM

Programmes of teacher education in most UK settings last for at least 1 year or a major part of a year and these 1-year programmes tend to be offered to graduates who already have a first degree. There are, however, still a number of settings where it is possible to undertake an undergraduate programme of 3 or 4 years that leads directly to a teaching qualification. In the case of either type of qualification it is usual to see the teacher education curriculum as consisting of several elements and the separation between these elements may vary. It is also the case that the balance between the elements will depend not only on whether this is a graduate or undergraduate programme, but also on what age phase the programme is preparing students to teach. We can categorise the curricular elements as follows:

- Subject studies
- Professional studies
- Professionally related subject studies

Subject studies is the element in the teacher education curriculum in which the intending teacher is supported to develop the appropriate subject knowledge to be able to teach the relevant curriculum to the children they will be working with. For a teacher in a secondary school, this will typically be one or sometimes two subjects and the knowledge will be that required to assist children to study for and sit the requisite public examinations in that subject. For a primary school teacher, although the teacher may specialise in a particular subject, perhaps in order to become a 'subject leader' in that specialism later, during their initial preparation they are going to need to be prepared to teach across the full curriculum, that is all subjects up to the level required for the age range they will teach. The emphasis therefore is very much on breadth of curriculum coverage, perhaps much more than depth. In Early Years settings (pre-school included) the subject knowledge required is likely to be less subject-specific and more about broad areas of learning, such as 'literacy' and 'numeracy'.

Professional studies is that part of the teacher education curriculum in which intending teachers study teaching and learning and learn about the school system that they are being prepared to teach in. This may or may not be informed by a range of background 'disciplines' in education, including philosophy, history, psychology and sociology (see Furlong and Lawn, 2010; Furlong, 2013). This element has been challenged recently, with opportunities for serious study of these aspects severely reduced in many contexts, especially in shorter courses, such as the 1-year programmes for graduates. As well as drawing on the disciplines of education, professional studies may also include aspects of professional enquiry, drawing on more recent traditions of 'teacher as researcher' (Stenhouse, 1975) or the enquiring teacher (Nias and Groundwater-Smith, 1988; Cochran-Smith and Lytle, 2009).

The element of professionally related subject studies has not always been recognised as a separate stream of study, but drawing on important work carried out in the US by Lee Shulman (1987), it has been widely accepted that there is something very particular about the educational significance of particular subjects. Shulman coined the term 'pedagogical content knowledge' (PCK) to indicate the need for teachers to be aware not only of the knowledge content of a subject per se, but to recognise the particular challenges of learning that subject. This, therefore, involves understanding the structure of the subject and the ways in which key concepts and ideas are best learnt by children. PCK is itself a concept that challenges the assumption that all subjects can be learnt in the same way and have equivalent structures (see Philpott, 2014).

If these are the main elements of a teacher education curriculum, we must now return to the question of how they are best taught and learnt and by whom and in what context.

PEDAGOGY IN TEACHER EDUCATION

We have already established that professional learning – learning to undertake a professional occupation – requires experiential processes as well as the accumulation of knowledge. Decisions about the balance between knowledge, concepts, skills and attitudes within a teacher education programme are likely to influence the question of how learning is organised. Reference has ready been made to the concept of clinical practice and perhaps the best way of illustrating the issues within teacher education pedagogy is to examine this approach. In their review of 'research-based clinical practice in teacher education', Burn and Mutton (2013) define clinical practice as follows:

…for beginning teachers working within an established community of practice, with access to the practical wisdom of experts, 'clinical practice' allows them to engage in a process of enquiry: seeking to interpret and make sense of the specific needs of particular students, to formulate and implement particular pedagogical actions and to evaluate the outcomes. (Burn and Mutton, 2013: 3)

We see that there is a crucial interaction between sites of learning, but we also see that the learning involved is essentially a social process. A student teacher cannot learn in isolation. S/he is dependent on being able to interact with other more experienced professionals, many of whom are likely to be school-based teacher educators (often referred to in schools as mentors or professional tutors). Traditionally, student teachers would be observed in some of their teaching sessions by a visiting tutor from their HEI, who would offer critical feedback aimed to identify strengths and areas for development. Increasingly, these elements of observation and feedback have been shared with school-based staff, although in many programmes external visits by HEI staff still play a part in the process.

In partnership-based programmes there will also be sessions in the HEI, led by HEI-based teacher educators who may well be research active in some aspect of educational studies and will be able to enrich the theoretical and research aspects of the students' learning. Furthermore, student teachers' learning may be greatly enhanced by being a part of a cohort of students who are all learning alongside each other. The opportunity to undertake peer observation and analysis is likely to be a very fruitful element in beginning teachers' learning.

Based on this model, the student teacher is certainly undertaking some conventional study, especially in developing knowledge of their subject, but this will be complemented by a very strong element of social and professional learning in relation to their professional studies and professionally related subject studies. Much of the latter learning can and often does take place in the school setting, with many schemes now delivering professional seminars for groups of trainees within the school setting. Another critical matter can be the range of school experiences that the student teacher may have. On longer programmes it is easier to ensure that the trainee will experience several different school settings; however on shorter (1 year) programmes it can often be difficult to ensure that the two different settings in which students are placed provide a sufficient range of experience. In some of the employment-based and/or 'school-led' routes that have developed recently, the intention is very much to prepare the student for one particular setting because it is anticipated that they will be employed within that setting. This may be seen as a relative weakness, in that the beginning teacher may be less well prepared to move on to other settings later in their career.

The extent to which the pedagogy within the teacher education programme is consistent with the pedagogy that the student teacher her/himself is developing is an interesting question, to which we will return later, but suffice to say that at this stage most teacher education pedagogy takes a strongly 'constructivist' view of professional learning and is increasingly one that is dependent on an interaction between knowledge and skills. The question of how professional values and dispositions are learnt is also critical because some aspect of these is invariably part of the standards against which teachers are to be assessed, but the actual teaching and learning of values and dispositions is philosophically very challenging because it involves a close connection between the personal and the professional. The question of whether values can be taught and, if so, how, is a challenging one (Mahony, 2009). In the real world of teacher education, 'professionalism' is still a term that is widely used and tends to override other considerations. This involves such diverse matters as developing respectful relationships with learners and with colleagues, being punctual and reliable in the school setting and dressing appropriately.

ASSESSMENT IN TEACHER EDUCATION

How should student teachers be assessed? This may seem a straightforward question, but we find that the answer depends on what kind of programme the student is on. At one extreme in England, there is what is called an 'Assessment Only' route into teaching. This is designed to enable people who have been working as unqualified teachers and have some experience to demonstrate that they have achieved the required standards to be recognised as a qualified teacher. They are therefore assessed only on their ability to demonstrate that they can meet those standards. Furthermore, it should be noted that in other parts of the UK and in many other settings, it is not possible to qualify as a teacher without some demonstration of a theoretical understanding of teaching as well as an ability to 'perform'. Most routes into teaching are therefore designed to lead to an academically related qualification in addition to basic teaching competence. In England, most schemes, such as Teach First and School Direct, in contrast to the Assessment Only route, lead not only to Qualified Teacher Status (QTS) but also to an accredited qualification, usually a Postgraduate Certificate in Education (PGCE). In order to achieve such a qualification, it is not only a requirement to demonstrate achievement of the standard for QTS, but the university validating the qualification will also require the student to submit some work for assessment against academic criteria. This may consist of a number of 'coursework assignments'. It is very unusual for student teachers on PGCE routes to be assessed through formal examinations, although this may continue to be the practice for parts of some degree entry routes into teaching.

The assessment of the performance element in all settings is a matter for professional judgement by those with the responsibility for making the decisions. Typically on partnership routes these judgements will be made by a combination of school-based and

HEI-based staff. They will observe the trainee's practice in the classroom, discuss it with him or her and analyse the records and plans that the trainee provides as evidence of their attending to the full range of criteria. The assessors are then likely to consult with each other and make a recommendation to a formal examination board, usually administered by the HEI concerned. The HEI will also have in place some quality assurance procedures designed to ensure that that judgements made are both internally consistent as well as consistent with the range of providers nationally. This will involve the deployment of some external examiners who have experience elsewhere.

Although the final assessment at the end of the programme is 'what matters' both for the individual concerned as well as for the sake of the system as a whole in which it is important to maintain appropriate quality for entry to the profession, the individuals are usually greatly supported through a process of formative assessment during the programme. As mentioned earlier under pedagogy, students would normally expect to be observed and to receive feedback during the early stages of their placements, helping them to ensure positive developments, especially in any perceived areas of weakness. The university-based elements of the programme may also include elements of formative assessment that help to improve the likelihood of success in the subsequent summative assessments.

CURRICULUM, PEDAGOGOY AND ASSESSMENT IN THE TEACHER EDUCATION CURRICULUM

We turn now to consider the three elements of curriculum, assessment and pedagogy as they are addressed in the curriculum experienced by teacher education students. In other words what are beginning teachers taught about these three message systems? How are they encouraged to appreciate their significance?

Underlying this is an interesting and important question about whether the way in which the student teacher experiences each of these as a student teacher is congruent with the way in which they experience each of them as a learner. Again, consideration is given to the UK example, particularly England, but the underlying principles are equally relevant in all teacher education settings.

Taking curriculum first, the most obvious way in which student teachers are exposed to curriculum during their programme is in becoming familiar with the actual curriculum they are expected to teach – this is likely to be defined by subject and by age range. As mentioned earlier, if they are a secondary teacher this will involve them learning about specific content in the particular subject that they are training to teach. If they are a primary teacher they may specialise in one subject but will have to include some coverage of the whole curriculum. In both cases, there may well be some 'cross-curricular elements' that they also need to study, which might include literacy or 'language across the curriculum', or it might be more thematic cross-curricular strands such as 'environmental issues' or 'citizenship'.

Although we may expect all student teachers to be introduced to these essential elements of 'curriculum content', the question to which there may be a more divergent answer is whether they are introduced to curricular concepts and indeed to curriculum theory. During the 1960s and 1970s, curriculum theory was seen as a key component of teacher education programmes. This was particularly the case in the US and in some European teacher education programmes. In the UK, where the tradition had been to study the discrete disciplines in education, the integrative subject of curriculum studies or curriculum theory was perhaps less wholeheartedly adopted, although education courses run by the Open University in this period did do a lot to promote the field. However, curriculum studies certainly fell out of favour as the more skills-based approach took hold from the 1980s onwards and has been the subject of some concern – in fact, some have asked 'whatever happened to curriculum theory?' (Priestley, 2011). Many student teachers today express some surprise at the idea of curriculum theory. Having gone through a schooling system themselves where the National Curriculum had been laid down for them, they arrive on the programme innocent of the possibility that the particular curriculum has been determined through a series of decisions made by policymakers. Concepts such as curriculum continuity and progression, curriculum differentiation and curriculum coherence may all be lost in the simple adherence to a prescribed curriculum to be 'delivered'.

The ideas of an objectives-based curriculum, a process-based curriculum and the questions about areas of learning and definitions of subject – or, as Bernstein (1972) put it, the classification and framing of educational knowledge – are all ideas at risk of being ignored if curriculum studies are absent from the teacher education curriculum. Much of the important work that links values to aims to curriculum objectives, which has underpinned educational theory for many years, may be judged to be essential if teachers are to grasp the significance of what they are doing in classrooms. Current debates about the extent to which knowledge should be the driving force for curriculum were addressed by Young (2007) and even more recently the idea of 'powerful knowledge' was promoted by Young and colleagues (Young et al., 2014). All of these – and related ideas – are crucial in the learning of beginning teachers.

Turning to pedagogy, there has been a similar tendency in recent years to reduce teaching about pedagogy to a simple and functionalist focus on the teaching standards. Programmes are required to ensure that students must be able to demonstrate their achievement of the standards; however. they are defined in particular jurisdictions. They typically cover aspects of teaching such as planning teaching and assessing learning, managing behaviour, ensuring differentiation and an ability

to meet the needs of all children. These are all important requirements, but they do not require students to study underlying theory about learning. Some years ago, the historian Brian Simon asked the question 'Why no pedagogy in England?' (Simon, 1981) and, although the word pedagogy is in greater use now than it was then, it is far from clear that there is any greater understanding of the importance of the processes of teaching and learning. In the 1960s and 1970s, student teachers were given the opportunity to look at the work of scientists such as Jean Piaget and Lev Vygotsky in order to assess its significance for work in the classroom. The work of Americans John Dewey through to Jerome Bruner was also frequently invoked, and often connected pedagogy with curriculum, but the opportunities for studying such work in English initial teacher education are now much reduced under pressure from the knowledge-based and skills-based emphases that have dominated teacher education since the 1980s.

Teaching about pedagogy has been replaced by the adoption of specific approaches such as particular techniques in the teaching of reading ('the National Literacy Strategy') or other ideas such as 'growth mindsets' or 'multiple intelligences', based on the research of particular scholars (in these cases, Carol Dweck and Howard Gardner). Other particular ideas have been promoted by government ministers at particular times, but have not given student teachers an opportunity to investigate underlying theories or research. For example, 'personalisation' was adopted as a particular mantra by the Labour-led Government in England in the early 2000s (Hartley, 2012). All this time, educational research was still being undertaken, but it was rarely leading to changes in teaching about pedagogy in teacher education courses.

If both curricular and pedagogical theories have tended to become restricted in how they have been taught and studied over recent years, it is perhaps in the field of assessment that there has been some more positive recent development in teacher education curricula. It would be reasonable to say that both curriculum theory and pedagogical theory were developed more thoroughly and earlier than assessment theory. Prior to the 1980s, most assessment research was essentially about testing and different approaches to testing. Important though it was, it was much more concerned with finding effective, fair and reliable examination methods than with the assessment elements of teaching itself. When new approaches to assessment were introduced in England after the 1988 Education Reform Act, teachers began to be more aware of different forms of assessment. Indeed the 'TGAT Report', written by Paul Black and colleagues to inform the development of assessment policy, very clearly spelt out four different purposes of assessment: formative, diagnostic, summative and evaluative (Task Group on Assessment and Testing (TGAT), 1987). Although the emphasis in the national assessment systems that followed was almost completely on summative elements, Black and his collaborator Dylan Wiliam went on to undertake research and promote understanding of wider processes, most specifically formative assessment or, as it became known, Assessment for Learning (AfL) (Black and Wiliam, 1990). The AfL approach was something that was gradually picked up as a very important element of good teaching, and it is fair to say that it now features strongly as an element of teacher education programmes across the UK and beyond.

This example of formative assessment becoming integrated or embedded within teacher education programmes is an excellent case of research informing practice, both in schools and in teacher education. Indeed, formative assessment has become embedded to the extent that it is now a key element of 'normal' pedagogy for many practitioners. It is also a subject of considerable investigation and sharing of practice amongst teachers in schools in the UK. It makes an uneasy bedfellow with the high stakes testing that is also increasingly part of many Western education systems.

CONCLUSION

This chapter has sought to explore how issues around curriculum, pedagogy and assessment are played out and how they connect with practices of teacher education. By providing an overview of the development of institutional teacher education and then identifying key themes that have emerged from that development, the scene was set for examining the connections in two different senses.

The first of these was to look at the organisation and practice of teacher education, especially initial teacher education, and to see what the major questions for curriculum, pedagogy and assessment processes are in teacher education programmes. The second sense of these connections was to look at the 'content' of teacher education programmes and to offer some assessment of how these three topics are typically addressed within these programmes.

The overall conclusions to be drawn from these two sets of analyses are as follows. If curriculum, pedagogy and assessment are the key message systems of schooling, then that is equally true of teacher education. We have seen how there has been a lot of change in how teacher education is organised and many of the key debates, both historically and contemporarily, have been concerned with one or more of these message systems. At present there is all too little opportunity for people entering the teaching profession to study any of these topics in much depth, such is the pressure for beginning teachers to be able to demonstrate their performance skills in the classroom. This has been influenced by the dominance of a technicist and craft model of teacher education, which has been particularly strong in England and in some parts of the US. This has increasingly led teacher education towards an apprenticeship model of learning at the cost of the intellectual elements of learning. In countries where an increasingly enquiry-oriented approach has been taken in teacher education (for example, Finland and Singapore are frequently cited), we see an association with a high level of pupil gains, or 'outputs' as the current discourse might put it (Tatto, 2013).

In the introduction to this chapter, two further underlying questions were suggested which are worthy of reconsideration now, following our review of the relevance of the three message systems in teacher education. The first was the nature of the relationship between schooling and teacher education. To what extent should one drive the other? It has to be said that there has been a strong tendency in recent years for schooling to drive the teacher education system. There has been very little educational innovation that has been led by teacher education. Indeed, there has not been much that has been led by schools; rather innovation that has emerged has tended to be led by politicians and policymakers who, since the late 1970s, have played an increasingly interventionist role in educational policy (Tomlinson, 2005). From the days when one could have expected fresh thinking and fresh ideas to emanate from research and theory being developed in university departments of education, in England at least, the current relationship between schools and universities has tended to stifle rather than foster such creativity. There is not a lot of high quality research directly concerned with teacher education happening in many of these universities; however, the results of the 2014 Research Excellence Framework (HEFCE, 2015) indicate that there is a considerable amount of world-leading educational research being undertaken across the UK. This makes it all the more alarming how little connection there appears to be between this research, teacher education and schools.

On the second question we can perhaps be a little more optimistic. This was the question of the continuing professional learning of teachers throughout their careers. Most of what has been discussed in this chapter has focused on initial or pre-service teacher education. There has been widespread recognition in most quarters that however weak or strong an initial teacher education programme is, there will still be a great need for continuing support for teachers in their professional development thereafter. It is here where we begin to see opportunities for a greater degree of agency on the part of teachers (Priestley et al., 2015) than has been the case where initial teacher education (ITE) is concerned. We see encouragement in many countries for teachers to undertake Masters courses with a strong enquiry element. Even in England, where ITE has been subject to such constraint, there appears to be support for teachers to become enquirers, to use research methods and techniques to gather and make use of evidence in their day-to-day work (BERA–RSA, 2014). We now see increasing reference to 'Evidence-Based Teaching' and a call for the creation of a College of Teaching, which would support such a notion as part of its rationale.

For the future, it remains very important that the three message systems continue to be the subject of critical scrutiny within teacher education and that there should be continuing examination of their links and congruence with what is happening in schools. Furthermore, it remains important to keep reviewing the nature of professional learning for teachers as a career-long process where the curricular, pedagogical and assessment needs and challenges may vary significantly over the professional life course. These three message systems are the lifeblood of teacher professionalism and teacher agency, and how they inform teacher education is crucial to the future health of teachers' professional learning and the contribution they can make, not only to the children they teach but also through them, to the wider society.

REFERENCES

BERA–RSA (British Educational Research Association–Royal Society for the Encouragement of the Arts, Manufacturing and Commerce) (2014) *Research and the Teaching Profession. Building the Capacity* for a Self-Improving Education System. Final Report of the BERA-RSA Inquiry into the Role of Research in Teacher Education. Available from https://www.bera.ac.uk/wp-content/uploads/2013/12/BERA-RSA-Research-Teaching-Profession-FULL-REPORT-for-web.pdf (accessed 22 July 2015).

Bernstein, B. (1972) 'On the classification and framing of educational knowledge', in M. Young (ed.), Knowledge and Control. London: Collier–Macmillan. pp. 47–69.

Bernstein, B. (1975) Towards a Theory of Educational Transmissions: Class, Codes and Control. Vol 3. London: Routledge.

Black, P. and Wiliam, D. (1990) Inside the Black Box. London: GL Assessment.

Burn, K. and Mutton, T. (2013) Review of 'Research-Informed Clinical Practice' in Initial Teacher Education. Research and Teacher Education: The BERA–RSA Inquiry. Available from https://www.bera.ac.uk/wp-content/uploads/2014/02/BERA-Paper-4-Research-informed-clinical-practice.pdf (accessed 22 July 2015).

Childs, A. and Menter, I. (2013) 'Teacher education in the 21st Century in England: a case study in neo-liberal policy', Revista Espanola de Educacion Camparada (Spanish Journal of Comparative Education), 22: 93–116.

Cochran-Smith, M. and Lytle, S.L. (2009) Enquiry as Stance: Practitioner Research for the Next Generation. New York, NY: Teachers College Press.

Cochran-Smith, M., Feiman-Nemser, S., McIntyre, J. and Demers, K. (eds) (2008) Handbook of Research in Teacher Education – Enduring Questions in Changing Contexts. 3rd edn. New York, NY: Routledge, Taylor & Francis and The Association of Teacher Educators.

Cook, C. (1984) 'Teachers for the inner city: change and continuity', in G. Grace (ed.), Education and the City. London: Robert Kennedy Publishing.

Cruickshank, M. (1970) History of the Training of Teachers in Scotland. London: University of London Press.

Dent, H. (1977) The Training of Teachers in England and Wales 1800 –1975. London: Hodder and Stoughton.

Department for Education (DfE) (2010) The Importance of Teaching: White Paper. London: DfE.

Department for Education and Science (DES) (1972) Teacher Education and Training (The James Report). London: HMSO.

Donaldson, G. (2011) Teaching Scotland's Future: A Report of the Review of Teacher Education in Scotland. Edinburgh: Scottish Government.

Furlong, J. (2013) Education – An Anatomy of the Discipline: Rescuing the University Project? Oxon, UK: Routledge.

Furlong, J. (2015) Teaching Tomorrow's Teachers, Options for the Future of Initial Teacher Education in Wales. Oxford: University of Oxford Department of Education.

Furlong, J. and Lawn, M. (eds.) (2010) Disciplines of Education: Their Roles in the Future of Education Research. London: Routledge.

Furlong, J., Barton, L., Miles, S., Whiting, C. and Whitty, G. (2000) Teacher Education in Transition: Reforming Professionalism? Buckingham, UK: Open University Press.

Hagger, H. and McIntyre, D. (2006) Learning Teaching from Teachers: Realizing the Potential of School-Based Teacher Education. Buckingham, UK: Open University Press.

Hartley, D. (2012) Education and the Culture of Consumption: Personalisation and the Social Order. London: Routledge.

HEFCE (2015) Research Excellence Framework 2014: Overview report by Main Panel C and Sub-panels 16 to 26. Available at http://www.ref.ac.uk/media/ref/content/expanel/member/Main%20Panel%20C%20overview%20report.pdf (accessed 22 July 2015)

Kennedy, A. (2013) 'Teacher professional learning', in T. Bryce, W. Humes, D. Gillies and A. Kennedy (eds.), Scottish Education. 4th edn. Edinburgh: Edinburgh University Press.

Mahony, P. (2009) 'Should "ought" be taught?', Teaching and Teacher Education, 25: 983–89.

Mahony, P. and Hextall, I. (2000) Reconstructing Teaching. London: RoutledgeFalmer.

Maclure, S. (1986) Educational Documents – England and Wales 1816 to the Present Day. London: Methuen.

McNamara, O., Murray, J. and Jones, M. (eds) (2013) Workplace Learning in Teacher Education, Professional Learning and Development in Schools and Higher Education. Dordrecht, Netherlands: Springer.

Nias, J. and Groundwater-Smith, S. (eds.) (1988) The Enquiring Teacher – Supporting and

Sustaining Teacher Research. London: Routledge.

Philpott, C. (2014) *Theories of Professional Learning.* St Albans, UK: Critical Publishing.

Priestley, M. (2011) 'Whatever happened to curriculum theory? Critical realism and curricular change', *Pedagogy, Culture and Society,* 19(2): 221–38.

Priestley, M., Biesta, G. and Robinson, S. (2015) *Teacher Agency: An Ecological Approach.* London: Bloomsbury.

Robinson, W. (2004) *Power to Teach – Learning through Practice.* London: RoutledgeFalmer.

Sahlberg, P. (2011) *Finnish Lessons: What Can the World Learn from Educational Change in Finland?* New York, NY: Teachers College Press.

Shulman, L. (1987) 'Knowledge and teaching: foundations of the new reform', *Harvard Educational Review,* 57(1): 1–22.

Simon, B. (1981) 'Why no pedagogy in England?', in B. Simon and W. Taylor (eds.), *Issues for the 80s: The Central Issues.* London: Batsford.

Stenhouse, L. (1975) *An Introduction to Curriculum Research and Development.* Oxford: Heinemann.

Task Group on Assessment and Testing (TGAT) (1987) *A Report.* London: Department for Education and Science.

Tatto, M.T. (2013) *The Role of Research In International Policy and Practice in Teacher Education. The BERA–RSA Inquiry.* Available from http://www.bera.ac.uk/wp-content/uploads/2014/02/BERA-Paper-2-International-Policy-and-Practice-in-Teacher-Education.pdf (accessed 22 July 2015).

Teacher Education Group (2015) *Teacher Education in Times of Change: Responding to Challenges across the UK and Ireland.* Bristol, UK: Policy Press.

Tomlinson, S. (2005) *Education in a Post-Welfare Society.* Buckingham, UK: Open University Press.

Young, M. (2007) *Bringing Knowledge Back In: From Social Constructivism to Social Realism in the Sociology of Education.* London: Routledge.

Young, M., Lambert, D., Roberts, C. and Roberts, M. (2014) *Knowledge and the Future School: Curriculum and Social Justice.* London: Routledge.

Index

Page numbers in **bold** indicate tables, in *italic* indicate figures and followed by a letter n indicate end of chapter notes.